CW0082193S

Who Sailed on
Titanic?

Who Sailed on
Titanic?
Debbie Beavis

Ian Allan

60th

ANNIVERSARY

First published 2002

ISBN 0 7110 2880 X

The essay 'Documenting Disaster' by Marian Smith, in Chapter 7, was originally published in *Voyage*, the quarterly journal of the Titanic International Society, PO Box 7007, Freehold, NJ 07728 and is reproduced here with the kind permission of Charles Haas, editor.

Published by Ian Allan Publishing

an imprint of Ian Allan Publishing Ltd, Hersham, Surrey KT12 4RG.
Printed by Ian Allan Printing Ltd, Hersham, Surrey KT12 4RG.

Code: 0203/B2

e&oe

Jacket photo montage by Gery Swiggum

Contents

Foreword

Rear Admiral John Lang
Chief Inspector of Marine Accidents, the United Kingdom

One of the most formidable tasks facing authorities that respond to major disasters is identifying who the victims might be. Even in well documented arenas such as air travel, when an aircraft crashes the process can be far from straightforward. Not only is it necessary to identify those on board but also, in certain circumstances, victims on the ground. In other situations such as a natural disaster, a fire in a road tunnel, an overcrowded ferry that capsizes on some isolated river in the undeveloped world or even a terrorist attack on a major landmark, the difficulties can become formidable. Nominal lists might contain misspellings, names might be recorded in different ways and, too often, there is no record at all. One of the more curious aspects of victim identification after a transport accident is the number of times a percentage of the deceased are found to be travelling under assumed names.

If the problems today are real enough, they were multiplied many times over in the past. Not only were records far from complete and compiled by hand but people were even less familiar with the conventions of address. An individual might have had his or her name recorded in different ways by different people so that in the aftermath of any tragedy that one person might be counted more than once.

One of the most memorable examples of the confusion that can arise is best demonstrated in the aftermath of what was, arguably, one of the worst disasters of all time, the sinking of the *Titanic* in April 1912. The events of that tragic night have been written about many times but professional researchers have noticed how often inaccurate information is repeated in one book after another when authors fail to check primary sources. This is clearly demonstrated whenever reference is made to the number of victims from the *Titanic*, let alone their identities.

It has taken one particular researcher, Debbie Beavis, to explore this subject in a way never previously attempted. Discovering that nobody had ever described how deaths at sea were recorded, or how accurate lists of survivors were compiled after an accident, she set out to find out exactly who was on board the *Titanic* on her fateful maiden, and last, voyage across the North Atlantic.

This book is a testament to her skills as a researcher as she checks and cross-checks the available information. She describes the many lists that were compiled of passengers and crew and it soon becomes very evident they contained many discrepancies. The authorities in 1912 were faced with the same problem as they tried to match up names recorded in many different hands, in varying styles and following different conventions.

But this book is more than just a record of determining who was on board *Titanic*. It is an inspiration to those who might wish to carry out their own research in trying to trace people who travelled by sea in some bygone age. It is also essential reading for anyone who could be faced with the task of identifying victims after a major disaster. Furnished with this book they will have a much greater understanding of the difficulties and pitfalls that await the unwary. Above all, the book is a joy to read.

Preface

During the night of 14/15 April 1912, *Titanic*, the world's largest passenger liner, struck an iceberg in mid-Atlantic and sank. Hundreds of passengers and crew lost their lives. Some, trapped in the hull or injured by falling debris, had no chance of saving themselves and went down with the ship. Many more fell or jumped into the water. In temperatures of -2° Centigrade, vital systems would have shut down within a few minutes and death was inevitable. The lucky few made it into lifeboats and were plucked to safety by the crew of the steamship *Carpathia*. With the arrival of the survivors into New York, and the retrieval of many bodies from the ocean over the next few weeks, the task began to compile an accurate list of every passenger who had been on board *Titanic* that night.

It rapidly became clear that this was not straightforward. Doubts were voiced about whether certain passengers had sailed at all. Several names seemed to have been omitted altogether and rumours of tickets changing hands for cash abounded, but there was rarely any absolute proof one way or the other. It was the names of the foreign steerage passengers that gave the investigators the biggest headache of all. In the English-speaking world, convention dictates that a person will have one or more given names, and a family name. On marriage, women adopt their husband's family name and the children follow suit. Much of the rest of the world has very different practices. It is beyond the scope of this book to explain Scandinavian, eastern European and Middle Eastern naming conventions. The processes would have been a mystery to most of the British clerks entering the names and details correctly on passenger lists prior to sailing, and to the investigators who later tried to match those same lists with the records of the non-English-speaking survivors and the deceased.

With the benefit of almost a century of research into the true identities of many of these people, and our own cosmopolitan society in which many of those previously alien names of a century ago no longer seem strange at all, it is easy to criticise the clerks for carelessness and inefficiency in recording the names at each stage – from the ticket numbers through to the identity of the survivors or of the deceased. Undoubtedly there is evidence of some very careless errors and clear lapses in concentration but in the context of the era in which they lived, the clerks generally made valiant attempts to decipher the foreign names written in unfamiliar handwriting styles. However, as each clerk at every stage of the recording process added his own interpretation to the previous one, the end result often resembles the party game of 'Chinese Whispers' or 'Telephone' and it is easy to understand the problems besetting those trying to compile an accurate list of passengers.

These problems are not only confined to *Titanic's* records. As a researcher into British passenger records of the late 19th and the 20th centuries, the naming patterns and the process of recording passenger names have long been a source of fascination to me. As the proliferation of *Titanic*-related material grew in the wake of the James Cameron movie *Titanic* I became increasingly concerned about the quality of the research behind many of the examples of so-called complete *Titanic* passenger lists. With no mention of the original sources but often with the same errors cropping up time after time, clearly many lists were simply copies of someone else's earlier transcription – without citations, how was the reader to verify the information? How had the original compiler arrived at a decision on the spelling of unfamiliar eastern European names? Why did the lists never include the accompanying biographical information so vital for an accurate identification? Unless the potential problems and the opportunities for further research were pointed out, wouldn't most readers blindly accept the accuracy of what they were offered without any thought or question, and wasn't there a danger of wrong or misleading information eventually being written in stone?

Some years before the blockbuster movie, I had obtained photocopies of the partially conserved Southampton section of the Board of Trade passenger departure list as part of my own general research into ocean travel. A few months later I had stumbled upon the Queenstown section lying almost untouched among the other Queenstown lists for April 1912 and copied that, too. I toyed briefly with the idea of transcribing both sets of information on to a computer database but there was little obvious public interest in *Titanic* at the time. I pushed the idea to the back of my mind until, some months later in March 1994 I received a gift of the John Eaton and Charles Haas book, *Titanic: Triumph and Tragedy*. The die was cast. I pulled the two sets of copies out of my files and transcribed them onto my computer. The following year I was skimming through some material at the Public Record Office in Kew when I found references to the crew agreement which apparently (and unusually) contained passengers' names. I examined the document but time interrupted my plan to transcribe it.

The idea was still simmering three years later when I made the acquaintance of Marian Smith, Senior Historian at the Immigration and Naturalization Service in Washington, D.C., and Sue Swiggum, a fellow researcher from Halifax, Nova Scotia. With the newly released Cameron movie a box office hit, and *Titanic* fever now at its height, we discovered that we each shared the same alarm at the variable quality of much of the available research. Sometime in early 1998 the idea of transcribing all the records onto one database was born. With the original archival source material held in various archives in Britain, America and Canada, a joint effort made absolute sense. Marian transcribed the New York arrival records including the then recently discovered *Carpathia* purser's list with its mysterious new passenger, Augusta Valentine. Sue transcribed the almost unknown Halifax arrival list, and other Canadian records.

I had a large amount of information already on my computer so I added the Canadian and American records to my original database, along with my transcriptions of the remaining British lists – the three separate records of deaths at sea and the White Star Line's two records: the Contract Ticket List and printed passenger list. Somehow the lot fell to me to write what we imagined would be a brief article comparing the various lists. Time passed and we each became involved in other projects until early last year when I quietly dusted the plan down and began writing. What began as an article quickly grew and over the last three years has become an in-depth study of all the various passenger lists compiled for RMS *Titanic* and what may be learned from them.

The first list of *Titanic's* passengers drawn up immediately following the disaster was altered and corrected several times, a process which involved difficult enquiries and lengthy correspondence in a world in which most communication was by postal letter. Would a comparison of similar records of other contemporary incidents with those of the *Titanic* indicate whether the process and accuracy of recording *Titanic's* passengers was representative at a time when communications technology as we know it today was in its infancy?

This comprehensive research based upon the original documents now enables direct comparisons between each of the primary sources. Viewed overall, this selection of different lists, each with its unique provenance, can teach a valuable lesson in the reliability or otherwise of these documents and open the way to a greater understanding of them in the broader field of passenger research. The information can be manipulated in order to generate

Preface

what might seem to be the nearest one can ever get to that elusive definitive list but I have made no attempt to alter, correct or guess when undertaking these comparisons for the sake of producing a tidy list of passengers. The names and all other essential identifying information from each list have been painstakingly transcribed exactly as they appear in the original record complete with as much accompanying data as space allowed and are reproduced in this book. Using the references in Appendix 1, readers may for the first time conduct their own across-the-board comparisons of each entry and are free at last to draw their own conclusions. They will discover that the list of those passengers appearing in every record in which they might be expected to appear, with spellings and all other details identical, is surprisingly short.

With all the names and details from each surviving primary source now computerised, no longer does this research need to be just a list of names of those who sailed on the ocean crossing. With the data re-sorted in order to show ethnic origins, port of arrival into the British Isles and the name of the steamship line that had carried them, the implications for further research are exciting! The sole and hitherto untapped source of this information is the Board of Trade's British passenger list. To date, no other study has been made of late 19th and 20th century British passenger lists. Until recently the existence of *Titanic's* was overlooked by researchers despite the valuable information it holds especially concerning the foreign passengers. With relatively little other documentary means with which to follow their journey, the exclusion of this British list and the unique information it contains represents a significant omission. Contemporary Board of Trade arrival lists have also been examined and offer a new dimension to *Titanic* research for several of the overseas passengers about whom little had previously been known.

For the first time, the various procedures for the registration of deaths at sea, the ticketing processes, and the compilation of the British pre-embarkation passenger records have been discussed at length. I hope that this study of the records compiled for RMS *Titanic* and others during the early years of the 20th century will provide a new insight into the transportation not only of *Titanic's* transmigrant passengers but of all foreigners arriving in Britain en route for the United States, Canada, South Africa, Australasia and other destinations in the years leading up to World War 1. For readers hoping to learn more of their own migrant ancestors, these and other sources explained here for the first time will prove to be valuable tools for their own research.

Debbie Beavis
Broadstairs, 2002

Introduction

With the haunting lament of Irish pipes floating across the still waters of Cork Bay, *Titanic*, the world's largest passenger ship, slipped out into St George's Channel and set a course for the Atlantic. Five days and three thousand miles ahead lay her goal – America!

Atlantic crossings in the days of wooden sailing ships had often been uncomfortable and dangerous. Violent storms struck without warning, snapping masts like matchwood, shredding canvas and sweeping giant waves across the decks, breaking hatches and flooding the accommodation below. Crew, cabin passengers and hapless emigrants huddled in steerage quarters were all entirely at the mercy of the wind and the waves and in the early years of Atlantic crossings the unpredictable ocean had claimed many lives. Despite the advent of larger, steam-driven vessels the wintry north Atlantic in the late 19th century could still be treacherous. Even the largest steamers faced the danger of being engulfed by towering grey walls of water or buffeted dangerously off course by fierce winds. As spring warmed the polar cap huge cathedrals of ice broke free and were swept south in the Labrador Current. Without the benefit of efficient warning systems passenger liner and berg not infrequently found themselves in the same shipping lane.

As the 19th century gave way to the 20th, technological advances in the world of shipbuilding resulted in bigger, faster and increasingly impressive ships entering the lucrative north Atlantic emigrant route. *Lusitania* and *Mauretania*, sleek greyhounds of the Cunard fleet, snatched the coveted Blue Riband for the fastest Atlantic crossing from rival German shipping lines. Competition was fierce among shipping companies in Britain, America, France and Germany for the prestige of owning the largest and most luxurious ship and led to unimagined splendour in the 1st class rooms on board these giants. The White Star Line's *Olympic* and *Titanic* reached new heights of opulence.

Titanic's maiden voyage carried an impressive list of glittering names including some of the world's richest and most powerful men. But out of sight of the affluent and privileged promenading on the topmost decks, safely concealed in the 3rd class accommodation way below were also several hundred of the poorest, most disadvantaged or displaced persons seeking to change their fortunes by emigrating to the United States and Canada. It was in this atmosphere of splendour and dreams that *Titanic* had begun her fateful voyage.

Whatever the explanation for the sequence of events which followed, the facts are brutally simple. The night was quiet, cold and moonless. Slicing effortlessly through the freezing waters, this dazzling new star powered her way westwards towards New York. Beyond the horizon, a jagged mountain of ice drifted into her path. Three hours later, *Titanic* was gone. The iceberg continued its leisurely drift southwards, leaving in its wake a sea of wreckage and shattered dreams.

The introduction of Marconi's wireless telegraphy to merchant vessels was potentially the greatest aid to saving lives at sea since sail gave way to steam. By 1912 the system was well established on virtually all transatlantic passenger ships but the presence of a wireless room on the big ocean liners was a novelty to the wealthy cabin passengers. Wireless operators, often working alone and sleeping only in catnaps, wasted considerable time each day in transmitting and receiving dozens of frivolous messages sent to impress friends and colleagues on shore.

Introducton

Titanic's loss of life was the greatest anywhere at sea at that time despite the presence on board of the latest Marconi wireless telegraphic equipment and not one but two experienced operators. Her wireless equipment had a range of 1,200 miles in the relative peace of a still Atlantic night but in daylight hours the level of traffic on now crowded airwaves reduced the range to around 400 miles. With the ever-increasing passenger carrying capacity of these Atlantic leviathans and the attendant shortfall in the number of lifeboats on board, the potential for huge loss of life was enormous should the ship founder in mid-ocean. No amount of state-of-the-art wireless equipment could help if receivers were switched off or if there were no ships in the immediate vicinity of the casualty. The survival time for anyone immersed in the icy waters of the north Atlantic could be measured in minutes.

The names of just over 700 survivors picked out of lifeboats by Cunard's SS *Carpathia* were relayed throughout the night and the following day to 21-year-old David Sarnoff, operating the Marconi wireless receiving station set high on Wanamaker's New York department store. The young man worked ceaselessly throughout the long day recording the names as accurately as possible but the signal from *Carpathia* was weak, and the constant interruptions from other radio stations attempting to intercept the messages were so intense that the resulting list contained many errors. Finally, so impossible was Sarnoff's task that President Taft himself intervened, demanding that all other radio stations should cease transmitting to allow the vital work to continue, and dispatched the USS *Chester* with its more powerful transmitters to *Carpathia's* assistance.

As New York awoke on the morning of 15 April 1912, news of the tragedy that continues to grip minds and imaginations 90 years after the event was already being shouted from the news-stands. In the confusion of those first few hours, a stunned world struggled to comprehend. Conflicting reports of the fate of the ship and her passengers and crew at first produced elation and relief which quickly turned to horror as the chilling truth became clear. *Titanic* had sunk. The sudden and dramatic loss of the ship they called 'almost unsinkable', endowed with the finest that technology could provide, and captained by the White Star Line's most senior officer, spread shockwaves across the world.

In a bizarre combination of shared grief and almost ghoulish voyeurism a horrified public demanded to know the smallest detail of the tragedy. The world's press was more than happy to oblige – tragedies have always sold newspapers. The film industry also immediately seized the opportunity to exploit the tragedy and only four weeks after the accident came the release of the first film version of the events, the Etienne Arnaud silent movie *Saved From The Titanic*. What made this movie especially noteworthy was the presence of its leading lady, Dorothy Gibson. Along with her mother, Miss Gibson, a young actress with the French Eclair Moving Picture Company, had been returning to America on board *Titanic* and was among the first to find a place in a lifeboat. Whether she found the writing some form of catharsis or simply a vehicle in which to transport herself into the limelight, within four weeks of the disaster she had somehow co-written the screenplay (casting herself in the role of heroine and wearing the very evening gown she had worn on the night of the disaster) and had become a box office star.

This was to be just one of many film and television versions, notably the 1953 major Hollywood production *Titanic* (directed by Jean Negulesco) and 1958's British film of the Walter Lord book *A Night To Remember* (directed by Roy Ward Baker).

In true crowd-pulling style these films invariably possess those essential Hollywood elements of romance, pathos and heroism in equal measure, unhappily sometimes at the expense of historical accuracy. The correctness of the information disseminated from such productions is variable. A popular theme often presents the totally erroneous belief that the ship was overbooked, and that the unfortunate upper-class hero was only able to obtain a ticket through some questionable negotiations with a poor emigrant from steerage. In truth the ship was nowhere nearly approaching fully-booked. Maiden voyages are traditionally undersubscribed, many cabin class passengers choosing to wait until any possible problems have emerged and been dealt with before they agree to set foot on board. Certainly in the case of *Titanic's* maiden voyage, berths were available in all classes and our hero could easily have obtained a ticket in far less dubious circumstances.

1997 saw the most spectacular movie version yet made of the tragedy with the release of James Cameron's multi-award-winning *Titanic*. His reconstructions of cabins and public rooms for each class were conducted with strict attention to detail and many of the costumes were antique period gowns. Cameron successfully interwove original archival cinefilm of *Titanic's* Southampton departure and his own stunning footage of the wreck itself lying on the seabed, around an improbable romantic liaison between a penniless emigrant from steerage and a young American débutante. The charisma of his central characters and the evocative final scenes played to hushed and tearful cinema audiences across the world did much to fan the flames of *Titanic* hysteria in a new and eager generation.

Advances in underwater exploration and video-photography have brought breathtaking, heartbreaking glimpses of the ship's past splendour to the screen. With easy access to the internet increasing, the number of *Titanic* websites continues to rise and a superficial search of the World Wide Web reveals scores of sites centring on Cameron's fictional theme. The passage of time may have done little to dispel the fascination with the events of that night but it has evidently blurred the line between fact and fiction. Despite all the careful attempts by Cameron and other documentary film-makers to introduce us to the real *Titanic*, for many people her passengers will always remain just actors in a celluloid romance.

In the world outside the cinema there is no room for the glamorising of an event which claimed the lives of so many. From the wealthiest socialite in 1st class to the poorest emigrant in 3rd the Atlantic drew no distinction. Those who played a real part that night, both those who survived and those who died, equally deserve to have their presence in this tragedy accurately recorded. Some internet sites have endeavoured to accomplish that and do so with varying degrees of accuracy. Head and shoulders above them stands Encyclopedia Titanica, edited by Philip Hind. With its vast collection of evidence, biographies, theories and articles presented by a growing number of respected *Titanic* historians, it is by far the most meticulously researched and informative site on the internet. Central to most of the other sites is a passenger list, marked to show who died and who survived. In many cases these lists incorporate or correct names extracted from a wide variety of second-hand sources. Errors and misunderstandings are perpetuated as easily as the truth and rarely do any of these sites offer any clue as to the origin of their passenger information let alone give a full citation of the primary or secondary source material.

Is it possible to say exactly who sailed on *Titanic*, and who died or survived that night? These are questions which have perplexed government investigators, lawyers, scholars and enthusiasts for almost a century. The sailing and ultimate sinking generated numerous lists of passengers' names, each compiled as an official record for a specific official purpose. It might reasonably be expected that these assorted lists would be identical, coming as they did either from the offices of the shipping line or from government sources on each side of the Atlantic. The reality is that any two or more entries for the same person are often far from identical and in some cases any comparisons are just as likely to confuse as to reveal.

The Registrar General of Shipping and Seamen (RGSS) in London was anxious to complete the necessary formalities to allow the registration of the deaths as soon as possible. Unless he received satisfactory evidence of the identity of the deceased passengers, the registrations could not go ahead. With the Inquiries into the disaster due to be held on each side of the Atlantic, but with their own investigations very far from complete, the Marine Department of the Board of Trade was under pressure urgently to submit an accurate list of passengers showing exactly who had survived and who had perished. The number of passengers was calculated and recalculated several times during those early weeks and still the figures would not agree. The British and US Senate Inquiries came and went and in final exasperation on 3 September 1912, the despairing memo from the Marine Department of the Board of Trade read, "We had better show 825 passengers as lost as the RGS has the names." Is it possible that the final tally was already known to be little more than an educated guess?

The list made available to the US Senate Inquiry was generally accepted at the time to be the most complete and accurate list available. In fact it was the only list available at that early stage in the investigation and drew largely upon information hastily compiled from the White Star Line's own passenger records; the benefit of almost a century of continuing research demonstrates its significant flaws. The official Board of Trade passenger list – the British government's record of those persons who actually departed on *Titanic* from the ports of Southampton and Queenstown and which one might suppose would be an entirely accurate record – appears to have been completely overlooked when compiling the final draft for the US Inquiry in 1912. No official passenger list, that is to say a list of passengers compiled by or for a British or French government department, ever existed for the Cherbourg departures. A list signed by the US consul at Cherbourg should have been produced but seems to have been lost with the ship.

The White Star Line's own printed passenger list went through several draft stages, apparently drawing information from various sources, but although it shows the corrected names, class of travel and in some cases port of embarkation, it contains few other details. Its own Contract Ticket List, presented as part of the court case for the Limitation of Liabilities is riddled with errors. The list drawn up on board *Carpathia* by the ship's purser and completed by immigration officials in New York and the typed list naturally show only the survivors. Both are valuable documents in their own right but both were compiled with details supplied by traumatised victims and in a state of considerable hiatus. The list of bodies positively identified and buried either at sea or in various cemeteries in Canada and elsewhere is very short. It is hardly surprising that both the Board of Trade and the US Senate investigators struggled to arrive at a correct list.

For decades, all ocean-bound vessels leaving the British Isles had been required to lodge an official list of all passengers sailing and RMS *Titanic* had been no exception. In that case, why was it now so difficult to produce an accurate list of her passengers? If there was a list of those who had embarked, then surely by process of elimination it must follow that if a name did not appear on the list of survivors picked up by *Carpathia*, then that person must have died? The research included in this book shows that the truth is considerably more complicated.

Author's Note

In order to understand the sometimes confusing numbers of passenger documents and the various government departments and others who were responsible for their compilation or collection, the reader may find the following glossary helpful.

The Passenger Records

1. The Board of Trade List – 2 sections: Southampton, BT27/780B; Queenstown, BT27/776

The passenger list required by the British government. It was compiled by the shipping line, signed by the Emigration Officer and the Master of the ship before departure, and submitted to the Customs office at the port. It was then sent to the Board of Trade Headquarters.

2. Form Inq.6 – MT9/920C

Compiled by the Superintendent of the Marine Office in Southampton. The first stage in the process of reporting and registering a death at sea. The necessary details concerning the death or deaths occurring on board were entered on to Form Inq[uiry] 6 and submitted to the Board of Trade.

3. List C&D – BT100/260

Compiled by the White Star Line's Southampton office. The second stage in the process was the provision of a Casualty and Deaths List, (List C&D). This list was drawn up on printed forms and submitted to the Registrar General of Shipping and Seamen, who was ultimately responsible for the registration of the deaths.

4. Register of Deaths At Sea – BT334/52

The final stage. The Registrar General of Shipping and Seamen's official register recording the name of the deceased, the ship name, geographical location of the death, and its cause.

5. BT32/5

Registers of Passenger Lists. Compiled by the Statistical Department of the Board of Trade. Upon receipt of a passenger list at the Board of Trade it was numbered, and the number and name of the ship only were entered in the register, in port order. This series contains no passenger names.

All the above records are held at the Public Record Office, Ruskin Avenue, Kew, England, where they are available on film, with the exception of BT32/5 and BT334/52, which are original documents.

6. United States Arrival Manifest – T715 Vol 4183

The list prepared by *Carpathia's* purser to submit to the immigration authorities as the ship steamed back to New York with *Titanic's* survivors.

7. Typed List — INS History Office, 425 1 Street NW, Room 1100, Washington DC 20536

Using the *Carpathia* Purser's original record, the passengers' names were typed into a list, by clerks at Ellis Island.

8. White Star Line Contract Ticket List – NRAN-21-SDNYCIVCAS-5512791

When, after the accident, the court case for the Limitation of Liabilities was held in New York City, the White Star Line was required to submit to the court its accounting records of tickets sold. The document is held at NARA-Northeast Region (New York City), 201 Varick Street, New York, NY 10014-4811.

9. White Star Line Passenger List – from Report of the Committee on Commerce, United States Senate, S.RES.283

Prepared by the White Star Line from its own passenger records, for submission to the Senate Investigators as Exhibit B.

10. Cave List — RG41, Vol 76A, No 14

A copy of the third draft of the 1st class passenger cabin allocations, which was found in the pocket of Cabin Steward Herbert Cave when his body was recovered from the sea.

11. Halifax Arrival Manifest — RG 76, Immigration, Reel No T-4706, National Archives of Canada

Although the ship was never destined for Halifax, Nova Scotia, it was a requirement of the Canadian authorities that, upon arrival in New York, those passengers intending to proceed to Canada should be inspected before being allowed entry. This record contains the names of only the non-Canadians. It seems that, due to the ordeal the passengers had suffered, the requirements for returning Canadians were waived.

12. List of Bodies Identified and Disposition of Same — VK, T53, D63

As each body was recovered, its details were recorded. The list contains the names of passengers and crew but for the purposes of this research, only the passenger names have been transcribed. Added to the names was a note detailing where the body had been buried, or to whom it was released, where each deceased person's effects had been sent and any other remarks.

Lists 10 and 12 are part of the collection held at the Nova Scotia Archives and Records Management Public Archives Site, 6016 University Avenue, Halifax, Nova Scotia B3H 1W4.

Correspondence

Chapter 6, British Records of Deaths at Sea, contains extracts from several files of correspondence in BT100/259, BT100/260, and MT9/920C held at the Public Record Office in Kew, England, concerning the process of compiling an accurate list of passengers. In order to help the reader unravel the various strands running through the correspondence, the following brief explanation may be useful.

An accurate record of passengers on board *Titanic* was required for three different official purposes:

1. To provide a list of deceased passengers (and crew) so that an entry could be made in the Board of Trade's Wreck Register.
2. To provide a list of all passengers as part of the evidence for the forthcoming Board of Trade Inquiry into the accident.
3. To provide a list of all deaths (of passengers and crew) to the Registrar General of Shipping and Seamen to allow him officially to register the deaths.

Although the ultimate responsibility for each of these areas was clearly defined, the means of obtaining the information was less so. Inevitably, each of the main players – the various departments of the Board of Trade, the White Star Line and the Registrar General of Shipping and Seamen – conferred at all times, and the result is a sometimes confusing collection of correspondence. In effect, the compilation of the final record of passengers lost or surviving was a joint effort with each party providing updated information to the others. List C&D in particular was forwarded for correction and update many times before finally being accepted. It was left only to the Registrar General of Shipping and Seamen to sift through all the information and to compile the final record in order to register the deaths.

Chapter 1

The Passengers – 1st Class, 2nd Class & 3rd Class Steerage

B y 1912, with a vast rail network spread throughout the British Isles, large numbers of travellers were routinely transported across the country to or from the major seaports in a relatively short time. Scandinavian and northern European arrivals into any one of Britain's northeastern ports could find themselves in Liverpool in as little as four hours. The frequency of trains from Scotland and the north of England, the West Country or the lesser English Channel ports made travel into central London relatively straightforward. Travellers bound for Southampton Docks, less than two hours down the line, left from the main Central London terminus, Waterloo station.

Passengers booked on steamships scheduled for midday departures from Southampton needed to be at the dockside as early as possible in the morning to enable the necessary formalities to be carried out before boarding. The train carrying *Titanic's* 2nd and 3rd class passengers had left Waterloo station at 7.30am and the 1st class passenger train had steamed away less than two hours later. Passengers travelling some distance had a choice of taking a very early train on the morning of departure, or, more likely, of arriving in the capital the previous day and staying in a hotel for the night. Some are known to have made the trip directly to Southampton the day before departure to give a more leisurely start to the day. The city's South Western Hotel provided comfortable accommodation close to the docks. In London the area around Waterloo station was not the most salubrious in 1912. The station was surrounded by industrial buildings and wharves but, for those who could afford it, the West End with its choice of large good hotels was only a few minutes away by taxicab.

There have never been passenger lists for rail travellers so there is no way of determining exactly how many took the boat trains and how many arrived during the morning at the port having made their own arrangements. A large number of 1st and 2nd class travellers certainly made the almost 80-mile trip from London to Southampton by rail, arriving right at *Titanic's* side in the few hours before departure. The system was no different for *Titanic's* passengers than for any others waiting to board the two or sometimes three trains heading for Southampton Docks – at Waterloo, all luggage was weighed and checked by station staff upon arrival, any excess baggage charges paid,[1] and the bags and trunks labelled to identify those which could be placed in the ship's hold or those required on the voyage.

By the time the 1st class passengers arrived at Waterloo the 2nd and 3rd class travellers were long gone, so there was little opportunity for chance encounters with 3rd class passengers. While formalities for all classes were being completed, the ladies booked in cabin classes were directed to the 1st and 2nd class waiting rooms set aside for their use near to Waterloo's platform 12, where they were able to freshen up, visit the toilets and relax in the warm for the short time until their respective trains were ready for boarding. The rail trip to Southampton took a little less than two hours. Upon arrival at the shipside, the 1st class travellers were escorted from the train, up the gangway and into the ship where the Chief Steward welcomed them.[2] Members of his staff were appointed to escort each party to their staterooms and cabins, and to familiarise them with the bell for summoning cabin service, the bathrooms, the telephone (internal system only) before leaving them to wander around the ship or to watch the crowds of well-wishers waiting on the quay. Those fortunate enough to have menservants and ladies' maids accompanying them would leave them to unpack the trunks, hang their clothes in the wardrobes and generally make their room ready for their return. Pampered from the moment they stepped on board, the 1st class cabin passengers had a dedicated team of hospitality staff at their beck and call. A quiet word or just a glance would bring a steward, hovering discreetly, rushing forward anxious to fulfil their every whim.

The 1st class passengers were accommodated in suites, staterooms or cabins on one of five upper decks,[3] the lower two of which were also shared with 2nd class travellers who, in smaller cabins, were accommodated on one of three decks. All cabin passengers were carefully protected from any possibility of chance contact with 3rd class passengers or crew. There was considerable variation in the prices paid for tickets within each class (the amount each passenger paid for his or her ticket is entered on the White Star Line's Contract Ticket List, discussed in detail in Chapter 5). The price depended upon the exact position within the ship, the number of berths in the cabin and the quality of the internal appointment of the accommodation. Merely holding a 1st class ticket did not automatically guarantee a passenger the degree of opulence that they may have glimpsed through open doors of nearby accommodation. Passengers travelling alone, or on cheaper tickets without a same-sex companion, could be expected to share a cabin with others in similar circumstances. The most expensive 1st class parlour suites, decorated in various period styles: Louis XVI, Renaissance and Queen Anne, were two-bedroomed extensive apartments with en suite bathrooms, separate drawing rooms or dining rooms, all beautifully appointed and richly furnished in polished woods, silks and brocades with a small private promenade deck.[4] Smaller suites, cabins and those for 2nd class passengers, though lacking in size and without the same degree of luxurious appointments, were nevertheless comfortably furnished for both sleeping and relaxing, the decor tasteful and elegant, amply justifying the cost of the ocean ticket and entirely befitting the prestige of travelling in cabin class on this huge vessel.

In the graceful saloons of the 1st class, the well bred and the well heeled rubbed shoulders with the well connected – the cream of British, American and European society. Never was the class system more evident in pre-war Britain than on board these ocean giants. Money talked – not only buying superior cabins but also privilege, exemplary service and gracious company. But among these pampered cabin passengers lay another unwritten class system in which the affluent or titled sought only the company of the very wealthiest and most influential 1st class travelling companions: Benjamin Guggenheim, the Astors, the Strausses and the Wideners among them. Whatever trappings their inherited or acquired wealth may have bought them, it did not buy them freedom. No less trapped in their position in society than their 3rd class counterparts, their regime was strict – be seen in all the right places, with the right people, dressed in the latest fashion. To show the least deviation from the accepted route through the society jungle would mean social suicide. In early April, the 'Season' at an end, the Americans and Canadians who had been visiting Europe began returning home in large numbers to prepare for the coming summer. What better opportunity for them to be seen, to mingle and to parade in the finest and latest French fashion than on board this jewel in the White Star Line's crown?

Dressing correctly was serious business for 1st class cabin passengers, and for ladies especially who brought a vast wardrobe, often far more than they could possibly have required. Rarely could they risk being seen wearing the same outfit twice and dressing for each occasion throughout the day was *de rigueur*. They dressed for breakfast, donning a topcoat and hat for a stroll around the deck afterwards. They dressed for luncheon, changed again for afternoons, which in good weather were often spent swathed in White Star Line rugs in deckchairs on the promenade deck. And they certainly dressed up for dinner – a different evening gown of the very latest Paris couture was a must for each night on board, complete with carefully chosen accessories: shoes, bag, hat, and the finest jewellery. The Cameron movie adhered closely to fashion detail, some of the gowns being antique models dating from 1912, portraying the new line for women: long jackets, straight, slim, ankle-length daywear; lace, satin and beaded slim-line creations with lavish flower corsages for evenings.[5] For men it was a little easier, perhaps not subject to quite the same critical scrutiny as the female passengers – smart lounge suits and shirts with an assortment of silk ties or cravats, dinner suits and warm outerwear, hats and gloves.

If social life on board *Titanic* revolved around being seen correctly attired and in conversation with the most socially acceptable companions, mealtimes on board provided the perfect backdrop. There were two main restaurants on *Titanic* for each class of traveller, together with a smart Parisian-style café, and various lounges where passengers, sipping afternoon tea and being seen, could sit watching the sea slide past.

Cabin class tickets did not necessarily include meals but there was a choice of suitable restaurants offering high-class cuisine for each class of traveller. Days at sea began with tea and toast for 1st class passengers, discreetly served by stewards in the private staterooms. Breakfasts and luncheons were lavish, each comprising many courses, with only a small restriction on choice for 2nd class dining saloon passengers. Dinners were sumptuous affairs, with fine china, crystal glasses and silver cutlery. The wealthiest diners took their evening meal in the exquisitely furnished à la carte restaurant. Private dinner parties could be hosted in the dining rooms of the parlour suites, or in a separate area of the 1st class dining saloon. Captain Smith, who normally dined in the à la carte restaurant, is reported to have attended a dinner party hosted by the Wideners on the evening of the 14 April.[6] The ephemera which survive as the only records now of those few short days aboard *Titanic* allow us to glimpse at the meals served in the dining saloon at luncheon or dinner, and the menus for the à la carte restaurant. The Café Parisien served dainty sandwiches and drinks during the day and cabin passengers could take after-dinner coffee either there or in the graceful reception rooms outside the dining saloons. Meals were served to the children in their staterooms – nice children should be seen but not heard, or so the old adage tells, but in the elegant dining rooms of Edwardian England, they were certainly neither.

Once out of the sight of land passengers turned to the diversions on board in order to while away the time between meals. The sea flat smooth, the weather fine and not uncommonly cold, most cabin class passengers donned overcoat and hat to spend an hour or so strolling around the deck after breakfast. The gymnasium was open early each morning; the surviving photographs[7] show cumbersome and heavy versions of modern-day gym equipment. Those intent on maintaining (or maybe discovering for the first time) a healthy body could receive advice and encouragement from the onboard gymnasium instructor. An energetic hour could be followed by a dip in the classically designed sea-water pool, one of the first to be made available to ocean liner passengers, or a visit to the exotically furnished Turkish baths – segregated between sexes. While the men were thus occupied the women indulged in more genteel pastimes, visiting the library or withdrawing to a quiet corner of the reading and writing room. After luncheon there was more time to wander on deck, doze an hour away in deckchairs with hot drinks to keep the Atlantic chill at bay, or to take tea and toast in the 1st class lounge. A newspaper, *The Atlantic Daily Bulletin*, was published daily in the print shop. It allowed the cabin passengers to keep up with the latest stock market news, racing results and society gossip received by wireless by the Marconi operators, who would also transmit and receive passengers' telegrams. There were deck games for the children, squash for adults, but much time was spent simply socialising in the various public rooms, listening to the orchestras or playing card or board games. Life was lived at a slow and gentle pace, the emphasis upon absolute comfort, luxury and relaxation in the palatial surroundings as this giant among ocean liners sped her way towards America.

Servants – maids, menservants, nursemaids, valets and drivers – accompanied many of the wealthiest passengers on their travel overseas. Often travelling in 2nd class cabins near their employers, more than 30 servants were believed to have been on board but they are not always easy to identify from the passenger lists. In most cases the Board of Trade's passenger list[8] omits their names entirely. The White Star Line's own list records the presence of some as unnamed maids or menservants, but the rest are listed among the other passengers' names with no way of distinguishing them. Most of them shared cabins, and ate in a dining room set aside for their use. When the time came to abandon the ship, most of the female servants survived. Most of the men; the valets, drivers and menservants, perished alongside their employers.

The presence of two groups of cabin class passengers, the orchestra and the postal clerks, caused some considerable confusion when the task began of recording numbers of lives saved and lost. At first it was unclear whether they were to be listed as crew or passengers and the ensuing debate in a series of letters between the Board of Trade and the Registrar of Shipping led to some recalculating and adjustments. It was finally decided that both groups should be included in the passenger figures, so the final numbers for passengers includes both groups of men.

There were two orchestras on board *Titanic* – eight men, all hired from the well-known Liverpool agency, C. W. & F. N. Black, who supplied staff to several shipping companies. All experienced musicians from other ocean liners, they were hired to play as a quintet and a trio. The trio, probably comprising Krins and Bricoux, and a pianist who may have been either Brailey or Taylor, played in the reception area outside the à la carte restaurant for passengers waiting to be seated, or drinking coffee after meals, and at various times in the Café Parisien. The quintet, led by Bandmaster Wallace Hartley, played in the 1st class lounge and the 1st class reception area. The men shared a large cabin and a ticket number. Many survivors reported that the men played to the very end, though the actual melody they were playing will never be finally confirmed. Reports that the men played the old hymn 'Nearer My God To Thee' are confusing; the hymn is traditionally sung to different melodies in America and Britain, but both American and British passengers reported hearing it. Whatever the truth, it seems as though these brave men did continue playing until the very end when all eight lost their lives.

Not only was *Titanic* an emigrant ship, but she was also licensed to carry the mails between her various ports of call. At both Cherbourg and Queenstown the tenders that carried passengers between the ship and the quay also carried sacks of mail. In a joint agreement, signed in 1905, transatlantic mail and passengers' letters carried on White Star Line and American Line ships were sorted at sea by members of the postal services of Britain and America. The five postal clerks on board *Titanic*, three American and two British men, all occupied 2nd class rooms. Shortly after the collision, water began flooding into the mailroom on G Deck where the men were busy sorting mail. Despite their valiant attempts to salvage the valuable registered mail by dragging it up to F Deck their task was impossible. All the mail was lost and none of the five men survived.

Titanic's 3rd class passengers outnumbered those in the two cabin classes by about one hundred. Most were emigrants and most of them boarded the ship in Southampton. With baggage stowed in the luggage compartment several hundred had been shepherded on to the early morning train from Waterloo that had arrived at the dockside shortly before 9.30am. Already gathered was a group of fellow travellers who had arrived during the preceding few days by sea or other rail services into Southampton and who had already spent one or more nights in lodgings or emigrant hostels in the city. As well as approximately 200 British 3rd class travellers gathered in the dock building and waiting for processing, there were almost 300 foreigners. By the time they had been joined later that day and the next by around 100 from Cherbourg and about the same again in Queenstown, their numbers had swelled to a little over 700. Their reasons for being there were many and varied. For some, the lure was the promise of regular, well-paid employment and the opportunity to forge a worthwhile life for themselves and their families. Some were escaping persecution – ethnic, religious and political. To these people America represented the freedom they could never know at home. Many were following in the footsteps of an earlier relative who had paved the way, found a job, a place to live and was often sending good money home. A number of passengers travelled on tickets purchased in advance for them by relatives or friends in America. The urge to join them and share in this land of plenty was often irresistible but the stories of rough Atlantic crossings and people herded like cattle into the bowels of the ships meant that many must have awoken on the morning of 10 April with considerable apprehension about the week which lay ahead.

Passing before the Medical Officer the 3rd class passengers flooded on board through the entrances on C and D Decks to begin the bewildering search for cabins in the maze of corridors below. Hard-pressed stewards struggled to direct non-English-speaking passengers in the right general direction according to the cabin and berth numbers stamped on their inspection cards.[9] Clutching papers, hand baggage and children, pushing through a tide of fellow travellers advancing from the opposite direction while desperately trying to keep the rest of the family in view, eventually all found their allotted accommodation and were then free to explore the 3rd class areas of the ship.

Later that morning, gradually gathering in apprehensive and bewildered groups in the 3rd class lounge on the Shelter Deck were a little under 500 passengers, a melting-pot of nationalities, languages and creeds: British families, Belgians, Bulgarians and Russians; olive-skinned Middle Eastern men and dark-eyed women; fair-haired, blue-eyed Scandinavians; unlikely companions but all united in a common desire for a better life on the other side of the Atlantic. The sight of the light and airy room equipped with tables and comfortable wooden seats in which they now found themselves must have come as an unexpected surprise to many of them but this General Room would soon establish itself as the centre of daytime socialising. Here they would join friends and make new ones, engage in conversation, play with the children and generally pass the time until they reached New York. The children quickly amused themselves capering on the deck among the hawsers and luggage cranes, playing marbles and games of chase. With no organised entertainment, the adults invented their own and James Cameron's vision of laughter, dancing and merrymaking may well not be too far removed from the reality of life in the General Room. For men wishing to escape the clamour, on the opposite side of the ship was the wood-panelled 3rd class smoking room. With its comfortable wooden chairs and tables, it was a male retreat, quiet and peaceful and hung in a permanent blue haze where friendships were forged over a cigarette and a game of cards.

If it had been the White Star Line's intention to establish new standards for 3rd class emigrant travel then it had certainly achieved that with *Titanic* and *Olympic*. Although naturally the 3rd class accommodation nowhere nearly approached the opulence of 1st class or the luxury of 2nd the two ships nevertheless broke new ground in the quality of the accommodation and facilities for 3rd class passengers. They were equipped with accommodation far superior to anything found before on an Atlantic emigrant ship.[10] No longer were all emigrants expected to endure the lack of privacy and the noisy, overcrowded and foetid conditions in the communal steerage quarters of the earliest emigrant ships, though *Titanic* still offered cheap small dormitory-style cabin accommodation for single males. Other cabins were compact but neat and comfortable, reportedly approaching the quality of 2nd class accommodation found on other transatlantic steamers. Sparsely but adequately furnished, they afforded little room for anything but bunks – tiers of two, mostly, brand new of course, with two, four or six to a cabin, and limited space for clothes and belongings. If they were a little cramped they were still clean and cheerful with white paintwork and the floors covered with bright linoleum. Even so there was little reason for the 3rd class passengers to remain in their cabins, and most of the day was spent in the General Room or the Smoke Room, and on deck in the small promenade area at the stern.

There were two 3rd class dining rooms, with two sittings at meal times. Photographs of the identical dining saloons on the *Olympic* show small tables, wooden chairs and crisp white tablecloths, again superior by far to anything they may have found on other transatlantic ships. Food was hearty and wholesome, if sounding a little strange to 21st century palates, and often quite extravagant compared to what some of the less fortunate emigrants were normally accustomed to.

Some passengers may not have been able to avail themselves of the hearty food on offer. However smart the ship, however comfortable the beds and whatever degree of luxury the passengers found themselves in, cabins could be stuffy, airless and claustrophobic. For many decades emigrant ships had been required to have a doctor on board. *Titanic* had a hospital, well equipped to handle most emergencies. There are no reports of the hospital having been used or the doctor being required but undoubtedly a problem for many on board, especially in the first few days, would have been seasickness. Not until later in the 20th century would ships regularly be fitted with stabilisers. *Titanic* certainly was not and, however calm the sea was reported to be by maritime standards, the very fact of being away from dry land, and with the constant throb of her engines, some passengers would have been aware of the crest and trough of every single wave with inevitable consequences. There were several stewardesses on board[11] who could have reassured the seasick passengers but anti-seasickness medication had not been invented in 1912 and beef tea or smelling salts were the only help available.

The suggestion that the 3rd class passengers were locked in at all times is an emotive and rather misleading description if the statement is not qualified by considering it in its historical context. It is certainly true that there were locked gates ensuring that they could not accidentally walk into areas where they could have come into contact with the ladies and gentlemen from the cabin classes. In the class-conscious world of Edwardian Britain few would have thought to question the presence of such gates. Members of the lower class would never have dreamt of daring to mingle with the middle classes let alone the aristocracy. *Titanic's* complement of wealthy passengers demanded not only luxurious accommodation but also peace of mind. Locked gates offered them that security, ensuring that while they were dining and socialising, no steerage passenger with other things in mind than the pattern on the carpet, could wander along the 1st class corridors. It is perhaps pertinent to note that it was not just 3rd class passengers who were restricted in their movements around the ship. The 2nd class passengers were similarly confined to their own areas and were strictly forbidden to enter certain 1st class zones. And of course the same system operates in 1st class and loyalty lounges at airports and railway stations today, though it is more likely to be a vigilant receptionist than a locked door which filters out anyone not entitled to enter. In 1912 on board *Titanic* it is true, however, that the existence of locked gates contributed to the huge loss of life just a few days after leaving Southampton.

Who Sailed on Titanic?

1   Eaton & Haas, *Titanic: Triumph and Tragedy*
2   Hyslop, Forsyth & Jemima, *Titanic Voices*
3   McCluskie, *Anatomy of the Titanic*
4   Marriott, *Titanic*
5   La Couturière Parisienne; www.marquise.de/1900/index.shtml
6   Eaton & Haas, *Titanic: Triumph & Tragedy*
7   McCluskie, *Anatomy of the Titanic*
8   BT27/780B; BT27/776 (PRO, Kew)
9   Sebak, *Titanic, 31 Norwegian Destinies*
10 McCluskie, *Anatomy of the Titanic*
11 BT100/260 (PRO, Kew)

Chapter 2

Transmigrants and Other Alien Passengers

The logistics of transferring over a thousand people along with baggage and supplies from four corners of the British Isles into a passenger liner by a set time on a particular day are awesome. Picture the same scenario happening every day of the week and one begins to appreciate the scale of the task which faced the shipping companies responsible for coordinating the arrangements. A large number of those people were foreigners, many of whom, tired, bewildered and disoriented, had already been travelling for days. Frequently speaking little or no English and at the mercy of anyone who chose to profit from their disadvantage, they were entirely dependent on others to guide them through the maze of bureaucracy standing between the familiar life they had left behind and the strange new world on the opposite side of the ocean.

Clerks working in the ticket offices of the various steamship lines had the huge daily task of entering the names and details for each of these passengers on to British passenger lists, in the format required by the Board of Trade, in the short time between the sale of the tickets and the departure of the ship. Add to this the difficulties they evidently experienced in attempting to decipher foreign names written in unfamiliar handwriting styles, and it requires little imagination to see how the accuracy of the records could be in doubt.

For many years of outbound passenger listing by the British authorities, anyone travelling overseas from Britain had been recorded with the same very basic information – usually only name, age and possibly occupation, and intended place of disembarkation. The only means of identifying the foreign passengers was by the presence of a tick in the column on the list. There was no way of identifying from where they came and whether those concerned were nationals of that country or had simply spent time there.

Legislation was tightened up in the early 1900s. Following the Aliens Act of 1905 and the Merchant Shipping Act of 1906 the information legally required to be entered on all Board of Trade British departure lists was extended. It was now necessary for clerks compiling the lists to include the nationality of the alien passengers (or the country of which they were citizens), and to enter the names in one of two separate sections according to their category. The two categories are set out on each passenger list form and are very distinct.

Category A – Transmigrants. Alien (non-British) passengers (other than 1st class passengers) who arrive in the United Kingdom having in their possession Prepaid Through Tickets and in respect of whom security has been given that they will proceed to places outside the United Kingdom.

This category of foreign passenger included those who had, either by choice or necessity, purchased a ticket for a steamship that departed not from their home country but from the British Isles. Their ticket was a through ticket, usually including the cost of their travel to Britain in order to board the ship, and often onwards later by rail to their final destination. They could stay in Britain only as long as it took them to reach a port such as Liverpool, London or Southampton, where they would embark on their intercontinental voyage on a steamer such as *Titanic*. Transmigrant records are discussed later in this chapter.

Who Sailed on Titanic?

Category B – Non Transmigrants. Alien passengers not included in A.

This category covers any other alien passenger, whether they were emigrating or visiting overseas for whatever purpose and regardless of from where they were travelling. When using British records it is important to note that anyone non-British was recorded as an alien. Any national of a British colony, possession or dominion was recorded as British. That meant that Canadians, Australians, New Zealanders, South Africans and, certainly in 1912 when the atlas was still very 'pink', passengers from various other small countries would be entered on the list as 'British'. Category B aliens also included those passengers who were born British (including Irish-born who often figure strongly in this category) but who had become naturalised citizens of another country, and who had returned to the homeland on a visit. Researchers can sometimes miss the entries of foreign passengers who had been living for a while in a British possession or colony but had not become British citizens. If they were travelling into or through Britain directly from that British colony they were sometimes, though wrongly, entered in the British section of the list.

Most of the (Category B) 1st class alien passengers on board *Titanic* were listed as citizens of the United States of America. As on any other similar passenger list of that era their last place of residence will be given as 'foreign countries' – assumed (perhaps erroneously) to be the United States; and their future intended residence specified as the United States. There is nothing to suggest that they were anything but Americans who had been abroad for a period and were now returning home.

Although without doubt some alien passengers on other ships did emigrate on 1st class tickets, very rarely are they positively identifiable as emigrants. None will appear as Category A transmigrants because it was not a requirement of the Board of Trade that 1st class alien passengers' names should be entered in that section, regardless of whether they may otherwise have at least partially fulfilled the criteria by their possession of pre-paid through tickets. No parallel should be drawn between holders of simple prepaid tickets, and holders of prepaid through tickets. The two classes of ticket were not the same.

Any 1st class alien passenger for whom an entry in Category B suggests that they may have been emigrants must be treated very cautiously. There are four 1st class passengers shown on the Board of Trade passenger list who, without the benefit of later research by others that suggests otherwise, might appear to be candidates for inclusion as 1st class emigrants.

The first two are Stahelin and Simonius. Travelling on 1st class tickets from Southampton they are shown as Germans. For each of them, their last permanent residence was shown as 'foreign countries' which was correct. Their future intended permanent residence was given as the United States, the term 'permanent residence' defined as being for a period of one year or more. For these men, knowing that in both cases their nationality was given as German and without more information, unwary researchers may be lured into assuming that the aforementioned 'foreign countries' meant Germany. In fact these two men were apparently Swiss not German[20], and it seems that they were not intending to remain in New York but were only visiting on business. Therefore their future intended permanent residences probably should not have been entered as the USA, but Switzerland. Later in the Board of Trade list, Bjornstrom-Steffenson is recorded as being Swedish, with his future intended permanent residence as America. He was indeed Swedish but had been working in the United States for some years. Quite correctly, his 'last residence of one year or more' was shown as 'foreign countries' but that was the United States and not, as one might have assumed, Sweden. His future intended permanent residence was also shown as America. He was not therefore a new emigrant; he was purely a non-naturalised resident of the United States returning to his American home. Finally the British passenger list shows Miss Amelia

Seiger, a German woman, last residence 'foreign countries' and future permanent residence again the United States. In fact, Miss Seiger (her first name is spelt in various ways in different documents) was actually Amelia Geiger, maid to Mrs Widener and travelling 1st class to assist her employer during the voyage. Again, she was a non-naturalised resident of the United States returning to America and certainly not an emigrant. Researchers into the passengers on board *Titanic* are fortunate in that a great deal of later research is available for most of these passengers and any assumptions may easily be checked. For anyone researching cases of 1st or any other class of emigration, great care must be taken with what at first may appear to be evidence.

To return to the subject of Category A transmigrant passengers, the new legislation in 1906 now meant that the information required to be shown on passenger lists also included the name of the shipping line that had brought them to Britain and the port into which they had arrived. By the middle of 1907, most pursers had been equipped with the latest style forms. For modern emigration researchers, the new regulations provide a treasure-trove. These regulations mean that today it is at last possible to identify alien passengers with a far greater degree of accuracy than ever before. Patterns of migration unfold. For those tracing immigrant ancestors it is now possible not only to discover the name of the ship carrying them from Britain to their final destination but with a little wider research it is sometimes possible to identify the name of the steamship which had carried them on the first part of their journey with a reasonable degree of accuracy.

There are several popular misconceptions about transmigrants: firstly that these were all 3rd class passengers from Scandinavia, Russia or Eastern Europe bound for the United States and Canada. Most were, but in fact transmigrants could be travelling from and to anywhere in the world: Australia, New Zealand, South Africa or even destinations much nearer to home, perhaps in France or Italy. Nor was *Titanic* particularly unusual in having twenty 2nd class transmigrants on board. Her sister ship, *Olympic*, which departed from Southampton exactly one week earlier,[1] had carried a total of 30. Secondly, not all transmigrants entered Britain on a small North Sea feeder ship or a cross-Channel ferry. Again, they could be travelling from anywhere, and among the transmigrants on *Titanic's* list are 10 men who had arrived into Southampton by ships of the Royal Mail Steam Packet Company. The RMSP Co operated vessels between Britain and South America, calling at various ports in between. Most of the men had boarded in Buenos Aires. Another, Nathan Goldsmith, arrived in Britain on a ship belonging to the Union Castle Steamship Company from South Africa. Admittedly these passengers did not fall into the usual transmigrant stereotype but nevertheless they were just as much transmigrants as all the others who had arrived on feeder ships and ferries. They were alien migrants. It was their type of ticket and the security given that they would not attempt to remain in Britain, that decided their transmigrant status, not their journey. Again, the term 'prepaid through tickets' referred to what would now be called 'package' tickets, combining all their travel, from their origin to their final destination, booked and paid for in one lump sum. The Brown family also travelled from South Africa in order to board *Titanic*. Although their journey was identical in every way to that of Nathan Goldsmith, including the ship bringing them from Cape Town to Southampton, they were British not aliens, so were not classed as transmigrants.

Although there are many exceptions such as those explained above, this indirect method of migration was nevertheless the way in which significant numbers of foreign migrants reached the United States of America and Canada in the 19th and early 20th centuries.

For earlier emigrants from Scandinavia and eastern Europe, the ordeal of an arduous journey often beginning by horse-drawn cart followed by a succession of trains, boats and more trains before a potentially unpleasant ocean passage was physically taxing for the youngest and fittest. For the elderly and the very young the physical and emotional demands were exhausting. Disease and illness spread like wildfire in the crowded and poorly ventilated steerage compartments and those undernourished at the outset of the journey were at serious risk of never actually arriving. On mercifully short North Sea crossings carrying transmigrants between Scandinavia and ports on the north-east coast of England, conditions on some of the ships had been of considerable concern.

Fortunately for the many thousands of passengers carried by these small steamships each year, successive Merchant Shipping Acts[2] introduced increasingly strict regulations governing the care and comfort of emigrants on these relatively short North Sea crossings. Steamship lines became legally required to offer more comfortable facilities and better quality food to their valuable emigrant passengers. Whilst the ships may not have been designed with comfort in mind and although the North Sea can be a cold, rough and hostile stretch of water especially during the winter months by 1912 the crossing had generally become a far less unpleasant experience.

On the Atlantic leg of the emigrants' journey, conditions also gradually improved. Steerage quarters were slowly replaced with dormitory-style accommodation divided between the sexes. By the dawn of the 20th century the White Star Line's latest ships, *Oceanic* and *Celtic* were offering both single-sex dormitories and individual cabins so that families travelling together could stay together.[3] No longer always confined below, there was often the provision of limited public rooms and a small area of deck on which to escape the claustrophobic conditions below, albeit often shared with cables, winches and other gear.

Little research has been undertaken into the subject of indirect migration. The role played by a host of lesser shipping lines which brought these travellers to Britain on the first part of their migration is eclipsed by research into the transatlantic steamship companies. Using only primary source material and the unique evidence obtained from the British Board of Trade passenger list, a great deal of new background material is available for all the transmigrants on board *Titanic*. How did they travel to Britain?

Many of the Scandinavian passengers arrived in the British Isles on board a vessel belonging to the Wilson Line of Hull. The Wilson Line was at the time the largest privately owned shipping line in the world.[4] Its fleet of small North Sea vessels regularly made several voyages each week carrying Scandinavian emigrants across to the port of Hull on Britain's northeast coast. Others arrived on DFDS or Great Eastern Railway ships into Harwich, or aboard one of many cross-Channel ferries making the short sea crossing from Europe into Southampton and Newhaven. A few, as mentioned earlier, had already travelled from the other side of the world to reach Britain and take up their passage on *Titanic*.

Only days before *Titanic* sailed, a coal strike that had devastated the British shipping industry for many weeks, had ended. The strike had not only brought chaos to Britain but also had major repercussions within the shipping industry as a whole. Many ocean liners had been stranded in port, unable to sail for lack of fuel, but also many of the feeder ships were unable to keep to their usual schedules. This posed a huge problem for the shipping lines as passengers were bumped from one ship to another and sometimes to a third. For the agents overseas, the problem was getting the emigrants on to the few surviving feeder ships in time for *Titanic's* departure. Only one Wilson Line ship left Norway for England in early April – the *Oslo*.[5]

Depending on the timetable for their onward journey, emigrants arriving at the east coast ports of Britain were escorted from the port and into the railway station waiting rooms until they were able to board the train taking them to the transatlantic departure port. It was in the shipping line's better financial interests to transfer transmigrant passengers across the country and on to the ship with as little delay as possible, but they usually needed to spend a night or more in a hostel or lodging house, all of which was included in the price of their through tickets. This transit stage would often take several days before the emigrants finally arrived at the steamer's side. By 1912, railway stations at the arrival ports were able to provide at least limited facilities.[6] Emigrants needed shelter from the weather, some kind of heating, and basic washing and toilet facilities whilst waiting for the trains taking them across the country to Liverpool on the west coast. Others travelled south to London or to Southampton, the latter reached via London's Liverpool Street and Waterloo stations. A number of *Titanic's* transmigrant passengers had apparently originally been booked on other ships which were then cancelled due to the coal strike and had begun trickling into Britain as much as 10 days before *Titanic's* departure. Postcards sent home[7] show that they had found themselves in Southampton with several days to spare. The White Star Line had to take responsibility for finding them suitable lodgings for this additional period, and to arrange for them to be fed. With no lodging house records and no railway passenger lists, exactly how many of them were already in Southampton and how many actually were on the boat train on the day of the sailing itself is unknown.

Jewish emigrants arriving in Britain were often cared for by one of the wide network of shelters or Jewish aid societies spread over the country. Although perhaps not approaching the size of London's Poor Jews Temporary Shelter in Mansell Street, Southampton nevertheless had a thriving Jewish community willing to care for Jews in transit, where necessary feeding them, housing them and looking after their spiritual needs until the vessels were ready for boarding. There was no requirement to state religious persuasion on the passenger lists either in Britain or the United States other than the American exclusion of 'polygamists' which was then a euphemism for Muslims and Mormons. This means that identifying specific religious groups on board *Titanic* is not possible with any degree of accuracy although the surnames of some passengers suggest strongly that they were probably Jewish. It seems highly probable that amongst the foreign passengers there were some for whom religious or dietary needs during their travel would have presented a significant problem and a large number may have felt extremely uncomfortable eating the food offered to them each day. Anyone who felt strongly enough about the food or its preparation may simply have had to go hungry if there was nothing suitable on the menu. The only exceptions to that are the Jewish passengers who were specifically catered for on board by the presence of a Jewish chef who prepared kosher food choices at each mealtime.[8]

Titanic's Board of Trade passenger list shows a total of 331 passengers who were recorded as transmigrants. All boarded in Southampton and all but 30 of them travelled as 3rd class passengers. The following chart shows the spread of nationalities, ports of arrival and the steamship line as recorded on the Board of Trade list.

Nationality	3rd Class	2nd Class	Total	Arrival Port	SS Co
Austrian	39	0	39	Southampton	L&SWR
Belgian	21	0	21	Harwich	GER
Bulgarian	31	0	31	Southampton	L&SW R
Danish	33	1	34	Harwich	United SS Co
	0	2	2	Southampton	RMSP Co
Finnish	52	6	58	Hull	Finnish SS Co
French	5	0	5	Southampton	L&SWR
Italian	1	0	1	Southampton	RMSP Co
Norwegian	18	0	18	Newcastle	Norwegian SS Co
	8	1	9	Hull	Wilson

Who Sailed on Titanic?

Nationality	3rd Class	2nd Class	Total	Arrival Port	SS Co
Portuguese	3	0	3	Southampton	RMSP Co
Russian	1	0	1	Southampton	Union Castle
Swedish	23	0	23	Harwich	United SS Co
	65	5	70	Hull	Wilson
Swiss	3	0	3	Southampton	L&SWR
Syrian	4	0	4	Southampton	RMSP Co
Turkish	1	0	1	Southampton	L&SWR
US/USC	0	2	2	Newhaven	LB&SCR
	2	1	3	Harwich	GER
	0	2	2	Hull	Finnish SS Co
	1	0	1	Newcastle	Norwegian SS Co

Southampton Arrivals

The majority travelled on one of the London & South Western Railway's cross-Channel ferries from Le Havre. They may have travelled on the *Normannia* or the *Hannonia*.[9] There are no passenger lists for ferry crossings, and no certain dates of arrival for the passengers travelling on the London & South Western Railway's ferries. However, the ships belonging to the L&SWR travelling from ports in the north of France (Cherbourg, St Malo or Le Havre) into Southampton in early April 1912 were: *Laura*, *Lydia*, *Princess Ena*, *Normannia* and *Hannonia*.[10]

Not all the Southampton arrivals travelled on that cross-Channel route. Ten passengers arrived into Southampton on the Royal Mail Steam Packet Company ship *Aragon*, which reached Southampton on 6 April.[11]

Newcastle Arrivals

A total of 22 transmigrants arrived at Newcastle on board ships of the Norwegian Steamship Company. All were Norwegians, though one had become a United States' citizen and had only been home to visit his family, so should not have been included.

Harwich Arrivals

A total of 81 transmigrants arrived at Harwich on a vessel belonging to one of two different shipping lines – a Great Eastern Railway steamer from Rotterdam, Antwerp or the Hook of Holland, or a vessel of the United Steamship Company (DFDS).

Ships of the Great Eastern Railway Company travelling into Harwich from Rotterdam, Antwerp and the Hook of Holland in April 1912 were: *Colchester*, *Amsterdam*, *Vienna*, *Dresden*, *Brussels*, *Copenhagen* and *St Petersburg*.[12]

A total of 21 Belgian transmigrants travelled across the North Sea this way, and further research may in the future pinpoint exactly which vessels they used. The United Steamship Company (DFDS) ships travelled from Denmark to Harwich or Parkeston, and in April 1912 the 23 Swedish, 34 Danish and 3 United States' citizens boarding the *Titanic* travelled on one of the following vessels: *Riberhuus*, *Nidaros*, *Viking*, *N. J. Fjord*, *Ficaria*, *Primula*, *Eos*, *Frejr*, *Tyr* and *J. C. La Cour*.[13]

Hull Arrivals

By far the greatest number of transmigrants arrived at the port of Hull – a total of 139 is recorded on the Board of Trade passenger list though that figure must be reduced by three in the light of later research. Seventy of them were Swedish. They, along with the nine

Norwegians, travelled on a Wilson Line steamer. The remaining 60 transmigrants were Finnish, including two United States' citizens, and travelled on a ship of the Finnish Steamship Company.

The effect of the coal strike upon the schedules of all North Sea feeder ships is open to further research.The Board of Trade list is apparently in error regarding at least 10 of the transmigrants. Per Kristian Sebak discovered that two reported on the Board of Trade list as having arrived at Newcastle on a Norwegian Steamship Company vessel actually arrived at Hull on a Wilson Line ship, and five reported to have arrived on a Wilson Line ship actually arrived at Newcastle on a Norwegian Line ship.[14]

Two men are recorded as transmigrants arriving in Newhaven on a cross-Channel ferry belonging to the London, Brighton and South Coast Railway. In fact, neither man should have been recorded in that section. The first man, Rene Levy, was French but had recently emigrated to Canada. The Board of Trade list erroneously records him as a United States citizen but does not list his future intended place of permanent residence. The second man was Edwin Wheeler, a British man from Bath, who had been valet to George W. Vanderbilt for some years. His nationality was also shown as American, and again no details of his future intended place of permanent residence was shown. He had recently been in France with the Vanderbilts. They had returned to the United States from Cherbourg on the *Olympic* one week before *Titanic's* departure. Reports that they cancelled their own *Titanic* passage at the last minute (as stated in the New York press) are probably untrue. There is no sign of any ticket transaction in their name (although the same can be said for others). It seems most likely that while they may have toyed with the idea of sailing on *Titanic*, this did not extend actually to purchasing tickets. Edwin Wheeler is believed to have taken charge of the car and most of their baggage. It seems that he may well have left his employers at Cherbourg and taken the ferry crossing to Britain, motoring down to Bath to visit his family for a few days before returning to Southampton where he boarded *Titanic*.

The passenger list for the Royal Mail Steam Packet vessel *Aragon*, which had brought several of *Titanic's* transmigrants into Southampton on 6 April, adds a little more to the information already known about them. With all spellings shown exactly as they appear on the Board of Trade arrival list, which may not always be identical with the way they are shown on *Titanic's*, these men are not recorded as transmigrants on the arrival list, as they almost certainly should have been.

Hans Christensen Givard, a farmer in the Argentine was shown as Danish. Also boarding in Buenos Aires was Martin Ponesell, another Dane, this time a blacksmith from the Argentine.

Usually recorded as Syrian, and about whom little has so far been published, was another group of transmigrants from Buenos Aires on the same ship: Assam Ali, 23; Abdla Asim, 35; Amed Ali, 24; and William Ali, 25. All four men were labourers who had been working for at least a year in Argentina and whose nationalities were all shown on the arrivals list as Turkish.

The Board of Trade arrivals list for the *Aragon* gives strangely contradictory information about Luigi Finoli, a 40-year-old American businessman. Most research suggests that he had been in America for some time, and had recently been visiting family in Italy[21], but the arrivals list for the *Aragon* shows that he actually embarked in Buenos Aires, and that his last place of permanent residence had been the Argentine. If he was returning to America from Italy, it is hard to see how he came to be aboard the *Aragon*. Whatever the truth, it seems that he probably should not have been included in the Transmigrant section of *Titanic's* list, thereby reducing the number of transmigrants by one. Also on board were Jose Jardim Netto, 21, Fernando Domingos Coelho, 20 and Goncalves Lanislav, 38. All three men were Portuguese labourers who had boarded the ship together in Madeira.

The Board of Trade list had shown that the transmigrants arrived at one of five British ports. With the figures adjusted accordingly to take into account all of this later research and notwithstanding the inconclusive status of a minority of the supposed transmigrants, the numbers of transmigrants arriving into each of only four ports now reads as follows:

Southampton	89
Newcastle	21
Hull	136
Harwich	81
Total	327

Alien Non-Transmigrant Arrivals into Britain

Using only the Board of Trade passenger departure list for *Titanic*, there is no way of knowing how the alien non-transmigrant passengers arrived in Britain. However, research in other Board of Trade passenger lists sheds new light on how some of them arrived to join *Titanic*, offering a small amount of additional information.

Nathan Goldsmith, a transmigrant, had arrived into Southampton on 5 April on board the Union Castle Line ship, *Garth Castle*[15] with a through ticket to Philadelphia. Among his travelling companions were two other names familiar to *Titanic* researchers: Simon Sather, shown as a 40-year-old miner, had apparently been living in South Africa for a period of at least 12 months, and Francisco Celotti, a 25-year-old fitter, previously believed to have spent time in London, was also on the ship. Interestingly, Francisco Celotti had a through ticket to San Francisco so possibly should have been in the Transmigrant section of *Titanic's* list.

Arriving on the Hamburg South American line ship, *Cap Arcona*[16] on 4 April, were the two Uruguayan Carran brothers, Francisco and Jose travelling from Buenos Aires.

Disembarking from the P&O steamship *Commonwealth*[17], were the hotelier T. W. S. Brown, and his wife and daughter. They had boarded in Cape Town, and disembarked in Plymouth on 1 April from where they would probably have taken a train to Southampton, rather than travelling directly into London.

Also arriving from South Africa on board a Union Castle ship, this time the *Kenilworth Castle*[18], was another group of *Titanic's* passengers. Anthony Abbing, shown as a 41-year-old blacksmith, an American citizen living in the Transvaal for the previous 12 months or more; Samuel Greenberg, a 51-year-old Russian merchant from the Cape Colony; and Moses Troupiansky, a 23-year-old Russian again from the Transvaal all disembarked on 6 April.

The Royal Mail ship *Aragon*, which brought 10 of *Titanic's* transmigrants, also brought Einar Windelin [sic], a 21-year-old Danish labourer who had spent at least the previous 12 months living in the Argentine. Much of this information differs slightly from what has previously been believed about some of the non-transmigrant passengers, sometimes clarifying exactly how long they had been in Britain before sailing on *Titanic*.

There is one further interesting passenger on board the *Aragon*. When *Titanic* arrived in Cherbourg, among the passengers disembarking was a passenger known only as Mr Brand.[19] With no other details whatsoever apparently known about this man, research has up to now proved very difficult. The passenger arrival list for the *Aragon* shows a passenger named as Carl Birger Brand, a teacher aged 41 from Sweden who had been living in Argentina for at least a year. His future intended permanent place of residence is noted only as 'Foreign Countries' but with the full name of this passenger known, it opens up an avenue to new research to discover if he is the hitherto mysterious Mr Brand.

Chapter 2

More of *Titanic's* non-transmigrant alien passengers may be lurking within the pages of other Board of Trade passenger lists. With the lists unindexed, the search to find them could be a long one.

1   BT27/780A (PRO, Kew)
2   Merchant Shipping Acts, 1894, 1906
3   Taylor, *The Distant Magnet*
4   Evans, 'Indirect Passage from Europe. Transmigration via the UK, 1836-1914', *Journal for Maritime Research,* June 2001
5   Sebak, *Titanic, 31 Norwegian Destinies*
6   Evans, 'Indirect Passage from Europe. Transmigration via the UK, 1836-1914', *Journal for Maritime Research,* June 2001
7   Sebak, *Titanic, 31 Norwegian Destinies*
8   BT100/260 (PRO, Kew)
9   Hyslop, Forsyth & Jemima, *Titanic Voices*
10 BT26/640 (PRO, Kew)
11 Finch, *Fleet Histories*
12 Finch, *Fleet Histories*
13 Finch, *Fleet Histories*
14 Sebak, *Titanic, 31 Norwegian Destinies*
15 BT26/540 (PRO, Kew)
16 BT26/540 (PRO, Kew)
17 BT26/532 (PRO, Kew)
18 BT26/540 (PRO, Kew)
19 White Star Line Contract Ticket List, NRAN-21-SDNYCIVCAS-5512791 (National Archives and Record Administration, New York City)
20 Encyclopedia Titanica, 1st class passenger Col Oberst Alfons Simonius-Blumer http:/www.encyclopedia-titanica.org/bio/p/1st/simonius_blumer_a.shtml
21 Encyclopedia Titanica, 3rd class passenger Luigi Finoli http:/www.encyclopedia-titanica.org/bio/p/3rd/finoli_l.shtml

Chapter 3
Cherbourg and Queenstown Passengers

During 9 and 10 April 1912 approximately 100 3rd class emigrants from across Europe and beyond arrived in straggling groups at the Gare St Lazare, the central Paris terminus for trains to the Atlantic coast ports. There were a handful of French nationals but many, exhausted and disoriented, had already endured days of arduous travel from as far away as the Balkans and the Middle East. Shepherded on to the boat train by Paris agents,[1] they headed for the port of Cherbourg, six hours to the northwest of Paris. Early arrivals would have been forced to find rooms in the busy port. Not until around 10 years after *Titanic's* sailing did the Hôtel d'Atlantique appear. Situated close to the docks, the much needed emigrant hotel was purpose built and funded by the main steamship lines to whom these passengers represented a lucrative trade.

Once at Cherbourg's Gare Maritime, in common with the increasing tide of emigrants using northern French ports, they were herded from the train and into the port building, where they underwent a brief medical check. Just as for the several hundred emigrants who boarded *Titanic* in Southampton, the shipping lines were financially responsible for the safe return home of any emigrant not considered acceptable for residency and who was consequently turned away by the United States immigration authorities. Poor health or disease were two of the main reasons for being refused entry at New York's emigrant arrival building on Ellis Island.

Although there is no documentary evidence to prove it, it would seem logical for the White Star Line to have operated the same system of recording passengers for the Cherbourg embarkations as it did for those boarding in Southampton and Queenstown. The names of passengers arriving at the dockside would first have been checked off on the shipping line's list of passengers. Assuming that all the paperwork was in order and they passed the doctor's close scrutiny, they would then have been given their travel documents and allowed to pass through into the dockside waiting rooms to await the arrival of the ship. The Cherbourg section of the White Star Line's list would probably have also been produced in the White Star Line's Southampton offices (see Chapter 5) and would have accompanied the ship to France in the care of the Purser. Some 274 passengers are believed to have boarded in Cherbourg, 142 1st class, 30 2nd class, and 102 3rd class. Although this was a far more manageable number for double-checking on the shipping line's lists, most of the 3rd class passengers neither spoke nor understood either English or French. The assorted ethnic naming patterns for many of these travellers meant that the entries on the passenger list may not have agreed at all with the passengers' papers. Often, the order in which the names were written alternated: first name followed by last name, or last name then first name, making identification slow and potentially confusing for the White Star Line's French staff.

Most of the 1st class and many of the 2nd class passengers were returning Americans and Canadians. Some had broken their journey in Paris,[2] and others had spent a night in one of several respectable hotels in Cherbourg. The majority of *Titanic's* wealthiest and most influential passengers boarded at the French port, including the Astors, Benjamin Guggenheim, Mrs Drake Cardeza, Sir Cosmo Duff Gordon and his elegant fashion designer wife, both of whom were travelling under assumed names, and the woman who later came to be known as the 'unsinkable Molly Brown', Margaret, the wife of a Colorado mining dollar billionaire. Segregated from the 2nd class and avoiding all contact with 3rd, they also watched and waited as dusk fell on the cool night. *Titanic*, delayed an hour following an incident in Southampton, anchored off Cherbourg a little after 6.30pm.

The French authorities did not systematically maintain records of all passengers leaving through French ports and very few survive.[3] Responsibility for the compilation of records of passengers arriving or departing lay almost entirely with the shipping companies and was for their use alone. Once the lists had served their immediate purpose most shipping lines saw no use for them and they were apparently discarded. There are no documentary records in any French archives relating to the embarkation by name of any of *Titanic's* Cherbourg passengers. Although *Titanic* was a British ship, neither was there any requirement for the names of passengers boarding in Cherbourg to be entered on the British Board of Trade list, which is discussed in detail in Chapter 4. The result is that without any official list compiled by a government department in either Britain or France for those who embarked at Cherbourg there is no way of cross-referencing the entries on the French section of the White Star Line's own passenger records. Almost a century later, extensive research by other *Titanic* scholars suggests, however, that the records of the White Star Line are essentially correct, although some question marks still remain.

The White Star Line had established a presence in Cherbourg as long ago as 1907 but although Cherbourg was a deep-water port long accustomed to handling transatlantic emigrant vessels, the quay was not long enough to accommodate the large *Olympic* Class ships. This, combined with the rapidly increasing numbers of transatlantic European emigrants using the White Star Line, persuaded the company to order two *transbordeurs* (tenders) specifically for boarding passengers at Cherbourg. The smaller tender, *Traffic*, and the larger *Nomadic*, both built at Harland and Wolff's shipyard in Belfast, entered service for the White Star Line in 1911. *Traffic* was lost during World War 2, but *Nomadic*, although altered, still bears some tell-tale signs of her White Star Line origins. She is currently berthed on the River Seine, in Paris.[4] Although now abandoned and deteriorating, she has had a busy and colourful career, ending her working life as a select floating restaurant near the Eiffel Tower. She now bears the scars of a severe gale in the French capital some years ago, and a great deal of work is needed in order to restore her to her former condition. At the time of writing, a campaign has been mounted to bring her back to Belfast for restoration as a floating museum but the latest information suggests that that is unlikely to happen. She is currently a virtual prisoner, riding too high in the water to allow her to pass under the low bridges of the Seine and there are grave fears that her hull may no longer be strong enough to support the ballast required to lower her. Sadly it seems that the future is bleak for *Nomadic*, the last surviving vessel of the White Star Line's fleet.

Nomadic was the first of the two tenders to reach *Titanic*, bringing ashore a number of cross-Channel passengers. The exact number of passengers who disembarked at Cherbourg that evening is uncertain but up to 24 has been quoted. Although they all boarded at Southampton both the Board of Trade passenger list and its corresponding summary sheet show only six passengers bound for Cherbourg. In most cases, only very brief information is given about these cross-Channel passengers, generally too little to allow positive identification, so this discrepancy in numbers is unlikely ever fully to be resolved.

Upon *Nomadic's* return to the quay, the cabin passengers prepared to make their way on board. *Traffic* followed shortly afterwards carrying the 3rd class passengers, the baggage and the mails. A little more than 90 minutes after her arrival in the French port, *Titanic* gave three blasts on her whistle, gently turned and set off for Queenstown.

Further wide discrepancies have been revealed between the White Star Line's passenger records and the official Board of Trade passenger list regarding the numbers on board when *Titanic* arrived off the French coast including, as previously mentioned, the exact number who had booked cross-Channel passages. This, together with the problems of accurately identifying many of the non-English-speaking passengers believed to have embarked at Cherbourg, meant that from the moment *Titanic* sailed from Cherbourg on her way to embark her final documented 120 passengers at Queenstown, no one can be absolutely certain of the exact number or names of all the passengers then on board.

A little before lunch, the 120 or so passengers waiting and watching at Queenstown's Pierhead were finally rewarded with the breathtaking view of *Titanic's* arrival in the shimmering waters of Cork Bay. Too large for Queenstown's harbour, she dropped anchor two miles out, but even at that distance she would have seemed huge to the crowds who had been gathering to watch her arrival. Wasting no time, the two Queenstown tenders, *America* and *Ireland*, steamed out to collect the mails and the small party of passengers disembarking there.[5] One of this group of passengers arriving at the Pierhead was a young priest, Francis Browne, whose unique collection of photographs of the ship at sea have since been published as the 'Father Browne collection', thus earning him a permanent place in history. As with passengers reportedly booked from Southampton to Cherbourg, the number of passengers recorded as having booked from Southampton to Queenstown is very different from the number of passengers named on the Board of Trade list which records one only – Mr E. Nichols. The White Star Line's Contract Ticket List shows that six tickets were purchased by a Mr Odell, but the identities of the travellers are not shown. Odell is believed not to have travelled, and it is understood that Father Browne was a member of the party, along with Mrs Odell and other relatives.

Ireland's railway network was extensive by 1912,[6] and many of *Titanic's* Irish passengers would have travelled by train from towns and villages across the country during the course of that morning and the previous day. Most of the passengers embarking for America were 3rd class, along with a small number of 2nd class. There were no recorded transmigrants, although one passenger is noted to be 'in transit' on the White Star Line Contract Ticket List, but that statement is unqualified. All except 11 (allowing for a handful of names crossed through) were recorded as British, with their last place of abode shown as Ireland. The 11 others were all recorded as American citizens but again with the last place of abode (by which was understood to be for the preceding 12 months or more) being Ireland. Later research by others suggests that most if not all of these 3rd class United States citizens were of Irish origin and had been spending time back in Ireland visiting family and friends. Each went through the same process of purchasing tickets, fulfilling criteria, and passing the medical inspection before being allowed to proceed. Among them was the tragic Rice family – the recently widowed Margaret and her five excited little boys who had been living in Ireland for the two years since Margaret's husband had died, all of whom were to lose their lives a few days later.

In accordance with regulations discussed in detail in Chapter 4, there is no surviving British Board of Trade arrivals list showing the names of passengers disembarking in Queenstown because the ship's voyage had not originated in a port outside Europe and therefore this was not required. The five pages of names partly comprising the Queenstown list contain their own fair selection of errors and anomalies. As mentioned earlier, several of the passengers recorded as disembarking in Ireland do not appear on the original Southampton list as having boarded there, while some passengers appear on both the Southampton and the Queenstown sections. Later research apparently suggests, for example, that the Minahan family boarded in Queenstown but they are listed in the Southampton section.[8]

As the two tenders ferried passengers back and forth between the ship and the Pierhead, the usual flotilla of tiny Queenstown bumboats joined them carrying enterprising Irish traders and laden with items for sale: finely woven Irish woollen cloths and delicate lace. The traders climbed on board the ship to conduct their business with well-practised patter, while local photographers scrambled for the best shot.[7] By 1.30pm on that April afternoon, with the Irish mail for New York loaded, and all passengers safely on board, *Titanic* slowly turned and set sail for disaster.

1   Destrais, *Le Titanic à Cherbourg*
2   BT334/52 Register of Deaths of Passengers at Sea (PRO, Kew)
3   Research, Bruce McNair
4   Destrais, *Le Titanic à Cherbourg*
5   Eaton & Haas, *Titanic: Triumph and Tragedy*
6   Railway Preservation Society of Ireland; http://website.lineone.net/~rpsi/rpsiir.htm
7   Eaton & Haas, *Titanic – Destination Disaster*
8   Encyclopedia Titanica 1st Class Passenger Dr William Edward Minahan http://www.encyclopedia-titanica.org/bio/p/1st/minahan_we.shtml

Chapter 4
The British Board of Trade Passenger List

B ritain first began keeping records of passengers departing from or arriving into the country by ship early in the 19th century. As the numbers of emigrants sailing to North America, South Africa, Australia, New Zealand and other developing countries across the world increased, there was a clear need for the British government to keep an accurate written account of passenger movements in and out of the country. The amount of information shown was variable. By the end of the 19th century, the names and brief details of all passengers, regardless of nationality, who passed through British ports, were recorded. The numbers of men, women and children on each ship were counted and the totals entered on to a separate recapitulation sheet, summarised on the final sheet of each list. The government statisticians later checked the figures against the lists and compiled their own records. The raw material was then filed, boxed and archived for future reference. There is little evidence to suggest that the lists were ever used again by the Board of Trade and for many years they lay unused and unseen. They were eventually deposited along with other Board of Trade records in the British national archives at the Public Record Office in Kew, where the descendants of these travellers are free to rummage through the boxes in a desperate search for their 'roots'.

Whilst elegantly clad cabin passengers dined off china plates with silver cutlery and crystal glasses, smoked, read and socialised in the lofty saloons of the transatlantic steamers, it was no picnic for 3rd class passengers on the earliest emigrant ships crossing the Atlantic or bound for Australia. Once on board, they were herded like cattle down into the stifling and reeking atmosphere of the steerage compartment. This area of the vessel was set aside for the machinery and equipment required for steering the ship, hence their being frequently referred to as the 'steerage passengers'. These poor unfortunates often warranted no more than a simple head-count to show how many were present on departure and subsequent landing. Many early passenger records, even including a few from the enlightened years at the dawn of the 20th century, list only the cabin passengers by name, adding the total number of steerage passengers almost as an afterthought.

To the Statistical Department of the Board of Trade only the numbers mattered. The identities did not count. Each successive Merchant Shipping Act amended the required information slightly until, by the early 1920s, sufficient biographical information was included about the British passengers on board, regardless of their class of travel, to allow positive identification of many passengers 80 or more years after they sailed. Unfortunately the amount of information required to be shown for the foreign passengers of any class never quite caught up so there will frequently be an element of doubt when attempting to identify anyone without an unusual name in the aliens' section of any list. By the late 1950s so many passengers were travelling by air that there seemed little point in continuing to keep track of the numbers and identities of ship passengers so in 1960 the last list was compiled, and the final box closed.

By the time *Titanic* sailed in 1912 the regulations governing the compilation of passenger lists were well defined. All surviving lists are held by the Public Record Office at Kew but the collection of lists dating from before 1890 was heavily weeded in the early years of the last century.

The lists are filed in one of two classes as follows: *BT26 – Passenger Lists, Inwards,*

Chapter 4

1878–88 and 1890–1960, and *BT27 – Passenger Lists, Outwards, 1890–1960.* The first of these gives the names of all passengers arriving at ports in the United Kingdom on ships whose voyages began at ports outside Europe and the Mediterranean Sea. Names of passengers who boarded these ships at European ports and disembarked in the UK are included. The second series gives the names of all passengers leaving from UK ports on ships whose eventual destinations were ports not in Europe or the Mediterranean Sea. Names of passengers who disembarked at European ports from these ships are included.

In each class, passenger lists for ships whose voyages both began and ended within the United Kingdom, Europe and the Mediterranean Sea are not included. These lists were originally kept for a period of only three weeks before being destroyed.

Within each of the above two classes, the passenger lists are filed in large boxes. They are arranged chronologically in annual sequences and then by port of departure or arrival. This filing system is not ideally suited for searching by today's generation of ancestor seekers. The decision governing the way in which they were to be filed was determined by the Statistical Department of the Board of Trade[1] many years ago, who may be forgiven for assuming then that they were the only ones likely ever to need to refer to the passenger lists. Little could they have foreseen that the genealogy bug would infect the world, and these old documents would suddenly become the focus of such great attention. The lists are unwieldy and fragile, and there are no effective finding aids. As a result of the eagerness, impatience or pure carelessness of many searchers the lists are now suffering badly from mishandling. Short of withdrawing all of them, there is little hope for their safe survival unless drastic action is taken to repack them into an order more suitable for easy searching. While there is no (yet traced) instruction explaining the original filing system it must be supposed to have been originally intended that they should be filed in numerical order. The Statistical Department of the Board of Trade was subsumed by other departments many years ago and the department now having responsibility for the lists advises that a change in the system would require a decision by Parliament and in reality therefore is unlikely to happen in the foreseeable future.

The Board of Trade passenger list for *Titanic* is more correctly two individual passenger lists, one for passengers boarding in Southampton and another for those embarking in Queenstown. Collectively it is the single most important record of passengers aboard *Titanic* held in British archives. However, despite the value of the unique information it contains, until recently it has apparently been overlooked in favour of the White Star Line's own passenger list.

By the time *Titanic* sailed, the British government's procedures for the compilation of accurate statistics showing the volume of passengers travelling the world via British ports had been well established for many years. From the ticket agents at the beginning of the chain, through the shipping line clerks responsible for entering details of ticket sales, and ending with the pursers who checked passengers on board, the emphasis was upon accurately recording passenger names. Once the ship had sailed taking with it one copy of the list for the purser's use, the second copy of the list recording those on board was sent to the offices of the Board of Trade where the next process began of transcribing the statistical data in preparation it for publication. It was a finely tuned system, with each stage depending upon the accuracy of the information provided by the previous stage. If the system broke down at any point in the process, for example if data were wrongly entered, names omitted, booking cancellations not deleted, then the system would collapse and there would be no way of determining exactly who was on board or who failed to sail. If this scenario seems familiar, it is because that is precisely what happened in *Titanic's* case.

The Board of Trade considered, and not without justification, that passenger lists were accurate representations of those who sailed on a particular ship on a particular day. The last sheet of each list at this time required both the ship's Master and each port's Emigration Officer to sign the following statement: 'We hereby Certify that the above is a correct List of the Names and Descriptions of all the Passengers who embarked at the Port of ... [Southampton in *Titanic's* case].' The same confirmation was repeated at each of the ship's ports of call until it left British waters. If the Board of Trade's own passenger list for *Titanic* is therefore such a valuable source for the identification of those who sailed on board, how could it have been apparently overlooked for so long?

Could it really have been simply forgotten, or was there some other reason why it was not used in the investigations following the sinking? If the Board of Trade considered it to be valuable and the government relied so firmly upon its statistics, then why was it filed away in a box in the archives of the Board of Trade for so many years without ever seeing the light of day? Why has the public been largely unaware of its existence for almost a century? Certainly the information it contains regarding a considerable number of passengers is distinctly at odds with that contained elsewhere. Could it be that despite the tight regulations governing its compilation it proved to contain too many errors to be of any use at all for the purpose of an investigation? Errors in the recording of information on individual passengers on a Board of Trade list would result in errors in the statistics extracted from that list. If the passenger list were shown to be seriously flawed, the government's figures would be proven unreliable with the possibility of considerable public embarrassment.

The real reason for the apparent silence surrounding the Board of Trade passenger list is probably very much simpler. It has been largely overlooked for all these years almost certainly because of a very significant omission. It contains only the names of those passengers who boarded in Southampton and Queenstown. Fully in accordance with Board of Trade requirements, it does not include the names of those who embarked in Cherbourg. Nor does it contain the names of any possible passengers who were already on board when the ship left Belfast. That information is available only from the records of the shipping line itself.

Using their own records of ticket sales, and cancellations or berths not taken up for any reason, the White Star Line compiled its own list of passengers' names and details. Once its own records were complete, it copied the names and any other information required by the British government on to the Board of Trade passenger sheets. Because both of these documents were apparently compiled from the same source material (see later), not only should both sets of names be correct but should differ only in the absence of the Cherbourg passengers from the Board of Trade's passenger list. The White Star Line's list[2] also included the cabin allotment and went through at least three drafts prior to the sailing. A few pages of the third draft of the 1st class list were found in the pocket of a saloon steward, Herbert Cave, when his body was recovered from the Atlantic. That list is now known as the Cave List and is held in the Provincial Archives of Nova Scotia, Canada.[3]

The Board of Trade list was unwieldy, with many over-sized sheets. A great deal of the unique additional information it contains would have been superfluous for the immediate purpose of establishing who had been on board at the time of the sinking, so it was therefore perfectly logical that the White Star Line's own briefer and more compact compilation would be given precedence over any other in the haste to identify every passenger on board *Titanic*. Very probably nobody ever examined the Board of Trade list closely enough in 1912 to discover that it contained many discrepancies and its accuracy certainly seems never to have been called publicly into question.

Back in London at the offices of the Statistical Department of the Board of Trade, with nobody showing any interest in it for the purposes of either Inquiry, *Titanic's* passenger list assumed no greater significance, and received no different treatment from any other list. The clerks painstakingly extracted the numbers of men, women and children recorded in the summary as having sailed, numbered the list in blue crayon, boxed it up along with all the other lists from April 1912 and archived it. The records were closed to the public in those days so if the authorities did not request sight of it and contemporary scholars did not cite it then it is hardly surprising that this valuable document simply passed into oblivion.

The Public Record Office in Kew is the repository for government departmental records, archived for safekeeping, to which the general public is given supervised access under secure conditions. When, many years after the sinking, the Board of Trade's archives were deposited at the Public Record Office, the two boxes containing *Titanic's* Southampton and Queenstown passenger lists were placed in the stacks along with all the others and became available to the public. As hobby genealogy increased in popularity, so the interest in tracing emigrant ancestors grew. The boxes of documents became more heavily used and inevitably, before long, the two *Titanic* lists surfaced. Despite the passing of time, fascination with the ship had barely waned at all, so the discovery of the two lists with their detailed information could have been a breakthrough for the many *Titanic* scholars but still their value seems not to have been fully appreciated. During the following years the Southampton section was roughly handled and suffered considerable damage to the pages. The shorter and therefore less handled Queenstown list remains in relatively good condition to this day. At some point, its value as an historical document finally realised, the Southampton list was removed from its box, restored and bound into a slim cardboard folder. It was then returned to the fray where it continued to be manhandled until the middle of 1998 when, in sudden apprehension of coach loads of film fans descending upon the PRO demanding to view it following the success of the Cameron movie, all documents relating to the incident were suddenly and hurriedly withdrawn from public access. The expected hordes swooped instead on Hollywood movie memorabilia and were largely uninterested in the real life material. In any event these fragile records, together with most other documents related to the incident in British archives, have deservedly been withdrawn from normal public access. The majority of them have been filmed and that is the only way they may now be viewed by the public.

What makes these two lists so immensely significant? Firstly, because although they do not include those passengers boarding in Cherbourg as already explained, the Board of Trade's stated intention was that they should be a precise and accurate listing of the people who actually sailed on *Titanic* from Southampton and Queenstown. This may or may not differ from the shipping line's own passenger list, or the Contract Ticket List showing ticket sales (which is discussed in Chapter 5) but that was of no consequence whatsoever to the Board of Trade. It was interested only in knowing who actually sailed, and not those who merely bought tickets. Secondly, the lists name the shipping line and the port of arrival for the alien transmigrants. This vital new evidence allows anyone researching those passengers to discover very easily, with the added help of other records, the method by which an alien passenger travelled from their home port into Britain. *Titanic's* list was not singled out for this special inclusion. The Aliens Act of 1905 had required more detailed information to be gathered concerning the alien transmigrants. The regulations were swiftly implemented and apart from some confusion during the transition stage before all the shipping lines received the new style forms, all lists dating from the end of 1906 or early 1907 should give this valuable additional information.

Compiling the British Passenger List
Anyone researching into the operations of the White Star Line or those of its agents in Britain and overseas is considerably hampered by the loss of the shipping company's own

archive. When the White Star Line was taken over by the Cunard Steamship Company in 1934, all the company's papers were reportedly destroyed. Certainly there appear to be no surviving records to shed light on the ticketing processes so one can only rely upon the clues gleaned from close examination of passenger lists, correspondence and other documents relating to the White Star Line and other major shipping lines both in Britain and overseas.

Once tickets had been purchased through any one of dozens of ticket agencies or offices of the steamship lines, the names and personal details of the prospective passengers were sent to the office of the shipping line. Exactly by what method the details were sent is not clear. The information may lie as yet undiscovered in the archives of shipping lines or telegraph offices but no procedure manuals appear to have survived to explain the process. What is certain, however, is that a large amount of vital information had to reach the offices of the steamship companies from scores of ticket agents situated across the world, reliably and in good time. The Board of Trade list had to be completed, and the shipping line needed to know passenger details for its own records, cabins had to be allocated, and arrangements made with suppliers to ensure the provisions were adequate. Board of Trade passenger lists were frequently signed and delivered to the port office one or two days in advance of the ship's departure. *Titanic's* Southampton list was signed by Captain Smith and the Emigration Officer, and stamped upon receipt in the office on 9 April, one whole day before the ship sailed and before any passengers had arrived at the quayside. One reason for the Captain putting his signature to the list was to confirm its accuracy, but if it was delivered 24 or even 48 hours before sailing, it could not necessarily be so unless the authorities were notified separately of last minute changes. Clearly they often were not.

Elias Johannesen Engesaeter, a young Norwegian, was booked to sail on *Titanic* and arrived in Newcastle two days before the liner was due to depart. Somewhere on the rail journey between Newcastle and Southampton, Elias was taken ill with appendicitis and missed the voyage. His name was not crossed off the British list, and at no time was his absence officially noted. To the great alarm of his family his name was later telegraphed by the Norwegian Consul General in New York to the Norwegian Foreign Office in Christiania as one of those lost.[4]

Part of the responsibility of the overseas agents was to ensure that all passengers reached their British port of departure in good time for their ocean passage. They did not, however, want passengers on through tickets to arrive at the dock too early, because the shipping lines were responsible for feeding and caring for their passengers as soon as their journeys began. The coal strike affecting British ports early in 1912 hit scheduled services badly and must have caused the agents considerable headaches rearranging cancelled passages.

Beginning a few days before *Titanic's* sailing a steady stream of passengers began arriving in Southampton, some arriving on the trains from Waterloo only a few hours before departure as we have seen. Booking details for transmigrants, whose tickets had often been arranged on their behalf by relatives already overseas, and for other passengers travelling on pre-paid tickets where time had not been of the essence, could easily have been sent to the shipping line or intermediate agents by letter post. The information needed to reach the shipping line sufficiently well in advance to allow it to compile its own records. Any last minute changes to the numbers and any bookings from distant agents where it was not possible to despatch the information in time would have been transmitted by telegraph.

By the last decade of the 19th century, a wide network of telegraph cables stretched across Europe. Submarine cables facilitated the rapid transfer of information between Britain and Europe and across the Atlantic seabed to North America. The steamship companies needed a fast and secure method of contacting their agents and, when time was short, or in cases of last-minute changes, the details of passengers and the classes of ticket purchased were transmitted by telegraph from the various agents across Britain and the Continent to the relevant shipping line office. Smaller, remote agents could have resorted to a combination of runners and telegraph from a central office. The Marconi Company archives in Britain have occasional fragmentary snippets of references suggesting the transmission of passenger details by telegraph,[5] and the headed notepaper in surviving correspondence between ticket agents and the shipping lines often includes the telegraphic address. The cost to the agents and shipping lines for these telegraphic transfers would not have been excessive particularly where an internal system of telegraphic communication was in operation between agents and the larger shipping companies and would in any case have been built in to the ticket price.

The full details of name, age and other necessary information for each passenger would have been received at the shipping offices by one or a combination of the methods discussed. There they were transcribed, tickets allocated from one of several number series, and the required details including contract ticket numbers entered on to the Board of Trade passenger list forms by several clerks.

The final drafts of the lists of passenger names, class, port of embarkation and cabin allocation were also produced by the shipping line's booking office and transported to the vessel. Where the paperwork for Queenstown passengers was prepared is not absolutely certain. The Board of Trade Queenstown section appears to have been written in a different hand from any of the several appearing on the Southampton section, and the shipping line and other details are entered by hand. The department dealing with the Southampton section has used the company's stamp and there are various other differences which suggest that it could have been compiled in a completely separate place. The differences may of course be nothing more than particular idiosyncrasies of the individual clerks so no great significance should be placed upon that. However, the ticket numbers for the Irish passengers, while not being absolutely consecutive with any of those for Southampton passengers, nevertheless fall within roughly similar numerical sequences. They are heavily interspersed with runs of Southampton numbers, as also are those for overseas passengers. A similar situation occurs with the ticket numbers for other White Star Line ships sailing within the same two-week period. The most logical conclusion is that regardless of where and through which agency the tickets were purchased, the numbers were probably all centrally allocated. Very probably, both sections of the British list were compiled in Southampton, signed together by Captain Smith and the Queenstown section taken to Queenstown on board *Titanic*. In Queenstown the emigration agent added his signature but the only date shown on the last sheet appears in the stamp at the Queenstown Customs Office two days after *Titanic* left there.

It is as well to be aware that most shipping lines by then were producing decorative lists of (mostly) cabin class passengers which were distributed to them as souvenir booklets. These were frequently produced in the on-board print room in the hours following departure. Some survive in private collections and public archives including a number (mostly for ships to India) in the Public Record Office's own collection. Even these last must be treated with caution, in view of the later problems in accurately identifying *Titanic's* passengers which seem not to be unique.

The designs of Board of Trade passenger list forms evolved over the years, reflecting changes in the information required. By the time *Titanic* sailed, all lists, no matter by which printer nor for which shipping line they were produced, conformed to the same basic design required by the British government to ensure accuracy of content. Two copies were supplied to the shipping line's representative at each port. Traditionally it is believed to have been the responsibility of the purser's department on each ship to ensure that the information given was accurate before offering it to the captain for signature. As discussed earlier, however, the lists were often already signed and in the office by the time passengers began arriving so there was already considerable potential for errors. The final list was produced after a series of transcriptions by a succession of clerks often wrestling with unfamiliar names. Errors, unnoticed at the time and by then largely undetectable, could easily have crept in.

Research suggests that the passenger lists must have been prepared in the shipping line's offices only a few days before the scheduled sailing of the vessel. Although in *Titanic's* case the tickets are in numerically ordered batches, the numbers were probably allocated in the order in which the ticket requests were received from the agents. The completed Board of Trade passenger list is not in full numerical order. The order in which names are entered on the list supports the hypothesis (for that is all it can ever be) that the names and details were already known by the shipping line long before the passengers arrived. A number of passengers' names are crossed through on the Board of Trade list indicating that there was a last-minute change of plan too late to notify the offices. There are also numerous instances of passengers reported to have purchased tickets, also apparently cancelled at the last minute, but whose names do not appear either in the British Board of Trade lists or the White Star Line's lists.

Correspondence between the shipping lines and the Board of Trade is attached to many of the lists in the Public Record Office's collection, suggesting that the checking of the lists was undertaken very conscientiously. The research indicates that the reality was otherwise.

Although the front of the list bears the date upon which *Titanic* departed from Southampton, the space left for the date on which the list was signed has been left blank. *Titanic's* purser could not have checked the list against the passengers who boarded because the stamp clearly shows that the list was in the Customs Office on the 9th, one day before the passengers arrived. Captain Smith and the Southampton Emigration Officer must have signed the list in blind faith, presumably relying upon last-minute changes being recorded later. There was very little time to check the paperwork against the passengers on the day of sailing. If anyone had compared the Board of Trade list with the White Star Line's list or checked it with the passengers on board they would have surely spotted considerable differences which should have been corrected. Perhaps the Board of Trade list was regarded as simply a piece of red tape which had to be completed at some point before the ship could sail. Most of the cancellations would have been notified sooner or later. Eventually the names of anyone rejected by the medical officer would have been noted on the list. Maybe the purser would have had this information to hand ready to alter the onboard passenger list during the voyage, which perhaps he could have substituted for the first copy now lying in the Customs Office. We shall never know for sure, but research suggests that they are unlikely.

In a process probably unquestioned since its inception, Captain Edward J. Smith verified by his signature that the list was an accurate representation of his passengers and that the provisions were sufficient for the stated number of adults on board – not when the passengers had been checked on board, not with reference to other documentation, but at some earlier stage, maybe one or even two days before sailing. Accurate or not, checked or not, one copy sailed with the ship whilst the other was submitted to the port office. It was placed in a pile along with those for other ships sailing that week. At approximately weekly intervals, the collection of lists from each office was parcelled up and sent to the Statistical Department of the Board of Trade in London. *Titanic's* list, assigned the number 276, was received at the Board of Trade on 24 April together with those of five other steamers: Hamburg South American Line's *Cap Finisterre*, Netherlands Royal Mail Line's *Prinses Juliana*, North German Lloyd's *Kaiser Wilhelm II*, Hamburg American's *Kaiserin Auguste Victoria* and the Royal Mail Steam Packet Company's *Clyde*. The number for *Titanic* was allotted and entered into the register, but her name is written in pencil presumably at a

Chapter 4

different time from the others. Could this be the point at which it was decided that *Titanic's* Board of Trade list was unsuitable for the purposes of any further investigation, leading to it being archived and from then onwards, its existence forgotten?

Checking the Passengers on Board

With no documentary evidence to explain the method of checking passengers on board *Titanic* or any other ocean liner at this period, one can only surmise. The most likely scenario involves a list compiled by and for the shipping line from the mass of transcribed information received from the various agents which included information required by the British and American governments and entered on to the respective passenger lists. This list would be the master copy from which would be created the shipping line's own list of all passengers, divided according to port of embarkation and class of travel. From that, a list would be drawn up showing the cabin allocation to ensure that families were kept together, and that, where possible, there was optimum occupancy in each cabin. The master list would normally have been retained by the White Star Line only until the voyage was complete. In the case of *Titanic's* untimely end, the same list would have formed the basis of the shipping line's record of passengers on board which it was required to submit to the Registrar General of Shipping and Seamen as part of the process of registering deaths at sea. It was also used as the blueprint for the final White Star Line passenger list used as an exhibit in the US Senate Inquiry. It would have been either discarded at the time, or archived by the White Star Line until its take-over by Cunard in 1934 when the whole of the company's archive was seemingly destroyed.

During the process of compiling an accurate list of passengers after the disaster as required by the various government departments both in Britain and the United States, the White Star Line's passenger list (discussed in Chapter 7) went through a series of drafts.[7] They were typeset, and alphabetised within each class. The final copy was fully formatted for presentation to the Senate Inquiry. Whether the White Star Line took the trouble to typeset its master list, and whether the three drafts of the final list presented to the Senate Inquiry were typeset only for the purpose of facilitating the checking and updating, is unknown. The likelihood is that the line had at least two copies of the master list, one for its own records and one for the purser, so it was almost certainly either typeset or hand-typed in duplicate.

Research confirms that any image of the purser seated at a desk at the ship's gangway patiently ticking off the passengers' names on the Board of Trade list as they prepared to board must be very far removed from the truth. Even for those lists which were not signed and delivered until after the ship had left, the early passenger lists are rarely in either numerical or alphabetical order and include many sheets so any such process would have been far too cumbersome when embarking and checking many hundreds of passengers in a relatively short period of time on to any of these giant steamers. The most probable candidate for use in the checking process was the list of passengers drawn up by the White Star Line from the master list. Certainly, if it were to have been divided and alphabetised by class, broad nationality and port of embarkation as were the later drafts, it would have presented a perfectly manageable list with which to work in restrictive circumstances and under pressure on the morning of departure. By the time *Titanic's* passengers boarded, one copy of the Board of Trade list was probably already locked away in the purser's office, and the other had been delivered to the port office 24 hours earlier.

Once the passengers had arrived at the quayside their tickets were easily checked against the White Star Line's list of passengers, and the 3rd class were filed past the Board of Trade doctor who conducted a brief visual examination. He paid the closest attention to the alien transmigrants, and anyone appearing to be unwell was pulled out of line for a further examination and possible rejection. During this process, the number of the allotted cabin was stamped on the boarding or inspection cards and, once declared medically fit, the passengers were allowed to board.

The remaining job falling to the purser would have been to note any alterations on his copy of the White Star Line's list of passengers – those rejected by the doctor, anyone not arriving at the dock, or any late additions. The purser's copy of the Board of Trade list went down with the ship so there is no way of knowing whether, during the course of the next few days, any alterations were cross-referenced between each list. Even if they were, the biggest downfall of this method is that it would rarely have exposed any problems already existing on the Board of Trade list – errors in recording sex, age, spellings, and omitted or additional names would not have been revealed unless the identical error had been picked up on the White Star List, which seems unlikely.

Circumstances suggest that the accuracy of the British Board of Trade passenger list was at this stage untested and probably nobody ever thought to check. The list does have ticks against many of the names, but comparisons with other contemporary lists which do not have marks suggest that they were not placed there as a means of demonstrating that the passenger had actually boarded but formed part of an entirely different clerical checking process. It is certainly unwise to assume that ticked, crossed or underscored names represent those who did or did not sail. The *Olympic, Titanic's* sister ship sailed exactly one week earlier, on 3 April.[8] That list also has ticks, crossings through and underscores. Some passengers who definitely boarded *Titanic* and died in the sinking also appear on *Olympic's* list. In several cases their *Olympic* entries are also ticked – if the ticks really were intended to signify that the passenger had been checked on board, then clearly the system was not working very efficiently. They are more likely to have been placed there in some other and undisclosed checking process.

For example Alfred Lowe's name appears on *Olympic's* list, but is crossed through and recorded as N.O.B (not on board). He later sailed on *Titanic* and drowned. Richard Nosworthy, a Cornish farm labourer, is entered and his name ticked then crossed through. His details have been left untouched and a scribbled note reads 'apparently to be included'. Richard did not sail on *Olympic*, and less than two weeks later he was dead. Helene, Viktor and Sallie Rosblum, ticked but names and details crossed through, were originally due to sail on *Olympic* – tragically, their booking was changed and they, too, died. Johannes Nysveen, recorded on *Olympic's* list as Johan Kysven, was ticked and crossed through. His wife heard some weeks after the tragedy that he had not, after all, sailed on *Olympic* but had lost his life in the disaster. Leo Zimmerman's name has been entered, not ticked, but crossed through – Leo later died on *Titanic*. Seventeen-year-old Bertha Ilett is recorded and ticked as travelling to New York on board the *Olympic* but the entry is wrong. Bertha's booking was also changed but she was one of the lucky ones that night.

It is unwise to assume that identical names, however unusual they may be, appearing on the Board of Trade lists of both *Olympic* and *Titanic* refer to a single individual. Among the passengers who died on *Titanic* was Camille Wittevrongel, a transmigrant. Scribbled on *Olympic's* list at the bottom of a page are a group of transmigrants, among them, ticked, is the name Camille Wittevrongel, travelling with a married woman of the same surname – was she his wife, and if so was he not the man who died on *Titanic* but simply someone of the same name? The ticket number for each voyage is different, and the *Olympic's* New York arrivals list indicates that a couple of this name really did sail on *Olympic*. Finally a slight question mark surrounds a traveller from 2nd class on the *Olympic*, travelling on ticket number 248717. August Meyer, a 48-year-old engineer, and a United States citizen, had been

Chapter 4

living in England for at least 12 months, according to the information on *Olympic*'s Board of Trade passenger list. *Titanic*'s passenger list records a German passenger August Meyer, a 2nd class passenger, travelling on ticket number 248723, having spent the last 12 months or more living in 'foreign countries'. The Register of Deaths At Sea in PRO reference BT334/52 indicates that Meyer had not spent the last year overseas at all but instead in the very English town of Harrow on the Hill! Undoubtedly he has a fairly common name, but given all the other anomalies and the closeness of the two ticket numbers, dare we be absolutely certain that the two men are not one and the same?

The Accuracy of the Lists

Often not until there is a tragedy of monumental proportions, when it suddenly becomes vital to know exactly who was present and who may now be missing, is the accuracy of surviving documents called into account. Different branches of an investigation each draw up their own records as part of the process of documenting a disaster. Only when those records are later compared are the shortcomings exposed.

The process of compiling passenger lists rolled along, year in and year out, apparently without anyone ever pausing to question the reliability of the documents or to consider the possible inadequacies of the process. During the course of the 1912 investigations into the *Titanic* disaster a number of lists of names were compiled for various purposes. Comparisons can now be made between the records compiled both before and after the tragedy. One of the most important of those compiled before it is the Board of Trade's official passenger list. Although each of the records may include differing amounts of information on each passenger, the common information on each should be consistent. Frequently, though, this is far from the case. Thankfully opportunities for comparisons are rare. Two other major marine disasters during the second decade of the 20th century involved large loss of life. These were the accidental loss of the Canadian Pacific steamship *Empress of Ireland* in 1914, and the Cunard Steamship Company's mail ship *Lusitania* as a result of a torpedo attack a year later. Both disasters happened when the two ships were eastbound and therefore there is no Board of Trade passenger list for either vessel to form a baseline with which to compare other records.

There were numerous small passenger losses in this period and chosen at random are the records of the *Veronese* and the *Mohegan*. Not a loss, but another opportunity to examine a large number of lists of names for the same vessel is provided by the New Zealand bound P&O Steam Navigation Company's steamship *Mongolia*. They were all relatively small ships but were all caught in the same system. Can anything be learnt from them about the process of dealing with the lists both before and after a sailing which can help promote a better understanding of *Titanic*'s list? What might they suggest about the accuracy of the records?

The Lamport & Holt Line vessel SS *Veronese* left London en route for Argentina on 16 January 1913 but soon afterwards foundered in a storm. A total of 19 passengers were lost, 14 of whom were Spanish nationals bound for Argentina. None of the 14 appeared on the Board of Trade list because they were picked up in Vigo after the ship left British waters. It does, however, provide an excellent illustration to prove that, if some mishap befell the vessel before it reached its destination, and before it was filed by the Statistical Department, the list was pulled from the bundle and marked up accordingly. In this instance the clerk has gone to great pains to invent four different symbols to record passengers: lost; returning to Liverpool on SS *Anselm* from Leixoes; proceeding to Buenos Aires aboard SS *Vandyck*; proceeding per SS *Darro*. These symbols are recorded on the list against the names, and annotated on the front. This is only one of many other examples which point to Board of

Trade passenger lists frequently being pulled back out of the piles and accidental loss recorded, even if in some ad hoc fashion, by the Statistical Department of the Board of Trade.

In 1898, 14 years before *Titanic* was lost, the small Atlantic Transport steamship *Mohegan*, 4,510 tons, was outbound from London on a voyage to New York. The Board of Trade passenger list records her 51 passengers by name, except for two: Mr King's valet, now known to be O'Rorke, and a nurse (later reported to be from Elstree but still unnamed), caring for the two King children. During a wild storm the vessel went aground on the Manacles Rocks off Falmouth on the Cornish coast. The list is annotated stating that the names of the 11 passengers (the clerk has miscounted as there were in fact 13) who were saved were removed from the list (they were shipwrecked in British waters and were no longer passengers so this was perfectly logical). The clerk has, however, crossed through not 11 passengers but 12, neglecting to remove the valet, Mr O'Rorke, the 13th man. The official inquiry published the names of all the passengers. However, it found not 51 but 53, now including a Mr Cordary and Dr Fellows, neither of whom appears on the Board of Trade passenger list. They both died, bringing the number to 13 saved and 40 lost. The Register of Deaths at Sea[9] includes yet another male passenger, Mr Horne, and three returning cattlemen having free passage. Those three caused the same difficulty, presumably, as *Titanic's* postal clerks – should they be included as passengers, or as crew? The Board of Trade listed them as passengers, bringing the final tally to 13 saved and 44 lost from a total of not 51 but 57 passengers in all.

The Peninsular & Oriental Steam Navigation Company's (P&O) ship SS *Mongolia* left London on 7 October 1910 with 292 passengers bound for Australia and New Zealand.[10] She arrived safely, but an examination of the various lists compiled at her ports of call illustrates the problems which can be encountered when several different people become involved in writing down the same names and details. The Board of Trade departure list now in the Public Record Office has been compared to the arrival and departure lists compiled under British jurisdiction by the authorities in Adelaide, Melbourne, Sydney and Auckland.[11] The results showed that at some point in the voyage, most passengers' details were recorded significantly differently from the entry on the Board of Trade departure list. Some details changed several times: spellings differed, names were omitted, families were split, nationalities and occupations were altered. Some passengers disappeared, only to reappear later. The German merchant and his wife who boarded in London arrived at their destination recorded as French music hall artistes. The ages of some passengers varied by as much as 40 years yet all the lists should have been produced from the same basic information – the P&O Steam Navigation Company's own records of those who had purchased tickets.

None of these examples attests directly to the accuracy of *Titanic's* various lists. However, they demonstrate clearly that the significant differences found when comparing the records for *Titanic* are far from unique and anyone using those or any other passenger list should consider carefully before accepting as fact whatever that passenger list contains.

The coal strike which had seriously affected the shipping industry in the early part of the year had just ended before *Titanic* was due to sail but had severely disrupted sailing schedules. Many ships were laid up and passages were either cancelled altogether or the passengers were distributed among other ships. A number of passengers found themselves on *Titanic* only as a result of the strike. Nysveen, the Norwegian passenger discussed earlier, was originally booked on the White Star Line ship *Megantic* from Liverpool. The sailing was cancelled, and he was rebooked on the *Olympic* then on *Titanic* with tragic consequences. The same happened to several more passengers. Inevitably as passengers were shuffled from one vessel to another, sometimes more than once, mistakes were bound to creep into the documentation and some passengers' names were missed out altogether whilst others had their names entered twice. Exactly how the financial implications were reconciled is not recorded but this must have presented a problem for the White Star Line's accounting department.

The Passenger List

Forget the neat and compact pages passed to successive celluloid Captain Smiths for signature – the real thing is a large, unwieldy document comprising 34 sheets, 27 for Southampton and 7 for Queenstown. Each sheet is divided into columns filled with data in varying degrees of illegibility. The most immediately striking feature of the Southampton section of the British list is its fragile condition, the pages creased, torn and crumbling. Unfortunately the first left-hand column containing the ticket numbers has largely disintegrated on many pages but still provides some interesting points.

Again, without the White Star Line archive we can only assume how the ticket numbers were allocated. Passengers travelling together often, but not always, shared the same ticket number, and it is difficult to spot any clear sequence – number patterns emerge fleetingly only to disappear just as quickly. The allocation of tickets, discussed in Chapter 5, needs further investigation if we are to understand exactly how the system operated.

The list was drawn up under the Merchant Shipping Act, 1906, and the Aliens Act, 1905, as the *Return of Passengers leaving the United Kingdom in ships bound for places out of Europe and not within the Mediterranean Sea.*

For the purposes of the Statistical Department of the Board of Trade, the passengers fell into three distinct categories – British, Alien Transmigrants and Alien Non-Transmigrants. Passengers who were not British subjects were recorded in one of these two alien sections – section A: Transmigrants, 'this is, alien passengers (other than first class passengers) who arrived in the United Kingdom, having in their possession Prepaid Through Tickets, and in respect of whom security has been given that they will proceed to places outside the United Kingdom'; or section B: 'Aliens other than included in A'.

The column headings on the sheets for British subjects read, from left to right:

- 1. The contract ticket number.
- 2. Names of Passengers.
- Unnumbered column subdivided into three for statistical purposes only – adults/children/infants. The status of each passenger is noted with a tick in the relevant column.
- 3. Class – Whether 1st, 2nd or 3rd.
- 4. Port at Which Passengers Contracted to Land – in this case, usually New York, with some passengers booked for Cherbourg and one for Queenstown.
- 5. Profession, Occupation or Calling of Passengers – with a note stating that in the case of First Class Passengers, this column need not be completed.
- 6. Ages of Passengers – wide section divided into 3 columns, each subdivided, with a note stating that except for First Class Passengers this should state the age at last birthday. The columns were: i. Adults of 12 years and upwards (with sub-divisions for those accompanied by husband or wife – male and female, and not accompanied by husband or wife – male and female [note that an entry in the 'not accompanied' column does not give proof of marital status]); ii. Children between 1 and 12 – male and female; iii. Infants – male and female.
- 7. Country of Last Permanent Residence – subdivided: England, Wales, Scotland, Ireland, British Possessions, Foreign Countries.

- 8. Country of Intended Future Permanent Residence – a footnote reads 'By permanent residence is to be understood residence for a year or more'.

Finally the number of passengers in each category is added, and the figure carried forward to the next sheet for the same class of passenger.

The sheets for Category B: Alien, Non-Transmigrants are identical in format except for column 7, which asks 'Country of which Citizen or Subject'.

The sheets for Category A: Alien, Transmigrants are slightly different. The column indicating profession or calling is omitted so column 5 now contains the ages of the passengers. Column 6 asks 'Country of which Citizen or Subject' and column 7 is headed 'Arrival into Britain'. It is subdivided into two: one column requests the name of the port at which the transmigrant arrived, and the other the name of the steamship line on which they travelled to Britain. The information in these two last columns is unique and has been overlooked up to now. The alien passengers are the subject of Chapter 3.

It was not to where the passenger himself was travelling, but rather where the ship itself was heading which determined the type of list compiled and whether it was quickly destroyed or was filed with the Board of Trade. Not all passenger lists were archived by the Board of Trade. Those passenger lists for ships on inter-European voyages (known as 3rd Schedules or 'PM3s') were kept for only three weeks, and this class included voyages between two British ports unless the ship was bound further afield. Passenger lists for ferry crossings between ports in the United Kingdom and mainland Europe were also not retained, a great disappointment for those researching passengers who used a cross-Channel ferry or North Sea feeder ship to reach the British Isles in order to board *Titanic*.

A ship's maiden voyage is customarily held to be the first voyage on which a ship carries fare-paying passengers. *Titanic* is reported to have left Belfast with at least one fare-paying passenger on board. There is no primary source documentary evidence to support it but, if this is true, then her maiden voyage actually began from Belfast and not from Southampton. If the maiden voyage did begin in Belfast, then there should have been a Belfast passenger list showing any embarkations because *Titanic* was proceeding to a port beyond Europe, but no list has been found. The passenger concerned, recorded in the *Belfast Newsletter* newspaper of April 1912 as Mr Wyckoff Derholf, aged 61, is reported to have booked a ticket from Belfast to New York.[11] No passenger of that exact name is recorded on the official list, but he is possibly the first class passenger Mr W. van der Hoef, recorded on the Board of Trade passenger list as having boarded in Southampton but who had a Belfast address.

It is too late now to rewrite the history books and so the maiden voyage is officially deemed to have begun on 10 April when the ship pulled away from the quayside in Southampton. That being the case, there will therefore be no surviving passenger list showing those passengers, fare-paying or not, who boarded in Belfast en route for Southampton because at that point *Titanic's* voyage was classed as a coastal voyage between two British ports. There are, however, entries showing the six passengers who boarded in Southampton and who disembarked in Cherbourg (because passengers disembarking at ports en route for an intercontinental voyage are shown on British lists) though curiously this is several fewer than were reported later to have disembarked there. The sole recorded passenger who had boarded in Southampton for the short trip to Queenstown, Mr E. Nichols, is shown on the outbound list from Southampton for the same reason. There would not, however, be a surviving arrival list at Queenstown because the ship's voyage had originated at another British port.

As *Titanic* steamed away from Southampton on 10 April the passenger list, signed in duplicate with one copy already on its way to the Board of Trade, showed that the number of passengers on board was 922.

1 BT27 Class List (PRO, Kew)
2 BT100/260 (PRO, Kew)
3 Nova Scotia Archives and Record Management, Halifax, NS.
4 Sebak, *Titanic, 31 Norwegian Destinies*
5 Gordon Bussey, Marconi Archives
6 BT32/5 (PRO, Kew)
7. BT100/260 (PRO, Kew)
8 BT27/780A (PRO, Kew)
9 BT334/14 (PRO, Kew)
10 BT27/676 (PRO, Kew)
11 Cameron, *Titanic, Belfast's Own*

Chapter 5
The White Star Line Contract Ticket List

From the moment *Titanic* sank, the White Star Line was bracing itself for the legal actions which were bound to follow.

On 19 April, Senator William Alden Smith took his place as Chairman of the Subcommittee of the Committee on Commerce of the United States' Senate to investigate the 'causes leading to the wreck of the White Star Liner *Titanic*'. After almost three weeks the investigation was brought to a close. The full and final report of the Committee on Commerce was published on 28 May. The White Star Line's passenger list was presented to the Investigation as Exhibit B and is discussed in detail in Chapter 7. Amongst its findings the investigation recommended that 'there should be additional legislation to secure the safety of life at sea'.

Meanwhile, on 23 April, the Lord Chancellor in London appointed the Right Honourable Lord Mersey, Wreck Commissioner, followed by the nomination a few days later of five assessors to head the planned investigation into the loss of *Titanic*. At the end of April the Board of Trade issued a request that a formal inquiry under the Merchant Shipping Acts 1894–1906, should be held to 'investigate the circumstances attending the loss of SS *Titanic*'. The case opened on 2 May at the Scottish Hall, Buckingham Gate, in Westminster, London. It later moved to Caxton Hall, and returned to the Scottish Hall for its final two days. The investigation centred on a list of 26 questions and a large number of witnesses were called, including Sir Walter J. Howell, the Assistant Secretary of the Board of Trade, and Head of the Marine Department. Chapter 6 contains a large amount of correspondence, some of which was between Sir Walter Howell and others. Lord Mersey presented his findings on 30 July 1912, setting out his view of the reasons for the loss of the vessel: 'The loss of the said ship was due to collision with an iceberg, brought about by the excessive speed at which the ship was being navigated.'

The (British) Merchant Shipping Act of 1894 had set out clear guidelines concerning the limits to which the owners of any vessel which was lost along with loss or injury of lives, cargo or property could be held liable. Unless negligence could be proven against the owners of any vessel, then the most the shipping line could be held liable for payment of compensation for the losses sustained in a sinking would be nominal – £15 per ton of the ship for loss of life, £8 per ton of the ship for loss of goods. On the other hand, if negligence was found to be the cause of the loss, then the claims against the line for damages and compensation would be enormous. The determining factor in deciding to what lengths the White Star Line was liable was whether it could be shown that either the shipping line or Captain Edward Smith himself had been guilty of negligence. The eyes of the world were turned to the two cases running concurrently in Britain and America. The first sign of victory for the claimants was the ruling in a British court, when in the case of Ryan v Oceanic Steam Navigation Company (the White Star Line) the jury found the company guilty of negligence. The White Star Line immediately launched an appeal but the decision was upheld, thus opening the flood gates for total claims amounting to more than £3 million (almost $17 million).

In a series of hearings lasting for several years, the Judge at the United States District Court in New York heard a number of cases in which claims for damages and compensation were brought by the survivors and the relatives of the deceased.[1] Because the Company was

British, he ruled that British law would be applied to the damages claim and eventually the case was brought to a close with settlement made on a pro-rata basis to each of the claimants.

In order to determine the amount payable, the value of *Titanic* was considered. The lifeboats and their equipment were the only items of any worth salvaged at that time from *Titanic*. Offset against that, and the money received previously for prepaid freight charges and passengers' ticket money were the costs already paid out by the White Star Line for railway fares and board for some of the passengers, which resulted in a total calculated figure of only £20,000 (under $100,000).

Vital as part of the evidence submitted by the White Star Line for consideration in the decision concerning the value of the *Titanic*, were its own records of tickets sold and monies received. This document, now generally known as the Contract Ticket List, is filed in the National Archives in New York.[2]

The document itself comprises a large number of folded ledger sheets, some interleaved, and within a paper cover entitled 'SS *Titanic* – Voyage 1. Sailed April 10th 1912'. The date stamp 23 November 1912 indicates the date at which it was first received as part of the records for the case of Limitation of Liability. These were once loose folded ledger sheets in the Accounts Department of the White Star Line's Liverpool offices. Holes were punched in the top and bottom left corners of the folded sheets. The normal method of keeping such large sheets filed together back in 1912 was a system of long metal bolts passing through holes punched in the corners of a document and held in place by screws on the underside of the pile and that is the most likely way these sheets were held, in order to provide easy access for the clerks when working on the figures. The photocopies available from the National Archives in New York require a little ingenuity in order to rearrange them into their original order but this must be done so that the figure work on each of the right-hand sheets may be matched up with its left-hand partner containing the names and other details. The overall impression is that the document is original, that is to say that it is the actual document compiled and written up by White Star Line clerks and not a copy made for the court hearings – the ring left by the ink bottle on the front cover is very suggestive of these sheets having been lying on a cluttered desk in a busy office whilst the figures were balanced, where it really did not matter too much about the ink blot because nobody was going to see it …

The document is in several sections, namely:

1st class, 7 sheets (of names); Cross Channel, 1 sheet; 2nd class, 6 sheets; Cross Channel, 1 sheet; 3rd class, 4 sheets; Scandinavians, 4 sheets; Continentals, 3 sheets; Continentals off Cherbourg, 3 sheets; British Pre-Paid: 1st class, 1 sheet; 2nd class, 1 sheet; 3rd class British, 1 sheet; 3rd class Foreign, 1 sheet; Queenstown: 2nd class, 1 sheet; 3rd class, 3 sheets.

The columns on each page are identical regardless of class of travel. This was after all an accounting ledger and the names were there only as a means of cross-reference. Against each name is entered the status of the passenger – adult, child or infant, and the Contract Ticket number. For those boarding in Southampton and Queenstown, this same ticket number should be entered on to the Board of Trade passenger list. The price paid for the ticket is entered into the column 'Ocean Fare'. The figures on the opposite page relate to monies received for commission and other passage money. There are occasional annotations – J. Bruce Ismay (Chairman of the White Star Line), his manservant and his secretary Harrison were travelling on complimentary tickets in 1st class, as was J. J. Ruechin. Thomas Andrews, Chisholm and Parr, part of the Harland & Wolff guarantee party, were travelling on Harland & Wolff's account which would have been settled direct. The column reading 'no. of Continental Ticket' generally does not contain a number but often gives clues about where the ticket may have been purchased. There are too many omissions to make this a reliable indication of where a ticket was purchased, however, and it would also be unwise to use the location where the ticket was purchased as an indication of where the passenger boarded. A handful of passengers appear more than once in the White Star Contract Ticket List. Mr Colley and Mr and Mrs Chaffey appear both in the main 1st class section and the British 1st class Prepaid, as do Mrs Jessie Trout and Mr G. Hunt in 2nd class, (though not the third British 2nd class Prepaid passenger, Robert Bateman) and Lockyer and Braund from 3rd class.

The most usual way for a prospective traveller to obtain a ticket for passage overseas was to write or call in person to the offices of a ticket agent or steamship line in towns and cities scattered across the globe. Some of these were general agents servicing several different transatlantic steamship lines. Others were dedicated to one particular company – the White Star Line employed many agents of its own to deal with thousands of bookings each year from parts of Scandinavia and other northern European locations, but in more remote areas such as Asia, South Africa and South America where there was less call for its services there were correspondingly fewer White Star Line agents. Many 1st or 2nd class passengers used the services of Thomas Cook & Son who had been successfully handling worldwide travel arrangements for many years. Although never heavily involved in the emigrant trade, in the early years of its operation Thomas Cook handled all classes of travel. By the 1890s Thomas Cook had moved up in the market and began targeting its advertising towards the wealthier traveller – several of *Titanic's* passengers left as their forwarding address one of the offices of Thomas Cook & Son.[3] It is perhaps as well to note at this point that Thomas Cook's archives contain no ticketing information, no booking references and no passenger lists whatsoever.

Some emigrants travelled on tickets obtained for them by relatives who had themselves emigrated earlier. They had made sufficient money to be able to afford to sponsor family back home and had now arranged the purchase of through tickets prepaid on their behalf from ticket agents in the United States and Canada. The requests and paperwork were submitted to the steamship company back in Britain so that tickets could be arranged for collection on sailing day. By 1912 transatlantic cable lines had been in regular business use for some decades but with no particular urgency there was plenty of time for the documentation to be sent by sea to the head office of the shipping line. Once confirmation of the travel arrangements had been received preparations could begin, but the whole process often took several months from the time the ticket was arranged to the arrival of the new migrant.

The shipping line did not simply hand over a ticket to anyone who arrived with money in their pocket. Prospective emigrants were usually required to obtain a passport or some other form of official documentation before they were given permission to leave their homeland, and in order to guarantee them free passage across other borders on their way to the port. Most countries also had immigration laws governing who would or would not be admitted. Responsibility was placed upon the ticket agents to verify that the passengers possessed all the necessary documentation allowing them to travel, and to identify anyone who would obviously be unacceptable to the immigration authorities at the chosen destination. Would-be migrants to America were required to answer a long list of questions designed to investigate their suitability for admission. The ticket agents worked under strict guidelines (in the case of *Titanic* and other ships carrying passengers to America, regulations laid down by the US government). Only when the agent for the shipping line had satisfied himself that the passenger had all the necessary papers and would be acceptable for residency in the country of their choice, would they be issued with travel documents. At the transatlantic departure port, once they had passed their medical check, the US consul stamped the paperwork and they were issued with their transatlantic steamship contract tickets. There was good reason for this apparent reluctance on the part of the shipping lines to hand over tickets to anyone who asked. Firstly, the shipping line was responsible for the care and sustenance of all passengers once their through-travel began and would therefore not wish to be liable for the cost of transporting sick or unsuitable candidates back to their home port. Secondly, both the master and the shipping line could be penalised heavily under the receiving country's immigration laws for attempting to disembark a passenger whom the immigration authorities found unfit for whatever reason.

An examination of the ticket numbers suggests the way in which they were allotted. The only two documents generally including them are the Board of Trade list and the Contract Ticket List. Neither document is in strict numerical order, probably because the tickets were allotted as the requests arrived from each agent, and entered accordingly. If the ticket numbers are extracted and sorted into order, patterns begin to form. They have been issued in blocks of numbers – the blocks may not contain all consecutive numbers with no omissions, and there are blocks missing, but nevertheless they are broadly speaking blocks of numbers. In many cases an examination of the ticket numbers on Board of Trade passenger lists for the *Olympic* and other White Star Line ships due to sail close to *Titanic's* departure, reveals the numbers missing from *Titanic's* ticket number blocks.

It is not at the moment clear exactly what, if any, significance there may be in the numbering with relation to the type of ticket purchased and the place where it was procured. Ticket numbers can comprise anything from one to seven digits but beyond that it is only possible at present to speak in generalisations. Although in the course of research, this author has examined a large number of Board of Trade passenger lists (all of which also include ticket numbers) it would be dangerous indeed to claim any in-depth understanding of the whole of the White Star Line's ticket processing on the evidence of what is necessarily a very small percentage of so many thousands of lists. With that proviso, in general it is possible to say that the low (one- to three-digit) numbers appear a little more likely to be for the short voyages: Southampton to Cherbourg, or for Southampton to Queenstown. It is difficult to find any strong pattern with the four-digit numbers except that many, but by no means all, were allotted to tickets purchased in Europe. The first digit (1, 2 or 3) of the five -digit numbers very often relates to the class of travel. Not until the six- and seven-digit numbers do they seem to settle into a distinct pattern whereby the first digit (1, 2 or 3) almost always relates to the class of travel. There are many inconsistencies, however.

Without the existence of other Contract Ticket Lists for cross-referencing both the ticket number and the location of the office where the ticket was arranged, or details of cabin allocation and any special circumstances which may have surrounded the booking or the passenger, it is impossible to draw any firm conclusions. Certainly the way is open for a greater examination of the whole practice of ticket issuing for both intermediate and ocean passages for all steamship companies. The number blocks of ticket allocations prove that the ticket numbers for the main ocean voyage must have been centrally allocated by the White Star Line in Britain and in cases where passengers sailed on a different ship from that on which they were originally booked, the ticket number usually appears not to have changed nor been reallocated. The exception to that is in cases where the passenger cancelled the booking, rather than simply transferring it, thereby receiving a refund on the original ticket. If they then decided to sail on another ship, they struck a completely new transaction complete with different ticket number. The image of an overseas ticket agent issuing tickets numbered according to the number on the Contract Ticket List is wrong. It is rare to find tickets remaining for ocean liners of that period but any which have survived, even those for prepaid through tickets for transmigrant passengers, suggest that the ticket for the intermediate voyage (into Britain) has its own ticket number which bears no relation to the contract ticket number for the ocean crossing.[4]

The White Star Line Contract Ticket List is exactly what its title claims that it is – a list of the ticket numbers and monies paid for the use of the shipping line and at the time it was compiled, nobody ever dreamed that it would come under the scrutiny which it has since received. Nor was it ever meant to be a precise listing of passengers and cannot possibly be put to that use now due to the many spelling errors and omissions. Most of the servants are unnamed, and a group of seamen travelling as passengers is omitted. Neither is the party of Chinese sailors recorded individually by name. The source of the information on the ticket list must surely be the lists of passengers who had purchased tickets and the details of which were also the source for compiling the passenger lists sent across to the White Star Line offices in the period leading up to the ship's departure. It is the only example known to exist for the main shipping lines of that period, which from a research point of view is disappointing.

Titanic's contract ticket list appears to have been made up either in the hours before the ship sailed or, much more likely, in the days following. In fact the tragedy may already have happened before the book-keepers had had the chance to compile it. The names of George Vanderbilt and his family, reported as cancelling their booking at the last minute (but see Chapter 2) and Elias Johannessen, who fell ill with appendicitis and was taken off the train en route for London on the 8th, are among those names not listed. Perhaps these are accidental and coincidental omissions but given the other major problems with the list it seems more likely that their absences were already known when the list was made up.

There are several persons who seem to have received a refund and it may be assumed that they did not sail on *Titanic*. The name of Frederick Miles has often been mentioned among these. For some time, he was believed to have sailed on the 2 May voyage of another White Star Line steamship, the *Cedric*, from Liverpool. Upon comparing the passenger list of the *Cedric*[5] with that of the *Titanic*, however, several significant differences are revealed, supporting the belief that the man on *Titanic's* list is not the same person as the man on the *Cedric's* list. Firstly, the man on *Titanic's* list was probably more correctly named Fred (sic) Niles. The Board of Trade list shows his name to be Niles, and the clerk entering names in that group was more prone to misreading a capital M as a capital W – in other words, if the name in front of him on the booking record had been Miles, he was more likely to mistake it for Wiles, than Niles. Add to that the fact that the name Niles is very much less common than Miles and one may assume that the clerk must have been very certain as he deliberately entered the name Niles on the Board of Trade list. There are so many basic spelling errors on the White Star ticket list, that no weight should be placed on the correctness or otherwise of any entry on that document. The fact that the two men were travelling on different ticket numbers is not necessarily important as it is known that his first booking had actually been cancelled; had he rebooked, he would have received a second ticket number. More significant is the fact that *Titanic's* Fred Niles was a 3rd class passenger, but the *Cedric's* Frederick Wm Miles was travelling 2nd class.

William Gillespie appears to have received a refund, apart from a small amount of commission money deducted. Marrius Petersen received a refund, too, and appears not to have sailed but is nevertheless recorded as having lost his life. The holder of ticket number 242154 is unnamed but also received a full refund. An interesting point is that others who were reported to have booked tickets are not shown in the ticket list. Several passengers shown on the Cave list do not appear in the Contract Ticket List. If George Vanderbilt or any other of his affluent friends who were reported to have booked tickets but changed their minds later had really done so, then this should have been reflected in this ledger. Equally, any booking transfers should also have been shown. None of the names are there, which suggests either very lax accounting procedures in the White Star Line office, or that the passengers may have planned to purchase tickets but never actually did so.

Thankfully the clerks entering names on the passenger lists were at least a little familiar with unusual or foreign names. The Queenstown section is written in a different hand to the Southampton one and the spelling has few problems. The rest of the list was written in a very neat and careful hand, but this was a man who simply could not decipher the handwriting on whatever document it was that he was transcribing on to these ledger sheets. The names of British origin are perfectly acceptable but although he clearly made a very brave attempt at reading the other names he was hopefully better suited to entering numbers. His endeavours produced such wonderful renamings as Frilly Madsen (Frittjof Madsen), Leo Zumcreman (Leo Zimmerman), Wille Tomble (Camille Wittevrongel) and Waslfspector (Wolf Spector). Although it was never intended to be any kind of a passenger list, it is a valuable and useful document in its own right but this transcription of the names from other White Star Line records is nothing short of abysmal. If no other records of passengers' names had been available, the errors in this transcription might never have come to light. Thankfully *Titanic* researchers have a great many other documents with which to cross-reference the names on the White Star ticket list but although it is an original 1912 document it is nevertheless a transcription and it teaches a very clear lesson. Regardless of how reliable the source of the original record may seem to be, never, ever, trust a transcription.

1   Petition of the Oceanic Steam Navigation Company Ltd, for Limitation of its Liability as Owner of the Steamship *Titanic*, United States District Court, Southern District, New York, NY. National Archives and Records Administration
2   National Archives and Records Administration, file NRAN-21-SDNYCIVCAS-5512791
3   Travel Archive, Thomas Cook
4   Sebak, *Titanic, 31 Norwegian Destinies*
5   BT27/754 (PRO, Kew)

Chapter 6
The British Records of Deaths at Sea

Included in the collection of indexes made available to the public by the General Registrar of England and Wales (and the equivalents in Scotland and Northern Ireland) are the Marine Registers, the large bound indexes to births and deaths at sea which date from the first registration in August 1837 to the present day. Most genealogical researchers are very familiar with them. They are full of names, but all too often also prove to be full of empty promises – the early records of deaths at sea were haphazardly kept and the indexes are a very poor reflection of the numbers of passengers and crew believed to have lost their lives that way. These indexes are only part of the story, however. The original report of the death would have been furnished by the master of the ship or the senior surviving officer to the Registrar of Shipping and Seamen upon his return to port. There will be an entry in the Marine indexes only if that information was forwarded to the General Registrar of the country concerned. In the early days many reports were not, and even for those which were, the quality of the information is variable. Anyone fortunate enough to find the entry they are looking for in the Marine Register indexes and who expects the certificate itself to reveal much more is probably in for a big disappointment. The available information often tells little more than the entry in the index but at least it is a tangible record of a long-lost forebear. The genealogical fraternity is by and large a philosophical group, if only because such disappointments are part and parcel of the family history game.

But for those actually living under the old system, it simply was not good enough. In those early days, sailing in a small wooden boat with canvas sails in a howling gale was a risky business and a large number of passengers really did lose their lives at sea – breadwinners, mothers with children, whole families sometimes wiped out without trace. The loss of life was appalling in itself, but something had to be done to tighten up the reporting and registering of those lost at sea – estates had to be settled, affairs wound up, probate granted. Bereaved families needed to have some legally acceptable evidence of the death so that husbands or wives could be free to marry again. The 19th century was a tough place for a single parent.

By 1850 the machinery was in place. The Mercantile Marine Act of that year required the masters of all merchant ships to record births and deaths occurring on board ship and the Merchant Shipping Act of 1854 tightened up this requirement further. On paper it was all perfectly straightforward. Any birth or death occurring on board was to be entered into the ship's log and submitted with the other ship's papers at the termination of its voyage – the round trip back to its British destination port. If the system ran smoothly, the entries relating to the birth or death (and marriage, though there were few) were extracted by the RGSS (Registrar General of Shipping & Seamen) and the details entered into the registers, now held at the Public Record Office in Kew. Although not all logs survived, some containing the original entries began appearing amongst the collection soon after 1854, but the records are still incomplete. Some entries not made at the time were forgotten, log books were not correctly submitted, the details were not extracted or indeed the ship sank taking with it the vital record. In other words, the system was there but life intervened and continued to do so for some years. Things gradually improved, and by the time *Titanic* sailed, the recording of births and deaths ran smoothly, mostly without incident, and still follows very closely that process today – names are recorded along with any additional information obtained from witnesses or from relatives or friends of the deceased, and the final details entered into the registers. Application may be made for a death certificate, and these days this includes the ship's name, map reference showing where the death occurred, and full details of the deceased.

Carpathia's arrival in New York was greeted with emotional scenes as thousands of New Yorkers crowded the harbour hoping for a glimpse of the *Titanic* survivors. The problem facing the officials waiting at the quay was how best to disembark more than 400 traumatised passengers quickly and smoothly, escort them past onlookers and the waiting hordes of journalists, through any immigration procedures and transport them to a place of safety as quickly as possible. Each survivor required assessment, medical attention and provision of warm clothing, and urgent arrangements had to be made as to their immediate future. Regardless of their mental and physical condition, it was also imperative to interview these passengers urgently in order to ascertain their identity, who their travelling companions had been and their possible fate.

Over the next few days, with the recovery of many bodies from the sea, and all hope gone of finding anyone else alive, relatives of those who died were finally forced to accept that their loved ones were not coming home, and the sorry business began of identification and obtaining the necessary certification to allow the deceased to be buried.

Amidst the waves of despair, the disbelief, the questions and the laying of blame, the Registrar General of Seamen in Britain steadily gathered the information arriving from all sources, and set about as accurately as possible adding the names and details of each person. Little by little the picture became clearer. Meanwhile, the Board of Trade needed urgently to finalise the details of the loss of the vessel for the Marine Department's Wreck Register and to prepare for the Commission of Inquiry to be held shortly in London. Both looked to the White Star Line to provide the first details of the passengers and crew lost and, on 26 April, Sir Walter Howell, the Assistant Secretary of the Board of Trade and head of the Marine Department sent a minute to the RGSS, Sir Henry Malan, formally requiring his response regarding the crew, and giving the number of passengers' lives lost as 815.[1]

Under British law, all deaths must be reported as soon as possible to the local Superintendent Registrar in the district where the death occurred. The details were recorded in locally held indexes and returns submitted to the General Registrar of England and Wales (or of Scotland and Ireland). In cases where the death occurred at sea a different but equally precise chain of events was set in motion.

In the event of a ship foundering with all its papers lost there was no logbook to submit to the RGSS, and therefore no record from which to extract the deaths. Nevertheless the formalities could not be waived. The shipping line, using its own copy of the crew list and passenger records and any other information at its disposal, would substitute a different document for the missing logbook entries of death – List C&D, the Casualty and Deaths list.

The master of any ship arriving in a British port normally proceeded immediately to the office of HM Customs & Excise to complete the necessary formalities and to deposit the ship's papers. If there had been a death on board the vessel, the master would instead report to the superintendent of the port's marine office where the matter would be recorded and first enquiries made. There were frequently witnesses to the incident, and if necessary the superintendent would take statements from any witnesses or anyone with information relevant to the death. Deaths would be recorded by hand on (printed) Form Inq.6, the forerunner of today's Form Inq.15, still used to record details of a death at sea.

Titanic's total loss and the large number of passenger and crew deaths meant that the established routine could not be followed without some direct guidance from the Board of Trade regarding the necessary documentation. The requirement to complete a Form Inq.6 for each separate passenger and crew member was temporarily waived following a statement by William Sanders of the Marine Department, Board of Trade, on 3 May:

'In conformity with the provisions of the M.S.A, & our Instructions to Superintendents, it will be necessary to obtain reports of all the crew & passengers lost from this vessel.

'I think we might now ask the Superintendent at Liverpool, or at Southampton, to prepare the required information.

'It would not appear necessary for the form Inq.6 to be used in each case, but a list might be substituted giving the required particulars as has previously been done in cases of missing vessels or in other cases where a large number of lives were lost.'

The Liverpool office might have seemed a logical choice as *Titanic* was registered there but on 6 May, perhaps with some relief, the Superintendent of the Marine Office on Merseyside wrote to his counterpart in Southampton:

'The White Star Line informs me that the List C&D will be dealt with by their Southampton office; it would therefore be as well for the particulars of deaths to be furnished by you.'

It made perfect sense for the job to fall to the Superintendent at Southampton because as the minute stated, the local office of the White Star Line was to have the task of compiling List C&D thereby simplifying correspondence between the two. On 13 May the completed Form Inq.6 was signed and stamped by A. Smith, the Marine Superintendent at the Mercantile Marine Office and despatched to the Assistant Secretary at the Board of Trade's London headquarters. Based upon information supplied to his office by the White Star Line, Smith had compiled what was to be the first official government record of the names of those who had died on board *Titanic*. Comprising 20 double sheets of blue lined paper, the names of passengers are entered on each left-hand sheet in alphabetical order within each class – surname, first name and initials, nationality and birthplace, age (except for 1st class) and sex. The right-hand sheet was partly typed – class of travel, port and date of embarkation, date and place of death, cause of death and finally last place of abode. Little else is ever heard of Form Inq.6. The Public Record Office file, MT9/920C (Marine Department, Correspondence), now includes the Form Inq.6 list of deceased passengers and crew. It also includes correspondence between the several departments within the Board of Trade: Marine, Solicitor's, and its various outstations including Southampton; and with the RGSS.

Running concurrently with MT9/920C are two other files, BT100/259 and BT100/260. BT100 is the Public Record Office class for logs and crew lists of 'Celebrated Ships' for which *Titanic* must surely qualify. BT100/259 mostly comprises correspondence between the Marine Office in Southampton, the Registrar General of Shipping and Seamen and the White Star Line's Southampton office.

BT100/260 is a little different. In accordance with the formalities discussed earlier, because *Titanic's* papers were lost along with the ship, there was no log in which to submit the names of passengers who had died during the voyage so a List C&D was drawn up – the second officially compiled record of deceased passengers. Whereas regulations were waived for the purposes of recording such a large number of passengers on Form Inq.6, no similar waiver seems to have been applied for the compilation of List C&D. It is a collection of over 60 sheets, each containing names and details of deceased passengers in tiny handwriting to allow the maximum number of names on each page. The pages are numbered from 1 to 60.

Extra sheets were added at a much later date for the purpose of adding names previously omitted – bandsmen and postal workers, and that of a passenger – Catherine McGowan. She had at first been reported lost but an order was given by the Registrar General of Shipping and Seamen on 11 June to strike her name, implying that she had actually been saved. Later reports confirmed that Catherine had died after all so a separate sheet was required to correct the error. The list was first drawn up and signed on 10 May, but remained in constant transit between the three offices until 15 August, as each new piece of updated information was added, and errors corrected.

It is quite proper to find List C&D in BT100/260 because it is the substitute for the official log, but what makes the file unique is that it also contains three separate partial draft copies of the White Star Line's own lists of passengers lost. The filmed copy of the drafts in BT100/260 is disjointed, out of order and haphazardly arranged. By printing each page and reorganising the disarranged sheets, the order in which they were originally compiled is revealed. The first draft was drawn up on 25 April by the White Star Line using as a basis its existing passenger records with the addition of the word 'saved' against the name of each passenger believed at that date to have survived – the list of 2nd class passengers is all that remains of that original draft. Still using copies of the same typeset draft, but including handwritten alterations up to 21st May, only the section showing 1st class passengers remains of the second draft. The draft corrected to 9 May is the only one complete, with alterations known up to that date. It comprises several sections:

A1	First class Passengers
B1	Second class Passengers
C1	Third class Passengers (other than Foreign) embarked at Southampton
D1	Third class Passengers embarked at Queenstown
E1	Third class Scandinavian and Continental Passengers embarked at Southampton
F1	Third class Passengers embarked at Cherbourg

Correspondence with agents overseas or with relatives and friends of the deceased gradually revealed the identity of the majority of those lost, but the shortcomings and inaccuracies contained within all surviving records of passengers' names made the job extremely difficult. The scale of the problem facing them 90 years ago may be imagined if one compares the Register of Deaths At Sea in BT334 dating from 1912 with the latest research. The latter is the result of many years of intense study, with the benefit of experience, the availability of later records, and not least of all, the speed of communications due to computer technology. The former, which is the final, corrected official record of the Registration of Deaths At Sea was the result of a few months of difficult enquiries, without the benefit in many cases even of a telephone. The clerks of 1912 did a magnificent job with the options available to them, but a glance at the Encyclopedia Titanica website exposes the shortcomings of the Register of Deaths At Sea.

As the weeks wore on, a steady stream of letters passed in both directions between the Board of Trade, the Wreck Investigators, the Registrar General of Shipping and Seamen and the White Star Line. Inevitably the task of compiling a List C&D was time consuming and at times frustrating. Some of the discrepancies related to maids, valets and other servants who had not all been named on the passenger lists, being described simply as maids or menservants. The bandsmen had been listed as passengers, travelling in 2nd class, and the status of the post clerks had caused confusion but most of the discrepancies related to spelling errors of passenger names. Nothing could be finalised until the problems could be resolved.

The correspondence in files MT9/920C, BT100/259 and BT100/260 graphically illustrates the frustrating process of gathering information in order for the Registrar General of Shipping and Seamen officially to register the deaths. The records referred to here are for the *Titanic*, but the process was practically the same for the registration of any other deaths at sea – the only difference lies in the huge numbers involved and the fact that, in most cases, similar records have not survived.

Many of the individual pieces of correspondence are signed by several persons, and the dating is haphazard – during the period of investigation, letters or memos previously read, signed and dated were removed from the file to be re-read, so were signed and dated again, and replaced in the file. At a later date, the folios were numbered and some pages are now not where they originally belonged. The result is a confusing collection of letters and minutes, and only when each piece of correspondence from each of the three files has been copied and rearranged in a logical sequence does one begin to follow the dialogue.

Unless otherwise shown, all correspondence discussed below may be found in file reference BT100/259.

The Registrar General of Shipping and Seamen wrote to the Superintendent of the Marine Office in Southampton on 20 May 1912:

'The name of the Bandmaster Hartley does not appear in the list of crew or passengers of the above named vessel and it is presumed the names of all the bandsmen have been similarly omitted. Please ascertain whether there were any other persons in a similar position and request the Owners to render additional Lists C&D with particulars of the deaths.

'On the printed list of 1st class passengers reference is made to 13 servants whose names are not given. Of these 9 appear to have been saved and enquiry should be made to ascertain the names of their employers with a view to the identification of the remaining four who were lost.

'It is observed that the cause of death is stated as Drowned in all cases. If in any case it is known that the death was caused by exposure or other violence and not by drowning a note should be made of the fact in order that the list may be corrected. It might also be ascertained whether "supposed drowned" would not be a more accurate statement with regard to many of the deaths.'

The Superintendent, A. Smith, replied at some length on 22 May:

'If the name of Wm Hartley, bandsman, has been omitted from the list of passengers this is an error. The company desire that the lists C&D may be returned so that the omission is rectified. Attached is a list of 2nd class passengers supplied by the company upon which the names of the bandsmen appear. They were not engaged as members of the crew.

'Attached is a list of the 1st class passengers corrected to date. It has been given to me by the company and has the latest information they possess as to the servants.

'There appears to be satisfactory evidence of death having been due to exposure only in one case – Hoyt Mr W. F. 1st class passenger, list A5. There is nothing at present to show that any of the other deaths was not due directly or indirectly to drowning. In view of all the circumstances however the company are willing to act on the suggestion that they should be put in the return as "supposed drowned".

'If the lists are returned the company will be pleased to alter them accordingly. If further evidence of the cause of death in any particular case is received a note of it will be made by the company.'

Chapter 6

On 30 May, the Registrar General of Shipping and Seamen returned the lists as requested, saying:

'The List C&D rendered for the Titanic are returned herewith with lists of discrepancies.

'On the attached list marked B are shown discrepancies between the printed list of passengers and the account given on List C&D.

'Five manservants [sic] are entered on List C&D but the printed list gives seven, those of Messrs Widener, Ismay, Carter, Straus, Astor, Moore and White. The names of the servants of Col Astor, Mr Straus and Mr Moore appear to have been since ascertained and might now be entered.

'The prefixes Mrs, Mrs &c should have been placed in brackets before the names.

The following discrepancies are not mentioned in the list marked B.

Name of Pass.	1st Printed List	2nd Printed List	C&D
Behr	Saved	Drowned	Not entered
Bjornstrom	Drowned	Saved	Entered
Dr Minahan	Saved	Drowned	Not entered

Carter's manservant is not entered on the second printed list.

'With regard to some of the foreign passengers there is doubt as to which is the forename and which is the surname. Special attention should be given to this and the Christian name or that which corresponds to it, placed first in all cases.

'The name of Washington A Roebling is incorrectly entered on the List C&D. Can it be stated what '2nd' means in his case?'
    (Signed Henry Malan, Registrar General, 30 May)

Apparently the Southampton Superintendent passed the lists on to the White Star Line office, because about a week later a representative of the White Star Line returned them to the Marine Superintendent of the Board of Trade, Southampton, stating:

'We regret that the lists C&D, and printed passenger lists showed discrepancies in consequence of deficient information when furnished. The lists C&D have been amended and as far as we can ascertain are correct. Please cancel the name of H. Bjornstrom from the printed lists, as this passenger has since been ascertained to be Mr H. Bjornstrom Steffansen who was saved.'

On the following day, 7 June, Henry Malan, the Registrar, clearly becoming impatient at the delay in settling the figures, also wrote to the Marine Superintendent at Southampton stating:

'Many urgent applications for certificates of death in respect of the Titanic 131428 have been received but cannot be dealt with until the lists of crew and passengers are completed. If both lists cannot yet be transmitted is it possible to complete and send the list of passengers only.'

On 12 June the Superintendent wrote again to the Registrar General of Shipping and Seamen returning lists C&D to his office but having clearly received further correspondence from the White Star Line office:

'The printed lists of passengers dated 21st May and all up to that date handed in with C&D have been found by the Company to be incorrect in some cases, and the company wish them to be cancelled. The Lists C&D herewith have been corrected as far as possible but the Company state information is still coming in from their agents which may lead to some further corrections, these they will notify as they receive them.

Attached Lists C&D show correct return of servants

Prefixes entered as directed

Behr is reported by the Company as saved

Bjornstrom should read H. Bjornstrom Steffanson, saved

Minaham is now entered on List C&D No 7A as supposed drowned

Carter's manservant (see corrected List C&D No 7)

'Numerous alterations of Christian and surname have been made by the Company on the List C&D and to the best of their knowledge are correct.

'I am informed that 2nd means in America that the deceased was the grandson of Washington A. Roebling and that the father of the same name is called "Junior".

'The additional Lists C&D numbers 7a and 60a are attached with seven additional names.

'The following names have been ruled out
1. Bjornstrom No 1 List C&D
2. Hanna Youseff No 60 List C&D
3. Georges Youseff No 60 List C&D
4. Katherine McGowan No 43 List C&D
5. Bert O'Donoghue No 46 List C&D
6. Thos Emmeth No 31 List C&D

'Numbers 1, 2, 3 and 4 above named have been ascertained by the company to have been saved, number 5 and 6 have been entered on List C&D incorrectly and are not known and entered on No 60a as: 5. Bridget Donohue and 6. Thos Smyth.'

Signed A. Smith, Supt 11 June 1912

The ruling out (on the List C&D) indicated that those passengers had in fact survived. Catherine McGowan's death was later confirmed, however.

Four weeks later, on 9 July, Henry Malan returned the Lists C&D to the Superintendent, Marine Office, Southampton:

'The Lists C&D are returned for the purposes of amendment in the cases of Mullin (544) Chisholm (22) and Thorn (103). All alterations should be attested.'

Smith replied to the Registrar on 10 July confirming:

'The Lists have been amended and attested as requested. A further letter is attached from the White Star Line requesting List C&D for 2 Second class Passengers named Mr Del Carlo and Mrs Edith C. Brown.'

On 10 July, a letter was sent from the White Star Passenger Department to Superintendent, Board of Trade confirming the identity of Thorne/Rosenshine explaining:

'Dear Sir
We return herewith List No 2 of 1 to 60 which you left us with this morning, and in same have altered the name of Mr 'Robert' Chisholm to Roderick Chisholm, and the name of Mr G. Thorne to C. Rosenshine.

'Mr Rosenshine booked in the name of Mr G. Thorne but we have since ascertained that his proper name was Rosenshine, and this has since been established by the recovery of the body and papers found on same.
    'We beg to ask that you will kindly return to us Lists C&D of the Second and Third class passengers by the *Titanic*, as we wish to amend same as under:-
    'Mrs Del Carlo, Second class, saved (shewn on lists as missing)
    'Mrs Brown Edith GJ, Second class, saved (shewn on lists as missing)
    'As regards the Third class lists, there are one or two queries which we have not yet cleared up, but hope to do so within the next few days, and this may necessitate alterations in the lists.'

Smith sent Lists C&D (9 and 11) to the Registrar General of Shipping and Seamen on 12 July saying:

'Lists C&D (9 and 11) are returned corrected and attested.

'The Company thank you for the proposal regarding the Lists for 3rd class passengers, as soon as they can obtain correct particulars which would necessitate their alteration, and to let the question stand over for a few days.'

On 3 August the Registrar wrote to the Superintendent at Southampton returning the lists of 2nd class passengers and a week later, the Superintendent returned the lists to the Registrar once more, stating:

'Lists C&D returned herewith. The White Star Line reports the death of Mrs Anna Lahtinen, 2nd class passenger who has been entered on an additional List C&D. The name Nasser (deceased) should be Nasralla. The Company has made the necessary alteration. Several changes in the spelling of the 3rd class passengers are reported. Perhaps you will be good enough to forward these lists for revision.'

On 15 August, by which time clearly the Registrar had forwarded the lists to the White Star Line who had in turn corrected them and returned them to the Marine Office at Southampton, the Superintendent at Southampton wrote again to the Registrar General of Shipping and Seamen:

'Lists of Third class passengers returned herewith, the owners having made the desired alterations. An additional List reporting another death is attached. List No 28 is also forwarded herewith.'

The 'additional list' referred to here is almost certainly the supplementary list finally correctly confirming the death of Catherine McGowan.

Who Sailed on Titanic?

List C&D, dated 15 August 1912 was signed and delivered up on that date and it appears from the records that the Registrar General of Shipping and Seamen accepted that as an accurate representation of those who had died.

With the correspondence now continuing in file MT9/920C, on 23 August he issued a statement reading:

'The loss of life as shown by the list of Crew and Passengers rendered by the owners is as follows:

Crew	673
Passengers	825
Total	1,498

Still concerned with accurate figures, the Marine Department of the Board of Trade wrote to the Board of Trade Solicitor's Department on 23 August:

'Have you any further information as to number of passengers lost. In Lord Mersey's report the number lost is given as 817.'

The Solicitor's Department replied, later that day:

'The figures given in the Report are the result of all the later information received by the owners. Many alterations had to be made in the lists first submitted by the Marine Department.'

On the following day the Marine Department sent a memo to the Receiver of Wreck at Liverpool, asking:

'The Receiver of Wreck, Liverpool is requested to communicate with the Owners of the Titanic as to the number of passengers lost.'

The reply came from the Receiver of Wreck four days later, dated Liverpool, 28 August:

'I forward herewith the answer received from the owners.

'The numbers given as lost in Report of Inquiry are 673 Crew and 817 passengers and these numbers will be shown in W. Abst.

'[to] Registrar General of Seamen, for his information. Please return the papers as soon as possible.'

The numbers obviously did not agree and the Registrar General of Shipping and Seamen pointed this out in his reply dated 31 August:

'The number of passengers supposed drowned is given by the Owners as 825 as follows:-

1st class	123
2nd class	166
3rd class	536
	825

Above: *Titanic*, attended by tugs, departs from Belfast for Southampton.
Robert McDougall collection

Below: Aerial view of the Floating Dock, Southampton, circa 1912.
Robert McDougall collection

Above: White Star liners in Southampton docks, before World War 1. *Robert McDougall collection*

Below: Aerial view of Southampton docks, including *Titanic's* sister shop *Olympic* moored at Ocean Dock, top right. *Robert McDougall collection*

Right: J. Bruce Ismay, White Star Line Chairman and Managing Director and *Titanic* survivor.
Robert McDougall collection

Below: The South Western Hotel, Southampton, used by Ismay and others before *Titanic* sailed.
Robert McDougall collection

Bottom: Quayside station at Hull, the first sight of England for many of *Titanic's* transmigrant passengers, shown on a postcard dated 1913.
Nicholas J. Evans collection

Above: View of Cherbourg Harbour, circa 1912. *Robert McDougall collection*

Below: View of the harbour at Queenstown, circa 1915, showing the railway station and the White Star Line jetty. *Robert McDougall collection*

Above: Queenstown's waterfront c1912, showing the two White Star tenders, *Ireland* and *America*.
Robert McDougall collection

Below: Coffins ready to be taken on board the *Minia*, in Halifax.
Maritime Museum of the Atlantic, Nova Scotia

These photographs were taken in the days following the 2001 exhumations.

Left: Fairview Lawn Cemetery, Halifax, Nova Scotia, where many of those who died when the *Titanic* sank are buried.
Sue & Gery Swiggum collection

Left: Gravestone of the unknown child buried in Fairview Lawn Cemetery.
Sue & Gery Swiggum collection

Below: Mount Olivet Cemetery in Halifax, Nova Scotia, burial site of the Roman Catholic victims of the *Titanic* disaster.
Sue & Gery Swiggum collection

ERECTED
TO THE MEMORY
OF AN
UNKNOWN CHILD
WHOSE REMAINS
WERE RECOVERED
AFTER THE
DISASTER TO
THE "TITANIC"
APRIL 15TH 1912

Above: Gravestone of William Harrison, J. Bruce Ismay's Secretary, in Fairview Lawn Cemetery.
Sue & Gery Swiggum collection

Right: The memorial in Sturt Park, Broken Hill, Australia to *Titanic's* bandmaster Wallace Hartley and the other members of the band. Hartley's body was recovered by the cable ship *Mackay Bennett*, and shipped back to Britain aboard *Arabic*. He was buried in his home town of Colne, Lancashire. *Author's collection*

The following pages are reproduced from the *Daily Graphic* 'Special Titanic in Memoriam Number, April 20 1912'. Published a week after the disaster, its pictures show a gallery of 'notable' passengers lost and saved as well as poignant scenes outside the White Star Line's offices in London and Southampton as friends and relatives of the passengers wait for news of the fate of their loved ones.

THE OCEAN GRAVE OF THE TITANIC.

LOST LINER'S TRAGEDY.

THE SAILING AND— THE END.

ICE, THE FOE.

SHOCK THAT RENT THE SHIP.

THE BRAVE DEAD.

WOMEN SAVED BY MEN'S SACRIFICE.

The largest ship in the world went to sea from Southampton harbour on the tenth of April, 1912.

People spoke of the tenth of April as a great day in the history of shipping, and they said ...y gave utterance to a truth more awful than could be conceived by living man.

It was a great day also in the history of Southampton, for many fathers of families had found employment on the Titanic, many women's faces were lightened because the shadow of need and poverty had been banished from their homes.

It was a day that no one who stood upon the quayside will ever forget. We who saw it saw a sight that will be unforgettable until our eyes are turned to dust.

We saw the start of the mightiest vessel in the world upon her solitary and uncompleted voyage. She was named Titanic and she has been Titanic in her sorrow. We saw her, the mightiest, finest product of human brains in the matter of ships to sail the sea, a gigantic vessel that realised in her being a floating city of treasured glories, riches, and luxury, as she first ploughed the grey fields of the ocean.

And her displacement of water, the foam, and the rush of her passage, was so tremendous that the stern ropes of another mighty liner parted and the New York, but for the ready aid of holding tugs, would have swung out aimlessly into the fairway.

THE HAPPY START.

We paused in our cheering then, chilled to a sudden silence at this first evidence of the great ship's untested powers for evil as for good. And our cheering now is hushed into sobbing, for within a week of her majestic passage from Southampton Harbour, the displacement of the Titanic has been so tremendous that she has drenched the bosom of the world in an ocean of tears.

Those of us who had come to wish the vessel "Good speed"—in the dark wisdom of Providence to wish "God speed" and "a fair journey" to those loved ones who were going out on the longest and loneliest voyage in Eternity—were up "by times" on that pleasant Wednesday morning, long before the stroke of noon when we knew Captain Smith would climb into his lofty perch on the navigating bridge and give the order to "let go" from the Trafalgar landing stage.

The air was busy with chatter, with "good for the present" and good wishes. We lived that morning in an atmosphere of pride. All these happy-faced Southampton women were proud that their men had entered into service on the greatest vessel ever built by man. They prattled of the Titanic with a sort of suggestion of proprietorship. Rumours and legends and tales of her glories luxuries and powers were bandied about in every street in Southampton. She was a caravanserai of marvels; a mighty treasure house of beauty and luxurious ease. In the phrase of the ...e, she was "the last word." The phrases of people are often true, because they are ...e edged.

Another phrase sticks now in the puzzle of a ...ing mind: "They're breaking all records this ..." And so they were. It had been determined that the Titanic should excel in luxury and equipment her sister vessel, the Olympic, which had sailed for New York a week before. And in a sort of desperate endeavour to achieve this we who had come to take a temporary parting from dear ones and friends were shown a new and latest marvel on the promenade deck of the Titanic. It was called the Café Parisien. Its walls were covered with a delicate trellis work around which trailed cool foliage. We looked at the soft-cushioned chairs, we regarded the comfort of the whole scene, and, feeling the suggestive atmosphere of the place, thought of those who would be taking coffee there after dinner with music lulling every sense, melting into the gentle roll and rhythm of the open sea. What a place in which to dream!—perhaps if one were young to hold a little romantic dalliance—what a place in which to forget the trials and harass of the world! What a place in which to sleep!

Some of us looked into the private suites that were to cost a mere trifle of £870 a voyage, and here we found snug dining-rooms, bedrooms that looked in themselves like little enchanted palaces of slumberous rest, and private promenade decks. Let us note that everyone spoke of "dining-rooms" and "bedrooms." The word "cabin" would have been an anachronism in this floating citadel of luxurious beauty. We examined the delicate glass and napery, the flowers and the fruit, the baths and the playing-courts, and the innumerable mechanical appliances that seemed to make personal effort or discomfort the only human impossibility on board.

There was one thing that no one looking even for a brief half-hour on this cushioned lap of luxury ever thought of giving a cursory glance or a thought. No one looked at the boats.

Punctually at noon Captain E. J. Smith, a typical figure of an English sailor as we knew him and imagined him in tougher, pre-Titanic days, took up his post of captainship on the navigating bridge. And as the bells sounded, the cheers of the multitudes went upward and hands and handkerchiefs were waved from quay and ship's side, and kisses were blown across and last familiar greetings exchanged.

So she went away with her human freight of two thousand two hundred and eight souls. We cheered to the last and waved our salutations, and that night I think there was not an unhappy woman in all Southampton. And to-night—who is to count the tear-stained faces or to cast a reckoning over the travail of these broken hearts, some here, some two thousand miles away, but all united beyond the cleavage of the pitiless seas, by the sacred companionship of sorrow!

THE NOBLE ELEMENT IN THE OCEAN TRAGEDY.

No element of tragedy seems to have failed to contribute its share to the overwhelming catastrophe of the Titanic. The forces of nature shook themselves free from the chains with which Man would bind them, burst in all their power from the limits in which he has sought to confine them, and dealt him a blow that has sent mourning through two nations. His last word in ship construction, equipped with every last device making for safety, or for aid in case of need, met at her maiden issue with the sea a challenge that broke her utterly and took her in toll with over twelve hundred of the lives she carried.

The magnitude of such a disaster leaves the mind as incapable of expressing the emotions aroused in it as its agencies were powerless to avert the catastrophe. For years we take our eager, heedless way, demanding more and more of life, increasingly impatient of its hindrances to our pleasure and our business, increasingly bold and cunning in overcoming them, and never pausing but to congratulate ourselves upon our triumphs. Every now and then comes some cataclysmic reminder that, if it is not possible to go too far and too fast, it is very possible to congratulate ourselves too well. For a brief moment we are brought to a full stop.

We trust the relatives of those who have perished may find some solace in the thought that though they have been called upon to suffer a grief almost unendurable to bear, they suffer it amidst that deepest sympathy which only when we are brought to face the realities of life can be aroused. For us, as for them, moreover, there is heartening thought in one thing that can be read into the disaster from the facts that have come to light. It is terribly clear that scenes of most dreadful horror must have taken place in the few hours between the Titanic's striking and her disappearance. And it is clear, from the fact that women and children form by far the greater majority of the saved, that in this dire emergency the imperilled rose to supreme heights of courage and devotion. Millionaire and steerage emigrant alike were called upon: alike they have presented us with that most inspiring of all spectacles—the inherent nobility of mankind.

WHAT WE THOUGHT—

So the Titanic went her away, and we went ours, and thought perhaps little about her, save thoughts of remembered joy in her strength and beauty, until on Tuesday morning came the news that smote upon our hearts with the thunder of doom. These were, of course, the first indefinite rumblings that woke fear in every human breast.

She had struck an iceberg; she had been rent; but she was unsinkable. She was heading slowly for shore, a great giant wounded thing in the wake of the Virginian. How our hopes died down until it seemed that the heart was burnt into a heap of dead cold ashes, only to rise, Phœnix-like, in jubilant and hopeful expectancy. Human lips have sobbed out strange prayers before to-day, but what volume of prayer went up to heaven in thankfulness to the Lord of Hosts who had brought the new wonder of wireless telegraphy out of the slow womb of time.

We thought of that unforgettable message speeding through the viewless air that is marked upon the chart sheets S.O.S. We picked up the common phrase of the operator and repeated to ourselves: "Save Our Souls," and thanked Providence for their salvation.

We pictured the scene. The lonely operator, composed with that old English valiance that has turned the blood of history into wine, calmly tapping out the cry of help. We saw the realisation of that message in the operator's cabin on other vessels. We saw the wonderful chain composed of those three words, stronger than stone or iron or tempered steel, stronger than wind or sea, suddenly dragging all the vessels within the sphere of hearing away from their allotted course, and sending them on the great adventure of succour and mercy. We pictured them racing along the railless roads of the open sea, rushing with insensate speed towards the spot of the catastrophe. We had leisure to imagine the scene, because we were told there had been a great deliverance; because we felt that man had fought his battle with the ocean and had won.

Then we knew that we had lost.

—AND WHAT WE LEARNT.

All the world knows how slowly those confessions of defeat came in upon us, how slowly the last flicker of an expiring hope was beaten down within our breasts, with what dilatory hands the veils were drawn from the implacable face of doom. Gradually the hush laid hold upon us, gradually a realisation of what had happened sank into our souls.

We knew that nothing but a miserable residue of the great human freightage had been saved to us. We knew that the enchanted floating palace, conceived by the brain of man and wrought by his hands, with all its mighty scheme of luxurious ease, health, and comfort, lay somewhere tangled in an old sea forest, two miles beneath the quiet surface of the sea. Little more do we know as I write. We can only hear the sobbing of the women at the street corners of Southampton, and find in them an eternal echo of the cheers with which we sent the Titanic out on her first, her last, her only voyage.

We know that among these women are many mothers. We know with thankfulness that though their faces are dark with sorrow they are untouched with the lightest shadow of shame. For though man has been beaten once again in his old fight with the sea, yet he has done one thing with all the glory and splendour of a victory.

He has taken the last gift of God and used it well. He has died as we all would die—for others.

Picturing that last dark awful moment, the last order of the captain, the last farewells—so different from these we exchanged at Southampton—the last tears and the last high human courage, all our sorrow is tempered by the thought that the women are alive to us and the children, and that the men died as we would have had them die, as we should like to have died ourselves had God steeled our hearts with a similar courage.

Knowing this, as we peer into the dark picture of that yet unrecorded scene, so deep with human anguish and yet so lighted with human grandeur, we may learn to endure the sobbings of the women and the cries of the fatherless that come up to us in every surge of the immemorial sea. Knowing this, we may take comfort in the great cry of a great poet in a sea-washed island that had born so many poets, and acclaim with him that:—

Nothing is here for tears, nothing to wail,
Or knock the breast, no weakness, no contempt,
Dispraise or blame, nothing but well and fair,
And what may quiet us in a death so noble.

A WIRELESS CABIN ON AN ATLANTIC LINER

Appalling as is the loss of life the death-roll would have been much longer but for the wireless telegraph. This picture shows a typical Marconi cabin on a large Atlantic liner, a cabin similar to that from which the signal "S.O.S." was despatched immediately after the Titanic had struck the iceberg.

THE OCEAN GRAVE OF THE TITANIC.

SECOND EDITION.

THE LINER DE LUXE.

SPLENDOUR THAT NOW LIES IN THE DEPTHS.

A MILLION AND A HALF.

RESTAURANT, RACQUET COURT AND PARISIAN CAFE.

Sister to the Olympic, the Titanic was the last word in ocean liners and the largest ship in the world. Her fittings were the most luxurious of any vessel afloat, including a restaurant, furnished in the Louis XVI. style, a reception-room of Jacobean style, and a squash racquet court.

The Titanic's displacement was 46,328 tons, 1,004 tons more than that of the Olympic. She cost over a million and a half. She was built by Messrs. Harland and Wolff at Belfast, and launched on May 31st, 1911. Her building took over a year, and her fitting-out nearly another year.

Some idea of the Titanic's enormous size may be gauged from the following figures:—

Total length, 882ft. 9in.
Breadth, 92½ft.
Height from keel to navigating bridge, 104ft.
Gross tonnage, 45,000.
Load draft, 34½ft.
Displacement, 60,000 tons.
Indicated horse-power of reciprocating engines, 30,000.
Shaft horse-power of turbine engine, 16,000.
Speed, 21 knots.

She carried ten decks, of which seven were passenger decks. The bridge deck extended over a length of 550ft. amidships, while the promenade and boat-decks were also over 500ft. long.

For first-class passengers there were thirty suite rooms on the bridge deck, and thirty-nine on the shelter deck, so arranged that they could be let in groups to form suites, including bedrooms, with baths, etc., with communicating doors. In all, the first-class accommodation comprised nearly 370 100 of which were single-berth rooms.

The Titanic was a floating town with accommodation for a population of over 3,000 people, made up as follows:—

Saloon passengers	750
Second-class passengers ...	500
Steerage passengers	1,100
Crew	800
Total	3,150

ENORMOUS FOOD STORES.

To feed this community she carried the following stores:—

Fresh meat	75,000lb.	Sweetbreads	1,000lb.
Fresh fish	11,000lb.	Coffee	2,200lb.
Salt fish	4,000lb.	Tea	800lb.
Bacon and ham	7,500lb.	Sugar	10,000lb.
Fresh butter	6,000lb.	Jams	1,120lb.
Poultry	8,000 head.	Flour	200 barrels.
Fresh eggs	40,000	Potatoes	40 tons.
Sausages	2,500lb.	Apples	180 boxes.

The ship was fitted with electrically-controlled watertight doors, and those giving communication between the various boiler-rooms and engine-rooms were arranged, as usual in White Star Line steamers, on the "drop system." They were of Messrs. Harland and Wolff's special design, of massive construction, and provided with oil cataracts.

Each door, according to the official description, was held in the open position by a friction clutch, which could instantly be released by means of a powerful electric magnet controlled from the captain's bridge, so that in the event of accident the captain, by simply moving an electric switch, could instantly close the doors throughout, thus, it was believed, practically making the vessel unsinkable.

As a further precaution, floats were provided beneath the floor level, which, in the event of water accidentally entering any of the compartments, would automatically lift and thereby close the doors opening into that compartment if they had not already been dropped.

The lifeboats attached to the liner were 30ft. long, and mounted on special davits on the boat deck. For purposes of wireless telegraphy the Titanic had two masts 205ft. above the average draught-line.

UNPARALLELED LUXURY.

Among the features of the Titanic may be mentioned the first-class promenades on the three top decks, which were exceptionally fine. In keeping with the public rooms were the large and beautiful first-class state-rooms, perhaps the most striking of these being the suite rooms decorated in different styles and periods, including the following:—Louis Seize, Empire, Adams, Italian Renaissance, Louis Quinze, Louis Quatorze, Georgian, Regence, Queen Anne, Modern Dutch, Old Dutch.

The Titanic's special features were the two promenade deck suites, with private promenades about fifty feet long—an absolutely novel feature—and the open-air Parisian café which adjoined the restaurant. The rates for these two suites during the busy season was to be £870 each.

The following is the official account of the Titanic's first-class dining saloon:—

"It is an immense room decorated in a style peculiarly English, reminiscent of early Jacobean times; but instead of the sombre oak of the sixteenth and seventeenth centuries, it is painted a soft, rich white, which, with the coved and richly-moulded ceilings and the spacious character of the apartment, would satisfy the most æsthetic critic.

"The furniture is of oak designed to harmonise with its surroundings."

THE DEAD CAPTAIN.

CAPTAIN SMITH'S CAREER.

FROM THE RAMMED OLYMPIC TO THE ILL-FATED TITANIC.

AN UNLUCKY RECORD.

By a remarkable coincidence Captain E. J. Smith, R.N.R., who was in command of the Titanic, was captain of the Olympic when, last September, she was in collision with the cruiser Hawke off Cowes.

As the vessel was subject to compulsory pilotage, the responsibility for her course was not Commander Smith's, but that of the Trinity pilot who was in charge.

Captain Smith entered the White Star service thirty-eight years ago, and has commanded in turn many of the White Star cracks, including the old Republic, the Britannic, and the Germanic, and for nine years was in command of the Majestic.

During the South African War he twice carried troops out in the Majestic, bringing back sick and wounded on the return trips. He was decorated by the King for his services.

He next commanded the Baltic, and then the Adriatic. Then, on the sailing of the Olympic, he was transferred to her, and finally to the Titanic.

He held an extra master's certificate, and was an honorary commander of the Royal Naval Reserve.

Other leading officers were Surgeon W. F. N. O'Loughlin, Assistant-Surgeon J. E. Simpson, Pursers H. W. McElroy and R. L. Barker, and Chief Steward A. Latimer.

CAPTAIN SMITH'S DEATH.

BRAVE MAN'S FIRST ORDER: "CLOSE THE EMERGENCY DOORS."

Mr. George A. Braden states: "I saw Captain Smith while I was in the water. He was standing on the deck all alone.

"Once he was swept down by a wave, but managed to get to his feet again.

"Then, as the boat sank, he was again knocked down by a wave, and then disappeared from view." —Reuter.

Robert Hichens, the Titanic's quartermaster, says Captain Smith's first word after the collision was: "Close the emergency doors."

"They're already closed, sir," replied Mr. Murdock, the first officer.

"Send for the carpenter, and tell him to sound the ship," said the captain, but the carpenter never came, for he had been killed in the first crash.

"I was at the wheel," continued the quartermaster, "until 12.25, when Second Officer Lightoller told me to take charge of a lifeboat and load it with ladies. I did so."

Captain Smith's self-sacrifice and heroism, even after the bridge had disappeared beneath the waves, has been commended by all.

Before he was literally washed from his post of duty he called through his megaphone, "Be British!" to the mass below. Later he was seen in the act of helping those struggling in the water, refusing an opportunity to save himself.

THE COMMANDER OF THE TITANIC AND THE BOWS OF HIS SHIP.

The portrait of Captain Smith was taken on board the Titanic on the day of the vessel's departure from Southampton. He was in command of the Olympic, the Titanic's sister ship, when, on her maiden voyage, she collided with H.M.S. Hawke.

SAVING A CHILD.

FURTHER ACCOUNTS OF CAPTAIN SMITH'S END.

Captain Smith, who is generally described as a typical British seaman of the old-fashioned type, is reported to have had a presentiment that the maiden voyage of the Titanic would be unlucky. He is also reported to have said that if anything serious happened to the ship he would go down with her.

All the survivors testify to the dead captain's valour and coolness in the last hour of trial.

Mr. Robert Davill, of Richmond, Virginia, said:—

"Captain Smith stuck to the bridge and behaved like a hero."

One fireman, who was on the bridge with the captain when the ship went down, said Captain Smith jumped into the water when the bridge was awash, and so far as is known no one saw him after that.

"I was on the bridge deck," said the fireman. The last boat was launched and the water began to break over the bridge on which Captain Smith stood. We were not able to launch the boat properly, so it was overturned, and was used as a raft.

When the water reached Captain Smith's knees and the last boat was at least 20ft. from the ship I was standing beside him.

"He gave one look all around, his face firm, and his lips hard set. He looked as if he might be trying to keep back the tears, as he thought of the doomed ship. I felt mightily like crying myself as I looked at him.

"It was the intention of the captain to put two little children on a boat, but when it overturned it was swept away. Many of those who had jumped as the ship went down, as I did, were saved by it.

"I looked around for the captain after I got to the overturned boat, but he was nowhere in sight.

"How did he act on the bridge while I was there? Always directing the lowering of the boats himself, and he was always shouting, 'Women and children first.' I think when he struck the water the cold made him let go his hold of the child, and he must have been swept away from the boats.

ICE AND FOG ROUTE.

DANGER ZONE IN THE NORTH ATLANTIC.

THE SAFE COURSE.

ROUTE THAT WOULD SKIRT THE PERIL.

The tragedy of the Titanic has drawn attention to the danger wilfully encountered by the great Atlantic liners of steaming over a course some 800 miles of which is known at certain periods of the year to be infected with ice-floes or icebergs.

Apart, too, from the presence of ice—which extends between March and August over a region chiefly surrounding Newfoundland, and at an average distance from it of nearly 1,000 miles—there is a coincident season during which fog or mist is prevalent over the North Atlantic. This is also chiefly concentrated over the Newfoundland area.

An inspection of the admirable monthly fog and mist maps for the North Atlantic, published by the Meteorological Office under the direction of their marine superintendent, Captain Hepworth, shows that the fog season prevails from April to September inclusive, while from October to March fog is seldom recorded on the steamer routes.

The maximum fog frequency of the North Atlantic in all months is found near the banks of Newfoundland, but, while it seldom exceeds 5 per cent. between October and February, it rises to as much as 40 per cent. in July.

In April fog begins to spread almost continuously across the ocean along the latitude of London, while the same month marks its first expansion southwards to a few miles south of latitude 40deg. Near Newfoundland fog forms 20 per cent. of the entries in April, but thereafter in May, June, and July it rises to 40 per cent. At the northerly confluence of the Gulf Stream and the Labrador current the risk from fog is eight[illegible] as great in mid-summer as in mid-winter.

LIMITS OF THE FOG BELT.

After July the southern limit of the fog-zone shifts to the north of latitude 40deg., and the ice-zone withdraws in the same direction. In July and August the route ordinarily followed by the liners condemns them to the danger and discomfort of fog during most of their passage, while in the latter month the contemplated change to a route a few degrees further south would enable vessels to be virtually fog-free a day or two after leaving Ireland up to their arrival at New York.

The prevalence of fog, or even mist, is a danger only second to that of ice, and when, as is frequently the case, they occur together, the presence of the former adds very greatly to the danger of the latter. A glance at the fog charts between April and September would be enough to warn any ordinary person from attempting a voyage across the Atlantic during these months by any of the existing routes. Quite apart from ice-fields or icebergs, derelicts or tramps present a sufficient danger.

From a rough calculation it would appear that between August and April a great circle-route from the Fastnet to longitude 47deg. W. and latitude 38deg. N. would secure freedom from both ice and fogs. During the remainder of the year—that is to say, during the iceberg and fog season—it would be much safer to adopt a route by which a great circle is sailed from the Fastnet to longitude 40deg. W. and latitude 38deg. N. The difference between such a route and the one ordinarily in vogue would not be more than about 370 miles, and the extra safety and comfort would be cheaply purchased.

The leading companies have given instructions to change the route of their steamers to one about three of four degrees further south, thus skirting the danger zone. It is a measure that must not be temporary—but permanent.

HEROIC COUPLES.

HUSBANDS AND WIVES WHO SACRIFICED THEMSELVES.

All the accounts of rescued passengers agree that Mrs. Isidore Straus refused to leave her husband.

Mr. Jacques Futrelle, the well-known American author, says Reuter, was also one of those who parted from his wife and steadfastly refused to accept a chance to enter a lifeboat when he knew that the Titanic was sinking. How he went to his death is told by Mrs. Futrelle, who said:—

"When the Titanic hit the iceberg there was the most appalling excitement, and who, after passing through such experiences, could blame those poor people for the panic which overwhelmed them! Jacques is dead, but he died like a hero, that I know. Three or four times after the crash I rushed up to him and clasped him in my arms, begging him to get into one of the lifeboats.

"'For God's sake, go!' he screamed, and tried to push me towards the lifeboat. I could see how he suffered.

"'It's your last chance, go!' he pleaded.

"Then one of the ship's officers forced me into a lifeboat and I gave up all hope that he could be saved."

SOME OF THE TITANIC'S NOTABLE PASSENGERS.

Lady Duff-Gordon ("Lucile").—She is known to be saved.
(Photographed by Bassano, Old Bond Street.)

Mr. and Mrs. Daniel Marvin, who were returning to New York from their honeymoon. Mr. Marvin is only nineteen years of age, and his bride is a year younger. Their parents are prominent New York people. Mrs. Marvin was saved.
(Photographed at the Dover Street Studios.)

Mrs. J. J. Astor, wife of Colonel J. J. Astor, the well-known millionaire.—She is known to be saved.

Isidor Straus, formerly a member of the United States Congress, and a partner in the New York firm of L. Straus and Son.

Master Harry Widener, son of the traction magnate who recently bought Rembrandt's " The Mill."

Mr. Cardoza, a partner in the firm of Cardoza Brothers, of Rio de Janeiro and New York.—Known to be saved.

Mrs. F. J. Swift, a New York society hostess.—Known to be saved.

Mr. J. J. Borebank, a well-known Californian horticulturist.

Major Archibald W. Butt, aide-de-camp to President Taft.

Mr. Charles Williams, the racquets champion, who was on his way to New York to meet G. Standing.

Mr. C. M. Hays, the president of the Grand Trunk Railway.

Mrs. H. B. Harris, daughter-in-law of an American theatre owner.—Known to be saved.

Mrs. C. E. H. Stengel, an American society hostess and wife of a well-known racehorse owner.—Known to be saved.

Miss Margaret Graham, a well-known Californian actress.—Known to be saved.

Mrs. G. M. Stone, well known in American society.—Known to be saved.

X

SOME OF THE TITANIC'S NOTABLE PASSENGERS.

Mr. Herbert Parsons, formerly Congressman for New York City.

Mr. Francis M. Warren, formerly United States Senator for Wyoming.

Mr. W. Van der Hoef, a prominent citizen of Minneapolis.

Mr. P. Marechal, a well-known resident of Washington.—Known to be saved.

Miss E. M. Eustis, well known in New York society.—Known to be saved.

Mrs. J. Snyder, well known in New York society.

Mrs. Figler, well known in New York society.

Mrs. Ettlinger, well known in New York society.

Mr. Christopher Head, ex-Mayor of Chelsea.

Colonel Archibald Gracie, a large cotton grower, of Jefferson County, Arkansas.

Mr. George Eastman.

Mr. J. H. Ross, a professor of Wisconsin University.

The Countess of Rothes.—Known to be saved. (Photographed by Lafayette, Bond Street.)

Miss Gladys Cherry, daughter of Lady Emily Cherry.—Known to be saved. (Photographed by Kate Pragnell.)

Mrs. F. M. Hoyt, wife of an ex-Governor of Washington.—Known to be saved.

Mrs. W. E. Carter, of Pennsylvania.

HELP FOR THE SUFFERERS: THE MUCH-DISCUSSED BOATS.

A MITE'S CONTRIBUTION TO THE LORD MAYOR'S FUND.

THE TITANIC'S LIFEBOATS ON THE DAVITS.

THE MAY FAMILY OF SOUTHAMPTON: THIS GROUP CONTAINS SIX OF THE SEVEN CHILDREN OF ONE OF THE TITANIC'S SAILORS. THEIR MARRIED BROTHER WAS ALSO ON BOARD, AND HIS WIFE, WITH HER TWO-MONTHS'-OLD BABY, IS SEEN ON THE RIGHT.   ("Daily Graphic" photographs.)

A LINE OF THE TITANIC'S BOATS.—THE LINER CARRIED SIXTEEN UNDER DAVITS AND FOUR ENGELHARDT BOATS, CAPABLE OF ACCOMMODATING 1,178 PERSONS IN ALL. ONLY 705, INCLUDING PASSENGERS AND CREW, HOWEVER, WERE SAVED.

A LINER THREADING HER WAY THROUGH A FIELD OF ICE IN THE NORTH ATLANTIC.

In this sketch a "Daily Graphic" artist has re-constructed from telegraphic descriptions the scene in the North Atlantic when a liner encounters one of the dreaded ice fields. The Carmania, which arrived at New York, reports that she ran through a field seventy miles in length.

The passengers state that twenty-five bergs were sighted in one cluster, and that some of them were no further than a hundred feet away from the vessel. The liner had to feel her way through the ice lane for hours. She finally put about, and steering south avoided further danger.

THE HOURS OF AWFUL SUSPENSE IN LONDON.

Relatives and friends of passengers on the Titanic studying the lists of the saved, and leaving the White Star Line offices at Oceanic House, Cockspur Street, after making anxious inquiries for news.

BREAKING THE NEWS OF THE TITANIC'S LOSS WITH OVER TWELVE HUNDRED LIVES TO LONDON.

Consternation reigned in London when the news of the Titanic's awful fate became known. All day long the City and West End offices of the White Star Company, over which the White Star flag floated at half-mast, were besieged by anxious relations and friends of those who sailed in the liner. The photograph on the left shows the flag at half-mast over Oceanic House, Cockspur Street. At the top, on the right, the scene inside the Cockspur Street offices is depicted, and below an anxious crowd is seen outside the City offices of the company.

THE ALLAN LINER VIRGINIAN, THE FIRST VESSEL TO RECEIVE THE TITANIC'S WIRELESS MESSAGE OF DISTRESS. UNFORTUNATELY SHE ARRIVED TOO LATE TO BE OF SERVICE.

aster Spedden, son of Mr. John Spedden, of
New York.

Mr. Harry Rogers, of Tavistock.

Mr. Thomas Andrews.

Mrs. W. D. Douglas, well known in American
society.—Known to be saved.

THE AGONISING WAIT FOR THE LIST OF THE LOST AT SOUTHAMPTON.

The majority of the Titanic's crew belonged to Southampton, and day after day the relations swarmed round the offices of the White Star Company in Canute Road anxiously awaiting tidings. As hour after hour passed and no list of the lost, or additions to the list of the saved were forthcoming, the distress of the people was pitiable to witness. The company erected a great board in readiness to receive the list as soon as it should come, and though repeatedly told that delay was inevitable, nothing could persuade the sufferers to leave this board.

THE ICEBERG ABOVE AND BELOW THE WATER.

The iceberg is one of those dangers to shipping against which the ingenuity of man cannot guard. It often rises from 150 to 300 feet above the sea level, and seven or eight times as much is under the surface of the water.

THE UPPER DECK OF THE TITANIC.

A view showing some of the lifeboats by which many of the survivors left the ship. Most of the boats were filled with women and children, and all these boats have been accounted for.

"Daily Graphic" photograph.)

MANSION HOUSE FUND OPENED FOR THE WIDOWS AND CHILDREN OF TITANIC SAILORS.

The Lord Mayor very promptly opened a fund at the Mansion House for the relief of the widows and orphans of those sailors of the Titanic who have gone down in the ship. In this picture the Lord Mayor's servants are seen fixing a public collecting box outside the Mansion House. The King and Queen, and Queen Alexandra were among the first to send donations to the fund.

The names are given in every case. Possibly the discrepancy in the numbers may be partly accounted for by the previous omission of the Postal Service.'

The Solicitor's Department of the Board of Trade sent a memo to the Marine Department dated 2 September asking for further information on this point. The Marine Department responded the following day, 3 September, stating:

'We had better show 825 passengers as lost, as the RGS has the names.'

A little over three weeks later, William Sanders of the Marine Department, Board of Trade, sent the following communication to Sir Walter Howell, Assistant Secretary of the Board of Trade, dated 27 September:

'The Report of the Inquiry by Lord Mersey gives the number of lives lost in the Titanic as 673 crew and 817 passengers but the Registrar General of Seamen while agreeing with the report as to the number of crew lost, gives the number of passengers lost as 825. As the Registrar General has the names of those lost, it would appear that the latter number is the correct one and should therefore be shown in the Wreck Abstract.'

Sir Walter Howell replied to his message on 27 September, agreeing to the proposal. Next Mr Hargreaves of the Marine Department, Board of Trade, wrote to the Registrar General of Shipping and Seamen on 2 October:

'We have a record of 821 passengers lost in the Titanic but it would appear that 825 passengers were drowned at the time of the casualty. The RGS suggests that the discrepancy in the numbers may be accounted for by the previous omission of members of the Postal Service. Request RGS to be so good as to forward particulars relating to the names, ages and nationality of the persons referred to.'

The list was immediately supplied by the Registrar General on 3 October. Then follows a minute signed by Sanders of the Marine Department, Board of Trade, and dated 23 October:

'It would appear from a later minute (attached) by Registrar General of Seamen that 826 passengers – instead of 825 – were lost. Show this number in the Wreck Abstract.'

This is followed by a note, in an unidentified hand:

'825 is correct. See subsequent paper.'

A minute from Hargreaves followed the same day reading:

'Our lists show 821 passengers lost – including the above the total will be 826 – see minutes with W.R 59 (Receiver of Wrecks register entry).'

One week later, correspondence from the Registrar General of Seamen was received, dated 30 October and reading:

'Attached is a list of the discrepancies between form Inq.6 and List C&D. The former contains the names of seven passengers who were saved, and the List C&D contains 10 names which do not appear on Inq.6, four of these however are given as unknown on Inq.6. As the List C&D was recently amended by the owners it may be presumed to represent the latest information available. The number of passengers lost according to the List C&D is 825.'

The following day, Mr Tull of the Board of Trade issued the instruction to record the necessary final corrections in the Death Register.

The third and last stage in the recording of deaths at sea was the formal Registration. At last prepared to accept the latest corrected version of List C&D, the Registrar General of Shipping and Seamen entered the names in the register. It was deposited some years ago as part of the Board of Trade archive at the Public Record Office with reference number BT334/52, the Register of Deceased Passengers. (The crew names are separately held.) Entered in month order, the *Titanic* entry appears under June 1912 and contains the most up-to-date and accurate information although it was compiled from List C&D which was not finally submitted until 15 August. It is ordered first by class and then alphabetically, page after page, a sad catalogue of names – date of death, 15.4.1912; Place of Death, About Lat 41.16N, Long 50.14W; Cause of death, supposed drowning.

Full transcriptions of entries from BT334/52, Form Inq.6 (MT9/920C) and List C&D (BT100/260) appear in Appendix 1.

1   MT9/920C (PRO, Kew)

Chapter 7
American Passenger Records

T he first pink rays of dawn danced on the Atlantic ripples and bounced from the peaks of a host of surrounding icebergs. It would have been an exquisite Atlantic morning had it not been for the sea of wreckage stretching in all directions. As the darkness lifted, several small lifeboats appeared, mostly drifting now, partly filled with frozen and terrified people scarcely able to row for numbness and exhaustion.

The small Cunard vessel *Carpathia*, with Captain Rostron in command, had been on her way eastwards to Trieste from New York with a full complement of passengers bound for Mediterranean ports. By chance her young wireless operator, about to turn in for the night, had, perhaps with some sixth sense, called up *Titanic* and received her distress call. Racing through the night, *Carpathia* covered the 58 miles to the coordinates given to her by *Titanic's* operator at great speed. Upon arrival, there should have been a grand ship but the searchers found nothing. She cruised gently onwards through ice-strewn waters, watching, listening — the faint glimmer of green lights guided her and by first light she began plucking to safety the traumatised occupants of the dozen tiny boats dotted among the ice.

Once on board, *Titanic's* passengers were fed and warmed. With great compassion *Carpathia's* crew and passengers wrapped them in blankets, gave them clothes, helped them with the children, and gave whatever small comfort they could. Rostron turned his ship around and headed back to a stunned New York. Later, in the radio shack, Harold Cottam was presented with the list of survivors prepared by *Carpathia's* Purser and his assistants. *Titanic's* surviving radio officer Bride was brought from his bed in *Carpathia's* sickbay to assist in the transmitting of the survivors' names. One man, Cottam, exhausted; a second man, Bride, suffering from frostbite and shock; a third man, David Sarnoff, in the radio room on top of the Wanamaker department store in New York, straining to pick out *Carpathia's* signal; the Purser and his clerks, trying to obtain accurate information from shocked and numb survivors just beginning to realise the enormity of the circumstances in which they suddenly found themselves. Among all this, how could anyone have been expected to get all the names right?

Many of the survivors were taken to St Vincent's Hospital, New York City. There they were nursed back to a degree of health sufficient for them to be discharged, and the immediate formalities allowing them to enter the United States were completed.

On 25 April, Sister Maria Isidore of St Vincent's Hospital, wrote to Commissioner Williams at the Bureau of Labor and Commerce:

'Permit us to express how much we appreciate your great kindness in sending Mr Sullivan to St Vincent's to conduct the investigation of discharges according to the legal requirements, in this period which has been so trying. We are more than grateful that in selecting an officer for this task you chose one, so quietly efficient and untiringly devoted to the noble work entrusted to him. To have spared us the confusion of trying to satisfy and care for so many foreigners for a long period while waiting the regular formalities of law was indeed an immense relief to our overworked Sisterhood and one for which we shall be ever most thankful to you.'[1]

Two days later, Commissioner Williams wrote to the Commissioner-General of Immigration in Washington, D.C.

'The alien survivors of the "Titanic" disaster are gradually becoming scattered. Of the 100, more or less, who went to St Vincent's Hospital for temporary care all but a handful have gone. Hardly anyone left without this office first obtaining most of the statutory data called for by the manifest. Inspector John M. Sullivan was sent to the hospital to facilitate the departure of these aliens, and judging from the enclosed copy of a letter which I have just received from Sister Marie Isadore he performed his duties with a great deal of tact.'

By late April all the survivors had been released from hospital, mostly wearing a donated set of clothes, virtually destitute and requiring financial assistance to enable them to find work and accommodation. Each was entitled to collect $25 to help them get back on their feet. Some had been collected by friends and relatives but single women and children under 16 years of age could not be sent out of the hospital alone, so were often collected by members of one of several immigrant aid societies, to be cared for until arrangements could be made for them to be sent on by train to their new destination. Others had returned to England, their hopes of a new life in America now shattered after the loss of loved ones and possessions.

The following essay by Marian Smith, Senior Historian of the Immigration and Naturalization Service in Washington, D.C., graphically illustrates the real problems facing *Carpathia's* Chief Purser, E. G. F Brown, as he struggled to fulfil the United States immigration procedures for the sudden influx of passengers on board. What procedure exactly should he follow? What happened to the survivors in the immediate aftermath? And how could it be that Titanic researchers had been unaware of the existence of Purser Brown's carefully drawn up list for almost 90 years?

Documenting Disaster, by Marian Smith

It is apparently a well-known fact that survivors of the *Titanic* disaster underwent no immigration inspection upon arrival in New York on 18 April 1912. The *Titanic* was lost, as were so many of her passengers and crew and all their belongings. Also lost were large sheets of paper in the care of the *Titanic's* Purser, entitled 'List or Manifest of Alien Passengers', official immigration forms commonly known as passenger lists. It is doubtful anyone at the scene was thinking of immigration regulations during the rescue of *Titanic* survivors from the icy North Atlantic, nor as those survivors climbed aboard the rescuing ship *Carpathia*. But once the *Carpathia* turned around and headed back toward New York, the port she had just left, it is sure her Purser began to wonder how these unusual passengers would be handled by immigration authorities.

United States immigration law applied not only to individual immigrants, but also to the master or owner of any vessel landing immigrants in the United States. If a non-US citizen arrived at a US port of entry and did not qualify for admission under immigration regulations, that person would be excluded (that is to say, barred from entry). But the law also imposed a fine on the vessel or ship company that carried an excludable individual to that port. For this reason much US immigration law enforcement was actually carried out by the shipping lines. It was the steamship companies' responsibility to ensure no tickets were sold or passage given to individuals who could not be admitted to the United States. To do so, they documented the immigrant's identity and answers to a long list of questions taken from immigration law. These documents, the passenger manifests, were certified by a US consul prior to embarkation from the foreign port and delivered to US immigration authorities upon arrival. Failure to submit a passenger manifest, even if the passenger was admissible, would itself subject a steamship company to heavy fines.

The *Carpathia's* Purser, E. G. F. Brown, could assume that all those survivors now aboard the rescue ship had been admissible, given the fact the White Star Line and US Consul allowed their embarkation. But the mere fact that so many lost their money when the Titanic went down meant they had already fallen into an excludable class — that of 'aliens likely to become a public charge'. Others were injured or sick from exposure and might be excluded on medical grounds. In any event, Brown had no manifest documenting these passengers to submit to US immigration authorities. In preparation to land the survivors in New York, he scrambled to create manifest records while the White Star Line appealed to the US government for an exception to regular immigration procedure.

On the morning of 15 April 1912, in New York City, attorney S. C. Neale of the International Mercantile Marine Company and representative of the White Star Line drafted a letter to US Commissioner-General of Immigration Daniel J. Keefe in Washington, D.C. Referring to 'the accident' and then under the impression all survivors would be landed in Halifax, Nova Scotia, Neale explained that the steamship company was 'very anxious to have the Department make some special arrangements for passing all the passengers destined to the United States at Halifax. This would be a very great accommodation... and would be greatly appreciated by the Company.' Neale argued further that 'in view of the unfortunate circumstances' he was sure the Immigration Service could 'see its way clear to extend such special facilities as are necessary to make this possible'. The attorney's letter estimated there would be 325 first class, 285 second class and 710 third class survivors, and that 10% of first class and 80% of second and third class passengers were aliens. Just after noon on the 15th, Commissioner-General Keefe sent a telegram to the US immigration office in Montreal instructing inspectors there to prepare to examine 1,300 persons at Halifax.[a]

By the next afternoon, 16 April, the question of how to admit *Titanic* passengers without the *Titanic* passenger list occupied Bureau of Immigration officials in Washington, D.C. Considering the 'unfortunate circumstances' cited by Mr Neale, it was decided not to apply the law in a strict fashion to Titanic survivors. At 3.55pm, Commissioner-General Keefe sent another telegram to Montreal, advising inspectors there to 'construe our laws liberally as possible'.[b] It is likely a message was sent at the same time to Capitol Hill, to the Committee on Immigration and Naturalization, requesting exemptions from immigration law requirements for *Titanic* survivors.

By that time it had become unclear whether any Titanic survivors would be landed at Halifax. The decision had been made by the next afternoon that *Carpathia* would arrive at New York. At 2.30pm on the 17th, Commissioner-General Keefe telephoned the Port Commissioner of Immigration at New York, William Williams, to instruct him on facilitating the landing of Titanic passengers. He followed the telephone call with a telegram to Williams, again advising inspectors to put the 'most liberal construction possible on immigration laws'. Immigration officials were clearly in communication with and receiving information from the White Star Line. Keefe also telegraphed the Chinese Inspector in Charge in New York City advising him that Chinese seamen would be among the survivors, and that those Chinese should be transferred to Ellis Island. Government officials also maintained contact with agents of the *Carpathia's* Cunard Line. A telegram of 18 April from Cunard's New York General Manager to the Captain of the *Carpathia* conveyed the government's decision that Customs and Immigration regulations would be modified as needed to facilitate landing *Titanic* passengers and crew.[c]

In New York, Williams determined to be present when the *Carpathia* arrived, forcing him to cancel dinner plans with Secretary of Commerce and Labor, Charles Nagel. In a series of notes and telegrams to the Secretary written 18 April, Williams explained the change in plans and said he wished to 'be on hand to receive the immigrants and supervise the work of caring for them'. He offered to leave a Customs House pass to allow Secretary Nagel access to the pier, should Nagel care to join him. Williams expected the *Carpathia* between 8 and 9pm, at a pier located at or near the foot of West 14th Street. While Williams invited Nagel to be present, he warned '[t]his is likely to be a terrible night there.'[d]

Meanwhile, aboard the *Carpathia*, Purser Brown learned that necessity is the mother of invention. His desk or file drawers were no doubt filled with many official forms and documents relating to the immigration regulations of a number of different countries. Only two weeks before he presented US passenger manifests to immigration officials in New York Harbor. For the current voyage he had prepared all the necessary paperwork to be submitted when delivering *Carpathia's* passengers to Mediterranean ports. But he apparently did not keep any large stock of forms on hand, for he was unable to locate enough US forms with which to record all the *Titanic* survivors now aboard the *Carpathia* and steaming again toward New York. He gathered all the blank US forms he could find, then took up other large, blank sheets of paper (perhaps the reverse of some other form) and found his ruler. Using the straight-edge and his familiarity with US passenger manifests, he did his best to re-create the documents he would be expected to deliver[e].

The *Carpathia* steamed into New York Harbor on the night of 18 April 1912, completing the *Titanic* survivors' interrupted journey. Little is known of what authorities met the ship. Under normal conditions, as it entered the harbor the steamship would have first been boarded by New York State Quarantine officers, then US Immigration and perhaps Public Health Service officers. Once past quarantine, immigration inspectors would examine first and second class passengers as the ship made its way to landing facilities on Manhattan or the New Jersey Shore. Popular reports mention only that tugs and other boats carrying press reporters came alongside the ship but none was allowed to board. The same accounts say that upon arrival at the dock it was medical personnel who first boarded the *Carpathia*. Whether immigration inspectors boarded the ship in the harbor or at the pier, under the law no passengers could disembark before the manifest was placed in the hands of immigration authorities. Days later, Port Commissioner William Williams wrote the following in a letter to the *Carpathia's* Cunard Steamship Company:

'In connection with the return to port of SS *Carpathia* as the result of the recent ocean tragedy, I wish to express my appreciation of her purser's work in presenting substantially correct manifests of the *Titanic's* passengers though he did not even have the benefit of the usual forms. I know that he must have worked under great disadvantages in preparing them. The result has been most useful to the Government.'

No account located to date fully recounts the passengers' immigration inspection. Newspapers reported that on 17 April Secretary Nagel advised Port Commissioner Williams to arrange for the survivors' inspection aboard the *Carpathia* and their release to friends and relatives at the Cunard pier. Those without friends or family in New York City would be lodged at Ellis Island until their relatives arrived or until able to resume their journey.[f] It does appear the majority of first and second class passengers were questioned and admitted aboard the *Carpathia*. Many in those groups were US citizens requiring no further processing, and a number of first class arrivals reportedly left the ship, got into their limousines or private rail cars, and got as far away from steamships as possible. As to the rest, it appears they were inspected and had their records completed over a period of several days.

Immigrant arrivals from third class, and some from second class, would normally have been taken to the immigration station on Ellis Island for processing. Yet the *Carpathia* landed immigrants at an unusually late hour — the Great Hall at the station was not open for business — and one third class survivor's report claims they 'did not have to go through Ellis Island, as all other immigrants did in those days'.[g]

Just as Port Commissioner Williams had come to the pier to supervise immigration operations there, it seems sure representatives of various immigrant aid societies were at the scene as well. Many of these groups maintained offices at Ellis Island and worked closely with immigration authorities on a daily basis. The evidence suggests the Women's Relief Committee may have been asked to oversee the placement of *Titanic* survivors in hospitals, immigrant homes, and with waiting relatives or friends. It is clear that some of the information found on third class manifest pages came to the government via the Women's Relief Committee.[h]

Even the six Chinese survivors, treated separately from other immigrants under the United States' Chinese Exclusion Act, were not taken to Ellis Island. Ah Lam, Bing Lee, Tang Lang, Hee Lang, Chip Chang and Foo Cheong were all employees of the Donaldson Steamship Company, on their way to New York to join the British steamship *Annetta*. Contrary to Commissioner-General Keefe's earlier instructions, the six sailors remained on the *Carpathia* until the next day, 19 April, when they were transferred to the *Annetta*. Once aboard that ship, they cleared New York Harbor on the 20th and set out into the Atlantic once again. Two additional Chinese *Titanic* passengers had been lost when that ship went down.[i] The *Carpathia* also departed New York again on the 19th, resuming her eastbound voyage.

Approximately one hundred of the survivors were placed in St Vincent's Hospital in New York City. Immigrant Inspector John M. Sullivan was assigned to inspect the immigrants there and did so beginning 19 April, finishing by the 24th. Some of the hospitalized survivors may have been well enough for release, but had to wait until formally admitted by Inspector Sullivan. 'We had to stay there from Thursday until Monday while everything was checked,' recalled second class passenger Bertha Lehmann, '[t]here seemed to be no end to the questions we had to answer'.[j]

By 25 April nearly all *Titanic* passengers had gone their separate ways, only a few remaining at St Vincent's. Though Port Commissioner Williams reported to Commissioner-General Keefe that '[h]ardly anyone left without this office first obtaining most of the statutory data called for by the manifest,' the government was obviously unable to process *Titanic* survivors in a normal fashion. On 20 April, 1912, Representative George Konig (D-Maryland) introduced a bill in the House of Representatives authorizing the Secretary of Commerce and Labor to 'suspend, in his judgement, in any particular case, the operation of any and all laws regulating the immigration of aliens into the United States, so far as any such law or laws may operate to exclude from entry into the United States any survivors of the wrecked steamship *Titanic*.'[k] While this Act would benefit any alien survivor who arrived without papers, money, or who was otherwise inadmissible under US immigration law, it would also relieve the US Immigration Service from its responsibility to bar the entry of any alien for whom there was not submitted a complete and accurate manifest.

The passenger list submitted by *Carpathia* purser E. G. F. Brown to immigration authorities at New York on the night of 18 April, 1912, consisted of at least five official manifest forms and at least 11 makeshift forms. On these forms he deposited what information he could elicit from approximately 477 shaken and sometimes hysterical survivors.[l] A largely successful effort was made to separate the records of those traveling in first, second and third class, and most passengers were separated between US citizens and non US citizens. Less information was required under law from the US citizens, so their records are less complete.

The original pages surviving on microfilm reveal some of the confusion that must have prevailed aboard *Carpathia*. Some survivors, well documented elsewhere, do not appear on this official government record. A few of those listed on the manifest are not listed elsewhere. Some are listed twice or more, indicating that they repeatedly attempted to have their name and existence noted. It may be that some survivors were unaware of the purser's purpose, or believed he had multiple purposes. They may have wanted to be recorded once for immigration purposes and again so their name could be broadcast to friends and loved ones at home. One survivor, recalling the purser's activity, said 'We were all gathered together, and our names taken for the newspapers.'[m]

First class passengers, as well as some second class and most US citizen passengers (approximately 150 persons) were recorded directly on to US Form 500, List or Manifest of Alien Passengers for the United States Immigration Officer. These were completed in the handwriting of at least two separate individuals. Though hurriedly written, the records are surprisingly neat and legible considering the circumstances. American citizen records contain only the passenger's name, age, sex, marital status and nationality. Alien passenger records contain their name, age, sex, marital status, occupation, nationality, last permanent residence, destination, names and addresses of friends or relatives at both the last permanent place of residence and destination, place of birth, and in most cases answers to legal questions ('Are you a Polygamist?') and a physical description. Two of the six pages contain mainly US citizens and thus contain little information.

Most second class survivors are listed on makeshift forms in the handwriting of two separate individuals, at least one of whom also completed first class manifests. Only one of these five pages contains a list of US citizens. Without the benefit of standard manifest lines and columns, often illegible records are crowded into these pages.

Further signs of confusion aboard the *Carpathia* are seen in records crossed out, written over, and incomplete entries. The fact that the records were submitted on a non-standard form later became a problem for clerks on Ellis Island when it came time to bind these smaller pages with other manifests. To solve the problem, clerks pasted the makeshift forms on to blank, standard-sized US Form 630, List of United States Citizens. Those clerks were oblivious to the fact that later researchers might misunderstand the listing of immigrant aliens under the 'List of United States Citizens' title.

Third class passenger records, when submitted by the purser, must have resembled the makeshift forms of second class manifests. It is unknown what happened to the original, makeshift pages, but they were most likely destroyed during the summer of 1912. Today the third class passengers are found listed neatly, in alphabetical order, on standard Forms 500, List or Manifest of Alien Passengers for the United States Immigration Officer. Information from the original list was transferred to the forms by personnel at Ellis Island, probably because the information would doubtless be needed in future for routine verification procedures. If the records were as crowded and sometimes sloppy as those of second class, verification clerks would have argued for a transcription of the records into legible form. The information would best be transferred to the proper form (Form 500) which would also be more easily bound into the manifest books. Finally, the fact that only third class manifest records were copied and alphabetized strongly suggests this transcription was done by and for the verification clerks (ie, record searchers).[n]

This writer has no doubt the third class, alphabetized manifest pages are a copy of what was submitted by Purser Brown. On 10 May, 1912, Commissioner-General Keefe requested Ellis Island provide him with a list of names of *Titanic* survivors. That list was typed at Ellis

Island between 10 and 14 May. The list was divided by class, and the names of first and second class passengers are given exactly, and in the same order, as on the manifest pages. Third class passengers, though, are listed in an entirely different order (not alphabetical). The entire list was typed directly from pages submitted by the purser. Only the third class pages were later copied (prior to 18 June, 1912) and so it is only those pages which now differ from the list sent to Commissioner-General Keefe on 14 May, 1912.°

A number of explanations have been offered to account for the filing of *Titanic's* passenger manifest under the date 18 June, 1912, rather than 18 April, the date of arrival. Some believe the manifest pages were loaned to Congressional investigators on Manhattan, whose hearings on the *Titanic* disaster ended on 17 June. If so, the records' return on June 18 explains their placement among Ellis Island records. The coincidence is compelling, if not conclusive. While this writer is not yet convinced official US immigration records were ever placed outside agency custody, it is reasonable to assume the manifest was not filed until all pending legal matters were settled. These may have been resolved on 17 or 18 June, 1912, as a result of, or in no way related to, the close of Congressional hearings. In either case, by that time, filing an 18 April manifest where it belonged would have posed a problem.

Records accumulated rapidly on Ellis Island. Passenger manifests were filed in large binders holding an average of 150 manifest pages. During spring months of peak immigration years, one or more volumes could be created each day. Unless one reserved space for the *Titanic* pages when binding records for 18 April, the insertion of those pages two months later would be no easy task. To open, shift the contents of, and rebind more than one hundred volumes dating 18 April to 18 June was apparently deemed unnecessary. The *Titanic* manifest was filed under date of 18 June, 1912, and clerks recorded the arrival of the *Carpathia* on that date in one of their reference catalogs. Annotations on the manifest itself reveal the Immigration Service, using the reference catalog, was able to easily locate the *Titanic* record on a regular basis from the 1920s through the early 1940s.

INS Special Agent Joseph Glovack recalls that as late as 1973, when he was a Verification Clerk at the INS New York District Office, veteran clerks were able to direct him to the *Titanic* passenger list. They told him to look for the *Carpathia*, rather than the *Titanic*, and to look in the reference catalog to find the arrival date (in this case the filing date, 18 June). He did so and was excited to find a record associated with the historic ship, though others around him 'just shrugged their shoulders' in response to the manifest. The catalog of which Agent Clovack spoke was later microfilmed and transferred to the National Archives, where it remains an unpublished, undescribed entry in Record Group 85. Thus the catalog, the one and only source linking *Carpathia* to the otherwise meaningless date of 18 June, 1912, was no longer available to the INS and did not become available to researchers.ᵖ

The National Archives published early 20th Century Ellis Island passenger manifests for researcher use in the 1980s. Because immigration manifests are a chronological series of records, researchers at the Archives would expect to find the *Titanic* filed under 18 April, 1912, or perhaps filed a few days later. The absence of any record on or near that date underlay conventional wisdom in recent years that no immigration record existed of the survivors' arrival aboard the *Carpathia*. It was a pleasant surprise, then, one day in late 1996 or early 1997 when a volunteer at the National Archives in Pittsfield, Massachusetts, looked up from her work with passenger list microfilm and said, 'Look what I found.' Volunteer Viola Sivik pointed out the *Titanic* manifest to archivist Walter Hickey, who recognized it had potential value for *Titanic* scholars but regarded it then as little more than a curiosity.

Recent interest in all things *Titanic* sparked the latest 'discovery' of the manifest. Unaware of Hickey's find, and intrigued by the popular movie, archivist Bill Doty prepared an exhibit of *Titanic*-related documents for the National Archives in Laguna Niguel, California. Having been told there was a list of survivors prepared aboard the *Carpathia*, Doty asked Richard Gelbke of the National Archives in New York City to locate the document among New York passenger manifests. Gelbke began a laborious search, beginning with records dated 18 April, 1912, and read each of 43 reels of microfilm until he found the *Titanic* manifest filed on 18 June, 1912.

That document may now take its place beside other records relating to the disaster. Whether information found on the manifest pages will make any significant contribution to understanding the *Titanic's* voyage or its passengers remains an open question. Researchers familiar with passenger lists know those records usually present as many mysteries as they solve.

Marian Smith
Washington, D.C

This essay was originally published in *Voyage*, the quarterly journal of the Titanic International Society, PO Box 7007, Freehold, NJ 07728 and is reproduced here with the kind permission of Charles Haas, editor.

New York Arrival Manifest

As with the British and Canadian records of *Titanic*, this valuable and fragile US manifest has been microfilmed. With some details stretching across two sheets, and far from perfect film quality, it is not the easiest of documents to examine. For the purpose of this book, for reasons of space the whole width of the manifest showing all its columns could not be included, but all identifying information from each passenger is shown. As with any transcription, careful comparisons must be made with the original record before any conclusions are drawn. A copy of the entire manifest has also been uploaded to the internet and is available for anyone with access to the World Wide Web.

As Marian Smith has shown, there would seem to be no doubt that it was the Purser's hand which drew up the sheets as closely as possibly to the correct manifest forms, but there is also no doubt that not all of the entries are in his handwriting. There are definitely four different hands, probably five. It is hardly surprising that he should have enlisted some help when trying to compile the manifest, but as he was evidently in charge of the whole exercise then it is also entirely reasonable that he should have put his name to it.

Using the order suggested by the numbers in heavy type at the bottom of the manifest sheets — which may or may not have been the original order in which it was compiled — the 17 sheets are made up as follows:

P57 Aliens entered directly on to Alien forms
P58 Aliens pasted on to US forms
P59 US citizens pasted on to US forms
P60 Aliens pasted on to US forms
P61 Aliens pasted on to US forms
P62 Aliens pasted on to US form
P63 Directly on to form, US on Aliens form
P64 Directly on to form, US on Aliens form
P65 Directly on to form, US on Aliens form
P66 Directly on to form, US and Aliens mixed on Aliens form
P67 Directly on to form, US and Aliens mixed on Aliens form
P68-73, directly on to forms, alphabetised Alien steerage.

Chapter 7

As described briefly in the essay above, the Alien section of a United States arrivals manifest builds into a fascinating biographical record, probably second to none other in the world in the depth of information required. They were asked a barrage of questions:

Full name, age, occupation, and whether they could read and write; nationality and race; country and town of last permanent residence and name of nearest relative or friend there; exact final destination; whether they had a ticket to their destination and by whom it had been purchased, and how much money they possessed; name of friend or relative in the United States and whether they had been to America before; if they had ever been in prison or an institution for the insane, or supported by charity; were a polygamist or anachist; their reason for coming to the US. and finally a full physical description.

There was very good reason for the questions asked of these new immigrants. With the doors to the Promised Land now wide open, the United States government operated an extremely strict vetting programme. All questions were compulsory, designed to weed out anyone unsuitable for whatever reason. Naturally the United States was not prepared to allow entry to anyone considered undesirable, or for other reasons such as ill-health likely to become a charge (that is anyone who was likely to be unable adequately to support themselves or their families thereby causing the United States government to accept responsibility for their welfare). Nor did it wish to allow anarchists, rogues or scoundrels, or anyone else who seemed programmed to become a nuisance. It was illegal for anyone to import workers without permission thereby denying Americans the same opening, and of course certain categories of female workers were wholly unwelcome in the United States! As a result, the government was highly suspicious of anyone seeming to be travelling on a ticket purchased by a prospective employer or 'friend', hence the searching questions.

Typed List

The list typed by Ellis Island clerks to which Marian Smith refers is headed 'List of Survivors of the SS Titanic Brought to This Port by the SS Carpathia.' It comprises only eight pages, with one column of names on each arranged as follows:

Page 1 First Cabin (un-numbered)
Page 2 First Cabin
Page 3 First Cabin
Page 4 Second Cabin
Page 5 Second Cabin
Page 6 Steerage
Page 7 Steerage
Page 8 Steerage

The typed list contains only names with no other information, though earlier errors have been corrected — several names wrongly entered as 1st class passengers have been corrected, as have the two entries for the same child ('Joseph Nigel' was actually Michael, the six-year-old son of Catherine Joseph).

In order to compare this typed list with the manifest, both sets have to be reordered — if the numbers in heavy print at the bottom of the manifest sheets are ignored, and sheets 1 and 2 of the printed list are reversed, the manifest can easily be reordered to fall exactly in line with the order of the names on the printed list.

White Star Line Passenger List (The Senate List)

This list perhaps more properly should be included in the chapter devoted to British passenger lists as it has its origins in the White Star Line office in Britain. However, it would have made more sense for it to be completed by the shipping line's New York office as it formed part of the evidence for the Senate committee inquiry. As part of the Senate Investigation into the loss of *Titanic*, a full list of passengers was required together with a separate listing of those who had survived. The information, dated 25 April 1912, was gathered by the White Star Line and submitted to the Investigation as Exhibit B. (The records of the crew formed Exhibit A.)

The White Star Line was already being pressed by the Board of Trade and the Registrar General of Shipping and Seamen in Britain to provide a correct list of all passengers who had died (see Chapter 6, Lists C&D), so the groundwork for this passenger list now required by the Senate subcommittee was already in progress. In order to compile this list, the White Star Line used its own records of passengers believed to have sailed, including addresses for cabin classes, and destination for some of the 3rd class. The line added any recently obtained information, including the onward travel plans of some survivors who had booked passages back out of the United States. It then typeset it and made it available to the Senate Investigators. Chapter 4 discusses the two subsequent drafts of this list produced by the White Star Line, which are now filmed and available in BT100/259. They added to, and in many instances corrected, the information included in this list. However, at the date it was presented to the Senate subcommittee, this White Star Line passenger list included the most recent information available.

The entries on the White Star Line list do not always agree with the information given by the United States arrivals manifest: some are omitted, some are briefer, and some are completely different. Several of the differences are certainly due to transcription errors at some stage of the process. Some details such as intended destinations are different almost certainly because, having survived the trauma, not surprisingly the passengers' plans may well have changed considerably from when they had set out a week or so earlier.

The list drawn up for the Senate Inquiry and later published comprises two sections for each class of passenger. Firstly there is a (roughly) alphabetical list of all passengers (excluding postal clerks). Next follows an alpha list of survivors. The alphabetical list of passengers includes addresses in Europe and North America and other notes, and whether the passenger was saved. (If a passenger is not specifically noted as 'saved' this does not necessarily mean that they were lost, merely that there was no information at the time the list was compiled.) Researchers must be aware that the alpha list of survivors is definitely not extracted from the main alphabetical list of passengers. There are significant differences in spelling, recording of names and the fate of the passengers. Four survivors' lists were compiled later.

It seems that whoever was responsible for obtaining the further details to present to the Senate Investigation may not have had access to the additional information from the United States arrival manifest before presenting the list to the investigators. The maids and menservants for the most part are not listed by name, again giving the list the tell-tale signs of having been compiled only from the White Star Line's information alone (which, as discussed earlier, also did not originally record them individually). In short, exactly the same fate which befell the Board of Trade passenger list, also befell the United States arrivals manifest. Because neither of those two valuable documents listed all the passenger names, and regardless of the fact that each contained other valuable information, both records were cast aside in favour of the White Star Line's own passenger records.

Chapter 7

l Letters, Sister Isidore, St Vincent's Hospital, to Port Commissioner Williams, April 25, 1912; Port Commissioner William Williams to Commissioner-General Keefe, 27 April, 1912. National Archives and Records Administration, Record Group 85, Accession 85-60A600, Box 412, File 53392/201.

a Letter, SC Neale, Counsel, International Mercantile Marine Company, to Commissioner-General of Immigration, 15 April, 1912; Telegram Commissioner-General Daniel J Keefe to US Commissioner of Immigration, Montreal, 15 April, 1912. National Archives and Records Administration, Record Group 85. Accession 85-60A600, Box 412, File 53392/201. (Unfortunately, File 53392/201 cannot now be located by either the National Archives nor the Immigration and Naturalization Service. Until it resurfaces, copies of any and all documents cited here and copied from that file may be obtained by writing the author at 425 1 Street NW, Room 1100, Washington DC 20536)

b Telegram, Commissioner-General Daniel J Keefe to US Commissioner of Immigration, Montreal, 16 April, 1912. National Archives and Records Administration, Record Group 85, Accession 85-60A600, Box 412, File 53392/201

c Telegram, Commissioner-General Daniel J Keefe to US Commissioner of Immigration, New York, 17 April, 1912; Telegram, Keefe to Chinese Inspector in Charge, New York, NY 18 April, 1912, 3:34pm. National Archives and Records Administration, Record Group 85, Accession 85-60A600, Box 412, File 53392/201; Telegram, Cunard General Manager Charles P. Sumner, New York, to Captain Rostron of the *Carpathia*, 18 April, 1912, 3:55am. The New York *American*, April 24, 1912 (and courtesy of John P. Eaton).

d Letter, Port Commissioner, William Williams to Secretary of Commerce and Labor Charles Nagel, 18 April, 1912; Telegram, Williams to Nagel, 18 April, 1912, National Archives and Records Administration, Record Group 85, Accession 85-60A600, Box 412, File 53392/201.

e Sixteen pages comprising the 'List or Manifest' of *Titanic* passenger survivors filed among the Passenger Arrival Records for the Port of New York, on microfilm at the National Archives in Washington, DC. Filed under date of 18 June, 1912. National Archives microfilm publication T715, Roll 1883 (Vol 4183).

f None actually went to Ellis Island because adequate shelter for all surviving passengers was arranged by local relief committees. Excerpt from unpublished manuscript *Titanic. Profile of a Disaster* by John P. Eaton.

g Statement of survivor Anna Turja's grandson, John Rudolph, published on the internet at http://www.execpc.com/~reva/html3.htm. (*Titanic, the Search for Answers* website of Garth W. Wangemann <http://www.execpc.com/~reva/html3.htm> There are numerous similar websites containing *Titanic* information and lists of passengers.

h See the manifest record of Joseph Nigel, National Archives microfilm publication T715, Roll 1883 (Vol 4183), third class, number stamp page 72, line 15

i Letter, HR Sisson, Chinese Inspector in Charge, New York, NY, to Commissioner-General of Immigration, 20 April, 1912. National Archives and Records Administration, Record Group 85, Accession 85-60A-600, Box 412, File 53392/201

j Statement of Bertha Lehmann Luhrs, as appeared in a December edition of the Brainerd Minnesota *Daily Despatch* in the late 1930s, and published at http://www.execpc.com/~reva/html3us4.htm

k HR 23572, 62c, 2s, April 10, 1912. It is doubtful this bill became law as no corresponding entry could be found in US Statutes At Large.

l The Cunard Line later reported the *Carpathia* delivered 201 1st class, 118 2nd class, and 179 3rd class passengers at New York on 18 April, 1912, a total of 490 passengers (as well as 207 crew members). 'Report of the Transatlantic Passenger Movements Calendar Year, 1912' (NY: James Kempster Printing, 1913) Table XXIII, p23

m Amy Stanley, in a letter later published in the Folkestone *Herald* (4 May, 1912, p3), reprinted at http://www.execpc.com/~reva/html3us4.htm

n The majority of verification activity at Ellis Island and other immigration stations always involved 3rd class or steerage passengers because that class carried the highest proportion of immigrants.

o Letters, Commissioner-General Daniel J. Keefe to Port Commissioner Williams, 10 May, 1912; Port Commissioner (NY) William Williams to Commissioner-General Keefe, 14 May, 1912; 'List of Survivors of the ss *Titanic*, Brought to This Port by the ss *Carpathia*', 8p. National Archives and Records Administration, Record Group 85, Accession 85-60A600, Box 412, File 53392/201

p Interview with INS Special Agent Joseph Glovack, 23 October, 1998. National Archives Record Group 85 (RG85) is the Records of the Immigration and Naturalization Service. The reference catalog used by Agent Glovack is the New York City Catalogues and Indexes of Ship Arrivals, 16 June, 1897 to 31 December, 1956, now in the Washington, DC National Archives, RG85, Undescribed Entry 13, 11 rolls of microfilm.

Chapter 8

Halifax and the Canadian Records

On board *Titanic* when she sailed were approximately 130 passengers travelling to Canada. Some were Canadian born, some were returning emigrants, and others were bound for Canada for the first time. They are largely unidentifiable on the Board of Trade list as most of those who boarded in Britain are recorded as British. A handful of names include 'Canada' in the column for 'future intended permanent residence' but this is disputable in several cases. Certainly a significant number from both the Southampton and Queenstown sections of the passenger list are recorded as bound for the United States when later research shows beyond all reasonable doubt that they were actually heading for locations across Canada. The intended future destination was not asked of the transmigrants at all, so if any of that category boarding in Southampton were heading for Canada, there is no way of knowing that by using information contained in the Board of Trade list. Anyone who may have been resident in Canada for the previous 12 months or more is similarly hiding and, like the Australian and South African passengers on board, the only clue is that their previous residence was 'British Possessions'.

Often overlooked, too, is the Canadian arrival manifest. The list has been filmed, and is now available at the Nova Scotia Archives & Records Management.[1] Although *Titanic* was never intending to call at Halifax, she was carrying passengers bound for Canada. In accordance with Canadian immigration laws, the names of passengers arriving at a port in the United States but who were ultimately bound for Canada have been entered on the form. In fact, instead of the names of a little over 40 survivors it lists only four 2nd class and five 3rd class. Normally, a list from this period would have included all passengers regardless of their status, title or class of travel. Whatever the reason for their arrival in Canada, everyone was entered – immigrants, Canadian citizens, those normally resident and visitors to the country. This Canadian list, however, seems to include only first-time immigrants and aliens. No correspondence appears to have survived to explain the shortfall of names but it may be that, given the immense problems facing passengers and clerks alike, normal regulations may have simply been waived for returning Canadians.

The list is signed by W. R. Klein, Civil Examiner, who was the Canadian Immigration Agent based in New York in 1912. Under normal circumstances, these Canadian arrivals manifests were partly filled in by the Purser on board ship and completed by the Civil Examiner in the port of arrival. Even if *Titanic's* Purser had compiled his section, it was clearly lost with the ship. It could be that *Carpathia's* Purser was unable to complete it, because it lacks the meticulous air he maintained in his work despite the pressure he was undoubtedly under at the time. The instructions to the Purser were to provide each passenger with a card indicating the number of sheet, and the line on which their name is to be found, and that columns 3, 29 and 30 were to be filled in by the Immigration Agent at the port of landing. Curiously, the front of the sheet is strongly suggestive of its having been filled in well before the arrival and possibly even before *Titanic* sank. The Immigration Agent was also required to complete the sailing details: ship name, line, port and date of departure, and date of arrival. Whoever filled it in has entered the name *Titanic* very boldly, before apparently as an afterthought squeezing in the words 'per SS *Carpathia*' between the lines. With *Titanic*, it is easy to create a mystery when one does not really exist. There are so many anomalies, so many unanswered questions. Maybe this page was filled in before *Titanic* sank; maybe it was filled in when the original reports stated that the liner was under tow bound for Halifax. Maybe the Immigration Agent was simply unable to figure exactly how he should represent these arrivals – *Titanic* or *Carpathia*? Perhaps he thought one thing then decided another and so hastily scribbled in the name of *Carpathia*. With nobody here to tell us, yet again we can only surmise. Whatever did happen and for whatever reason, the Canadian list omits a significant number of names.

The passenger details are also very brief, and only sketchy details have been included. For the 3rd class passengers, the list includes the name, age and sex for each one, and their marital status. The question 'have you ever been to Canada before?' has been left blank for each, and the next column headed 'if so, when, where and for how long' contains instead the identity of the person to whom they were immediately going.

There are also errors and omissions in the 3rd class list. The two Jarred-Nicola children, Jumila and Elias are recorded as bound 'to mother'. They were ultimately destined to join their mother in Florida but their brother met them in New York and took them to Canada to stay with him for a while. The two children had to endure another sea voyage from New York to the Canadian port of Yarmouth. Of the five 3rd class passengers listed we know that all except Marian Assaf could read and write, but the adjacent column inquiring whether their stay in Canada was to be permanent was not completed for any of the five. Nationality and destination were filled in for all of them, and the nature of their occupations before they left their homelands, but no further information is given so we have no clues as to what they planned to do once in Canada, or whether they had worked in various stated occupations (thereby rendering them more useful in the eyes of the Canadian government), or their religious denomination. The column which should have contained the initials of the Civil Examiner is ticked but not initialled, but presumably it was Civil Examiner Klein's acknowledgement that he had fulfilled his responsibilities.

The 2nd class section with its four names: Antoine Mallet and her baby son Andre, Matilda Weisz and Mildred Brown asks the same questions and omits the same answers, though adjacent to Mrs Mallet is written 'last permanent residence Montreal'.

Normally a Canadian manifest bore the signature of the master confirming the number of passengers, and the affirmation by the ship's surgeon that he had, during the passage, 'made a general inspection of the passengers' but obviously neither of these was appropriate in the case of *Titanic*.

Tragically, the majority of *Titanic's* passengers who arrived in Halifax had been recovered from the Atlantic by one of the four recovery vessels sent out to retrieve the bodies from the icy waters. In the hours following the tragedy, the White Star Line's agents in Halifax, Nova Scotia, had acted swiftly to set in motion arrangements for the recovery of the victims. A cable-laying ship, the *Mackay-Bennett* belonging to the Commercial Cable Company was immediately chartered by the White Star Line and preparations began to equip her for the grim task of searching for and retrieving bodies.[2] A volunteer crew was signed on with double pay to compensate them for the sights which would face them. Funeral Directors Messrs John Snow and Company were engaged to arrange the burials and to oversee the supply of canvas and over 100 plain wooden coffins. Shortly before the departure of the *Mackay-Bennett*, tons of crushed ice were brought on board, with gallons of formaldehyde to preserve the bodies. A team of embalmers called in from all over the province joined the ship bringing with them the most basic tools of their trade. Finally Canon Kenneth Hind of Halifax joined Captain Larnder and his crew on the day of departure.[3]

In the aftermath of the tragedy most ships had moved to a more southerly lane well out of the path of the ice, but some ships passing through the same ice field as *Titanic* radioed the coordinates of any bodies and wreckage they had noticed in their path to the cable ship captain as he steamed out into the Atlantic. When the *Mackay-Bennett* reached the main area of wreckage five days after the sinking the crew were greeted by scenes of unspeakable horror. Wreckage was spread out all around the small vessel and floating amongst it were dozens of bodies, buoyed up by lifejackets, many apparently asleep amidst this field of carnage. Among them they found the body of a tiny fair-haired boy, who came to be known as the 'unknown child'.

Each body was taken from the water and stripped of clothing. Personal possessions and valuables were placed in a canvas bag, anything showing a name or other means of identification was carefully preserved. The bodies, bloated and discoloured from many days in the water, some damaged by crushing or as the result of falling from *Titanic's* decks as she began her final plunge, and many badly mutilated by marine creatures, were carefully checked for any distinguishing marks, and physical characteristics were precisely recorded: hair colour, eyes, estimated weight, height and age; anything which might aid later identification.

Bodies of the crew, or those considered too badly disfigured to be identified or too decomposed to be embalmed, were wrapped in canvas and weighted. In a dignified service conducted by Canon Hinds, they were returned to the deep.

The embalming of *Titanic's* passengers was very far removed from the methods and purpose of the technique first introduced by the Ancient Egyptians. The men on the *Mackay-Bennett* performed no long-term mystical preservation process to ease the bodies into the after-life. The team of 40 men worked fast and without ceremony. Nor was there time to put to any great use the artistic techniques currently being perfected in mortuaries and funeral parlours to enhance and restore the bodies of the deceased in preparation for viewing. By injecting large quantities of a formaldehyde-based solution into the stomach cavities of the bodies they had pulled from the water and packing them with ice, they were able to do little more than to sanitise and stabilise them for the short time until they could return them to Halifax for formal identification and burial.[4]

As the days passed it became clear that the *Mackay-Bennett* could not possibly do the job alone. The more time elapsed, the less likely it was that bodies would be found, and that, even if they were, they would be in any state to be identified. The strain was telling on both the crew and the embalmers and the weather was increasingly poor. The embalming techniques used on the victims were never intended to last for long, and Larnder urgently needed to return to Halifax with his tragic cargo. A week later, with a fresh supply of coffins finally available, a second cable ship, the *Minia* of the Anglo-American Telegraph Company, set sail under Captain Carteret to relieve the crew of the *Mackay-Bennett*.[5]

Early in May, a third vessel was despatched to search a wider area. The *Montmagny*, a fisheries vessel, located a further three bodies but with the weather turning foul and the likelihood of finding any other bodies increasingly remote, she returned to Halifax. The fourth ship to join the search was the *Algerine*, which departed from St John's loaded with coffins but returned with just one body, bringing the total number of bodies recovered to 328, 119 of whom had been buried at sea. Some returned in canvas body-bags, some, including any 1st class passengers, in a simple wooden coffin. A full and moving account of the search for the bodies is published in the *Titanic* classic, *Titanic: Triumph and Tragedy* by Eaton & Haas.

The city of Halifax greeted the return of *Titanic's* silent passengers with a solemn display of respect and grief. Public buildings, businesses and private homes alike were draped in the mourning colours of black and purple.

As first the *Mackay-Bennett*, later the *Minia* and the *Montmagny* arrived in Halifax, and the *Algerine* to her dock in St John's, the well-rehearsed process unfolded. The ships, docking deeper into the harbour than normal to allow for the unusual activity, unloaded their sad cargo on to the waiting horse-drawn hearses. Gradually the coffins and body-bags, and those to whom no such basic luxury was afforded, arrived at the Mayflower Curling Rink, chosen for its proximity to the dock and for the facilities and space it offered.

Here, the bodies waited. Further embalming was carried out where necessary, both to sanitise and to ease in any way possible the shock of the waiting relatives. On the opposite side of the rink the distraught families of the deceased waited. Eventually they were allowed to approach the coffins to begin the grim and distressing task of identifying their loved ones. The most urgent cases, those where decomposition was advancing rapidly, were buried almost immediately. Sadly, those travelling from Britain and Ireland were rarely able to reach Halifax in time to view the deceased. Photographs were taken of anyone not immediately claimed for future possible identification purposes and now form part of the *Titanic* collection in the Nova Scotia Archives and Records Management.

Some bodies were claimed by relatives and taken away for private burial. Other relatives, perhaps unable to bear the cost of transporting the coffin to the cemetery of their choice, gave instructions regarding the place of burial. Those not claimed, or for whom no special instructions were received, were buried in the cemetery considered most appropriate. There were three cemeteries set aside to receive victims: the non-sectarian Fairview Lawn Cemetery, the Jewish Baron de Hirsch Cemetery, and the Catholic Mount Olivet Cemetery. Burials began on 3 May, the first to be interred being those most urgently requiring burial for sanitary reasons. Over the ensuing days, a total of 150 were buried in the three cemeteries. In several cases there were problems of identity, the most well known being the burial in the Jewish cemetery of Michael Navratil who, due to the alias he was using as he fled across the Atlantic with his two small sons, was at first assumed to be Jewish whereas he was in fact Roman Catholic.

The Nova Scotia Archives and Records Management has also retained the printed records of deceased passengers in two series: *Titanic*, dead identified and *Titanic*, dead unidentified.[6] During the years since their passing, using the collection of records compiled for *Titanic*, the identity of some of the previously unidentified was established. Others remain unidentified and it is doubtful whether that will ever change for most of them. The records compiled in 1912 of *Titanic's* dead, identified and unidentified, form part of the research for this book.

In May 2001 three exhumations were carried out in Halifax's Fairview Lawn Cemetery and an attempt was made to remove slivers of thigh bone from each set of remains, in the hope of obtaining DNA samples. Advances in the world of technology now mean that DNA testing can prove genetic links between two or more persons otherwise separated by several generations. If the same scientific procedures could be applied to the remains of *Titanic's* victims and compared with DNA obtained from living people, then perhaps the identity of some still lying in unmarked graves could finally be decided. With circumstantial evidence and personal property already suggesting the identity of at least two people in Fairview Lawn, City officials were first approached several years earlier by a clergyman on behalf of a woman orphaned by the disaster. Unable to rest, she needed confirmation that one of the unidentified bodies was that of her parent. After considerable deliberation, the Halifax authorities finally acceded to the woman's request. Two other families were also contacted and asked if they wished to take part in the investigation by donating a sample of DNA in the hope that their relative might also at last be confirmed among the dead in Halifax.

The two adult victims involved in the exhumations, a young man and a woman, had been tentatively identified some time earlier but without scientific assistance there was no way of advancing the theory. The third exhumation was that of perhaps the most famous of all *Titanic's* victims, the unknown child. There has long been controversy over the baby's identity. Aged about two years with blond hair, he could be tiny Eugene Rice, or the angel-faced Swedish baby, Gosta Palsson.

The Northern Ontario Heritage Foundation and a Californian bio-tech company jointly funded the exhumations in an investigation which lasted several days. Behind white canvas tenting to preserve the privacy and dignity of the procedure, the graves were opened and the three coffins were unsealed. First indications were that the samples were not all of a suitable standard for testing, but samples were removed where possible, the coffins resealed and prayers said over the grave. Finally the soil was replaced and the samples despatched to Lakehead University scientific laboratory for analysis expected to take six months. At the time of writing, families who have already waited 90 long years for the answers must wait a little longer.

1   RG76 Reel T-4706 (Nova Scotia Archives and Record Management)
2   Eaton & Haas, *Titanic: Triumph and Tragedy*
3   Eaton & Haas, *Titanic – Destination Disaster*
4   Threader, Fredk Payne Funeral Directors, Isleworth
5   Eaton & Haas, *Titanic: Triumph and Tragedy*
6   List of Bodies Identified and Disposal of Same (Nova Scotia Archives and Record Management)

Chapter 9
Final Thoughts

With the research finally completed and the names and details transcribed from each of the lists of passengers held in archives in Britain, Canada and the United States, the job of comparing and matching each name from each list began. Although the original intention had been to compile a definitive list of passengers, once the research got underway it immediately became clear that this would be an impossible task. Much of the evidence uncovered over many years of research by a variety of scholars suggests that most of the surviving lists have significant errors. Some have more than others, but none is absolutely correct. This book has tried to put that into context and explain how such a situation may have arisen.

The transcriptions included in this book have been undertaken as conscientiously as possible. The temptation to correct what often seemed to be a simple mistake in the spelling of a very obvious name was almost overwhelming at times, especially when it seemed that the apparent error must surely have been a simple slip of the pen of the particular clerk. However, if this research was to be valid then the temptation to correct had to be resisted. Some of the comparisons were perfectly obvious, with the spelling and details almost the same for each list in which the passenger appeared. Many of the others were eventually matched but on some lists, a small handful of names defied comparison.

Some passenger names remain unresolved. Missing names from the White Star Line passenger list, the Board of Trade List, or the several records of deaths at sea (especially where no body was every found) are probably simple errors. But with no evidence, no body found and no travelling companions to tell the tale, there is no absolute proof that the passenger ever sailed.

A mystery surrounds an Australian *Titanic* passenger, Arthur McCrae. A grave stone in a Sydney cemetery for an Allan McCrie records a 'beloved son, lost on *Titanic*'. However, it has been established that the two men are unconnected, and the man who lies in the cemetery in Australia did not sail on *Titanic*.

Equally intriguing is the case of Augusta Valentine. Augusta, as mentioned briefly in Chapter 7, made two appearances on the United States arrival manifest. Neither entry is complete, and one is overwritten. However, the Purser or his clerk began writing her name. He then apparently changed his mind, crossed it out and wrote it again on a different sheet. He still did not complete the entry but this time he did not cross it out. When the list was typed later, Augusta's name was included on the list. Was she really a 30-year-old United States' citizen and a survivor of *Titanic*? No other details have been entered for her either by the Purser or by the immigration officers in New York, but the same could be said for a number of other people who have been accepted as having survived the sinking. Could she have been one of those who wandered away before formalities were completed? If she did not exist, where did the Purser obtain her name and why did he write it not once but twice? Did Mrs Carter's maid, Augusta Serreplan speak indistinctly when asked her name, resulting in the Purser mishearing her? Or could she be Mrs Ada Clarke, whose husband's middle name was Valentine? Or was she a passenger on *Carpathia*'s passenger list, on her way back from New York to Europe who just happened to be confused with *Titanic's* passengers in the chaos of that first day?

Another possible passenger, John Borap, also appears on the same United States arrival manifest and the later typed list. No further details are known for this man either and he is another whose entry on the list remains unresolved.

Hilda Mary Slayter was a young Canadian woman who had been living in England for a while. On the Southampton section of the Board of Trade list, there is an entry for a young woman named Marion Slayter, a British woman aged 24, with her last place of residence shown to be England. On the Queenstown section of the list, there is an entry for Miss H M Slater, no age given, with her last place of residence shown as Ireland. Both women have the same ticket number. At the end of the day, if this is ever to be unravelled, they will probably turn out to be the same woman. However, with the names and details different, and in one case entirely at odds with what the real Hilda Slayter's name was, it is wholly unsafe to deny all possibility that the real mistake lies with the ticket number, and that they were actually two different women.

The Reverend Charles Kirkland also appears on both sections of the Board of Trade list, though his details are identical on each section.

A large number of passengers have also been proved later (often because they survived to tell their own stories) to have boarded in Southampton. They do not however appear on the Board of Trade list at all. Some of them are servants, but others are 1st and 2nd class passengers. The Minahan family are reported as boarding in Queenstown but are shown on the Southampton section.

The White Star Line's Contract Ticket list has similar omissions. Most of the servants are not listed by name, and a group of seamen is also omitted. The list or errors and anomalies goes on, proving even more strongly that a definitive list is unfeasible.

Battling against faded ink, poor photocopies and almost illegible, unfamiliar handwriting made transcribing difficult and tedious at times. Records which have already suffered from several transcriptions or mistranscriptions by various different clerks in government departments or shipping lines staff, have now been exposed to yet one more transcription for the purposes of this latest research. The transcriptions included in this book are my own interpretations of each entry. That may be very different from how another reader may interpret them. Almost a century ago, exactly the same problem was a contributory factor to the problems faced by the governments and the White Star Line in their rush to produce an accurate list in the immediate aftermath of the tragedy.

No matter how much more research is undertaken, nobody will ever be absolutely certain exactly who died on *Titanic*. Several passengers were travelling under an alias. Have they all been exposed? A handful remain curiously unidentified. After 90 years of publicity nobody has come forward to claim them. Could they be paying the ironic price of an overly-successful attempt to conceal their true identity? In 1987 a cross-Channel car ferry, *Herald of Free Enterprise*, sank just outside Zeebrugge with the loss of almost 200 lives. The body of one man was reportedly claimed by two 'wives', one on each side of the English Channel, neither of whom knew of the existence of the other. How many passengers on *Titanic* were living double lives? Others apparently on board died without trace along with their travelling companions. Given the secrets some passengers are known to have carried, can we be quite certain that these missing people ever boarded *Titanic* at all? However sure we may be of who was or who was not on board and whatever each of these official documentary sources may suggest, in fact they offer no proof at all, only circumstantial evidence.

Only *Titanic* knows the truth, and there are some answers she will never give up.

Appendix 1
The Research

T he research has been arranged in such a way as to allow the reader to track any passenger through each of the lists in which the name appears.

Every name appearing on any archival list has been entered into a 'master' list. It was important to use the most recently researched evidence regarding the actual identity of each passenger and the spelling of their names. In order to complete the list I have drawn on names from all documentary sources in this book. In instances of very complicated names, or where recent additional information has been made available, I have used the names and spellings as they appear on the Encyclopedia Titanica website with the permission of the editor, Philip Hind. The list includes those who may not have sailed after all, and also the anomalies such as Augusta Valentine, John Borap and the possibly two Slater/Slayter women. Each name on the Master List has been numbered. The Master List is now in both alphabetical and numerical order.

The names and number of each passenger on the Master List are entered in columns across a grid on the Passengers Identification table. The next three columns headed by letters of the alphabet, show:

A. Port at which each passenger may have boarded *Titanic*
B. Class of travel -1st, 2nd or 3rd
C. Lost or saved. Passengers lost are marked L. Where saved, the cell is blank.
The remaining columns represent each document as follows:
D. White Star Contract Ticket
E. Board of Trade Passenger List
F. Register of Deaths At Sea
G. Inq.6
H. C&D (Casualty & Deaths)
J. United States Arrival
K. Typed
L. White Star Line's Passenger List
M. Cave
N. Bodies Identified
O. Halifax Arrivals

In order to track each passenger, firstly locate then on the Passenger Identification table and note the master list number. That is their Identification Number which remains with that passenger in each list in this book. Working across the columns, note the list or list in which that passenger's name appears.

Turn to the transcription for each list. Recorded on the left in bold type are the ID numbers from the Master List. Locate the number for the passenger you are tracking in order to access their details on that list. This can be repeated for each list on which the passenger appears.

The passenger names on each individual list transcription are no longer in the order in which they were transcribed. Should you wish to reconstruct the order of the original transcription, it may be accomplished by referring to the number next to the bold type number on each list. That represents their position on the original list, before it was renumbered in Master List order.

Passenger Identification Table

Column A

Port of Embarkationl recorded in 1912

        S ~ Southampton

        C ~ Cherbourg

        Q ~ Queenstown

        CC ~ Cross-Channel and Southampton to Queenstown

Column B

Class of Travel recorded in 1912

        1 ~ 1st Class

        2 ~ 2nd Class

        3 ~ 3rd Class

        CC ~ Cross Channel

	Surname	Forename(s)	A	B	C	D	E	F	G	H	J	K	L	M	N	O
1	Abbing	Anthony	S	3	L	X	X	X	X	X			X			
2	Abbott	Eugene Joseph	S	3	L	X	X	X	X	X			X			
3	Abbott	Rosa	S	3		X	X				X	X	X			
4	Abbott	Rossmore Edward	S	3	L	X	X	X	X	X			X		X	
5	Abelseth	Karen Marie	S	3		X	X				X	X	X			
6	Abelseth	Olais Jorgensen	S	3		X	X				X	X	X			
7	Abelson	H	C	2		X					X	X	X			
8	Abelson	Samuel	C	2	L	X		X	X	X			X			
9	Abrahamsson	Abraham August	S	3		X	X				X	X	X			
10	Abrahim	Mary Sofia Joseph	C	3		X					X	X	X			
11	Adahl	Mauritz Nils	S	3	L	X	X	X	X	X			X		X	
12	Adams	John	S	3	L	X	X	X	X	X			X		X	
13	Ahlin	Johanna	S	3	L	X	X	X	X	X			X			
14	Ahmed	Ali	S	3	L	X	X	X	X	X			X			
15	Aks	Frank Philip	S	3		X	X				X	X	X			
16	Aks	Leah	S	3		X	X				X	X	X			
17	Albimona	Nassef Cassem	C	3	L	X					X	X	X			
18	Aldworth	Charles Augustus	S	2	L	X	X	X	X	X			X			
19	Alexander	William	S	3	L	X	X	X	X	X			X			
20	Alhomaki	Ilmari Rudolf	S	3	L	X	X	X	X	X			X			
21	Ali	William	S	3	L	X	X	X	X	X			X		X	
22	Allen	Elisabeth Walton	S	1		X	X				X	X	X	X		
23	Allen	William Henry	S	3	L	X	X	X	X	X			X			
24	Allison	Bessie Waldo	S	1	L	X	X	X	X	X			X	X		
25	Allison	Helen Loraine	S	1	L	X	X	X	X	X			X	X		
26	Allison	Hudson Joshua	S	1	L	X	X	X	X	X			X	X		X
27	Allison	Hudson Trevor	S	1	L	X					X	X	X			
28	Allum	Owen George	S	3	L	X	X	X	X	X			X			X
29	Andersen	Albert Karvin	S	3	L	X	X	X	X	X			X			X
30	Andersen-Jensen	Carla Christine	S	3		X	X				X	X	X			
31	Anderson	Harry	S	1		X	X				X	X	X	X		
32	Andersson	Alfrida	S	3	L	X	X	X	X	X			X			
33	Andersson	Anders Johan	S	3	L	X	X	X	X	X			X			
34	Andersson	August Edvard	S	3		X	X				X	X	X			
35	Andersson	Ebba Iris	S	3	L	X	X	X	X	X			X			
36	Andersson	Ellis Anna	S	3	L	X	X	X	X	X			X			
37	Andersson	Erna Alexandra	S	3		X	X				X	X	X			
38	Andersson	Ida Augusta	S	3	L	X	X	X	X	X			X			
39	Andersson	Ingeborg Constanzia	S	3	L	X	X	X	X	X			X			
40	Andersson	Johan Samuel	S	3	L	X	X	X	X	X			X			
41	Andersson	Sigrid Elisabeth	S	3	L	X	X	X	X	X			X			
42	Andersson	Sigvard Harald	S	3	L	X	X	X	X	X			X			

Column C	Fate L = Lost (as shown on Senate List)
Column D	White Star Contract Ticket List
Column E	Board of Trade Passenger List BT27/780B, BT27/776
Column F	Form Inq.6 MT9/920C
Column G	List C&D BT100/260
Column H	Register of Deaths of Passengers and Seamen at Sea BT334/52
Column J	List or Manifest of Survivors, RMS *Carpathia*, Port of New York
Column K	Purser's Typed List of Survivors, RMS *Carpathia*, Port of New York
Column L	White Star Line passenger list, Senate Investigation Exhibit B
Column M	Cave List - 3rd Draft of 1st Class Passenger List
Column N	List of Bodies Identified, and Disposition of Same (Bound for Halifax)
Column O	Passengers Bound for Halifax (List of Bodies)

	Surname	Forename(s)	A	B	C	D	E	F	G	H	J	K	L	M	N	O
43	Andreasson	Paul Edvin	S	3	L	X	X	X	X	X			X			
44	Andrew	Frank Thomas	S	2	L	X		X	X	X			X			
45	Andrew	Edgardo Samuel	S	2	L	X	X	X	X	X			X			
46	Andrews	Kornelia Theodosia	S	1		X							X	X		
47	Andrews	Thomas	S	1	L	X	X	X	X	X			X	X		
48	Angheloff	Minko	S	3	L	X	X	X	X	X			X			
49	Angle	Florence Mary	S	2		X	X				X	X	X			
50	Angle	William	S	2	L	X	X	X	X	X			X			
51	Appleton	Charlotte Lamson	S	1		X	X						X	X		
52	Arnold-Franchi	Josef	S	3	L	X	X	X	X	X			X			
53	Arnold-Franchi	Josefine	S	3	L	X	X	X	X	X			X			
54	Aronsson	Ernst Axel	S	3	L	X	X	X	X	X			X			
55	Artagaveytia	Ramon	C	1	L	X		X	X	X			X		X	
56	Ashby	John	S	2	L	X	X	X	X	X			X			
57	Asim	Adola	S	3	L	X	X	X	X	X			X			
58	Asplund	Carl Edgar	S	3	L	X	X	X	X	X			X		X	
59	Asplund	Carl Oscar	S	3	L		X	X	X	X			X			
60	Asplund	Clarence Gustaf	S	3	L	X	X	X	X	X			X			
61	Asplund	Edvin Rojj Felix	S	3		X	X				X	X	X			
62	Asplund	Filip Oscar	S	3	L	X	X	X	X	X			X			
63	Asplund	Johan Charles	S	3		X	X				X	X	X			
64	Asplund	Lillian Gertrud	S	3		X	X					X	X			
65	Asplund	Selma Augusta	S	3		X	X					X	X			
66	Assaf	Gerios	C	3	L	X		X	X	X			X			
67	Assaf	Marian	C	3		X					X	X	X			X
68	Assam	Ali	S	3	L	X	X	X	X	X			X			
69	Astor	John Jacob	C	1	L	X		X	X	X			X		X	
70	Astor	Madeleine Talmadge	C	1		X					X	X	X			
71	Attala	Sleiman	C	3	L	X		X	X	X			X			
72	Aubert	Leontine Pauline	C	1		X					X	X	X	X		
73	Augustsson	Albert	S	3	L	X	X	X	X	X			X			
74	Ayoub	Banoura	C	3		X					X	X	X			
75	Baccos	Raffull	C	3	L	X		X	X	X			X			
76	Backstrom	Karl Alfred	S	3	L	X	X	X	X	X			X			
77	Backstrom	Maria Mathilda	S	3		X	X				X	X	X			
78	Baclini	Eugenie	C	3		X					X	X	X			
79	Baclini	Helene Barbara	C	3		X					X	X	X			
80	Baclini	Latifa Qurban	C	3		X					X	X	X			
81	Baclini	Marie Catherine	C	3		X					X	X	X			
82	Badman	Emily Louisa	S	3		X	X				X	X	X			
83	Badt	Mohamed	C	3	L	X		X	X	X			X			
84	Bailey	Percy Andrew	S	2	L	X	X	X	X	X			X			

Who Sailed on Titanic?

	Surname	Forename(s)	A	B	C	D	E	F	G	H	J	K	L	M	N	O
85	Baimbrigge	Charles Robert	S	2	L	X	X	X	X	X			X			
86	Balkic	Cerin	S	3	L	X	X	X	X	X			X			
87	Ball	Ada	S	2		X	X					X	X	X		
88	Banfield	Frederick James	S	2	L	X	X	X	X	X			X			
89	Barbara	Catherine	C	3	L	X		X	X	X			X			
90	Barbara	Saude	C	3		X		X	X	X			X			
91	Barber	Ellen	S	1		X					X	X	X	X		
92	Barkworth	Algernon Henry	S	1		X	X				X	X	X	X		
93	Barry	Julia	Q	3	L	X	X	X	X	X			X			
94	Barton	David John	S	3	L	X	X	X	X	X			X			
95	Bateman	Robert James	S	2	L	X	X	X	X	X			X		X	
96	Baumann	John D	S	1	L	X		X	X	X			X		X	
97	Baxter	Helene DeLaudeniere	S	1		X	X				X	X	X	X		
98	Baxter	Quigg Edmond	S	1	L	X	X	X	X	X			X	X		
99	Bazzani	Albine	C	1		X							X	X		
100	Beane	Edward	S	2		X	X					X	X	X		
101	Beane	Ethel	S	2		X	X					X	X	X		
102	Beattie	Thomson	C	1	L	X		X	X	X			X	X		
103	Beauchamp	Henry James	S	2	L	X	X	X	X	X			X			
104	Beavan	William Thomas	S	3	L	X	X	X	X	X			X			
105	Becker	Marion Louise	S	2		X	X					X	X	X		
106	Becker	Nellie	S	2		X	X					X	X	X		
107	Becker	Richard	S	2		X	X					X	X	X		
108	Becker	Ruth Elizabeth	S	2		X	X					X	X	X		
109	Beckwith	Richard Leonard	S	1		X	X					X	X	X	X	
110	Beckwith	Sallie	S	1		X	X					X	X	X	X	
111	Beesley	Lawrence	S	2		X	X					X	X	X		
112	Behr	Karl Howell	C	1	L	X						X	X	X	X	
113	Bengtsson	John Viktor	S	3	L	X	X	X	X	X			X			
114	Bentham	Lillian	S	2		X	X					X	X	X		
115	Berglund	Karl Ivar	S	3	L	X	X	X	X	X			X			
116	Berriman	William John	S	2	L	X	X	X	X	X			X			
117	Betros	Seman	C	3	L			X	X	X			X			
118	Betros	Tannous	C	3	L			X	X	X			X			
119	Bidois	Rosalie	C	1		X						X	X	X		
120	Bing	Lee	S	3		X	X					X	X	X		
121	Bird	Ellen	S	1		X	X					X	X	X	X	
122	Birkeland	Hans Martin	S	3	L	X	X	X	X	X			X			
123	Birnbaum	Jakob	C	1	L	X		X	X	X			X	X		
124	Bishop	Dickinson	C	1		X							X	X		
125	Bishop	Helen Walton	C	1		X							X	X		
126	Bissette	Amelia	C	1		X						X	X	X		
127	Bjorklund	Ernst Herbert	S	3	L	X	X	X	X	X			X			
128	Bjornstrom-Steffansson	Mauritz Hakan	S	1		X	X					X	X	X		
129	Blackwell	Stephen Weart	S	1	L	X	X	X	X	X			X	X	X	
130	Blank	Henry	C	1		X						X	X	X	X	
131	Bonnell	Caroline	S	1		X	X					X	X	X	X	
132	Bonnell	Elizabeth	S	1		X	X					X	X	X	X	
133	Borap	John	UNKNOWN									X				
134	Borebank	John James	S	1	L	X	X	X	X	X			X	X		
135	Bostandyeff	Guentcho	S	3	L	X	X	X	X	X			X			
136	Botsford	William Hull	S	2	L	X	X	X	X	X			X			
137	Boulos	Akar	C	3	L			X	X	X			X			
138	Boulos	Hanna	C	3	L			X	X	X			X			
139	Boulos	Nourelain	C	3		X						X	X			
140	Boulos	Sultana	C	3	L			X	X	X			X			
141	Bourke	Catherine	Q	3	L	X	X	X	X	X			X			
142	Bourke	John	Q	3	L	X	X	X	X	X			X			
143	Bourke	Mary	Q	3	L	X	X	X	X	X			X			
144	Bowen	David John	S	3	L	X	X	X	X	X			X			
145	Bowen	Grace Scott	C	1		X						X	X	X		
146	Bowenur	Solomon	S	2	L	X	X	X	X	X			X			
147	Bowerman	Elsie Edith	S	1		X	X					X	X	X	X	
148	Bracken	James	S	2	L	X	X	X	X	X			X			
149	Bradley	Bridget Delia	Q	3		X	X					X	X	X		
150	Bradley	George	S	1		X	X					X	X	X		
151	Brady	John Bertram	S	1	L	X	X	X	X	X			X	X		

Passenger Identification Table

	Surname	Forename(s)	A	B	C	D	E	F	G	H	J	K	L	M	N	O
152	Braf	Elin Ester	S	3	L	X	X	X	X	X			X			
153	Brailey	Theodore Ronald	S	2	L	X	X	X	X	X						
154	Brand		CC	CC		X										
155	Brandeis	Emil	C	1	L	X		X	X	X			X	X	X	
156	Braund	Lewis Richard	S	3	L	X	X	X	X	X			X			
157	Braund	Owen Harris	S	3	L	X	X	X	X	X			X			
158	Brewe	Arthur Jackson	C	1	L	X		X	X	X			X			
159	Bricoux	Roger Marie	S	2		X	X	X	X	X						
160	Brito	Jose Joaquim	S	2	L	X	X	X	X	X			X			
161	Brobeck	Karl Rudolf	S	3	L	X	X	X	X	X			X			
162	Brocklebank	William Alfred	S	3	L	X	X	X	X	X			X			
163	Brown	Amelia	S	2		X	X				X	X	X			X
164	Brown	Caroline Lane	S	1		X	X						X	X		
165	Brown	Edith Eileen	S	2		X	X				X		X			
166	Brown	Elizabeth Catherine	S	2		X	X				X	X	X			
167	Brown	Margaret Tobin	C	1		X							X			
168	Brown	Thomas William	S	2	L	X	X	X	X	X			X			
169	Browne	Francis M	CC	CC		X										
170	Bryhl	Dagmar Jenny	S	2		X	X				X	X	X			
171	Bryhl	Kurt Arnold	S	2	L	X	X	X	X	X			X			
172	Buckley	Daniel	Q	3		X	X				X	X	X			
173	Buckley	Katherine	Q	3	L	X	X	X	X	X			X		X	
174	Bucknell	Emma Eliza	C	1		X							X	X		
175	Burke	Jeremiah	Q	3	L	X	X	X	X	X			X			
176	Burns	Elizabeth	S	1		X	X				X	X	X	X		
177	Burns	Mary Delia	Q	3	L	X	X	X	X	X			X			
178	Buss	Kate	S	2		X	X				X	X	X			
179	Butler	Reginald Fenton	S	2	L	X	X	X	X	X			X		X	
180	Butt	Archibald	S	1	L	X	X	X	X	X			X	X		
181	Byles	Thomas Roussel	S	2	L	X	X	X	X	X			X		X	
182	Bystrom	Karolina	S	2		X	X				X	X	X			
183	Cacic	Jego Grga	S	3	L	X	X	X	X	X			X			
184	Cacic	Luka	S	3	L	X	X	X	X	X			X			
185	Cacic	Manda	S	3	L	X	X	X	X	X			X			
186	Cacic	Marija	S	3	L	X	X	X	X	X			X			
187	Cairns	Alexander	S	1	L	X		X	X	X						
188	Calderhead	Edward Pennington	S	1		X	X				X	X	X	X		
189	Caldwell	Albert Francis	S	2		X	X				X	X	X			
190	Caldwell	Alden Gates	S	2		X	X				X	X	X			
191	Caldwell	Sylvia Mae	S	2		X	X				X	X	X			
192	Calic	Petar	S	3	L	X	X	X	X	X			X			
193	Cameron	Clear Annie	S	2		X	X				X	X	X			
194	Campbell	William	S	2	L	X	X	X	X	X			X			
195	Canavan	Mary	Q	3	L	X	X	X	X	X			X			
196	Canavan	Patrick	Q	3	L	X	X	X	X	X			X			
197	Candee	Helen Churchill	C	1		X					X	X	X			
198	Cann	Ernest Charles	S	3	L	X	X	X	X	X			X			
199	Caram	Joseph	C	3	L	X		X	X	X			X			
200	Caram	Maria Elias	C	3	L	X		X	X	X			X			
201	Carbines	William	S	2	L	X	X	X	X	X			X			
202	Cardeza	Charlotte Wardle	C	1		X					X	X	X	X		
203	Cardeza	Thomas Drake	C	1		X					X	X	X	X		
204	Carfirth	John	S	3	L	X	X	X	X	X			X			
205	Carlson	Frans Olof	S	1	L	X		X	X	X			X			
206	Carlsson	August Sigfrid	S	3	L	X	X	X	X	X			X			
207	Carlsson	Carl Robert	S	3	L	X	X	X	X	X			X			
208	Carr	Jane	Q	3	L	X	X	X	X	X			X			
209	Carrau	Francisco M	S	1	L	X	X	X	X	X			X			
210	Carrau	Jose Pedro	S	1	L	X	X	X	X	X			X			
211	Carter	Ernest Courtenay	S	2	L	X	X	X	X	X			X			
212	Carter	Lilian Hughes	S	2	L	X	X	X	X	X			X			
213	Carter	Lucile P	S	1		X	X				X	X	X	X		
214	Carter	Lucile P (Mrs)	S	1		X	X				X	X	X	X		
215	Carter	William Ernest	S	1		X	X				X	X	X	X		
216	Carter	William Thornton	S	1		X	X				X	X	X	X		
217	Carver	Alfred	S	1	L		X	X	X	X			X			
218	Case	Howard Brown	S	1	L	X	X	X	X	X			X	X		
219	Cassebeer	Eleanor Genevieve	C	1		X					X	X	X			

	Surname	Forename(s)	A	B	C	D	E	F	G	H	J	K	L	M	N	O
220	Cavendish	Julia Florence	S	1		X	X					X	X	X	X		
221	Cavendish	Tyrell William	S	1	L	X	X	X	X	X				X	X	X	
222	Celotti	Francesco	S	3	L	X	X	X	X	X				X			
223	Chaffee	Carrie Constance	S	1		X	X					X	X	X	X		
224	Chaffee	Herbert Fuller	S	1	L	X	X	X	X	X				X	X		
225	Chambers	Bertha	S	1		X	X							X			
226	Chambers	Norman Campbell	S	1		X	X							X			
227	Chapman	Charles Henry	S	2	L	X	X	X	X	X				X		X	
228	Chapman	John Henry	S	2	L	X	X	X	X	X				X		X	
229	Chapman	Sara Elizabeth	S	2	L	X	X	X	X	X				X			
230	Charters	David	Q	3	L	X	X	X	X	X				X			
231	Chaudanson	Victorine	C	1		X						X	X	X			
232	Cherry	Gladys	S	1		X	X					X	X	X	X		
233	Chevre	Paul Romaine	C	1		X						X	X	X	X		
234	Chibnall	Edith Martha	S	1		X	X					X	X	X	X		
235	Chip	Chang	S	3		X	X					X	X	X			
236	Chisholm	Roderick Robert	S	1	L	X	X	X	X	X				X	X		
237	Christmann	Emil	S	3	L	X	X	X	X	X				X			
238	Christy	Alice Frances	S	2		X	X					X	X	X	X		
239	Christy	Julie Rachel	S	2		X	X					X	X	X	X		
240	Chronopoulos	Apostolos	C	3	L	X		X	X	X				X			
241	Chronopoulos	Demetrios	C	3	L	X		X	X	X				X			
242	Clark	Ada Maria	S	2		X	X					X	X	X			
243	Clark	Charles Valentine	S	2	L	X	X	X	X	X				X			
244	Clark	Virginia Estelle	C	1		X						X	X	X	X		
245	Clark	Walter Miller	C	1	L	X		X	X	X				X	X		
246	Clarke	John Frederick	S	2	L	X	X	X	X	X							
247	Cleaver	Alice	S	1		X						X	X	X	X		
248	Clifford	George Quincy	S	1	L	X	X	X	X	X				X	X		
249	Coelho	Domingos Fernandeo	S	3	L	X	X	X	X	X				X			
250	Cohen	Gurshon	S	3		X	X					X	X	X			
251	Colbert	Patrick	Q	3	L	X	X	X	X	X				X			
252	Coleff	Peju	S	3	L	X	X	X	X	X				X			
253	Coleff	Satio	S	3	L	X	X	X	X	X				X			
254	Coleridge	Reginald Charles	S	2	L	X	X	X	X	X				X			
255	Collander	Erik Gustaf	S	2	L	X	X	X	X	X				X			
256	Collett	Sidney	S	2		X	X					X	X	X			
257	Colley	Edward Pomeroy	S	1	L	X	X	X	X	X				X	X		
258	Collis		CC	CC		X											
259	Collyer	Charlotte	S	2		X	X					X	X	X			
260	Collyer	Harvey	S	2	L	X	X	X	X	X				X			
261	Collyer	Marjorie Charlotte	S	2		X	X					X	X	X			
262	Compton	Alexander Taylor	C	1	L	X		X	X	X				X	X		
263	Compton	Mary Eliza	C	1		X						X	X	X	X		
264	Compton	Sara Rebecca	C	1		X						X	X	X	X		
265	Conlon	Thomas Henry	Q	3	L	X	X	X	X	X				X			
266	Connaghton	Michael	Q	3	L	X	X	X	X	X				X			
267	Connolly	Kate	Q	3		X	X					X	X	X			
268	Connolly	Kate	Q	3	L	X	X	X	X	X				X			
269	Connors	Patrick	Q	3	L	X	X	X	X	X				X		X	
270	Cook	Jacob	S	3	L	X	X	X	X	X				X			
271	Cook	Selena	S	2		X	X					X	X	X			
272	Cor	Bartol	S	3	L	X	X	X	X	X				X			
273	Cor	Ivan	S	3	L	X	X	X	X	X				X			
274	Cor	Liudevik	S	3	L	X	X	X	X	X				X			
275	Corbett	Irene	S	2	L	X	X	X	X	X				X			
276	Corey	Mary Phyllis	S	2	L	X	X	X	X	X				X			
277	Corn	Harry	S	3	L	X	X	X	X	X				X			
278	Cornell	Malvina Helen	S	1		X	X							X	X		
279	Corr	Ellen	Q	3		X	X					X	X	X			
280	Cotterill	Henry	S	2	L	X	X	X	X	X				X			
281	Coutts	Neville Leslie	S	3		X	X					X	X	X			
282	Coutts	William Loch	S	3		X	X					X	X	X			
283	Coutts	Winnie	S	3		X	X					X	X	X			
284	Coxon	Daniel	S	3	L	X	X	X	X	X				X			
285	Crafton	John Bertram	S	1	L	X	X	X	X	X				X			
286	Craig	Norman C													X	X	
287	Crease	Ernest James	S	3	L	X	X	X	X	X				X			

	Surname	Forename(s)	A	B	C	D	E	F	G	H	J	K	L	M	N	O
288	Cribb	John Hatfield	S	3	L	X	X	X	X	X			X			
289	Cribb	Laura	S	3		X	X				X	X	X			
290	Crosby	Catherine Elizabeth	S	1		X	X						X	X		
291	Crosby	Edward Gifford	S	1	L	X	X	X	X	X			X	X	X	
292	Crosby	Harriette	S	1		X							X			
293	Cumings	Florence Briggs	C	1		X					X	X	X			
294	Cumings	John Bradley	C	1	L	X		X	X	X			X			
295	Cunningham	Alfred Fleming	S	2	L	X	X	X	X	X			X			
296	Daher	Shedid	C	3	L	X		X	X	X			X		X	
297	Dahl	Charles Edward	S	3		X	X				X	X	X			
298	Dahlberg	Gerda Ulrika	S	3	L	X	X	X	X	X			X			
299	Dakic	Branko	S	3	L	X	X	X	X	X			X			
300	Daly	Eugene Patrick	Q	3		X	X				X	X	X			
301	Daly	Margaret Marcella	Q	3		X	X				X	X	X			
302	Daly	Peter Dennis	S	1		X	X				X	X	X	X		
303	Danbom	Anna Sigrid	S	3	L	X	X	X	X	X			X			
304	Danbom	Ernst Gilbert	S	3	L	X	X	X	X	X			X		X	
305	Danbom	Gilbert Sigvard	S	3	L	X	X	X	X	X			X			
306	Daniel	Robert Williams	S	1	L	X	X				X	X	X			
307	Daniels	Sarah	S	1		X					X	X	X	X		
308	Danoff	Yoto	S	3	L	X	X	X	X	X			X			
309	Dantcheff	Ristiu	S	3	L	X	X	X	X	X			X			
310	Davidson	Orian Hays	S	1		X	X				X	X	X	X		
311	Davidson	Thornton	S	1	L	X	X	X	X	X			X	X		
312	Davies	Alfred	S	3	L	X	X	X	X	X			X			
313	Davies	Charles Henry	S	2	L	X	X	X	X	X			X			
314	Davies	Elizabeth Agnes	S	2		X	X				X	X	X			
315	Davies	Evan	S	3	L	X	X	X	X	X			X			
316	Davies	H V	CC	CC		X										
317	Davies	John Morgan	S	2		X	X				X	X	X			
318	Davies	John Samuel	S	3	L	X	X	X	X	X			X			
319	Davies	Joseph	S	3	L	X	X	X	X	X			X			
320	Davies	K	CC	CC		X										
321	Davis	Mary	S	2		X	X				X	X	X			
322	Davison	Mary	S	3		X	X				X	X	X			
323	Davison	Thomas Henry	S	3	L	X	X	X	X	X			X			
324	de Grasse	J	CC	CC		X										
325	de Messemaeker	Anna	S	3		X	X				X	X	X			
326	de Messemaeker	Guillaume Joseph	S	3		X	X				X	X	X			
327	de Mulder	Theodoor	S	3		X	X				X	X	X			
328	de Pelsmaeker	Alfons	S	3	L	X	X	X	X	X			X			
329	Deacon	Percy William	S	2	L	X	X	X	X	X			X			
330	Dean	Bertram Frank	S	3	L	X	X	X	X	X			X			
331	Dean	Bertram Vere	S	3		X	X				X	X	X			
332	Dean	Elizabeth Gladys	S	3		X	X				X	X	X			
333	Dean	Eva Georgette	S	3		X	X				X	X	X			
334	Del Carlo	Argene Genovesi	C	2		X					X	X	X			
335	Del Carlo	Sebastiano	C	2	L	X		X	X	X			X		X	
336	Delalic	Regjo	S	3	L	X	X	X	X	X			X			
337	Demetri	Marinko	S	3	L	X	X	X	X	X			X			
338	Denbury	Herbert	S	2	L	X	X	X	X	X			X			
339	Denkoff	Mitto	S	3	L	X	X	X	X	X			X			
340	Dennis	Samuel	S	3	L	X	X	X	X	X			X			
341	Dennis	William	S	3	L	X	X	X	X	X			X			
342	Dequemin	Joseph	S	3		X	X				X	X	X			
343	Devaney	Margaret Delia	Q	3		X	X				X	X	X			
344	Dibden	William	S	2	L	X	X	X	X	X			X			
345	Dick	Albert Adrian	S	1		X	X				X	X	X	X		
346	Dick	Vera Gillespie	S	1		X	X				X	X	X	X		
347	Dika	Mirko	S	3	L	X	X	X	X	X			X			
348	Dimic	Jovan	S	3	L	X	X	X	X	X			X			
349	Dintcheff	Valtcho	S	3	L	X	X	X	X	X			X			
350	Dodge	Ruth Vidaver	S	1		X	X				X	X	X	X		
351	Dodge	Washington	S	1		X	X				X	X	X	X		
352	Dodge	Washington (Master)	S	1		X	X				X	X	X	X		
353	Doharr	Tannous	C	3	L	X		X	X	X			X			
354	Doling	Ada Julia	S	2		X					X	X	X			
355	Doling	Elsie	S	2		X					X	X	X			

	Surname	Forename(s)	A	B	C	D	E	F	G	H	J	K	L	M	N	O
356	Donohoe	Bridget	Q	3	L	X	X	X	X	X			X			
357	Dooley	Patrick	Q	3	L	X	X	X	X	X			X			
358	Dorking	Edward Arthur	S	3		X	X				X	X	X			
359	Douglas	Mahala Dutton	C	1		X					X	X	X	X		
360	Douglas	Mary Helene	S	1		X	X				X	X	X	X		
361	Douglas	Walter Donald	C	1	L	X		X	X	X			X	X	X	
362	Dowdell	Elizabeth	S	3		X	X				X	X	X			
363	Downton	William James	S	2	L	X	X	X	X	X			X			
364	Doyle	Elizabeth	Q	3	L	X	X	X	X	X			X			
365	Drazenovic	Jozef	C	3	L	X		X	X	X			X			X
366	Drew	Lulu Thorne	S	2		X	X				X	X	X			
367	Drew	Marshall Brines	S	2		X	X				X	X	X			
368	Drew	James Vivian	S	2	L	X	X	X	X	X			X			
369	Driscoll	Bridget	Q	3		X	X				X	X	X			
370	Dropkin	Jennie	S	3		X	X				X	X	X			
371	Duff Gordon	Lucy	C	1		X					X	X	X	X		
372	Duff Gordon	Cosmo	C	1		X					X	X	X	X		
373	Dulles	William Crothers	C	1	L	X		X	X	X			X	X	X	
374	Duran	Asuncion	C	2		X					X	X	X			
375	Duran	Florentina	C	2		X					X	X	X			
376	Dwan	Frank	Q	3	L	X	X	X	X	X			X			
377	Dyker	Adolf Fredrik	S	3	L	X	X	X	X	X			X			
378	Dyker	Anna Elisabeth	S	3		X	X				X	X	X			
379	Earnshaw	Olive	C	1		X					X	X	X	X		
380	Eastman	Anne K				X							X	X		
381	Ecimovic	Jeso	S	3	L	X	X	X	X	X			X			
382	Edvardsson	Gustaf Hjalmar	S	3	L	X	X	X	X	X			X			
383	Eitemiller	George Floyd	S	2	L	X	X	X	X	X			X			
384	Eklund	Hans Linus	S	3	L	X	X	X	X	X			X			
385	Ekstrom	Johan	S	3	L	X	X	X	X	X			X			
386	Elias	Dibo	C	3	L	X		X	X	X			X			
387	Elias	Joseph	C	3	L	X		X	X	X			X			
388	Elias	Joseph	C	3	L	X		X	X	X			X			
389	Elias	Tannous	C	3	L	X		X	X	X			X			
390	Elsbury	William James	S	3	L	X	X	X	X	X			X			
391	Emanuel	Virginia Ethel	S	3		X	X				X	X	X			
392	Emir-Farres	Chehab	C	3	L	X		X	X	X			X			
393	Enander	Ingvar	S	2	L	X	X	X	X	X			X			
394	Endres	Caroline Louise	C	1		X					X	X	X	X		
395	Estanislau	Manuel Gonvalves	S	3	L	X	X	X	X	X			X			
396	Eustis	Elizabeth Mussey	S	1		X	X				X	X	X	X		
397	Evans	Edith Corse	C	1	L	X		X	X	X			X	X		
398	Evans	E	CC	CC		X										
399	Everett	Thomas James	S	3	L	X	X	X	X	X			X		X	
400	Ewards	J D	CC	CC		X										
401	Ewards		CC	CC		X										
402	Fahlstrom	Arne Jones	S	2	L	X	X	X	X	X			X			
403	Farrell	James	Q	3	L	X	X	X	X	X			X		X	
404	Farthing	John	S	1	L	X	X	X	X	X			X	X		
405	Faunthorpe	Elizabeth	S	2		X	X				X	X	X			
406	Faunthorpe	Harry	S	2	L	X	X	X	X	X			X		X	
407	Fillbrook	Joseph Charles	S	2	L	X	X	X	X	X			X			
408	Finoli	Luigi	S	3		X	X				X	X	X			
409	Fischer	Eberhard	S	3	L	X	X	X	X	X			X			
410	Flegenheim	Antoinette	S	1		X					X	X	X			
411	Fleming	Honora	Q	3	L	X	X	X	X	X			X			
412	Fleming	Margaret	C	1		X							X	X		
413	Fletcher	N	CC	CC		X										
414	Flynn	James	Q	3	L	X	X	X	X	X			X			
415	Flynn	John	Q	3	L	X	X	X	X	X			X			
416	Flynn	John Irwin	S	1		X	X				X	X	X	X		
417	Foley	Joseph	Q	3	L	X	X	X	X	X			X			
418	Foley	William	Q	3	L	X	X	X	X				X			
419	Foo	Choong	S	3		X	X				X	X	X			
420	Ford	Arthur	S	3	L	X	X	X	X	X			X			
421	Ford	Dollina Margaret	S	3	L	X	X	X	X	X			X			
422	Ford	Edward Watson	S	3	L	X	X	X	X	X			X			
423	Ford	Margaret Ann	S	3	L	X	X	X	X	X			X			

Passenger Identification Table

	Surname	Forename(s)	A	B	C	D	E	F	G	H	J	K	L	M	N	O
424	Ford	Robina Maggie	S	3	L	X	X	X	X	X			X			
425	Ford	William Neal Thomas	S	3	L	X	X	X	X	X			X			
426	Foreman	Benjamin Laventall	C	1	L	X		X	X	X			X	X		
427	Forman	J	CC	1		X	X									
428	Forman	Mrs	CC	1		X	X									
429	Fortune	Alice Elizabeth	S	1		X	X				X	X	X	X		
430	Fortune	Charles Alexander	S	1	L	X	X	X	X	X			X	X		
431	Fortune	Ethel Flora	S	1		X	X					X	X	X		
432	Fortune	Mabel Helen	S	1		X	X					X	X	X		
433	Fortune	Mark	S	1	L	X	X	X	X	X			X	X		
434	Fortune	Mary	S	1		X	X					X	X	X		
435	Fox	Patrick	Q	3	L	X	X	X	X	X			X			
436	Fox	Stanley Hubert	S	2	L	X	X	X	X	X			X		X	
437	Francatelli	Laura	C	1		X						X	X	X		
438	Franklin	Charles	S	3	L	X	X	X	X	X			X			
439	Franklin	Thomas Parnham	S	1	L	X	X	X	X	X			X	X		
440	Frauenthal	Clara Heinsheimer	S	1		X						X	X	X		
441	Frauenthal	Henry William	S	1		X						X	X	X		
442	Frauenthal	Isaac Gerald	C	1		X						X	X	X		
443	Frolicher	Hedwig Margaritha	C	1		X						X	X	X	X	
444	Frolicher-Stehli	Margaritha	C	1		X						X	X	X	X	
445	Frolicher-Stehli	Maximilian	C	1		X						X	X	X	X	
446	Frost	Anthony Wood	S	2	L	X		X	X	X			X			
447	Fry	Richard	S	1	L	X		X	X	X			X			
448	Funk	Annie Clemmer	S	2	L	X	X	X	X	X			X			
449	Futrelle	Jacques Heath	S	1	L	X	X	X	X	X			X			
450	Futrelle	Lily May	S	1		X	X					X	X	X		
451	Fynney	Joseph	S	2	L	X		X	X	X			X		X	
452	Gale	Harry	S	2	L	X		X	X	X			X			
453	Gale	Shadrach	S	2	L	X		X	X	X			X			
454	Gallagher	Martin	Q	3	L	X	X	X	X	X			X			
455	Garside	Ethel	S	2		X	X					X	X	X		
456	Gaskell	Alfred	S	2	L	X		X	X	X			X			
457	Gavey	Lawrence	S	2	L	X		X	X	X			X			
458	Gee	Arthur	S	1	L	X	X	X	X	X			X	X	X	
459	Gerios	Youssef	C	3	L	X		X	X	X			X		X	
460	Gheorgheff	Stanio	C	3	L	X		X	X	X			X			
461	Gibson	Dorothy	C	1		X						X	X	X		
462	Gibson	Pauline	C	1		X						X	X	X		
463	Gieger	Amalie	S	1		X	X					X	X	X	X	
464	Giglio	Victor	C	1	L	X		X	X	X			X	X		
465	Gilbert	William	S	2	L	X	X	X	X	X			X			
466	Giles	Edgar	S	2	L	X	X	X	X	X			X			
467	Giles	Frederick Edward	S	2	L	X	X	X	X	X			X			
468	Giles	Ralph	S	2	L	X	X	X	X	X			X		X	
469	Gilinski	Eliezer	S	3	L	X	X	X	X	X			X		X	
470	Gill	John	S	2	L	X	X	X	X	X			X		X	
471	Gillespie	William Henry	S	2	L	X	X	X	X	X			X			
472	Gilnagh	Mary Katherine	Q	3		X	X					X	X	X		
473	Givard	Hans Kristensen	S	2	L	X	X	X	X	X			X		X	
474	Glynn	Mary Agatha	Q	3		X	X					X	X	X		
475	Goldenburg	Nella	C	1		X						X	X	X	X	
476	Goldenburg	Samuel	C	1		X						X	X	X	X	
477	Goldschmidt	George	C	1	L	X		X	X	X			X	X		
478	Goldsmith	Emily Alice	S	3		X	X					X	X	X		
479	Goldsmith	Frank John	S	3	L	X	X	X	X	X			X			
480	Goldsmith	Frank John William	S	3	L	X	X					X	X	X		
481	Goldsmith	Nathan	S	3	L	X	X	X	X	X			X			
482	Goodwin	Augusta	S	3	L	X	X	X	X	X			X			
483	Goodwin	Charles Edward	S	3	L	X	X	X	X	X			X			
484	Goodwin	Charles Frederick	S	3	L	X	X	X	X	X			X			
485	Goodwin	Harold Victor	S	3	L	X	X	X	X	X			X			
486	Goodwin	Jessie Allis	S	3	L	X	X	X	X	X			X			
487	Goodwin	Lillian Amy	S	3	L	X	X	X	X	X			X			
488	Goodwin	Sidney Leonard	S	3	L	X	X	X	X	X			X			
489	Goodwin	William Frederick	S	3	L	X	X	X	X	X			X			
490	Gracie	Archibald	S	1		X	X					X	X	X	X	
491	Graham	Edith	S	1		X	X					X	X	X	X	

	Surname	Forename(s)	A	B	C	D	E	F	G	H	J	K	L	M	N	O
492	Graham	George Edward	S	1	L	X	X	X	X	X			X	X	X	
493	Graham	Margaret Edith	S	1		X	X					X	X	X	X	
494	Green	George Henry	S	3	L	X	X	X	X	X			X			
495	Greenberg	Samuel	S	2	L	X	X	X	X	X			X		X	
496	Greenfield	Blanche Strouse	C	1		X						X	X	X	X	
497	Greenfield	William Bertram	C	1	L	X						X	X	X	X	
498	Gronnestad	Daniel	S	3	L	X	X	X	X	X			X			
499	Guest	Robert	S	3	L	X	X	X	X	X			X			
500	Guggenheim	Benjamin	C	1	L		X	X	X	X			X	X		
501	Gustafsson	Alfred Ossian	S	3	L	X	X	X	X	X			X			
502	Gustafsson	Anders Vilhelm	S	3	L	X	X	X	X	X			X		X	
503	Gustafsson	Johan Birger	S	3	L	X	X	X	X	X			X			
504	Gustafsson	Karl Gideon	S	3	L	X	X	X	X	X			X			
505	Gwinn	William L	S	2	L			X	X	X						
506	Haas	Aloisia	S	3	L	X	X	X	X	X			X			
507	Hagland	Ingvald Olai	S	3	L	X	X	X	X	X			X			
508	Hagland	Konrad Mathias	S	3	L	X	X	X	X	X			X			
509	Hakkarainen	Elin Matilda	S	3		X	X				X	X	X			
510	Hakkarainen	Pekka Pietari	S	3	L	X	X	X	X	X			X			
511	Hale	Reginald	S	2	L	X	X	X	X	X			X		X	
512	Hamatainen	Wiljo	S	2		X	X				X	X	X			
513	Hamatainene	Anna	S	2		X	X				X	X	X			
514	Hampe	Leon Jerome	S	3	L	X	X	X	X	X			X			
515	Hanna	Mansour	C	3	L	X		X	X	X			X			
516	Hannah	Borak	C	3	L	X		X	X	X	X	X	X	X		
517	Hansen	Claus Peter	S	3	L	X	X	X	X	X			X			
518	Hansen	Henrik Juul	S	3	L	X	X	X	X	X			X			
519	Hansen	Henry Damsgaard	S	3	L	X	X	X	X	X			X		X	
520	Hansen	Jennie Louise	S	3		X	X				X	X	X			
521	Harbeck	William	S	2	L	X	X	X	X	X			X		X	
522	Harder	Dorothy Annan	C	1		X						X	X	X	X	
523	Harder	George Achilles	C	1		X						X	X	X	X	
524	Hargadon	Catherine	Q	3	L	X	X	X	X	X			X			
525	Harknett	Alice Pheobe	S	3	L	X	X	X	X	X			X			
526	Harmer	Abraham	S	3	L	X	X	X	X	X			X			
527	Harper	Annie Jessie	S	2		X	X				X	X	X			
528	Harper	Henry Sleeper	C	1		X						X	X	X	X	
529	Harper	John	S	2	L	X	X	X	X	X			X			
530	Harper	Myra Haxtun	C	1		X						X	X	X	X	
531	Harrington	Charles	S	1	L	X	X	X	X	X			X			
532	Harris	George	S	2		X	X				X	X	X			
533	Harris	Henry Birkhardt	S	1	L	X	X	X	X	X			X	X		
534	Harris	Rene	S	1		X	X					X	X	X	X	
535	Harris	Walter	S	2	L	X	X	X	X	X			X			
536	Harrison	William	S	1	L	X	X	X	X	X			X		X	
537	Hart	Benjamin	S	2	L	X	X	X	X	X			X			
538	Hart	Esther Ada	S	2		X	X				X	X	X			
539	Hart	Eva Miriam	S	2		X	X				X	X	X			
540	Hart	Henry	Q	3	L	X	X	X	X	X			X			
541	Hartley	William	S	2	L	X	X	X	X	X						
542	Hassab	Hammad	C	1		X						X	X	X	X	
543	Hassan	Houssein	C	3	L	X		X	X	X			X			
544	Hawksford	Walter James	S	1		X	X					X	X	X	X	
545	Hays	Charles Melville	S	1	L	X	X	X	X	X			X	X	X	
546	Hays	Clara Jennings	S	1		X	X					X	X	X	X	
547	Hays	Margaret Bechstein	C	1		X						X	X	X	X	
548	Head	Christopher	S	1	L	X	X	X	X	X			X	X		
549	Healy	Hanora	Q	3	L	X	X						X			
550	Hedman	Oskar Arvid	S	3		X	X				X	X	X			
551	Hee	Ling	S	3		X	X				X	X	X			
552	Hegarty	Hanora	Q	3	L	X	X	X	X	X			X			
553	Heikkinen	Laina	S	3		X	X				X	X	X			
554	Heininen	Wendla Maria	S	3	L	X	X	X	X	X			X			
555	Hellstrom	Hilda Maria	S	3		X	X				X	X	X			
556	Hendekovic	Ignaz	S	3	L	X	X	X	X	X			X		X	
557	Henriksson	Jenny Lovisa	S	3	L	X	X	X	X	X			X			
558	Henry	Delia	Q	3	L	X	X	X	X	X			X			
559	Herman	Alice	S	2		X	X				X	X	X			

Passenger Identification Table

	Surname	Forename(s)	A	B	C	D	E	F	G	H	J	K	L	M	N	O
560	Herman	Jane Laver	S	2		X	X				X	X	X			
561	Herman	Kate	S	2		X	X				X	X	X			
562	Herman	Samuel	S	2	L	X	X	X	X	X			X			
563	Hewlett	Mary Dunbar	S	2		X	X				X	X	X			
564	Hickman	Leonard Mark	S	2	L	X	X	X	X	X			X			
565	Hickman	Lewis	S	2	L	X	X	X	X	X			X		X	
566	Hickman	Stanley George	S	2	L	X	X	X	X	X			X			
567	Hilliard	Herbert Henry	S	1	L	X	X	X	X	X			X	X		
568	Hiltunen	Marta	S	2	L	X	X	X	X	X			X			
569	Hipkins	William Edward	S	1	L	X	X	X	X	X			X	X		
570	Hippach	Ida Sophia	S	1		X	X						X	X		
571	Hippach	Jean Gertrude	S	1		X	X						X	X		
572	Hirvonen	Helga	S	3	L	X	X				X	X	X			
573	Hirvonen	Hildur	S	3		X	X				X		X			
574	Hocking	Elizabeth	S	2		X	X				X	X	X			
575	Hocking	Ellen	S	2		X	X				X	X	X			
576	Hocking	Richard George	S	2	L	X	X	X	X	X			X			
577	Hocking	Samuel James	S	2	L	X		X	X	X			X			
578	Hodges	Henry	S	2	L	X	X	X	X	X			X		X	
579	Hogeboom	Anna Louisa	S	1		X							X	X		
580	Hold	Annie	S	2		X	X				X	X	X			
581	Hold	Stephen	S	2	L	X	X	X	X	X			X			
582	Holden	J Stuart											X	X		
583	Holm	John Fredrik	S	3	L	X	X	X	X	X			X			
584	Holthen	Johan Martin	S	3	L	X	X	X	X	X			X			
585	Holverson	Alexander Oskar	S	1	L	X	X	X	X	X			X		X	
586	Holverson	Mary Aline	S	1		X	X				X	X	X			
587	Homer	Harry	S	1		X	X				X	X	X			
588	Honkanen	Eliina	S	3		X	X				X	X	X			
589	Hood	Ambrose	S	2	L	X	X	X	X	X			X			
590	Horgan	John	Q	3	L	X	X	X	X	X			X			
591	Hosono	Masabumi	S	2		X	X				X	X	X			
592	Howard	Benjamin	S	2	L	X	X	X	X	X			X			
593	Howard	Ellen	S	2	L	X	X	X	X				X			
594	Howard	May Elizabeth	S	3		X	X				X	X	X			
595	Hoyt	Frederick Maxfield	S	1		X	X				X	X	X	X		
596	Hoyt	Jane Anne	S	1		X	X				X	X	X	X		
597	Hoyt	William Fisher	C	1	L	X		X	X	X			X			
598	Humblen	Adolf Mathias	S	3	L	X	X	X	X	X			X		X	
599	Hume	John Law	S	2	L	X	X	X	X	X			X			
600	Hunt	George Henry	S	2	L	X	X	X	X	X			X			
601	Hyman	Abraham	S	3		X	X				X	X	X			
602	Icard	Amelie	S	1		X	X				X	X	X	X		
603	Ilett	Bertha	S	2		X	X				X	X	X			
604	Ilieff	Ylio	S	3	L	X	X	X	X	X			X			
605	Ilmakangas	Ida Livija	S	3	L	X	X	X	X	X			X			
606	Ilmakangas	Pieta Sofia	S	3	L	X	X	X	X	X			X			
607	Isham	Ann Elizabeth	C	1	L	X		X	X	X			X	X		
608	Ismay	Joseph Bruce	S	1		X	X				X	X	X			
609	Ivanoff	Kanio	S	3	L	X	X	X	X	X			X			
610	Jacobsohn	Amy Frances	S	2		X	X				X	X	X			
611	Jacobsohn	Sidney Samuel	S	2	L	X	X	X	X	X			X			
612	Jalsevac	Ivan	C	3		X					X	X	X			
613	Jansson	Carl Olof	S	3		X	X				X	X	X			
614	Jardim	Jose Neto	S	3	L	X	X	X	X	X			X			
615	Jarvis	John Denzil	S	2	L	X	X	X	X	X			X			
616	Jefferys	Clifford Thomas	S	2	L	X	X	X	X	X			X			
617	Jefferys	Ernest William	S	2	L	X	X	X	X	X			X			
618	Jenkin	Stephen Curnow	S	2	L	X	X	X	X	X			X			
619	Jensen	Hans Peder	S	3	L	X	X	X	X	X			X			
620	Jensen	Niels Peder	S	3	L	X	X	X	X	X			X			
621	Jensen	Svend Lauritz	S	3	L	X	X	X	X	X			X			
622	Jermyn	Annie	Q	3		X	X				X	X	X			
623	Jerwan	Marie Marthe	C	2		X					X	X	X			
624	Johannesen	Bernt Johannes	S	3		X	X				X	X	X			
625	Johannessen	Elias	S	3	L	X	X						X			
626	Johanson	Jakob Alfred	S	3	L	X	X	X	X	X			X		X	
627	Johansson	Erik	S	3	L	X	X	X	X	X			X		X	

Who Sailed on Titanic?

	Surname	Forename(s)	A	B	C	D	E	F	G	H	J	K	L	M	N	O
628	Johansson	Gustaf Joel	S	3	L	X	X	X	X	X			X		X	
629	Johansson	Karl Johan	S	3	L	X	X	X	X	X			X			
630	Johansson	Nils	S	3	L	X	X	X	X	X			X			
631	Johansson	Oscar Leander Palmquist	S	3		X	X				X	X	X			
632	Johnson	Alfred	S	3	L		X	X	X	X			X			
633	Johnson	Eleanor Ileen	S	3		X	X				X	X	X			
634	Johnson	Elisabeth Vilhelmina	S	3		X	X				X	X	X			
635	Johnson	Harold Theodor	S	3		X	X				X	X	X			
636	Johnson	Malkolm Joackim	S	3	L	X	X	X	X	X			X		X	
637	Johnson	William Cahoon	S	3	L	X	X	X	X	X			X			
638	Johnston	Andrew Emslie	S	3	L	X	X	X	X	X			X			
639	Johnston	Catherine Nellie	S	3	L	X	X	X	X	X			X			
640	Johnston	Eliza	S	3	L	X	X	X	X	X			X			
641	Johnston	William Andrew	S	3	L	X	X	X	X	X			X			
642	Jones	Charles Cresson	S	1	L	X	X	X	X	X			X		X	
643	Jonkoff	Lalio	S	3	L	X	X	X	X	X			X			
644	Jonsson	Carl	S	3	L	X	X				X	X	X			
645	Jonsson	Nils Hilding	S	3	L	X	X	X	X	X			X			
646	Joseph	Anna	C	3	L	X		X	X	X			X			
647	Joseph	Catherine	C	3		X					X	X	X			
648	Joseph	Michael	C	3	L	X		X	X	X	X	X	X			
649	Julian	Henry Forbes	S	1	L	X	X	X	X	X			X	X		
650	Jussila	Eiriik	S	3		X	X				X	X	X			
651	Jussila	Katriina	S	3	L	X	X	X	X	X			X			
652	Jussila	Mari Aina	S	3	L	X	X	X	X	X			X			
653	Kallio	Nikolai Erland	S	3	L	X	X	X	X	X			X			
654	Kalvik	Johannes Halvorsen	S	3	L	X	X	X	X	X			X			
655	Kantor	Miriam	S	2		X	X				X	X	X			
656	Kantor	Sinai	S	2	L	X	X	X	X	X			X		X	
657	Karajic	Milan	S	3	L	X	X	X	X	X			X			
658	Karlsson	Einar Gervasius	S	3		X	X				X	X	X			
659	Karlsson	Julius Konrad	S	3	L	X	X	X	X	X			X			
660	Karlsson	Nils August	S	3	L	X	X	X	X	X			X			
661	Karnes	Claire Bennett	S	2	L	X	X	X	X	X			X			
662	Karun	Franz	C	3		X					X	X	X			
663	Karun	Manca	C	3		X					X	X	X			
664	Kassem	Fared	C	3	L	X		X	X	X			X			
665	Katavelas	Vassilios	C	3	L	X		X	X	X			X		X	
666	Keane	Andrew	Q	3	L	X	X	X	X	X			X			
667	Keane	Daniel	Q	2	L	X	X	X	X	X			X			
668	Keane	Nora	Q	2		X	X				X	X	X			
669	Keefe	Arthur	S	3	L	X	X	X	X	X			X			
670	Keeping	Edwin	S	1	L	X	X	X	X	X			X	X	X	
671	Kelley	James	Q	3	L	X	X	X	X	X			X		X	
672	Kelly	Anna Katherine	Q	3		X	X				X	X	X			
673	Kelly	Florence	S	2		X	X				X	X	X			
674	Kelly	James	S	3	L	X	X	X	X	X			X			
675	Kelly	Mary	Q	3		X	X				X	X	X			
676	Kennedy	John	Q	3		X	X				X	X	X			
677	Kent	Edward Austin	C	1	L	X		X	X	X			X	X	X	
678	Kenyon	Frederick	S	1	L	X	X	X	X	X			X	X		
679	Kenyon	Marion	S	1		X	X				X	X	X			
680	Khalil	Betros	C	3	L	X		X	X	X			X			
681	Khalil	Zahie Maria	C	3	L	X		X	X	X			X			
682	Kiernan	John	Q	3	L	X	X	X	X	X			X			
683	Kiernan	Philip	Q	3	L	X	X	X	X	X			X			
684	Kilgannon	Thomas	Q	3	L	X	X	X	X	X			X			
685	Kimball	Edwin Nelson	S	1		X	X				X	X	X	X		
686	Kimball	Gertrude	S	1		X	X				X	X	X	X		
687	Kink	Anton	S	3		X	X				X	X	X			
688	Kink	Louise	S	3		X	X				X	X	X			
689	Kink	Louise	S	3		X	X				X	X	X			
690	Kink	Vincenz	S	3	L	X	X	X	X	X			X			
691	Kink	Maria	S	3	L	X	X	X	X	X			X			
692	Kirkland	Charles Leonard	Q	2	L	X	X	X	X	X			X			
693	Klaber	Herman	S	1	L	X	X	X	X	X			X	X		
694	Klasen	Gertrud Emilia	S	3	L	X	X	X	X	X			X			

	Surname	Forename(s)	A	B	C	D	E	F	G	H	J	K	L	M	N	O
695	Klasen	Hulda Kristina	S	3	L	X	X	X	X	X			X			
696	Klasen	Klas Albin	S	3	L	X	X	X	X	X			X			
697	Kneese		CC	CC		X										
698	Knight	Robert	S	2	L	X	X	X	X	X			X			
699	Kraeff	Theodor	C	3	L	X		X	X	X			X			
700	Krekorian	Nesham	C	3		X					X	X	X			X
701	Kreuchen	Emilie	S	1		X	X				X	X	X	X		
702	Krins	George	S	2	L	X	X	X	X	X			X			
703	Kvillner	Johan Henrik	S	2	L	X	X	X	X	X			X	X		
704	Lahoud	Sarkis	C	3	L	X		X	X	X			X			
705	Lahtinen	Anna Sylfven	S	2	L	X	X	X	X	X			X			
706	Lahtinen	William	S	2	L	X	X	X	X	X			X			
707	Laitinen	Kristina Sofia	S	3	L	X	X	X	X	X			X			
708	Laleff	Kristo	S	3	L	X	X	X	X	X			X			
709	Lam	A H	S	3		X	X				X	X	X			
710	Lam	Len	S	3	L	X	X	X	X	X			X			
711	Lamb	John Joseph	Q	2	L	X	X	X	X	X			X			
712	Landergren	Aurora Adelia	S	3		X	X				X	X	X			
713	Lane	Patrick	Q	3	L	X	X	X	X	X			X			
714	Lang	Fang	S	3		X	X				X	X	X			
715	Laroche	Joseph Philippe	C	2	L	X		X	X	X			X			
716	Laroche	Juliette Marie	C	2		X					X	X	X			
717	Laroche	Louise	C	2		X					X	X	X			
718	Laroche	Simonne Marie	C	2		X					X	X	X			
719	Larsson	August Viktor	S	3	L	X	X	X	X	X			X			
720	Larsson	Bengt Edvin	S	3	L	X	X	X	X	X			X			
721	Larsson-Rondberg	Edvard	S	3	L	X	X	X	X	X			X			
722	Laund	W	S	3		X										
723	Lawrence	A	S	1		X	X							X		
724	Leader	Alice Farnham	S	1		X	X				X	X	X	X		
725	Leeni	Fahim	C	3		X					X	X	X			
726	Lefebre	Frances	S	3	L	X	X	X	X	X			X			
727	Lefebre	Henry Forbes	S	3	L	X	X	X	X	X			X			
728	Lefebre	Ida	S	3	L	X	X	X	X	X			X			
729	Lefebre	Jeannie	S	3	L	X	X	X	X	X			X			
730	Lefebre	Mathilde	S	3	L	X	X	X	X	X			X			
731	Lehmann	Bertha	C	2		X					X	X	X			
732	Leinonen	Antti Gustaf	S	3	L	X	X	X	X	X			X			
733	Leitch	Jessie	S	2		X	X				X	X	X			
734	Lemberopoulos	Peter	C	3	L	X		X	X	X			X		X	
735	Lemore	Amelia	S	2		X	X				X	X	X			
736	Lennon	Denis	Q	3	L	X	X	X	X	X			X			
737	Lennon	Mary	Q	3	L	X	X	X	X	X			X			
738	Lenox-Conyngham	Alice	CC	CC		X	X									
739	Lenox-Conyngham	Denis	CC	CC		X	X									
740	Lenox-Conyngham	Eileen	CC	CC		X	X									
741	Lenox-Conyngham	Mrs	CC	CC		X	X									
742	Leonard	Lionel	S	3	L		X	X	X	X			X			
743	Leroy	Bertha	C	1		X					X	X	X	X		
744	Lester	James	S	3	L	X	X	X	X	X			X			
745	Lesueur	Gustave	C	1		X					X	X	X	X		
746	Levy	Rene Jacques	S	2	L	X	X	X	X	X			X			
747	Lewis	Charlton T Mrs	S	1		X							X	X		
748	Lewy	Ervin	C	1	L	X		X	X	X			X			
749	Leyson	Robert William	S	2	L	X	X	X	X	X			X		X	
750	Lievens	Rene Aime	S	3	L	X	X	X	X	X			X			
751	Lindahl	Agda Thorilda	S	3	L	X	X	X	X	X			X			
752	Lindblom	Augusta Charlotta	S	3	L	X	X	X	X	X			X			
753	Lindeberg-Lind	Erik Gustaf	S	1	L	X	X	X	X	X			X			
754	Lindell	Edvard Bengtsson	S	3	L	X	X	X	X	X			X			
755	Lindell	Elin Gerda	S	3	L	X	X	X	X	X			X			
756	Lindquist	Eino William	S	3		X	X				X	X	X			
757	Lindstrom	Sigrid Posse	C	1		X					X	X	X			
758	Linehan	Michael	Q	3	L	X	X	X	X	X			X			
759	Lines	Elizabeth Lindsey	S	1		X							X	X		
760	Lines	Mary Conover	S	1		X							X	X		
761	Ling	Lee	S	3	L	X	X	X	X	X			X			
762	Linhart	Wenzel	S	3	L	X	X	X	X	X			X		X	

	Surname	Forename(s)	A	B	C	D	E	F	G	H	J	K	L	M	N	O
763	Linnane	John	Q	2	L	X	X	X	X	X			X			
764	Lithman	Simon	S	3	L	X	X	X	X	X			X			
765	Lobb	Cordelia	S	3	L	X	X	X	X	X			X			
766	Lobb	William Arthur	S	3	L	X	X	X	X	X			X			
767	Lockyer	Edward Thomas	S	3	L	X	X	X	X	X			X		X	
768	Long	Milton Clyde	S	1	L	X	X	X	X	X			X	X	X	
769	Longley	Gretchen Fiske	S	1		X							X	X		
770	Loring	Joseph Holland	S	1	L	X	X	X	X	X			X			
771	Louch	Alice Adelaide	S	2		X	X				X	X	X			
772	Louch	Charles Alexander	S	2	L	X	X						X		X	
773	Lovell	John Hall	S	3	L	X	X	X	X	X			X			
774	Lowe	Alfred	S	3		X	X									
775	Lulic	Nicola	S	3		X	X				X	X	X			
776	Lundahl	Johann Svensson	S	3	L	X	X	X	X	X			X			
777	Lundin	Olga Elida	S	3		X	X					X	X	X		
778	Lundstrom	Thure Edvin	S	3		X	X					X	X	X		
779	Lurette	Eugenie	C	1		X						X	X	X	X	
780	Lyntakoff	Stanko	S	3	L	X	X	X	X	X			X			
781	Mack	Mary	S	2	L	X	X	X	X	X			X		X	
782	MacKay	George William	S	3	L	X	X	X	X	X			X			
783	Madigan	Margaret	Q	3		X	X					X	X	X		
784	Madill	Georgette Alexandra	S	1		X	X					X	X	X		
785	Madsen	Fridtjof	S	3		X	X					X	X			
786	Maenpaa	Matti Alexanteri	S	3	L	X	X	X	X	X			X			
787	Maguire	J	S	1	L	X	X	X	X	X			X		X	
788	Mahon	Bridget Delia	Q	3	L	X	X	X	X	X			X			
789	Mahon	John	Q	3	L	X	X	X	X	X			X			
790	Maioni	Roberta	S	1		X	X						X	X		
791	Maisner	Simon	S	3	L	X	X	X	X	X			X			
792	Makinen	Kalle Edvard	S	3	L	X	X	X	X	X			X			
793	Malachard	Noel	C	2	L	X		X	X	X			X			
794	Malaki	Attala	C	3	L	X		X	X	X			X			
795	Mallet	Albert	C	2	L	X		X	X	X			X			
796	Mallet	Antoinine	C	2		X					X	X	X			X
797	Mallet	Andre	C	2		X					X	X	X			X
798	Mamee	Hanna	C	3		X					X	X	X		X	
799	Mangan	Mary	Q	3	L	X	X	X	X	X			X		X	
800	Mangiavacchi	Serafino Emilio	C	2	L	X		X	X	X			X			
801	Mannion	Margaret	Q	3		X	X				X	X	X			
802	March	John Starr	S	2	L			X	X	X					X	
803	Mardirosian	Sarkis	C	3	L	X		X	X	X			X			
804	Marechal	Pierre	C	1		X					X	X	X	X		
805	Markoff	Marin	S	3	L	X		X	X	X			X			
806	Markun	Johann	C	3	L	X		X	X	X			X			
807	Marvin	Daniel Warner	S	1	L	X	X	X	X	X			X	X		
808	Marvin	Mary Graham	S	1		X	X				X	X	X	X		
809	Maskey		S	3		X										
810	Masselmani	Fatima	C	3		X					X	X	X			
811	Matinoff	Nicola	C	3	L	X		X	X	X			X			
812	Matthews	William John	S	2	L	X	X	X	X	X			X			
813	May	Richard	CC	CC		X										
814	May	Stanley	CC	CC		X										
815	Maybery	Frank Hubert	S	2	L	X	X	X	X	X			X			
816	Mayne	Berthe	C	1		X					X	X	X	X		
817	McCaffry	Thomas Francis	C	1	L	X		X	X	X			X	X	X	
818	McCarthy	Catherine	Q	3		X	X					X	X			
819	McCarthy	Timothy	S	1	L	X	X	X	X	X			X	X	X	
820	McCormack	Thomas Joseph	Q	3		X	X				X	X	X			
821	McCoy	Agnes	Q	3		X	X				X	X	X			
822	McCoy	Alicia	Q	3		X	X				X	X	X			
823	McCoy	Bernard	Q	3		X	X				X	X	X			
824	McCrae	Arthur Gordon	S	2	L	X	X	X	X	X			X		X	
825	McCrie	James Matthew	S	2	L	X	X	X	X	X			X			
826	McDermott	Bridget Delia	Q	3		X	X				X	X	X			
827	McEvoy	Michael	Q	3	L	X	X	X	X	X			X			
828	McGough	James Robert	S	1		X	X				X	X	X	X		
829	McGowan	Anna	Q	3		X	X				X	X	X			
830	McGowan	Katherine	Q	3	L	X	X	X	X	X			X			

Passenger Identification Table

	Surname	Forename(s)	A	B	C	D	E	F	G	H	J	K	L	M	N	O
831	McGowan	Cath	Q	3		X	X				X	X	X			
832	McKane	Peter David	S	2	L	X	X	X	X	X			X			
833	McMahon	Martin	Q	3	L	X	X	X	X	X			X			
834	McNamee	Eileen	S	3	L	X	X	X	X	X			X		X	
835	McNamee	Neil	S	3	L	X	X	X	X	X			X			
836	McNeill	Bridget	Q	3	L	X	X	X	X	X			X			
837	Meanwell	Marion Ogden	S	3	L	X	X	X	X	X			X			
838	Meek	Annie Louise	S	3	L	X	X	X	X	X			X			
839	Mellinger	Elizabeth Anne	S	2		X	X				X	X	X			
840	Mellinger	Madeleine Violet	S	2		X	X				X	X	X			
841	Mellors	William John	S	2		X	X				X	X	X			
842	Melody	A	S	3		X	X						X			
843	Meo	Alfonzo	S	3	L	X	X	X	X	X			X		X	
844	Mernagh	Robert	Q	3	L	X	X	X	X	X			X			
845	Meyer	August	S	1	L	X	X	X	X	X			X			
846	Meyer	Edgar Joseph	C	1	L	X		X	X	X			X			
847	Meyer	Leila Saks	C	1		X					X	X	X			
848	Midtsjo	Karl Albert	S	3		X	X				X	X	X			
849	Miles	Frank	S	3	L	X	X	X	X	X			X			
850	Miles	Frederick	S	3		X	X						X			
851	Millet	Francis Davis	S	1	L	X		X	X	X			X	X	X	
852	Milling	Jacob Christian	S	2	L	X	X	X	X	X			X		X	
853	Minahan	Daisy	S	1		X	X				X	X	X	X		
854	Minahan	Lillian	S	1		X	X				X	X	X	X		
855	Minahan	William Edward	S	1	L	X	X	X	X	X			X	X	X	
856	Mineff	Ivan	S	3	L	X	X	X	X	X			X			
857	Minkoff	Lazar	S	3	L	X	X	X	X	X			X			
858	Mionoff	Stoytcho	S	3	L	X	X	X	X	X			X			
859	Mitchell	Henry Michael	S	2	L	X	X	X	X	X			X			
860	Mitkoff	Mito	S	3	L	X	X	X	X	X			X			
861	Mock	Philipp Edmund	C	1		X					X	X	X			
862	Mockler	Ellen Mary	Q	3		X	X				X	X	X			
863	Moen	Sigurd Hansen	S	3	L	X	X	X	X	X			X		X	
864	Molson	Harry Markland	S	1	L	X	X	X	X	X			X	X		
865	Montvila	Juozas	S	2	L	X	X	X	X	X			X			
866	Moor	Biele	S	3		X	X				X	X	X			
867	Moor	Meier	S	3		X	X				X	X	X			
868	Moore	Clarence Bloomfield	S	1	L	X	X	X	X	X			X			
869	Moore	Leonard Charles	S	3	L	X	X	X	X	X			X			
870	Moran	Bertha Bridget	Q	3		X	X				X	X	X			
871	Moran	Daniel James	Q	3	L	X	X	X	X	X			X			
872	Moran	James	Q	3	L	X	X	X	X	X			X			
873	Moraweck	Ernest	S	2	L	X	X	X	X	X			X			
874	Morley	Henry Samuel	S	2	L	X	X	X	X	X			X			
875	Morley	William	S	3	L	X	X	X	X	X			X			
876	Morrow	Thomas Rowan	Q	3	L	X	X	X	X	X			X			
877	Moss	Albert	S	3		X	X				X	X	X			
878	Moubarek	Gerios	C	3		X					X	X	X			
879	Moubarek	Halim Gonios	C	3		X					X		X			
880	Moubarek	Omine	C	3		X					X	X	X			
881	Moussa	Mantoura Boulos	C	3	L	X		X	X	X			X			
882	Moutal	Rahamin Haim	S	3	L	X	X	X	X	X			X			
883	Mudd	Thomas Charles	S	2	L	X	X	X	X	X			X			
884	Mullen		CC	CC		X										
885	Mullen	Katherine	Q	3		X	X				X	X	X			
886	Mulvihill	Bertha	Q	3		X	X				X	X	X			
887	Murdlin	Joseph	S	3	L	X	X	X	X	X			X			
888	Murphy	Catherine	Q	3		X	X				X	X	X			
889	Murphy	Margaret Jane	Q	3		X	X				X	X	X			
890	Murphy	Nora	Q	3		X	X				X	X	X			
891	Myhrman	Pehr Fabian	S	3	L	X	X	X	X	X			X			
892	Myles	Thomas Francis	Q	2	L	X	X	X	X	X			X			
893	Naidenoff	Penko	S	3	L	X	X	X	X	X			X			
894	Najib	Adele Kiamie	C	3		X					X	X	X			
895	Nakid	Marie	C	3		X					X	X	X			
896	Nakid	Said	C	3		X					X	X	X			
897	Nakid	Waika	C	3		X					X	X	X			
898	Nancarrow	William Henry	S	3	L	X	X	X	X	X			X			

	Surname	Forename(s)	A	B	C	D	E	F	G	H	J	K	L	M	N	O
899	Nankoff	Minko	S	3	L	X	X	X	X	X			X			
900	Nasr	Mustafa	C	3	L	X		X	X	X			X			
901	Nasser	Adele	C	2		X					X	X	X			
902	Nasser	Nicholas	C	2	L	X		X	X	X			X		X	
903	Natsch	Charles	C	1	L	X		X	X	X			X	X		
904	Naughton	Hannah	Q	3	L	X	X	X	X	X			X			
905	Navratil	Edmond Roger	S	2		X	X				X	X	X			
906	Navratil	Michael	S	2	L	X	X	X	X	X			X		X	
907	Navratil	Michel Marcel	S	2		X	X				X	X	X			
908	Nenkoff	Christo	S	3	L	X	X	X	X	X			X			
909	Nesson	Israel	S	2	L	X	X	X	X	X			X			
910	Newell	Arthur Webster	C	1	L	X		X	X	X			X	X	X	
911	Newell	Madeleine	C	1		X					X	X	X	X		
912	Newell	Marjorie	C	1		X					X	X	X	X		
913	Newsom	Helen	S	1		X	X				X	X	X	X		
914	Nicholls	Joseph Charles	S	2	L	X	X	X	X	X			X		X	
915	Nichols	E	CC	CC		X	X									
916	Nicholson	Arthur Ernest	S	1	L	X	X	X	X	X			X		X	
917	Nicola-Yarred	Elias	C	3		X					X	X	X			X
918	Nicola-Yarred	Jamila	C	3		X					X	X	X			X
919	Nieminen	Manta Josefina	S	3	L	X	X	X	X	X			X			
920	Niklasson	Samuel	S	3	L	X	X	X	X	X			X			
921	Nilsson	August Ferdinand	S	3	L	X	X	X	X	X			X			
922	Nilsson	Berta Olivia	S	3		X	X				X	X	X			
923	Nilsson	Helmina Josefina	S	3		X	X				X	X	X			
924	Nirva	Iisakki Aijo	S	3	L	X	X	X	X	X			X			
925	Niskanen	Juha	S	3		X	X				X	X	X			
926	Noel		CC	CC		X										
927	Noel	G J	CC	CC		X										
928	Norman	Robert Douglas	S	2	L	X	X	X	X	X			X		X	
929	Nosworthy	Richard Cater	S	3	L	X	X	X	X	X			X			
930	Nourney	Alfred	C	2		X					X	X	X			
931	Novel	Mansouer	C	3	L	X		X	X	X			X		X	
932	Nye	Elizabeth	S	2		X	X				X	X	X			
933	Nysten	Anna	S	3	L	X	X				X	X	X			
934	Nysveen	Johan Hansen	S	3	L	X	X	X	X	X			X			
935	O'Brien	Johanna	Q	3		X	X				X	X	X			
936	O'Brien	Thomas	Q	3	L	X	X	X	X	X			X			
937	O'Brien	Timothy	Q	3	L	X	X	X	X	X			X			
938	O'Connell	Patrick Denis	Q	3	L	X	X	X	X	X			X			
939	O'Connor	Maurice	Q	3	L	X	X	X	X	X			X			
940	O'Connor	Patrick	Q	3	L	X	X	X	X	X			X			
941	Odahl	Nils Martin	S	3	L	X	X	X	X	X			X			
942	Odell	Jack	CC	CC		X										
943	Odell	Kate	CC	CC		X										
944	Odell	Lilly	CC	CC		X										
945	O'Dwyer	Ellen	Q	3		X	X				X	X	X			
946	Ohman	Velin	S	3		X	X				X	X	X			
947	O'Keefe	Patrick	Q	3		X	X				X	X	X			
948	O'Leary	Hanora	Q	3		X	X				X	X	X			
949	Oliva y Ocana	Hermina	C	1		X							X	X		
950	Olsen	Artur Karl	S	3		X	X				X	X	X			
951	Olsen	Henry Margido	S	3	L	X	X	X	X	X			X		X	
952	Olsen	Karl Siegwart	S	3	L	X	X	X	X	X			X			
953	Olsen	Ole Martin	S	3	L	X	X	X	X	X			X			
954	Olsson	Elina	S	3	L	X	X	X	X	X			X			
955	Olsson	Nils Johan	S	3	L	X	X	X	X	X			X			
956	Olsson	Oscar Wilhelm	S	3		X	X				X	X	X			
957	Olsvigen	Thor Andersen	S	3	L	X	X	X	X	X			X		X	
958	Omont	Alfred Fernand	C	1		X					X	X	X			
959	Oreskovic	Jelka	S	3	L	X	X	X	X	X			X			
960	Oreskovic	Luka	S	3	L	X	X	X	X	X			X			
961	Oreskovic	Marija	S	3	L	X	X	X	X	X			X			
962	Osborne	D	CC	CC		X										
963	Osen	Olaf Elon	S	3	L	X	X	X	X	X			X			
964	Osman	Mara	S	3		X	X				X	X	X			
965	Ostby	Engelhart Cornelius	S	1	L	X	X	X	X	X			X	X	X	
966	Ostby	Helene Ragnhild	S	1		X	X				X	X	X	X		

Passenger Identification Table

	Surname	Forename(s)	A	B	C	D	E	F	G	H	J	K	L	M	N	O
967	O'Sullivan	Bridget	Q	3	L	X	X	X	X	X			X			
968	Otter	Richard	S	2	L	X	X	X	X	X			X			
969	Ovies	Servando Jose	C	1	L	X		X	X	X			X	X	X	
970	Oxenham	Percy Thomas	S	2		X	X				X	X	X			
971	Padron Manent	Julian	C	2		X					X	X	X			
972	Pain	Alfred	S	2	L	X	X	X	X	X			X			
973	Pallas y Castello	Emilio	C	2		X					X	X	X			
974	Palsson	Alma Cornelia	S	3	L	X	X	X	X	X			X		X	
975	Palsson	Gosta Leonard	S	3	L	X	X	X	X	X			X		X	
976	Palsson	Paul Folke	S	3	L	X	X	X	X	X			X			
977	Palsson	Stina Viola	S	3	L	X	X	X	X	X			X			
978	Palsson	Torborg Danira	S	3	L	X	X	X	X	X			X			
979	Panula	Eino Viljami	S	3	L	X	X	X	X	X			X			
980	Panula	Ernesti Arvid	S	3	L	X	X	X	X	X			X			
981	Panula	Jaako Arnold	S	3	L	X	X	X	X	X			X			
982	Panula	Juha Niilo	S	3	L	X	X	X	X	X			X			
983	Panula	Maria Emilia	S	3	L	X	X	X	X	X			X			
984	Panula	Urho Abraham	S	3	L	X	X	X	X	X			X			
985	Parker	Clifford Richard	S	2	L	X	X	X	X	X			X			
986	Parkes	Francis	S	2	L	X	X	X	X	X			X			
987	Parr	William Henry	S	1	L	X	X	X	X	X			X	X		
988	Parrish	Lutie Davis	S	2		X	X						X			
989	Partner	Austen	S	1	L	X	X	X	X	X			X	X	X	
990	Pasic	Jakob	S	3	L	X	X	X	X	X			X			
991	Patchett	George	S	3	L	X	X	X	X	X			X			
992	Paulner	Uscher	C	3	L	X		X	X	X			X			
993	Pavlovic	Stefo	S	3	L	X	X	X	X	X			X			
994	Payne	Vivian Ponsonby	S	1	L	X	X	X	X	X			X	X		
995	Peacock	Alfred Edward	S	3	L	X	X	X	X	X			X			
996	Peacock	Edith	S	3	L	X	X	X	X	X			X			
997	Peacock	Treasteall	S	3	L	X	X	X	X	X			X			
998	Pearce	Ernest	S	3	L	X	X	X	X	X			X			
999	Pears	Edith Wearne	S	1		X	X				X	X	X	X		
1000	Pears	Thomas Clinton	S	1	L	X	X	X	X	X			X	X		
1001	Pedersen	Olaf	S	3	L	X	X	X	X	X			X			
1002	Peduzzi	Joseph	S	3	L	X	X	X	X	X			X			
1003	Pekoniemi	Edvard	S	3	L	X	X	X	X	X			X			
1004	Peltomaki	Nikolai Johannes	S	3	L	X	X	X	X	X			X			
1005	Penasco	Maria Josefa	C	1		X					X	X	X	X		
1006	Penasco	Victor	C	1	L	X		X	X	X			X	X		
1007	Pengelly	Frederick William	S	2	L	X	X	X	X	X			X			
1008	Perkin	John Henry	S	3	L	X		X	X	X			X			
1009	Pernot	Rene	C	2	L	X		X	X	X			X			
1010	Perreault	Mary	S	1		X					X	X	X	X		
1011	Persson	Ernst Ulrik	S	3		X	X				X	X	X			
1012	Peruschitz	Joseph Benedikt	S	2	L	X	X	X	X	X			X			
1013	Peters	Katie	Q	3	L	X	X	X	X	X			X			
1014	Petersen	Marius	S	3	L	X	X	X	X	X			X			
1015	Petranec	Matilda	S	3	L	X	X	X	X	X			X			
1016	Petroff	Nedialco	S	3	L	X	X	X	X	X			X			
1017	Petroff	Pastcho	S	3	L	X	X	X	X	X			X			
1018	Petterson	Johan Emil	S	3	L	X	X	X	X	X			X			
1019	Pettersson	Ellen Natalia	S	3	L	X	X	X	X	X			X			
1020	Peuchen	Arthur Godfrey	S	1		X	X				X	X	X	X		
1021	Phillips	Alice Frances	S	2		X	X				X	X	X			
1022	Phillips	Escott Robert	S	2	L	X	X	X	X	X			X			
1023	Phillips	Kate Florence	S	2		X	X				X	X	X			
1024	Pinsky	Rosa	S	2		X	X				X	X	X			
1025	Plotcharsky	Vasil	S	3	L	X	X	X	X	X			X			
1026	Pokmic	Mate	S	3	L	X	X	X	X	X			X			
1027	Pokmic	Tome	S	3	L	X	X	X	X	X			X			
1028	Ponesell	Martin	S	2	L	X	X	X	X	X			X			
1029	Portaluppi	Emilio Ilario	C	2		X					X	X	X			
1030	Porter	Walter Chamberlain	S	1	L	X	X	X	X	X			X	X	X	
1031	Potter	Lily Alexenia	C	1		X					X	X	X	X		
1032	Pulbaum	Franz	C	2	L	X		X	X	X			X			
1033	Quick	Jane	S	2		X	X				X	X	X			
1034	Quick	Phyllis May	S	2		X	X				X	X	X			

Who Sailed on Titanic?

	Surname	Forename(s)	A	B	C	D	E	F	G	H	J	K	L	M	N	O
1035	Quick	Winifred Vera	S	2		X	X				X	X	X			
1036	Radeff	Alexander	S	3	L	X	X	X	X	X			X			
1037	Rasmussen	Lena	S	3	L	X	X	X	X	X			X			
1038	Razi	Raihed	C	3	L	X		X	X	X			X			
1039	Reed	James George	S	3	L	X	X	X	X	X			X			
1040	Reeves	David	S	2	L	X	X	X	X	X			X			
1041	Rekic	Tido	S	3	L	X	X	X	X	X			X			
1042	Remesch	Miss	CC	CC		X										
1043	Renouf	Lillian	S	2		X	X				X	X	X			
1044	Renouf	Peter Henry	S	2	L	X	X	X	X	X			X			
1045	Reuchlin	Jonkheer	C	1	L	X		X	X	X			X	X		
1046	Reynaldo	Encarnacion	S	2		X	X				X	X	X			
1047	Reynolds	Harold J	S	3	L	X	X	X	X	X			X		X	
1048	Rheims	George Alexander	C	1		X					X	X	X			
1049	Rice	Albert	Q	3	L	X	X	X	X	X			X			
1050	Rice	Arthur	Q	3	L	X	X	X	X	X			X			
1051	Rice	Eric	Q	3	L	X	X	X	X	X			X			
1052	Rice	Eugene	Q	3	L	X	X	X	X	X			X			
1053	Rice	George Hugh	Q	3	L	X	X	X	X	X			X			
1054	Rice	Margaret	Q	3	L	X	X	X	X	X			X			
1055	Richard	Emile	C	2	L	X		X	X	X			X			
1056	Richards	Emily	S	2		X	X				X	X	X			
1057	Richards	George Sibley	S	2		X	X				X	X	X			
1058	Richards	William Rowe	S	2		X	X				X	X				
1059	Ridsdale	Lucy	S	2		X	X				X	X	X			
1060	Riihivuori	Susanna	S	3	L	X	X	X	X	X			X			
1061	Ringhini	Sante	C	1	L	X		X	X	X			X	X	X	
1062	Rintamaki	Matti	S	3	L	X	X	X	X	X			X			
1063	Riordan	Hannah	Q	3		X	X				X	X	X			
1064	Risien	Emma	S	3	L	X	X	X	X	X			X			
1065	Risien	Samuel Beard	S	3	L	X	X	X	X	X			X			
1066	Robbins	Victor	C	1	L	X		X	X	X			X			
1067	Robert	Elisabeth Walton	S	1		X	X				X	X		X		
1068	Robins	Alexander	S	3	L	X	X	X	X	X			X		X	
1069	Robins	Grace Charity	S	3	L	X	X	X	X	X			X		X	
1070	Roebling	Washington Augustus	S	1	L	X	X	X	X	X			X	X		
1071	Rogers	Reginald Harry	S	2		X	X	X	X	X			X			
1072	Rogers	William John	S	3	L	X	X	X	X	X			X			
1073	Romaine	Charles	S	1		X	X						X			
1074	Rommetvedt	Knud Paust	S	3	L	X	X	X	X	X			X			
1075	Rood	Hugh Roscoe	S	1	L	X	X	X	X	X			X	X		
1076	Rosblom	Helena Wilhelmina	S	3	L	X	X	X	X	X			X			
1077	Rosblom	Salli Helena	S	3	L	X	X	X	X	X			X			
1078	Rosblom	Viktor Richard	S	3	L	X	X	X	X	X			X			
1079	Rosenbaum	Edith Louise	C	1		X					X	X	X			
1080	Rosenshine	George	S	1		X		X	X	X			X		X	
1081	Ross	John Hugo	S	1	L	X		X	X	X			X	X		
1082	Roth	Sarah A	S	3		X	X				X	X	X			
1083	Rothes	Lucy Noel	C	1		X	X				X	X	X	X		
1084	Rothschild	Elizabeth Jane	C	1		X					X	X	X			
1085	Rothschild	Martin	C	1	L	X		X	X	X			X			
1086	Rouse	Richard Henry	S	3	L	X	X	X	X	X			X			
1087	Rowe	Alfred	S	1	L	X	X	X	X	X			X		X	
1088	Rugg	Emily	S	2		X	X				X	X	X			
1089	Rush	Alfred George	S	3	L	X	X	X	X	X			X			
1090	Ryan	Edward	Q	3		X	X				X	X	X			
1091	Ryan	Patrick	Q	3	L	X	X	X	X	X			X			
1092	Ryerson	Arthur Larned	C	1	L	X		X	X	X			X			
1093	Ryerson	Emily Borie	C	1		X					X	X	X			
1094	Ryerson	Emily Maria	C	1		X					X	X	X			
1095	Ryerson	John Borie	C	1		X					X	X	X			
1096	Ryerson	Susan Parker	C	1		X					X	X	X			
1097	Saad	Amin	C	3	L	X		X	X	X			X			
1098	Saad	Khalil	C	3	L	X		X	X	X			X			
1099	Saade	Jean Nassr	C	3	L	X		X	X	X			X			
1100	Saalfeld	Adolphe	S	1		X	X				X	X	X	X		
1101	Sadlier	Matthew	Q	3	L	X	X	X	X	X			X			
1102	Sadowitz	Harry	S	3	L	X	X	X	X	X			X			

Passenger Identification Table

#	Surname	Forename(s)	A	B	C	D	E	F	G	H	J	K	L	M	N	O
1103	Saether	Simon Sivertsen	S	3	L	X	X	X	X	X			X		X	
1104	Sage	Annie Elizabeth	S	3	L	X	X	X	X	X			X			
1105	Sage	Anthony William	S	3	L	X	X	X	X	X			X		X	
1106	Sage	Constance Gladys	S	3	L	X	X	X	X	X			X			
1107	Sage	Dorothy Florence	S	3	L	X	X	X	X	X			X			
1108	Sage	Douglas Bullen	S	3	L	X	X	X	X	X			X			
1109	Sage	Elizabeth Ada	S	3	L	X	X	X	X	X			X			
1110	Sage	Frederick	S	3	L	X	X	X	X	X			X			
1111	Sage	George John	S	3	L	X	X	X	X	X			X			
1112	Sage	John George	S	3	L	X	X	X	X	X			X			
1113	Sage	Stella Anne	S	3	L	X	X	X	X	X			X			
1114	Sage	Thomas Henry	S	3	L	X	X	X	X	X			X			
1115	Sagesser	Emma	C	1		X						X	X	X	X	
1116	Salander	Karl Johan	S	3	L	X	X	X	X	X			X			
1117	Salkjelsvik	Anna Kristine	S	3		X	X				X	X	X			
1118	Salomon	Abraham Lincoln	S	1		X						X	X	X		
1119	Salonen	Johan Werner	S	3	L	X		X	X	X			X			
1120	Samaan	Elias	C	3	L	X		X	X	X			X			
1121	Samaan	Hanna	C	3	L	X		X	X	X			X			
1122	Samaan	Youssef	C	3	L	X		X	X	X			X			
1123	Sandstrom	Agnes Charlotta	S	3		X	X				X	X	X			
1124	Sandstrom	Beatrice Irene	S	3		X	X				X	X	X			
1125	Sandstrom	Marguerite Rut	S	3		X	X				X	X	X			
1126	Sap	Julius	S	3		X	X				X	X	X			
1127	Saundercock	William Henry	S	3	L		X	X	X	X			X			
1128	Sawyer	Frederick Charles	S	3	L	X	X	X	X	X			X		X	
1129	Scanlan	James	Q	3	L	X	X	X	X	X			X			
1130	Schabert	Emma	C	1		X						X	X	X		
1131	Scheerlinckx	Jean	S	3		X	X				X	X	X			
1132	Schmidt	August	S	2	L	X	X	X	X	X			X			
1133	Sdycoff	Todor	S	3	L	X	X	X	X	X			X			
1134	Sedgwick	Charles Frederick	S	2	L	X	X	X	X	X			X			
1135	Serreplan	Auguste	C	1		X						X	X	X		
1136	Seward	Frederick Kimber	S	1		X	X						X			
1137	Sharp	Percival James	S	2	L	X	X	X	X	X			X			
1138	Shaughnessy	Patrick	Q	3	L	X	X	X	X				X			
1139	Shawah	Youssef Ibrahim	C	3		X							X			
1140	Shellard	Frederick William	S	3	L	X	X	X	X	X			X			
1141	Shelley	Imanita	S	2		X	X									
1142	Shine	Ellen Natalia	Q	3		X	X				X	X	X			
1143	Shorney	Charles Joseph	S	3	L	X	X	X	X	X			X			
1144	Shutes	Elizabeth Weed	S	1		X	X					X	X	X	X	
1145	Silven	Lyyli Karolina	S	2		X	X					X	X	X		
1146	Silverthorne	Spencer Victor	S	1		X	X					X	X	X	X	
1147	Silvey	Alice	C	1		X						X	X	X	X	
1148	Silvey	William Baird	C	1	L	X		X	X	X			X		X	
1149	Simmons	John	S	3	L	X	X	X	X	X			X			
1150	Simonius-Blumer	Oberst Alfons	S	1		X	X					X	X	X		
1151	Sincock	Maude	S	2		X	X					X	X	X		
1152	Sinkkonen	Anne	S	2		X	X					X	X	X		
1153	Sirayanian	Orsen	C	3	L	X		X	X	X			X			
1154	Sirota	Maurice	S	3	L	X	X	X	X	X			X			
1155	Sivic	Husein	S	3	L	X	X	X	X	X			X			
1156	Sivola	Antti Wilhelm	S	3	L	X	X	X	X	X			X			
1157	Sjoblom	Anna Sofia	S	3		X	X				X	X	X			
1158	Sjostedt	Ernest Adolf	S	2	L	X	X	X	X	X			X			
1159	Skoog	Anna Bernhardina	S	3	L	X	X	X	X	X			X			
1160	Skoog	Harald	S	3	L	X	X	X	X	X			X			
1161	Skoog	Karl Thorsten	S	3	L	X	X	X	X	X			X			
1162	Skoog	Mabel	S	3	L	X	X	X	X	X			X			
1163	Skoog	Margit Elizabeth	S	3	L	X	X	X	X	X			X			
1164	Skoog	Wilhelm	S	3	L	X	X	X	X	X			X			
1165	Slabenoff	Petco	S	3	L	X	X	X	X	X			X			
1166	Slayter	Marion	S	2		X	X									
1167	Slayter	Hilda Mary	Q	2		X	X					X	X	X		
1168	Slemen	Richard James	S	2	L	X	X	X	X	X			X			
1169	Slocovski	Selman Francis	S	3	L	X	X	X	X	X			X			
1170	Sloper	William Thompson	S	1		X	X					X	X	X		

	Surname	Forename(s)	A	B	C	D	E	F	G	H	J	K	L	M	N	O
1171	Smart	John Montgomery	S	1	L	X	X	X	X	X			X			
1172	Smiljanic	Mile	S	3	L	X	X	X	X	X			X			
1173	Smith	James Clinch	C	1	L	X		X	X	X			X	X		
1174	Smith	John Richard Jago	S	2	L			X	X	X			X			
1175	Smith	Lucian Philip	CC	CC	L	X		X	X	X			X			
1176	Smith	Marion Elsie	S	2		X	X				X	X	X			
1177	Smith	Mary Eloise	CC	CC		X					X	X	X			
1178	Smith	Richard William	S	1	L	X	X	X	X	X			X	X		
1179	Smith	Thomas	Q	3	L	X	X	X	X	X			X			
1180	Smyth	Julia	Q	3		X	X				X	X	X			
1181	Snyder	John Pilsbury	S	1		X	X				X	X	X	X		
1182	Snyder	Nellie	S	1		X	X				X	X	X	X		
1183	Sobey	Samuel James	S	2	L	X	X	X	X	X			X			
1184	Soholt	Peter Andreas	S	3	L	X	X	X	X	X			X			
1185	Somerton	Francis William	S	3	L	X	X	X	X	X			X			
1186	Spector	Woolf	S	3	L	X	X	X	X	X			X			
1187	Spedden	Frederic Oakley	S	1		X	X				X	X	X	X		
1188	Spedden	Margaretta Corning	S	1		X	X				X	X	X	X		
1189	Spedden	Robert Douglas	S	1		X	X				X	X	X	X		
1190	Spencer	Marie Eugenie	C	1		X					X	X	X	X		
1191	Spencer	William Augustus	C	1	L	X		X	X	X			X	X		
1192	Spinner	Henry John	S	3	L	X	X	X	X	X			X			
1193	Stahelin-Maeglin	Max	S	1		X	X				X	X	X			
1194	Staneff	Ivan	S	3	L	X	X	X	X	X			X			
1195	Stankovic	Ivan	C	3	L	X	X	X	X	X			X			
1196	Stanley	Amy Zillah	S	3		X	X				X	X	X			
1197	Stanley	Edward Roland	S	3	L	X	X	X	X	X			X			
1198	Stanton	Samuel Ward	C	2	L	X		X	X	X			X			
1199	Stead	William Thomas	S	1	L	X	X	X	X	X			X	X		
1200	Stengel	Annie May	C	1		X					X	X	X			
1201	Stengel	Charles Emil	C	1		X					X	X	X			
1202	Stephenson	Martha Eustis	S	1		X	X				X	X	X	X		
1203	Stevens	G	CC	CC		X										
1204	Stewart	Albert	C	1	L	X		X	X	X			X			
1205	Stokes	Philip Joseph	S	2	L	X	X	X	X	X			X		X	
1206	Stone	Martha Evelyn	S	1		X	X						X	X		
1207	Storey	Thomas	S	3	L		X	X	X	X			X			X
1208	Stoytcheff	Ilia	S	3	L	X	X	X	X	X			X			
1209	Strandberg	Ida Sofia	S	3	L	X	X	X	X	X			X			
1210	Stranden	Juho	S	3		X	X				X	X	X			
1211	Straus	Isidor	S	1	L	X	X	X	X	X			X	X	X	
1212	Straus	Rosalie Ida	S	1	L	X	X	X	X	X			X	X	X	
1213	Strilic	Ivan	S	3	L	X	X	X	X	X			X			
1214	Strom	Elna Matilda	S	3	L	X	X	X	X	X			X			
1215	Strom	Telma Matilda	S	3	L	X	X	X	X	X			X			
1216	Sunderland	Victor Francis	S	3		X	X				X	X				
1217	Sundman	Johan Julian	S	3		X	X				X	X	X			
1218	Sutehall	Henry	S	3	L	X	X	X	X	X			X			
1219	Sutton	Charles	S	3		X	X									
1220	Sutton	Frederick	S	1	L	X		X	X	X			X	X		
1221	Sutton	Henry	S	3		X	X									
1222	Svensson	Johan	S	3	L	X	X	X	X	X			X			
1223	Svensson	Johan Cervin	S	3		X	X				X	X	X			
1224	Svensson	Olof	S	3	L	X	X	X	X	X			X			
1225	Swane	George	S	2	L	X	X	X	X	X			X		X	
1226	Sweet	George Frederick	S	2	L	X	X	X	X	X			X			
1227	Swift	Margaret Welles	S	1		X	X				X	X	X			
1228	Taussig	Emil	S	1	L	X	X	X	X	X			X	X		
1229	Taussig	Ruth	S	1		X	X						X	X		
1230	Taussig	Tillie Mandelbaum	S	1		X	X						X	X		
1231	Taylor	Elmer Zebley	S	1		X	X				X	X	X	X		
1232	Taylor	Juliet Cummins	S	1		X	X				X	X	X	X		
1233	Taylor	Percy Cornelius	S	3	L	X	X	X	X	X			X			
1234	Tenglin	Gunnar Isidor	S	2		X	X				X	X	X			
1235	Thayer	John Borland	C	3	L	X		X	X	X			X	X		
1236	Thayer	John Borland jnr	C	1		X					X	X	X	X		
1237	Thayer	Marian Longstreth	C	1		X					X	X	X	X		
1238	Theobald	Thomas Leonard	S	1	L	X	X	X	X	X			X			X

Passenger Identification Table

	Surname	Forename(s)	A	B	C	D	E	F	G	H	J	K	L	M	N	O
1239	Thomas	Assad Alexander	C	3		X					X	X	X			
1240	Thomas	Charles	C	3	L	X		X	X	X			X			
1241	Thomas	John	C	3	L	X		X	X	X			X			
1242	Thomas	Tannous	C	3	L			X	X	X			X			
1243	Thomas	Thamine	C	3		X					X	X	X			
1244	Thomson	Alexander Morrison	S	3	L	X	X	X	X	X			X			
1245	Thorne	Gertrude Maybelle	C	1		X					X	X	X			
1246	Thorneycroft	Florence Kate	S	3		X	X				X	X	X			
1247	Thorneycroft	Percival	S	3	L	X	X	X	X	X			X			
1248	Tikkanen	Juho	S	3	L	X	X	X	X	X			X			
1249	Tobin	Roger	Q	3	L	X	X	X	X	X			X			
1250	Todoroff	Lalio	S	3	L	X	X	X	X	X			X			
1251	Tomlin	Ernest Portage	S	3	L	X	X	X	X	X			X		X	
1252	Toomey	Ellen	S	2		X	X				X	X	X			
1253	Torber	Ernst Wilhelm	S	3	L	X	X	X	X	X			X			
1254	Torfa	Assad	C	3	L	X		X	X	X			X			
1255	Tornquist	William Henry	S	3		X	X				X	X			X	
1256	Toufik	Nakli	C	3	L	X		X	X	X			X			
1257	Touma	Georges Youssef	C	3		X					X	X	X			
1258	Touma	Hanna Youssef	C	3		X					X	X	X			
1259	Touma	Maria Youssef	C	3		X					X	X	X			
1260	Tovey		CC	CC		X										
1261	Trembisky	Berk	S	3		X	X				X	X	X			
1262	Troupiansky	Moses Aaron	S	2	L	X	X	X	X	X			X			
1263	Trout	Jessie	S	2		X	X				X	X	X			
1264	Troutt	Edwina Celia	S	2		X	X				X	X	X			
1265	Tucker	Gilbert Milligan	S	1		X	X				X	X	X	X		
1266	Turcin	Stjepan	S	3	L	X		X	X	X			X			
1267	Turja	Anna Sofia	S	3		X	X				X	X	X			
1268	Turkula	Hedwig	S	3		X	X				X	X	X			
1269	Turpin	Dorothy Ann	S	2	L	X	X	X	X	X			X			
1270	Turpin	William John	S	2	L	X	X	X	X	X			X			
1271	Uruchurtu	Manuel E	C	1	L	X		X	X	X			X			
1272	Uzelas	Jovo	S	3	L	X	X	X	X	X			X			
1273	Valentine	Augusta		1								X	X			
1274	van Billiard	Austin Blyler	S	3	L	X		X	X	X			X		X	
1275	van Billiard	James William	S	3	L	X		X	X	X			X			
1276	van Billiard	Walter John	S	3	L	X		X	X	X			X		X	
1277	Van de Velde	Johannes Joseph	S	3	L	X	X	X	X	X			X			
1278	Van den Steen	Leo Peter	S	3	L	X	X	X	X	X			X			
1279	Van der Hoef	Wyckoff	S	1	L	X	X	X	X	X			X	X	X	
1280	Van Impe	Catherine	S	3	L	X	X	X	X	X			X			
1281	Van Impe	Jean Baptist	S	3	L	X	X	X	X	X			X			
1282	Van Impe	Rosalie Paula	S	3	L	X	X	X	X	X			X			
1283	van Melkebeke	Philemon	S	3	L	X	X	X	X	X			X			
1284	Vande Walle	Nestor Cyriel	S	3	L	X	X	X	X	X			X			
1285	Vandercruyssen	Victor	S	3	L	X	X	X	X	X			X			
1286	Vanderplanke	Augusta Marie	S	3	L	X	X	X	X	X			X			
1287	Vanderplanke	Emelia Marie	S	3	L	X	X	X	X	X			X			
1288	Vanderplanke	Julius	S	3	L	X	X	X	X	X			X			
1289	Vanderplanke	Leo Peter	S	3	L	X	X	X	X	X			X			
1290	Vartanian	David	C	3		X					X	X	X			X
1291	Veale	James	S	2	L	X	X	X	X	X			X			
1292	Vendel	Olof Edvin	S	3	L	X	X	X	X	X			X			
1293	Vestrom	Hulda Amanda	S	3	L	X	X	X	X	X			X			
1294	Vovk	Janko	S	3	L	X	X	X	X	X			X			
1295	Waelens	Achille	S	3	L	X	X	X	X	X			X		X	
1296	Walcroft	Nellie	S	2		X	X				X	X	X			
1297	Walker	William Anderson	S	1	L	X	X	X	X	X			X	X		
1298	Ward	Anna	C	1		X					X	X	X	X		
1299	Ware	Florence Louise	S	2		X	X				X	X	X			
1300	Ware	Frederick	S	3	L	X	X	X	X	X			X			
1301	Ware	John James	S	2	L	X	X	X	X	X			X			
1302	Ware	William Jeffery	S	2	L	X	X	X	X	X			X			
1303	Warren	Anna Sophia	C	1		X					X	X	X	X		
1304	Warren	Charles William	S	3	L	X	X	X	X	X			X			
1305	Warren	Frank Manley	C	1	L	X		X	X	X			X	X		
1306	Watson	Ennis Hastings	S	2	L	X	X	X	X	X			X			

	Surname	Forename(s)	A	B	C	D	E	F	G	H	J	K	L	M	N	O
1307	Watt	Elizabeth Inglis	S	2		X	X				X	X	X			
1308	Watt	Robertha Josephine	S	2		X	X				X	X	X			
1309	Webber	James	S	3	L	X	X	X	X	X			X			
1310	Webber	Susan	S	2		X	X				X	X	X			
1311	Weir	John	S	1	L	X	X	X	X	X			X			
1312	Weisz	Leopold	S	2	L	X	X	X	X	X			X		X	
1313	Weisz	Mathilde Francoise	S	2		X	X				X	X	X			X
1314	Wells	Addie	S	2		X	X				X	X	X			
1315	Wells	Joan	S	2		X	X				X	X	X			
1316	Wells	Ralph Lester	S	2		X	X				X	X	X			
1317	West	Ada Mary	S	2		X	X				X	X	X			
1318	West	Barbara Joice	S	2		X	X				X	X	X			
1319	West	Constance Mirium	S	2		X	X				X	X	X			
1320	West	Edwy Arthur	S	2	L	X	X	X	X	X			X			
1321	Whabee	Shawneene Abi-Saab	C	3	L	X		X	X	X	X	X	X			
1322	Wheadon	Edward	S	2	L	X	X	X	X	X			X			
1323	Wheeler	Edwin Charles	S	2	L	X	X	X	X	X			X			
1324	White	Ella Holmes	S	1		X	X				X	X	X	X		
1325	White	Percival Wayland	S	1	L	X	X	X	X	X			X	X		
1326	White	Richard Fraser	S	1	L	X	X	X	X	X			X	X	X	
1327	Wick	George Dennick	S	1	L	X	X	X	X	X			X			
1328	Wick	Mary Hitchcock	S	1		X	X				X	X	X			
1329	Wick	Mary Natalie	S	1		X	X				X	X	X			
1330	Widegren	Charles Peter	S	3	L	X	X	X	X	X			X			
1331	Widener	Eleanor Elkins	S	1		X	X				X	X	X	X		
1332	Widener	George Dunton	S	1	L	X	X	X	X	X			X	X		
1333	Widener	Harry Elkins	S	1	L	X	X	X	X	X			X	X		
1334	Wiklund	Carl Johan	S	3	L	X	X	X	X	X			X			
1335	Wiklund	Jakob Alfred	S	3	L	X	X	X	X	X			X		X	
1336	Wilhelms	Charles	S	2		X	X				X	X	X			
1337	Wilkes	Ellen	S	3		X	X				X	X	X			
1338	Wilkinson	Ada	S	2		X	X									
1339	Wilkinson	Mary	S	2		X	X									
1340	Willard	Constance	S	1		X	X				X	X	X			
1341	Willer	Aaron	C	3	L	X		X	X	X			X			
1342	Willey	Edward	S	3	L	X	X	X	X	X			X			
1343	Williams	Charles Duane	C	1	L	X		X	X	X			X			
1344	Williams	Charles Eugene	S	2		X	X				X	X	X			
1345	Williams	Howard Hugh	S	3	L	X	X	X	X	X			X			
1346	Williams	Leslie	S	3	L	X	X	X	X	X			X		X	
1347	Williams	Richard Norris	C	1		X					X	X	X			
1348	Williams-Lambert	Fletcher Fellows	S	1	L	X	X	X	X	X			X	X		
1349	Williamson	James Bertram	S	2	L			X	X	X						
1350	Wilson	Helen Alice	S	1		X	X				X	X	X	X		
1351	Windelov	Einar	S	3	L	X	X	X	X	X			X			
1352	Wirz	Albert	S	3	L	X	X	X	X	X			X		X	
1353	Wiseman	Phillippe	S	3	L	X	X	X	X	X			X			
1354	Wittevrongel	Camille	S	3	L	X	X	X	X	X			X			
1355	Wolten	H	CC	CC		X										
1356	Wood	Frank P											X	X		
1357	Wood	Frank P Mrs											X	X		
1358	Woodward	John Wesley	S	2	L	X	X	X	X	X						
1359	Woody	Oscar S	S	2	L			X	X	X					X	
1360	Woolner	Hugh	S	1		X	X				X	X	X	X		
1361	Wright	George	S	1	L	X	X	X	X	X			X			
1362	Wright	Marion	S	2		X	X				X	X	X			
1363	Yazbeck	Antoni	C	3	L	X		X	X	X			X			
1364	Yazbeck	Selini	C	3		X					X	X	X			
1365	Young	Marie Grice	C	1		X							X	X		
1366	Yousif	Wasli	C	3	L	X		X	X	X			X			
1367	Yousseff	Gerios	C	3	L	X		X	X	X			X			
1368	Yrois	Henriette	S	2	L	X	X	X	X	X			X			
1369	Zabour	Hileni	C	3	L	X		X	X	X			X			
1370	Zabour	Thamine	C	3	L	X		X	X	X			X			
1371	Zakarian	Mapriededer	C	3	L	X		X	X	X			X		X	
1372	Zakarian	Ortin	C	3	L	X		X	X	X			X			
1373	Zimmermann	Leo	S	3	L	X	X	X	X	X			X			

White Star Line Contract Ticket List

Note that an asterisk against an amount in the Ocean Fare column denotes a total cost shared between two or more passengers travelling together

Master No	Old No	Surname	First Name	Class	Contract Ticket	Continental Ticket	Ocean Fare £	s	d	Refunds	Remarks
1	715	Abbing	Anthony	3	5547		7	11	0		USC
2	789	Abbott	Rosa	3	2673		20*	5	0		
3	791	Abbott	E	3	2673		20*	5	0		
4	790	Abbott	R	3	2673		20*	5	0		
5	899	Abelsith	Karen	3	348125		7	13	0		
6	896	Abelseth	Olanes	3	348122		7	13	0		
7	596	Abelson	H	2	3381	Paris	24*	0	0		
8	595	Abelson	S	2	3381	Paris	24*	0	0		
9	849	August	Abrahamson	3	3101284		7	18	6		
10	1129	Mary	Joseph	3	2657		7	4	7		
11	828	Adahl	Maurits	3	7076		7	5	0		
12	728	Adams	J	3	341826		8	1	0		
13	1087	Aklan	Johamma	3	7546		5	0			
14	641	Ahmed	Ali	3	3101311		7	1	0		
15	660	Aks	Filly	3	392091		9*	7	0		
16	659	Aks	Leah	3	392091		9*	7	0		
17	1188	Belmenby	Nassef	3	2699		18*	15	9		
18	429	Aldsworth	C	2	248744		13	0	0		
19	1325	Alexander		3	3474	34269	7	17	9		
20	852	Alhomaki	Ilmari	3	3101287		7	18	6		
21	642	Ali	William	3	3101312		7	1	0		
22	303	Allen	E W	1	24160		211*	6	9		
23	725	Allen	M	3	373450		8	1	0		
24	68	Allison	H J	1	113781		151*	16	0		
25	69	Allison	H J	1	113781		151*	16	0		
26	70	Allison	H J	1	113781		151*	16	0		
27	71	Allison	Master	1	113781		151*	16	0		
28	1322	Allum		3	12223	111580	8	6	0		
29	807	Anderson	Albert	3					0		
30	810	Anderson	Carla	3	350046		7	17	1		
31	38	Anderson	H	1	19952		26	11	0		
32	963	Anderson	Alfrida	3	347082		31*	5	6		
33	962	Anderson	Anders	3	347082		31*	5	6		
34	925	Wennerstrom		3	350043		7	15	11		
35	966	Anderson	Ebba	3	347082		31*	5	6		
36	968	Anderson	Ellis	3	347082		31*	5	6		
37	875	Anderson	Erna	3	3101281		7	18	6		
38	983	Anderson	Ida	3	347091		7	15	6		
39	965	Anderson	Ingeberg	3	347082		31*	5	6		
40	947	Anderson	Samuel	3	347075		7	15	6		
41	964	Anderson	Sigrid	3	347082		31*	5	6		
42	967	Anderson	Sigvand	3	347082		31*	5	6		
43	905	Andreason	Paul	3	347466		7	17	1		
44	495	Andrew	Frank	2	3405		10	10	0		
45	361	Andrews	Edgar	2	231945		11	10	0		
46	266	Andrews	C T	1	13502		77*	19	2		
47	100	Andrews	T	1	112050		0	0			A/C H&W
48	1011	Angheloff	Minko	3	349202		7	17	11		
49	470	Angle		2	226875		26*	0	0		
50	469	Angle	William	2	226875		26*	0	0		
51	119	Appleton	E D	1	11769	Paris	51*	9	7		
52	1046	Arnold	Josef	3	349237		17*	16	0		Swiss
53	1047	Arnold	Josephine	3	349237		17*	16	0		Swiss
54	825	Aranson	Ernest	3	349911		7	15	6		

Master No	Old No	Surname	First Name	Class	Contract Ticket	Continental Ticket	£	s	d	Refunds	Remarks
55	197	Artageytia	R	1	17609	Paris	49	10	1		
56	388	Ashby	John	2	244346		13	0	0		
57	640	Asim	Adola	3	3101310		7	1	0		
58	949	Asplund	Charles	3	347077		31*	7	9		
58	953	Asplund	Carl	3	347077		31*	7	9		
60	952	Asplund	Gustaf	3	347077		31*	7	9		
61	955	Asplund	Felix	3	347077		31*	7	9		
62	951	Asplund	Oscar	3	347077		31*	7	9		
63	929	Asplund	Johen C	3	350054		7	15	11		
64	954	Asplund	Lillian	3	347077		31*	7	9		
65	950	Asplund	Selma	3	347077		31*	7	9		
66	1181	Gerios	Assaf	3	2692		7	4	6		
67	1185	Assaf	Marian	3	2696		7	4	6		
68	639	Assam	Ali	3	3101309		7	1	0		
69	211	Astor	J J	1	17757		247*	10	6		
70	213	Astor		1	17757		247*	10	6		
71	1183	Slieman	Atalla	3	2694		7	4	6		
72	141	Aubert	N	1	17477	Paris	69*	6	0		
73	907	San	Albert	3	347468		7	17	1		
74	1174	Banoura	Ayoub	3	2687		7	4	7		
75	1165	Rafoul	Baccos	3	2679		7	4	6		
76	873	Backstrom	Karl	3	3101278		15*	17	0		
77	874	Backstrom	Marie	3	3101279		15*	17	0		
78	1147	Eugenie	Baclini	3	2666		19*	5	2		
79	1148	Helene	Baclini	3	2666		19*	5	2		
80	1145	Latife	Baclini	3	2666		19*	5	2		
81	1146	Marie	Baclini	3	2666		19*	5	2		
82	779	Badman	Emily	3	31416		8	1	0		
83	1103	Mohamed	Badt	3	2623		7	4	6		
84	547	Bailey	Percy	2	29108		11	10	0		
85	531	Barmbrigge	C R	2	31030		10	10	0		
86	1055	Balkic	Ceru	3	349248		7	17	11		Austrian
87	494	Balls	Ada E	2	28551		13	0	0		
88	570	Banfield	F J	2	34068		10	10	0		
89	1179	Catherine	Barbara	3	2691		14*	9	1		
90	1180	Saude	Barbara	3	2691		14*	9	1		
91	24	Cavendish's Maid		1	19877	London	78*	17	0		
92	255	Barksworth	A H	1	27042		30	0	0		
93	1194	Barry	Julia	3	330844		7	12	7		
94	793	Barton	David	3	324669		8	1	0		
95	1313	Bateman		2	1166	19426	12	10	6		
96	345	Bauman	J	1	17318		25	18	6		
97	151	Baxter	James	1	17558	Paris	247*	10	5		
98	152	Baxter	Quigg	1	17558	Paris	247*	10	5		
99	290	Buckell's Maid		1	11813	Cherbourg	75*	14	8		
100	471	Beane	Ed	2	2908		26*	0	0		
101	472	Beane	Ethel	2	2908		26*	0	0		
102	263	Beattie	T	1	13050		75*	4	10		
103	393	Beauchamp	H J	2	244358		26*	0	0		
104	703	Bevan	W T	3	323951		8	1	0		
105	441	Beeker	child	2	230136		39*	0	0		
106	440	Beeker	A O	2	230136		39*	0	0		
107	442	Beeker	child	2	230136		39*	0	0		
108	443	Beeker	child	2	230136		39*	0	0		
109	107	Beckwith	R L	1	11751	London	52*	11	1		
110	108	Beckwith		1	11751	London	52*	11	1		
111	416	Beesley	L	2	248698		13	0	0		
112	281	Behr	H H	1	111369		31	0	0		
113	939	Benson	John	3	347068		7	15	6		
114	522	Bentham	L W	2	28404		13	0	0		
115	832	Bergland	Ivar	3	4348		9	7	0		
116	483	Berriman	William	2	28425		13	0	0		
117	1102	Behos	Semon	3	2622		4	0	3		
118	1115	Tannous	Betrous	3	2648		7	4	7		
119	214	Astor's Maid		1	17757		247*	10	6		
120	1314	Chinamen		3	1601		56*	9	11		
121	147	Strauss's Maid		1	17483	London	221*	15	7		
122	901	Birkland	Hans	3	312992		7	15	6		

White Star Line Contract Ticket List

Master No	Old No	Surname	First Name	Class	Contract Ticket	Continental Ticket	£	s	d	Refunds	Remarks
123	277	Jacob	B	1	13905		26	0	0		
124	259	Bishop	D H	1	11967	Paris	91*	1	7		
125	260	Bishop		1	11967	Paris	91*	1	7		
126	222	White's Maid		1	17760		135*	12	8		
127	982	Bjorklund	Ernst	3	347090		7	15	0		
128	278	Bjornstrom	H	1	110564	London	26	11	0		
129	75	Blacknell	S W	1	113784		35	10	0		
130	282	Blank	Henry	1	112277	Paris	31	0	0		
131	74	Bonnell	L	1	113783		26	11	0		
132	308	Bonnell	E	1	36928		164*	17	4		
134	244	Borebank	J J	1	110489		26	11	0		
135	1033	Bostandyef	Giecutcho	3	349224		7	17	11		
136	446	Botsforn	W H	2	237670		13	0	0		
137	1164	Akar	Boulos	3	2678		15*	4	11		
138	1142	Hanne	Boulos	3	2664		7	4	6		
139	1163	Nourelain	Boulos	3	2678		15*	4	11		
140	1162	Sultani	Boulos	3	2678		15*	4	11		
141	1243	Bourke	Catherine	3	364849		15*	10	0		
142	1242	Bourke	John	3	364849		15*	10	0		
143	1241	Bourke	Mary	3	364848		7	15	0		
144	749	Bowen	David	3	54636		16*	2	0		
145	194	Bowen		1	17608	Paris	262*	7	6		
146	459	Boweneer	S	2	211535	London	13	0	0		
147	45	Cowerman Chibnall	E	1	113505		55*	0	0		
148	496	Bracken	J H	2	220267	London	13	0	0		
149	1234	Brady	Bridget	3	334914		7	14	6		
150	247	Brayton	G	1	111427		26	11	0		
151	17	Brady	J B	1	113054	London	30	10	0		
152	910	Braf	Elin	3	347471		7	17	1		
153	372	Bradey	W	2	250654	Bandsmen					
154	322	Brand		CC	8	S to C	1	10	0		
155	168	Brandeis	E	1	17591	Paris	50	9	11		
156	806	Braund		3	3460			10	0		
157	769	Braund	Owen	3	21171		7	5	0		
158	288	Brewe	A J	1	112379	Paris	39	12	0		
159	373	Breicoux	R	2	250654	Bandsmen					
160	395	Brito	Jose de	2	244360		13	0	0		
161	926	Broberk	Carl	3	350045		7	15	11		
162	671	Brocklebank	William	3	364512		8	1	0		
163	424	Brown	Mildred	2	248733		13	0	0		
164	118	Brown	J M	1	11769	Paris	51*	9	7		
165	508	Brown	E	2	29750		39*	0	0		
166	507	Brown	E C	2	29750		39*	0	0		
167	198	Brown	J J	1	17610	Paris	27	14	5		
168	506	Brown	T S	2	29750	London	39*	0	0		
169	327	Odell	H	CC	84	S to Q	24*	0	0	4	
170	611	Bryhl	D	2	236853		26*	0	0		
171	610	Bryhl	C	2	236853		26*	0	0		
172	1199	Buckley	Daniel	3	330920		7	12	7		
173	1285	Buckley	Katherine	3	329944		7	5	8		
174	289	Buckell	W	1	11813	Cherbourg	75*	14	8		
175	1287	Burke	Jerimah	3	365222		6	15	0		
176	9	O'Speddon's Nurse		1	16966		*134	10	0		
177	1207	Burns	Mary	3	330963		7	12	7		
178	558	Buss	Kate	2	27849		13	0	0		
179	493	Butler	Reginald	2	234686		13	0	0		
180	15	Brill	A W	1	113050	London	26	11	0		
181	387	Byles	T R D	2	244310		13	0	0		
182	609	Bystrom	K	2	236852	E.C. Port	13	0	0		
183	1075	Grgo	Cacic	3	315091		8	13	3		
184	1073	Luka	Cacic	3	315089		8	13	3		
185	1071	Nanda	Cacic	3	315087		8	13	3		
186	1068	Teko	Cecie	3	315084		8	13	3		
187	89	Carter's Valet		1	113798		31*	0	0		
188	140	Calderhead	E P	1	17476	London	26	5	9		
189	426	Caldwell	A F	2	248738		29*	0	0		
190	428	Caldwell	A G	2	248738		13	0	0		
191	427	Caldwell	S M	2	248738		29*	0	0		

Who Sailed on Titanic?

Master No	Old No	Surname	First Name	Class	Contract Ticket	Continental Ticket	£	s	d	Refunds	Remarks
192	1070	Petar	Calic	3	315086		8	13	3		
193	376	Cameron	Clear	2	13528		21*	0	0		
194	434	Campbell	W	2	239853						A/C H&W
195	1240	Concannon	Mary	3	364846		7	15	0		
196	1247	Cannavan	Patrick	3	364858		7	15	0		
197	188	Cardell	C	1	17606	Paris	27	8	11		
198	759	Cann	Ernest	3	2152		8	1	0		
199	1176	Joseph	Caran	3	2689		14*	9	2		
200	1177	Maria	Caran	3	2689		14*	9	2		
201	482	Carbines	William	2	28424		13	0	0		
202	204	Cardeza	J M N	1	17755	Paris	512*	6	7		
203	206	Cardeza	T D	1	17755	Paris	512*	6	7		
204	797	Garfith	John	3	358585		14*	10	0		
205	4	Carlson	F	1	695		5	0	0		Special
206	924	Carlsson	August	3	350042		7	15	11		
207	890	Carlson	Carl	3	350409		7	17	1		
208	1264	Carr	Jeanie	3	368364		7	15	0		
209	20	Carran	F H	1	113059	London	47*	2	0		
210	21	Carran	J P	1	113059	London	47*	2	0		
211	389	Carter	E C	2	244252		26*	0	0		
212	390	Carter	E C	2	244252		26*	0	0		
213	58	Carter	L	1	113760		120*	0	0		
214	59	Carter	L	1	113760		120*	0	0		
215	57	Carter	W E	1	113760		120*	0	0		
216	60	Carter	W T	1	113760		120*	0	0		
218	25	Case	H B	1	19924		26	0	0		
219	230	Cassebeer	H A	1	17770	Paris	27	14	5		
220	23	Cavendish		1	19877	London	78*	17	0		
221	22	Cavendish	J W	1	19877	London	78*	17	0		
222	717	Celloti	Francesco	3	343275		8	1	0		
223	317	Chaffee		1	5734		22*	0	0		
224	316	Chaffee	H F	1	5734		22*	0	0		
225	96	Chambers		1	113806	London	53*	2	0		
226	95	Chambers	N	1	113806	London	53*	2	0		
227	423	Chapman	C	2	248731		13	10	0		
228	512	Chapman	J H	2	29037		26*	0	0		
229	513	Chapman	E	2	29037		26*	0	0		
230	1223	Charters	David	3	13032		7	14	8		
231	196	Ryerson's Maid		1	17608	Paris	262*	7	6		
232	236	Cherry	G	1	110152		86*	10	0		
233	173	Chevre	Paul	1	17594	Paris	29	14	0		
234	44	Cowerman Chibnall	M	1	113505		55*	0	0		
235	1315	Chinamen		3	1601		56*	9	11		
236	101	Chrisholm	R Roderick	1	112051		0	0			A/C H&W
237	718	Christman	Emil	3	343276		8	1	0		
238	448	Christy	Alice	2	237789		30*	0	0		
239	449	Christy	Julie	2	237789		30*	0	0		
240	1166	Apostolos	Chionopoulous	3	2680		14*	9	1		
241	1167	Dennehious	Chionopoulous	3	26880		14*	9	1		
242	351	Clark	Ada M	2	2003		26*	0	0		
243	350	Clark	Charles V	2	2003		26*	0	0		
244	272	Clark	Mrs	1	13508		136*	15	7		
245	271	Clark	W M	1	13508		136*	15	7		
246	370	Clarke	F C	2	250654	Bandsmen					
247	72	Allison's Nurse		1	113781		151*	16	0		
248	241	Clifford	G	1	110465		52*	0	0		
249	637	Coelho	Donigos	3	3101307		7	1	0		
250	775	Cowen	Curshow	3	3540		8	1	0		
251	1289	Colbert	Patrick	3	371109		7	5	0		
252	1019	Coliff	Peyo	3	349210		7	17	11		
253	1018	Coliff	Fotio	3	349209		7	17	11		
254	406	Coleridge	R C	2	14263		10	10	0		
255	613	Collander	Erik	2	248740		13	0	0		
256	478	Collett	S	2	28034		10	10	0		
257	315	Colley	E P	1	5727		6	0	0		
258	323	Collis		CC	7	S to C			0		
259	466	Collyer	C	2	31921		26*	5	0		
260	465	Collyer	H	2	31921		26*	5	0		

White Star Line Contract Ticket List

Master No	Old No	Surname	First Name	Class	Contract Ticket	Continental Ticket	Ocean Fare £	s	d	Refunds	Remarks
261	467	Collyer	M	2	31921		26*	5	0		
262	208	Compton	A T	1	17756	Paris	83*	3	2		
263	210	Compton	A T	1	17756	Paris	83*	3	2		
264	209	Compton	S R	1	17756	Paris	83*	3	2		
265	1224	Conlin	Thomas Henry	3	21332		7	14	8		
266	1236	Connaughton	Michael	3	335097		7	15	0		
267	1210	Connolly	Kate	3	330972		7	12	7		
268	1301	Connolly	Katie	3	370373		7	15	0		
269	1296	Connors	Patrick	3	370369		7	15	0		
270	774	Cook	Jacob	3	3536		8	1	0		
271	407	Rogers	Selina	2	14266		10	10	0		
272	1039	Bartol	Cor	3	349229		7	17	11		Austrian
273	1038	Ivan	Cor	3	349229		7	17	11		Austrian
274	1040	Ludovick	Cor	3	349229		7	17	11		Austrian
275	451	Corbett	J C	2	237249		13	0	0		
276	382	Corey	P C	2	13534		21*	0	0		
277	658	Corn	Harry	3	392090		8	1	0		
278	120	Cornell	R C	1	11770	Paris	25	14	10		
279	1260	Corr	Ellen	3	367231		7	15	0		
280	546	Cotterill	Harry	2	29107		11	10	0		
281	724	Coutts	Leslie	3	37671		15*	18	0		
282	723	Coutts	William	3	37671		15*	18	0		
283	722	Coutts	Winnie	3	37671		15*	18	0		
284	668	Coxan	Daniel	3	364500		7	5	0		USC London
285	82	Crafton	John B	1	113791		26	11	0		
287	1324	Crease		3	3464	23885	8	3	2		
288	742	Cribb	John	3	371362		16*	2	0		
289	743	Cribb	John	3	371362		16*	2	0		
290	99	Crosby		1	5735	London	71*	0	0		
291	98	Crosby	J E G	1	WE	London	71*	0	0		
292	258	Crosby	H	1	112901		26	11	0		
293	180	Cumming		1	17599	Paris	71*	5	8		
294	179	Cumming	J B	1	17599	Paris	71*	5	8		
295	433	Cunningham	Alfred	2	239853						A/C H&W
296	1187	Shedid	Daher	3	2698		7	4	6		
297	706	Dake	Charles	3	7598		8	1	0		
298	1342	Dahlberg		3	7552	62762	10	10	4		
299	1037	Dakic	Branko	3	349228		10	3	5		Austrian
300	1273	Daly	Eugene	3	382651		7	15	0		
301	1272	Daly	Marcella	3	382650		6	19	0		
302	18	Daly	P D	1	113055	London	26	11	0		
303	959	Danbom	Sigrid	3	347080		14*	8	0		
304	958	Danbom	Ernest	3	347080		14*	8	0		
305	960	Danbom	Gillbert	3	347080		14*	8	0		
306	94	Daniel	R W	1	113804		30	10	0	30	
307	73	Allison's Maid		1	113781		151*	16	0		
308	1028	Danof	Toto	3	349219		7	17	11		
309	1012	Dantchof	Hristo	3	349203		7	17	11		
310	250	Davidson		1	12750		52*	0	0		
311	249	Davidson	T	1	12750		52*	0	0		
312	764	Davies	Alfred	3	48871		24*	3	0		
313	357	Davies	Charles	2	14879		73*	10	0		
314	485	Davis	Agnes	2	33112		36*	15	0		
315	803	Davies	Evan	3	23568		8	1	0		
316	627	Davies	H V	CC	406		2*	0	0		
317	488	Davis	J M	2	33112		36*	15	0		
318	765	Davies	John	3	48871		24*	3	0		
319	766	Davies	Joseph	3	48873		8	1	0		
320	628	Davies	K	CC	406		2*	0	0		
321	445	Davis	Mary	2	237668		13	0	0		
322	788	Davison	Mary	3	386525		16*	2	0		
323	787	Davison	Thomas	3	386525		16*	2	0		
324	625	de Grasse	J	CC	651		1	0	0		
325	989	Anna	de Messematter	3	345572		17*	8	0		
326	988	Jultoure	de Messematter	3	345572		17*	8	0		
327	1002	Theodore	de Mulder	3	345774		9	10	0		
328	1004	Alfons	Pelsmaker	3	345778		9	10	0		
329	355	Deacon	Percy	2	14879		73*	10	0		

111

Who Sailed on Titanic?

Master No	Old No	Surname	First Name	Class	Contract Ticket	Continental Ticket	Ocean Fare £	s	d	Refunds	Remarks
330	688	Dean	Bertram	3	2315	London	20*	11	6		
331	690	Dean	Bertram	3	2315	London	20*	11	6		
332	691	Dean	Vera	3	2315	London	20*	11	6		
333	689	Dean	Hetty	3	2315	London	20*	11	6		
334	593	Del Carlo		2	2167	Cherbourg	27*	14	5		
335	592	Del Carlo	Sebastiane	2	2167	Cherbourg	27*	14	5		
336	1057	Delalic	Regyo	3	349250		7	17	11		Austrian
337	1048	Dinistri	Marki	3	349238		7	17	11		Macedonian
338	530	Denbony	Herbert	2	31029		31*	10	0		
339	1034	Denkof	Mito	3	349225		7	17	11		
340	770	Dennis	Samuel	3	21172		7	5	0		
341	773	Dennis	William	3	21175		7	5	0		
342	634	Dugemon	Joseph	3	752		7	11	0		
343	1205	Devaney	Margaret	3	330958		7	12	7		
344	358	Dibden	W	2	14879		73*	10	0		
345	232	Dick	A A	1	17474		57*	0	0		
346	233	Dick		1	17474		57*	0	0		
347	1041	Dika	Mirko	3	349232		7	17	11		Austrian
348	1072	Toan	Dinic	3	315088		8	13	3		
349	1035	Dinitchef	Valteho	3	349226		7	17	11		
350	294	Dodge		1	33638		81*	17	2		
351	293	Dodge	W	1	33638		81*	17	2		
352	295	Dodge		1	33638		81*	17	2		
353	1173	Tannous	Dahour	3	2686		7	4	7		
354	359	Doling		2	231919		23*	0	0		
355	360	Doling		2	231919		23*	0	0		
356	1246	Donohue	Bridget	3	364856		7	15	0		
357	1304	Dooley	Patrick	3	370376		7	15	0		
358	745	Dorkings	Arthur	3	10482		8	1	0		
359	226	Douglas		1	17761		106*	8	6		
360	153	Douglas	F C	1	17558	Paris	247*	10	5		
361	225	Douglas	W D	1	17761		106*	8	6		
362	672	Dowdell	Elizabeth	3	364516		12*	9	6		
363	520	Downton	W J	2	28403		26*	0	0		
364	1267	Doyle	Elizabeth	3	368702		7	15	0		
365	1093	Drazenavic	Josip	3	349241		7	17	11		
366	501	Drew	L T	2	28220		32*	10	0		
367	502	Drew	M B	2	28220		32*	10	0		
368	500	Drew	J V	2	28220		32*	10	0		
369	1220	Driscoll	Bridget	3	14311		7	15	0		
370	654	Drapkin	Jenie	3	392083		8	1	0		
371	112	Morgan		1	11755	Paris	39	12	0		
372	148	"Morgan, Duff Gordon"		1	17485	Paris	56*	18	7		
373	161	Dulles	W C	1	17580	Paris	29	14	0		
374	588	Durran	A	2	2149	Cherbourg	13	17	2		
375	587	Durran	F	2	2148	Cherbourg	13	17	2		
376	1239	Divan	Frank	3	336439		7	15	0		
377	943	Dyken	Adolph	3	347072		13*	18	0		
378	944	Dyken	Elisabeth	3	347072		13*	18	0		
379	117	Earnshaw	B	1	11767	Paris	83*	3	2		
381	1074	Toso	Ecuuovic	3	315090		8	13	3		Croatian
382	826	Edvardson	Gustaf	3	349912		7	15	6		
383	509	Eiteniler	G F	2	29751		13	0	0		
384	946	Eklund	Hams	3	347074		7	15	6		
385	932	Elstrom	Johan	3	347061		6	19	6		
386	1158	Debo	Elias	3	2674		7	4	6		
387	1178	Joseph	Elias	3	2690		7	4	7		
388	1159	Elias	Joseph	3	2675		7	4	7		
389	1184	Tanouso	Elias	3	2695		7	4	7		
390	776	Elsbury	James	3	3902		7	5	0		
391	673	Emanuel	Ethel	3	364516		12*	9	6		
392	1112	Chehab	Emir F	3	2631		7	4	6		
393	612	Enander	T	3	236854		13	0	0		
394	215	Endus	C	1	17757		247*	10	6		
395	636	Goncalves	Manoel	3	3101306		7	1	0		
396	310	Eustis	E M	1	36947		78*	5	4		
397	150	Evans	E	1	17531	Paris	31	13	7		

White Star Line Contract Ticket List

Master No	Old No	Surname	First Name	Class	Contract Ticket	Continental Ticket	Ocean Fare £	s	d	Refunds	Remarks
398	626	Evans		CC	88		1	0	0		
399	727	Everett	Thomas	3	6212		15*	2	0		
400	340	Ewards	J D	CC	87	S to C	3*	0	0		
401	341	Ewards		CC	87	S to C	3*	0	0		
402	606	Fahlstrom	H J	2	236171		13	0	0		
403	1261	Farrell	James	3	367232		7	15	0		
404	145	Strauss's Valet		1	17483	London	221*	15	7		
405	519	Faunthorpe	L	2	2926		26*	0	0		
406	518	Faunthorpe	H	2	2926		26*	0	0		
407	564	Fillbrook	C	2	15185		10	10	0		
408	638	Luigi	Finole	3	3101308		7	1	0		
409	923	Percher	Clerland	3	350036		7	15	11		
410	178	Flegenheim	A	1	17598	Paris	31	13	8		
411	1248	Fleming	Norah	3	364859		7	15	0		
412	127	Thayer's Maid		1	17421		110*	17	8		
413	324	Fletcher	N	CC	405	S to C	1	10	0		
414	1245	Flynn	James	3	364851		7	15	0		
415	1263	Flynn	John	3	368323		6	19	0		
416	138	Flynn	J I	1	17474	London	26	5	9		
417	1196	Foley	Joseph	3	330910		7	12	7		
418	1249	Foley	William	3	365235		7	15	0		
419	1316	Chinamen		3	1601		56*	9	11		
420	768	Ford	Arthur	3	1478		8	1	0		
421	682	Ford	D M	3	6608		34*	7	6		
422	683	Ford	E W	3	6608		34*	7	6		
423	681	Ford	Margaret	3	6608		34*	7	6		
424	685	Ford	Maggie	3	6608		34*	7	6		
425	684	Ford	T M	3	6608		34*	7	6		
426	16	Foreman	B L	1	113051	Paris	27	15	0		
427	337	Forman	J	CC	85	S to C	3*	0	0		
428	338	Forman		CC	85	S to C	3*	0	0		
429	35	Fortune	A	1	19950		263*	0	0		
430	37	Fortune	C	1	19950		263*	0	0		
431	34	Fortune	E	1	19950		263*	0	0		
432	36	Fortune	M	1	19950		263*	0	0		
433	32	Fortune	F	1	19950		263*	0	0		
434	33	Fortune		1	19950		263*	0	0		
435	1266	Fox	Patrick	3	368573		7	15	0		
436	557	Fox	Stanley H	2	229236		13	0	0		
437	149	"Morgan, Duff Gordon's Maid"		1	17485	Paris	56*	18	7		
438	643	Franklin	Charles	3	3101314		7	5	0		
439	66	Franklin	T P	1	113778		26	11	0		
440	200	Fraventhal		1	17611	Paris	133*	13	3		
441	199	Fraventhal	H W	1	17611	Paris	133*	13	3		
442	229	Fraunthal	T G	1	17765	Paris	27	14	5		
443	276	Frolicher	M	1	13568		49	10	0		
444	275	Stehli		1	13567		79*	4	0		
445	274	Stehli	M F	1	13567		79*	4	0		
446	435	Frost	A	2	239854						A/C H&W
447	105	Ismay's Manservant		1	112058	Complimentary					
448	447	Funk	Annie	2	237671		13	0	0		
449	92	Futrelle	J	1	113802	London	53*	2	0		
450	93	Futrelle	M	1	113802		53*	2	0		
451	438	Fynney	J	2	239865		26*	0	0		
452	572	Gale	Harry	2	28664		21*	0	0		
453	573	Gale	S	2	28664		21*	0	0		
454	1230	Gallagher	Martin	3	36864		7	14	10		
455	414	Garside	E	2	243880		13	0	0		
456	439	Gaskell	A	2	239865		26*	0	0		
457	527	Gavey	L	2	31028		10	10	0		
458	257	Gee	A	1	111320		26	0	0		
459	1110	Gerios	Youssef	3	2628		7	4	6		
460	1095	Gheorgef	Stamio	3	349254		7	17	11		
461	286	Gibson		1	112378	Paris	59*	8	0		
462	287	Gibson		1	112378	Paris	59*	8	0		
463	50	Widener's Maid		1	113503		211*	10	0		
464	172	Guglio	Victor	1	17593	Paris	79*	4	0		

Master No	Old No	Surname	First Name	Class	Contract Ticket	Continental Ticket	Ocean Fare £	s	d	Refunds	Remarks
465	505	Gilbert	William	2	30769		10	10	0		
466	480	Giles	Edgar	2	28133		11	10	0		
467	481	Giles	Fred	2	28134		11	10	0		
468	419	Giles	Ralph	2	248726		13	10	0		
469	786	Gilinskie	Leslie	3	14973		8	1	0		
470	463	Gill	John	2	233866		13	0	0		
471	561	Gillespie	William	2	12233		13	0	0	11	
472	1225	Gilmagh	Kate	3	35851		7	14	8		
473	391	Gward	Hans K	2	250646		13	0	0		
474	1238	Glynn	Mary	3	335677		7	15	0		
475	130	Goldenburg		1	17453		89*	2	1		
476	129	Goldenburg	E L	1	17453		89*	2	1		
477	203	Goldschmidt	G B	1	17754	Paris	34	13	1		
478	739	Goldsmith	Emily	3	363291		20*	10	6		
479	738	Goldsmith	Frank	3	363291		20*	10	6		
480	740	Goldsmith	Frank	3	363291		20*	10	6		
481	650	Goldsmith	Natham	3	3101263		7	17	0		
482	731	Goodwin	Augusta	3	2144		46*	18	0		
483	733	Goodwin	Charles	3	2144		46*	18	0		
484	730	Goodwin	Frederick	3	2144		46*	18	0		
485	736	Goodwin	Harold	3	2144		46*	18	0		
486	735	Goodwin	Jessie	3	2144		46*	18	0		
487	732	Goodwin	Lillian	3	2144		46*	18	0		
488	737	Goodwin	Sidney	3	2144		46*	18	0		
489	734	Goodwin	Wm	3	2144		46*	18	0		
490	67	Gracie	A	1	113780		28	10	0		
491	162	Graham	W G	1	17582	London	153*	9	3		
492	103	Graham		1	112053		30	0	0		
493	163	Graham	M	1	17582	London	153*	9	3		
494	799	Green	George	3	21440		8	1	0		
495	365	Greenburg	Samuel	2	250647		13	0	0		
496	219	Greenfield	L D	1	17759		63*	7	2		
497	220	Greenfield	W B	1	17759		63*	7	2		
498	1084	Gromestade	Damel	3	8471		4	4			
499	780	Guest	Robert	3	376563		8	1	0		
500	171	Guggenheim	B	1	17593	Paris	79*	4	0		
501	1339	Gustafson		3	7554	113528	9	16	11		
502	871	Gustafson	Anders	3	3101276		7	18	6		
503	872	Gustafson	Johan	3	3101277		7	18	6		
504	940	Gustafson	Gideon	3	347069		7	15	6		
506	1045	Haas	Alaisia	3	349236		8	17	0		Swiss
507	916	Hagland	Ingvald	3	65303		6	19	4		
508	917	Hagland	Konrad	3	65304		6	19	4		
509	845	Hakwianine	Elen	3	3101279		15*	17	0		
510	844	Hakwianine	Pekka	3	3101279		15*	17	0		
511	497	Hale	Reginald	2	250653		13	0	0		
512	616	Hamatainen	Master	2	250649		14*	10	0		
513	615	Hamatainen	A	2	250649		14*	10	0		
514	996	Leon	Uampe	3	345769		9	10	0		
515	1182	Hanna	Mansour	3	2693		7	4	7		
516	1141	Hanne	Moubarch	3	2663		7	4	7		
517	814	Hansen	Claus	3	350026		14*	2	2		
518	813	Julet	Henrik	3	350025		7	17	1		
519	816	Hansen	Henry	3	350026		7	17	1		
520	815	Hansen	Jenny	3	350026		14*	2	2		
521	430	Harbeck	W H	2	248746		13	0	0		
522	114	Harder		1	11765	Paris	55*	8	10		
523	113	Harder	G	1	11765	Paris	55*	8	10		
524	1214	Hargadon	Kate	3	30631		7	14	8		
525	686	Harknett	Alice	3	6609		7	11	0		
526	713	Harmer	Abraham	3	374887		7	5	0		
527	422	Harper	Maria	2	248727		33*	0	0		
528	158	Harper	H S	1	17572	Paris	76*	14	7		
529	420	Harper	John	2	248727		33*	0	0		
530	159	Harper		1	17572	Paris	76*	14	7		
531	87	Moore's Valet		1	113796		42*	8	0		
532	402	Harris	George	2	751		10	10	0		
533	313	Harris	H B	1	36973		83*	9	6		

White Star Line Contract Ticket List

Master No	Old No	Surname	First Name	Class	Contract Ticket	Continental Ticket	Ocean Fare £	s	d	Refunds	Remarks
534	314	Harris		1	36973		83*	9	6		
535	403	Harris	W	2	14208	London	10	10	0		
536	106	Harrison	W H	1	112059	Complimentary					
537	378	Hart	Benjamin	2	13529		26*	5	0		
538	379	Hart	Esther	2	13529		26*	5	0		
539	380	Hart	Eva M	2	13529		26*	5	0		
540	1213	Hart	Henry	3	394140		6	17	2		
541	371	Hartley	W	2	250654	Bandsmen					
542	160	Harper's Valet		1	17572	Paris	76*	14	7		
543	1189	Belmenby	Hassan	3	2699		18*	15	9		
544	10	Hawksford	W J	1	16988		30	0	0		
545	251	Hays	C H	1	12749		93*	10	0		
546	252	Hays		1	12749		93*	10	0		
547	116	Hayes	M	1	11767	Paris	83*	3	2		
548	12	Head	C	1	113038	London	42	10	0		
549	1303	Healy	Nora	3	370375		7	15	0		
550	981	Hedman	Oscar	3	347089		6	19	6		
551	1317	Chinamen		3	1601		56*	9	11		
552	1286	Hegarty	Nora	3	365226		6	15	0		
553	847	Heikkinen	Laina	3	3101282		7	18	6		
554	855	Heininen	Wendla	3	3101290		7	18	6		
555	1088	Hellstrom	Hilda	3	7548		5	0	0		
556	1050	Zguaq	Hendekovic	3	349243		7	17	11		Austrian
557	973	Henrikson	Jenny	3	347086		7	15	6		
558	1271	Henry	Delia	3	382649		7	15	0		
559	555	Herman	Alice	2	220845		65*	0	0		
560	553	Herman	Jane	2	220845		65*	0	0		
561	554	Herman	Kate	2	220845		65*	0	0		
562	552	Herman	Samuel	2	220845		65*	0	0		
563	417	Hewlitt	M D	2	248706		16	0	0		
564	352	Hickman	Leonard	2	14879		73*	10	0		
565	353	Hickman	L	2	14879		73*	10	0		
566	354	Hickman	Stanley	2	14879		73*	10	0		
567	132	Hilliard	H H	1	17463	Soton	51*	9	7		
568	617	Hilltunen	M	2	250650		13	0	0		
569	1	Hipkins	W E	1	680		50	0	0		
570	280	Hippach	J	1	111361		57*	19	7		
571	279	Hippach	J S	1	111361		57*	19	7		
572	869	Hervonin	Helga	3	3101298		12*	5	9		
573	870	Hervonin	Hildu	3	3101298		12*	5	9		
574	541	Hocking	Eliza	2	29105		23*	0	0		
575	542	Hocking	Nellie	2	29105		23*	0	0		
576	540	Hocking	George	2	29105		11	10	0		
577	571	Hoaking	S J	2	242963		13	0	0		
578	362	Hodges	Henry P	2	250643		13	0	0		
579	268	Hogeboom	J G	1	13502		77*	19	2		
580	476	Hold	A	2	26707		26*	0	0		
581	475	Hold	Stephen	2	26707		26*	0	0		
583	827	Hbm	John F	3	7075		6	9	0		
584	809	Holten	Johan	3	4001		22	10	6		
585	79	Holverson	A O	1	113789		52*	0	0		
586	80	Holverson		1	113789		52*	0	0		
587	246	Haven	H	1	111426		26	11	0		
588	848	Honkonen	Eluna	3	3101283		7	18	6		
589	356	Hood	Ambrose	2	14879		73*	10	0		
590	1305	Horgan	John	3	370377		7	15	0		
591	450	Hosono	M	2	237798		13	0	0		
592	473	Howard	B	2	24065		26*	0	0		
593	474	Howard	E T	2	24065		26*	0	0		
594	794	Howard	Mary	3	39186		8	1	0		
595	29	Hoyt	F	1	19943		100*	0	0		
596	30	Hoyt		1	19943		100*	0	0		
597	181	Hoyt	W J	1	17600	Paris	30	13	11		
598	895	Humblin	Adolf	3	348121		7	13	0		
599	367	Hume	J	2	250654	Bandsmen					
600	621	Hunt	G	2	1585		1	10	0		
601	1326	Hyman		3	3470	52285	7	17	9		
602	56	Stone's Maid		1	113572		80*	0	0		

Who Sailed on Titanic?

Master No	Old No	Surname	First Name	Class	Contract Ticket	Continental Ticket	Ocean Fare £	s	d	Refunds	Remarks
603	533	Ilett	Bertha	2	14885		10	10	0		
604	1029	Jlief	Ylio	3	349220		7	17	11		
605	838	Ilmakangas	Ida	3	3101270		7	18	6		
606	839	Ilmakangas	Pista	3	3101271		7	18	6		
607	174	Isham	E A	1	17595	Paris	28	14	3		
608	104	Ismay	J B	1	112058	Complimentary					
609	1010	Ivanoff	Ronic	3	349201		7	17	11		Bulgarian
610	413	Jacobsohn		2	243847		27*	0	0		
611	412	Jacobsohn	S S	2	243847		27*	0	0		
612	1092	Jalsevac	Yovan	3	349240		7	17	11		
613	921	Jansen	Carl O	3	350034		7	15	11		
614	635	Jardin	Jose	3	3101305		7	1	0		
615	464	Jarvis	J D	3	237565		15	0	0		
616	528	Jeffreys	Clifford	2	31029		31*	10	0		
617	529	Jeffreys	Ernest	2	31029		31*	10	0		
618	484	Jenkin	Stephen	2	33111		10	10	0		
619	817	Ginum	Ham	3	350050		7	17	1		
620	812	Jenum	Niths R	3	350048		7	1	1		
621	811	Jenum	Svent C	3	350047		7	17	1		
622	1222	Jermyn	Annie	3	14313		7	15	0		
623	601	Tervan	A T	2	Basle	Cherbourg	13	15	10		
624	919	Johamesen	Bernt	3	65306		8	2	3		
626	876	Johnson	Jakob A	3	3101264		6	9	11		
627	927	Johansson	Erik	3	350052		7	15	11		
628	1086	Johansen	Gustaf	3	7540			5	0		
629	934	Johnsson	Carl	3	347063		7	15	6		
630	906	Johnson	Nils	3	347467		7	17	1		
631	941	Johanson	Oscar	3	347070		7	15	6		
633	912	Johnson	Elianara	3	347742		11*	2	8		
634	911	Johnson	Elis	3	347742		11*	2	8		
635	913	Johnson	Harold	3	347742		11*	2	8		
636	933	Johnsson	Malkom	3	347062		7	15	6		
638	677	Johnstone	A E	3	6607		23*	9	0		
639	680	Johnstone	H	3	6607		23*	9	0		
640	678	Johnstone		3	6607		23*	9	0		
641	679	Johnstone	William	3	6607		23*	9	0		
642	3	Jones	C E	1	694		26	0	0		Special
643	1013	Yonkoff	Lazom	3	349204		7	17	11		
644	891	Jenson	Carl	3	350417		7	17	1		
645	889	Jonsson	Niels	3	350408		7	17	1		
646	1152	Anna	Peter	3	2668		22*	7	2		
647	1150	Catherine	Peter	3	2668		22*	7	2		
648	1151	Mike	Peter	3	2668		22*	7	2		
649	14	Julian	H J	1	113044	London	26	0	0		
650	851	Jussila	Eerik	3	3101286		7	18	6		
651	1336	Jussila		3	4136	113515	9	16	10		
652	1337	Jussila		3	4137	113516	9	16	10		
653	842	Kallio	Mikvali	3	3101274		7	2	6		
654	1328	Kaling		3	8475	6998	8	8	1		
655	398	Kantor		2	244367		26*	0	0		
656	397	Kantor	S	2	244367		26*	0	0		
657	1053	Karafic	Milan	3	349246		7	17	11		Austrian
658	928	Carlsson	Egnar	3	350053		7	15	11		
659	904	Carlsan	Julius	3	347465		7	17	1		
660	930	Karlsson	Nels	3	350060		10	10	5		
661	383	Karnes	J F	2	13534		21*	0	0		
662	1097	Karm	Frang	3	349256		13*	8	4		Croatian
663	1098	Karm	Anna	3	349256		13*	8	4		Syrienne
664	›1190	Kassen	Fared	3	2700		7	4	7		
665	1169	Vasselion	Catavelar	3	2682		7	4	7		
666	1219	Keane	Andy	3	12460		7	15	0		
667	1310	Keane	Daniel	2	233734		12	7	0		
668	1309	Keane	Nora A	2	226593		12	7	0		
669	709	Keepe	Arthur	3	323592		7	5	0		
670	49	Widener's Valet		1	113503		211*	10	0		
671	721	Kelled	James	3	363592	London	8	1	0		
672	1218	Reilly	Anne Kate	3	9234		7	15	0		
673	453	Kelly	F	2	223596	London	13	10	0		

White Star Line Contract Ticket List

Master No	Old No	Surname	First Name	Class	Contract Ticket	Continental Ticket	£	s	d	Refunds	Remarks
674	1197	Kelly	James	3	330911		7	12	7		
675	1221	Kelly	Mary	3	14312		7	15	0		
676	1269	Kennedy	John	3	368783		7	15	0		
677	121	Kent	E A	1	11771	Paris	29	14	0		
678	133	Kenyon	F R	1	17464	Soton	51*	17	3		
679	134	Kenyon		1	17464	Soton	51*	17	3		
680	1133	Betros	Khalil	3	2660		14*	9	1		
681	1134	Lahie	Khalil	3	2660		14*	9	1		
682	1255	Kiernan	John	3	367227		7	15	0		
683	1257	Kiernan	Philip	3	367229		7	15	0		
684	1231	Kilgannon	Thomas	3	36865		7	14	9		
685	110	Kimball	E	1	11753		52*	11	1		
686	111	Kimball		1	11753	London	52*	11	1		
687	1062	Anton	Kink	3	315151		22*	0	6		Croatian
688	1063	Louis	Kink	3	315151		22*	0	6		Croatian
689	1064	Louis	Kink	3	315151		22*	0	6		
690	1060	Vincenz	Kink	3	315151		22*	0	6		Croatian
691	1061	Maria	Kink	3	315151		22*	0	6		Croatian
692	1308	Kirkland	C L	2	219533		12	7	0		
693	11	Klafer	H	1	113028	London	26	11	0		
694	886	Klasen	Gertrude	3	350404		12*	3	8		
695	885	Klasen	Huldo	3	350404		12*	3	8		
696	884	Klasen	Klas	3	350404		7	17	1		
697	623	Kneese		CC	47		2*	0	0		
698	436	Knight	R	2	239855						A/C H&W
699	1094	Kraef	Thodor		349253		7	17	11		Bulgarian
700	1126	Nicham	Krikorian	3	2654		7	4	7		
701	304	Robert's Maid		1	24160		211*	6	9		
702	366	Krins	G	2	250654	Bandsmen					
703	605	Kvillner	J H	2	18723	E.C. Port	10	10	0		
704	1104	Sarkis	Lahoud	3	2624		7	4	6		
705	620	Lahtinen		2	250651		26*	0	0		
706	619	Lahtinen	W	2	250651		26*	0	0		
707	1334	Laitinen		3	4135	100576	9	11	9		
708	1026	Lalef	Kristo	3	349217		7	17	11		
709	1318	Chinamen		3	1601		56*	9	11		
710	1319	Chinamen		3	1601		56*	9	11		
711	1306	Lamb	J J	3	240261		10	14	2		
712	829	Landegrin	Aurora	3	7077		7	5	0		
713	1216	Lane	Patrick	3	7935		7	15	0		
714	1320	Chinamen		3	1601		56*	9	11		
715	579	Laroche	Joseph	2	2123	Cherbourg	41*	11	7		
716	580	Laroche		2	2123	Cherbourg	41*	11	7		
717	582	Laroche	Louise	2	2123	Cherbourg	41*	11	7		
718	581	Laroche	S	2	2123	Cherbourg	41*	11	7		
719	1341	Larson		3	7545	36851	9	9	8		
720	938	Larsson	Bengt	3	347067		7	15	6		
721	936	Larsson	Edward	3	347065		7	15	6		
722	758	Laund	W	3	2151		8	1	0		
724	135	Leader	F A	1	17465	Soton	25	18	7		
725	1100	Fahim	Leeni	3	2620		7	4	6		
726	1329	Lefebre		3	4133	7973	25*	9	4		
727	1330	Lefebre		3	4133	7973	25*	9	4		
728	1331	Lefebre		3	4133	7973	25*	9	4		
729	1332	Lefebre		3	4133	7973	25*	9	4		
730	1333	Lefebre		3	4133	7973	25*	9	4		
731	602	Lehmann	B	2	1748	Cherbourg	12	0	0		
732	857	Leinonen	Antli	3	3101292		7	18	6		
733	421	Leitch	Jessie	2	248727		33*	0	0		
734	1170	Peter	Leneberopailos	3	2683		6	8	9		
735	532	Laneori	A	2	3426	London	10	10	0		
736	1298	Lennon	Dennis	3	370371		15*	10	0		
737	1299	Lennon	Mary	3	370371		15*	10	0		
738	336	Connyngham	A L	CC	74	S to C	1	10	0		
739	334	Connyngham		CC	74	S to C	3*	0	0		
740	335	Connyngham		CC	74	S to C	3*	0	0		
741	333	Connyngham	L	CC	74	S to C	3*	0	0		
743	227	Douglas's Maid		1	17761		106*	8	6		

Who Sailed on Titanic?

Master No	Old No	Surname	First Name	Class	Contract Ticket	Continental Ticket	Ocean Fare £	s	d	Refunds	Remarks
744	763	Lester	James	3	48871		24*	3	0		
745	207	Cardeza's Valet		1	17755	Paris	512*	6	7		
746	590	Levy	R J	2	2163	Port.	12	17	6		
748	201	Levy	E G	1	17612	Paris	27	14	5		
749	566	Leyson	R W	2	29566		10	10	0		
750	1007	Rene	Lievens	3	345781		9	10	0		
751	942	Lindhal	Agdar	3	347071		7	15	6		
752	945	Lindbom	August	3	347073		7	15	0		
753	234	Lingrey	Edgar J	1	17475	London	26	11	0		
754	823	Lindell	Edvard B	3	349910		15*	11	0		
755	824	Lindell	Elen	3	349910		15*	11	0		
756	850	Lindgit	Eino	3	3101285		7	18	6		
757	285	Lindstroem	O A	1	112317	Paris	27	14	5		
758	1209	Linehan	Michael	3	330971		7	12	7		
759	169	Lines	Ernest H	1	17592	Paris	59*	8	0		
760	170	Lines	Mary C	1	17592	Paris	59*	8	0		
761	1321	Chinamen		3	1601		56*	9	11		
762	987	Lenhart	Menzel	3	345775		9	10	0		Austrian
763	1312	Lingane	John	2	235529		12	7	0		
764	632	Lethman	Simon	3	251		7	11	0		
765	752	Lobb	Cordelia	3	3336		16*	2	0		
766	751	Lobb	William	3	3336		16*	2	0		
767	804	Lockyer		3	1222		5	0			
768	43	Long	M C	1	113501		30	0	0		
769	267	Longley	G T	1	13502		77*	19	2		
770	91	Loring	J H	1	113801		45	10	0		
771	549	Louch	A A	2	3085		26*	0	0		
772	548	Louch	Charles	2	3085		26*	0	0		
773	771	Lovell	John	3	21173		7	5	0		
775	1082	Vikola	Lulic	3	315098		8	13	3		
776	914	Laindahl	John	3	347743		7	1	1		
777	908	Lunden	Olga	3	347469		7	17	1		
778	883	Lindstrom	Juri	3	350403		7	11	7		
779	157	Spencer's Maid		1	17569	Paris	146*	10	5		
780	1044	Lyntcakof	Stanko	3	235		7	17	11		Bulgarian
781	348	Mack	Mary	2	3		10	10	0		
782	708	Mackay	George	3	42795		7	11	0		
783	1297	Madigan	Maggie	3	370370		7	15	0		
784	302	Mavill	G A	1	24160		211*	6	9		
785	831	Madsen	Frilly	3	17369		7	2	10		
786	843	Maenya	Malli	3	3101275		7	2	6		
787	243	McGuire	J E	1	110469		26	0	0		
788	1201	Mahon	Delia	3	330924		7	12	7		
789	1215	Mahan	John	3	3130		7	15	0		
790	237	Mairore	R	1	110152		86*	10	0		
791	756	Maisner	Simon	3	2816		8	1	0		
792	836	Makiner	Halle	3	3101268		7	18	6		
793	598	Malachard	H N	2	237735	Paris	15	0	11		
794	1109	Malaki	Attalie	3	2627		14*	9	2		
795	576	Mallett	A	2	2079	Paris	37*	1	0		
796	577	Mallett	Mrs	2	2079	Paris	37*	1	0		
797	578	Mallett	Master	2	2079	Paris	37*	1	0		
798	1161	Hanna	Meme	3	2677		7	4	7		
799	1244	Mangan	Mary	3	364850		7	15	0		
800	608	Mangivacchi	E	1	2861	Paris	15	11	7		
801	1232	Mamion	Margaret	3	36866		7	14	9		
803	1127	Larkis	Mirdirosian		3	2655	7	4		7	American
804	122	Marcchal	Pierre	1	11774	Paris	29	14	0		
805	1022	Harkof	Harin	3	349213		7	17	11		
806	1099	Markin	Johann	3	349257		7	17	11		
807	62	Marvin	D W	1	113773		53*	2	0		
808	63	Marvin		1	113773		53*	2	0		
809	805	Maskey		3	1595			0			
810	1116	Fatma	Musutmanami	3	2649		7	4	6		
811	1096	Matinof	Vuolia	3	349255		7	17	11		
812	504	Matthews	W J	2	28228		13	0	0		
813	328	Odell		CC	84	S to Q	24*	0	0		
814	329	Odell		CC	84	S to Q	24*	0	0		

White Star Line Contract Ticket List

Master No	Old No	Surname	First Name	Class	Contract Ticket	Continental Ticket	Ocean Fare £	s	d	Refunds	Remarks
815	411	Maybery	Frank H	2	239059		16	0	0		
816	143	de Villiers	B	1	17482	Paris	49	10	1		
817	262	McCaffery	T	1	13050		75*	4	10		
818	1282	McCarthy	Katie	3	383123		7	15	0		
819	131	McCarthy	T J	1	17463	Soton	51*	9	7		
820	1256	McCormack	Thomas	3	367228		7	15	0		
821	1252	McCoy	Agnes	3	367226		23*	5	0		
822	1253	McCoy	Alice	3	367226		23*	5	0		
823	1254	McCoy	Bernard	3	367226		23*	5	0		
824	457	McCraie	A G	2	237216		13	10	0		
825	458	McCrie	J M	2	233478	London	13	0	0		
826	1203	McDermott	Delia	3	330932		7	15	8		
827	1228	McEvoy	Michael	3	36568		15*	10	0		
828	137	McGough	R	1	17473	London	26	5	9		
829	1200	McGowan	Annie	3	330923		7	15	7		
830	1217	McGowan	Catherine	3	9232		7	15	0		
831	1202	McGowan	Mary	3	330931		7	12	7		
832	521	McKane	P D	2	28403		26*	0	0		
833	1300	McMahon	Martin	3	370372		7	15	0		
834	784	McNanee	Eileen	3	376566		16*	2	0		
835	783	McNanee	Neil	3	376566		16*	2	0		
836	1295	McNeil	Bridget	3	370368		7	15	0		
837	656	Meanwel	Marion O	3	392087		8	1	0		
838	767	Meek	Annie	3	343095		8	1	0		
839	363	Mellinger	Elizabeth	2	250644		19*	10	0		
840	364	Mellinger	child	2	250644		19*	10	0		
841	401	Mellers	William	2	751		10	10	0		
843	795	Meo	Alfonso	3	11206		8	1	0		
844	1268	Meneagh	Robert	3	368703		7	15	0		
845	418	Meyer	August	2	248723		13	0	0		
846	185	Meyer	Edgar J	1	17604	Paris	82*	3	5		
847	186	Meyer		1	17604	Paris	82*	3	5		
848	984	Midbsle	Carl	3	345501		7	15	6		
849	761	Mills	Frank	3	359306		8	1	0		
850	662	Miles	Frederick	3	392095		7	5	0	5	
851	273	Muller	F D	1	13509		26	11	0		
852	607	Milling	J	2	234360		13	0	0		
853	28	Minaham	D	1	19928		90*	0	0		
854	27	Minaham		1	19928		90*	0	0		
855	26	Minaham	W E	1	19928		90*	0	0		
856	1042	Cuisef	Ivan	3	349233		7	17	11		Bulgarian
857	1020	Minkoff	Lazar	3	349211		7	17	11		
858	1016	Mihof	Stoytcho	3	340207		7	17	11		
859	568	Mitchell	Henry	3	24580		10	10	0		
860	1030	Milkof	Mito	3	349221		7	17	11		
861	320	Mock	P E	1	13236		57*	15	0		
862	1212	Mocklare	Ellen	3	330980		7	12	7		
863	897	Moen	Sigurd	3	348123		7	13	0		
864	77	Markland Molson	H	1	113787		30	10	0		
865	460	Mantvila	J	2	211536	London	13	0	0		
866	663	Moore	Beile	3	392096		12*	9	6		
867	664	Moore	Meir	3	392096		12*	9	6		
868	86	Moore	Clarence	1	113796		42*	8	0		
869	792	Moore	Leonard	3	54510		8	1	0		
870	1292	Moran	Bertha	3	371110		24*	3	0		
871	1290	Moran	Daniel J	3	371110		24*	3	0		
872	1193	Moran	James	3	330877		6	19	2		
873	604	Moraweck	E	2	29011	Hook-Holland	14	0	0		
874	374	Marshall	Henry	2	250655		26*	0	0		
875	669	Morley	William	3	364506		8	1	0		
876	1270	Morrow	Thomas	3	372622		7	15	0		
877	900	Mass	Albert	3	312991		7	15	6		
878	1136	Gerios	Moubarek	3	2661		15*	4	11		Syrienne
879	1137	Halim	Moubarek	3	2661		15*	4	11		Syrienne
880	1135	Amine	Moubarek	3	2661		15*	4	11		Syrienne
881	1107	Mantoma	Moussa	3	2626		7	4	7		
882	707	Moutal	Rahamin	3	374746		8	1	0		
883	349	Mudd	Thomas E	2	3		10	10	0		

Who Sailed on Titanic?

Master No	Old No	Surname	First Name	Class	Contract Ticket	Continental Ticket	Ocean Fare £	s	d	Refunds	Remarks
884	631	Mullen		CC	404		1	0	0		
885	1226	Mullen	Kate	3	35852		7	14	8		
886	1280	Mulvihill	Bertha E	3	382653		7	15	0		
887	719	Mirdlin	Joseph	3	3235		8	1	0		
888	1259	Murphy	Kate	3	367230		15*	10	0		
889	1258	Murphy	Mary J	3	367230		15*	10	0		
890	1229	Murphy	Norah	3	36568		15*	10	0		
891	956	Mylrinan	Oliver	3	347078		7	15	0		
892	1307	Myles	F T	2	240276		9	13	9		
893	1015	Naidenof	Penko	3	349206		7	17	11		
894	1149	Adeli	Nafib	3	2667		7	4	6		
895	1125	Marie	Nahed	3	2653		15*	14	10		
896	1123	Said	Nahed	3	2653		15*	14	10		
897	1124	Madia	Nahed	3	2653		15*	14	10		
898	755	Nancorron	William	3	3338		8	1	0		
899	1027	Vanhof	Minko	3	349218		7	17	11		Bulgarian
900	1122	Nasr	Mustafa	3	2652		7	4	7		
901	600	Nasser		2	237736	Paris	30*	1	5		
902	599	Nasser	N	2	237736	Paris	30*	1	5		
903	175	Natcsh	Charles	1	17596	Paris	29	14	0		
904	1250	Naughton	Hannagh	3	365237		7	15	0		
905	409	Hoffman	child	2	230080		26*	0	0		
906	408	Hoffman		2	230080		26*	0	0		
907	410	Hoffman	child	2	230080		26*	0	0		
908	1043	Nenkoff	Christo	3	349234		7	17	11		Bulgarian
909	399	Nesson	Israel	2	244368		13	0	0		
910	296	Newell	A	1	35273		113*	5	6		
911	298	Newell	M	1	35273		113*	5	6		
912	297	Newell		1	35273		113*	5	6		
913	109	Newsom	H	1	11752		26	5	8		
914	486	Nicholls	J C	2	33112		36*	15	0		
915	342	Nichols	E	CC	103	S to Q	4	0	0		
916	2	Nicholson	A J	1	693		26	0	0		
917	1121	Elias	Nicola	3	2651		11*	4	10		
918	1120	Tamille	Nicola	3	2651		11*	4	10		
919	868	Meiminen	Manta	3	3101297		7	18	6		
920	750	Niklasen	Sander	3	363611		8	1	0		
921	892	Nilsson	August	3	350410		7	17	1		
922	937	Millssom	Barta	3	347066		7	15	6		
923	909	Nilsen	Helmina	3	347470		7	17	1		
924	840	Nirva	Ishal	3	3101272		7	2	6		
925	854	Niskamen	John	3	3101289		7	18	6		
926	326	Noel		CC	48	S to C	3*	0	0		
927	325	Noel	G T	CC	48	S to C	3*	0	0		
928	550	Norman	R D	2	218629		13	10	0		
929	760	Nosworthy	Richard	3	39886		7	16	0		
930	591	Drachstedt		2	2166	Cherbourg	13	17	3		
931	1186	Norel	Mansour	3	2697		7	4	7		
932	565	Nye	Eliz	2	29395		10	10	0		
933	961	Ingstrom	Anna	3	347081		7	15	0		
934	986	Nysven	Johan	3	345364		6	4	9		
935	1294	O'Brien	Hannah	3	370365		15*	10	0		
936	1293	O'Brien	Thomas	3	370365		15*	10	0		
937	1211	O'Brien	Denis	3	330979		7	12	7		
938	1233	O'Connell	Patrick D	3	334912		7	14	8		
939	1251	O'Connor	Patrick	3	366713		7	15	0		
940	1288	O'Connor	Maurice	3	371060		7	15	0		
941	1345	Odahl		3	7267	7884	9	4	6		
942	330	Odell		CC	84	S to Q	24*	0	0		
943	331	Odell		CC	84	S to Q	24*	0	0		
944	332	Odell		CC	84	S to Q	24*	0	0		
945	1206	O'Dwyer	Nellie	3	330959		7	12	7		
946	972	Olman	Velm	3	347085		7	15	6		
947	1265	O'Keeffe	Patrick	3	368402		7	15	0		
948	1198	O'Leary	Norah	3	330919		7	12	7		
949	218	Penasco's Maid		1	17758		108*	18	0		
950	830	Olsen	Arfthur	3	17368		3	3	5		USC
951	808	Olsen	Henry	3	Bergen				0		

White Star Line Contract Ticket List

Master No	Old No	Surname	First Name	Class	Contract Ticket	Continental Ticket	Ocean Fare £	s	d	Refunds	Remarks
952	1344	Olsen		3	4579	35933	8	8	1		
953	915	Olson	M	3	265302		7	6	3		
954	888	Olssm	Elida	3	350407		7	17	1		
955	903	Olsan	John	3	347464		7	17	1		
956	957	Johannsen	Oscar	3	347079		7	15	6		
957	1343	Andersen		3	6563	103992	9	4	6		
958	318	Ormont	A F	1	12998		25	14	10		
959	1069	Teko	Ores	3	315085		8	13	3		
960	1078	Luka	Ores	3	315094		8	13	3		
961	1080	Maria	Ores	3	315096		8	13	3		
962	629	Osborne	D	CC	516		2*	0	0		
963	1085	Osen	Elan	3	7534		5	0			
964	1051	Osman	Mara	3	349244		8	13	8		Austrian
965	51	Ostby	E C	1	113509		61*	19	7		
966	52	Ostby	H R	1	113509		61*	19	7		
967	1195	O'Sullivan	Bridget	3	330909		7	12	7		
968	499	Otter	Richard	2	28213		13	0	0		
969	154	Ovies	S	1	17562	Paris	27	14	5		
970	405	Oxenham	T	2	14260		10	10	0		
971	585	Padro	Julian	2	2146	Cherbourg	13	17	3		
972	386	Pain	Alfred	2	244278		10	10	0		
973	586	Pallas	Emilio	2	2147	Cherbourg	13	17	2		
974	818	Paulson	Alma	3	349909		21*	1	6		
975	822	Paulson	Gosta	3	349909		21*	1	6		
976	820	Paulson	Paul	3	349909		21*	1	6		
977	821	Paulson	Stma	3	349909		21*	1	6		
978	819	Paulson	Torbrig	3	349909		21*	1	6		
979	866	Penula	William	3	3101295		39*	13	9		
980	863	Penula	Ernest	3	3101295		39*	13	9		
981	864	Penula	Eona	3	3101295		39*	13	9		
982	862	Penula	Juha	3	3101295		39*	13	9		
983	860	Penula	Maria	3	3101295		39*	13	9		
984	865	Penula	Wihu	3	3101295		39*	13	9		
985	523	Parker	E R	2	14888		10	10	0		
986	432	Parker	Frank	2	239853	Free a/c Harland					
987	102	Parr	H W	1	112052		0	0			A/C H&W
988	455	Parish	L D	2	230433	London	26*	0	0		
989	13	Partner	A	1	113043	London	28	10	0		
990	1081	Takob	Pasic	3	315097		8	13	3		
991	798	Potchill	George	3	358585		14*	10	0		
992	1192	Uscher	Paulmer	3	3411		8	14	3		
993	1049	Pavlovic	Stefo	3	349242		7	17	11		Austrian
994	253	Payne	V	1	12749		93*	10	0		
995	646	Peacock	Alfred E	3	3101315		13*	15	6		
996	644	Peacock	Treastall	3	3101315		13*	15	6		
997	645	Peacock	Treastall	3	3101315		13*	15	6		
998	716	Pearce	Ernest	3	343271		7	0	0		
999	65	Pears	Edith	1	113776		66*	12	0		
1000	64	Pears	Thomas	1	113776		66*	12	0		
1001	985	Peterson	Olaf	3	345498		7	15	6		
1002	757	Peduzzi	Joseph	3	2817		8	1	0		
1003	859	Pekonmi	E	3	3101294		7	18	6		
1004	856	Peltomaki	Nikolai	3	3101291		7	18	6		
1005	217	Penasco		1	17758		108*	18	0		
1006	216	Penasco	Victor	1	17758		108*	18	0		
1007	574	Pengelly	F	2	28665		10	10	0		
1008	772	Perkin	John	3	21174		7	5	0		
1009	583	Pernot	Rene	2	2131	Paris	15	1	0		
1010	254	Hays' Maid		1	12749		93*	10	0		
1011	969	Person	Ernst	3	347083		7	15	6		
1012	444	Peruschitz	J M	2	237393		13	0	0		
1013	1204	Peters	Katie	3	330935		7	17	9		
1014	704	Peterson	Maruis	3	342441		8	1	0	6	
1015	1052	Petranic	Matilda	3	349245		7	17	11		Austrian
1016	1021	Petroff	Vedelco	3	349212		7	17	11		
1017	1024	Petrof	Pentcho	3	349215		7	17	11		
1018	948	Petersen	Johan	3	347076		7	15	6		
1019	974	Peterson	Ellen	3	347087		7	15	6		

Master No	Old No	Surname	First Name	Class	Contract Ticket	Continental Ticket	Ocean Fare £	s	d	Refunds	Remarks
1020	76	Peuchen	Arthur	1	113786		30	10	0		
1021	347	Phillips	Alice	2	2		21*	0	0		
1022	346	Phillips	Robert	2	2		21*	0	0		
1023	375	Marshall	Kate	2	250655		26*	0	0		
1024	511	Pinsky	Rosa	2	234604		13	0	0		
1025	1036	Plotchaisky	Vasil	3	349227		7	17	11		
1026	1079	Mate	Pocrenic	3	315095		8	13	3		
1027	1076	Pame	Pocrenic	3	315092		8	13	3		
1028	392	Ponesell	Martin	2	250647		13	0	0		
1029	603	Portaluppi	E	2	34644		12	14	9		
1030	242	Porter	W C	1	110465		52*	0	0		
1031	115	Potter	T	1	11767	Paris	83*	3	2		
1032	594	Pulbaum	Frank	2	2168	Paris	15	0	8		
1033	534	Quick	Jane	2	26360		26*	0	0		
1034	536	Quick	P M	2	26360		26*	0	0		
1035	535	Quick	W F	2	26360		26*	0	0		
1036	1032	Radef	Abrandre	3	349223		7	17	11		
1037	918	Solvang	Lena	3	65305		8	2	3		
1038	1111	Raihid	Razi	3	2629		7	4	7		
1039	796	Reed	George	3	362316		7	5	0		
1040	514	Reeves	David	2	17248		10	10	0		
1041	1056	Rekic	Tido	3	349249		7	17	11		Austrian
1042	624	Remesch		CC	47		2*	0	0		
1043	526	Renouf	L	2	31027		21*	0	0		
1044	525	Renouf	P H	2	31027		21*	0	0		
1045	39	Ruechin	J J P	1	19972	Comp	13	0	0		see L'pool C
1046	456	Reynaldo	E	2	230434		13	0	0		
1047	705	Reynolds	Harold	3	342684		8	1	0		
1048	189	Rheims	George	1	17607	Paris	39	12	0		
1049	1275	Rice	Albert	3	382652		29*	2	6		
1050	1278	Rice	Arthur	3	382652		29*	2	6		
1051	1277	Rice	Eric	3	382652		29*	2	6		
1052	1279	Rice	Eugene	3	382652		29*	2	6		
1053	1276	Rice	George	3	382652		29*	2	6		
1054	1274	Rice	Margaret	3	382652		29*	2	6		
1055	584	Richard	Emile	2	2133	Paris	15	0	11		
1056	543	Richards	E	2	29106		18*	15	0		
1057	545	Richards	S G	2	29106		18*	15	0		
1058	544	Richards	W R	2	29106		18*	15	0		
1059	404	Ridsdale	Lucy	2	14258		10	10	0		
1060	861	Penula	Samni	3	3101295		39*	13	9		
1061	223	White's Manservant		1	17760		135*	12	8		
1062	841	Rinkamaki	Natti	3	3101273		7	2	6		
1063	1235	Reordan	Hannah	3	334915		7	14	5		
1064	666	Pisien	Emma	3	364498		14*	10	0		
1065	665	Pisien	Samuel	3	364498		14*	10	0		
1066	212	Astor's Valet		1	17757		247*	10	6		
1067	301	Robert	E W	1	24160		211*	6	9		
1068	753	Robins	Alex	3	3337		14*	10	0		
1069	754	Robins	Charley	3	3337		14*	10	0		
1070	167	Roebling	W A	1	17590	London	50	9	11		
1071	477	Rogers	Harry	2	28004		10	10	0		
1072	802	Rogers	John	3	23567		8	1	0		
1073	248	Rolmane	E	1	111428		26	11	0		
1074	902	Rummveldt	K P	3	312993		7	15	6		
1075	61	Rood	Hugh R	1	113767	London	50	0	0	5	Restaurant Rebate
1076	880	Rosblom	Helene	3	370129		20*	4	3		
1077	882	Rosblom	Salli	3	370129		20*	4	3		
1078	881	Rosblom	Viktor	3	370129		20*	4	3		
1079	202	Rosenbaum		1	17612	Paris	27	14	5		
1080	165	Thorn	G	1	17585	Paris	79*	4	0		
1081	261	Ross	J H	1	13049		40	2	6		
1082	710	Roth	Sarah	3	342712		8	1	0		
1083	235	Rothes		1	110152		86*	10	0		
1084	184	Rothschild		1	17603	Paris	59*	8	0		
1085	183	Rothschild	M	1	17603	Paris	59*	8	0		
1086	785	Rowse	Henry	3	3594		8	1	0		

Master No	Old No	Surname	First Name	Class	Contract Ticket	Continental Ticket	£	Ocean Fare s	d	Refunds	Remarks
1087	81	Rowe	Alfred	1	113790		26	11	0		
1088	524	Rugg	Emily	2	31026		10	10	0		
1089	746	Rush	George	3	20589		8	1	0		
1090	1283	Ryan	Edward	3	383162		7	15	0		
1091	1291	Ryan	Patrick	3	371110		24*	3	0		
1092	190	Ryerson	A	1	17608	Paris	262*	7	6		
1093	191	Ryerson		1	17608	Paris	262*	7	6		
1094	192	Ryerson		1	17608	Paris	262*	7	6		
1095	193	Ryerson		1	17608	Paris	262*	7	6		
1096	195	Ryerson		1	17608	Paris	262*	7	6		
1097	1155	Saad	Amin	3	2671		7	4	7		
1098	1156	Saad	Khalil	3	2672		7	4	6		
1099	1160	Massr	Saad	3	2676		7	4	6		
1100	40	Saalfeld	A	1	19988		30	10	0		
1101	1262	Sadler	Matthew	3	367655		7	14	7		
1102	1323	Sadowitz		3	1588	16997	7	11	10		
1103	649	Sather	Simon	3	3101262		7	5	0		
1104	693	Sage	Annie	3	2343		69*	11	0		
1105	699	Sage	William	3	2343		69*	11	0		
1106	701	Sage	Constance	3	2343		69*	11	0		
1107	698	Sage	Dorothy	3	2343		69*	11	0		
1108	696	Sage	Douglas	3	2343		69*	11	0		
1109	700	Sage	Ada	3	2343		69*	11	0		
1110	697	Sage	Fredrk	3	2343		69*	11	0		
1111	695	Sage	George	3	2343		69*	11	0		
1112	692	Sage	John	3	2343		69*	11	0	8	
1113	694	Sage	Stella	3	2343		69*	11	0		
1114	702	Sage	Thomas	3	2343		69*	11	0		
1115	142	Aubert's Maid		1	17477	Paris	69*	6	0	4	Restaurant Rebate
1116	1090	Salander	Carl	3	7266			12	0		
1117	894	Salkfilvik	Anna	3	343120		7	13	0		
1118	245	Salomon	A L	1	111162		26	0	0		
1119	867	Salonin	Werner	3	3101296		7	18	6		
1120	1139	Elias	Samaan	3	2662		21*	13	7		
1121	1138	Hanna	Samaan	3	2662		21*	13	7		
1122	1140	Youssef	Samaan	3	2662		21*	13	7		
1123	833	Sandstrom	Agnes E	3	9549		16*	14	0		
1124	835	Sandstrom	Irene	3	9549		16*	14	0		
1125	834	Sandstrom	Ruth	3	9549		16*	14	0		
1126	995	Jubs	Sop	3	345768		9	10	0		Belgium
1128	711	Sawyer	Fredk	3	342826		8	1	0		
1129	1227	Scanlon	James	3	36209		7	14	6		
1130	319	Schabert	P	1	13236		57*	15	0		
1131	1005	Jean	Scherlench	3	345779		9	10	0		
1132	415	Smith	A	2	248659		13	0	0		
1133	1031	Sdyeof	Todor	3	349222		7	17	11		
1134	396	Sedgwick	E F	2	244361		13	0	0		
1135	88	Carter's Maid		1	113798		31*	0	0		
1136	84	Seward	Fred. K	1	113794		26	11	0		
1137	394	Sharpe	Percival	2	244358		26*	0	0		
1138	1302	Shaughnessy	Patrick	3	370374		7	15	0		
1139	1108	Youssef	Braukim	3	2627		14*	9	2		
1140	726	Shellard	Frederick	3	6212		15*	2	0		
1141	454	Shelley	J	2	230433	London	26*	0	0		
1142	1208	Shine	Ellen	3	330968		7	12	7		
1143	712	Shorney	Charles	3	374910		8	1	0		
1144	164	Shutes	E W	1	17582	London	153*	9	3		
1145	618	Silven	L	2	250652		13	0	0		
1146	139	Silverthorne		1	17475	London	26	5	9		
1147	270	Silvey	A M	1	13507		55*	18	0		
1148	269	Silvey	W B	1	13507		55*	18	0		
1149	653	Simmons	John	3	392082		8	1	0		
1150	264	Simonius	O A	1	13213	London	35	10	0		
1151	487	Sincock	Maude	2	33112		36*	15	0		
1152	614	Sinkkonen	A	2	250648		13	0	0		
1153	1153	Arsen	Sirayamen	3	2669		7	4	7		
1154	661	Scroter	Maurice	3	392092		8	1	0		

Who Sailed on Titanic?

Master No	Old No	Surname	First Name	Class	Contract Ticket	Continental Ticket	£	s	d	Refunds	Remarks
1155	1058	Sivic	Kusen	3	349251		7	17	11		Austrian
1156	846	Sihvola	Antle	3	3101280		7	18	6		
1157	877	Goblom	Anna	3	3101265		6	9	11		
1158	452	Sjostedt	G	2	237442		13	10	0		
1159	976	Skoog	Anna	3	347088		27*	18	0		
1160	979	Skoog	Earald	3	347088		27*	18	0		
1161	977	Skoog	Carl	3	347088		27*	18	0		
1162	978	Skoog	Mabel	3	347088		27*	18	0		
1163	980	Skoog	Margaret	3	347088		27*	18	0		
1164	975	Skoog	William	3	347088		27*	18	0		
1165	1023	Stabenof	Petco	3	349214		7	17	11		
1167	1311	Slayter	H M	2	234818		12	7	0		
1168	498	Slemen	R J	2	28206		10	10	0		
1169	655	Slocovski	Selman	3	392086		8	1	0		
1170	78	Sloper	W J	1	113788		35	10	0		
1171	83	Smart	John M	1	113792		26	11	0		
1172	1083	Mili	Smiljamic	3	315037		8	13	3		Austrian
1173	228	Clinch Smith	J	1	17764	Paris	30	13	11		
1175	343	Smith	L P	CC	13695		60*	0	0		
1176	510	Smith	M	2	31418		13	0	0		
1177	344	Smith		CC	13695		60*	0	0		
1178	19	Smith	R W	1	113056	London	26	0	0		
1179	1284	Smith	Thomas	3	384461		7	15	0		†

†Note reads transferred from *Cymric* 7 April Withdrawn

Master No	Old No	Surname	First Name	Class	Contract Ticket	Continental Ticket	£	s	d	Refunds	Remarks
1180	1237	Smyth	Julia	3	335432		7	14	8		
1181	291	Snyder	J	1	21228		82*	5	4		
1182	292	Snyder		1	21228		82*	5	4		
1183	569	Sobey	Hayden	2	29178		13	0	0		
1184	898	Soholt	Peter	3	348124		7	13	0		
1185	714	Somerton	Francis	3	18509		8	1	0		
1186	720	Waslfspector		3	3236		8	1	0		
1187	5	O'Speddon	F	1	16966		*134	10	0		
1188	6	O'Speddon		1	16966		*134	10	0		
1189	7	O'Speddon	R	1	16966		*134	10	0		
1190	156	Spencer		1	17569	Paris	146*	10	5		
1191	155	Spencer	W A	1	17569	Paris	146*	10	5		
1192	729	Skinner	Henry	3	369942		8	1	0		
1193	265	Stahelin	M	1	13214		30	10	0		
1194	1017	Stanef	Ivan	3	349208		7	17	11		
1195	1091	Stankovic	Yovan	3	349239		8	13	9		Austrian
1196	687	Harknett	Amy	3	2314		7	11	0		
1197	801	Stanley	E R	3	45380		8	1	0		
1198	597	Stanton	S W	2	237734	Paris	15	0	11		
1199	54	Stead	W T	1	113514		26	11	0		
1200	124	Stengal		1	11778	Paris	55*	8	10		
1201	123	Stengal	C E H	1	11778	Paris	55*	8	10		
1202	309	Stepenson	W B	1	36947		78*	5	4		
1203	321	Stevens	G	CC	50	S to C			0		
1204	187	Stewart	A	1	17605	Paris	27	14	5		
1205	384	Stokes	Phillip J	2	13540		10	10	0		
1206	55	Stone	G M	1	113572		80*	0	0		
1208	1014	Stoytchof	Julia	3	349205		7	17	11		
1209	1089	Stranberg	Ida	3	7553			5	0		
1210	853	Stranden	Julio	3	3101288		7	18	6		
1211	144	Strauss	S	1	17483	London	221*	15	7		
1212	146	Strauss		1	17483	London	221*	15	7		
1213	1067	Ivan	Strilic	3	315083		8	13	3		
1214	970	Strom	Elma	3	347084		10*	9	3		
1215	971	Strom	Selma	3	347084		10*	9	3		
1216	657	Sunderland	Victor F	3	292089		8	1	0		
1217	837	Sundmam	Johan	3	3101269		7	18	6		
1218	651	Sutehall	Henry	3	392076		7	1	0		USC
1220	311	Sullon	F	1	36963		32	6	5		
1222	931	Ivernson	Johan	3	347060		7	15	6		
1223	1340	Svenson		3	7538	114028	9	4	6		
1224	922	Svennon	Olaf	3	350035		7	15	11		
1225	425	Swane	George	2	248734		13	0	0		
1226	556	Sweet	George	2	220845		65*	0	0		

White Star Line Contract Ticket List

Master No	Old No	Surname	First Name	Class	Contract Ticket	Continental Ticket	Ocean Fare £	s	d	Refunds	Remarks
1227	136	Swift	F J	1	17466	Soton	25	18	7		
1228	238	Taussig	E	1	110413		79*	13	0		
1229	240	Taussig	R	1	110413		79*	13	0		
1230	239	Taussig	E	1	110413		79*	13	0		
1231	41	Taylor	E J	1	19996		52*	0	0		
1232	42	Taylor		1	19996		52*	0	0		
1232	1171	Tannous	Thomas	3	2684		7	4	6		
1233	368	Taylor	P E	2	250654	Bandsmen					
1234	920	Torgling	Gunnar	3	350033		7	15	11		
1235	125	Thayer	J B	1	17421		110*	17	8		
1236	128	Thayer	J B jnr	1	17421		110*	17	8		
1237	126	Thayer		1	17421		110*	17	8		
1238	741	Theobald	Thomas	3	363294		8	1	0		
1239	1106	Assad	Thomas	3	2625		8*	10	4		
1240	1101	Thomas	Charles	3	2621		6	8	9		
1241	1168	Thomas	John	3	2681		6	8	9		
1243	1105	Taman	Thomas	3	2625		8*	10	4		
1244	778	Thomson	Alex	3	32302		8	1	0		
1245	166	Thorn		1	17585	Paris	79*	4	0		
1246	782	Thorneycroft	Kate	3	376564		16*	2	0		
1247	781	Thorneycroft	Percival	3	376564		16*	2	0		
1248	858	Tikkanen	Juho	3	3101293		7	18	6		
1249	1281	Tobin	Roger	3	383121		7	15	0		
1250	1025	Todorof	Lalio	3	349216		7	17	11		
1251	667	Tomlin	Ernest	3	364499		8	1	0		
1252	381	Toomey	Ellen	2	13531		10	10	0		
1253	670	Tober	Ernest	3	364511		8	1	0		
1254	1157	Torfa	Assad	3	2673		7	4	7		
1256	1113	Toufik	Nahil	3	2641		7	4	7		
1257	1119	Yousef	Georges	3	2650		15*	4	11		
1258	1117	Yousef	Hamine	3	2650		15*	4	11		
1259	1118	Yousef	Marian	3	2650		15*	4	11		
1260	630	Tovey		CC	516		2*	0	0		
1261	652	Trembisky	Beck	3	392078		8	1	0		
1262	468	Troupiansky	M A	2	233639		13	0	0		
1263	622	Trant	G	2	240929		1	10	0		
1264	479	Troutt	E C	2	34218		10	10	0		
1265	231	Tucker	G M	1	2543	Paris	28	10	9		
1266	1054	Turcui	Stefan	3	349247		7	17	11		Austrian
1267	1335	Turja		3	4138	111991	9	16	10		
1268	1338	Turkula		3	4134	43138	9	11	9		
1269	563	Turpin	D A	2	11668		21*	0	0		
1270	562	Turpin	W J	2	11668		21*	0	0		
1271	182	Uruchuotu	M R	1	17601	Paris	27	14	5		
1272	1077	Tero	Uze	3	315093		8	13	3		
1274	674	Billmard	A von	3	851		14*	10	0		
1275	675	Billmard	James	3	851		14*	10	0		
1276	676	Billmard	Walter	3	851		14*	10	0		
1277	1006	Joseph	Pande	3	345780		9	10	0		
1278	1008	Leo	Steen	3	345783		9	10	0		
1279	256	Van der Hoef	W A	1	111240	London	33	10	0		
1280	1001	Catherine	Van Impe	3	345773		24*	3	0		
1281	999	Jacob	Van Impe	3	345773		24*	3	0		
1282	1000	Rosalie	Van Impe	3	345773		24*	3	0		
1283	1003	Philma	Melkeluk	3	345777		9	10	0		
1284	997	Nestor	Vande	3	345770		9	10	0		
1285	994	Victor	Perprufssi	3	345765		9	0	0		
1286	992	Augusta	Vander	3	345764		18*	0	0		
1287	990	Emnhie	Vander	3	345763		18*	0	0		
1288	991	Jubs	Vander	3	345763		18*	0	0		
1289	993	Lion	Vander	3	345764		18*	0	0		
1290	1130	David	Vartanian	3	2658		7	4	6		
1291	503	Veale	James	2	28221		13	0	0		
1292	893	Wendall	Olaff	3	350416		7	17	1		
1293	887	Vestrom	Hulda	3	350406		7	17	1		
1294	1059	Vork	Janko	3	349252		7	17	11		Austrian
1295	1009	Achille	Waelens	3	345767		9	0	0		
1296	377	Walcroft	Nellie	2	13528		21*	0	0		

Master No	Old No	Surname	First Name	Class	Contract Ticket	Continental Ticket	£	s	d	Refunds	Remarks
1297	312	Walker	W A	1	36967		34	0	5		
1298	205	Cardeza's Maid		1	17755	Paris	512*	6	7		
1299	462	Ware	F L	2	31352		21*	0	0		
1300	762	Ware	Fred	3	359309		8	1	0		
1301	461	Ware	J J	2	31352		21*	0	0		
1302	575	Ware	W J	2	28666		10	10	0		
1303	284	Warren		1	110813	Paris	75*	5	0		
1304	744	Warren	Charles	3	49867		7	11	0		
1305	283	Warren	F M	1	110813	Paris	75*	5	0		
1306	437	Watson	E	2	239856						A/C H&W
1307	559	Watt	Mrs	2	33595	London	15*	15	0		
1308	560	Watt	Miss	2	33595		15*	15	0		
1309	647	Webber	James	3	3101316		8	1	0		USC
1310	515	Webber	Susie	2	27267		13	0	0		
1311	90	Weir	J	1	113800		26	11	0		
1312	516	Weisz	L	2	228414		26*	0	0		
1313	517	Weisz	M	2	228414		26*	0	0		
1314	537	Wells	A D	2	29103		23*	0	0		
1315	538	Wells	J	2	29103		23*	0	0		
1316	539	Wells	R L	2	29103		23*	0	0		
1317	490	West	E M	2	33112		27*	15	0		
1318	492	West	B J	2	33112		27*	15	0		
1319	491	West	E M	2	33112		27*	15	0		
1320	489	West	E A	2	33112		27*	15	0		
1321	1175	Chahini	Georges	3	2688		7	4	7		
1322	567	Wheadon	E H	2	24579		10	10	0		
1323	589	Wheeler	E	2	2159	Port. Southampton	12	17	6		
1324	221	White	J S	1	17760		135*	12	8		
1325	299	White	P W	1	35281		77*	5	9		
1326	300	White	R F	1	35281		77*	5	9		
1327	305	Wick	G D	1	36928		164*	17	4		
1328	306	Wick		1	36928		164*	17	4		
1329	307	Wick	M	1	36928		164*	17	4		
1330	935	Wichelgn	Charles	3	347064		7	15	0		
1331	47	Widener		1	113503		211*	10	0		
1332	46	Widener	G	1	113503		211*	10	0		
1333	48	Widener	H	1	113503		211*	10	0		
1334	878	Wickland	Karl	3	3101266		6	9	11		
1335	879	Wickland	Jakob	3	3101267		6	9	11		
1336	385	Wilhelm	Charles	2	244270		13	0	0		
1337	777	Wilkes	Ellen	3	363272		7	0	0		CSV
1340	85	Willard	Constance	1	113795		26	11	0		
1341	1191	Abi	Weller	3	3410		8	14	3		Russe
1342	633	Willey	Edward	3	751		7	11	0		
1343	176	Williams	D	1	17597	Paris	61*	7	7		
1344	400	Williams	C	2	244373		13	0	0		
1345	800	Williams	Harry	3	2466		8	1	0		
1346	748	Williams	Leslie	3	54636		16*	2	0		
1347	177	Williams	R M	1	17597	Paris	61*	7	7		
1348	53	Williams	F F L	1	113510		35	0	0		
1350	8	O'Speddon's Maid		1	16966		*134	10	0		
1351	648	Windilow	Einai	3	3101317		7	5	0		
1352	1065	Albert	Wirz	3	315154		8	13	3		
1353	747	Wiseman	Philip	3	34244		7	5	0		
1354	998	Tomble	Wille	3	345771		9	10	0		
1355	339	Wotten	H	CC	86	S to C	1	10	0		
1358	369	Woodward	J W	2	250654	Bandsmen					
1360	31	Woolner	F	1	19947		35	10	0		
1361	97	Wright	G	1	113807		26	11	0		
1362	551	Wright	Marion	2	220844		13	10	0		
1363	1131	Yazbeck	Antoni	3	2659		14*	9	1		
1364	1132	Yazbeck	Silem	3	2659		14*	9	1		
1365	224	Young	M	1	17760		135*	12	8		
1366	1114	Wazli	Yousif	3	2647		7	4	6		
1367	1172	Gerious	Youssouf	3	2685		7	4	7		
1368	431	Yroies	H	3	248747						
1369	1144	Labour	Hiliem	3	2665		14*	9	1		
1370	1143	Labour	Tamine	3	2665		14*	9	1		

White Star Line Contract Ticket List

Master No	Old No	Surname	First Name	Class	Contract Ticket	Continental Ticket	£	Ocean Fare s	d	Refunds	Remarks
1371	1128	Mapre	Zacharian	3	2656		7	4	6		
1372	1154	Artin	Lakarian	3	2670		7	4	6		
1373	1066	Leo	Zumcreman	3	3	315082		7	17	6	
	see 315	Colley		1	5727	17387	19	11	9		
	see 316	Chaffee		1	5734	11947	39*	3	6		
	see 316	Chaffee		1	5734	11947	39*	3	6		
	see 622	Trout		2	240929	11030	11	12	0		
	see 621	Hunt		2	1585	49642	10	15	6		
	see 806	Braund		3	3460	67062	6	10	11		
	see 804	Lockyer		3	12222	111280	7	12	7		
	see 1088	Hellstrom		3	7548	103135	8	14	3		
	see 1089	Strandberg		3	7553	115626	9	11	9		
	see 1086	Johanson		3	7540	4940	8	8	1		
	see 1087	Ahlin		3	7546	3611	9	4	6		
	see 1085	Osen		3	7534	36144	8	19	4		
	see 1084	Gonnestad		3	8471	50035	8	2	11		

Also shown on Cross Channel sheets, cargo plus dogs

Meanwell 5.00	1 Canary	
Noel 5.00 2 Cycles		
E West 7.00	8 Cases	
E West 10.00	1 Crated Cycle	
Dulbes 1.19.7	1 Dog	868
Harper 1.19.7	1 Dog	869

Refunds also given for the following unnamed passengers:

345776	10	11	6	9
Rejected, probably Emma Duynejouck				
345782	11	1	6	10
Rejected, probably Henri Vander Steeen				
242154	29			27

Board of Trade Passenger Lists fc
Southampton & Queenstown

Master No	Old No	Surname	First Name	Class	Occupation	Sex/ Status	Age	Country of which a citizen
1	551	Abbing	Anthony	3	Blacksmith	M/U	42	USA
2	547	Abbott	Eugene	3	Scholar	M/U	13	USA
3	545	Abbott	Rosa	3	Wife	F/U	36	USA
4	546	Abbott	Rossmore	3	Jeweller	M/U	16	USA
5	784	Abelseth	Karen	3	F/U		16	Norwegian
6	781	Abelseth	Olais	3		M/U	25	Norwegian
9	899	Abrahamson	August	3		M/U	20	Finns
11	635	Adahl	Maurits	3		M/U	30	Denmark
12	84	Adams	John	3	Farm Labr	M/U	26	British
13	643	Aklin	Johanna	3		F/U	40	Sweden
14	927	Ahmed	Ali	3		M/U	24	Syrian
15	571	Aks	Filly	3	Infant	FI	8m	Russia
16	570	Aks	Leah	3	Wife	F/U	21	Russia
18	367	Aldworth	Chas	2		M/U	30	British
19	40	Alexander	William	3	Gen Labr	M/U	23	British
20	902	Jussila	Ilmari	3		M/U	20	Finns
21	928	Ali	William	3		M/U	25	Syrian
22	462	Allen	Miss E W	1		F/U	/	USA
23	106	Allen	William	3	Toolmaker	M/U	35	British
24	144	Allison	Miss	1		FC	/	British
25	143	Allison	Mrs	1		F/A	/	British
26	142	Allison	H J	1		M/A	/	British
27	145	Allison	Master	1		MI	/	British
28	4	Allum	Owen G	3	Gardener	M/U	18	British
29	618	Andersen	Albert	3		M/U	33	Norway
30	854	Andersen	Carta	3		M/U	19	Dane
31	417	Anderson	H	1		M/U	/	USA
32	746	Anderson	Alfrida	3		F/A	40	Sweden
33	745	Anderson	Anders	3		M/A	39	Sweden
34	852	Wennertion	August	3		M/U	28	Dane
35	749	Anderson	Ebba	3		FC	6	Sweden
36	751	Anderson	Ellis	3		MC	2	Sweden
37	896	Anderson	Erna	3		F/U	17	Finns
38	766	Andersson	Tala Auguste	3		M/U	38	Sweden
39	748	Anderson	Ingeborg	3		FC	9	Sweden
40	730	Andersen	Samuel	3		M/U	26	Sweden
41	747	Anderson	Sigrid	3		FC	11	Sweden
42	750	Anderson	Sigvard	3		MC	4	Sweden
43	769	Andreasan	Paul Edvin	3		M/U	20	Sweden
45	313	Andrew	Edgar	2		M/U	16	British
47	176	Andrews	Thos	1		M/U	/	British
48	786	Angheloff	Muika	3		M/U	26	Bulgarian
49	305	Angle	Mary	2		F/A	32	British
50	304	Angle	Wm	2		M/A	34	British
51	384	Appleton	E D	1		F/U	/	USA
52	821	Arnold	Josef	3		M/A	25	Switzerland
53	822	Arnold	Josephine	3		F/A	24	Switzerland
54	842	Aranstan	Ernst Axel	3		M/U	24	Sweden
56	498	Ashby	John	2		M/U	57	USA
57	926	Asim	Adola	3		M/U	35	Syrian
58	736	Asplund	Carl	3		MC	5	Sweden
59	732	Asplund	Charles	3		M/A	40	Sweden
60	735	Asplund	Gustaf	3		MC	9	Sweden
61	738	Asplund	Felix	3		MC	3	Sweden
62	734	Asplund	Oscar	3		MC	11	Sweden
63	860	Asplund	Johan	3		M/U	23	Dane
64	737	Asplund	Lillian	3		FC	5	Sweden
65	733	Asplund	Selma	3		F/A	37	Sweden
68	925	Assam	Ali	3		M/U	23	Syrian

Key

Sex/Status
M/U — Male unaccompanied by wife
M/A —Male accompanied by wife
F/U — Female unaccompanied by husband
F/A — Female accompanied by husband

MC— Male child
FC — Female child
MI — Male infant
FI — Female infant

Ticket Numbers
F denotes partially or wholly illegible

Last Permanent Residence	Ticket No	Embarked	UK port of arrival	Steamship Line
England	5547	S		
England	2673	S		
England	2673	S		
England	2673	S		
	348125	S	Newcastle	Norwegian SS Co
	348122	S	Newcastle	Norwegian SS Co
	3101284	S	Hull	Finland SS Co
	7076	S	Harwich	United SS Co
England	341826	S		
	7546	S	Hull	Wilson Line
	3101311	S	Southampton	RM SP Co
England	392091	S		
England	392091	S		
England	248744	S		
England	3474	S		
	3101287	S	Hull	Finland SS Co
	3101312	S	Southampton	RM SP Co
Foreign Countries	24160	S		
England	373450	S		
England	113871	S		
England	113781	S		
England	113781	S		
England	113871	S		
England	f223	S		
	4001	S	Newcastle	Norwegian SS co
	350046	S	Harwich	United SS Co
Foreign Countries	19952	S		
	347082	S	Hull	Wilson Line
	347082	S	Hull	Wilson Line
	350043	S	Harwich	United SS Co
	347082	S	Hull	Wilson Line
	347082	S	Hull	Wilson Line
	3101281	S	Hull	Finland SS Co
	347091	S	Hull	Wilson Line
	347082	S	Hull	Wilson Line
	347075	S	Hull	Wilson Line
	347082	S	Hull	Wilson Line
	347082	S	Hull	Wilson Line
	347466	S	Harwich	United SS Co
England	231945	S		
England	112050	S		
	349202	S	Southampton	L&SW Rly Co
England	226875	S		
England	226875	S		
Foreign Countries	11769	S		
	349237	S	Southampton	L&SW Rly Co
	349237	S	Southampton	L&SW Rly Co
	349911	S	Harwich	United SS Co
England	244346	S		
	3101310	S	Southampton	RM SP Co
	347077	S	Hull	Wilson Line
	347077	S	Hull	Wilson Line
	347077	S	Hull	Wilson Line
	347077	S	Hull	Wilson Line
	347077	S	Hull	Wilson Line
	350054	S	Harwich	United SS Co
	347077	S	Hull	Wilson Line
	347077	S	Hull	Wilson Line
	3101309	S	Southampton	RM SP Co

Master No	Old No	Surname	First Name	Class	Occupation	Sex/ Status	Age	Country of which a citizen
73	771	Augustan	Albert	3		M/U	23	Sweden
76	891	Backstom	Karl	3		M/A	32	Finns
77	892	Backstom	Marie	3		F/A	33	Finns
82	65	Badman	Emily	3	Servant	F/U	18	British
84	265	Bailey	Percy	2		M/U	18	British
85	276	Baimbrigge	Chas R	2		M/U	23	British
86	830	Balkic	Cerin	3		M/U	26	Austria
87	248	Balls	Ada	2		F/U	36	British
88	289	Banfield	Frederick	2		M/U	28	British
92	179	Barkworth	A H	1		M/U	/	British
93	930	Barry	Julia	3	Spinster	F/U	27	British
94	83	Barton	David	3	Gen Labr	M/U	22	British
95	195	Bateman	Robert	2		M/U	52	British
97	398	Baxter	James	1		F/U	/	USA
98	399	Baxter	Quigg	1		M/U	/	USA
100	499	Beane	Edward	2		M/A	27	USA
101	500	Beane	Ethel	2		F/A	22	USA
103	338	Beauchamp	Hy J	2		M/U	28	British
104	82	Beavan	William	3	Gen Labr	M/U	19	British
105	311	Becker	Marion	2		FC	4	British
106	309	Becker	Alice	2		F/U	40	British
107	312	Becker	Richard	2		MC	1	British
108	310	Becker	Ruth	2		F/U	12	British
109	378	Beckwith	R C	1		M/A	/	USA
110	379	Beckwith	Mrs	1		F/A	/	USA
111	341	Beesley	Lawrence	2		M/U	26	British
113	722	Bensen	John	3		M/U	26	Sweden
114	245	Bentham	Lilian	2		F/U	19	British
115	631	Bergland	Ivar	3		M/U	20	Finland
116	247	Berriman	Wm	2		M/U	23	British
120	596	Lee	Bing	3	Seaman	M/U	32	China
121	150	Bird	Ellen	1		F/U		British
122	662	Birkiland	Hans	3		M/U	21	Norway
127	765	Bjorklund	Ernst	3		M/U	18	Sweden
128	370	Bjornstrom	H	1		M/U	/	Sweden
129	377	Blackwell	S W	1		M/U	/	USA
131	467	Bonnell	Caroline	1		F/U	/	USA
132	141	Bonnell	Lily	1		F/U	/	British
134	146	Borebank	J J	1		M/U	/	British
135	808	Bostandyeff	Guentcho	3		M/U	26	Bulgarian
136	532	Botzford	W Hull	2		M/U	30	USA
141	984	Bourke	Cath	3	H Wife	F/A	32	British
142	983	Bourke	John	3	Farmer	M/A	40	British
143	982	Burke	Mary	3	Spinster	F/U	30	British
144	80	Bowen	David	3	Pugilist	M/U	26	British
146	531	Bowenur	Solomon	2		M/U	42	USA
147	157	Bowerman	E	1		F/U	/	British
148	536	Bracken	Jas H	2		M/U	27	USC
149	978	Bradley	Brgt	3	Spinster	F/U	21	British
150	489	Brayton	Geo	1		M/U	/	USA
151	441	Brady	John B	1		M/U	/	USA
152	774	Braf	Elin Ester	3		F/U	20	Sweden
153	359	Brailey	J	2		M/U	24	British
156	37	Braund	Lewis	3	Farm Labr	M/U	29	British
157	57	Braund	Owen	3	Ironmonger	M/U	22	British
159	534	Breicoux	R	2		M/U	28	French
160	510	Brito	Jose de	2		M/U	40	Portugal
161	853	Brobek	Cauk	3		M/U	22	Dane
162	100	Brocklebank	William	3	Groom	M/U	35	British
163	348	Brown	Mildred	2		F/U	24	British
164	383	Brown	J M	1		F/U	/	USA
165	366	Brown	Eliz	2		F/U	18	British
166	365	Brown	Eliza	2		F/A	40	British
168	364	Brown	Tom	2		M/A	45	British
170	615	Brejhe	Dagmar	2		F/U	20	Swedish
171	614	Brejhe	Curt	2		M/U	25	Swedish
172	936	Buckley	Daniel	3	FarmLabr	M/U	a	British
173	929	Buckley	Kath	3	Spinster	F/U	20	British

Last Permanent Residence	Ticket No	Embarked	UK port of arrival	Steamship Line
	347468	S	Harwich	United SS Co
	3101278	S	Hull	Finland SS Co
	3101278	S	Hull	Finland SS Co
England	31416	S		
England	29108	S		
England	31030	S		
	349248	S	Southampton	L&SW Rly Co
England	28551	S		
England	34068	S		
England	27042	S		
Ireland	30884	Q		
England	324669	S		
England	1166	S		
Foreign Countries	17558	S		
Foreign Countries	17558	S		
England	2908	S		
England	2908	S		
England	244358	S		
England	323951	S		
England	230136	S		
England	230136	S		
England	230136	S		
England	230136	S		
Foreign Countries	11751	S		
Foreign Countries	11751	S		
England	248698	S		
	347068	S	Hull	Wilson Line
England	28404	S		
	4348	S	Hull	Finnish SS Co
England	28425	S		
England	1601	S		
England	19483	S		
	312992	S	Newcastle	Norwegian SS co
	347090	S	Hull	Wilson Line
Foreign Countries	110564	S		
Foreign Countries	113784	S		
Foreign Countries	36928	S		
England	113783	S		
England	110489	S		
	349224	S	Southampton	L&SW Rly Co
England	237670	S		
Ireland	364849	Q		
Ireland	364849	Q		
Ireland	364848	Q		
England	54636	S		
England	211535	S		
England	113505	S		
England	220367	S		
Ireland	334914	Q		
Foreign Countries	111427	S		
Foreign Countries	113054	S		
	347471	S	Harwich	United SS Co
England	250653	S		
England	3460	S		
England	21171	S		
England	250654	S		
Foreign Countries	244360	S		
	350045	S	Harwich	United SS Co
England	364512	S		
England	248733	S		
Foreign Countries	11769	S		
England	29750	S		
England	29750	S		
England	29750	S		
	236853	S	Hull	Wilsons
	236853	S	Hull	Wilsons
Ireland	30920	Q		
Ireland	29944	Q		

Who Sailed on Titanic?

Master No	Old No	Surname	First Name	Class	Occupation	Sex/ Status	Age	Country of which a citizen
175	989	Burke	Jeremiah	3	Agr Labr	M/U	19	British
176	167	Burns	Eliz M	1		F/U	/	British
177	939	Burns	Mary	3	Spinster	F/U	18	British
178	238	Buss	Kate	2		F/U	36	British
179	316	Butler	Reg	2		M/U	25	British
180	440	Butt	A	1		M/U	/	USA
181	337	Byles	Thos	2		M/U	43	British
182	613	Bejstrom	Karolina	2		F/U	42	Swedish
183	674	Cacic	Gego	3		M/U	18	Austria
184	672	Cacac	Luka	3		M/U	38	Austria
185	670	Calic	Manda	3		F/U	21	Austria
186	667	Cacic	Maria	3		F/U	30	Austria
188	395	Calderhead	E P	1		M/U	/	USA
189	526	Caldwell	Albert Frances	2		M/A	26	USA
190	528	Caldwell	Alden G	2		MI	9m	USA
191	527	Caldwell	Sylvia M	2		F/A	26	USA
192	669	Calic	Peter	3		M/U	17	Austria
193	206	Cameron	Clear	2		F/U	31	British
194	327	Campbell	Wm	2		M/U	21	British
195	981	Canavan	Mary	3	Spinster	F/U	21	British
196	987	Cannivan	Pat	3	Gen Labr	M/U	21	British
198	16	Cann	Ernest	3	Miners Labr	M/U	21	British
201	246	Carbines	Wm	2		M/U	19	British
204	126	Garfirth	John	3	Shoemaker	M/U	?	British
206	851	Carlssan	August	3		M/U	28	Dane
207	870	Carlson	Carl	3		M/U	24	Dane
208	1004	Carr	Janie	3	Spinster	F/U	37	British
209	491	Carran	F M	1		M/U	/	USA
210	492	Carran	J P	1		M/U	/	USA
211	333	Carter	Ernest	2		M/A	54	British
212	334	Carter	Lilian	2		F/A	44	British
213	432	Carter	L	1		F/U	/	USA
214	431	Carter	Mrs	1		F/A	/	USA
215	430	Carter	William	1		M/A	/	USA
216	433	Carter	W T	1		MC	/	USA
217	580	Carver	Albert	3	Seaman	M/U	28	USA
218	405	Case	Howard B	1		M/U	/	USA
220	153	Cavendish	Mrs	1		F/A	/	British
221	152	Cavendish	F W	1		M/A	/	British
222	556	Celotti	Francesco	3	Stoker	M/U	24	Italiga
223	376	Chaffee	Mrs	1		F/A	/	USA
224	375	Chaffee	Herbert F	1		M/A	/	USA
225	494	Chambers	Mrs	1		F/A	/	USA
226	493	Chambers	N G	1		M/A	/	USA
227	347	Chapman	Chas	2		M/U	25	British
228	253	Chapman	John	2		M/A	30	British
229	254	Chapman	Eliza	2		F/A	28	British
230	951	Charten	David	3	Gen Labr	M/U	21	British
232	181	Cherry	Gladys	1		F/U	/	British
234	156	Chibnall	E M	1		F/U	/	British
235	594	Chang	Chip	3	Seaman	M/U	32	China
236	177	Chisholm	Robert	1		M/U	/	British
237	557	Christman	Emil	3	Clerk	M/U	29	Germany
238	320	Christy	Alice	2		F/U	40	British
239	321	Christy	Juli	2		F/U	25	British
242	198	Clarke	Ada	2		F/A	28	British
243	197	Clarke	Chas V	2		M/A	29	British
246	357	Clarke	F C	2		M/U	30	British
248	447	Clifford	Geo Q	1		M/U	/	USA
249	923	Coelho	Donigos	3		M/U	20	Portuguese
250	41	Cohen	Gurshon	3	Compositor	M/U	19	British
251	1030	Colbert	Pat	3	Gen Labr	M/U	24	British
252	794	Coleff	Peyo	3		M/U	36	Bulgarian
253	793	Coleff	Satis	3		M/U	24	Bulgarian
254	217	Coleridge	Reginald	2		M/U	29	British
255	617	Collander	Erik	2		M/U	28	Finland
256	240	Collett	Stuart	2		M/U	24	British
257	151	Colley	E P	1		M/U	/	British

Last Permanent Residence	Ticket No	Embarked	UK port of arrival	Steamship Line
Ireland	365222	Q		
England	16966	S		
Ireland	30963	Q		
England	27849	S		
England	234686	S		
Foreign Countries	113050	S		
England	244310	S		
	236852	S	Hull	Wilsons
	315091	S	Southampton	LSW Ry Co
	815089	S	Southampton	LSW Ry Co
	815087	S	Southampton	LSW Ry Co
	815084	S	Southampton	LSW Ry Co
Foreign Countries	17476	S		
England	248738	S		
England	248738	S		
England	248738	S		
	815086	S	Southampton	LSW Ry Co
England	13528	S		
Ireland	239853	S		
Ireland	364846	Q		
Ireland	364858	Q		
England	f2122	S		
England	28424	S		
England	358585	S		
	350042	S	Harwich	United SS Co
	350409	S	Harwich	United SS Co
Ireland	368364	Q		
Foreign Countries	113059	S		
Foreign Countries	113059	S		
England	244252	S		
England	244252	S		
Foreign Countries	113760	S		
Foreign Countries	113760	S		
Foreign Countries	113760	S		
Foreign Countries	113760	S		
England	370160	S		
Foreign Countries	19924	S		
England	19877	S		
England	19877	S		
British Possessions	343275	S		
Foreign Countries	5734	S		
Foreign Countries	5734	S		
Foreign Countries	113806	S		
Foreign Countries	113806	S		
Scotland	248731	S		
England	29037	S		
England	29037	S		
Ireland	A513032	Q		
England	110152	S		
England	113505	S		
England	1601	S		
England	112051	S		
England	343276	S		
England	237789	S		
England	237789	S		
England	2003	S		
England	2003	S		
England	250653	S		
Foreign Countries	110468	S		
	3101307	S	Southampton	RM SP Co
England	3540	S		
Ireland	371109	Q		
	349210	S	Southampton	L&SW Rly Co
	349209	S	Southampton	L&SW Rly Co
England	14268	S		
	248740	S	Hull	Finnish SS Co
England	28034	S		
Ireland	5727	S		

Who Sailed on Titanic?

Master No	Old No	Surname	First Name	Class	Occupation	Sex/ Status	Age	Country of which a citizen
259	281	Collyer	Charlotte	2		F/A	31	British
260	280	Collyer	Harvey	2		M/A	32	British
261	282	Collyer	Marjorie	2		FC	8	British
265	952	Conlin	Thomas H	3	Gen Labr	M/U	31	British
266	979	Connaghton	Michl	3	Farm Labr	M/U	31	British
267	942	Connolly	Kate	3	Spinster	F/U	30	British
268	1022	Connolly	Kate	3	Spinster	F/U	22	British
269	959	Connor	Pat	3	Farm Labr	M/U	a	British
270	588	Cook	Jacob	3	Carpenter	M/U	43	Russian
271	218	Rogers	Selina	2		F/U	20	British
272	814	Cor	Bartol	3		M/U	35	Austria
273	813	Cor	Ivan	3		M/U	27	Austria
274	815	Cor	Ludovik	3		M/U	19	Austria
275	497	Corbett	Irene C	2		F/U	30	USA
276	211	Corey	Phyllis	2		F/U	30	British
277	569	Corn	Henry	3	Upholsterer	M/U	30	Russia
278	385	Cornell	R C	1		F/U	/	USA
279	1003	Corr	Ellen	3	Spinster	F/U	16	British
280	264	Cotterill	Harry	2		M/U	20	British
281	69	Coutts	Leslie	3	Child	MC	3	British
282	68	Coutts	William	3	Child	MC	9	British
283	67	Coutts	Winnie	3	Wife	F/U	36	British
284	562	Coxon	Daniel	3	Gn. Dealer	M/U	59	USA
285	481	Crafton	John B	1		M/U	/	USA
287	38	Crease	Ernest J	3	Tinsmith	M/U	19	British
288	104	Cribb	John	3	Butler	M/U	44	British
289	105	Cribb	Alice	3	Shop Asst	F/U	16	British
290	148	Crosby	Mrs	1		F/A	/	British
291	147	Crosby	Ed G	1		M/A	/	British
295	326	Cunningham	Alf	2		M/U	21	British
297	130	Dahl	Charles	3	Carpenter	M/U	45	British
298	645	Dahlberg	Gerda	3		F/U	22	Sweden
299	812	Dakie	Branko	3		M/U	19	Austria
300	1009	Daly	Eugene	3	Agr Labr	M/U	29	British
301	1038	Daly	Marcella	3	HKeeper	F/U	30	USA
302	172	Daly	P D	1		M/U	/	British
303	742	Danborn	Sigrid	3		F/A	27	Sweden
304	741	Danborn	Ernest	3		M/A	34	Sweden
305	743	Danborn	Gillbert	3		FC	4	Sweden
306	474	Daniel	Robt W	1		M/U	/	USA
308	803	Danoff	Joto	3		M/U	27	Bulgarian
309	787	Danbuhoff	Christo	3		M/U	25	Bulgarian
310	137	Davidson	Mr	1		M/A	/	British
311	138	Davidson	Mrs	1		F/A	/	British
312	75	Davies	Alfred	3	Caster	M/U	24	British
313	224	Davies	Charles	2		M/U	21	British
314	283	Davis	Agnes	2		F/U	49	British
315	64	Davies	Evan	3	Miner	M/U	22	British
317	286	Davis	John	2		MC	8	British
318	76	Davies	John	3	Ironworker	M/U	21	British
319	77	Davis	Joseph	3	Ironworker	M/U	17	British
321	319	Davis	Mary	2		F/U	24	British
322	115	Davison	Mary	3	Wife	F/A	32	British
323	114	Davison	Thomas	3	Blacksmith	M/A	32	British
325	702	de Messemaeker	Emma	3		F/A	36	USA
326	701	de Messemaeker	Guillaume	3		M/A	36	USA
327	706	de Mulder	Theodor	3		M/U	30	Belgium
328	709	de Pelsmaker	Alfons	3		M/U	17	Belgium
329	222	Deacon	Percy	2		M/U	20	British
330	18	Dean	Bertram	3	Farmer	M/A	25	British
331	20	Dean	Bertram	3	Child	MC	2	British
332	21	Dean	Vera	3	Infant	FI	2m	British
333	19	Dean	Hetty	3	Wife	F/A	31	British
336	832	Delalic	Regzo	3		M/U	25	Austria
337	823	Dimitri	Marinko	3		M/U	23	Turkey
338	275	Denborny	Herbert	2		M/U	25	British

Last Permanent Residence	Ticket No	Embarked	UK port of arrival	Steamship Line
England	31921	S		
England	31921	S		
England	31921	S		
Ireland	21332	Q		
Ireland	335097	Q		
Ireland	30972	Q		
Ireland	370373	Q		
Ireland	370369	Q		
England	3536	S		
England	14266	S		
	349230	S	Southampton	L&SW Rly Co
	349229	S	Southampton	L&SW Rly Co
	349231	S	Southampton	L&SW Rly Co
England	232749	S		
England	13534	S		
England	392090	S		
Foreign Countries	11770	S		
Ireland	367231	Q		
England	29107	S		
England	37671	S		
England	37671	S		
England	37671	S		
England	364500	S		
Foreign Countries	113791	S		
England	3464	S		
England	371362	S		
England	371362	S		
British Possession	5735	S		
British Possession	5735	S		
Ireland	239853	S		
England	7598	S		
	7552	S	Hull	Wilson Line
	349228	S	Southampton	L&SW Rly Co
Ireland	382651	Q		
Ireland	382650	Q		
England	113055	S		
	347080	S	Hull	Wilson Line
	347080	S	Hull	Wilson Line
	347080	S	Hull	Wilson Line
Foreign Countries	113804	S		
	349219	S	Southampton	L&SW Rly Co
	349203	S	Southampton	L&SW Rly Co
British Possession	12750	S		
British Possession	12750	S		
England	48871	S		
England	14879	S		
England	33112	S		
Wales	23568	S		
England	33112	S		
England	48871	S		
England	48873	S		
England	237668	S		
England	386525	S		
England	386525	S		
	345772	S	Harwich	GE Ry Co
	345772	S	Harwich	GE Ry Co
	345774	S	Harwich	GE Ry Co
	345718	S	Harwich	GE Ry Co
England	14879	S		
England	2315	S		
England	2315	S		
England	2315	S		
England	2315	S		
	349250	S	Southampton	L&SW Rly Co
	349238	S	Southampton	L&SW Rly Co
England	31029	S		

Who Sailed on Titanic?

Master No	Old No	Surname	First Name	Class	Occupation	Sex/ Status	Age	Country of which a citizen
339	809	Denkoff	Mito	3		M/U	30	Bulgarian
340	58	Dennis	Samuel	3	Farmer	M/U	23	British
341	61	Dennis	William	3	Farmer	M/U	26	British
342	2	Dugemin	Joseph	3	Stone Mason	M/U	24	British
343	937	Devany	Margt	3	Spinster	F/U	19	British
344	225	Dibden	Wm	2		M/U	19	British
345	442	Dick	A A	1		M/A	/	USA
346	443	Dick	Mrs	1		F/A	/	USA
347	816	Mirko	Dika	3		M/U	17	Austria
348	671	Dimic	Jovan	3		M/U	42	Austria
349	810	Dintiheff	Valtcho	3		M/U	43	Bulgarian
350	456	Dodge	Mrs	1		F/A	/	USA
351	457	Dodge	W	1		MC	/	USA
352	455	Dodge	W	1		M/A	/	USA
356	986	Donohue	Brgt	3	Spinster	F/U	20	British
357	1027	Dooley	Pat	3	Gen Labr	M/U	32	British
358	55	Dorkings	Edward	3	Groom	M/U	19	British
360	400	Douglas	F C	1		F/U	/	USA
362	101	Dowdell	Elizabeth	3	Housekeeper	F/U	27	British
363	518	Downton	William J	2		M/U	54	USA
364	1005	Doyle	Eliz	3	Spinster	F/U	24	British
366	502	Drew	Lulu T	2		F/A	29	USA
367	503	Drew	Marshall B	2		MC	8	USA
368	501	Drew	James V	2		M/A	30	USA
369	963	Driscoll	Brgt	3	Spinster	F/U	27	British
370	567	Drapkin	Jenie	3	Box Maker	F/U	23	Russia
376	954	Divan	Frank	3	Agr Labr	M/U	65	British
377	726	Dyker	Adolph	3		M/A	23	Sweden
378	727	Dyker	Elizabeth	3		F/A	22	Sweden
381	673	Ecimovic	Toso	3		M/U	17	Austria
382	843	Edvarosler	Austoy	3		M/U	18	Sweden
384	729	Eklund	Hans	3		M/U	16	Sweden
385	715	Ekstrom	Johan	3		M/U	46	Sweden
390	550	Elsbury	James	3	Farmer	M/U	47	USA
391	102	Emanuel	Ethel	3	Child	FC	5	British
393	616	Enander	Ingvar	2		M/U	21	Swedish
395	922	Goncalves	Manoel	3		M/U	38	Portuguese
396	469	Eustis	E M	1		F/U	/	USA
399	44	Everett	Thomas	3	Craneman	M/U	36	British
402	612	Fahlstrom	Arne T	2		M/U	28	Norwegian
403	1002	Farrell	James	3	Agr Labr	M/U	26	British
404	149	Farthing	John	1		M/U	/	British
405	200	Fannthorpe	Lizzie	2		F/A	35	British
406	199	Fannthorpe	Harry	2		M/A	40	British
407	228	Fillbrook	Chas	2		M/U	19	British
408	924	Finole	Luigi	3		M/U	41	Italian
409	850	Pirctur	Clerhard	3		M/U	19	Dane
411	988	Fleming	Nora	3	Spinster	F/U	21	British
414	985	Flynn	James	3	Gen Labr	M/U	27	British
415	1017	Flynn	John	3	Agr Labr	M/U	42	British
416	393	Flynn	J T	1		M/U	/	USA
417	933	Foley	Joseph	3	Agr Labr	M/U	19	British
418	991	Foley	Wm	3	Farm Labr	M/U	20	British
419	593	Cheong	Foo	3	Seaman	M/U	32	China
420	5	Ford	Arthur	3	Carpenter	M/U	22	British
421	50	Ford	Daisy	3	Servant	F/U	21	British
422	51	Ford	Ernest	3	Blacksmith	M/U	18	British
423	49	Ford	Margaret	3	Wife	F/U	48	British
424	53	Ford	Maggie	3	Child	FC	9	British
425	52	Ford	William	3	Messenger	M/U	16	British
427	495	Forman	Mr	1		M/A	/	Austria
428	496	Forman	Mrs	1		F/A	/	Austria
429	414	Fortune	Alice	1		F/U	/	USA
430	416	Fortune	Charles	1		M/U	/	USA
431	413	Fortune	Ethel	1		F/U	/	USA
432	415	Fortune	Mabel	1		F/U	/	USA
433	411	Fortune	Mark	1		M/A	/	USA
434	412	Fortune	Mrs	1		F/A	/	USA

Last Permanent Residence	Ticket No	Embarked	UK port of arrival	Steamship Line
	349225	S	Southampton	L&SW Rly Co
England	21172	S		
England	21175	S		
England	752	S		
Ireland	30958	Q		
England	14879	S		
Foreign Countries	17474	S		
Foreign Countries	17474	S		
	349232	S	Southampton	L&SW Rly Co
	815088	S	Southampton	LSW Ry Co
	349226	S	Southampton	L&SW Rly Co
Foreign Countries	33638	S		
Foreign Countries	33638	S		
Foreign Countries	33638	S		
Ireland	364856	Q		
Ireland	370376	Q		
England	10482	S		
Foreign Countries	17558	S		
England	364516	S		
England	28403	S		
Ireland	368702	Q		
England	28220	S		
England	28220	S		
England	28220	S		
Ireland	14311	Q		
England	392083	S		
Ireland	336439	Q		
	347072	S	Hull	Wilson Line
	347072	S	Hull	Wilson Line
	315090	S	Southampton	LSW Ry Co
	349912	S	Harwich	United SS Co
	347074	S	Hull	Wilson Line
	347061	S	Hull	Wilson Line
England	3902	S		
England	364516	S		
	236854	S	Hull	Wilsons
	3101306	S	Southampton	RM SP Co
Foreign Countries	36947	S		
England	6212	S		
	236171	S	Hull	Wilsons
Ireland	367232	Q		
Foreign Countries	19483	S		
England	2926	S		
England	2926	S		
England	15185	S		
	3101308	S	Southampton	RM SP Co
	350036	S	Harwich	United SS Co
Ireland	364859	Q		
Ireland	364851	Q		
Ireland	368323	Q		
Foreign Countries	17474	S		
Ireland	30910	Q		
Ireland	365235	Q		
England	1601	S		
England	f178	S		
England	6608	S		
England	6608	S		
England	6608	S		
England	6608	S		
England	6608	S		
Foreign Countries	85	S		
Foreign Countries	85	S		
Foreign Countries	19950	S		
Foreign Countries	19950	S		
Foreign Countries	19950	S		
Foreign Countries	19950	S		
Foreign Countries	19950	S		
Foreign Countries	19950	S		

Who Sailed on Titanic?

Master No	Old No	Surname	First Name	Class	Occupation	Sex/ Status	Age	Country of which a citizen
435	1025	Fox	Pat	3	Gen Labr	M/U	26	British
436	530	Fox	Stanley H	2		M/U	30	USA
438	122	Franklin	Charles	3	Carpenter	M/U	38	British
439	162	Franklin	T P	1		M/U	/	British
448	535	Funk	Annie	2		F/U	37	USC
449	475	Futrelle	J	1		M/A	/	USA
450	476	Futrelle	Mrs	1		F/A	/	USA
452	249	Gale	Harry	2		M/U	38	British
453	250	Gale	Shadrack	2		M/U	33	British
454	974	Gallagher	Martin	3	Agr Labr	M/U	25	British
455	332	Garside	Ethel	2		F/U	24	British
457	272	Gavey	Lawrence	2		M/U	26	British
458	183	Gee	Arthur	1		M/U	/	British
463	424	Seiger	Amelia	1		F/U	/	Germany
465	504	Gilbert	William	2		M/U	45	USA
466	241	Giles	Edgar	2		M/U	21	British
467	242	Giles	Fred	2		M/U	22	British
468	343	Giles	Ralph	2		M/U	22	British
469	553	Gilinsky	Leslie	3	Locksmith	M/U	22	Russia
470	315	Gill	John	2		M/U	24	British
471	205	Gillespie	Wm	2		M/U	34	British
472	969	Gilnagh	Katie	3	Spinster	F/U	18	British
473	598	Givard	Hans	2		M/U	30	Denmark
474	980	Glynn	Mary	3	Spinster	F/U	19	British
478	94	Goldsmith	Emily	3	Wife	F/A	31	British
479	93	Goldsmith	Frank	3	Turner	M/A	33	British
480	95	Goldsmith	Frank	3	Child	MC	9	British
481	877	Goldsmith	Nathan	3		M/U	41	Russian
482	8	Goodwin	Augusta	3	Wife	F/A	43	British
483	10	Goodwin	Charles	3	Scholar	M/U	14	British
484	7	Goodwin	Frederick	3	Engr Labr	M/A	42	British
485	13	Goodwin	Harold	3	Child	MC	9	British
486	12	Goodwin	Jessie	3	Child	FC	10	British
487	9	Goodwin	Lillian	3	Servant	F/U	16	British
488	14	Goodwin	Sidney	3	Child	MC	2	British
489	11	Goodwin	William	3	Child	MC	11	British
490	438	Gracie	Archibald	1		M/U	/	USA
491	401	Graham	Wm G	1		F/U	/	USA
492	175	Graham	Mr	1		M/U	/	British
493	402	Graham	M	1		F/U	/	USA
494	62	Green	George	3	Farrier	M/U	40	British
495	529	Greenberg	Samuel	2		M/U	25	Russia
498	648	Gronnestaf	Daniel	3		M/U	32	Norway
499	109	Guest	Robert	3	Gen Labr	M/U	23	British
501	647	Gustafsen	Alfred	3		M/U	20	Sweden
503	890	Gustafson	Johan	3		M/U	28	Finns
504	723	Gustafssen	Gideon	3		M/U	19	Sweden
506	820	Haas	Alaisia	3		F/U	24	Bulgaria
507	656	Hagland	Ingvald	3		M/U	28	Norway
508	657	Hagland	Konrad	3		M/U	20	Norway
509	894	Hakkwainen	Elin	3		F/A	27	Finns
510	893	Hakkwainen	Pekka	3		M/A	28	Finns
511	353	Hale	Reg	2		M/U	30	British
512	603	Hamatainen	Wiljo	2		MI	6m	Finnish
513	602	Hamatainen	Anna	2		F/U	32	Finnish
514	698	Mampe	Leon	3		M/U	20	Belgium
517	845	Hansen	Claus	3		M/A	41	Dane
518	844	Futel	Henric	3		M/U	26	Dane
519	861	Hansen	Henry	3		M/U	21	Dane
520	846	Hansen	Jenny	3		F/A	40	Dane
521	539	Harbeck	Wm	2		M/U	30	USC
524	958	Hargardon	Kate	3	Spinster	F/U	17	British
525	54	Harknett	Alice	3	Servant	F/U	21	British
526	564	Harmer	Abraham	3	Jeweller	M/U	25	Russia
527	346	Harper	Nina	2		FC	6	British
529	344	Harper	John	2		M/U	28	British
531	485	Harrington	Chas	1		M/U	/	USA
532	505	Harris	George	2		M/U	30	USA

138

Last Permanent Residence	Ticket No	Embarked	UK port of arrival	Steamship Line
Ireland	368573	Q		
England	229236	S		
England	3101314	S		
England	113778	S		
England	237671	S		
Foreign Countries	113803	S		
Foreign Countries	113803	S		
England	28664	S		
England	28664	S		
Ireland	36864	Q		
England	243880	S		
England	31028	S		
England	11320	S		
Foreign Countries	113503	S		
England	30769	S		
England	28133	S		
England	28134	S		
England	248726	S		
England	14973	S		
England	233866	S		
Ireland	12233	S		
Ireland	35851	Q		
	250646	S	Southampton	RM SP Co
Ireland	335677	Q		
England	363291	S		
England	363291	S		
England	363291	S		
	3101263	S	Soton	UC SS Co
England	2144	S		
England	2144	S		
England	2144	S		
England	2144	S		
England	2144	S		
England	2144	S		
England	2144	S		
England	2144	S		
Foreign Countries	113780	S		
Foreign Countries	17582	S		
England	112053	S		
Foreign Countries	17582	S		
England	21440	S		
Foreign Countries	250645	S		
	8471	S	Hull	Wilson Line
England	376563	S		
	7554	S	Hull	Wilson Line
	3101277	S	Hull	Finland SS Co
	347069	S	Hull	Wilson Line
	349236	S	Southampton	L&SW Rly Co
	65303	S	Hull	Wilson Line
	65304	S	Hull	Wilson Line
	3101279	S	Hull	Finland SS Co
	3101279	S	Hull	Finland SS Co
England	250653	S		
	250649	S	Hull	Finnish SS Co
	250649	S	Hull	Finnish SS Co
	345769	S	Harwich	GE Ry Co
	350026	S	Harwich	United SS Co
	350025	S	Harwich	United SS Co
	350059	S	Harwich	United SS Co
	350026	S	Harwich	United SS Co
England	248746	S		
Ireland	Aa330631	Q		
England	6609	S		
England	374887	S		
England	248727	S		
England	248727	S		
Foreign Countries	113796	S		
England	752	S		

Who Sailed on Titanic?

Master No	Old No	Surname	First Name	Class	Occupation	Sex/ Status	Age	Country of which a citizen
533	373	Harris	Henry B	1		M/A	/	USA
534	214	Harris	Walter	2		M/U	30	British
535	374	Harris	Mrs	1		F/A	/	USA
536	133	Harrison	W H	1		M/U	/	British
537	208	Hart	Benjamin	2		M/A	30	British
538	209	Hart	Esther	2		F/A	29	British
539	210	Hart	Eva	2		FC	6	British
540	950	Hart	Henry	3	Gen Labr	M/U	28	British
541	358	Hartley	Wm	2		M/U	31	British
544	168	Hawksford	W J	1		M/U	/	British
545	134	Hays	Chas M	1		M/A	/	British
546	135	Hays	Mrs	1		F/A	/	British
548	169	Head	C	1		M/U	/	British
549	1024	Healy	Nora	3	Spinster	F/U	a	British
550	764	Hadman	Oskar	3		M/U	27	Sweden
551	595	Ling	Slee	3	Seaman	M/U	24	China
552	990	Hegarty	Nora	3	Spinster	F/U	20	British
553	897	Hakkinen	Saina	3		F/U	26	Finns
554	905	Heininen	Wendla	3		F/U	23	Finns
555	644	Hillstrom	Hilda	3		F/U	21	Sweden
556	825	Hendekovic	Ignaz	3		M/U	28	Austria
557	756	Henrikssos	Jenny	3		F/U	28	Sweden
558	1008	Henery	Delia	3	Spinster	F/U	23	British
559	301	Herman	Alice	2		F/U	24	British
560	299	Herman	Jane	2		F/A	48	British
561	300	Herman	Kate	2		F/U	24	British
562	298	Herman	Samuel	2		M/A	49	British
563	342	Hewlett	Mary	2		F/U	29	British
564	219	Hickman	Leonard	2		M/U	24	British
565	220	Hickman	Lewis	2		M/U	32	British
566	221	Hickman	Stanley	2		M/U	20	British
567	387	Hilliard	H H	1		M/U	/	USA
568	604	Hiltunen	M	2		F/U	28	Finnish
569	174	Hipkins	W E	1		M/U	/	British
570	452	Hippach	J	1		F/U	/	USA
571	451	Hippach	T	1		F/U	/	USA
572	919	Hervonen	Helga	3		F/U	22	Finns
573	920	Hervonen	Hildwe	3		FC	2	Finns
574	259	Hocking	Eliza	2		F/U	53	British
575	260	Hocking	Nellie	2		F/U	20	British
576	258	Hocking	Geo	2		M/U	21	British
578	350	Hodges	Hy P	2		M/U	50	British
580	507	Hold	Annie	2		F/A	36	USA
581	506	Hold	Stephen	2		M/A	42	USA
583	634	Holm	John	3		M/U	43	Denmark
584	620	Holten	Johan	3		M/U	28	Norway
585	472	Holverson	O A	1		M/A	/	USA
586	473	Holverson	Mrs	1		F/A	/	USA
587	488	Haven	H	1		M/U	/	USA
588	898	Honkonen	Eluma	3		F/U	27	Finns
589	223	Hood	Ambrose	2		M/U	22	British
590	1028	Horgan	John	3	Gen Labr	M/U	a	British
591	508	Hosono	Masatumi	2		M/U	32	Japan
592	230	Howard	Benj	2		M/A	63	British
593	231	Howard	Ellen	2		F/A	60	British
594	70	Howard	May	3	Laundrymaid	F/U	27	British
595	409	Hoyt	F M	1		M/A	/	USA
596	410	Hoyt	Mrs	1		F/A	/	USA
598	780	Humblen	Adolf O	3		M/U	42	Norwegian
599	354	Hume	J	2		M/U	28	British
600	196	Hunt	Geo	2		M/U	30	British
601	39	Hyman	Abraham	3	Framemaker	M/U	34	British
602	429	Icard	Miss	1		F/U	/	USA
603	226	Ilett	Bertha	2		F/U	17	British
604	804	Ylieff	Ylio	3		M/U	32	Bulgarian
605	884	Kmakangas	Ida	3		F/U	27	Finns
606	885	Ilmakangas	Pista	3		F/U	25	Finns
608	132	Ismay	J Bruce	1		M/U	/	British

Last Permanent Residence	Ticket No	Embarked	UK port of arrival	Steamship Line
Foreign Countries	36973	S		
England	14208	S		
Foreign Countries	36973	S		
England	112059	S		
England	13529	S		
England	13529	S		
England	13529	S		
Ireland	F	Q		
England	250653	S		
England	16988	S		
British Possession	12749	S		
British Possession	12749	S		
England	113038	S		
Ireland	370375	Q		
	347089	S	Hull	Wilson Line
England	1601	S		
Ireland	365226	Q		
	3101282	S	Hull	Finland SS Co
	3101290	S	Hull	Finland SS Co
	7548	S	Hull	Wilson Line
	349243	S	Southampton	L&SW Rly Co
	347086	S	Hull	Wilson Line
Ireland	382649	Q		
England	220845	S		
England	220845	S		
England	220845	S		
England	220845	S		
England	248706	S		
England	14879	S		
England	14879	S		
England	14879	S		
Foreign Countries	17463	S		
	250650	S	Hull	Finnish SS Co
England	680	S		
Foreign Countries	111361	S		
Foreign Countries	111361	S		
	3101298	S	Hull	Finland SS Co
	3101298	S	Hull	Finland SS Co
England	29105	S		
England	29105	S		
England	29104	S		
England	250643	S		
England	26707	S		
England	26707	S		
	7075	S	Harwich	United SS Co
	4001	S	Newcastle	Norwegian SS co
Foreign Countries	113789	S		
Foreign Countries	113789	S		
Foreign Countries	111426	S		
	3101283	S	Hull	Finland SS Co
England	14879	S		
Ireland	370377	Q		
Foreign Countries	237798	S		
England	24065	S		
England	24065	S		
England	39186	S		
Foreign Countries	19943	S		
Foreign Countries	19943	S		
	348121	S	Newcastle	Norwegian SS Co
England	250653	S		
England	1585	S		
England	3470	S		
Foreign Countries	113752	S		
England	14885	S		
	349220	S	Southampton	L&SW Rly Co
	3101270	S	Hull	Finland SS Co
	3101271	S	Hull	Finland SS Co
England	112058	S		

Who Sailed on Titanic?

Master No	Old No	Surname	First Name	Class	Occupation	Sex/ Status	Age	Country of which a citizen
609	785	Joanoff	Kouis	3		M/U	20	Bulgarian
610	331	Jacobsohn	Amy	2		F/A	34	British
611	330	Jacobsohn	Sydney	2		M/A	40	British
613	848	Jansson	Carl	3		M/U	22	Dane
614	921	Jardin	Jose	3		M/U	21	Portuguese
615	318	Jarvis	John	2		M/U	47	British
616	273	Jefferys	Clifford	2		M/U	24	British
617	274	Jefferys	Ernest	2		M/U	22	British
618	509	Jenkin	Stephen	2		M/U	32	USA
619	857	Genen	Peter	3		M/U	21	Dane
620	856	Jenim	Withn	3		M/U	48	Dane
621	855	Jenim	Iven	3		M/U	17	Dane
622	965	Jerymin	Annie	3	Spinster	F/U	22	British
624	659	Johanneson	Bernt	3		M/U	29	Norway
625	660	Johannessen	Elias	3		M/U	23	Norway
626	878	Johnson	Jakob	3		M/U	34	Finns
627	858	Johansson	Erik	3		M/U	20	Dane
628	641	Johansen	Gustaf	3		M/U	33	Sweden
629	717	Johnson	Carl	3		M/U	32	Sweden
630	770	Johansan	Nils	3		M/U	30	Sweden
631	724	Johanson	Oscar	3		M/U	26	Sweden
632	576	Johnson	Alfred	3	Seaman	M/U	49	Sweden
633	777	Jahnson	Eleanaia	3		FI	11	Sweden
634	775	Jahnson	Elis	3		F/U	29	Sweden
635	776	Jahnson	Harald	3		MC	4	Sweden
636	716	Johnsson	Malkolm	3		M/U	30	Sweden
637	578	Johnson	William	3	Seaman	M/U	19	USA
638	45	Johnston	Albert	3	Plumber	M/A	34	British
639	48	Johnston	Carrie	3	Child	FC	8	British
640	46	Johnston	Lily	3	Wife	F/A	34	British
641	47	Johnston	William	3	Child	MC	9	British
642	369	Jones	C C	1		M/U	/	USA
643	788	Yonkoff	Lazoi	3		M/U	23	Bulgarian
644	873	Jansen	Carl	3		M/U	25	Dane
645	869	Jonsson	Neils	3		M/U	26	Dane
649	171	Julian	H F	1		M/U	/	British
650	901	Jussila	Eirukc	3		M/U	32	Finns
651	628	Jussila	Katriina	3		F/U	20	Finland
652	629	Jussila	Mari	3		F/U	21	Finland
653	888	Kallia	Mikolai	3		M/U	17	Finns
654	649	Kalvig	Johannes	3		F/U	21	Norway
655	543	Kantor	Miriam	2		F/A	24	Russian
656	542	Kantor	Schua	2		M/A	34	Russian
657	828	Karajic	Milan	3		F/U	30	Austria
658	859	Karlsson	Ejnar	3		M/U	21	Dane
659	768	Carlsan	Julius	3		M/U	33	Sweden
660	862	Karlnon	Pelskey	3		M/U	22	Dane
661	212	Karnes	Jessie	2		F/U	28	British
666	966	Keane	Andy	3	Agr Labr	M/U	23	British
667	1035	Keane	Danl	2	Gent	M/U	35	British
668	1034	Keane	Nora A	2	Spinster	F/U	35	British
669	81	Keefe	Arthur	3	Farmer	M/U	39	British
670	158	Keeping	E H	1		M/U	/	British
671	934	Keely	James	3	Agr Labr	M/U	44	British
672	962	Kelly	Annie K	3	Spinster	F/U	18	British
673	303	Kelly	Florence	2		F/U	45	British
674	97	Kelly	James	3	Painter	M/U	19	British
675	964	Kelly	Mary	3	Spinster	F/U	22	British
676	1007	Kennedy	John	3	Farm Labr	M/U	21	British
678	388	Kenyon	F R	1		M/A	/	USA
679	389	Kenyon	Mrs	1		F/A	/	USA
682	997	Kiernan	John	3	Gen Labr	M/U	25	British
683	999	Kiernan	Philip	3	Gen Labr	M/U	20	British
684	975	Kilgannon	Thos	3	Agr Labr	M/U	21	British
685	381	Kimball	E N	1		M/A	/	USA
686	382	Kimball	Mrs	1		F/A	/	USA
687	684	Kink	Anton	3		M/A	29	Austria
688	685	Kink	Louise	3		F/A	26	Austria

Board of Trade Passenger Lists for Southampton & Queenstown

Last Permanent Residence	Ticket No	Embarked	UK port of arrival	Steamship Line
	349201	S	Southampton	L&SW Rly Co
England	243847	S		
England	243847	S		
	350034	S	Harwich	United SS Co
	3101305	S	Southampton	RM SP Co
England	237565	S		
England	31029	S		
England	31029	S		
England	33111	S		
	350050	S	Harwich	United SS Co
	350048	S	Harwich	United SS Co
	350047	S	Harwich	United SS Co
Ireland	14313	Q		
	65306	S	Hull	Wilson Line
	312988	S	Newcastle	Norwegian SS co
	3101264	S	Hull	Finland SS Co
	350052	S	Harwich	United SS Co
	7540	S	Hull	Wilson Line
	347063	S	Hull	Wilson Line
	347467	S	Harwich	United SS Co
	347070	S	Hull	Wilson Line
England	370160	S		
	347472	S	Harwich	United SS Co
	347472	S	Harwich	United SS Co
	347472	S	Harwich	United SS Co
	347062	S	Hull	Wilson Line
England	370160	S		
Scotland	6607	S		
Scotland	6607	S		
Scotland	6607	S		
Scotland	6607	S		
Foreign Countries	694	S		
	349204	S	Southampton	L&SW Rly Co
	350417	S	Harwich	United SS Co
	350408	S	Harwich	United SS Co
England	113044	S		
	3101286	S	Hull	Finland SS Co
	4136	S	Hull	Finnish SS Co
	4137	S	Hull	Finnish SS Co
	3101274	S	Hull	Finland SS Co
	8475	S	Hull	Wilson Line
England	244368	S		
England	244368	S		
	349246	S	Southampton	L&SW Rly Co
	350053	S	Harwich	United SS Co
	347465	S	Harwich	United SS Co
	350060	S	Harwich	United SS Co
England	13534	S		
Ireland	12460	Q		
Ireland	233734	Q		
Ireland	226593	Q		
England	323592	S		
England	113503	S		
Ireland	30911	Q		
Ireland	9234	Q		
England	223596	S		
Ireland	363592	S		
Ireland	14312	Q		
Ireland	368783	Q		
Foreign Countries	17464	S		
Foreign Countries	17464	S		
Ireland	367227	Q		
Ireland	367229	Q		
Ireland	36865	Q		
Foreign Countries	11753	S		
Foreign Countries	11753	S		
	315153	S	Southampton	LSW Ry Co
	315153	S	Southampton	LSW Ry Co

Who Sailed on Titanic?

Master No	Old No	Surname	First Name	Class	Occupation	Sex/ Status	Age	Country of which a citizen
689	686	Kink	Louise	3		FC	4	Austria
690	682	Kink	Vincenz	3		M/U	27	Austria
691	683	Kink	Maria	3		F/U	22	Austria
692	1037	Kirkland	Chas L	2	Gent	M/U	a	British
693	439	Klaber	Hermann	1		M/U	/	USA
694	866	Klassen	Gertud	3		FC	1	Dane
695	865	Klassen	Hilda	3		F/U	36	Dane
696	864	Klassen	Klas	3		M/U	18	Dane
698	328	Knight	Robt	2		M/U	39	British
701	463	Krenchen	Amelia	1		F/U	/	USA
702	533	Krins	Geo	2		M/U	34	Belgian
703	610	Kvillner	Johan H	2		M/U	31	Swedish
705	606	Lahtinen	Anna	2		F/A	26	USC
706	605	Lahtinen	Wm	2		M/A	30	USC
707	627	Laitinen	Sofia	3		F/U	37	Finland
708	801	Laleff	Kristo	3		M/U	23	Bulgarian
709	590	Ah	Lam	3	Seaman	M/U	38	China
710	592	Len	Lam	3	Seaman	M/U	23	China
711	1047	Lamb	J	2	Gent	M/U	a	USA
712	636	Landegrin	Aurora	3		F/U	23	Denmark
713	967	Lane	Patrick	3	Agr Labr	M/U	17	British
714	591	Fang	Lang	3	Seaman	M/U	26	China
719	642	Larson	Viktor	3		M/U	29	Sweden
720	721	Larson	Bengt	3		M/U	29	Sweden
721	719	Lasson	Edward	3		M/U	22	Sweden
723	435	Lawrence	A	1		M/U	/	USA
724	390	Leader	F A	1		F/U	/	USA
726	621	Lefebre	Frances	3		F/U	39	France
727	624	Lefebre	Henry	3		MC	4	France
728	625	Lefebre	Ida	3		FC	2	France
729	623	Lefebre	Jeanne	3		FC	6	France
730	622	Lefebre	Mathilde	3		FC	11	France
732	907	Sunonen	Antti	3		M/U	32	Finns
733	345	Leitch	Jessie	2		F/U	24	British
735	291	Lancore	Amelia	2		F/U	34	British
736	1019	Lennon	Denis	3	Gen Labr	M/U	21	British
737	1020	Lennon	Mary	3	Spinster	F/U	20	British
738	186	Conyngham	L	1		F/U	/	British
739	188	Conyngham	Master	1		MC	/	British
740	187	Conyngham	Miss	1		FC	/	British
741	189	Conyngham	Miss	1		F/U	/	British
742	579	Leonard	Lionel	3	Seaman	M/U	36	USA
744	74	Lester	James	3	Dipper	M/U	26	British
746	609	Levy	R J	2		M/U	28	USA
749	268	Leyson	Wm R	2		M/U	25	British
750	712	Lierkens	Rene	3		M/U	24	Belgium
751	725	Lindahl	Agda	3		F/U	25	Sweden
752	728	Lindblom	August	3		M/U	45	Sweden
754	840	Lindell	Edvard	3		M/A	36	Sweden
755	841	Lindell	Elin	3		F/A	30	Sweden
756	900	Lindqvist	Eino	3		M/U	32	Finns
758	941	Lenihan	Michl	3	Agr Labr	M/U	21	British
761	597	Lee	Ling	3	Seaman	M/U	28	China
762	707	Wenzel	Zinhart	3		M/U	27	Belgium
763	1046	Lingane	John	2	Gent	M/U	a	USA
764	544	Lithman	Simon	3	Baker	M/U	20	Russia
765	35	Lobb	Cordelia	3	Wife	F/A	26	British
766	34	Lobb	William	3	Engineer	M/A	30	British
767	3	Lockyer	Edward	3	Grocer's Asst	M/U	21	British
768	420	Long	Milton C	1		M/U	/	USA
770	477	Loring	J H	1		M/U	/	USA
771	202	Louch	Alice	2		F/A	42	British
772	201	Louch	Charles	2		M/A	50	British
773	59	Lovell	John	3	Farmer	M/U	20	British
774	107	Lowe	Alfred	3	Fitter	M/U	37	British
775	681	Sulic	Vicola	3		F/U	27	Austria
776	778	Lundall	John	3		M/U	51	Sweden
777	772	Lundin	Olga	3		F/U	23	Sweden

144

Last Permanent Residence	Ticket No	Embarked	UK port of arrival	Steamship Line
	315153	S	Southampton	LSW Ry Co
	315151	S	Southampton	LSW Ry Co
	315152	S	Southampton	LSW Ry Co
Ireland	219533	Q		
Foreign Countries	113028	S		
	350405	S	Harwich	United SS Co
	350405	S	Harwich	United SS Co
	350404	S	Harwich	United SS Co
Ireland	239855	S		
Foreign Countries	24160	S		
England	250654	S		
	18723	S	Hull	Wilsons
	250651	S	Hull	Finnish SS Co
	250651	S	Hull	Finnish SS Co
	4135	S	Hull	Finnish SS Co
	349217	S	Southampton	L&SW Rly Co
England	1601	S		
England	1601	S		
Ireland	240261	Q		
	7077	S	Harwich	United SS Co
Ireland	7935	Q		
England	1601	S		
	7545	S	Hull	Wilson Line
	347067	S	Hull	Wilson Line
	347065	S	Hull	Wilson Line
Foreign Countries	113770	S		
Foreign Countries	17465	S		
	4133	S	Southampton	LSW Ry Co
	4133	S	Southampton	LSW Ry Co
	4133	S	Southampton	LSW Ry Co
	4133	S	Southampton	LSW Ry Co
	4133	S	Southampton	LSW Ry Co
	3101292	S	Hull	Finland SS Co
England	248727	S		
England	34260	S		
Ireland	370371	Q		
Ireland	370371	Q		
England	74	S		
England	74	S		
England	74	S		
England	74	S		
England	370160	S		
England	48871	S		
	2163	S	Newhaven	LB & SE
England	29566	S		
	345781	S	Harwich	GE Ry Co
	347071	S	Hull	Wilson Line
	347073	S	Hull	Wilson Line
	349910	S	Harwich	United SS Co
	349910	S	Harwich	United SS Co
	3101285	S	Hull	Finland SS Co
Ireland	30971	Q		
England	1601	S		
	345775	S	Harwich	GE Ry Co
Ireland	235529	Q		
England	251	S		
England	3336	S		
England	3336	S		
England	f222	S		
Foreign Countries	113501	S		
Foreign Countries	113801	S		
England	3085	S		
England	3085	S		
England	21173	S		
England	373930	S		
	315098	S	Southampton	LSW Ry Co
	347473	S	Harwich	United SS Co
	347469	S	Harwich	United SS Co

Master No	Old No	Surname	First Name	Class	Occupation	Sex/ Status	Age	Country of which a citizen
778	863	Linststrom	Tun	3		M/U	32	Dane
780	819	Lyntakoff	Stanko	3		M/U	44	Bulgaria
781	192	Mack	Mary	2		F/U	30	British
782	72	Mackay	George	3	Butler	M/U	20	British
783	968	Madigan	Maggie	3	Spinster	F/U	a	British
784	461	Nadill	G A	1		F/U	/	USA
785	654	Madsen	Frittjof	3		M/U	22	Norway
786	889	Maenyal	Matti	3		M/U	22	Finns
787	449	Maguire	J E	1		M/U	/	USA
788	946	Mahon	Delia	3	Spinster	F/U	18	British
789	960	Mechan	John	3	Gen Labr	M/U	22	British
790	182	Maioni	R	1		F/U	/	British
791	589	Waisner	Simon	3	Tailor	M/U	34	Russian
792	882	Wakiner	Hallo	3		M/U	29	Finns
799	1045	Mangan	Mary	3	Spinster	F/U	a	USA
801	976	Mannion	Margt	3	Spinster	F/U	24	British
805	797	Markoff	Marin	3		M/U	35	Bulgarian
807	436	Marvin	D W	1		M/A	/	USA
808	437	Marvin	Mrs	1		F/A	/	USA
812	244	Matthews	Wm J	2		M/U	30	British
815	322	Mayberry	Frank	2		M/U	20	British
818	1012	McCarthy	Katie	3	Spinster	F/U	24	British
819	386	McCarthy	T J	1		M/U	/	USA
820	998	McCormack	Thomas	3	Gen Labr	M/U	20	British
821	994	McCoy	Agnes	3	Spinster	F/U	28	British
822	995	McCoy	Alice	3	Spinster	F/U	26	British
823	996	McCoy	Bernard	3	Gen Labr	M/U	24	British
824	363	McCrae	Arthur	2		M/U	33	British
825	314	McCrie	James	2		M/U	20	British
826	948	McDermott	Delia	3	Spinster	F/U	a	British
827	972	McElroy	Michl	3	Farm Labr	M/U	20	British
828	392	McGough	J K	1		M/U	/	USA
829	947	McGovern	Mary	3	Spinster	F/U	20	British
830	945	McGowan	Annie	3	Spinster	F/U	18	British
831	961	McGowan	Cath	3	Spinster	F/U	35	British
832	519	McKane	Peter D	2		M/U	46	USA
833	1021	McMahon	Martin	3	Agr Labr	M/U	20	British
834	113	McNamee	Eileen	3	Wife	F/A	19	British
835	112	McNamee	Neal	3	Provision M	M/A	27	British
836	957	O'Neill	Brgt	3	Spinster	F/U	a	British
837	119	Meanwell	Marian	3	Milliner	F/U	63	British
838	88	Meēk	Annie	3	Wife	F/U	31	British
839	351	Mellinger	Eliz	2		F/U	30	British
840	352	Mellinger	Mary	2		FC	4	British
841	194	Mellers	William	2		M/U	19	British
842	486	Melody	A	1		M/U	/	USA
843	552	Meo	Alfonso	3	Musician	M/U	45	Italy
844	1006	Mornagh	Robert	3	Farm Labr	M/U	26	British
845	520	Meyer	August	2		M/U	30	Germany
848	690	Miatsjo	Carl	3		M/U	22	Norway
849	90	Miles	Frank	3	Engineer	M/U	23	British
850	585	Niles	Fred	3	Clerk	M/U	44	USC
852	600	Milling	Jacob	2		M/U	48	Denmark
853	408	Minehan	Daisy	1		F/U	/	USA
854	407	Minehan	Mrs	1		F/A	/	USA
855	406	Minehan	W E	1		M/A	/	USA
856	817	Museff	Ivan	3		M/U	24	Bulgaria
857	795	Minkoff	Lazas	3		M/U	21	Bulgarian
858	791	Mihoff	Stayliko	3		M/U	28	Bulgarian
859	233	Mitchell	Henry	2		M/U	71	British
860	805	Mitkoff	Mito	3		M/U	23	Bulgarian
862	944	Mocklare	Ellie	3	Spinster	F/U	20	British
863	782	Moen	Sigurd H	3		M/U	25	Norwegian
864	139	Molson	H M	1		M/U	/	British
865	525	Mantvila	Joseph	2		M/U	27	Russia
866	582	Moor	Beile	3	Tailoress	F/U	27	USA
867	583	Moor	Nein	3	Child	FC	7	USA
868	484	Moore	C	1		M/U	/	USA

Last Permanent Residence	Ticket No	Embarked	UK port of arrival	Steamship Line
	350403	S	Harwich	United SS Co
	349235	S	Southampton	L&SW Rly Co
England	3	S		
Scotland	42795	S		
Ireland	370370	Q		
Foreign Countries	24160	S		
	17369	S	Newcastle	Norwegian SS co
	3101275	S	Hull	Finland SS Co
Foreign Countries	110469	S		
Ireland	F	Q		
Ireland	Aa43130	Q		
England	110152	S		
England	2816	S		
	3101268	S	Hull	Finland SS Co
Ireland	364850	Q		
Ireland	36866	Q		
	349213	S	Southampton	L&SW Rly Co
Foreign Countries	113773	S		
Foreign Countries	113773	S		
England	28228	S		
England	239059	S		
Ireland	383123	Q		
Foreign Countries	17463	S		
Ireland	367228	Q		
Ireland	367226	Q		
Ireland	367226	Q		
Ireland	367226	Q		
Scotland	237216	S		
England	233478	S		
Ireland	F	Q		
Ireland	36568	Q		
Foreign Countries	17473	S		
Ireland	F	Q		
Ireland	F	Q		
Ireland	9232	Q		
England	28403	S		
Ireland	370372	Q		
Ireland	376566	S		
Ireland	376566	S		
Ireland	370368	Q		
England	392087	S		
England	343095	S		
England	250644	S		
England	250644	S		
England	751	S		
Foreign Countries	111424	S		
England	11206	S		
Ireland	368703	Q		
Foreign Countries	248723	S		
	345501	S	Newcastle	Norwegian SS Co
England	359306	S		
England	392095	S		
	234360	S	Harwich	United SS Co
Foreign Countries	19928	S		
Foreign Countries	19928	S		
Foreign Countries	19928	S		
	349233	S	Southampton	L&SW Rly Co
	349211	S	Southampton	L&SW Rly Co
	349207	S	Southampton	L&SW Rly Co
England	24580	S		
	349221	S	Southampton	L&SW Rly Co
Ireland	30980	Q		
	348123	S	Newcastle	Norwegian SS Co
England	113787	S		
Foreign Countries	211536	S		
England	392096	S		
England	392096	S		
Foreign Countries	113796	S		

Master No	Old No	Surname	First Name	Class	Occupation	Sex/ Status	Age	Country of which a citizen
869	78	Moore	Leonard	3	Bricklayer	M/U	19	British
870	1033	Moran	Bertha	3	Spinster	F/U	a	British
871	1031	Moran	Danl J	3	Gen Labr	M/U	a	British
872	931	Moran	James	3	Gen Labr	M/U	22	British
873	611	Moraweck	Ernest	2		M/U	30	USA
874	360	Marshall	Henry	2		M/A	33	British
875	99	Morley	William	3	Carpenter	M/U	34	British
876	1026	Morrow	Thos	3	Gen Labr	M/U	30	British
877	661	Moss	Albert	3		M/U	29	Norway
882	584	Moutal	Rahasmin	3	Traveller	M/U	28	Turk
883	193	Mudd	Thos C	2		M/U	28	British
885	970	Mullen	Katie	3	Spinster	F/U	20	British
886	1010	Mulvihill	Bertha E	3	Spinster	F/U	24	British
887	574	Murdlin	Joseph	3	Chemist	M/U	22	Russia
888	1001	Murphy	Kate	3	Spinster	F/U	18	British
889	1000	Murphy	Mary J	3	Spinster	F/U	20	British
890	973	Murphy	Norah	3	Spinster	F/U	32	British
891	739	Myhrman	Oliver	3		M/U	18	Sweden
892	1048	Myles	F T	2	Gent	M/U	a	USA
893	790	Vaiducoff	Penko	3		M/U	22	Bulgarian
898	36	Nancarrow	William	3	Mason	M/U	34	British
899	802	Vankoff	Minko	3		M/U	32	Bulgarian
904	992	Naughton	Hannah	3	Spinster	F/U	21	British
905	308	Hoffman	Fred	2		MC	2	British
906	306	Hoffman	Charles	2		M/U	32	British
907	307	Hoffman	John	2		MC	4	British
908	818	Nenkoff	Christe	3		M/U	22	Bulgaria
909	541	Nesson	Israel	2		M/U	26	Russian
913	380	Newsom	Helen	1		F/U	/	USA
914	284	Nicholls	Joseph	2		M/U	19	British
915	185	Nichols	E	1		M/U	/	British
916	131	Nicholson	A S	1		M/U	/	British
919	918	Nieminen	Mansa	3		F/U	30	Finns
920	559	Niklasen	Sander	3	Gn.Laborer	M/U	28	Sweden
921	871	Nilsson	August	3		M/U	21	Dane
922	720	Nilsson	Berta	3		F/U	18	Sweden
923	773	Nilsan	Helmina	3		F/U	26	Sweden
924	886	Nirva	Tlak	3		M/U	41	Finns
925	904	Mikanen	John	3		M/U	39	Finns
928	296	Norman	Robert	2		M/U	28	British
929	71	Nosworthy	Richard	3	Farm Labr	M/U	20	British
932	267	Nige	Elizabeth	2		F/U	29	British
933	744	Myster	Anna	3		F/U	22	Sweden
934	688	Nyoven	Johan	3		M/U	61	Norway
935	956	O'Brien	Mrs	3	H Wife	F/A	26	British
936	955	O'Brien	Thomas	3	Agr Labr	M/A	27	British
937	943	O'Brien	Denis	3	FarmLabr	M/U	21	British
938	977	O'Connell	Pat D	3	Gen Labr	M/U	17	British
939	1029	O'Connor	Maurice	3	Gen Labr	M/U	a	British
940	993	O'Connor	Pat	3	Farmer	M/U	24	British
941	638	Adahl	Martin	3		M/U	23	Sweden
945	938	O'Dwyer	Nellie	3	Spinster	F/U	23	British
946	755	Olman	Velin	3		M/U	22	Sweden
947	1018	O'Keefe	Pat	3	Agr Labr	M/U	22	British
948	935	O'Leary	Norah	3	Spinster	F/U	17	British
950	653	Olsen	Arthur	3		M/U	42	Norway
951	619	Olsen	Henry	3		M/U	28	Norway
952	632	Olsen	Carl	3		M/U	42	USA
953	655	Olsen	Ole	3		M/U	27	Norway
954	868	Olson	Elida	3		F/U	31	Dane
955	767	Olsan	John	3		M/U	28	Sweden
956	740	Johanson	Oscar	3		M/U	32	Sweden
957	633	Andersen	Thor	3		M/U	20	Norway
959	668	Oreskovic	Teko	3		M/U	23	Austria
960	677	Oreskovic	Luka	3		M/U	20	Austria
961	679	Oreskovic	Maria	3		F/U	20	Austria
963	639	Osen	Elon	3		F/U	17	Sweden
964	826	Osman	Mara	3		F/U	31	Austria

Board of Trade Passenger Lists for Southampton & Queenstown

Last Permanent Residence	Ticket No	Embarked	UK port of arrival	Steamship Line
England	54510	S		
Ireland	371110	Q		
Ireland	371110	Q		
Ireland	30887	Q		
	29011	S	Harwich	Gt Eastern
England	250655	S		
England	364506	S		
Ireland	372622	Q		
	312991	S	Newcastle	Norwegian SS co
Foreign Countries	374746	S		
England	3	S		
Ireland	35852	Q		
Ireland	382653	Q		
England	3235	S		
Ireland	367231	Q		
Ireland	367230	Q		
Ireland	36568	Q		
	347078	S	Hull	Wilson Line
Ireland	240276	Q		
	349206	S	Southampton	L&SW Rly Co
England	3338	S		
	349218	S	Southampton	L&SW Rly Co
Ireland	365237	Q		
England	230080	S		
England	230080	S		
England	230080	S		
	349234	S	Southampton	L&SW Rly Co
England	244368	S		
Foreign Countries	11752	S		
England	33112	S		
England	103	S		
England	693	S		
	3101297	S	Hull	Finland SS Co
England	363611	S		
	350410	S	Harwich	United SS Co
	347066	S	Hull	Wilson Line
	347470	S	Harwich	United SS Co
	3101272	S	Hull	Finland SS Co
	3101289	S	Hull	Finland SS Co
Scotland	218629	S		
England	39886	S		
England	29395	S		
	347081	S	Hull	Wilson Line
	345364	S	Hull	Wilson Line
Ireland	370365	Q		
Ireland	370365	Q		
Ireland	30979	Q		
Ireland	334912	Q		
Ireland	371060	Q		
Ireland	366713	Q		
	7267	S	Harwich	United SS Co
Ireland	30959	Q		
	347085	S	Hull	Wilson Line
Ireland	368402	Q		
Ireland	30919	Q		
	17368	S	Newcastle	Norwegian SS co
	4001	S	Newcastle	Norwegian SS co
	4579	S	Newcastle	Norwegian
	65302	S	Hull	Wilson Line
	350407	S	Harwich	United SS Co
	347464	S	Harwich	United SS Co
	347079	S	Hull	Wilson Line
	6563	S	Newcastle	Norwegian
	815085	S	Southampton	LSW Ry Co
	315094	S	Southampton	LSW Ry Co
	315096	S	Southampton	LSW Ry Co
	7534	S	Hull	Wilson Line
	349244	S	Southampton	L&SW Rly Co

Master No	Old No	Surname	First Name	Class	Occupation	Sex/ Status	Age	Country of which a citizen
965	425	Ostby	E C	1		M/U	/	USA
966	426	Ostby	Helen	1		F/U	/	USA
967	932	O'Sullivan	Bgt	3	Spinster	F/U	22	British
968	511	Otter	Richard	2		M/U	39	USA
970	216	Oxenham	P Thos	2		M/U	22	British
972	336	Pain	Alfred	2		M/U	40	British
974	835	Paulsson	Alma	3		F/U	29	Sweden
975	839	Paulsson	Gosta	3		FC	2	Sweden
976	837	Paulsson	Paul	3		MC	5	Sweden
977	838	Paulsson	Stina	3		FC	3	Sweden
978	836	Paulsson	Torbrig	3		MC	8	Sweden
979	916	Pannea	William	3		MI	1	Finns
980	913	Pannea	Erneste	3		M/U	17	Finns
981	914	Pannea	Eina	3		M/U	16	Finns
982	912	Pannea	Iuka	3		M/U	18	Finns
983	910	Pannea	Mareia	3		F/U	40	Finns
984	915	Pannea	Urhu	3		FC	3	Finns
985	227	Parker	Clifford	2		M/U	28	British
986	325	Parkes	Frank	2		M/U	18	British
987	178	Parr	W H	1		M/U	/	British
988	523	Parrish	L Davis	2		F/U	50	USA
989	170	Partner	Austin	1		M/U	/	British
990	680	Pasic	Jakob	3		M/U	21	Austria
991	127	Potchett	George	3	Shoemaker	M/U	19	British
993	824	Pavlovic	Stefo	3		M/U	32	Austria
994	136	Payne	V	1		M/U	/	British
995	125	Peacock	Alfred	3	Child	MI	7m	British
996	123	Peacock	Treasteall	3	Wife	F/U	36	British
997	124	Peacock	Treasteall	3	Child	FC	4	British
998	89	Pearce	Ernest	3	Farmer	M/U	32	British
999	161	Pears	Edith	1		F/A	/	British
1000	160	Pears	Thos	1		M/A	/	British
1001	689	Petersen	Olaf	3		M/U	29	Norway
1002	586	Peduzzi	Joseph	3	Waiter	M/U	24	Italian
1003	909	Pekonemi	E	3		M/U	32	Finns
1004	906	Peltomaki	Nkolai	3		M/U	25	Finns
1007	251	Pengelly	Fredrick	2		M/U	20	British
1008	60	Perkin	John	3	Farmer	M/U	22	British
1011	752	Persson	Ernst	3		M/U	25	Sweden
1012	537	Pernschitz	Joseph	2		M/U	40	German
1013	949	Peters	Katie	3	Spinster	F/U	a	British
1014	555	Petersen	Marius	3	Dairyman	M/U	24	Denmark
1015	827	Petranec	Matilda	3		F/U	31	Austria
1016	796	Pelroff	Vedeleo	3		M/U	19	Bulgarian
1017	799	Petroff	Pastelo	3		M/U	29	Bulgarian
1018	731	Peterson	Johan	3		M/U	25	Sweden
1019	757	Petersson	Ellen	3		F/U	18	Sweden
1020	140	Peuchen	A	1		M/U	/	British
1021	191	Phillips	Alice	2		F/U	21	British
1022	190	Phillips	Robert	2		M/U	42	British
1023	361	Marshall	Kate	2		F/A	24	British
1024	540	Pinsky	Rosa	2		F/U	29	Russian
1025	811	Plovhavsky	Vasil	3		M/U	27	Bulgarian
1026	678	Pacruic	Mate	3		M/U	17	Austria
1027	675	Pacruic	Tame	3		M/U	24	Austria
1028	599	Ponesell	Martin	2		M/U	24	Denmark
1030	448	Chamberlain	W F	1		M/U	/	USA
1033	234	Quick	Jane	2		F/U	33	British
1034	236	Quick	Phyllis	2		FC	2	British
1035	235	Quick	Winifred	2		FC	8	British
1036	807	Radeff	Alexander	3		M/U	27	Bulgarian
1037	658	Solvang	Lena	3		F/U	63	Norway
1039	92	Reed	James	3	Butcher	M/U	19	British
1040	229	Reeves	David	2		M/U	36	British
1041	831	Kekic	Tido	3		M/U	38	Austria
1043	271	Renouf	Lillie	2		F/A	30	British
1044	270	Renouf	Peter	2		M/A	34	British
1046	521	Reynalds	Encarnacion	2		F/U	28	Spain

Last Permanent Residence	Ticket No	Embarked	UK port of arrival	Steamship Line
Foreign Countries	113509	S		
Foreign Countries	113509	S		
Ireland	30909	Q		
England	28213	S		
England	14260	S		
England	244278	S		
	349909	S	Harwich	United SS Co
	349909	S	Harwich	United SS Co
	349909	S	Harwich	United SS Co
	349909	S	Harwich	United SS Co
	349909	S	Harwich	United SS Co
	3101295	S	Hull	Finland SS Co
	3101295	S	Hull	Finland SS Co
	3101295	S	Hull	Finland SS Co
	3101295	S	Hull	Finland SS Co
	3101295	S	Hull	Finland SS Co
	3101295	S	Hull	Finland SS Co
England	14888	S		
Ireland	239853	S		
England	112052	S		
England	230433?	S		
England	113043	S		
	315097	S	Southampton	LSW Ry Co
England	358585	S		
	349242	S	Southampton	L&SW Rly Co
British Possession	12749	S		
England	310315	S		
England	310315	S		
England	310315	S		
England	343271	S		
England	113776	S		
England	113776	S		
	345498	S	Newcastle	Norwegian SS Co
England	2817	S		
	3101294	S	Hull	Finland SS Co
	3101291	S	Hull	Finland SS Co
England	28665	S		
England	21174	S		
	347083	S	Hull	Wilson Line
England	237393	S		
Ireland	F	Q		
England	342441	S		
	349245	S	Southampton	L&SW Rly Co
	349212	S	Southampton	L&SW Rly Co
	349215	S	Southampton	L&SW Rly Co
	347076	S	Hull	Wilson Line
	347087	S	Hull	Wilson Line
British Possession	113786	S		
England	2	S		
England	2	S		
England	250655	S		
England	234604	S		
	349227	S	Southampton	L&SW Rly Co
	315095	S	Southampton	LSW Ry Co
	315092	S	Southampton	LSW Ry Co
	250647	S	Southampton	RM SP Co
Foreign Countries	110468	S		
England	26360	S		
England	26360	S		
England	26360	S		
	349223	S	Southampton	L&SW Rly Co
	65305	S	Hull	Wilson Line
Wales	362316	S		
England	17248	S		
	349249	S	Southampton	L&SW Rly Co
England	31027	S		
England	31027	S		
Foreign Countries	230434	S		

Who Sailed on Titanic?

Master No	Old No	Surname	First Name	Class	Occupation	Sex/Status	Age	Country of which a citizen
1047	85	Reynolds	Harold	3	Baker	M/U	21	British
1049	1040	Rice	Albert	3	Child	MC	10	USA
1050	1043	Rice	Arthur	3	Child	MC	4	USA
1051	1042	Rice	Eric	3	Child	MC	7	USA
1052	1044	Rice	Eugene	3	Child	MC	2	USA
1053	1041	Rice	George	3	Child	MC	9	USA
1054	1039	Rice	Margt	3	HKeeper	F/U	39	USA
1056	261	Richards	Emily	2		F/U	25	British
1057	263	Richards	S Geo	2		MI	8m	British
1058	262	Richards	Wm	2		MC	3	British
1059	215	Ridsdale	Lucy	2		F/U	26	British
1060	911	Pannea	Sanni	3		M/U	21	Finns
1062	887	Rentamaki	Natti	3		M/U	35	Finns
1063	1015	Riordan	Hanna	3	Spinster	F/U	20	British
1064	561	Risien	Emma	3	Wife	F/A	58	USA
1065	560	Risien	Samuel	3	Hotel Prop	M/A	68	USA
1067	460	Robert	E W	1		F/U	/	USA
1068	548	Robins	Alexander	3	Mason	M/A	50	USA
1069	549	Robins	Charity	3	Wife	F/A	48	USA
1070	404	Roebling	Washington	1		M/U	/	USA
1071	239	Rogers	Harry	2		M/U	18	British
1072	63	Rogers	William	3	Miner	M/U	29	British
1073	490	Rolmane	C	1		M/U	/	USA
1074	663	Rummetvedt	Kristian	3		M/U	49	Norway
1075	434	Rood	Hugh R	1		M/U	/	USA
1076	874	Rosblom	Helen	3		F/U	41	Finns
1077	876	Rosblom	Salli	3		FC	2	Finns
1078	875	Rosblom	Viktor	3		M/U	18	Finns
1082	86	Roth	Sarah	3	Tailoress	F/U	29	British
1083	180	Rothes	Countess	1		F/U	/	British
1086	42	Rouse	Richard G	3	Farm Labr	M/U	53	British
1087	480	Rowe	Alfred	1		M/U	/	USA
1088	269	Rugg	Emily	2		F/U	22	British
1089	56	Lush	Alfred	3	Porter	M/U	17	British
1090	1013	Ryan	Edwd	3	Gen Labr	M/U	23	British
1091	1032	Ryan	Pat	3	Gen Labr	M/U	a	British
1100	155	Saalfeld	Adolph	1		M/U	/	British
1101	1016	Sadlier	Matt	3	Agr Labr	M/U	20	British
1102	6	Sadowitz	Harry	3	Fur cutter	M/U	17	British
1103	572	Sather	Simon	3	Miner	M/U	25	USA
1104	23	Sage	Annie	3	Wife	F/A	44	British
1105	29	Sage	William	3	Child	MC	11	British
1106	31	Sage	Constance	3	Child	FC	7	British
1107	28	Sage	Dorothy	3	Scholar	F/U	13	British
1108	26	Sage	Douglas	3	Baker	M/U	18	British
1109	30	Sage	Ada	3	Child	FC	9	British
1110	27	Sage	Frederick	3	Cook	M/U	16	British
1111	25	Sage	George	3	Barman	M/U	19	British
1112	22	Sage	John	3	Tradesman	M/A	44	British
1113	24	Sage	Stella	3	Dressmaker	F/U	20	British
1114	32	Sage	Thomas	3	Child	MC	4	British
1116	637	Salander	Carl	3		M/U	24	Sweden
1117	779	Saljilsvik	Anna	3		F/U	23	Norwegian
1119	917	Salonen	Werner	3		M/U	29	Finns
1123	650	Sandstrom	Agnes	3		F/U	27	Sweden
1124	652	Sandstrom	Beatrice	3		FC	1	Sweden
1125	651	Sandstrom	Margarete	3		FC	4	Sweden
1126	697	Sop	Jules	3		M/U	25	Belgium
1127	15	Saundercock	William	3	Miners Labr	M/U	20	British
1128	87	Sawyer	Frederick	3	Gardener	M/U	23	British
1129	971	Scanlan	James	3	Farm Labr	M/U	20	British
1131	710	Scheerlinck	Jean	3		M/U	29	Belgium
1132	513	Smith	Augustus	2		M/U	26	Austria
1133	806	Sayloff	Todor	3		M/U	42	Bulgarian
1134	340	Sedgwick	Chas	2		M/U	25	British
1136	482	Seward	F	1		M/U	/	USA
1137	339	Sharp	Percival	2		M/U	27	British
1138	1023	Shaughnessy	Pat	3	Farm Labr	M/U	20	British

Last Permanent Residence	Ticket No	Embarked	UK port of arrival	Steamship Line
England	342684	S		
Ireland	382652	Q		
Ireland	382652	Q		
Ireland	382652	Q		
Ireland	382652	Q		
Ireland	382652	Q		
Ireland	382652	Q		
England	29106	S		
England	29106	S		
England	29106	S		
England	14258	S		
	3101295	S	Hull	Finland SS Co
	3101273	S	Hull	Finland SS Co
Ireland	334915	Q		
England	364498	S		
England	364498	S		
Foreign Countries	24160	S		
England	3337	S		
England	3337	S		
Foreign Countries	17590	S		
England	28004	S		
Wales	23567	S		
Foreign Countries	111428	S		
	312993	S	Newcastle	Norwegian SS co
Foreign Countries	113767	S		
	370129	S	Hull	Finland SS
	370129	S	Hull	Finland SS
	370129	S	Hull	Finland SS
England	342712	S		
England	110152	S		
England	3594	S		
Foreign Countries	113790	S		
England	31026	S		
England	20589	S		
Ireland	383162	Q		
Ireland	371110	Q		
England	19988	S		
Ireland	367655	Q		
England	1588	S		
British Possessions	3101262	S		
England	2343	S		
England	2343	S		
England	2343	S		
England	2343	S		
England	2343	S		
England	2343	S		
England	2343	S		
England	2343	S		
England	2343	S		
England	2343	S		
England	2343	S		
	7266	S	Harwich	United SS Co
	348120	S	Newcastle	Norwegian SS Co
	3101296	S	Hull	Finland SS Co
	9549	S	Hull	Wilson Line
	9549	S	Hull	Wilson Line
	9549	S	Hull	Wilson Line
	345768	S	Harwich	GE Ry Co
England	f2121	S		
England	342826	S		
Ireland	36209	Q		
	345719	S	Harwich	GE Ry Co
Foreign Countries	248659	S		
	349222	S	Southampton	L&SW Rly Co
England	244361	S		
Foreign Countries	113794	S		
England	244358	S		
Ireland	370374	Q		

Who Sailed on Titanic?

Master No	Old No	Surname	First Name	Class	Occupation	Sex/ Status	Age	Country of which a citizen
1140	43	Shellard	Frederick	3	Painter	M/U	52	British
1141	522	Shelley	Imanita	2		F/U	25	USA
1142	940	Shine	Ellen	3	Spinster	F/U	18	British
1143	108	Shorney	Charles	3	Valet	M/U	22	British
1144	403	Shutes	E W	1		F/U	/	USA
1145	607	Silver	Lyyli	2		F/U	24	Finnish
1146	394	Silverthorne	Mr	1		M/U	/	USA
1149	116	Simmons	John	3	Gen Labr	M/U	39	British
1150	372	Simonens	O A	1		M/U	/	German
1151	285	Sincock	Maude	2		F/U	21	British
1152	601	Sinkkonen	Anna	2		F/U	30	Finnish
1154	121	Scrotor	Maurice	3	Tailor	M/U	20	British
1155	833	Sevic	Husen	3		M/U	40	Austria
1156	895	Sckvola	Antte	3		M/U	21	Finns
1157	879	Goblorn	Anna	3		F/U	18	Finns
1158	512	Sjostedt	Ernest A	2		M/U	28	Sweden
1159	759	Skoog	Anna	3		F/A	43	Sweden
1160	762	Skoog	Harald	3		MC	4	Sweden
1161	760	Skoog	Carl	3		MC	10	Sweden
1162	761	Skoog	Mabel	3		FC	9	Sweden
1163	763	Skoog	Margret	3		FC	2	Sweden
1164	758	Skoog	William	3		M/A	39	Sweden
1165	798	Stabenoff	Peko	3		M/U	42	Bulgarian
1166	317	Slayter	Marion	2		F/U	24	British
1167	1036	Slater	H M	2	Spinster	F/U	a	British
1168	243	Slemen	Richard J	2		M/U	35	British
1169	568	Slocovski	Selman	3	Merchant	M/U	20	Russia
1170	479	Sloper	W T	1		M/U	/	USA
1171	483	Smart	John M	1		M/U	/	USA
1172	664	Smiljanic	Mile	3		M/U	37	Austria
1176	279	Smith	Marion	2		F/U	40	British
1178	173	Smith	R W	1		M/U	/	British
1179	1014	Smith	Thomas	3	Gen Labr	M/U	24	British
1180	953	Smyth	Julia	3	Spinster	F/U	a	British
1181	453	Snyder	John	1		M/A	/	USA
1182	454	Snyder	Mrs	1		F/A	/	USA
1183	266	Sobey	Hayden	2		F/U	25	British
1184	783	Soholt	Peter	3		M/U	19	Norwegian
1185	554	Somerton	Frances	3	Wife	F/U	31	USA
1186	587	Spector	Woolf	3	G.Labr	M/U	23	Russian
1187	163	Spedden	F O	1		M/A	/	British
1188	164	Spedden	Mrs	1		F/A	/	British
1189	166	Spedden	R	1		MC	/	British
1192	103	Skinner	Henry	3	Grocer	M/U	32	British
1193	371	Stahelin	Max	1		M/U	/	German
1194	792	Staneff	Ivan	3		M/U	23	Bulgarian
1196	17	Stanley	Amy	3	Servant	F/U	24	British
1197	73	Stanley	Ernest	3	Porter	M/U	21	British
1199	159	Stead	W T	1		M/U	/	British
1202	468	Stephenson	W B	1		F/U	/	USA
1205	213	Stokes	Philip	2		M/U	25	British
1206	428	Stone	M Geo	1		F/U	/	USA
1207	581	Storey	Tom	3	Seaman	M/U	51	USA
1208	789	Stoytchoff	Ylia	3		M/U	19	Bulgarian
1209	646	Strandberg	Ida	3		F/U	22	Sweden
1210	903	Stranden	Jako	3		M/U	31	Finns
1211	396	Straus	Isidor	1		M/A	/	USA
1212	397	Straus	Mrs	1		F/A	/	USA
1213	666	Strilic	Ivan	3		M/U	27	Austria
1214	753	Strom	Elma	3		F/U	28	Sweden
1215	754	Strom	Selma	3		FC	2	Sweden
1216	120	Sunderland	Victor	3	Farmer	M/U	20	British
1217	883	Sundman	Johan	3		M/U	44	Finns
1218	565	Mitchell	Henry	3	Coach Painter	M/U	26	USA
1219	117	Sutton	Charles	3	Goldsmith	M/U	25	British
1220	470	Sutton	F	1		F/U	/	USA
1221	118	Sutton	Henry	3	Engineer	M/U	22	British
1222	714	Svensson	Johan	3		M/U	74	Sweden

Last Permanent Residence	Ticket No	Embarked	UK port of arrival	Steamship Line
England	6212	S		
England	230433?	S		
Ireland	30968	Q		
England	374910	S		
Foreign Countries	17582	S		
	250652	S	Hull	Finnish SS Co
Foreign Countries	17475	S		
England	392082	S		
Foreign Countries	13213	S		
England	33112	S		
	250648	S	Hull	Finnish SS Co
England	392092	S		
	349251	S	Southampton	L&SW Rly Co
	3101280	S	Hull	Finland SS Co
	3101265	S	Hull	Finland SS Co
Foreign Countries	237442	S		
	347088	S	Hull	Wilson Line
	347088	S	Hull	Wilson Line
	347088	S	Hull	Wilson Line
	347088	S	Hull	Wilson Line
	347088	S	Hull	Wilson Line
	347088	S	Hull	Wilson Line
	349214	S	Southampton	L&SW Rly Co
England	234818	S		
Ireland	234818	Q		
England	28206	S		
England	392086	S		
Foreign Countries	113788	S		
Foreign Countries	113792	S		
	815037	S	Southampton	LSW Ry Co
England	31418	S		
England	113056	S		
Ireland	384461	Q		
Ireland	335432	Q		
Foreign Countries	21228	S		
Foreign Countries	21228	S		
England	29178	S		
	348124	S	Newcastle	Norwegian SS Co
England	18509	S		
England	3236	S		
England	16966	S		
England	16966	S		
England	16966	S		
England	369943	S		
Foreign Countries	13214	S		
	349208	S	Southampton	L&SW Rly Co
England	2314	S		
England	45380	S		
England	113514	S		
Foreign Countries	36947	S		
England	13540	S		
Foreign Countries	113752	S		
England	370160	S		
	349205	S	Southampton	L&SW Rly Co
	7553	S	Hull	Wilson Line
	3101288	S	Hull	Finland SS Co
Foreign Countries	17483	S		
Foreign Countries	17483	S		
	815083	S	Southampton	LSW Ry Co
	347084	S	Hull	Wilson Line
	347084	S	Hull	Wilson Line
England	392089	S		
	3101269	S	Hull	Finland SS Co
England	392076	S		
England	392085	S		
Foreign Countries	36963	S		
England	392085	S		
	347060	S	Hull	Wilson Line

Who Sailed on Titanic?

Master No	Old No	Surname	First Name	Class	Occupation	Sex/ Status	Age	Country of which a citizen
1223	640	Svenson	Cervin	3		M/U	14	Sweden
1224	849	Strennsan	Olaf	3		M/U	24	Dane
1225	349	Swane	Geo	2		M/U	26	British
1226	302	Sweet	Geo	2		M/U	14	British
1227	391	Swift	F J	1		F/U	/	USA
1228	444	Taussig	Emil	1		M/A	/	USA
1229	446	Taussig	Miss	1		F/U	/	USA
1230	445	Taussig	Mrs	1		F/A	/	USA
1231	418	Taylor	E Z	1		M/A	/	USA
1232	419	Taylor	Mrs	1		F/A	/	USA
1233	355	Taylor	P C	2		M/U	32	British
1234	847	Tongliz	Aunnan	3		M/U	25	Dane
1238	96	Theobald	Thomas	3	Groom	M/U	34	British
1244	66	Thomson	Alex	3	Stonecutter	M/U	36	British
1246	111	Thorneycroft	Florence	3	Wife	F/A	33	British
1247	110	Thorneycroft	Percival	3	Gen Labr	M/A	36	British
1248	908	Tikkanen	Juho	3		M/U	32	Finns
1249	1011	Tobin	Roger	3	Farmer	M/U	20	British
1250	800	Todoroff	Lalio	3		M/U	23	Bulgarian
1251	98	Tomlin	Ernest	3	Student	M/U	22	British
1252	514	Toomey	Ellen	2		F/U	50	USA
1253	563	Torber	Ernest	3	Florist	M/U	41	Germany
1255	577	Turnguist	Wm	3	Seaman	M/U	25	USA
1261	566	Trembisky	Berk	3	Leather Worker	M/U	32	Russia
1262	524	Troupiansky	Moses A	2		M/U	23	Russia
1263	362	Trant	Jessie	2		F/U	30	British
1264	290	Troutt	Celia	2		F/U	20	British
1265	829	Turcin	Stefan	3		M/U	36	Austria
1267	630	Turja	Anna	3		F/U	18	Finland
1268	626	Turkula	Hedwig	3		F/U	20	Finland
1269	204	Jurpin	Dorothy	2		F/A	27	British
1270	203	Jurpin	Wm	2		M/A	29	British
1272	676	Uzelas	Toso	3		M/U	17	Austria
1277	711	Velde	Joseph Vande	3		M/U	36	Belgium
1278	713	Steen	Leo Vander	3		M/U	28	Belgium
1279	450	Van der Hoef	W	1		M/U	/	USA
1280	705	Van Impe	Catherine	3		FC	10	Belgium
1281	703	Van Impe	Jacob	3		M/A	36	Belgium
1282	704	Van Impe	Rosalie	3		F/A	30	Belgium
1283	708	Melkebuk	Philemon V	3		M/U	23	Belgium
1284	699	Nande Walle	Nestor	3		M/U	25	Belgium
1285	695	Vereruysse	Victor	3		M/U	47	Belgium
1286	693	Planke	Augusta Vander	3		F/U	18	Belgium
1287	692	Planke	Emilie Vander	3		F/A	31	Belgium
1288	691	Planke	Jules Vander	3		M/A	31	Belgium
1289	694	Planke	Leon Vander	3		M/U	16	Belgium
1291	515	Veale	James	2		M/U	30	USA
1292	872	Wendal	Olaf	3		M/U	21	Dane
1293	867	Vestrom	Hulda	3		F/U	14	Dane
1294	834	Vook	Janko	3		M/U	21	Austria
1295	696	Welens	Adulle	3		M/U	22	Belgium
1296	207	Walcroft	Nellie	2		F/U	35	British
1297	471	Walker	W Anderson	1		M/U	/	USA
1299	278	Ware	Florence	2		F/A	28	British
1300	91	Ware	Frederick	3	Fitter	M/U	34	British
1301	277	Ware	John	2		M/A	30	British
1302	252	Ware	Wm J	2		M/U	23	British
1304	128	Warren	Charles	3	Bricklayer	M/U	30	British
1306	329	Watson	Ennis	2		M/U	18	British
1307	287	Watt	Bessie	2		F/U	32	British
1308	288	Watt	Bertha	2		FC	6	British
1309	573	Webber	James	3	Miner	M/U	66	USA
1310	237	Webber	Susie	2		F/U	30	British
1311	478	Weir	J	1		M/U	/	USA
1312	516	Weisz	Leopold	2		M/A	28	Hungary
1313	517	Weisz	Mathilde	2		F/A	26	Hungary
1314	255	Wells	Addie	2		F/U	29	British
1315	256	Wells	Joan	2		FC	4	British

Last Permanent Residence	Ticket No	Embarked	UK port of arrival	Steamship Line
	7538	S	Hull	Wilson Line
	350035	S	Harwich	United SS Co
England	248734	S		
England	220845	S		
Foreign Countries	17466	S		
Foreign Countries	110413	S		
Foreign Countries	110413	S		
Foreign Countries	110413	S		
Foreign Countries	19996	S		
Foreign Countries	19996	S		
England	250653	S		
	350033	S	Harwich	United SS Co
England	363291	S		
England	32302	S		
England	376564	S		
England	376564	S		
	3101293	S	Hull	Finland SS Co
Ireland	383121	Q		
	349216	S	Southampton	L&SW Rly Co
England	364499	S		
England	1351	S		
England	364511	S		
England	370160	S		
England	392078	S		
Foreign Countries	233639	S		
England	240929	S		
England	34218	S		
	349247	S	Southampton	L&SW Rly Co
	4138	S	Hull	Finnish SS Co
	4134	S	Hull	Finnish SS Co
England	11668	S		
England	11668	S		
	315093	S	Southampton	LSW Ry Co
	345780	S	Harwich	GE Ry Co
	345783	S	Harwich	GE Ry Co
Foreign Countries	111240	S		
	345773	S	Harwich	GE Ry Co
	345773	S	Harwich	GE Ry Co
	345773	S	Harwich	GE Ry Co
	345717	S	Harwich	GE Ry Co
	345770	S	Harwich	GE Ry Co
	345765	S	Harwich	GE Ry Co
	345764	S	Harwich	GE Ry Co
	345763	S	Harwich	GE Ry Co
	345763	S	Harwich	GE Ry Co
	345764	S	Harwich	GE Ry Co
England	28221	S		
	350416	S	Harwich	United SS Co
	350406	S	Harwich	United SS Co
	349252	S	Southampton	L&SW Rly Co
	345767	S	Harwich	GE Ry Co
England	13528	S		
Foreign Countries	36967	S		
England	31352	S		
England	359309	S		
England	31352	S		
England	28666	S		
England	49867	S		
Ireland	239856	S		
England	33595	S		
England	33595	S		
England	3101316	S		
England	27267	S		
Foreign Countries	113800	S		
Foreign Countries	228414	S		
Foreign Countries	228414	S		
England	29103	S		
England	29103	S		

Who Sailed on Titanic?

Master No	Old No	Surname	First Name	Class	Occupation	Sex/ Status	Age	Country of which a citizen
1316	257	Wells	Ralph	2		MC	2	British
1317	293	West	Ada	2		F/A	33	British
1318	295	West	Barbara	2		FC	10	British
1319	294	West	Constance	2		FC	4	British
1320	292	West	Arthur	2		M/A	36	British
1322	232	Wheadon	Ed H	2		M/U	66	British
1323	608	Wheeler	Edwin	2		M/U	24	USA
1324	487	White	J	1		M/U	/	USA
1325	458	White	Percival	1		M/U	/	USA
1326	459	White	R F	1		M/U	/	USA
1327	464	Wick	Geo D	1		M/A	/	USA
1328	465	Wick	Mrs	1		F/A	/	USA
1329	466	Wick	Mary	1		F/U	/	USA
1330	718	Widegrin	Charles	3		M/U	44	Sweden
1331	422	Widener	Mrs	1		F/A	/	USA
1332	421	Widener	Geo D	1		M/A	/	USA
1333	423	Widener	Harry	1		M/U	/	USA
1334	880	Wiklund	Carl	3		M/U	21	Finns
1335	881	Wiklund	Jakob	3		M/U	18	Finns
1336	335	Wilhelms	Chas	2		M/U	32	British
1337	558	Wilkes	Ellen	3	Wife	F/U	40	USA
1338	324	Wilkinson	Ada	2		F/U	18	British
1339	323	Wilkinson	Mary	2		F/U	40	British
1340	184	Willard	Constance	1		F/U	/	British
1342	1	Willey	Edward	3	Farm Labourer	M/U	18	British
1344	368	Williams	Chas	2		M/U	24	British
1345	33	Williams	Harry	3	Carman	M/U	28	British
1346	79	Williams	Leslie	3	Pugilist	M/U	28	British
1348	427	Lambert Williams	F F	1		M/U	/	USA
1350	165	Wilson	Alice	1		F/U	/	British
1351	575	Windelov	Eimar	3	Dairyman	M/U	21	Denmark
1352	687	Wirz	Albert	3		M/U	28	Austria
1353	129	Wiseman	Philip	3	Merchant	M/U	54	British
1354	700	Wellewrongel	Camille	3		M/U	36	Belgium
1358	356	Woodward	J W	2		M/U	27	British
1360	154	Woolner	Hugh	1		M/U	/	British
1362	297	Wright	Marion	2		F/U	30	British
1368	538	Yvois	Harriet	2		F/U	24	French
1373	665	Zimmermann	Leo	3		M/U	29	Switzerland

Key

Sex/Status

M/U — Male unaccompanied by wife
M/A —Male accompanied by wife
F/U — Female unaccompanied by husband
F/A — Female accompanied by husband
MC— Male child
FC — Female child
MI — Male infant
FI — Female infant

Ticket Numbers
F denotes partially or wholly illegible

Last Permanent Residence	Ticket No	Embarked	UK port of arrival	Steamship Line
England	29103	S		
England	34651	S		
England	34651	S		
England	34651	S		
England	34651	S		
England	24579	S		
	2159	S	Newhaven	LB & SE
Foreign Countries	111424	S		
Foreign Countries	35281	S		
Foreign Countries	35281	S		
Foreign Countries	36928	S		
Foreign Countries	36928	S		
Foreign Countries	36928	S		
	347064	S	Hull	Wilson Line
Foreign Countries	113503	S		
Foreign Countries	113503	S		
Foreign Countries	113503	S		
	3101266	S	Hull	Finland SS Co
	3101267	S	Hull	Finland SS Co
England	244270	S		
England	363272	S		
Scotland	239827	S		
Scotland	239827	S		
England	113795	S		
England	751	S		
England	244373	S		
England	2466	S		
England	54636	S		
Foreign Countries	113510	S		
England	16966	S		
Foreign Countries	3101317	S		
	315154	S	Southampton	LSW Ry Co
England	34244	S		
	345771	S	Harwich	GE Ry Co
England	250653	S		
England	19947	S		
England	220844	S		
England	248747	S		
	815082	S	Southampton	LSW Ry Co

Inq.6

Master list No	Old list No	Surname	Name(s)	Sex	Age	Nationality	Embarked	Class	Last Abode
1	289	Abbing	Anthony	M	42	US	Southampton	3	Southampton
2	290	Abbott	Eugene	M	13	US	Southampton	3	London
4	291	Abbott	Ross M	M	16	US	Southampton	3	London
8	122	Abelson	Samson	M		Russian	Cherbourg	2	Paris
11	292	Adahl	Mauritz	M	30	Swedish	Southampton	3	Copenhagen
12	293	Adams	J	M		British	Southampton	3	Yeovil
13	294	Ahlin	Johanna	M	40	Swedish	Southampton	3	Gothenburg
14	295	Ahmed	Ali	M	24	Syria	Southampton	3	Buenos Aires
18	123	Aldworth	C	M			Southampton	2	London
19	296	Alexander	Wm	M	23	British	Southampton	3	Gt Yarmouth
20	297	Alhomaki	Ilman	M	20	Finland	Southampton	3	Finland
21	298	Ali	Wm	M	25	Syria	Southampton	3	Buenos Aires
23	299	Allen	Wm	M	35	British	Southampton	3	Birmingham
24	1	Allison	H J	M		British	Southampton	1	152 Abbey Road, West Hampstead, London
25	3	Allison		F			Southampton	1	152 Abbey Road, West Hampstead, London
26	2	Allison	H J (Mrs)	F			Southampton	1	152 Abbey Road, West Hampstead, London
28	300	Allum	Owen Geo	M	18	British	Southampton	3	London
29	302	Anderson	Albert	M	33	Norway	Southampton	3	Bergen
32	305	Anderson	Alfrida	F	40	Swedish	Southampton	3	Gothenburg
33	304	Anderson	Anders	M	39	Swedish	Southampton	3	Gothenburg
35	308	Anderson	Ebba	F	6	Swedish	Southampton	3	Gothenburg
36	310	Anderson	Ellis	M	2	Swedish	Southampton	3	Gothenburg
38	312	Andersson	Ida A	F	38	Swedish	Southampton	3	Gothenburg
39	307	Anderson	Ingeborg	F	9	Swedish	Southampton	3	Gothenburg
40	311	Anderson	Samuel	M	26	Swedish	Southampton	3	Gothenburg
41	306	Anderson	Sigrid	F	11	Swedish	Southampton	3	Gothenburg
42	309	Anderson	Sigvard	M	4	Swedish	Southampton	3	Gothenburg
43	313	Andreason	Paul C	M	20	Swedish	Southampton	3	Gothenburg
44	125	Andrew	Frank	M	25	British	Southampton	2	Redruth
45	124	Andrew	Edgar	M	16	British	Southampton	2	Southampton
47	4	Andrews	Thos	M			Southampton	1	Harland & Wolff, Belfast

Master list No	Old list No	Surname	Name(s)	Sex	Age	Nationality	Embarked	Class	Last Abode
48	314	Angheloff	Minko	M	26	Bulgarian	Southampton	3	Basle
50	126	Angle	Wm	M		British	Southampton	2	14 Mill St, Warwick
52	315	Arnold	Joseph	M	25	Swiss	Southampton	3	Basle
53	316	Arnold	Josephine	F	24	Swiss	Southampton	3	Basle
54	317	Aronsson	Ernest Axel	M	24	Swedish	Southampton	3	Helsingborg
55	5	Artagaveytia	Ramon	M			Cherbourg	1	London
56	127	Ashby	John	M	57	American	Southampton	2	London
57	325	Asim	Adola	M	35	Syria	Southampton	2	Buenos Aires
58	320	Asplund	Carl	M	5	Swedish	Southampton	3	Sweden
59	318	Asplund	Charles	M	40	Swedish	Southampton	3	Sweden
60	321	Asplund	Gustaf	M	9	Swedish	Southampton	3	Sweden
62	319	Asplund	Oscar	M	11	Swedish	Southampton	3	Sweden
66	323	Assaf	Gerios	M	21	Syria	Cherbourg	3	Syria
68	324	Assam	Ali	M	23	Syria	Southampton	3	Buenos Aires
69	6	Astor	J J	M		American	Cherbourg	1	
71	327	Attala	Sleiman	M	30	Canada	Cherbourg	3	Syria
73	328	Augustsan	Albert	M	23	Swedish	Southampton	3	Sweden
75	329	Baccos	Rafael	M	20	Syria	Cherbourg	3	Syria
76	330	Backstrom	Karl	M	32	Finland	Cherbourg	3	Finland
83	331	Badt	Mahomed	M	40	Syria	Cherbourg	3	Syria
84	128	Baily	Percy	M	18	English	Southampton	2	Penzance
85	129	Barmbrigge	Chas R	M	23		Southampton	2	Guernsey, Rothais Marne
86	332	Balkic	Cerin	M	26	Austrian	Southampton	2	Austria
88	130	Banfield	Fred J	M	28		Southampton	2	30 Grenville Rd, Plymo
89	333	Barbara	Catherine	F	45	Syria	Cherbourg	3	Syria
90	334	Barbara	Saide	F	18	Syria	Cherbourg	3	Syria
93	335	Barry	Julia	F	27	British	Queenstown	3	Ireland
94	336	Barton	David	M	52	British	Southampton	3	
95	131	Bateman	R J	M		American	Southampton	2	Rendences Rd, Staplehill, Bristol
96	7	Baumann	J	M		American	Cherbourg	1	Grand Hotel, Paris
98	8	Baxter	Quigg	M		American	Cherbourg	1	Elysee Palace Hotel, Paris
102	9	Beattie	T	M		American	Southampton	1	Hotel Majestic, Nice
103	132	Beauchamp	H J	M			Southampton	2	London
104	338	Beavan	W T	M	19	US	Southampton	3	London
113	339	Benson	Jn Victor	M	26	Swedish	Southampton	3	Sweden
115	340	Berglund	Ivar	M	20	Finland	Southampton	3	Sweden
116	133	Berriman	Wm	M	23		Southampton	2	St Ives
117	740	Seman	Betros	M	10	Syria	Cherbourg	3	Syria
118	341	Betros	Tannous	M	20	Belgian	Cherbourg	3	Syria
122	345	Birkland	Hans	M	21	Norway	Southampton	3	Norway
123	54	Jakob	Birnbaum	M		Austrian	Cherbourg	1	11 Rue Membling, Antwerp
127	346	Bjorklund	Ernest	M	18	Swedish	Southampton	3	Sweden

Master list No	Old list No	Surname	Name(s)	Sex	Age	Nationality	Embarked	Class	Last Abode
128	10	Bjornstrom	H SAVED	M		American	Southampton	1	
129	11	Blackwell	Stephen Weart	M		British	Southampton	1	
134	12	Borebank	J J	M			Southampton	1	
135	347	Bostandyeff	Grentcho	M	26	Bulgarian	Southampton	3	Bulgaria
136	134	Botsford	W Hull	M		American	Southampton	2	c/o Cook
137	349	Borlos	Akar	M	9	Syria	Cherbourg	3	Syria
138	348	Borlos	Hanna	F	18	Syria	Cherbourg	3	Syria
140	362	Boulos	Sultani	F	40	Syria	Cherbourg	3	Syria
141	351	Bourke	Catherine	F		British	Queenstown	3	Queenstown
142	350	Bourke	Jno	M		British	Queenstown	3	Queenstown
143	360	Burke	Mary	F		British	Queenstown	3	Queenstown
144	352	Bowen	David	M		British	Southampton	3	
146	135	Bowenur	Solomon	M		American	Southampton	2	c/o Cook
148	136	Bracken	J H	M	27	American	Southampton	2	London
151	13	Brady	J B	M		British	Southampton	1	
152	353	Braf	Elin E	M	20	Swiss	Southampton	3	Sweden
153	287	Brailey		M		British	Southampton	2	c/o J & S Black, Liverpool
155	14	Brandeis	E	M			Cherbourg	1	Elysee Palace Hotel, Paris
156	354	Braund	L R	M	29	British	Southampton	3	Holdsworthy
157	355	Braund	O P	M	22	British	Southampton	3	Holdsworthy
158	15	Brewe	Arthur Jackson	M		American	Cherbourg	1	
159	288	Breicoux	R	M		French	Southampton	2	c/o J & S Black, Liverpool
160	137	Brito	Jose D	M		Portugal	Southampton	2	c/o S Duarte, 34 Mulgrave, Hove
161	356	Brobek	Carl R	M	22	Denmark	Southampton	3	Copenhagen
162	357	Brocklebank	Wm	M	35	British	Southampton	3	London
166	139	Brown	SAVED (Mrs)	F		British	Southampton	2	London SAVED
168	138	Brown	S	M		British	Southampton	2	London
171	140	Bryhe	Curt	M	20	Swedish	Southampton	2	Gottenborg, C/o Ludvig Shara,
173	358	Bucksley	Catherine	F		British	Queenstown	3	Queenstown
175	359	Burke	Jeremiah	M		British	Queenstown	3	Queenstown
177	361	Burns	Mary	F	18	British	Queenstown	3	Queenstown
179	141	Butler	Regd	M	25	British	Southampton	2	Portsmo Grenada Hotel
180	16	Butt	Archibald W	M		American	Southampton	1	
181	142	Byles	T R D	M		British	Southampton	2	101 Ridgway, London
183	363	Cacic	R	M	18	Austrian	Southampton	3	Austria
184	364	Cacic	Luka	M	38	Austrian	Southampton	3	Austria
185	365	Cacic	Manda	F	21	Austrian	Southampton	3	Austria
186	377	Cacic	Maria	F	30	Austrian	Southampton	3	Austria
187	119	Male	? ms Carter	M			Southampton		
192	366	Calic	Peter	M	17	Austrian	Southampton	3	Austria
194	277	Campbell	Wm	M	21	British	Southampton	2	Belfast c/o Harland & Wolff
195	367	Canavan	Mary	F		British	Queenstown	3	Queenstown

Master list No	Old list No	Surname	Name(s)	Sex	Age	Nationality	Embarked	Class	Last Abode
196	369	Cannavan	Pat	M		British	Queenstown	3	Queenstown
198	368	Cann	Ernest	M		British	Southampton	3	Southampton
199	371	Caram	Joseph	M		Canada	Cherbourg	3	Paris
200	372	Caram	Maria	F		Canada	Cherbourg	3	Paris
201	143	Carbines	Wm	M	19	British	Southampton	2	St Ives, Nangivey
204	454	Garfirth	John	M	22	British	Southampton	3	Wellingboro
205	17	Carlson	Frank	M		American	Southampton	1	
206	375	Carlsson	August Sigfrid	M		Denmark	Southampton	3	Copenhagen
207	373	Carlsson	Carl R	M		Denmark	Southampton	3	Copenhagen
208	370	Car	Jeannie	F		British	Queenstown	3	Queenstown
209	18	Carran	F M	M		American	Southampton	1	
210	19	Carran	J P	M		American	Southampton	1	
211	144	Carter	E C	M	54	British	Southampton	2	London
212	145	Carter	Lillian	M	44	British	Southampton	2	London
217	378	Carver	A	M		British	Southampton	3	Southampton
218	20	Case	Howard B	M		American	Southampton	1	Vaccuum Oil Co, London
221	21	Cavendish	T W	M		American	Southampton	1	23 Chesham Place, London
222	379	Celotti	Francesco	M	24	Italian	Southampton	3	Cape Town
224	22	Chaffee	H F	M		American	Southampton	1	
227	148	Chapman	Charles	M		British	Southampton	2	Mr Wheeler's Yard, W Drayton
228	146	Chapman	J A	M	30	British	Southampton	2	Liscarn, Devon
229	147	Chapman	E (Mrs)	F	28	British	Southampton	2	Liscarn, Devon
230	380	Chartens	David	M		British	Queenstown	3	Queenstown
236	23	Chisholm	Robt	M		British	Southampton	1	Harland & Wolff, Belfast
237	381	Christmans	Emil	M	29	German	Southampton	3	London
240	382	Chronopoulos	Apostolos	M	26	Greek	Cherbourg	3	Greece
241	383	Chronopoulos	Demetrios	M	18	Greek	Cherbourg	3	Greece
243	149	Clarke	Chas V	M	29	British	Southampton	2	Soton
245	24	Clark	W M	M		American	Cherbourg	1	c/o Anex Co, Rome
246	285	Clarke	F C	M		British	Southampton	2	c/o J & S Black, Liverpool
248	25	Clifford	Geo Quincey	M		American	Southampton	1	c/o Kings Hotel, King St, Cheapside,
249	384	Coelho	Fernandes Domingos	M	20	Portugal	Southampton	3	Portugal
251	385	Colbert	Patrick	M		British	Queenstown	3	Queenstown
252	387	Coleff	Peya	M	36	Bulgarian	Southampton	3	Bulgaria
253	386	Coleff	Tatio	M	24	Bulgarian	Southampton	3	Bulgaria
254	150	Coleridge	R C	M	29	British	Southampton	2	232 Strand
255	151	Collander	Erik	M		Finn	Southampton	2	Finskaa, Helsinfors
257	26	Colley	E P	M		British	Southampton	1	Farmath Rathger, Dublin
260	152	Collyer	Harvey	M	32	British	Southampton	2	Mount Hill, Basingstoke
262	27	Compton	A T jnr	M			Cherbourg	1	Hotel Dysart, Paris
265	388	Conlin	Thos H	M		British	Queenstown	3	Queenstown
266	389	Connaghten	Michael	M		British	Queenstown	3	Queenstown

163

Who Sailed on Titanic?

Master list No	Old list No	Surname	Name(s)	Sex	Age	Nationality	Embarked	Class	Last Abode
268	390	Connolly	Kate	F		British	Queenstown	3	Queenstown
269	391	Connors	Pat	M		British	Queenstown	3	Queenstown
270	392	Cook	Jacob	M	43	Russian	Southampton	3	Russia
272	393	Cor	Bartol	M	35	Austrian	Southampton	3	Austria
273	394	Cor	Ivan	M	27	Austrian	Southampton	3	Austria
274	395	Cor	Ludovik	M	19	Austrian	Southampton	3	Austria
275	153	Corbett	Irene C	F	30	American	Southampton	2	York Road, London
276	154	Corey	C P	F		American	Southampton	2	London
277	396	Corn	Harry	M	30	Russian	Southampton	3	London
280	155	Cotterill	Harry	M	20	British	Southampton	2	26 Adelaide St, Penzance
284	397	Coxon	Daniel	M	US		Southampton	3	USA
285	28	Crafton	J B	M		American	Southampton	1	Victoria Hotel London
287	398	Crease	Ernest Jos	M	19	British	Southampton	3	Bristol
288	399	Cribb	In Harfield	M	44	British	Southampton	3	Bournemouth
291	29	Crosby	Ed G	M			Southampton	1	Grand Trunk Rly
294	30	Cummings	In Bradley	M			Cherbourg	1	c/o Morgan Herfes, Paris
295	276	Cunningham	A	M		British	Southampton	2	Belfast c/o Harland & Wolff
296	401	Daher	Shedid	M	21	Syria	Cherbourg	3	Syria
298	402	Dahlberg	Gerda	M	22	Swedish	Southampton	3	Gothenburg
299	403	Dalic	Branko	M	19	Austrian	Southampton	3	Austria
303	405	Danborn	Sigrid	M	27	Swedish	Southampton	3	Gothenburg
304	404	Danborn	Ernest	M	34	Swedish	Southampton	3	Gothenburg
305	406	Danborn	Gillbert	M	4m	Swedish	Southampton	3	Gothenburg
308	407	Danoff	Toto	M	27	Bulgarian	Southampton	3	Bulgaria
309	408	Dantchoff	Christo	M	25	Bulgarian	Southampton	3	Bulgaria
311	31	Davidson	Thornton	M			Cherbourg	1	Cherbourg
312	411	Davies	Alf J	M	24	British	Southampton	3	W Bromwich
313	156	Davies	Charles	M	21	British	Southampton	2	Lyndhurst, Hants
315	410	Davies	Evan	M	22	British	Southampton	3	Pontadowe
318	412	Davies	John	M	21	British	Southampton	3	W Bromwich
319	413	Davis	Joseph	M	17	British	Southampton	3	W Bromwich
323	409	Davison	Thos N	M	32	British	Southampton	3	Liverpool
328	669	Pelsmaker	Alfonse de	M	17	Belgian	Southampton	3	Antwerp
329	157	Deacon	Percy	M	20	British	Southampton	2	Lyndhurst, Hants
330	414	Dean	Bertram F	M	25	British	Southampton	3	Southampton
334	159	Del Carlo	SAVED (Mrs)	F			Cherbourg	2	Paris c/o Braischim Luces, Italy
335	158	Del Carlo	Sebastiani	M			Cherbourg	2	Paris c/o Braischim Luces, Italy
336	415	Delalic	Regyo	M	25	Austrian	Southampton	3	Austria
337	421	Dimitri	Marinko	M	23	Macedonia			Austria
338	160	Denbon	Herbert	M	25	British	Southampton	2	Les Sauvages, St Samorain
339	417	Denkoff	Mito	M	30	Bulgarian	Southampton	3	Bulgaria
340	416	Dennis	Samuel	M	28	British	Southampton	3	Holsworthy, St Mary, Bude

Master list No	Old list No	Surname	Name(s)	Sex	Age	Nationality	Embarked	Class	Last Abode
341	423	Dennis	Wm	M	26	British	Southampton	3	Holsworthy, St Mary, Bude
344	161	Dibden	Wm	M	19	British	Southampton	2	Bramshaw, Hants
347	419	Dika	Mirko	M	17	Austrian	Southampton	3	Austria
348	420	Dimic	Jovan	M	42	Austrian	Southampton	3	Austria
349	422	Dintcheff	Valteto	M	43	Bulgarian	Southampton	3	Bulgaria
353	400	Daher	Tannus	M	28	Syria	Cherbourg	3	Syria
356	637	O Donoghue	Bert Saved	M		British	Queenstown	3	Ireland,Queenstown
357	424	Dooley	Pat	M		British	Queenstown	3	Queenstown
361	32	Douglas	W A	M		American	Cherbourg	1	c/o Boyd Neel, 6 Rue Tamsin, Paris
363	162	Downton	W J	M	54	British	Southampton	2	c/o Mrs Donaille, Nearvale Church, Guernsey
364	425	Doyle	Elin	F		British	Queenstown	3	Queenstown
365	426	Dragenovic	Josif	M	33	Austrian	Southampton	3	Austria
368	163	Drew	Jas	F	M	American	Southampton	2	Penrhyn, Cornwall
373	33	Dulles	W C	M		American	Cherbourg	1	Hotel France, Paris
376	418	Dewar	Frank	M		British	Queenstown	3	Queenstown
377	427	Dyker	Adolf	M	23	Swedish	Southampton	3	Gothenburg
381	428	Eceinovic	Joso	M	17	Swiss	Southampton	3	Basle
382	429	Edwardsson	Gustaf F	M	18	Swedish	Southampton	3	Helsingborg
383	164	Eitemiller	G F	F	16	Swedish	Southampton	2	Bonnington Hotel, Soton
384	430	Eklund	Hans	M	46	Swedish	Southampton	3	Gothenburg
385	431	Ekstrom	Johan	M	29	Swedish	Southampton	3	Gothenburg
386	432	Elias	Dibo	M	39	Syria	Cherbourg	3	Syria
387	520	Joseph	Joseph	M	18	Syria	Cherbourg	3	Syria
388	434	Elias	Joseph	M	20	Syria	Southampton	3	Syria
389	435	Elias	Tanous	M	47	Syria	Cherbourg	3	Syria
390	436	Elsbury	James	M	29	British	Southampton	3	Taunton
392	165	Chehal	Emir Farres	M	21	Syria	Cherbourg	3	Syria
393	468	Enander	Ingvar	M	38	Swedish	Southampton	2	127a, Sveagation, Gothenburg
395	34	Goncalves	Manoel	M		Portugal	Southampton	3	Brazil
397	437	Evans	E	F	36	American	Cherbourg	1	Hotel Majestic, Paris
399	166	Everett	Thos B	M		British	Southampton	3	Bristol
402	439	Fahlstrom	Arne J	M		Norway	Southampton	2	Slendal, Christiania
403	121	Farrell	James	M		British	Southampton	3	Queenstown
404		Male	? valet						
406	167	Fannthorpe	Harry	M		British	Southampton	2	Lpool
407	168	Fillbrook	Chas	M	19	British	Southampton	2	16 Charles Street, Truro
409	440	Fischer	Eberhard	M	19	Denmark	Southampton	3	Copenhagen
411	488	Hemming	Nora	F		British	Queenstown	3	Queenstown
414	443	Flynn	James	M		British	Queenstown	3	Queenstown
415	444	Flynn	John	M		British	Queenstown	3	Queenstown
417	441	Foley	Joseph	M	19	British	Queenstown	3	Queenstown

Master list No	Old list No	Surname	Name(s)	Sex	Age	Nationality	Embarked	Class	Last Abode
418	442	Foley	Wm	M		British	Queenstown	3	Queenstown
420	445	Ford	Arthur	M	22	British	Southampton	3	Bridgewater
421	447	Ford	D M	F	21	British	Southampton	3	London
422	448	Ford	E W	M	18	British	Southampton	3	London
423	446	Ford	Margaret	F	48	British	Southampton	3	London
424	450	Ford	Maggie	F	9	British	Southampton	3	London
425	449	Ford	M T M	M	16	British	Southampton	3	London
426	35	Forman	B L	M		British	Southampton	1	
430	37	Fortune	Chas	M		American	Southampton	1	Hotel Metropole, London
433	36	Fortune	Mark	M		American	Southampton	1	Hotel Metropole, London
435	452	Fox	Patrick	M		British	Queenstown	3	Queenstown
436	169	Fox	Stanley	M		American	Southampton	2	c/o Morrisons Broking Offices, Victoria St Birmingham
438	451	Franklin	Charles	M	38	British	Southampton	3	Southampton
439	38	Franklin	T P	M		British	Southampton	1	17 Cheapside, London EC
446	278	Frost	A	M	37	British	Southampton	2	Belfast c/o Harland & Wolff
447	118	Male	? ms Ismay			Southampton			
448	170	Funk	Annie	F		American	Southampton	2	c/o Cook Ludgate Circus
449	39	Futrelle	J	M		American	Southampton	1	44 Gloster Terr, Hyde Park, W
451	171	Fynney	Jos	M		American	Southampton	2	Browns Bdgs, Lpool
452	172	Gale	Harry	M		British	Southampton	2	School Road, Jarrow, Barrow
453	173	Gale	Shadrack	M		British	Southampton	2	nr St Dominics, Cornwall
454	453	Gallagher	Martin	M	38	British	Queenstown	3	Queenstown
456	174	Gaskell	Alfd	M		British	Southampton	2	20 Dexters, Liverpool
457	175	Gavey	Lawrence	M		British	Southampton	2	Basirestil, Guernsey
458	40	Gee	Arthur	M		British	Southampton	1	Morningside Riley A. St Annes
459	813	Youssef	Gerios	M		Syria	Cherbourg	3	Syria
460	456	Gheorgheff	Stanio	M	26	Bulgarian	Cherbourg	3	Bulgaria
464	41	Giglio	Victor	M	?		Cherbourg	1	57 Ave Montaigne, Paris
465	176	Gilbert	William	M		British	Southampton	2	Carleens Village, Cornwall
466	177	Giles	Edgar	M		British	Southampton	2	Porthleven
467	178	Giles	Fred	M		British	Southampton	2	Porthleven
468	179	Giles	Ralph	M		British	Southampton	2	10 Gunderstone Rd, W Kensington
469	457	Gilinskie	Leslie	M	22	Russian	Southampton	3	Wales
470	180	Gill	John	M		British	Southampton	2	3 Griffin Rd, Clevedon, Somerset
471	181	Gillespie	Wm H	M	34	British	Southampton	2	Coffee Palace, Abbeyleix
473	182	Givard	Hans K	M		Danish	Southampton	2	Soton
477	42	Goldshmidt	Geo B	M		American	Cherbourg	1	Hotel Continental, Paris
479	458	Goldsmith	Frank J	M	33	British	Southampton	3	England
481	459	Goldsmith	Nathan	M	41	Russian	Southampton	3	Cape Town
482	460	Goodwin	Augusta	F	43	British	Southampton	3	High St, Melksham
483	463	Goodwin	Charles E	M	40	British	Southampton	3	High St, Melksham

Master list No	Old list No	Surname	Names)	Sex	Age	Nationality	Embarked	Class	Last Abode
484	461	Goodwin	Frederick	M	40	British	Southampton	3	High St, Melksham
485	466	Goodwin	Harold V	M	9	British	Southampton	3	High St, Melksham
486	465	Goodwin	Jessie A M	F	10	British	Southampton	3	High St, Melksham
487	462	Goodwin	Lillias A	F	16	British	Southampton	3	High St, Melksham
488	467	Goodwin	Sidney A	M	6	British	Southampton	3	High St, Melksham
489	464	Goodwin	Wm F	M	11	British	Southampton	3	High St, Melksham
492	43	Graham	?	M		British	Southampton	1	c/o T Eaton & Co, London
494	469	Green	George	M	40	British	Southampton	3	Gunnerslake
495	183	Greenberg	Saml	M		Russian	Southampton	2	Soton
498	470	Gronnestad	Daniel D	M	32	Norwegian	Southampton	3	Norway
499	471	Guest	Robert	M	23	British	Southampton	3	London
500	44	Guggenheim	Benj	M		American	Cherbourg	1	37 Ave Montaigne, Paris
501	472	Gustafson	Alfred	M	20	Swedish	Southampton	3	Sweden
502	473	Gustafson	Anders	M	37	Finn	Southampton	3	Finland
503	474	Gustafson	Johan	M	28	Finn	Southampton	3	Finland
504	475	Gustafsson	Gideon	M	19	Swedish	Southampton	3	Sweden
506	476	Haas	Alaisia	F	24	Swiss	Southampton	3	Switzerland
507	479	Hagland	Ingvald C	M	28	Norwegian	Southampton	3	Norway
508	480	Hagland	Konrad R	M	20	Norwegian	Southampton	3	Norway
510	481	Halkurainen	Pekka	M	28	Finn	Southampton	3	Finland
511	184	Hale	Reginald	M	30	British	Southampton	2	Rodney Stoke in Cheddar
514	620	Nampe	Leon	M		Belgian	Southampton	3	Antwerp
515	584	Mansour	Hanna	M	35	Syria	Cherbourg	3	Syria
516	611	Moubarek	Hanna	F	25	Syria	Cherbourg	3	Syria
517	482	Hansen	Claus	M	41	US	Southampton	3	Copenhagen
518	525	Jutel	Henrik H	M	26	Dane	Southampton	3	Copenhagen
519	483	Hansen	Hy D	M	21	Denmark	Southampton	3	Copenhagen
521	185	Harbeck	Wm H	M		American	Southampton	2	London
524	477	Hagarden	Kate	F		British	Queenstown	3	Queenstown
525	484	Harknett	Alice	F	21	British	Southampton	3	London
526	485	Harmer	Abraham	M	25	Russian	Southampton	3	Manchester
529	186	Harper	John	M		British	Southampton	2	3 Claud Villa, Denmark Hill, London
533	45	Harris	Hy B	M		American	Southampton	1	Savoy Hotel, London
535	187	Harris	Walker	M		British	Southampton	2	47 Granville Road, Walthamstow
536	46	Harrison	W H	M		British	Southampton	1	
537	188	Hart	Benj	M		British	Southampton	2	
540	486	Hart	Henry	M		British	Queenstown	3	Queenstown
541	286	Hartley	Wm	M		British	Southampton	2	c/o J & S Black, Liverpool
543	495	Honsolfring	Kassan M	M		British	Cherbourg	3	
545	47	Hays	C M	M		British	Southampton	1	Grand Trunk Rly
548	48	Head	Christopher	M		British	Southampton	1	
552	478	Hagarty	Nora	F		British	Queenstown	3	Queenstown

Master list No	Old list No	Surname	Name(s)	Sex	Age	Nationality	Embarked	Class	Last Abode
554	487	Heininen	Wendla	F	23	Finn	Southampton	3	Finland
556	489	Hendekovic	Ignas	M	28	Austrian	Southampton	3	Austria
557	491	Henriksson	Jenny	F	28	Swedish	Southampton	3	Gothenburg
558	490	Henery	Delia	F		British	Queenstown	3	Queenstown
562	189	Herman	Samuel	M		British	Southampton	2	Yeovil
564	190	Hickman	Leonard	M	24	British	Southampton	2	Lyndhurst, Hants
565	191	Hickman	Lewis	M	32	British	Southampton	2	Lyndhurst, Hants
566	192	Hickman	Stanley	M	20	British	Southampton	2	Lyndhurst, Hants
567	49	Hilliard	Herbert H	M		British	Southampton	1	Hotel Chatham, Paris
568	193	Hilkinen	Martha	F		Finnish	Southampton	3	Helsingfors
569	50	Hipkins	W E	M		British	Southampton	1	c/o W & T Avery, Birmingham
576	194	Hocking	George	M	21	British	Southampton	2	26 St Mary's, Penzance
577	195	Hocking	Samuel J	M		British	Southampton	2	3 Four St, Devonport
578	196	Hodges	Henry P	M	50	British	Southampton	2	Highfield Lane, Soton
581	198	Hold	Stephen	M	42	US	Southampton	2	Fritham, Hants
583	492	Holm	Jn F A	M	43	US	Southampton	3	Copenhagen Hkanen
584	493	Holken	Johan	M	28	Norwegian	Southampton	3	Norway
585	51	Holverson	A O	M		American	Southampton	1	Picadilly Hotel, London
589	199	Hood	Ambrose	M	22	US	Southampton	2	85 Cheltenham St, Swindon
590	494	Horgan	John	M		British	Queenstown	3	Queenstown
592	200	Howard	Benjamin	M	63	British	Southampton	2	85 Cheltenham St, Swindon
593	201	Howard	Ellen T	F	60	British	Southampton	2	85 Cheltenham St, Swindon
597	52	Hoyt	W F	M		American	Cherbourg	1	c/o 123 Pall Mall, London
598	496	Humblen	Adolf	M	42	Norwegian	Southampton	3	Arlesund
599	282	Hume	J	M		British	Southampton	2	c/o J & S Black, Liverpool
600	202	Hunt	George	M		British	Southampton	2	Ashtead nr Epsom
604	497	Ilieff	Ilio	M	32	Bulgarian	Southampton	3	Bulgaria
605	498	Ilmakangas	Ida	F	27	Finn	Southampton	3	Finland
606	499	Ilmakangas	Pista	F	25	Finn	Southampton	3	Finland
607	53	Isham	A E	F		American	Cherbourg	1	c/o Rue de la Varenne, Paris
609	503	Ivanoff	Konis	M	20	Bulgarian	Southampton	3	Bulgaria
611	203	Jacobsohn	Sidney S	M		British	Southampton	2	7 Pembridge Sq, London
614	504	Jardin	Jose H	M		Portugal	Southampton	3	Brazil
615	204	Jarvis	Jno D	M	21	British	Southampton	2	The ... Stony Gate
616	205	Jefferys	Clifford	M		British	Southampton	2	Rossley Half Way House, Guernsey
617	206	Jefferys	Ernest	M		British	Southampton	2	Rossley Half Way House, Guernsey
618	207	Jenkin	Stephen	M		US	Southampton	2	St Ives
619	505	Jensen	Hans P	M	21	Dane	Southampton	3	Denmark
620	506	Jensen	Nils L	M	48	US	Southampton	3	Denmark
621	507	Jensen	Svens L	M	17	Dane	Southampton	3	Denmark
626	512	Johnson	Jakob A	M	34	Finn	Southampton	3	Finland
627	510	Johanson	Enk	M	20	Dane	Southampton	3	Denmark

Master list No	Old list No	Surname	Name(s)	Sex	Age	Nationality	Embarked	Class	Last Abode
628	508	Johanson	Gustaf	M	33	Swedish	Southampton	3	Sweden
629	511	Johnson	Carl	M	32	Swedish	Southampton	3	Sweden
630	509	Johanson	Milo	M	30	Swedish	Southampton	3	Sweden
632	521	Johnson	A	M		British	Southampton	3	8 Kingsley Rd, Southampton
636	513	Johansson	Malkolm	M	30	Swedish	Southampton	3	Sweden
637	522	Johnson	W	M		British	Southampton	3	8 Kingsley Rd, Southampton
638	514	Johnston	A E	M	34	British	Southampton	3	London
639	517	Johnston	C H	F	8	British	Southampton	3	London
640	515	Johnston	Mrs	F	34	British	Southampton	3	London
641	516	Johnston	Wm A	M	9	British	Southampton	3	London
642	55	Jones	C C	M		American	Southampton	1	c/o Junction Hotel, Dorchester
643	518	Jonkoff	Lazore	M	23	Bulgarian	Southampton	3	Bale
645	519	Jonsson	Niels H	M	26	Dane	Southampton	3	Denmark
646	677	Peter	Anna	F	2	Syria	Cherbourg	3	Syria
648	676	Peter	Niki	M	4	Syria	Cherbourg	3	Syria
649	56	Julian	H	F	M	American	Southampton	1	Finland
651	523	Jussila	Katrina	M	20	Finn	Southampton	3	Finland
652	524	Jussila	Mari	F	21	Finn	Southampton	3	Finland
653	526	Kallio	Nikolai	M	17	Finn	Southampton	3	Finland
654	527	Kalvig	Johannes	M	21	Norwegian	Southampton	3	Stavanger
656	208	Kantor	Sehua	M	34	Russian	Southampton	2	c/o White Star Line, London
657	528	Karafic	Milan	M	30	Swiss	Southampton	3	Basle
659	374	Carlson	Julino	M		Swedish	Southampton	3	Malmo
660	529	Karlsson	Nils A	M	22	Dane	Southampton	3	Copenhagen
661	209	Karres	J F	F			Southampton	2	
664	438	Fared	Kassem	M	18	Syria	Cherbourg	3	Syria
665	376	Catavelas	Vassilios	M		Greek	Cherbourg	3	Paris
666	533	Kerane	Andy	M		British	Queenstown	3	Queenstown
667	210	Keane	Daniel	M			Southampton	2	c/o E Ludlow, Limerick
669	530	Keefe	Arthur	M	39	US	Southampton	3	USA
670	117	Keeping	Arthur msWidener	M			Southampton		
671	531	Kelley	James	M	44	British	Southampton	3	Kirk St, Carlake
674	532	Kelly	James	M	19	British	Queenstown	3	Queenstown
677	57	Kent	Ed A	M		American	Cherbourg	1	Hotel Continental, Paris
678	58	Kenyon	F R	M		American	Southampton	1	Hotel Delatamise, Paris
680	541	Khalil	Betros	M	25	Syria	Cherbourg	3	Syria
681	543	Khalil	Zahic	F	20	Syria	Cherbourg	3	Syria
682	539	Kiernan	John	M		British	Queenstown	3	Queenstown
683	535	Kiernan	Phillip	M		British	Queenstown	3	Queenstown
684	534	Kilgannon	Thos	M		British	Queenstown	3	Queenstown
690	536	Kink	Vincenz	M	27	Swiss	Southampton	3	Basle
691	537	Kink	Maria	F	22	Swiss	Southampton	3	Basle

Master list No	Old list No	Surname	Name(s)	Sex	Age	Nationality	Embarked	Class	Last Abode
692	211	Kirkland	Chas L	M		American	Queenstown	2	
693	59	Klaber	Herman	M			Southampton	1	
694	542	Klasen	Gertrude	F	1	Swedish	Southampton	3	Sweden
695	540	Klasen	Hulda K E	F	36	Swedish	Southampton	3	Sweden
696	538	Klasen	Klas A	M	18	Denmark	Southampton	3	Copenhagen
698	279	Knight	R	M	39	British	Southampton	2	Belfast c/o Harland & Wolff
699	545	Kraeff	Thodor	M		Bulgarian	Cherbourg	3	Bale
702	281	Krins	George	M		Belgian	Southampton	2	c/o J & S Black, Liverpool
703	212	Kvilner	Jn Hy	M	31	Swedish	Southampton	2	Gothenburg
704	546	Lahond	Sarkis	M	30	Syria	Cherbourg	3	Syria
706	213	Lahtinen	Wm	M		US	Southampton	3	Helsingfors
707	547	Laitiners	Sofia	F	37	Finn	Southampton	3	Finland
708	548	Laleff	Kristo	M	23	Bulgarian	Southampton	3	Bale
710	549	Lam	Len	M	23	Chinese	Southampton	3	London
711	214	Lamb	J J	M		British	Queenstown	2	Enniskerry, Glencrea
713	550	Lane	Patk	M		British	Queenstown	3	Queenstown
715	215	Larouch	Joseph	M		French	Cherbourg	2	131 Grand Rue ..... Paris
719	552	Larson	Viktor	M	29	Swedish	Southampton	3	Sweden
720	551	Larson	Benj E	M	29	Swedish	Southampton	3	Sweden
721	553	Larsson	Edward	M	22	Swedish	Southampton	3	Sweden
726	554	Lefebre	Francis	F	39	French	Southampton	3	Havre
727	557	Lefebre	Henry	M	4	French	Southampton	3	Havre
728	558	Lefebre	Ida	F	2	French	Southampton	3	Havre
729	556	Lefebre	Jeannie	F	6	French	Southampton	3	Havre
730	555	Lefebre	Mathilde	F	39	French	Southampton	3	Havre
732	559	Leinonen	Antti	M	23	Finn	Southampton	3	Finland
734	560	Lemberopoulos	Peter Leni	M	30	Greek	Cherbourg	3	Marseilles
736	561	Lemon	Denis	M		British	Queenstown	3	Queenstown
737	562	Lemon	Mary	F		British	Queenstown	3	Queenstown
742	563	Leonard	L	M		British	Southampton	3	Soton
744	564	Lester	James	M		British	Southampton	3	West Bromwich, 29 Harwood Street
746	216	Levy	R J	M		American	Cherbourg	2	Grand Hotel, Paris
748	61	Leroy	E G	M		Wales	Southampton	1	42 Rue de la Pulitier, Paris
749	217	Leyson	Robert D N	M	25	Belgian	Southampton	2	171 Cromwell Road, So Kensington
750	819	Nievens	Rene	M	24	Belgian	Southampton	3	Antwerp
751	565	Lindahl	Agda	F	25	Dane	Southampton	3	Gothenburg
752	566	Lindblom	August	M	45	Dane	Southampton	3	Gothenburg
753	62	Lingrey	Ed	M			Southampton	1	
754	567	Lindell	Ed B	M	36	Swedish	Southampton	3	Malmo
755	568	Lindell	Elin J	F	30	Swedish	Southampton	3	Malmo
758	569	Linehan	M	M	21	British	Queenstown	3	Kingstown, Ireland
761	570	Ling	Lee	M	28	Chinese	Southampton	3	

Master list No	Old list No	Surname	Name(s)	Sex	Age	Nationality	Embarked	Class	Last Abode
762	798	Wenzel	Finhart	M	27	Austrian	Southampton	3	Antwerp
763	218	Lingan	John	M		Russian	Queenstown	2	Regent Street
764	571	Lithman	Simon	M	20	Russian	Southampton	3	17 Drummond St, Edinboro
765	573	Lobb	Cordelia	F	26	British	Southampton	3	St Austell, Cornwall
766	572	Lobb	Wm A	M	30	British	Southampton	3	St Austell, Cornwall
767	574	Lockyer	Edward	M	21	British	Southampton	3	London
768	63	Long	Milton C	M		American	Southampton	1	Hotel Engadine, Kolm, St Moritz
770	64	Loring	J H	M		American	Southampton	1	28 Park Lane, London
772	219	Louch	Charles	M	50	British	Southampton	2	Weston Supermare
773	575	Lovell	John	M	20	British	Southampton	3	Holsworthy
776	576	Lindahl	John	M	51	US	Southampton	3	Malmo
780	577	Lyntakoff	Stanko	M	44	Bulgarian	Southampton	3	Bale
781	220	Mack	Mary (Mrs)	F	50	British	Southampton	2	Bitterne Park, Soton
782	578	Mackay	G W	M	30	British	Southampton	3	London
786	579	Maenpaa	Matti	F	22	Finn	Southampton	3	Finland
787	65	Maguire	J E	M		American	Southampton	1	Kings Hotel, Cheapside
788	580	Mahon	Delia	F	18	British	Queenstown	3	Ireland Qtown
789	596	Mechan	John	M		British	Queenstown	3	Queenstown
791	581	Maisner	Suilon	M	34	Russian	Southampton	3	London
792	582	Makinen	Kalle	M	29	Finn	Southampton	3	Finland
793	221	Malachan	Noel	M					c/o T Cook
794	326	Attala	Malake	F	17	Syria	Cherbourg	3	Syria
795	222	Mallet	A	M			Cherbourg	2	6 Rue Corn..ville, Paris
799	583	Mangen	Mary	F		British	Queenstown	3	Ireland Qtown
800	223	Maqiavacchi	Emilie	F			Cherbourg	2	c/o T Cook, Paris
803	586	Mardirosiam	Sarkis	M	25	Syria	Cherbourg	3	Syria
805	587	Markoff	Maria	F	35	Bale	Cherbourg	3	Bale
806	588	Marehun	Johannes	M	20	Austrian	Cherbourg	3	Austria
807	66	Marvin	D W	M		American	Southampton	1	58 Acor Lane, Brixton, SW
811	589	Matinoff	Ziola	M		Bulgarian	Cherbourg	3	Bale
812	226	Matthews	W J	M		British	Southampton	2	St Austell, Cornwall
815	227	Maybery	Frank H	M		Colonial	Southampton	2	1 White Grass Road, Weston S Mare
817	67	McCaffoy	T	M			Southampton	1	Hotel Majestic, Nice
819	68	McCarthy	Tim J	M	33	British	Southampton	1	Hotel Chatham, Paris
824	228	McCrae	A G	M		British	Southampton	2	c/o Bank of Australasia
825	229	McCrie	James	M		British	Southampton	2	Strand Palace Hotel
827	590	McElroy	M E	M		British	Queenstown	3	Queenstown
830	591	McGowan	Katherine	F		British	Queenstown	3	Queenstown
832	230	McKane	Peter D	M	46	British	Southampton	2	Guernsey
833	592	McMahon	Martin	M		British	Queenstown	3	Queenstown
834	594	McNamee	Eileen	F	19	British	Southampton	3	London
835	593	McNamee	Neal	M	27	British	Southampton	3	London

171

Master list No	Old list No	Surname	Name(s)	Sex	Age	Nationality	Embarked	Class	Last Abode
836	643	O Neil	Bridget	F		British	Queenstown	3	Charlesville, Ireland
837	595	Meanwell	Marion	F	63	British	Southampton	3	England, c/o L... Leadenhall St
838	597	Meek	A L	F	31	British	Southampton	3	Cardiff
843	599	Mew	Alfonso	M	48	Italian	Southampton	3	
844	623	Nemagh	Robert	M		British	Queenstown	3	Queenstown
845	231	Meyer	August	M		German	Southampton	2	26 Kildas Road, Harrow on the Hill
846	69	Meyer	Edgar J	M		American	Cherbourg	1	Hotel Majestic, Paris
849	601	Miles	Frank	M	23	British	Southampton	3	103 King George St, Greenwich
851	70	Millet	Frank D	M		American	Cherbourg	1	
852	232	Milling	Jacob L	M	48	Danish	Southampton	2	Odense, Copenhagen
856	602	Mineff	Ivan	M	24	Bulgarian	Southampton	3	Bale
857	603	Minkoff	Lazar	M	21	Bulgarian	Southampton	3	Bale
858	600	Mikoff	Stoyliko	M	28	Bulgarian	Southampton	3	Basle
859	233	Mitchell	Henry	M	71	British	Southampton	3	Upland Road, Guernsey
860	604	Mitkoff	Milo	M	23	Bulgarian	Southampton	3	Bale
863	605	Moen	Sigard H	M	25	Norwegian	Southampton	3	Norway
864	71	Molsom	H Markland	M		British	Southampton	1	c/o Athenaem Club, London
865	224	Mantvila	Joseph	M	27	Russian	Southampton	3	21 The Oval, Hackney Rd
868	72	Moore	Clarence	M		American	Southampton	1	Almonds Hotel, Clifford St, London
869	606	Moor	Leo Chas	M	22	British	Southampton	3	London
871	609	Morgan	Danl J	M		British	Queenstown	3	Ireland, Queenstown
872	607	Moran	Jas	M	22	British	Queenstown	3	Ireland, Cork
873 Bru...	234	Morawick	Ernest	M	US	British	Southampton	2	c/o Karlmorawick, Hotel S Ca...
874	225	Marshall	M	M		British	Southampton	2	6 Bristol St, Birmingham
875	608	Morley	Wm	M	34	British	Southampton	3	London, Petworth, Sussex
876	610	Marrow	Thos	M		British	Queenstown	3	Ireland, Queenstown
881	612	Moussa	Mantourd	F	35	Syria	Cherbourg	3	Syria
882	613	Moutal	Rahamin	M	28	Turkish	Southampton	3	London, Hammersmith
883	235	Mudd	Thos C	M	16	British	Southampton	2	
887	614	Murdlin	Joseph	M	22	Russian	Southampton	3	London
891	616	Myhriman	Oliver	M	18	Norwegian	Southampton	3	Gothenburg
892	236	Myles	Thos F	M	US		Queenstown	2	Fermoy
893	617	Naidenoff	Penko	M	22	Bulgarian	Southampton	3	Basel
898	619	Nancarrow	Wm Hy	M	34	British	Southampton	3	Cornwall, c/o Mansell and Rowse
899	621	Nankoff	Ninko	M	32	Bulgarian	Southampton	3	Bulgaria
900	615	Nasr	Mustafa	M	20	Syria	Cherbourg	3	Syria
902	237	Nasser	Nicolas	M		Turkish	Cherbourg	2	c/o Cook, Paris
903	73	Natsch	Chas	M		American	Cherbourg	1	
904	622	Naughton	Hannah	F		British	Queenstown	3	Queenstown
906	197	Hoffman	M				Southampton	2	Shipton
908	624	Nenkoff	Christo	M	22	Bulgarian	Southampton	3	Basel

Master list No	Old list No	Surname	Name(s)	Sex	Age	Nationality	Embarked	Class	Last Abode
909	238	Nesson	Brail	M	26	Russian	Southampton	2	London
910	74	Newell	A W	M	19	American	Cherbourg	1	Hotel St James and Albany, Paris
914	239	Nicholls	Joseph C	M		British	Southampton	2	St Ives
916	75	Nicholson	A S	M	30	British	Southampton	1	Claremont, Shanklin, London
919	625	Nanta	Meminen	F		Finn	Southampton	3	Finland
920	626	Niklasen	Sander	M	21	Swedish	Southampton	3	c/o Druado, Hull
921	627	Nilssen	August F	M	41	Swedish	Southampton	3	Copenhagen
924	629	Nirva	Isak	M	28	Finn	Southampton	3	Finland
928	240	Norman	Robt D	M	20	British	Southampton	2	Glasgow
929	630	Nosworthy	Ruben C	M	22	British	Southampton	3	Newton Abbott
931	585	Mansour	Noel	M	61	Syria	Cherbourg	3	Syria
934	628	Nysven	Johan	M		Norwegian	Southampton	3	Christiania
936	632	O Brien	Thos	M	21	British	Queenstown	3	Queenstown
937	631	O Brien	Dennis	M		British	Queenstown	3	Queenstown
938	634	O Connell	Pat D	M		British	Queenstown	3	Queenstown
939	633	O Connor	Maurice	M		British	Queenstown	3	Queenstown
940	635	O Connor	Pat	M		British	Queenstown	3	Queenstown
941	636	Odahl	Mauritz	M	23	Swedish	Southampton	3	Sweden
951	639	Olsen	Hy	M	28	Norwegian	Southampton	3	Norway
952	638	Olsen	Carl	M	42	US	Southampton	3	Norway
953	640	Olsen	Ole A	M	27	Norwegian	Southampton	3	Norway
954	642	Olsson	Elida	F	31	Copenhagen	Southampton	3	Copenhagen
955	641	Olsen	John	M	28	Norwegian	Southampton	3	Norway
957	303	Anderson	Thor	M	20	Norway	Southampton	3	Christiania
959	645	Oreskovic	Suko	M	20	Swiss	Southampton	3	Basel
960	644	Oreskovic	Luka	M	23	Swiss	Southampton	3	Basel
961	646	Oreskovic	Maria	F	20	Swiss	Southampton	3	Basel
963	647	Olsson	Elon	M	17	Norwegian	Southampton	3	Gothenburg
965	76	Ostby	E C	M	22	American	Southampton	1	Brown Shipley, Pall Mall
967	648	O Sullivan	Bridget	F		US	Queenstown	3	USA and Queenstown
968	241	Otter	Richard	M	39	US	Southampton	2	Southampton
969	77	Ovies	S	M		French	Cherbourg	1	30 Faubourg Poissiniere, Paris
972	242	Pain	Alfred	M	29	Swedish	Southampton	2	Helsingborg
974	657	Paulsson	Alma C	F	2	Swedish	Southampton	3	Helsingborg
975	661	Paulsson	Gosta	M	5	Swedish	Southampton	3	Helsingborg
976	659	Paulsson	Paul	M	3	Swedish	Southampton	3	Helsingborg
977	660	Paulsson	Stina	F	8	Swedish	Southampton	3	Helsingborg
978	658	Paulsson	Torberg	F	11m	Swedish	Southampton	3	Helsingborg
979	655	Panula	Wm	M	17	Finn	Southampton	3	Finland
980	652	Panula	Ernesti	M	16	Finn	Southampton	3	Finland
981	653	Panula	Eira	F	18	Finn	Southampton	3	Finland
982	651	Panula	Yuka	M		Finn	Southampton	3	Finland

Master list No	Old list No	Surname	Name(s)	Sex	Age	Nationality	Embarked	Class	Last Abode
983	649	Panula	Maria	F	40	Finn	Southampton	3	Finland
984	654	Panula	Urthu	F	3	Finn	Southampton	3	Finland
985	243	Parker	Clifford R	M			Southampton	2	Guernsey, St Andrews
986	275	Parks	Frank	M	18	British	Southampton	2	Belfast c/o Harland & Wolff St Anne's On Sea
987	78	Parr	M H W	M		British	Southampton	1	Harland & Wolff, Belfast
989	79	Partner	Austin	M		British	Southampton	1	
990	656	Pasic	Jakob	M	21	Austrian	Southampton	3	Austria
991	689	Potchett	Geo	M	19	British	Southampton	3	Woollaston nr Wellington
992	337	Baulner	Uscher	M	16	Russian	Cherbourg	3	Paris
993	662	Pavlovic	Stifo	M	32	Austrian	Southampton	3	Austria
994	80	Payne	V	M		British	Southampton	1	Grand Trunk Rly, London
995	665	Peacock	Alfred E	M	7M	British	Southampton	3	35 Orchard Place, Soton
996	663	Peacock	Treasteall	F	26	British	Southampton	3	35 Orchard Place, Soton
997	664	Peacock	Treasteall	F	4	British	Southampton	3	35 Orchard Place, Soton
998	666	Pearce	E	M	32	British	Southampton	3	10 Bedford Place, Soton
1000	81	Pears	Thos	M		British	Southampton	1	Mevagissey, Isleworth, Middlesex
1001	675	Pettersen	Olaf	M	29	Norwegian	Southampton	3	Norway
1002	667	Pedrizzi	Joseph	M	24	Italian	Southampton	3	1 Ash Grove, Hackney
1003	668	Pekonimi	E	M	32	Finn	Southampton	3	Finland
1004	670	Peltomaki	Nikolai	M	25	Finn	Southampton	3	Finland
1006	82	Penasco	Victor	M		American	Cherbourg	1	Hotel Majestic, Paris
1007	244	Pengelly	T	M	20	British	Southampton	2	Gunnislake
1008	671	Perkin	Jn Hy	M	22	British	Southampton	3	Holsworthy
1009	245	Pernot	Rene	M			Cherbourg	2	Paris
1012	246	Peruschitz	Jos	M	M	German	Southampton	2	London
1013	672	Peters	Katie	F	9	British	Queenstown	3	Co..hir.. Tipperary
1014	681	Petersen	Marius	M	24	Dane	Southampton	3	London
1015	678	Petranic	Matilda	F	30	Austrian	Southampton	3	Basel
1016	680	Petroff	Nedeco	M	19	Bulgarian	Southampton	3	Bulgaria
1017	679	Pentcho	Petroff	M	29	Bulgarian	Southampton	3	Bulgaria
1018	673	Peterson	Johan	M	25	Swedish	Southampton	3	Gothenburg
1019	674	Petersson	Ellen	F	18	Swedish	Southampton	3	Gothenburg
1022	247	Phillips	Robt	M	45	British	Southampton	2	Ilfracombe
1025	686	Plotchersky	Vasil	M	27	Bulgarian	Southampton	3	Bale
1026	688	Pocruic	Mate	M	17	Austrian	Southampton	3	Austria
1027	687	Pocruic	J	M	24	Austrian	Southampton	3	Austria
1028	248	Ponesell	Martin	M		Danish	Southampton	2	Soton
1030	83	Porter	Walter C	M			Southampton	1	Kings Hotel, Cheapside, London
1032	249	Pulbaum	Frank	M			Cherbourg	2	Paris
1036	690	Radeff	Alexander	M	27	Bulgarian	Southampton	3	Bale
1037	757	Soloang	Lena J	M	63	Norwegian	Southampton	3	Norway

Inq.6

Master list No	Old list No	Surname	Name(s)	Sex	Age	Nationality	Embarked	Class	Last Abode
1038	691	Raihid	Razi	M	30	Syria	Cherbourg	3	Syria
1039	692	Reed	Jas Geo	M	19	Welsh	Southampton	3	Cardiff
1040	250	Reeves	Dd	M	36	British	Southampton	2	Brighton
1041	693	Rakic	Tido	M	38	Austrian	Southampton	3	Bale
1044	251	Renouf	Peter H	M	34		Southampton	2	Guernsey
1045	84	Reuchlin	Jonkleer J G	M		Dutch	Cherbourg	1	c/o Holland American Line
1047	694	Reynolds	Harold	M	21	British	Southampton	3	London
1049	696	Rice	Albert	M		British	Queenstown	3	Queenstown
1050	699	Rice	Arthur	M		British	Queenstown	3	Queenstown
1051	698	Rice	Eric	M		British	Queenstown	3	Queenstown
1052	700	Rice	Eugene	M		British	Queenstown	3	Queenstown
1053	697	Rice	George	M		British	Queenstown	3	Queenstown
1054	695	Rice	Margaret	F		British	Queenstown	3	Queenstown
1055	252	Richard	Emile	M			Cherbourg	2	Paris
1060	650	Panfield	Sanni	M	21	Finn	Southampton	3	Finland
1061	120	Male	? valet	M			Southampton	1	
1062	701	Rinlamaki	Natti	M	35	Finn	Southampton	3	Finland
1064	703	Risien	Emma	F	58	US	Southampton	3	London
1065	702	Risien	Saml	M	68	US	Southampton	3	London
1068	704	Robins	Alexdr	M	50	British	Southampton	3	Cornwall
1069	705	Robins	Charity	M	48	British	Southampton	3	Cornwall
1070	85	Roebling	Washington A 2nd	M		American	Southampton	1	129 Pall Mall, London
1071	253	Rogers	Harry	M	18	British	Southampton	2	Tavistock
1072	706	Rogers	Wm Jno	M	29	British Pontadawe	Southampton	3	Pantadawe, S Wales
1074	711	Rummelvedt	K P	M	49	Norwegian Bergen	Bergen	3	Bergen
1075	86	Rood	Hugh R	M		American	Southampton	1	Ritz Hotel, London
1076	707	Rosblom	Helene	F	41	Finn	Southampton	3	Finland
1077	709	Rosblom	Salli	F	2	Finn	Southampton	3	Finland
1078	708	Rosblom	Viktor	M	18	Finn	Southampton	3	Finland
1080	104	Thorne	G	M		American	Cherbourg	1	17 Faubourg Poissoniere, Paris
1081	87	Ross	J Hugo	M		American	Southampton	1	Savoy Hotel, London
1085	88	Rothschild	M	M		American	Cherbourg	1	Grand Hotel, Paris
1086	710	Rouse	Rd Hy	M	53	British	Southampton	3	Sittingbourne
1087	89	Rowe	Alfred	M		American	Southampton	1	c/o Petersham B, Gloster Rd, London
1089	712	Rusto	Alfred G J	M	17	British London	Southampton	3	London
1091	713	Ryan	Pat	M		British	Queenstown	3	Queenstown also at 301
1092	90	Ryerson	A	M		American	Cherbourg	1	Hotel Langhem, Paris
1097	301	Saad	Amin	M	30	Syria	Cherbourg	3	Syria
1098	544	Khalil	Saad	M	25	Syria	Cherbourg	3	Syria
1099	714	Saade	Jean N	M	20	Syria	Southampton	3	Syria
1101	715	Sadlier	Matt	M	17	British	Queenstown	3	Queenstown
1102	716	Sadowitz	Harry	M	17	British	Southampton	3	London

175

Master list No	Old list No	Surname	Name(s)	Sex	Age	Nationality	Embarked	Class	Last Abode
1103	735	Sather	Simon	M	25	US	Southampton	3	Capetown
1104	720	Sage	Annie	F	44	British	Southampton	3	246 Gladstone Rd, Peterboro
1105	726	Sage	Wm	M	11	British	Southampton	3	246 Gladstone Rd, Peterboro
1106	728	Sage	Constance	F	7	British	Southampton	3	246 Gladstone Rd, Peterboro
1107	725	Sage	Dorothy	F	13	British	Southampton	3	246 Gladstone Rd, Peterboro
1108	723	Sage	Douglas	M	18	British	Southampton	3	246 Gladstone Rd, Peterboro
1109	727	Sage	Ada	F	9	British	Southampton	3	246 Gladstone Rd, Peterboro
1110	724	Sage	Fredk	M	16	British	Southampton	3	246 Gladstone Rd, Peterboro
1111	722	Sage	George	M	19	British	Southampton	3	246 Gladstone Rd, Peterboro
1112	719	Sage	John	M	44	British	Southampton	3	London, 246 Gladstone Rd, Peterboro
1113	721	Sage	Stella	F	20	British	Southampton	3	246 Gladstone Rd, Peterboro
1114	729	Sage	Thos	M	4	British	Southampton	3	246 Gladstone Rd, Peterboro
1116	730	Salander	Carl	M	24	Swedish	Southampton	3	Gothenburg
1119	731	Salloneri	Werner	M	29	Finn	Southampton	3	Finland
1120	733	Samaan	Elias	M	18	Syria	Cherbourg	3	Syria
1121	732	Samaan	Hanna	M	40	Syria	Cherbourg	3	Syria
1122	734	Samaan	Youssef	M	16	Syria	Cherbourg	3	Syria
1127	736	Saundercock	Wm H	M	20	British	Southampton	3	Soton
1128	737	Sawyer	Fredk	M	23	British	Southampton	3	Woolwich
1129	738	Scanlan	James	M		British	Queenstown	3	Queenstown
1132	258	Smith	August	M		Austrian	Southampton	3	London
1133	739	Sydloff	B Fodor	M	4	Bulgarian	Southampton	3	Basel
1134	254	Sedgewick	C F	M			Southampton	2	London
1137	255	Sharp	Percival	M			Southampton	2	London
1138	741	Shaughnessy	Pat	M		British	Queenstown	3	Queenstown
1140	742	Shellard	Fred	M	52	British	Southampton	3	Bristol
1143	743	Shorney	Chas J	M	22	British	Southampton	3	Brighton
1148	91	Silvey	Wm B	M		British	Cherbourg	1	
1149	745	Simmons	Jno	M	39	British	Southampton	3	England
1153	718	Sirayaman	Orsen	M	22	US	Cherbourg	3	Marseille
1154	717	Sirota	Maurice	M	20	British	Southampton	3	London
1155	746	Sikic	Husen	M	40	Austrian	Southampton	3	Bale
1156	744	Scloold	Antti	M	21	Finn	Southampton	3	Finland
1158	256	Sjostedt	Ernest A	M		Swedish	Southampton	2	London
1159	748	Skoog	Anna	F	43	Swedish	Southampton	3	Sweden
1160	751	Skoog	Harold	M	4	Swedish	Southampton	3	Sweden
1161	749	Skoog	Carl	M	10	Swedish	Southampton	3	Sweden
1162	750	Skoog	A	F	9	Swedish	Southampton	3	Sweden
1163	752	Skoog	Margaret	F	2	Swedish	Southampton	3	Sweden
1164	747	Skoog	Wm	M	39	Swedish	Southampton	3	Sweden
1165	753	Slabenoff	Peter	M	42	Bulgarian	Southampton	3	Bale
1168	257	Sleeman	Rd J	M	35	British	Southampton	2	Soton

Master list No	Old list No	Surname	Name(s)	Sex	Age	Nationality	Embarked	Class	Last Abode
1169	754	Slocovski	Selenan	M	20	Russian	Southampton	3	London
1171	92	Smart	Jn	M	M	American	Southampton	1	3 Wood End Cottage, Kildale.... York
1172	755	Smilganic	Nile	M	37	Austrian	Southampton	3	Basel
1173	93	Smith	J Clinch	M		American	Cherbourg	1	4 Villa Said, Paris
1175	95	Smith	L P	M			Cherbourg	1	??nephews London
1178	94	Smith	R W	M		British	Southampton	1	??nephews London
1183	259	Sobey	Hayden	M	25	British	Southampton	2	Plymo
1184	756	Sobolt	Peter	M	19	Norwegian	Southampton	3	Norway
1185	758	Somerton	Francis	F	31	US	Southampton	3	Cheltenham
1186	759	Spector	Woolf	M	23	Russian	Southampton	3	London
1191	96	Spencer	W A	M		American	Cherbourg	1	33 Avenue Hy Martin, Paris
1192	760	Spinner	Henry Jno	M	32	British	Southampton	3	Worcester
1194	761	Staneff	Ivan	M	23	Bulgarian	Southampton	3	Bale
1195	762	Stankovic	Jovan	M	33	Austrian	Cherbourg	3	Bale
1197	763	Stanley	E R	M	21	British	Southampton	3	Swanage
1198	260	Stanton	S Ward	M		US	Cherbourg	2	Paris
1199	97	Stead	W T	M		British	Southampton	1	5 Smith Sq, Westminster
1204	98	Stewart	A A	M		American	Cherbourg	1	Hotel Cortin 1e, Paris
1205	261	Stokes	Phillip J	M	25	British	Southampton	2	London
1207	765	Tory	T	M		British	Southampton	3	
1208	766	Stoytchoff	Ilia	M	19	Bulgarian	Southampton	3	Bale
1209	767	Svandberg	Ida	F	19	Swedish	Southampton	3	Sweden
1211	99	Straus	Isidor	M		American	Southampton	1	Hotel Bristol, Paris
1212	100	Straus	Isidor (Mrs)	F		American	Southampton	1	Hotel Bristol, Paris
1213	768	Strilic	Ivan	M	27	Austrian	Southampton	3	Basel
1214	769	Strom	Elma	F	28	Swedish	Southampton	3	Sweden
1215	770	Strom	Selma	F	2	Swedish	Southampton	3	Sweden
1218	771	Sutchall	Hy	M	26	US	Southampton	3	London
1220	101	Sutton	Fredk	M		British	Southampton	1	
1222	772	Svensson	Johan	M	74	Swedish	Southampton	3	Sweden
1224	773	Svenssen	Olaf	M	24	Swedish	Southampton	3	Sweden
1225	262	Swane	George	M		British	Southampton	2	154 Abbey Road, London
1226	263	Sweet	George	M	14	British	Southampton	2	Yeovil
1228	102	Tanssiq	Emil	M		Austrian	Southampton	1	Vienna
1233	283	Taylor	P C	M		British	Southampton	2	c/o J & S Black, Liverpool
1235	103	Thayer	J B	M		American	Cherbourg	1	
1238	774	Theobald	Thos	M	34	British	Southampton	3	Rochester
1240	775	Thomas	Charles	M	31	Syria	Cherbourg	3	Marseille
1241	776	Thomas	Jno	M	34	Syria	Cherbourg	3	Marseille
1242	777	Thomas	Tannous J	M	16	Syria	Southampton	3	Marseille
1244	780	Thomson	Alex	M		British	Southampton	3	Scotland
1247	778	Thorneycroft	Percival	M	36	British	Southampton	3	London

177

Master list No	Old list No	Surname	Name(s)	Sex	Age	Nationality	Embarked	Class	Last Abode
1248	779	Mikanen	Juto	M	32	Finnish	Southampton	3	Finland
1249	781	Tobin	Roger	M		British	Queenstown	3	London
1250	782	Todoroff	Lalio	M	23	Bulgarian	Southampton	3	Bale
1251	783	Tomlin	Ernest P	M	22	British	Southampton	3	London
1253	784	Torber	Ernest	M	41	German	Southampton	3	London
1254	322	Assad	Zorfa	M	20	Syria	Cherbourg	3	Syria
1256	618	Nakle	Unfik	M	17	Syria	Cherbourg	3	Syria
1257	812	Youssef	George SAVED	M	6	Syria	Cherbourg	3	Syria
1258	811	Youssef	Hancie SAVED	F	30	Syria	Cherbourg	3	Syria
1262	264	Tronpiansky	Moses A	M	23	Russian	Southampton	3	London
1266	785	Turcin	Stefan	M	36	Austrian	Southampton	3	Bale
1269	265	Turpin	Dorothy	F	27	British	Southampton	2	Plymouth
1270	266	Turpin	Wm J	M	29	British	Southampton	2	Plymouth
1271	105	Uruchurtu	M R	M		American	Cherbourg	1	Grand Hotel, Paris
1272	786	Tovo	Uzelas	M	17	Austrian	Southampton	3	Basel
1274	342	Billiard	A Van	M		US	Southampton	3	London
1275	343	Billiard	James	M		US	Southampton	3	London
1276	344	Billiard	Walter	M		US	Southampton	3	London
1277	787	Van de Velde	Joseph	M	36	Belgian	Southampton	3	Antwerp
1278	764	Steen	Leo	M	28	Belgian	Southampton	3	Antwerp
1279	106	Van der Hoef	Wijkoff	M		American	Southampton	1	5 College Park, E Belfast
1280	502	Impe	Catharin Van	F	10	Belgian	Southampton	3	Belgium
1281	500	Impe	Jacob Van	M	36	Belgian	Southampton	3	Belgium
1282	501	Impe	Rosalie Van	F	30	Belgian	Southampton	3	Belgium
1283	598	Melebuk	Philemon	M	23	Belgian	Southampton	3	Antwerp
1284	792	Van de Walle	Nestor	M	28	Belgian	Southampton	3	Antwerp
1285	788	Vereraysse	Victor	M	47	Belgian	Southampton	3	Antwerp
1286	682	Planke	August Vander	M	18	Belgian	Southampton	3	Antwerp
1287	685	Planke	Emilie	F	31	Belgian	Southampton	3	Antwerp
1288	684	Planke	Jules	M	31	Belgian	Southampton	3	Antwerp
1289	683	Planke	Leon	M	16	Belgian	Southampton	3	Antwerp
1291	267	Veale	James	M		US	Southampton	2	Falmouth
1292	797	Wendel	Olaf Edwin	M	21	Swedish	Southampton	3	Copenhagen
1293	789	Vestrom	Hulda A A	F	14	Swedish	Southampton	3	Sweden
1294	790	Vook	Jinko	M	21	Austrian	Southampton	3	Bale
1295	791	Walteus	Achille	M	22	Belgian	Southampton	3	Antwerp
1297	107	Walker	W Anderson	M		British	Southampton	1	Manchester
1300	793	Ware	Fred	M	34	British	Southampton	3	Greenwich
1301	268	Ware	Jn James	M		British	Southampton	2	Bristol
1302	269	Ware	Wm J	M	23	British	Southampton	2	Gunnerslake
1304	794	Warren	Wm Chas	M	30	British	Southampton	3	Portsmouth
1305	108	Warren	F M	M		American	Cherbourg	1	Paris

Master list No	Old list No	Surname	Name(s)	Sex	Age	Nationality	Embarked	Class	Last Abode
1306	280	Watson	Ennis	M	18	British	Southampton	2	Belfast c/o Harland & Wolff
1309	795	Webber	Jas	M	66	US	Southampton	3	Southampton
1311	109	Weir	J	M		American	Southampton	1	London
1312	270	Weisz	Leopold	M	36	Hungary	Southampton	2	Birmingham
1320	271	West	E A	M	42	British	Southampton	2	Bournemouth
1321	455	Georgeo	Chahini	M	66	Syria	Cherbourg	3	Syria
1322	272	Wheadon	Edward	M		British	Southampton	2	Guernsey
1323	273	Wheeler	Edwin	M		British	Southampton	2	Paris
1325	110	White	Percival W	M		British	Southampton	1	65 Bridge St, Wednesbury
1326	111	White	Rd F	M		British	Southampton	1	65 Bridge St, Wednesbury
1327	112	Wick	Geo D	M		American	Southampton	1	
1330	799	Widegrin	Chas	M	44	Norwegian	Southampton	3	Norway
1332	113	Widener	Geo D	M		American	Southampton	1	Hotel Ritz, London
1333	114	Widener	Hy	M		American	Southampton	1	Hotel Ritz, London
1334	809	Wiklund	Karl	M	21	Finn	Southampton	3	Finland
1335	800	Wiklund	Jakobt	M	18	Finn	Southampton	3	Finland
1341	796	Weller	Abi	M	37	Russian	Cherbourg	3	Paris
1342	801	Willey	Ed	M	18	British	Southampton	3	England
1343	115	Williams	Duane	M		Canadian	Cherbourg	1	Guernsey
1345	802	Williams	Hy	M	28	British	Southampton	3	19 Eleanor S, Tony Pandy
1346	803	Williams	Leslie	M		British	Southampton	3	6 West Bickerhall Mansions, Gloster Place, London W
1348	60	Lambert Williams	Fletcher Fellows	M		American	Southampton	1	
1351	804	Windolov	Eina	M	21	Denmark	Southampton	3	Capetown
1352	805	Wiry	Albert	M	28	Swedish	Southampton	3	Basel
1353	806	Wiseman	Philip	M	54	British	Southampton	3	London
1354	807	Witkwrongel	Carille	M	36	Belgian	Southampton	3	Antwerp
1358	284	Woodward	J W	M		British	Southampton	2	c/o J & S Black, Liverpool
1361	116	Wright	George	M		Canadian	Southampton	1	Geneva, Suisse
1363	808	Zanbeek	Antoni	M	27	Syria	Cherbourg	3	Syria
1366	810	Yousiff	Wazli	M	25	Syria	Cherbourg	3	Syria
1367	814	Youssef	Gerios	M	45	Syria	Cherbourg	3	Syria
1368	274	Yrois	H (Miss)	F		French	Southampton	2	London
1369	816	Zabour	Hileni	F	16	Syria	Cherbourg	3	Syria
1370	815	Zabour	Tamime	F	19	Syria	Cherbourg	3	Syria
1371	818	Zakarian	Maprider	M		Syria	Cherbourg	3	Syria
1372	817	Zakarian	Artem	M	27	Syria	Cherbourg	3	Syria
1373	820	Zimmermann	L C U	M	29	Swiss	Southampton	3	Basel

List C&D

Master No	Old List No	Surname	First Name (s)	Title	Class	Sex	Age	Occupation
1	285	Abbing	Anthony		3	m	42	Blacksmith
2	286	Abbot	Eugene		3	m	13	Scholar
4	287	Abbot	Rossmore		3	m	16	Jeweller
8	123	Abelson	Samson	Mr	2	m		Russian
11	288	Adahl	Maurits		3	m	30	Labourer
12	289	Adams	John		3	m		Farm Labourer
13	290	Ahlin	Johanna	Mrs	3	f	30	Wife
14	291	Ahmett	Ali		3	m	24	Labourer
18	124	Aldworth	Augustus	Mr	2	m		
19	292	Alexander	William		3	m	23	Labourer
20	293	Alhomaki	Ilmari		3	m	20	Labourer
21	294	Ali	William		3	m	25	Labourer
23	295	Allen	William		3	m	35	Tool maker
24	1	Allison	H J	Mr	1	m		
25	3	Allison		Miss	1	f		
26	2	Allison	H J	Mrs	1	f		
28	296	Allum	Owen George		3	m	18	Gardener
29	298	Andersen	Albert		3	m	33	Engineer
32	301	Anderson	Alfrida	Mrs	3	f	40	Wife
33	300	Anderson	Anders		3	m	39	Labourer
35	304	Anderson	Ebba	Miss	3	f	6	Child
36	306	Anderson	Ellis		3	m	2	Child
38	308	Andersson	Ida Augusta	Mrs	3	f	38	Wife
39	303	Anderson	Ingeborg	Miss	3	f	9	Child
40	307	Anderson	Samuel		3	m	26	Labourer
41	302	Anderson	Sigrid	Miss	3	f	11	Child
42	305	Anderson	Sigvard	M	3	m	4	Child
43	309	Andreasan	Paul Edvin		3	m	29	Labourer
44	126	Andrew	Frank	Mr	2	m	25	Miner
45	125	Andrew	Edgar	Mr	2	m	16	
47	4	Andrews	Thomas	Mr	1	m		Ship builder
48	310	Angelhoff	Minko		3	m	26	Labourer
50	127	Angle	William B	Mr	2	m		
52	311	Arnold	Josef		3	m	25	Labourer
53	312	Arnold	Josephine	Mrs	3	f	24	Wife
54	313	Aronsson	Axel A		3	m	24	Labourer
55	5	Artagaveytia	Ramon	Mr	1	m		
56	128	Ashby	John	Mr	2	m	57	
57	321	Asim	Adola		3	m	35	Labourer
58	317	Asplund	Carl		3	m	5	Child
59	314	Asplund	Charles		3	m	40	Labourer
60	316	Asplund	Gustaf		3	m	9	Child
62	315	Asplund	Oscar		3	m	11	Child
66	319	Assaf	Gerios		3	m	21	Farmhand
68	320	Assam	Ali		3	m	23	Labourer
69	6	Astor	J J	Mr	1	m		Col in American Army
71	323	Attala	Sleiman		3	m	30	Journalist
73	324	Augustsan	Albert		3	m	23	Labourer
75	325	Baccos	Rafoul		3	m	20	Farmhand
76	326	Backstrom	Carl Anton		3	m	32	Labourer
83	327	Badt	Mohamed		3	m	40	Farmer
84	129	Bailey	Percy	Mr	2	m	18	Butcher's Assistant
85	130	Baimbrigge	Chas R	Mr	2	m	23	Horse Trainer
86	328	Balkic	Cerin		3	m	26	Labourer
88	131	Banfield	Frederick J	Mr	2	m	28	Miner
89	329	Barbara	Catherine	Mrs	3	f	45	Housekeeper
90	330	Barbara	Saude	Miss	3	f	18	Housekeeper
93	331	Barry	Julia	Miss	3	f	27	Housekeeper
94	332	Barton	David	Mr	3	m		
95	132	Bateman	Robert J	Mr	2	m	52	
96	7	Baumann	J J	Mr	1	m		
98	8	Baxter	Quigg	Mr	1	m		
102	9	Beattie	T	Mr	1	m		

List C&D

Nationality	Last Abode	Address
USA	Southampton	
USA	London	Salvation Army, London
USA	London	Salvation Army, London
Russian	Paris	
Sweden	Copenhagen	
English	Yeovil	Heath Cottage, Alum Chine Rd, Bournemouth
Sweden	Gothenburg	
Syria	Buenos Aires	
	London	
England	Gt Yarmouth	10 Belvedere Place, Kitchener Rd, Gt Yarmouth
Finland	Finland	
Syria	Buenos Aires	
England	Birmingham	c/o F Hunt, 78 Queens Rd, Erdington, Birmingham
	152 Abbey Rd, West Hampstead,London NW	
	152 Abbey Rd, West Hampstead,London NW	
	152 Abbey Rd, West Hampstead,London NW	
	London	22 Oswald Rd, Southall
Norway	Bergen	
Sweden	Gothenburg	
Sweden	Gothenburg	
Sweden	Gothenburg	
Sweden	Gothenburg	
Sweden	Gothenburg	
Sweden	Gothenburg	
Sweden	Gothenburg	
Sweden	Gothenburg	
Sweden	Gothenburg	
Sweden	Gothenburg	
English	Redruth	Pencoys Four Lanes
	Southampton	
Irish	Harland & Wolff, Belfast	
Bulgaria	Basle	
English	Warwick	14 Mill St, Warwick
Switzerland	Basle	
Switzerland	Basle	
Sweden	Helsingborg	
	26 Rue Pasquier, Paris	
USA Citzen	London	
Syrian	Buenos Ayres	
Swede	Sweden	
Swede	Sweden	
Swede	Sweden	
Swede	Sweden	
Syrian	Syria	
Syrian	Buenos Ayres	
USC	Hotel Ritz, Paris	
Syrian	Syria	
Swede	Sweden	
Syrian	Syria	
Finn	Finland	
Syrian	Syria	
English	Penzance	25 Swavas St
English	Guernsey	Robais Manor
Austria	Austria	
English	Plymouth	30 Grenville Road
Syrian	Syria	
Syrian	Syria	
Irish	Ireland	c/o J K O Connor & Son, Castle Island, Co Kerry
English		Belle Vue Cottages, Wicken, Cambridge
	Southampton	Rendennis Road, Staple Hill, Bristol
USC	Grand Hotel, Paris	
USC	Elysee Palace Hotel, Paris	
USC	Hotel Majestic, Nice	

Who Sailed on Titanic?

Master No	Old List No	Surname	First Name (s)	Title	Class	Sex	Age	Occupation
103	133	Beauchamp	Henry James	Mr	2	m		
104	334	Beavan	William Thomas	Mr	3	m	19	Labourer
113	335	Benson	John Viktor	Mr	3	m	26	Labourer
115	336	Berglund	Ivar	Mr	3	m	20	Labourer
116	134	Berriman	Wm	Mr	2	m	23	
117	731	Seman	Betros	Master	3	m	10	Child
118	337	Betros	Tannous	Mr	3	m	20	Shoemaker
122	341	Birkeland	Hans	Mr	3	m	21	Sailor
123	52	Birnbaum	Jakob	Mr	1	m		
127	342	Bjorklund	Ernst	Mr	3	m	18	Labourer
129	10	Blackwell	Stephen Weart	Mr	1	m		
133		Beauchamp	Henry James	Mr	2	m		
134	11	Borebank	J J	Mr	1	m		
135	343	Bostandyeff	Guentcho	Mr	3	m	26	Labourer
136	135	Botsford	W Hull	Mr	2	m		
137	345	Boulos	Akar	Master	3	m	9	Child
138	344	Boulos	Hanna	Mr	3	m	18	Labourer
140	358	Boulos	Sultani	Mrs	3	f	40	wife
141	347	Bourke	Catherine	Mrs	3	f		
142	346	Bourke	John	Mr	3	m		
143	356	Burke	Mary	Miss	3	f		
144	348	Bowen	David	Mr	3	m		Boxer
146	136	Bowenur	Solomon	Mr	2	m	42	Merchant
148	137	Bracken	James H	Mr	2	m	27	Stockman
151	12	Brady	John B	Mr	1	m		
152	349	Braf	Elin Ester	Miss	3	f	20	Maid
153	282	Brailey	Ronald	Mr	2	m		
155	13	Brandeis	E	Mr	1	m		
156	350	Braund	Lewis B	Mr	3	m	29	Farm Labourer
157	351	Braund	Owen Harris	Mr	3	m	22	Ironmonger
158	14	Brewe	Arthur Jackson	Mr	1	m		
159	283	Bricoux	Roger	Mr	2	m		
160	138	Brito	Jose	Mr	2	m		
161	352	Brobek	Carl R	Mr	3	m	22	Farm Labourer
162	353	Brocklebank	William	Mr	3	m	35	Groom
168	139	Brown	Thomas Wm Solomon	Mr	2	m		
171	140	Bryhe	Curt	Mr	2	m	20	
173	354	Bucksley	Katherine	Miss	3	f		
175	355	Burke	Jeremiah	Mr	3			
177	357	Burns	Mary	Miss	3	f	18	
179	141	Butler	Reginald	Mr	2	m	25	Mechanical Engineer
180	15	Butt	Archibald W	Mr	1	m		Major in American Army
181	142	Byles	Thos R D	Mr	2	m		Minister of Religion
183	359	Cacic	Grigo	Mr	3	m	18	Farmer
184	360	Cacic	Luka	Mr	3	m	38	Farmer
185	361	Cacic	Manda	Miss	3	f	21	Farm Girl
186	362	Cacic	Maria	Miss	3	f	30	Farm Girl
187	117	Cairns	Alexander	Mr	1	m		Carter's Manservant
192	363	Calic	Petar	Mr	3	m	17	Farmhand
195	364	Canavan	Mary	Miss	3	f		
196	366	Canavan	Patrick	Mr	3	m		
198	365	Cann	Ernest	Mr	3	m		
199	368	Caram	Joseph	Mr	3	m	28	Merchant
200	369	Caram	Maria	Mrs	3	f	20	Housekeeper
201	143	Carbines	Wm	Mr	2	m	19	Miner
204	450	Garfirth	John	Mr	3	m	22	Shoe Op
205	16	Carlson	Frank	Mr	1	m		
206	372	Carlsson	August Sigfrid	Mr	3	m	28	Farmer
207	370	Carlson	Carl R	Mr	3	m	24	Labourer
208	367	Car	Janie	Mrs	3	f		
209	17	Carran	F M	Mr	1	m		
210	18	Carran	J P	Mr	1	m	19	
211	144	Carter	Ernest C	Mr	2	m	54	Minister of Religion
212	145	Carter	Lilian	Mrs	2	f	44	Housewife
217	374	Carver	A	Mr	3			
218	19	Case	Howard B	Mr	1	m		
221	20	Cavendish	T W	Mr	1	m		
222	375	Celotti	Francesco	Mr	3	m	24	Stoker

List C&D

Nationality	Last Abode	Address
	London	
USA	London	95 Richmond Rd, Gillingham
Swede	Sweden	
Finn	Sweden	
	St Ives	Hellesover St
Syria	Syria	
Syrian	Syria	
Norwegian	Norway	
Austrian	11 Rue Membling, Antwerp	
Swede	Sweden	
USC		
	London	
USC		
Bulgarian	Bulgaria	
USC	London	c/o T Cook & Son, Ludgate Circus
Syrian	Syria	
Syrian	Syria	
Syria	Syria	
Ireland	Queenstown	
Ireland	Queenstown	
English	England	
English	England	c/o Dean and Davron, Cardiff
USC	London	
USC	London	
Eng		
Sweden	Sweden	
English	London	71 Lancaster Rd
	Elysee Palace Hotel, Paris	
English	Holsworthy	
English	Holsworthy	
USC		
French	France	
Portuguese	London	c/o Mr Fred Duarte, 34 Mulgrave Street, Liverpool
Denmark	Copenhagen	
English	London	Alpha Villa, Bromfield Hill, Nr Chelmsford
British	London	
Swedish	Gothenburg	c/o Mr G Lustig, Skara, Stadsfiskal
English	England	
English	England	
Irish	Queenstown	c/o James Young, Ballis O Dare
British	Portsmouth	Granada Hotel, Southsea
USC		
	London	c/o Mrs Byles, 101 The Ridgway, Wimbledon
Austrian	Austria	
Austrian	Austria	
Austrian	Austria	
Austrian	Austria	
	Liverpool	
Austrian	Austria	
Irish	Queenstown	
Irish	Queenstown	
English	Southampton	
Canadian	Paris	
Canadian	Paris	
English	St Ives	Nangivey
England	Wellingborough	Henwick Rd, Wollaston, Nr Wellingborough
USC		
Dane	Copenhagen	
Dane	Copenhagen	
Irish	Queenstown	
USC		
USC		
English	London	
English	London	
English	Southampton	
USC	Vacuum Oil Co London	
USC	23 Chesham Place	
Italian	Capetown	

Who Sailed on Titanic?

Master No	Old List No	Surname	First Name (s)	Title	Class	Sex	Age	Occupation
224	21	Chaffee	Herbert F	Mr	1	m		
227	148	Chapman	Charles	Mr	2	m		
228	146	Chapman	John H	Mr	2	m	30	Farmer
229	147	Chapman	Eliz	Mrs	2	f	28	Housewife
230	376	Chartens	David	Mr	3	m		
236	22	Chisholm	Roderick	Mr	1	m		
237	377	Christmann	Emil	Mr	3	m	29	Clerk
240	378	Chronopoulos	Apostolos	Mr	3	m	26	Labourer
241	379	Chronopoulos	Demetrios	Mr	3	m	18	Labourer
243	149	Clarke	Charles V	Mr	2	m	29	
245	23	Clark	Walter M	Mr	1	m		
246	280	Clarke	John Frederick Preston	Mr	2	m		
248	24	Clifford	George Quincey	Mr	1	m		
249	380	Coelho	Domingos Fernandes	Mr	3	m	20	Labourer
251	381	Colbert	Patrick	Mr	3	m		
252	383	Coleff	Peyo	Mr	3	m	36	Labourer
253	382	Coleff	Fotio	Mr	3	m	24	Labourer
254	150	Coleridge	Reginald C	Mr	2	m	29	Advt. Consultant
255	151	Collander	Erik	Mr	2	m		
257	25	Colley	E P	Mr	1	m		
260	152	Collyer	Harvey	Mr	2	m	32	Grocer
262	26	Compton	A T Jnr	Mr	1	m		
265	384	Conlin	Thomas H	Mr	3	m		
266	385	Connaghten	Michael	Mr	3	m		
268	386	Connolly	Kate	Miss	3	f		
269	387	Connors	Patrick	Mr	3	m		
270	388	Cook	Jacob	Mr	3	m	43	Wood Carver
272	389	Cor	Bartol	Mr	3	m	25	Labourer
273	390	Cor	Ivan	Mr	3	m	27	Labourer
274	391	Cor	Ludovik	Mr	3	m	19	Labourer
275	153	Corbett	Irene C	Mrs	2	f	30	Musician
276	154	Corey	Percy C	Mrs	2	f		
277	392	Corn	Harry	Mr	3	m	30	Upholsterer
280	155	Cotterill	Harry	Mr	2	m	20	Carpenter
284	393	Coxon	Daniel	Mr	3	m		
285	27	Crafton	John B	Mr	1	m		
287	394	Crease	Ernest James	Mr	3	m	19	Tinsmith
288	395	Cribb	John Hatfield	Mr	3	m	44	Butler
291	28	Crosby	Edward G	Mr	1	m		
294	29	Cummings	John Bradley	Mr	1	m		
295	272	Cunningham	Alf	Mr	2	m	21	Fitter
296	397	Daher	Shedid	Mr	3	m	22	
298	398	Dahlberg	Gerda	Miss	3	f	22	Wife
299	399	Dakic	Branko	Mr	3	m	19	Labourer
303	401	Danbom	Sigrid	Mrs	3	f	27	Wife
304	400	Danbom	Ernst	Mr	3	m	34	Labourer
305	402	Danbom	Gillbert	Master	3	m	4m	Child
308	403	Danoff	Yoto	Mr	3	m	27	Labourer
309	404	Dantchoff	Kristo	Mr	3	m	25	Labourer
311	30	Davidson	Thornton	Mr	1	m		
312	407	Davies	Alfred	Mr	3	m	24	Coster
313	156	Davies	Chas	Mr	2	m	21	
315	406	Davies	Evan	Mr	3	m	22	Miner
318	408	Davies	John	Mr	3	m	21	Ironworker
319	409	Davis	Joseph	Mr	3	m	17	Ironworker
323	405	Davison	Thomas	Mr	3	m	32	Smith
328	661	Pelsmaker	Alfons de	Mr	3	m	17	Farm Labourer
329	157	Deacon	Percy	Mr	2	m	20	
330	410	Dean	Bertram F	Mr	3	m	25	Farmer
335	158	del Carlo	Sebastiani	Mr	2	m		
336	411	Delalic	Regyo	Mr	3	m	25	Labourer
337	418	Dimitri	Marinko	Mr	3	m	23	Labourer
338	159	Denbury	Herbert	Mr	2	m	25	
339	414	Denkoff	Mito	Mr	3	m	30	Labourer
340	412	Dennis	Samuel	Mr	3	m	23	Farming
341	413	Dennis	William	Mr	3	m	26	Farming
344	160	Dibden	Wm	Mr	2	m	19	

List C&D

Nationality	Last Abode	Address
USC		
English		McWheeler's Yard, West Drayton
English	Liskeard	c/o George & Co, Liskeard, Cornwall
English	Liskeard	c/o George & Co, Liskeard, Cornwall
Ireland	Queenstown	
Irish	Harland & Wolff, Belfast	
Germany	London	
Greek	Greece	
Greek	Greece	
English	Southampton	
USC	c/o Amexco, Rome	
English	Liverpool	5 Milldown Rd
USC	c/o Kings House, King St, Cheapside, London	
Portugal	Portugal	
English	Queenstown	
Bulgaria	Bulgaria	
Bulgaria	Bulgaria	
English	London	232 Strand
Finnish	London	Finska A A Helsingfors
Irish	Fermath Rathgow, Dublin	
English		Mt Hill, Basingstoke
	Hotel Dysart, Paris	
English	Queenstown	
English	Queenstown	
English	Queenstown	40 Bank Place, Tipperary
English	Queenstown	
Russia	Russia	
Austrian	Austria	
Austrian	Austria	
Austrian	Austria	
USA citizen	London	York Road
	London	
Russia	Russia	
English	Penzance	26 Adelaide St
USA	USA	38 Rochford St, Kentish Town, London
USC	Victoria Hotel, London	
English	Bristol	2 Hollybrook Place, Bedminster, Bristol
English	Bournemouth	Helenita, Saltern Rd, Parkstone, Dorset
	Grand Trunk Rlwy, London SW	
	c/o Morgan Harjes, Paris	
English	Belfast	Harland & Wolff's men
Syria	Syria	
Sweden	Gothenburg	
Austrian	Austria	
Sweden	Gothenburg	
Sweden	Gothenburg	
Sweden	Gothenburg	
Bulgaria	Bulgaria	
Bulgaria	Bulgaria	
USC		
English	W Bromwich	29 Harwood St, W Bromwich
	Lyndhurst, Hants	c/o Mr D Davies, Brook Hill, Lyndhurst, N Forest
Welsh	Pontardawe	c/o Mrs Rogers, Yrisymond Farm, Glais, Nr Swansea
English	W Bromwich	29 Harwood St, W Bromwich
English	W Bromwich	Moxtoke Cottage, West Bromwich
English	Liverpool	10 Park St, Woodlands, Chippenham
Belgium	Antwerp	
	Lyndhurst, Hants	
English	Southampton	Bartley Farm, Netley Marsh
	Paris	c/o Branchim, Lucco, Italy
Austrian	Austria	
Macedonian	Austria	
English	Guernsey	Les Sauvages, St Sampson's
Bulgarian	Bulgaria	
English	Holsworthy	Leigh Farm, Week St Mary Nr Bude
English	Holsworthy	Leigh Farm, Week St Mary Nr Bude
	Lyndhurst, Hants	Bramshaw, Witham, N Forest

Master No	Old List No	Surname	First Name (s)	Title	Class	Sex	Age	Occupation
347	416	Dika	Mirko	Mr	3	m	17	Labourer
348	417	Dimic	Jovan	Mr	3	m	42	Farmer
349	419	Dintcheff	Valtcho	Mr	3	m	43	Labourer
353	396	Daher	Tannous	Mr	3	m	28	
356	810	Donohue	Bridget	Miss	3	f		
357	420	Dooley	Patrick	Mr	3	m		
361	31	Douglas	W D	Mr	1	m		
363	161	Downton	Wm Jas	Mr	2	m	54	
364	421	Doyle	Elisabeth	Miss	3	f		
365	422	Dragenovic	Josip	Mr	3	m	33	Labourer
368	162	Drew	James V	Mr	2	m		
373	32	Dulles	William C	Mr	1	m		
376	415	Divan	Frank	Mr	3	m		
377	423	Duyker	Adolph	Mr	3	m	23	Labourer
381	424	Ecimovic	Joso	Mr	3	m	17	Farmer
382	425	Edwardsson	Gustaf Hjalmar	Mr	3	m	18	Labourer
383	163	Eitemiller	George Floyd	Mr	2	m		
384	426	Eklund	Hans	Mr	3	m	16	Labourer
385	427	Ekstrom	Johan	Mr	3	m	46	Labourer
386	428	Elias	Dibo	Mr	3	m	29	Labourer
387	429	Elias	Joseph	Mr	3	m	39	Labourer
388	514	Joseph	Elias	Mr	3	m	18	Labourer
389	430	Elias	Tannous	Mr	3	m	20	Labourer
390	431	Elsbury	James	Mr	3	m	47	Farmer
392	432	Emir	Farres Chehab	Mr	3	m	29	Labourer
393	164	Enander	Ingvar	Mr	2	m	21	
395	464	Goncalves	Manuel Estanislas	Mr	3	m	38	Labourer
397	33	Evans	E	Miss	1	f		
399	433	Everett	Thomas J	Mr	3	m	36	Craneman
402	165	Fahlstrom	Arne T	Mr	2	m		
403	435	Farrell	James	Mr	3	m		
404	119	Farthing	John	Mr	1	m		Straus's Manservant
406	166	Faunthorpe	Harry	Mr	2	m		
407	167	Fillbrook	Chas	Mr	2	m	19	Decorator
409	436	Fischer	Eberhard	Mr	3	m	19	Farming
411	483	Fleming	Nora	Miss	3	f		
414	439	Flynn	James	Mr	3	m		
415	440	Flynn	John	Mr	3	m		
417	437	Foley	Joseph	Mr	3	m	19	
418	438	Foley	Wm	Mr	3	m		
420	441	Ford	Arthur	Mr	3	m	22	Carpenter
421	443	Ford	D M	Miss	3	f	21	Domestic
422	444	Ford	E W	Mr	3	m	18	Blacksmith
423	442	Ford	Margaret	Mrs	3	f	48	Poultry Farming
424	446	Ford	Maggie	Miss	3	f	9	Child
425	445	Ford	W T N	Mr	3	m	16	PO Messenger
426	34	Foreman	B L	Mr	1	m		
430	36	Fortune	Charles	Mr	1	m		
433	35	Fortune	Mark	Mr	1	m		
435	448	Fox	Patrick	Mr	3	m		
436	168	Fox	Stanley H	Mr	2	m		
438	447	Franklin	Charles	Mr	3	m	38	Carpenter
439	37	Franklin	T P	Mr	1	m		
446	273	Frost	Anthony Wood	Mr	2	m	37	Foreman fitter
447	116	Fry	Richard	Mr	1	m		Ismay's Manservant
448	169	Funk	Annie	Miss	2	f	37	Missionary
449	38	Futrelle	J	Mr	1	m		
451	170	Fynney	Jos	Mr	2	m		
452	171	Gale	Harry	Mr	2	m	38	Miner
453	172	Gale	Shadrack	Mr	2	m	33	Miner
454	449	Gallagher	Martin	Mr	3	m		
456	173	Gaskell	Alfred	Mr	2	m		
457	174	Gavey	Lawrence	Mr	2	m	26	
458	39	Gee	Arthur	Mr	1	m		
459	802	Youssef	Gerios	Mr	3	m	26	Labourer
460	452	Gheorgheff	Stanko	Mr	3	m		Labourer

Nationality	Last Abode	Address
Austrian	Austria	
Austrian	Austria	
Bulgarian	Bulgaria	
Syria	Syria	
British	Queenstown	
Ireland	Queenstown	
USC	c/o Boyd Neel, 1 Rue Damion, Paris	
English	Guernsey	c/o Mrs Domaille, Nr Vale Church
Ireland	Queenstown	
Austria	Austria	
USC		Contstantine, Penryn, Cornwall
USC	Hotel France & Choisneul, Paris	
Irish	Queenstown	
Sweden	Gothenburg	
Switzerland	Basel	
Sweden	Helsingborg	
	London	Bonnington Hotel, Southampton Row
Sweden	Gothenburg	
Sweden	Gothenburg	
Syria	Syria	
Syria	Syria	
Syrian	Syria	
Syria	Syria	
England	Taunton	c/o J E Kingsbury
Syria	Syria	
Swedish	Gothenburg	27A Svengatan Gothenberg
Portuguese	Brazil	
USC	Hotel Majestic, Paris	
England	Bristol	7 Treefield Place, Nina Road, Bristol
Norwegian	Christiania	Slemdal, Christiania
Irish	Queenstown	
English	Liverpool	
English	Truro	16 Charles Street
Dane	Copenhagen	
Irish	Queenstown	
Irish	Queenstown	
Irish	Queenstown	
Irish	Queenstown	
Irish	Queenstown	
England	Bridgwater	9 Victoria Rd, Bridgwater
England	London	
England	London	
England	London	
England	London	
England	London	
Eng		
USC	Hotel Metropole, London	
USC	Hotel Mctropole, London	
Irish	Queenstown	
USC	Birmingham	c/o Morrison's Booking Office, 6 Victoria Square
England	Southampton	
Eng	17 Cheapside, London EC	
English	Belfast	Harland & Wolff's men
	Liverpool	
USC	London	c/o T Cook & Son, Ludgate Circus
USC	44 Gloucester Terrace, Hyde Park, London W	
	Liverpool	Brown's Bldgs
English		School Road, Harrowbarrow, Nr St Dominee, Cornwall
English		School Road, Harrowbarrow, Nr St Dominee, Cornwall
Ireland	Queenstown	
	Liverpool	20 Dexter Street
British	Guernsey	Bas Courtil Banks
Eng	Morningside, Riley Avenue, St Annes on Sea	
Syrian	Syria	
Bulgaria	Bulgaria	

Who Sailed on Titanic?

Master No	Old List No	Surname	First Name (s)	Title	Class	Sex	Age	Occupation
464	40	Giglio	Victor	Mr	1	m		
465	175	Gilbert	Wm	Mr	2	m	45	
466	176	Giles	Edgar	Mr	2	m	21	Carpenter
467	177	Giles	Fred	Mr	2	m	22	Carpenter
468	178	Giles	Ralph	Mr	2	m		
469	453	Gilinsky	Leslie	Mr	3	m	22	Locksmith
470	179	Gill	John	Mr	2	m	24	Chauffeur
471	180	Gillespie	Wm	Mr	2	m	34	Law Clerk
473	181	Givard	Hans K	Mr	2	m		
477	41	Goldschmidt	George B	Mr	1	m		
479	454	Goldsmith	Frank J	Mr	3	m	33	Turner
481	455	Goldsmith	Nathan	Mr	3	m	41	Bootmaker
482	457	Goodwin	Augusta	Mrs	3	f	43	Wife
483	459	Goodwin	Charles E	Mr	3	m	14	Child
484	456	Goodwin	Frederick	Mr	3	m	40	Eng Labourer
485	462	Goodwin	Harold	Master	3	m	9	Child
486	461	Goodwin	Jessie A M	Miss	3	f	10	Child
487	458	Goodwin	Lillian A	Miss	3	f	15	Child
488	463	Goodwin	Sidney	Master	3	m	6	Child
489	460	Goodwin	Wm T	Master	3	m	11	Child
492	42	Graham	George E	Mr	1	m		
494	465	Green	George	Mr	3	m	40	Farrier
495	182	Greenberg	Saml	Mr	2	m		
498	466	Gronnestad	Daniel	Mr	3	m	32	Labourer
499	467	Guest	Robert	Mr	3	m	23	Labourer
500	43	Guggenheim	Benjamin	Mr	1	m		
501	468	Gustafson	Alfred	Mr	3	m	20	Labourer
502	469	Gustafson	Anders	Mr	3	m	37	Labourer
504	470	Gustafsson	Gideon	Mr	3	m	18	Labourer
505	816	Gwinn	Wlliam L	Mr	3	m	c37	American Sea Post Clerk
506	471	Hass	Alouisia	Miss	3		24	Labourer
507	474	Hagland	Ingvald O	Mr	3	m	28	Labourer
508	475	Hagland	Konrad R	Mr	3	m	10	Labourer
510	476	Hakkarainen	Pekka	Mr	3	m	28	Labourer
511	183	Hale	Reginald	Mr	2	m	30	
514	613	Hampe	Leon	Mr	3	m		Painter
515	578	Mansour	Hanna	Mr	3	m	35	Journalist
516	604	Moubarak	Hanna	Mr	3	m	25	Farm Labourer
517	477	Hansen	Claus	Mr	3	m	41	Barber
518	519	Jutel	Henrik	Mr	3	m	26	Farmer
519	478	Hansen	Harry Dangaard	Mr	3	m	21	Manufacturer
521	184	Harbeck	Wm	Mr	2	m		
524	472	Hargadon	Kate	Miss	3	f		
525	479	Harknett	Alice	Miss	3	f	21	Servant
526	480	Harmer	Abraham	Mr	3	m	25	Jeweller
529	185	Harper	John	Mr	2	m		
531	118	Harrington	Charles	Mr	1	m		Moore's Manservant
533	44	Harris	Henry B	Mr	1	m		
535	186	Harris	Walter	Mr	2	m		
537	187	Hart	Benjamin	Mr	2	m		
540	481	Hart	Henry	Mr	3	m		
541	281	Hartley	Wm	Mr	2	m		
545	45	Hays	Charles M	Mr	1	m		
548	46	Head	Christopher	Mr	1	m		
552	473	Hegarty	Nora	Miss	3	f		
554	482	Heininen	Wendla	Miss	3	f	23	Servant
556	484	Hendekovic	Ignas	Mr	3	m	28	Labourer
557	486	Henriksson	Jenny	Miss	3	f	28	Domestic
558	485	Henery	Delia	Miss	3	f		
562	188	Herman	Samuel	Mr	2	m	49	Farmer
564	189	Hickman	Leonard	Mr	2	m	24	
565	190	Hickman	Lewis	Mr	2	m	32	
566	191	Hickman	Stanley	Mr	2	m	20	
567	47	Hilliard	Herbert Henry?	Mr	1	m		
568	192	Hiltunen	Martta	Miss	2	f		
569	48	Hipkins	W E	Mr	1	m		
576	193	Hocking	Geo	Mr	2	m	21	
577	194	Hocking	Samuel	Mr	2	m		Painter

List C&D

Nationality	Last Abode	Address
	57 Avenue Montaigne, Paris	
		Carleens, Breage, Cornwall
English	Portleven	Wheat Unity Road
English	Portleven	Wheat Unity Road
	London	10 Gunterstone Road, West Kensington
Russia	Wales	36 Glaneynon Terrace
English	Bristol	3 Griffin Road, Clevedon
Irish	Abbey Leix	Coffee Palace
Danish	Southampton	
USC	Hotel Continentale, Paris	
England	England	c/o Curtis & Sons, Rochester
Russia	Capetown	c/o Curtis & Sons, Rochester
England	Bath	Watsons Court, High St, Melksham
England	Bath	Watsons Court, High St, Melksham
England	Bath	Watsons Court, High St, Melksham
England	Bath	Watsons Court, High St, Melksham
England	Bath	Watsons Court, High St, Melksham
England	Bath	Watsons Court, High St, Melksham
England	Bath	Watsons Court, High St, Melksham
England	Bath	Watsons Court, High St, Melksham
Eng	c/o T Eaton & Co, London	
English	Gunnislake	1 Lyon's Cottage, Dorking
Russian	Southampton	
Norwegian	Norway	
English	London	c/o Pickfords, Gresham St
USC	57 Avenue Montaigne, Paris	
Swede	Sweden	
Finn	Finland	
Finn	Finland	
American	4 Commercial Rd, Southampton	Asbury Park, New Jersey, USA
Swiss	Switzerland	
Norwegian	Norway	
Norwegian	Norway	
Finn	Finland	
English	Westbury	Rodneystoke, Nr Cheddar
Belgium	Antwerp	
Syrian	Syria	
Syrian	Syria	
USA	Copenhagen	
Denmark	Copenhagen	
Dane	Copenhagen	
USC	London	
British	Queenstown	
English	London	c/o W S Hill, Cockspur St
Russia	Manchester	36 Strong Street, Lower Droughton
English	London	3 Claud Villa, Denmark Hill
USC	Savoy Hotel, London	
English	London	47 Granville Rd, Hoe St, Walthamstow
English	London	
Ireland	Queenstown	
English	Dewsbury	Surreyside, West Park St
Eng	Grand Trunk Rly, London SW	
Eng		
British	Queenstown	
Finland	Finland	
Austria	Austria	
Sweden	Gothenburg	
Irish	Queenstown	
English	Yeovil	
	Lyndhurst, Hants	Fritham, New Forest
	Lyndhurst, Hants	Fritham, New Forest
	Lyndhurst, Hants	Fritham, New Forest
Eng	Hotel Chatham, Paris	
Finnish	Helsingfors	
Eng	W&T Avery, Birmingham	
English	Penzance	26 St Mary Street
	Plymouth	3 Fore Street, Devonport

Who Sailed on Titanic?

Master No	Old List No	Surname	First Name (s)	Title	Class	Sex	Age	Occupation
578	195	Hodges	Henry P	Mr	2	m	50	Musical Instrument Vendor
581	196	Hold	Stephen	Mr	2	m	42	Independent
583	487	Holm	John F A	Mr	3	m	43	Farmer
584	488	Holten	Johan	Mr	3	m	28	2nd Mate
585	49	Holverson	A O	Mr	1	m		
589	197	Hood	Ambrose	Mr	2	m	22	
590	489	Horgan	John	Mr	3	m		
592	198	Howard	Benjamin	Mr	2	m	63	Retired
593	199	Howard	Ellen T	Mrs	2	f	60	Wife
597	50	Hoyt	W F	Mr	1	m		
598	490	Humblen	Adolf O	Mr	3	m	42	Farmer
599	277	Hume	John Law	Mr	2	m		
600	200	Hunt	George	Mr	2	m		
604	491	Ilieff	Ilio	Mr	3	m	32	Labourer
605	492	Ilmakangas	Ida	Miss	3	f	29	Servant
606	493	Ilmakangas	Pista Sofia	Miss	3	f	25	Servant
607	51	Isham	A E	Miss	1	f		
609	497	Ivanoff	Koino	Mr	3	m	20	Labourer
611	202	Jacobsohn	Sydney S	Mr	2	m		
614	498	Jardin	Jose Netto	Mr	3	m	21	Labourer
615	203	Jarvis	John D	Mr	2	m	47	Engineer
616	204	Jefferys	Clifford	Mr	2	m	24	
617	205	Jefferys	Ernest	Mr	2	m	22	
618	206	Jenkin	Stephen	Mr	2	m	32	Miner
619	499	Jensen	Hans Peter	Mr	3	m	21	
620	500	Jensen	Niels R	Mr	3	m	48	Farmer
621	501	Jensen	Svenst L	Mr	3	m	17	Farmer
626	506	Johnson	Jakob Alfred	Mr	3	m	34	Labourer
627	504	Johansson	Erik	Mr	3	m	20	Labourer
628	502	Johanson	Gustaf	Mr	3	m	33	
629	505	Johnson	Carl	Mr	3	m	32	Labourer
630	503	Johanson	Nils	Mr	3	m	30	Labourer
632	515	Johnson	A	Mr	3	m		
636	507	Johnsson	Malkolm	Mr	3	m	30	Labourer
637	516	Johnson	W	Mr	3	m		
638	508	Johnston	A E	Mr	3	m	34	Plumber
639	511	Johnston	C H	Miss	3	f	8	Child
640	509	Johnston		Mrs	3	f	34	Wife
641	510	Johnston	Wm A	Master	3	m	9	Child
642	53	Jones	C C	Mr	1	m		
643	512	Jonkoff	Lazore	Mr	3	m	23	Labourer
645	513	Jonsson	Niels	Mr	3	m	26	Labourer
646	669	Peter	Anna	Miss	3	f	2,7m	Child
648	668	Peter	Miki	Master	3	m	4	Child
649	54	Julian	H F	Mr	1	m		
651	517	Jussila	Katriine	Miss	3	f	20	Servant
652	518	Jussila	Marie	Miss	3	f	21	Servant
653	520	Kallio	Nicolai	Mr	3	m	17	Labourer
654	521	Kalvig	Johannes H	Mr	3	m	21	Labourer
656	207	Kantor	Sekua	Mr	2	m	34	
657	522	Karajio	Milau	Mr	3	m	30	Labourer
659	371	Carlsan	Julius	Mr	3	m	33	Labourer
660	523	Karlsson	Nils Aug	Mr	3	m	22	Farmer
661	208	Karnes	T Frank	Mrs	2	f		
664	434	Kassem	Fared	Mr	3	m	18	Farming
665	373	Catavelas	Vassilios	Mr	3	m	19	Farmer
666	527	Keane	Andy	Mr	3	m		
667	209	Keane	Daniel	Mr	2	m		
669	524	Keefe	Arthur	Mr	3	m	39	Farmer
670	115	Keeping	Edwin Herbert	Mr	1	m		Widener's Manservant
671	525	Kelley	James	Mr	3	m	44	Labourer
674	526	Kelly	James	Mr	3	m	19	Painter
677	55	Kent	Edward A	Mr	1	m		
678	56	Kenyon	F R	Mr	1	m		
680	535	Khalil	Betros	Mr	3	m	25	Farm Labourer
681	537	Khalil	Zahic	Miss	3	f	20	Farm Labourer
682	529	Kiernan	John	Mr	3	m		
683	530	Kiernan	Philip	Mr	3	m		

List C&D

Nationality	Last Abode	Address
English	Southampton	Highfield Lane
USC	Shipton	
USA	Copenhagen	
Norway	Norway	
USC	Piccadilly Hotel, London	
	Lyndhurst, Hants	Fritham, New Forest
Ireland	Queenstown	
English	Swindon	85 Cheltenham St
English	Swindon	85 Cheltenham St
USC	c/o Brown Shipley & Co, 123 Pall Mall, London	
Norway	Aalesund	
Scotch	Dumfries	42 George St
British	London	Ashtead, nr Epsom
Bulgarian	Bulgaria	
Finn	Finland	
Finn	Finland	
USC	86 Rue de Varenne, Paris	
Bulgarian	Bulgaria	
	London	7 Pembridge Square
Portuguese	Brazil	
English	Leicester	The Crest, Stoneygate
English	Guernsey	Rossly, Halfway Banks
English	Guernsey	Rossly, Halfway Banks
American	St Ives	Nanjivey, St Ives
Dane	Denmark	
USA	Denmark	
Dane	Denmark	
Finnish	Finland	
Dane	Denmark	
Swede	Sweden	
Swede	Sweden	
Swede	Sweden	
English	Southampton	8 Kingsley Rd, Millbrook
Swede	Sweden	
English	Southampton	8 Kingsley Rd, Millbrook
English	London	6 Newton Terrace, Paisley
Scotland	London	6 Newton Terrace, Paisley
English	London	6 Newton Terrace, Paisley
Scotland	London	6 Newton Terrace, Paisley
USC	c/o Foot Dorchester or Junction Hotel	
Bulgarian	Bale	
Dane	Denmark	
Syria	Syria	
Syria	Syria	
USC		
Finnish	Finland	
Finnish	Finland	
Finland	Finland	
Norway	Stavanger	
Russian	London	c/o W S Line, Leadenhall Street EC
Switzerland	Basel	
Swede	Malmo	
Dane	Copenhagen	
Syria	Syria	
Greek	Paris	
Ireland	Queenstown	
		E Ludlow, Limerick
USA	USA	
English	London	W Kelly, Kirk St, Carlake
Irish	Queenstown	
USC	Hotel Continentale, Paris	
USC	Hotel de la Tamise	
Syrian	Syria	
Syrian	Syria	
Ireland	Queenstown	
Ireland	Queenstown	

Who Sailed on Titanic?

Master No	Old List No	Surname	First Name (s)	Title	Class	Sex	Age	Occupation
684	528	Kilgannon	Thomas	Mr	3	m		
690	531	Kink	Vincenz	Mr	3	m	27	Magazineer
691	532	Kink	Maria	Miss	3	f	22	Maid
692	210	Kirkland	Chas L	Mr	2	m		Minister of religion
693	57	Klaber	Herman	Mr	1	m		
694	536	Klasen	Gertrude	Miss	3	f	1	Child
695	534	Klasen	Hulda K E	Mrs	3	f	36	Housewife
696	533	Klasen	Klas A	Mr	3	m	18	Farm Labourer
698	274	Knight	Robert	Mr	2	m	39	Fitter
699	539	Kraeff	Thodor	Mr	3	m		Labourer
702	276	Krins	Geo	Mr	2	m		
703	211	Kvillner	Johan Henrik	Mr	2	m	31	Mech, Engr
704	540	Lahoud	Sarkis	Mr	3	m	30	Labourer
705	284	Lahtinen	Anna	Mrs	2	f		wife
706	212	Lahtinen	Wm	Mr	2	m		Minister of religion
707	541	Laitinen	Sofia	Miss	3	f	37	Servant
708	542	Laleff	Hristo	Mr	3	m	23	Labourer
710	543	Lam	Len	Mr	3	m	23	Seaman
711	213	Lamb	John Joseph	Mr	2	m		
713	544	Lane	Patrick	Mr	3	m		
719	546	Larson	Viktor	Mr	3	m	29	Labourer
720	545	Larson	Bengt Edvin	Mr	3	m	29	Labourer
721	547	Larsson	Edvard	Mr	3	m	22	Labourer
726	548	Lefebre	Frances	Mrs	3	f	39	Wife
727	551	Lefebre	Henry	Master	3	m	4	Child
728	552	Lefebre	Ida	Miss	3	f	2	Child
729	550	Lefebre	Jeannie	Miss	3	f	6	Child
730	549	Lefebre	Mathilde	Miss	3	f	11	Child
732	553	Leinonen	Antii	Mr	3	m	23	Labourer
734	554	Lemberopoulos	Peter	Mr	3	m	30	Labourer
736	555	Lennon	Denis	Mr	3	m		
737	556	Lennon	Mary	Mrs	3	f		
742	557	Leonard	L	Mr	3	m		
744	558	Lester	James	Mr	3	m		Dipper
746	214	Levy	Rene J	Mr	2	m		
748	59	Lewy	E G	Mr	1	m		
749	215	Leyson	Robert W N	Mr	2	m	25	Engineer
750	808	Lievens	Aime Rene	Mr	3	m	24	Farmer
751	559	Lindahl	Agda	Miss	3	f	25	Wife
752	560	Lindblom	August	Mr	3	m	45	Labourer
753	60	Lingrey	Edward A	Mr	1	m		
754	561	Lindell	Edvard B	Mr	3	m	36	Labourer
755	562	Lindell	Elin G	Mrs	3	f	30	Wife
758	563	Linehan	Michael	Mr	3	m	21	Farm Labourer
761	564	Ling	Lee	Mr	3	m	28	
762	789	Wenzel	**hart	Mr	3	m	27	Baker
763	216	Lingan	John	Mr	2	m		
764	565	Lithman	Simon	Mr	3	m	20	Baker
765	567	Lobb	Cordelia	Mrs	3	f	26	Housewife
766	566	Lobb	William A	Mr	3	m	30	Engineer
767	568	Lockyer	Edward	Mr	3	m	21	Grocer's Assistant
768	61	Long	Milton C	Mr	1	m		
770	62	Loring	J H	Mr	1	m		
772	217	Louch	Chas	Mr	2	m	50	Saddler
773	569	Lovell	John	Mr	3	m	20	Farmer
776	570	Lundahl	John	Mr	3	m	37	Labourer
780	571	Lyntakoff	Stanko	Mr	3	m	44	Labourer
781	218	Mack	Mary	Mrs	2	f	50	
782	572	Mackay	Geo W	Mr	3	m	30	Butler
786	573	Maenpaa	Matti	Miss	3	f	22	
787	63	Maguire	J E	Mr	1	m		
788	574	Mahon	Delia	Miss	3	f	18	
789	589	Mechan	John	Mr	3	m		
791	575	Maisner	Simon	Mr	3	m	34	Tailor
792	576	Makinen	Kalle	Mr	3	m	29	Labourer
793	219	Malachard	Noel	Mr	2	m		
794	322	Attala	Malaki	Miss	3	f	17	Servant
795	220	Mallet	Andre	Mr	2	m		

List C&D

Nationality	Last Abode	Address
Ireland	Queenstown	
Switzerland	Basel	
Switzerland	Basel	
USC		
Swede	Sweden	
Swede	Sweden	
Denmark	Copenhagen	
English	Belfast	Harland & Wolff's men
Bulgarian	Bale	
Belgian		
Swedish	Gothenburg	Vattenverker Trollhattan, Sweden
Syrian	Syria	
USA	Helsingfors	
USC	Helsingfors	
Finnish	Finland	
Bulgarian	Bale	
Chinese	London	
British	Enniskerry	Wood View Cottage, Glencrea
Irish	Queenstown	
Swede	Sweden	
Swede	Sweden	
Swede	Sweden	
France	Havre	
France	Havre	
France	Havre	
France	Havre	
France	Havre	
Finland	Finland	
Greece	Marseille	
Irish	Queenstown	
Irish	Queenstown	
English	Southampton	
English	West Bromwich	29 Harwood St
	Paris	Grand Hotel
USC	12 Rue le Peletier, Pris	
Welsh	London	171 Cromwell Rd, South Kensington
Belgium	Antwerp	
Denmark	Gothenburg	
Denmark	Gothenburg	
Sweden	Malmo	
Sweden	Malmo	
Ireland	King Williamstown	c/o P Fitzpatrick, King Williamstown
China		
Austria	Antwerp	
Russia	Scotland	c/o Kucher, Edinburgh, 17 Drummond St
English	Cornwall	
English	Cornwall	c/o Daniel & Rowse, St Austell, Cornwall
English	London	57 Lyall Mews
USC	Hotel Engadine, Kulm, St Moritz	
USC	28 Park Lane, London W	
British	Weston Super Mare	Regent St, Weston
English	Holsworthy	
USA	Malmo	
Bulgarian	Bale	
English	Southampton	Bittern Park
Scotch	London	
Finnish	Finland	
USC	Kings House, Kiing St, Cheapside London	
Irish	Ireland	
Irish	Queenstown	
Russian	London	29 Houndsditch
Finnish	Finland	
	Paris	c/o T Cook & Son
Syrian	Syria	
	Paris	6 Rue Cornmaille

Who Sailed on Titanic?

Master No	Old List No	Surname	First Name (s)	Title	Class	Sex	Age	Occupation
799	577	Mangen	Mary	Miss	3	f		
800	221	Maniavacchi	Emilio	Mr	2	m		
802	815	Marsh	John Starr	Mr	3	m	c50	American Sea Post Clerk
803	580	Mardirosian	Sarkis	Mr	3	m	25	Farm Labourer
805	581	Markoff	Marin	Mr	3	m	35	Labourer
806	582	Markun	Johann	Mr	3	m	20	Labourer
807	64	Marvin	D W	Mr	1	m		
811	583	Matinoff	Nicol	Mr	3	m		
812	224	Matthews	Wm T	Mr	2	m		
815	225	Maybery	Frank H	Mr	2	m		
817	65	McCaffry	T	Mr	1	m		
819	66	McCarthy	Timothy	Mr	1	m		
824	226	McCrae	Arthur G	Mr	2	m	33	Mining Engr
825	227	McCrie	James M	Mr	2	m		
827	584	McEvoy	Michael	Mr	3	m		
830	817	McGowan	Catherine		3	f		
832	228	McKrae?	Peter D	Mr	2	m	46	
833	585	Mcmahon	Martin	Mr	3	m		
834	587	McNamee	Eileen	Mrs	3	f	19	Wife
835	586	McNamee	Neal	Mr	3	m	27	Provision Man
836	635	McNeill	Bridget	Miss	3	f		
837	588	Meanwell	Marion Ogden	Mrs	3	f	63	Milliner
838	590	Meek	Annie	Mrs	3	f	31	Housewife
843	592	Meo	Alfonse	Mr	3	m	48	Musician
844	616	Mernagh	Robert	Mr	3	m		
845	229	Meyer	August	Mr	2	m		
846	67	Meyer	Edgar J	Mr	1	m		
849	594	Miles	Frank	Mr	3	m	23	Engineer
851	68	Millet	Frank D	Mr	1	m		
852	230	Milling	Jacob C	Mr	2	m	48	Machine Inspector
855	122	Minehan	W E	Mr	1	m		US Merchant
856	595	Mineff	Ivan	Mr	3	m	24	Labourer
857	596	Minkoff	Lazar	Mr	3	m	21	Labourer
858	593	Mikoff	Stoytcho	Mr	3	m	28	Labourer
859	231	Mitchell	Henry	Mr	2	m	71	Retired
860	597	Mitkoff	Milo	Mr	3	m	23	Labourer
863	598	Moen	Sigurd H	Mr	3	m	25	Joiner
864	69	Molson	H Markland	Mr	1	m		
865	222	Mantvila	Joseph	Mr	2	m	27	Priest
868	70	Moore	Clarence	Mr	1	m		
869	599	Moore	Leonard Charles	Mr	3	m	19	Bricklayer
871	602	Moran	Daniel	Mr	3	m		
872	600	Moran	James	Mr	3	m	22	
873	232	Moraweck	Ernest	Mr	2	m		Doctor
874	223	Marshall	Henry	Mr	2	m		
875	601	Morley	Wm A	Mr	3	m	34	Carpenter
876	603	Marrow	Thomas	Mr	3	m		
881	605	Moussa		Mrs	3	f	35	Housewife
882	606	Moutal	Rahamin	Mr	3	m	28	Traveller
883	233	Mudd	Thos C	Mr	2	m	16	
887	607	Murdlin	Joseph	Mr	3	m	22	Chemist
891	609	Myhrman	Oliver	Mr	3	m	18	Labourer
892	234	Myles	Thomas F	Mr	2	m		
893	610	Naidenoff	Penko	Mr	3	m	22	Labourer
898	612	Nancarrow	William Henry	Mr	3	m	34	Mason
899	614	Nankoff	Minko	Mr	3	m	32	Labourer
900	608	Mustafa	Nasr	Mr	3	m	20	Farm Labourer
902	235	Nasser	Nicolas	Mr	2	m		
903	71	Natsch	Charles	Mr	1	m		
904	615	Naughton	Hannah	Miss	3	f		
906	201	Hoffman	Louis	Mr	2	m		
908	617	Nenkoff	Christo	Mr	3	m	22	Labourer
909	236	Nesson	Israel	Mr	2	m	26	Electrician
910	72	Newell	A W	Mr	1	m		
914	237	Nicholls	Joseph Charles	Mr	2	m	19	Miner
916	73	Nicholson	A E	Mr	1	m		

List C&D

Nationality	Last Abode	Address
Irish	Ireland	
	Paris	c/o T Cook & Son, Florence
American	13 East Park Tce, Southampton	Emmett Street, Newark, New Jersey, USA
Syrian	Syria	
Bulgarian	Bale	
Austrian	Austria	
USC	58 Acre Lane, Brixton SW	
Bulgarian	Bale	
English	Southampton	Penwithick, St Austell, Cornwall
British Colonial	London	1 Whitecross Road, Weston Super Mare
	Hotel Majestic, Nice	
Irish	Hotel Chatham, Paris	
Scotch	Southampton	c/o Bank of Australasia, Threadneedle St, EC
British	London	Strand Palace Hotel
Irish	Ireland	
Ireland	Terry, **asbrook, Crossmolina	
English	Guernsey	Highland Vale
Ireland	Queenstown	
Ireland	London	Mr & Mrs O Leary, Kingston House, Wlton Road, Salisbury
Ireland	London	Mr & Mrs O Leary, Kingston House, Wlton Road, Salisbury
Irish	Charlesville	c/o Patrick Hayes, Broadford
English	England	c/o W S Hill, Leadenhall St
Irish	Queenstown	89 Windsor Road, Penarth
Italy	England	
Irish	Queenstown	
German	London	26 Kildas Rd, Harrow on Hill
USC	Hotel Majestic, Paris	
English	Greenwich	103 King George Street
USC		
Danish	Copenhagen	Odense
USC		
Bulgaria	Basel	
Bulgarian	Bale	
Bulgaria	Basel	
British	Guernsey	Upland Rd
Bulgarian	Bale	
Norwegian	Norway	
Eng	c/o Junior Athaenium Club, Picadilly, W	
Russian	London	21 The Oval, Hackney
USC	Almonds Hotel,Clifford St, London W	
English	London	134 Acre Road, Kingston on Thames
Irish	Ireland	
Irish	Ireland	c/o James Barton & son, Cork
USC	Berlin	c/o Karl Moraweck, Hotel Slavia, Brunn, Austria
English		6 Bristol St, Birmingham
English	London	Lods Bridge, Petworth, Sussex
Irish	Ireland	
Syrian	Syria	
Turk	London	27 Beauclere Rd, Hammersmith
English	Holesworth, Suffolk	Huntingfield
Russian	London	
Norway	Gothenburg	
USC	Fermoy	
Bulgarian	Basel	
English	Cornwall	c/o Daniel & Rowse, Cornwall
Bulgarian	Bulgaria	
Syrian	Syria	
Turkish	Paris	c/o T Cook & Son
USC		
Irish	Queenstown	
Bulgarian	Basel	
Russian	London	
USC	Hotel St James & Albany, Paris	
English	St Ives	Stennach Villas
Eng	Claremont, Shanklin, IoW	

Who Sailed on Titanic?

Master No	Old List No	Surname	First Name (s)	Title	Class	Sex	Age	Occupation
919	618	Nieminen	Mannta	Miss	3	f	30	Servant
920	619	Niklasen	Sander	Mr	3	m		Labourer
921	620	Nilsson	August F	Mr	3	m		Labourer
924	622	Nirva	Isak Aijo	Mr	3	m	41	Labourer
928	238	Norman	Robert Douglas	Mr	2	m	28	Elect. Engr
929	623	Nosworthy	Richard C	Mr	3	m	20	Labourer
931	579	Mansour	Notel	Mr	3	m	20	Journalist
934	621	Nysven	Johan	Mr	3	m	61	Farmer
936	625	O Brien	Thos	Mr	3	m		Labourer
937	624	O Brien	Dennis	Mr	3	m	21	Labourer
938	627	O Connell	Patrick	Mr	3	m		Labourer
939	626	O Connor	Maurice	Mr	3	m		Labourer
940	628	O Connor	Patrick	Mr	3	m		Labourer
941	629	Odahl	Martin	Mr	3	m	23	Labourer
951	631	Olsen	Henry	Mr	3	m	28	Donkeyman
952	630	Olsen	Carl	Mr	3	m	42	Labourer
953	632	Olsen	Ole M	Mr	3	m	27	Labourer
954	634	Olsson	Elida	Miss	3	f	31	Maiden
955	633	Olsen	John	Mr	3	m	28	Labourer
957	299	Andersen	Thor		3	m	20	Labourer
959	637	Oreskovic	Jeko	Mr	3	m	20	Farmer
960	636	Oreskovic	Luka	Mr	3	m	23	Farmer
961	638	Oreskovic	Maria	Miss	3	f	20	Farmhand
963	639	Osen	Elon	Mr	3	m	17	Farm Labourer
965	74	Ostby	E C	Mr	1	m		
967	640	O Sullivan	Bridget	Miss	3	f	32	Servant
968	239	Otter	Richard	Mr	2	m	39	Stone Cutter
969	75	Ovies	S	Mr	1	m		
972	240	Pain	Alfred	Mr	2	m		Doctor
974	649	Paulsson	Alma C	Mrs	3	f	29	Housewife
975	653	Paulsson	Gosta	Miss	3	f	2	Child
976	651	Paulsson	Paul	Master	3	m	5	Child
977	652	Paulsson	Stina	Miss	3	f	3	Child
978	650	Paulsson	Torborg	Miss	3	f	8	Child
979	647	Panula	William	Master	3	m	11	Child
980	644	Panula	Ernesti	Mr	3	m	17	Labourer
981	645	Panula	Eino	Mr	3	m	16	Farm Labourer
982	643	Panula	Jeko	Mr	3	m	18	Labourer
983	641	Panula	Maria	Mrs	3	f	40	Wife
984	646	Panula	Urhu	Miss	3	f	3	Child
985	241	Parker	Clifford R	Mr	2	m		Clerk
986	271	Parkes	Frank	Mr	2	m	18	Plumber
987	76	Parr	H W	Mr	1	m		
989	77	Partner	Austin	Mr	1	m		
990	648	Pasic	Jakob	Mr	3	m	21	Farmer
991	681	Potchet	Geo	Mr	3	m	19	Shoe Operative
992	333	Usscher	Pullnent	Mr	3	m	16	Plumber
993	654	Pavlovic	Stefo	Mr	3	m	32	Labourer
994	78	Payne	V	Mr	1	m		
995	657	Peacock	Alfred	Master	3	m	7m	Infant
996	655	Peacock	Treastall	Mrs	3	f	26	Wife
997	656	Peacock	Treastall	Miss	3	f	4	Child
998	658	Pearce	Ernest	Mr	3	m	32	Farmer
1000	79	Pears	Thomas	Mr	1	m		
1001	667	Pettersen	Olaf	Mr	3	m	29	Labourer
1002	659	Peduzzi	Joseph	Mr	3	m	24	Waiter
1003	660	Pekonemi	Edvard	Mr	3	m	32	Labourer
1004	662	Peltomaki	Nikolai	Mr	3	m	25	Labourer
1006	80	Penasco	Victor	Mr	1	m		
1007	242	Pengelly	Fredk	Mr	2	m	20	Miner
1008	663	Perkin	John Henry	Mr	3	m	22	Farmer
1009	243	Pernot	Rene	Mr	2	m		Chauffeur
1012	244	Peruschitz	Joseph M	Mr	2	m		Monk
1013	664	Peters	Katie	Miss	3	f	9	Child
1014	673	Petersen	Marius	Mr	3	m	24	Dairyman
1015	670	Petranec	Matilda	Miss	3	f	30	Servant
1016	672	Petroff	Nedelco	Mr	3	m	19	Labourer
1017	671	Petroff	Pentcho	Mr	3	m	29	Labourer

List C&D

Nationality	Last Abode	Address
Finland	Finland	
Sweden	Hull	c/o P Drusdo, Hull
Sweden	Copenhagen	
Finnish	Finland	
Scotch	Glasgow	c/o A E G Electric Co, So Wellington St
English	Newton Abbot	11 Fisher road
Syrian	Syria	
Norway	Christiania	
Irish	Queenstown	
Irish	Queenstown	
Irish	Queenstown	
Irish	Queenstown	
Irish	Queenstown	
Swede	Sweden	
Norwegian	Norway	
American	Norway	
Norwegian	Norway	
Sweden	Copenhagen	
Norwegian	Norway	
Norway	Christiania	
Switzerland	Basel	
Switzerland	Basel	
Switzerland	Basel	
Norway	Gothenburg	
USC	Brown Shipley, Pall Mall, London	
USA	USA	
USC	Southampton	Southwell, Portland, Dorset
French	c/o Foulds & Co, 30 Faubourg Poissoniere, Paris	
Sweden	Helsingborg	
Sweden	Helsingborg	
Sweden	Helsingborg	
Sweden	Helsingborg	
Sweden	Helsingborg	
Child	Finland	Finland
Finland	Finland	
Finland	Finland	
Finland	Finland	
Finland	Finland	
Finland	Finland	
English	Guernsey	Fernleigh, St Andrews
English	Belfast	Harland & Wolff's men
Eng	Harland & Wolff, Belfast	
Eng		
Austrian	Austria	
English	England	Hanwick Road, Wollaston, Nr Wellingboro
Russian	Paris	
Austrian	Austria	
Eng	Grand Trunk Rly Co, London	
English	Southampton	Mrs Elkins, 35 Orchard Place
English	Southampton	Mrs Elkins, 35 Orchard Place
English	Southampton	Mrs Elkins, 35 Orchard Place
English	England	10 Bedford Place
Eng	Ineragissey, Isleworth, Middlesex	
Norway	Norway	
Italian	London	1 Ashgrove, Hackney
Finnish	Finland	
Finland	Finland	
Spanish	Hotel Majestic, Paris	
English	Gunnislake	Chilworthy Beam
English	Holsworthy	c/o Hawkins
	Paris	12 Rue Lesneur
German	London	c/o P Jaricot, St Augustine's College, Ramsgate
Irish	Ireland	c/o Clarke & Co, Cahir,Tipperary
Dane	London	73 West End Road, Southall
Austrian	Basel	
Bulgarian	Bulgaria	
Bulgarian	Bulgaria	

Who Sailed on Titanic?

Master No	Old List No	Surname	First Name (s)	Title	Class	Sex	Age	Occupation
1018	665	Peterson	Johan	Mr	3	m	25	Labourer
1019	666	Petersson	Ellen	Mrs	3	f	18	Wife
1022	245	Phillips	Robert	Mr	2	m	45	
1025	678	Plotchersky	Vasil	Mr	3	m	27	Labourer
1026	680	Pocruic	Mate	Mr	3	m	17	Farmer
1027	679	Pocruic	Tome	Mr	3	m	24	Farmer
1028	246	Ponesell	Martin	Mr	2	m		
1030	81	Porter	Walter Chamberlain	Mr	1	m		
1032	247	Pulbaum	Frank	Mr	2	m		
1036	682	Radeff	Alexander	Mr	3	m	27	Labourer
1037	748	Solvang	Lena Jacobson	Mrs	3	m	63	
1038	683	Rachid	Razi	Mr	3	m	30	Labourer
1039	684	Reed	Jas Geo	Mr	3	m	19	Butcher
1040	248	Reeves	David	Mr	2	m	36	Carpenter
1041	685	Rekic	Tido	Mr	3	m	38	Labourer
1044	249	Renouf	Peter Henry	Mr	2	m	34	Carpenter
1045	82	Reuchlin	Jonkleer J G	Mr	1	m		
1047	686	Reynolds	Harold	Mr	3	m	21	Baker
1049	688	Rice	Albert	Master	3	m		Child
1051	690	Rice	Eric	Master	3	m		Child
1052	691	Rice	Eugene	Master	3	m		Child
1053	689	Rice	George	Master	3	m		Child
1054	687	Rice	Margaret	Mrs	3	f		
1055	250	Richard	Emile	Mr	2	m		
1060	642	Panula	Sanni	Mr	3	m	21	Labourer
1061	120	Regheim	Sante	Mr	1	m		White's Manservant
1062	692	Rintamaki	Matti	Mr	3	m	33	Labourer
1064	694	Risien	Emma	Mrs	3	f	58	Hotel keeper
1065	693	Risien	Samuel	Mr	3	m	68	Hotel keeper
1066	121	Robbins		Mr	1	m		Astor's Manservant
1068	695	Robins	Alexander	Mr	3	m	50	Mason
1069	696	Robins	Charity	Mrs	3	f	48	Housewife
1070	83	Roebling	Washington A 2nd	Mr	1	m		
1072	697	Rogers	William John	Mr	3	m	29	Miner
1074	702	Rummetvedt	Kristian P	Mr	3	m	49	Tailor
1075	84	Rood	Hugh R	Mr	1	m		
1076	698	Rosblom	Helene	Mrs	3	f	41	Wife
1077	700	Rosblom	Salli	Miss	3	f	2	Child
1078	699	Rosblom	Viktor	Mr	3	m	18	Labourer
1080	102	Rosenshine	G	Mr	1	m		
1081	85	Ross	J Hugo	Mr	1	m		
1085	86	Rothschild	M	Mr	1	m		
1086	701	Rouse	Richard Henry	Mr	3	m	53	Labourer
1087	87	Rowe	Alfred	Mr	1	m		
1089	703	Rush	Alfred Geo	Mr	3	m	17	Porter
1091	704	Ryan	Patrick	Mr	3	m		
1092	88	Ryerson	Arthur	Mr	1	m		
1097	297	Saad	Amin		3	m	30	Farm Labourer
1098	538	Saad	Khalil	Mr	3	m	25	Farm Labourer
1099	705	Saade	Jean Nassr	Mr	3	m	20	Farm Labourer
1101	706	Sadlier	Matt	Mr	3	m		
1102	707	Sadowitz	Harry	Mr	3	m	17	Fur Cutter
1103	726	Sather	Simon	Mr	3	m	25	Miner
1104	711	Sage	Annie	Mrs	3	f	44	Wife
1105	717	Sage	William	Master	3	m	11	Child
1106	719	Sage	Constance	Miss	3	f	7	Child
1107	716	Sage	Dorothy	Miss	3	f	13	Scholar
1108	714	Sage	Douglas	Mr	3	m	18	Baker
1109	718	Sage	Ada	Miss	3	f	9	Child
1110	715	Sage	Frederick	Mr	3	m	16	Assistant Cook
1111	713	Sage	George	Mr	3	m	19	Barman
1112	710	Sage	John	Mr	3	m	44	Tradesman
1113	712	Sage	Stella	Miss	3	f	20	Dressmaker
1114	720	Sage	Thomas	Master	3	m	4	Child
1116	721	Salander	Carl	Mr	3	m	24	Labourer
1119	722	Salonen	Werner	Mr	3	m	29	Labourer
1120	724	Samaan	Elias	Mr	3	m	18	Labourer

List C&D

Nationality	Last Abode	Address
Sweden	Gothenburg	
Sweden	Gothenburg	
English	Ilfracombe	
Bulgarian	Bale	
Austrian	Austria	
Austrian	Austria	
Danish	Southampton	
	Kings House, King St, Cheapside, London	
	Paris	Luna Park
Bulgarian	Bale	
Norwegian	Norway	
Syria	Syria	
Welsh	Cardiff	Mr Reed, Platform Tavern, Town Quay, Soton
English	Brighton	Hayes Lane, Slinfold, Sussex
Austrian	Bale	
English	Guernsey	Rossley Halfway Banks
Dutch	Holland American Line	
English	London	10 Courthill Rd, Lewisham
Ireland	Queenstown	W T Kerrigan, The Square, Athlone, Ireland
Ireland	Queenstown	W T Kerrigan, The Square, Athlone, Ireland
Ireland	Queenstown	W T Kerrigan, The Square, Athlone, Ireland
Ireland	Queenstown	W T Kerrigan, The Square, Athlone, Ireland
Ireland	Queenstown	W T Kerrigan, The Square, Athlone, Ireland
	Paris	St Jean d'Angeleys, Charente
Finland	Finland	
Finland	Finland	
USA	London	154 Camden St, Camden Gardens
USA	London	154 Camden St, Camden Gardens
USA	Cornwall	c/o Daniel & Rowse, St Austell, Cornwall
USA	Cornwall	c/o Daniel & Rowse, St Austell, Cornwall
USC	Brown Shipley, 123 Pall Mall, London	
Welsh	Pontardawe	c/o Mrs Rogers, Ynisy Mont Farm, Glais, Nr Swansea
Norwegian	Bergen	
USC	Ritz Hotel, London W	
Finnish	Finland	
Finnish	Finland	
Finnish	Finland	
USC	17 Faubourg Poissoniere, Paris	
USC	Savoy Hotel, London	
USC	Grand Hotel, Paris	
English	Sittingbourne	30 New Road
USC	6 Petersham Place, Gloucester Rd, London	
English	London	37 Palace Road, Upper Norwood
Irish	Queenstown	
USC	Hotel Langham, Paris	
Syria	Syria	
Syrian	Syria	
Syrian	Syria	
Irish	Queenstown	
English	London	
USA	Capetown	
English	London	246 Gladstone Rd, Peterborough
English	London	246 Gladstone Rd, Peterborough
English	London	246 Gladstone Rd, Peterborough
English	London	246 Gladstone Rd, Peterborough
English	London	246 Gladstone Rd, Peterborough
English	London	246 Gladstone Rd, Peterborough
English	London	246 Gladstone Rd, Peterborough
English	London	246 Gladstone Rd, Peterborough
English	London	246 Gladstone Rd, Peterborough
English	London	246 Gladstone Rd, Peterborough
English	London	246 Gladstone Rd, Peterborough
Sweden	Gothenburg	
Finland	Finland	
Syria	Syria	

Master No	Old List No	Surname	First Name (s)	Title	Class	Sex	Age	Occupation
1121	723	Samaan	Hanna	Mr	3	m	40	Labourer
1122	725	Samaan	Toussef	Mr	3	m	16	Labourer
1127	727	Saundercock	William Henry	Mr	3	m	20	Labourer
1128	728	Sawyer	Frederick	Mr	3	m	23	Gardener
1129	729	Scanlan	James	Mr	3	m		
1132	255	Smith	Augustus	Mr	2	m		
1133	730	Sydcoff	Todor	Mr	3	m	25	Labourer
1134	251	Sedgwick	Charles Frederick Waddington	Mr	2	m		
1137	252	Sharp	Percival	Mr	2	m		
1138	732	Shaughnessy	Patrick	Mr	3	m		
1140	733	Shellard	Frederick	Mr	3	m	62	Painter
1143	734	Shorney	Charles J	Mr	3	m	22	Valet
1148	89	Silvey	William B	Mr	1	m		
1149	736	Simmons	John	Mr	3	m	39	Labourer
1153	709	Sirayamin	Arsen	Mr	3	m	22	Farmer
1154	708	Siriota	Maurice	Mr	3	m	20	Tailor
1155	737	Sivic	Husen	Mr	3	m	40	Labourer
1156	735	Sihvola	Antti	Mr	3	m	21	Labourer
1158	253	Sjostedt	Ernest A	Mr	2	m		
1159	739	Skoog	Anna	Mrs	3	f	43	Labourer
1160	742	Skoog	Harald	Master	3	m	4	Labourer
1161	740	Skoog	Carl	Master	3	m	10	Labourer
1162	741	Skoog	Mabel	Miss	3	f	9	Labourer
1163	743	Skoog	Margret	Miss	3	f	2	Labourer
1164	738	Skoog	Wm	Mr	3	m	39	Labourer
1165	744	Slabenoff	Petco	Mr	3	m	42	Labourer
1168	254	Slemen	Richard J	Mr	2	m	35	
1169	745	Slocovski	Saleman	Mr	3	m	20	Merchant
1171	90	Smart	John M	Mr	1	m		
1172	746	Smilganic	Mile	Mr	3	m	37	Farm Labourer
1173	91	Smith	J Clinch	Mr	1	m		
1174	812	Smith	John Richard Jago	Mr	3	m	35	British Post Clerk
1175	93	Smith	L P	Mr	1	m		
1178	92	Smith	R W	Mr	1	m		
1179	811	Smyth	Thomas	Mr	3	m		
1183	256	Sobey	Hayden	Mr	2	m	25	Quarryman
1184	747	Soholt	Peter	Mr	3	m	19	Joiner
1185	749	Somerton	Francis	Mrs	3	f	31	Wife
1186	750	Spector	Woolf	Mr	3	m	23	
1191	94	Spencer	W A	Mr	1	m		
1192	751	Spinner	Henry John	Mr	3	m	32	Grocer
1194	752	Staneff	Ivan	Mr	3	m	23	Labourer
1195	753	Stankovic	Jovan	Mr	3	m	33	Labourer
1197	754	Stanley	Ernest Rowland	Mr	3	m	21	Hotel Porter
1198	257	Stanton	S Ward	Mr	2	m		
1199	95	Stead	W T	Mr	1	m		
1204	96	Stewart	A A	Mr	1	m		
1205	258	Stokes	Phillip ReadasJ	Mr	2	m	25	Bricklayer
1207	756	Storey	T	Mr	3	m		
1208	757	Stoytchoff	Ilia	Mr	3	m	19	Labourer
1209	758	Strandberg	Ida	Miss	3	f	19	
1211	97	Strauss	Isidor	Mr	1	m		
1212	98	Strauss		Mrs	1	f		
1213	759	Strilic	Ivan	Mr	3	m	27	Farmer
1214	760	Strom	Elma	Mrs	3	f	28	Wife
1215	761	Strom	Selma	Miss	3	f	2	Child
1218	762	Sutchall	Henry	Mr	3	m	26	Coach Trimmer
1220	99	Sutton	Frederick	Mr	1	m		
1222	763	Svensson	Johan	Mr	3	m	74	
1224	764	Svenssen	Olaf	Mr	3	m	24	Farmer
1225	259	Swane	Geo	Mr	2	m		
1226	260	Sweet	Geo	Mr	2	m	14	Farm Labourer
1228	100	Taussig	Emil	Mr	1	m		
1233	278	Taylor	Percy Cornelius	Mr	2	m		
1235	101	Thayer	J B	Mr	1	m		
1238	765	Theobald	Thos	Mr	3	m	34	Groom
1240	766	Thomas	Charles	Mr	3	m	31	Dealer

List C&D

Nationality	Last Abode	Address
Syria	Syria	
Syria	Syria	
English	Southampton	
English	Woolwich	2 Acres Cottages, Slade Green, Kent
Ireland	Queenstown	
Austrian	London	Berwick St N
Bulgarian	Basel	
	London	
	London	
Irish	Queenstown	
English	Bristol	520 Gloucester Rd, Harfield
English	Brighton	c/o Thomas Cook & Son
English	England	W S Line, Leadenhall Street
American	Marseille	
English	London	57 Mile End Rd, London
Austrian	Bale	
Finland	Finland	
Swedish	London	Hjo Sweden
Swede	Sweden	
Swede	Sweden	
Swede	Sweden	
Swede	Sweden	
Swede	Sweden	
Swede	Sweden	
Bulgarian	Bale	
English	Southampton	Landrake by St Germans, Cornwall
Russian	London	c/o W S Line, Leadenhall Street
USC	3 Woodend Cottage, Kildale, via Grosmont, York	
Austrian	Basel	
USC	4 Villa Said, Paris	
British	45 Atherley Rd, Southampton	Trebarvethh, H Keverne, Cornwall
Eng	Reinach & Nephews, London	
British	Queenstown	
English	Plymouth	Porthalow Nr Helston, Cornwall
Norwegian	Norway	
American	Cheltenham	c/o Cook & Son, Cheltenham
Russian	London	
USC	33 Avenue Hy Martin, Paris	
English	Worcester	
Bulgarian	Bale	
Bulgarian	Bale	
English	Swanage	
USC	Paris	
Eng	5 Smith Square, Westminster	
USC	Hotel Continentale, Paris	
English	London	91 Hawstedd Rd, Catford
English		
Bulgarian	Bale	
Swede	Sweden	
USC	Hotel Bristol, Paris	
USC	Hotel Bristol, Paris	
Austrian	Basel	
Swede	Sweden	
Swede	Sweden	
USC	London	
Eng		
Swede	Sweden	
Swede	Sweden	
	London	154 Abbey Rd NW
English	Yeovil	
Austrian	Vienna	
English	London	9 Fentiman Rd, Clapham
USC		
English	Rochester	c/o Curtiss & Sons
Syrian	Marseille	

Who Sailed on Titanic?

Master No	Old List No	Surname	First Name (s)	Title	Class	Sex	Age	Occupation
1241	767	Thomas	John	Mr	3	m	34	Dealer
1242	768	Thomas	Tannous J	Mr	3	m	16	Student
1244	771	Thomson	Alexander	Mr	3	m		
1247	769	Thorneycroft	Percival	Mr	3	m	36	Labourer
1248	770	Tikkanen	Jutio	Mr	3	m	32	Labourer
1249	772	Tobin	Rger	Mr	3	m		
1250	773	Todoroff	Lalio	Mr	3	m	23	Labourer
1251	774	Tomlin	Ernest Portage	Mr	3	m	22	Student
1253	775	Torber	Ernest	Mr	3	m	41	Gardener
1254	318	Assad	Torfa		3	m	20	Farmhand
1256	611	Nakle	Toufik	Mr	3	m	17	Labourer
1262	261	Troupiansky	Moses Aaron	Mr	2	m	23	Shop Assistant
1266	776	Turcin	Stefan	Mr	3	m	36	Labourer
1269	262	Turpin	Dorothy Ann	Mrs	2	f	27	Housewife
1270	263	Turpin	Wm John	Mr	2	m	29	Carpenter
1271	103	Uruchurtu	M R	Mr	1	m		
1272	777	Uselas	Jovo	Mr	3	m	17	Farmer
1274	338	Billiard	Austin Van	Mr	3	m		
1275	339	Billiard	James Van	Master	3	m		Child
1276	340	Billiard	Walter Van	Master	3	m		Child
1277	778	Van der Velde	Joseph	Mr	3	m	36	Farmer
1278	755	Steen	Leon van den	Mr	3	m	28	Farmer
1279	104	Van der Hoef	Wyckoff	Mr	1	m		
1280	496	Impe	Catherine Van	Miss	3	f	10	Child
1281	494	Impe	Jacob Van	Mr	3	m	36	Farmer
1282	495	Impe	Rosalie Van	Mrs	3	f	39	Housewife
1283	591	Melkebuk	Philemon Van	Mr	3	m	23	Farmer
1284	783	Van der Walle	Nestor	Mr	3	m	28	Merchant
1285	779	Vererysse	Victor	Mr	3	m	47	Farmer
1286	674	Planke	Augusta Van der	Miss	3	f	18	Servant
1287	677	Planke	Emilie Van der	Mrs	3	f	31	Wife
1288	676	Planke	Jules Van der	Mr	3	m	31	Farmer
1289	675	Planke	Leon Van der	Mr	3	m	16	Farm Labourer
1291	264	Veale	Jas		2	m		
1292	788	Wendel	Olof Edvin	Mr	3	m	21	Labourer
1293	780	Vestrom	Hulda A	Miss	3	f	14	Servant
1294	781	Vook	Janko	Mr	3	m	21	Labourer
1295	782	Waelens	Achille	Mr	3	m	22	Farm Labourer
1297	105	Walker	W Anderson	Mr	1	m		
1300	784	Ware	Frederick	Mr	3	m	34	Motor Fitter
1301	265	Ware	John Jas	Mr	2	m		Builder
1304	785	Warren	Charles William	Mr	3	m	30	Bricklayer
1305	106	Warren	F M	Mr	1	m		
1306	275	Watson	Ennis	Mr	2	m	18	Electrician
1309	786	Webber	James	Mr	3	m	66	Miner
1311	107	Weir	J	Mr	1	m		Colonel in American army
1312	266	Weisz	Leopold	Mr	2	m		
1320	267	West	E Arthur	Mr	2	m	36	
1321	451	Georges	Chahini	Mrs	3	f	42	Wife
1322	268	Wheadon	Edward H	Mr	2	m	66	Farmer
1323	269	Wheeler	Edwin	Mr	2	m		
1325	108	White	Percival W	Mr	1	m		
1326	109	White	Richard J	Mr	1	m		
1327	110	Wick	George D	Mr	1	m		
1330	790	Widegrin	Charles	Mr	3	m	44	Labourer
1332	111	Widener	George D	Mr	1	m		
1333	112	Widener	Harry	Mr	1	m		
1334	792	Wiklund	Karl Johan	Mr	3	m	21	Labourer
1335	791	Wiklund	Jakobt Alfred	Mr	3	m	18	Labourer
1341	787	Weller	Abe	Mr	3	m	37	Tailor
1342	793	Willey	Edward	Mr	3	m	18	Farm Labourer
1343	113	Williams	Duane	Mr	1	m		
1345	794	Williams	Harry	Mr	3	m	28	Carman
1346	795	Williams	Leslie	Mr	3	m		Boxer
1348	58	Lambert-Williams	Fletcher Fellows	Mr	1	m		
1349	813	Williamson	James Bertram	Mr	3	m	35	British Post Clerk
1351	796	Windelov	Einar	Mr	3	m	21	Dairyman

List C&D

Nationality	Last Abode	Address
Syrian	Marseille	
Syrian	Marseille	
Scotch	Scotland	
English	London	Crundell, 14 Walter St, Penge
Finnish	Finland	
English	London	
Bulgarian	Bale	
English	London	1 Sanders Rd, London
German	London	112 Walton St, Kensington
Syrian	Syria	
Syrian	Syria	
Russian	London	African Hotel, Southampton
Austrian	Bale	
British	Plymouth	59 Chaddlewood Avenue
British	Plymouth	59 Chaddlewood Avenue
USC	Grand Hotel, Paris	
Austrian	Basel	
USA	London	W Bartlett, 4 Armitage Mansions, Golder's Green
USA	London	W Bartlett, 4 Armitage Mansions, Golder's Green
USA	London	W Bartlett, 4 Armitage Mansions, Golder's Green
Belgium	Antwerp	
Belgian	Antwerp	
USC	5 College Park E Belfast	
Belgium	Belgium	
Belgium	Belgium	
Belgium	Belgium	
Belgium	Antwerp	
Belgium	Antwerp	
Belgium	Antwerp	
Belgian	Antwerp	
Belgian	Antwerp	
Belgian	Antwerp	
Belgian	Antwerp	
USC	Southampton	Port Navis, Falmouth
Sweden	Copenhagen	
Swede	Sweden	
Austrian	Bale	
Belgium	Antwerp	
	Manchester	
English	Greenwich	
English	Bristol	13 Salthrop Rd, Morley Square, Bishopston
English	Portsmouth	
USC	Paris	
English	Belfast	Harland & Wolff's men
American	Southampton	
USC	London	
Hungarian	Birmingham	c/o Bromsgrove Guild, Bromsgrove
English	Bournemouth	Newhorn, Truro, Cornwall
Syria	Syria	
English	Guernsey	La Couture
	Paris	4 Melcome Road, Durley Park, Bath
Eng	65 Bridge Street, Wednesbury	
Eng	65 Bridge Street, Wednesbury	
USC		
Norway	Nilsson	
USC	Hotel Ritz, London	
USC	Hotel Ritz, London	
Finland	Finland	
Finland	Finland	
Russian	Paris	
English	England	
Canadian	Geneva, Suisse	
English	Guernsey	
English	Cardiff	Mrs E Williams, 19 Eleanor St, Tonypandy
USC	6 West Bickerhall Mansions, Gloucester Place, London W	
British	93 Clovelly Rd, Southampton	Botanic Rd, Dublin
Denmark	Capetown	

Who Sailed on Titanic?

Master No	Old List No	Surname	First Name (s)	Title	Class	Sex	Age	Occupation
1352	797	Wirz	Albert	Mr	3	m	28	Farmer
1353	798	Wiseman	Philip	Mr	3	m	54	Merchant
1354	799	Wittewrongel	Camille	Mr	3	m	36	Farmer
1358	279	Woodward	John Wesley	Mr	2	m		
1359	814	Woody	Oscar S	Mr	3	m	41	American Sea Post Clerk
1361	114	Wright	George	Mr	1	m		
1363	800	Yazbeck	Antoni	Mr	3	m	27	Labourer
1366	801	Yousif	Wazli	Mr	3	m	25	Farmer
1367	803	Youssef	Gerios	Mr	3	m	45	Shoemaker
1368	270	Yrois	Henriette	Miss	2	f		
1369	805	Zabour	Hileni	Miss	3	f	16	Housekeeper
1370	804	Zabour	Tamini Camozic	Miss	3	f	19	Housekeeper
1371	807	Zakarian	Mapreder	Mr	3	m		
1372	806	Zakarian	Artin	Mr	3	m	27	Labourer
1373	809	Zimmerman	Leo	Mr	3	m	29	Farmer

List C&D

Nationality	Last Abode	Address
Sweden	Basel	
English	London	
Belgium	Antwerp	
English	Oxford	The Fris, Windmill Rd, Headington
American	Parkers Hotel, Southampton	Clifton Springs, Fairfax County, Virginia, USA
Canadian		
Syria	Syria	
Syrian	Syria	
Syrian	Syria	
French	London	5 Rue des Pyramides, Paris
Syrian	Syria	
Syrian	Syria	
Syrian	Syria	
Swiss	Basel	

Register of Deaths of Passengers

Master List No	Old List No	Surname	First Name(s)	Sex	Class	Age	Occupation	Nationality	Last Abode
1	290	Abbing	Anthony	M	3	42	Blacksmith	USA	Southampton
2	291	Abbott	Eugene J	M	3	13	Scholar	USA	London, Salvation Army London
4	292	Abbott	Rossmore E	M	3	16	Jeweller	USA	London, Salvation Army London
8	124	Abelson	Samson	M	2			Russian	Paris
11	293	Adahl	Maurits	M	3	30	Labourer	Sweden	Copenhagen
12	294	Adams	John	M	3		Farm Labourer	English	Yeovil, (Heath Cottage, Alum Chine Rd, Bournemouth)
13	295	Ahlin	Johanna	F	3	40	Wife	Sweden	Gothenburg
14	296	Ahmed	Ali	M	3	24	Labourer	Syria	Buenos Aires
18	125	Aldworth	Augustus	M	2				London
19	298	Alexander	William	M	3	23	Labourer	England	10 Belvedere Place, Kitchener Rd, Gt Yarmouth
20	299	Alhomaki	Ilmari	M	3	20	Labourer	Finland	Finland
21	300	Ali	William	M	3	25	Labourer	Syria	Buenos Aires
23	301	Allen	William	M	3	35	Tool Maker	England	c/o F Hunt, 78 Queens Road, Erdington, Birmingham
24	2	Allison	H J (Mrs)	F	1				152 Abbey Road, West Hampstead, London NW
25	3	Allison	(Miss)	F	1				152 Abbey Road, West Hampstead, London NW
26	1	Allison	H J	M	1				152 Abbey Road, West Hampstead, London NW
28	302	Allum	Owen George	M	3	18	Gardener	England	London, 22 Oswald Rd, Southall
29	303	Andersen	Albert	M	3	33	Engineer	Norway	Bergen
32	306	Anderson	Alfrida	F	3	40	Wife	Sweden	Gothenburg
33	305	Anderson	Anders	M	3	39	Labourer	Sweden	Gothenburg
35	309	Anderson	Ebba	F	3	6		Sweden	Gothenburg
36	311	Anderson	Ellis	M	3	2		Sweden	Gothenburg
38	313	Andersson	Ida Augusta	F	3	38	Wife	Sweden	Gothenburg
39	308	Anderson	Ingleborg	F	3	9		Sweden	Gothenburg
40	312	Anderson	Samuel	M	3	26	Labourer	Sweden	Gothenburg
41	307	Anderson	Sigrid	F	3	11	Child	Sweden	Gothenburg
42	310	Anderson	Sigvard	M	3	4		Sweden	Gothenburg
43	314	Andreason	Paul Edvin	M	3	2	Labourer	Sweden	Gothenburg
44	127	Andrew	Frank	M	2	25	Miner	English	Pencoys, Four Lanes, Redruth
45	126	Andrew	Edgar	M	2	16			Southampton
47	4	Andrews	Thomas	M	1		Ship Builder	Irish	Harland & Wolff, Belfast
48	315	Angheloff	Minko	M	3	20	Labourer	Bulgaria	Basle

Master List No	Old List No	Surname	First Name(s)	Sex	Class	Age	Occupation	Nationality	Last Abode
50	128	Angle	Wm	M	2	25	Labourer	English	14 Mill St, Warwick
52	316	Arnold	Joseph	M	3	24		Switzerland	Basle
53	317	Arnold	Josephine	F	3	24	Wife	Switzerland	Basle
54	318	Aronsson	Ernst Axel A	M	3		Labourer	Sweden	Helsingfors
55	5	Artagaveytia	Ramon	M	1				26 Rue Pasquier, Paris
56	129	Ashby	John	M	2	57	Labourer	USC	London
57	324	Asim	Adola	M	3	35		Syrian	Buenos Aires
58	322	Asplund	Carl	M	3	5	Child	Swede	Sweden
59	319	Asplund	Charles	M	3	40	Labourer	Swede	Sweden
60	321	Asplund	Gustaf	M	3	9	Child	Swede	Sweden
62	320	Asplund	Oscar	M	3	11	Child	Swede	Sweden
66	454	Gerios	Assaf	M	3	21	Farmhand	Syrian	Syria
68	323	Assam	Ali	M	3	23	Labourer	Syrian	Buenos Aires
69	6	Astor	J J	M	1		Col in American Army	USC	Hotel Ritz, Paris
71	750	Sleiman	Attala	M	3	30	Journalist	Canadian	Syria
73	326	Augustson	Albert	M	3	28	Labourer	Swede	Sweden
75	327	Baccos	Rafoul	M	3	20	Farmhand	Syrian	Syria
76	328	Backstrom	Carl Anton	M	3	32	Labourer	Finn	Finland
83	329	Badt	Mohamed	M	3	40	Farmer	Syrian	Syria
84	130	Bailey	Percy	M	2	18	Butcher's Assistant	English	25 Guavas St, Penzance
85	131	Baimbrigge	Chas R	M	2	23	Horse Trainer	English	Robais Manor, Guernsey
86	330	Balkic	Cerin	M	3	26	Labourer	Austria	Austria
88	132	Banfield	Frederick J	M	2	28	Miner	English	30 Grenville Rd, Plymouth
89	331	Barbara	Catherine	F	3	45	Housekeeper	Syrian	Syria
90	332	Barbara	Saude	F	3	18	Housekeeper	Syrian	Syria
93	333	Barry	Julia	M	3	27	Housekeeper	Irish	Ireland, c/o T K O'Connor & Son, Castle Island, Co Kerry
94	335	Barton	David	M	3			English	Bellevue Cottages, Wicken, Cambridge
95	133	Bateman	Robert J	M	2	52			Southampton, (Pendennis Road, Staple Hill, Bristol)
96	7	Baumann	J	M	1				Grand Hotel, Paris
98	8	Baxter	Quigg	M	1			USC	Elysee Palace Hotel, Paris
102	9	Beattie	T	M	1			USC	Hotel Majestic, Nice
103	134	Beauchamp	Henry James	M	2			USC	London
104	336	Beavan	William Thomas	M	3	19	Labourer	USA	London, 95 Richmond Rd, Gillingham
113	337	Benson	John Viktor	M	3	26	Labourer	Swede	Sweden
115	338	Berglund	Ivar	M	3	20	Labourer	Finn	Sweden
116	135	Berriman	Wm	M	3	23	Miner		Hellesover St, St Ives
117	734	Seman	Betros	M	3	10	Child	Syria	Syria
118	339	Betros	Tannous	M	3	20	Shoe Maker	Syrian	Syria
122	343	Birkeland	Hans	M	3	21	Sailor	Norwegian	Norway
123	57	Jakob	Birnbaum	M	1			Austrian	11 Rue Membling, Antwerp

Master List No	Old List No	Surname	First Name(s)	Sex	Class	Age	Occupation	Nationality	Last Abode
127	344	Bjorklund	Ernst	M	3	18	Labourer	Swede	Sweden
129	10	Blackwell	Stephen Weart	M	1			USC	
134	11	Borebank	J J	M	1			English	
135	345	Bostandyeff	Guentcho	M	3	26	Labourer	Bulgarian	Bulgaria
136	136	Botsford	W Hull	M	2			USC	c/o T Cook & Son, Ludgate Circus, London
137	347	Boulos	Akar	M	3	9	Child	Syria	Syria
138	346	Boulos	Hanna	M	3	18	Labourer	Syria	Syria
140	348	Boulos	Sultani	F	3	40	Wife	Syria	Syria
141	350	Bourke	Catherine	F	3			Ireland	Queenstown
142	349	Bourke	John	M	3			Ireland	Queenstown
143	359	Burke	Mary	F	3			English	England
144	351	Bowen	David	M	3		Boxer	English	England c/o Dean & Dawson, Cardiff
146	137	Bowenur	Solomon	M	2	42	Merchant	USC	London
148	138	Bracken	James H	M	2	27	Stockman	USC	London
151	12	Brady	John B	M	1				Elysee Palace Hotel, Paris
152	352	Braf	Elin Ester	F	3	20	Maid	Sweden	Sweden
153	139	Brailey	Ronald	M	2			English	71 Lancaster Rd, London
155	13	Brandeis	E	M	1				
156	353	Braund	Lewis	M	3	29	Farm Labourer	English	Holsworthy
157	354	Braund	Owen Harris	M	3	22	Ironmonger	English	Holsworthy
158	14	Brewe	Arthur Jackson	M	1			USC	
159	140	Bricoux (Breicoux)	Roger	M	2			French	France
160	141	Brito	Jose de	M	2			Portuguese	London c/o Mr Fred Duarte, 34 Mulgrave St, Liverpool
161	355	Brobek	Carl R	M	3	22	Farm Labourer	Denmark	Copenhagen
162	356	Brocklebank	William	M	3	35	Groom	English	London,(Alpha Villa, Bromfield Hill, Nr Chelmsford)
168	142	Brown	Thomas Wm Solomon	M	2		British	London	
171	143	Bryhl	Curt	M	2	20		Swedish	Gothenburg, c/o Mr G Lustig, Skara, Stadfiskel
173	357	Buckley	Katherine	F	3			English	England
175	358	Burke	Jeremiah	M	3			English	England
177	360	Burns	Mary	F	3	18		Irish	Queenstown, c/o Jas Young, Ballisodare
179	144	Butler	Reginald	M	2	25	Mechl Engineer	British	Portsmouth, Grenada Hotel, Southsea
180	15	Butt	Archibald W	M	1		Major in American Army	USC	
181	145	Byles	Thos R D	M	2		Minister of Religion		London c/o Mrs Byles, 101 The Ridgway, Wimbledon
183	361	Cacic	Grigo	M	3	18	Farmer	Austrian	Austria
184	362	Cacic	Luka	M	3	38	Farmer	Austrian	Austria
185	363	Cacic	Manda	F	3	21	Farm Girl	Austrian	Austria
186	364	Cacic	Maria	F	3	30	Farm Girl	Austrian	Austria
187	16	Cairns	Alexander	M	1		Carter's Manservant		
192	365	Calic	Petar	M	3	17	Farmhand	Austrian	Austria

Master List No	Old List No	Surname	First Name(s)	Sex	Class	Age	Occupation	Nationality	Last Abode
194	146	Campbell	Wm	M	2	21	Joiner	English	Harland & Wolff, Belfast
195	366	Canavan	Mary	F	3			Irish	Queenstown
196	368	Canavan	Patrick	M	3			Irish	Queenstown
198	367	Cann	Ernest	M	3			English	Southampton
199	370	Caram	Joseph	M	3	28	Merchant	Canadian	Paris
200	371	Caram	Maria	F	3	20	Housekeeper	Canadian	Paris
201	147	Carbines	Wm	M	2	19	Miner	English	Nangivey, St Ives
204	452	Garfirth	John	M	3	22	Shoe Op	English	Wellingboro, Henwick Rd, Woollaston, nr Wellingboro
205	17	Carlson	Frank	M	1			USC	
206	374	Carlsson	August Sigfrid	M	3	28	Farmer	Dane	Copenhagen
207	372	Carlson	Carl R	M	3	24	Labourer	Dane	Copenhagen
208	369	Car	Janie	F	3			Irish	Queenstown
209	18	Carron	F M	M	1			USC	
210	19	Carron	J P	M	1			USC	
211	148	Carter	Ernest C	M	2	54	Minister of Religion	English	London
212	149	Carter	Lilian	F	2	44	Housewife	English	London
217	375	Carver	A	M	3			English	Southampton
218	20	Case	Howard B	M	1			USC	Vaccuum Oil Co, London
221	21	Cavendish	T W	M	1			USC	23 Chesham Place, London
222	376	Celotti	Francesco	M	3	24	Stoker	Italian	Cape Town
224	22	Chaffee	Herbert	F M	1			USC	
227	152	Chapman	Charles	M	2			English	M C Wheelers Yard, West Drayton
228	150	Chapman	John H	M	2	30	Farmer	English	c/o George & Co, Liskeard, Cornwall
229	151	Chapman	Eliz.	F	2	28	Housewife	English	c/o George & Co, Liskeard, Cornwall
230	377	Charters	David	M	3			Ireland	Queenstown
236	23	Chisholm	Roderick	M	1			Irish	Harland & Wolffe, Belfast
237	378	Christmann	Emil	M	3	29	Clerk	Germany	London
240	379	Chronopoulos	Apostolos	M	3	26	Labourer	Greek	Greece
241	380	Chronopoulos	Demetrios	M	3	18	Labourer	Greek	Greece
243	153	Clarke	Charles V	M	2	29			Southampton
245	24	Clark	Walter M	M	1			USC	c/o Amerco, Rome
246	154	Clarke	John Frederick Preston	M	2			English	Southdown Road, Liverpool
248	25	Clifford	George Quiney	M	1	20		USC	c/o Kings House, Kings St, Cheapside, London
249	381	Coelho	Domingos Fernandes	M	3		Labourer	Portugal	Portugal
251	382	Colbert	Patrick	M	3			English	Queenstown
252	384	Coleff	Peyo	M	3	36	Labourer	Bulgaria	Bulgaria
253	383	Coleff	Fotio	M	3	24	Labourer	Bulgaria	Bulgaria
254	155	Coleridge	Reginald C	M	2	29		English	232 Strand, London
255	156	Collander	Erik	M	2	29	Advt Consultant	Finnish	London, Finska A.A. Helsingfors

Master List No	Old List No	Surname	First Name(s)	Sex	Class	Age	Occupation	Nationality	Last Abode
257	26	Colley	E P	M	1			Irish	Fermath, Rathgow, Dublin
260	157	Collyer	Harvey	M	2	32	Grocer	English	Mt Hill, Basingstoke
262	27	Compton	A T jnr	M	1				Hotel Dysart, Paris
265	385	Conlin	Thos H	M	3			English	Queenstown
266	386	Connaghton	Michael	M	3			English	Queenstown
268	387	Connolly	Kate	F	3			English	Queenstown 40 Bank Place, Tipperary
269	388	Connors	Patrick	M	3			English	Queenstown
270	389	Cook	Jacob	M	3	43	Wood Carver	Russia	Russia
272	390	Cor	Bartol	M	3	35	Labourer	Austria	Austria
273	391	Cor	Ivan	M	3	27	Labourer	Austria	Austria
274	392	Cor	Ludovik	M	3	19	Labourer	Austria	Austria
275	158	Corbett	Irene C	F	2	30	Musician	USC	York Rd, London
276	159	Corey	Percy C (Mrs)	F	2				London, 26 Adelaide St
277	393	Corn	Harry	M	3	30	Upholsterer	Russia	London
280	160	Cotterill	Harry	M	2	20	Carpenter	English	Penzance, Harland & Wolff's man
284	394	Coxon	Daniel	M	3			USA	USA (38 Rochford St, Kentish Town, London)
285	28	Crafton	John B	M	1			USC	Victoria Hotel, London
287	395	Crease	Ernest James	M	3	19	Tinsmith	English	Bristol, 2 Hollybrook Place, York St, Bedminster, Bristol
288	396	Cribb	John Hatfield	M	3	44	Butler	English	Bournemouth, Helenita, Saltern Road, Parkstone Dorset
291	29	Crosby	Edward G	M	1				Grand Trunk Rly, London SW
294	30	Cummings	John Bradley	M	1				c/o Morgan Harjes, Paris
295	161	Cunningham	Alf	M	2	21	Fitter	English	Belfast
296	397	Daher	Shedid	M	3	22		Syria	Syria
298	399	Dahlberg	Gerda	F	3	22	Wife	Sweden	Gothenburg
299	400	Dakic	Branko	M	3	19	Labourer	Austria	Austria
303	403	Danbom	Sigrid	F	3	27	Wife	Sweden	Gothenburg
304	401	Danbom	Ernst	M	3	34	Labourer	Sweden	Gothenburg
305	402	Danbom	Gillbert	M	3	4m	Child	Sweden	Gothenburg
308	404	Danoff	Toto	M	3	27	Labourer	Bulgaria	Bulgaria
309	405	Dantchoff	Kristo	M	3	25	Labourer	Bulgaria	Bulgaria
311	31	Davidson	Thornton	M	1			USC	
312	406	Davies	Alfred J	M	3	24	Coster	English	W Bromwich, 29 Harwood St
313	162	Davies	Chas	M	2	21			c/o Mrs Davies, Brook Hill, Lyndhurst, Hants
315	407	Davies	Evan	M	3	22	Miner	Welsh	Pontardawe, c/o Mrs Rogers, Ynisymond Farm, Glais,nr Swansea
318	408	Davies	John	M	3	21	Ironworker	English	W Bromwich, 29 Harwood St
319	409	Davis	Joseph	M	3	17	Ironworker	English	West Bromwich, Moxtoke Cottage,
323	410	Davison	Thomas H	M	3	32	Smith	English	Liverpool, 10 Park St, Woodlands,Chippenham
328	668	Pelsmaker	Alfons de	M	3	17	Farm Labourer	Belgium	Antwerp
329	163	Deacon	Percy	M	2	20			Lyndhurst, Hants
330	411	Dean	Bertram F	M	3	25	Farmer	English	Southampton, Bartley Farm, Netley Marsh
335	164	Del Carlo	Selastiani	M	2				Paris, c/o Brauchim, Lucco, Italy
336	412	Delalic	Regyo	M	3	25	Labourer	Austrian	Austria

Master List No	Old List No	Surname	First Name(s)	Sex	Class	Age	Occupation	Nationality	Last Abode
337	419	Dimitri	Marinko	M	3	23	Labourer	Macedonian	Austria
338	165	Denbury	Herbert	M	2	25		English	Les Sauvages, St Sampsons, Guernsey
339	413	Denkoff	Mito	M	3	30	Labourer	Bulgarian	Bulgaria
340	414	Dennis	Samuel	M	3	23	Farming	English	Holsworthy, Leigh Farm, Wick St Mary, nr Bude
341	415	Dennis	William	M	3	27	Farming	English	Holsworthy, Leigh Farm, Wick St Mary, nr Bude
344	166	Dibden	Wm	M	2	19		English	Lyndhurst, Hants, c/o Mrs Domaille, Nr Vale Church
347	417	Dika	Mirko	M	3	17	Labourer	Austrian	Austria
348	418	Dimic	Jovan	M	3	42	Farmer	Austrian	Austria
349	420	Dintcheff	Valtcho	M	3	43	Labourer	Bulgarian	Bulgaria
353	398	Daher	Tannous	M	3	28		Syria	Syria
356	421	Donohue	Bridget	F	3			British	Queenstown
357	422	Dooley	Patrick	M	3			Ireland	Queenstown
361	32	Douglas	W D	M	1			USC	c/o boyd Neel, 1 Rue Damion, Paris
363	167	Downton	Wm Jas	M	2	54		English	Guernsey
364	423	Doyle	Elizabeth	M	3			Ireland	Queenstown
365	424	Drazenovic	Josip	M	3	33	Labourer	Austria	Austria
368	168	Drew	James V	M	2			USC	Constantine, Penryn, Cornwall
373	33	Dulles	William C	M	1			USC	Hotel France & Choisneul, Paris
376	416	Devan	Frank	M	3			Irish	Queenstown
377	425	Dyker	Adolph	M	3		Labourer	Sweden	Gothenburg
381	426	Ecimovic	Joso	M	3		Farmer	Switzerland	Basel
382	427	Edvardsson	Gustaf Hjalmar	M	3		Labourer	Sweden	Helsingborg
383	169	Eitemiller	George Floyd	M	2				Bonnington Hotel, Southampton Row, London
384	428	Eklund	Hans	M	3		Labourer	Sweden	Gothenburg
385	429	Ekstrom	Johan	M	3		Labourer	Sweden	Gothenburg
386	430	Elias	Dibo	M	3		Labourer	Syria	Syria
387	431	Elias	Joseph	M	3		Labourer	Syria	Syria
388	524	Elias	Elias	M	3	18	Labourer	Syrian	Syria
389	432	Elias	Tannous	M	3		Labourer	Syria	Syria
390	433	Elsbury	James	M	3		Farmer	English	Taunton c/o J E Kingsbury
392	434	Emir	Farres Chehab	M	3		Labourer	Syria	Syria
393	170	Enander	Ingvar	M	2	21		Swedish	27a Svengstan, Gothenburg
395	468	Goncalves	Manuel Estanislaw	M	3	38	Labourer	Portuguese	Brazil
397	34	Evans	E (Miss)	F	1			USC	Hotel Majestic, Paris
399	435	Everett	Thomas	M	3		Craneman	English	Bristol, 7 Treefield Place, Nina Road
402	171	Fahlstrom	Arne T	M	3			Norwegian	Christiania
403	436	Farrell	James	M	3			Irish	Queenstown
404	39	Farthing	John	M	1		M/s to Straus		
406	172	Faunthorpe	Harry	M	2			English	Liverpool
407	173	Fillbrook	Chas	M	2	19	Decorator	English	16 Charles St, Truro
409	437	Fischer	Eberhard	M	3		Farming	Dane	Copenhagen
411	438	Fleming	Norah	F	3			Irish	Queenstown

Master List No	Old List No	Surname	First Name(s)	Sex	Class	Age	Occupation	Nationality	Last Abode
414	441	Flynn	James	M	3			Irish	Queenstown
415	442	Flynn	John	M	3			Irish	Queenstown
417	439	Foley	Joseph	M	3			Irish	Queenstown
418	440	Foley	William	M	3			Irish	Queenstown
420	443	Ford	Arthur	M	3		Carpenter	English	Bridgwater, 9 Victoria Rd
421	444	Ford	D M	F	3		Domestic	English	London
422	445	Ford	E W	M	3		Blacksmith	English	London
423	447	Ford	Margaret	F	3		Poultry Farming	English	London
424	446	Ford	Maggie	F	3		Child	English	London
425	448	Ford	W T N	M	3		P.O Messenger	English	London
426	35	Foreman	B L	M	1			English	Hotel Metropole, London
430	37	Fortune	Charles	M	1			USC	Hotel Metropole, London
433	36	Fortune	Mark	M	1			USC	Hotel Metropole, London
435	450	Fox	Patrick	M	3			Irish	Queenstown
436	174	Fox	Stanley H	M	2			USC	c/o Morrisons Booking Office, 6 Victoria Sq, Birmingham
438	449	Franklin	Charles	M	2		Carpenter	English	Southampton
439	38	Franklin	T P	M	1			English	17 Cheapside, London EC
446	175	Frost	Anthony Wood	M	2	37	Foreman Fitter	English	Belfast, Harland & Wolff's man
447	40	Fry	Richard	M	1		M/s to Ismay	English	Liverpool
448	176	Funk	Annie	F	2	37	Missionary	USC	c/o T Cook & Son, Ludgate Circus, London
449	41	Futrelle	J	M	1			USC	44 Gloucester Terrace, Hyde Park, London W
451	177	Fynney	Jos	M	2			English	Browns Bdgs, Liverpool
452	178	Gale	Harry	M	2	38	Miner	English	School Rd, Harrowbarrow Nr St Dominee, Cornwall
453	179	Gale	Shadrack	M	2	33	Miner	English	School Rd, Harrowbarrow Nr St Dominee, Cornwall
454	451	Gallagher	Martin	M	3			Ireland	Queenstown
456	180	Gaskell	Alfred	M	2			English	20 Dexter St, Liverpool
457	181	Gavey	Lawrence	M	2	26		British	Bas Courtil Banks, Guernsey
458	42	Gee	Arthur	M	1			English	Morningside, Riley Avenue, St Anne's on Sea
459	455	Gerios	Youssef	M	3		Labourer	Syrian	Syria
460	456	Gheorgheff	Stanio	M	3	26	Labourer	Bulgaria	Bulgaria
464	43	Giglio	Victor	M	1				57 Avenue Montaigne, Paris
465	182	Gilbert	Wm	M	2	45		English	Carleens Buage, Cornwall
466	183	Giles	Edgar	M	2	21	Carpenter	English	Wheat Unity Road, Portleven
467	184	Giles	Fred	M	2	22	Carpenter	English	Wheat Unity Road, Portleven
468	185	Giles	Ralph	M	2	22			10 Gunterstone Rd, West Kensington, London
469	457	Gilinsky	Leslie	M	3	24	Locksmith	Russia	Wales, 36 Glancynon Terrace
470	186	Gill	John	M	2		Chauffeur	English	3 Griffin Rd, Clevedon, Bristol
471	187	Gillespie	Wm	M	2	34	Law Clerk	Irish	Coffee Palace, Abbeyleix
473	188	Givard	Hans K	M	1			Danish	Hotel Continental, Paris
477	44	Goldsmith	George B	M	3			English	Southampton
479	458	Goldsmith	Frank	M	3	33	Turner	English	England c/o Curtis & Sons, Rochester
481	459	Goldsmith	Nathan	M	3	41	Bootmaker	Russia	Cape Town

Master List No	Old List No	Surname	First Name(s)	Sex	Class	Age	Occupation	Nationality	Last Abode
482	460	Goodwin	Augusta	F	3	43	Wife	English	Bath, Watsons Court, High St, Melksham
483	461	Goodwin	Charles E	M	3	14	Child	English	Bath, Watsons Court, High St, Melksham
484	462	Goodwin	Frederick	M	3	40	Engr Labourer	English	Bath, Watsons Court, High St, Melksham
485	463	Goodwin	Harold V	M	3	9	Child	English	Bath, Watsons Court, High St, Melksham
486	464	Goodwin	Jessie A M	F	3	10	Child	English	Bath, Watsons Court, High St, Melksham
487	465	Goodwin	Lillian A	F	3	16	Child	English	Bath, Watsons Court, High St, Melksham
488	466	Goodwin	Sidney L	M	3	6	Child	English	Bath, Watsons Court, High St, Melksham
489	467	Goodwin	William F	M	3	11	Child	English	Bath, Watsons Court, High St, Melksham
492	45	Graham	George E	M	1			English	c/o T Eaton & Co, London
494	469	Green	George	M	3	40	Farrier	English	Gunnislake, (1 Lyons Cottage, Dorking)
495	189	Greenberg	Saml	M	2			Russian	Southampton
498	470	Gronnesta	Daniel D	M	3	32	Labourer	Norwegian	Norway
499	471	Guest	Robert	M	3	23	Labourer	English	London, c/o Pickfords, Gresham St
500	46	Guggenheim	Benjamin	M	1			USC	57 Avenue Montaigne, Paris
501	472	Gustafson	Alfred	M	3	20	Labourer	Swede	Sweden
502	473	Gustafson	Anders	M	3	37	Labourer	Finn	Finland
503	474	Gustafson	Johan	M	3	28	Labourer	Finn	Finland
504	475	Gustafsson	Gideon	M	3	19	Labourer	Swede	Sweden
505	476	Gwinn	William L	M	3	abt 37	American Sea Post Clerk	American	4 Commercial Rd, Southampton
506	477	Haas	Aloisia	M	3	24	Labourer	Swiss	Switzerland
507	479	Hagland	Ingvald O	M	3	28	Labourer	Norwegian	Norway
508	480	Hagland	Konrad R	M	3	20	Labourer	Norwegian	Norway
510	481	Hakkarainen	Pekko	M	3	28	Labourer	Finn	Finland
511	190	Hale	Reginald	M	2	30		English	Westbury, Rodneystoke, Nr Cheddar
514	482	Hampe	Leon	M	3	35	Painter	Belgium	Antwerp
515	483	Hanna	Mansour	M	3	25	Journalist	Syrian	Syria
516	615	Moubarek	Hanna	M	3	41	Farm Labourer	Syrian	Syria
517	484	Hansen	Claus	M	3	26	Barber	USA	Copenhagen
518	527	Jutel	Henrik Hanson	M	3	21	Farmer	Denmark	Copenhagen
519	485	Hansen	Henry Damgaard	M	2		Manufacturer	Dane	Copenhagen
521	191	Harbeck	Wm H	M	3			USC	London
524	478	Hargadon	Kate	F	3			British	Queenstown
525	486	Harknett	Alice	F	3	21	Servant	English	London, c/o W S Hill, Cockspur St
526	487	Harmer	Abraham	M	3	25	Jeweller	Russia	Manchester, 36 Strong St, Lower Broughton
529	192	Harper	John	M	2			English	3 Claud Villa, Denmark HIll, London
531	47	Harrington	Charles	M	1		M/s to Moore		
533	48	Harris	Henry B	M	1			USC	Savoy Hotel, London
535	193	Harris	Walter	M	2			English	47 Granville Rd, Hoe St, Walthamstow, London
536	49	Harrison	W H	M	1			English	
537	194	Hart	Benjamin	M	2			English	London
540	488	Hart	Henry	M	3			Ireland	Queenstown

Master List No	Old List No	Surname	First Name(s)	Sex	Class	Age	Occupation	Nationality	Last Abode
541	195	Hartley	Wm	M	2			English	Surreyside, West Park St, Dewsbury
543	489	Hassan	Haussein G N	M	3				Grand Trunk Rly, London SW
545	50	Hays	Charles M	M	1			English	
548	51	Head	Christopher	M	3			English	
552	490	Hegarty	Nora	F	3	23	Servant	British	Queenstown
554	491	Heininen	Wendla	F	3		Servant	Finland	Finland
556	492	Hendekovic	Ignaz	M	3	28	Labourer	Austria	Austria
557	494	Henriksson	Jenny	F	3	28	Domestic	Sweden	Gothenburg
558	493	Henery	Delia	F	3			Irish	Queenstown
562	196	Herman	Samuel	M	2	49	Farmer	English	Yeovil
564	197	Hickman	Leonard	M	2	24			Lyndhurst, Hants, Fritham, New Forest
565	198	Hickman	Lewis	M	2	32			Lyndhurst, Hants, Fritham, New Forest
566	199	Hickman	Stanley	M	2	20			Lyndhurst, Hants, Fritham, New Forest
567	52	Hilliard	Herbert Henry	M	1				Hotel Chatham, Paris
568	200	Hiltunen	Martta	F	2			English	Helsingfors
569	53	Hipkins	W E	M	1			Finnish	W & T Avery, Birmingham
576	201	Hocking	Geo	M	2	21	Baker	English	26 St Mary St, Penzance
577	202	Hocking	Samuel J	M	2		Painter	English	Plymouth, 3 Fore St, Devonport
578	203	Hodges	Henry P	M	2	50	Musical Instrument Vendor	English	Highfield Lane, Southampton
581	204	Hold	Stephen	M	2	42	Independent	USC	Shipton
583	495	Holm	John F A	M	3	43	Farmer	USA	Copenhagen
584	496	Holten	Johan	M	3	28	2nd Mate	Norway	Norway
585	54	Holverson	A O	M	1			USC	Picadilly Hotel, London W
589	205	Hood	Ambrose	M	2	22			Lyndhurst, Hants, Fritham, New Forest
590	497	Horgan	John	M	3			Ireland	Queenstown
592	206	Howard	Benjamin	M	2	63	Retired	English	85 Cheltenham St, Swindon
593	207	Howard	Ellen T	F	2	60	Wife	English	85 Cheltenham St, Swindon
597	55	Hoyt	W F	M	1			USC	c/o Brown Shipley & Co, 123 Pall Mall, London.
598	498	Humblen	Adolf O	M	3	42	Farmer	Norway	Aalesund
599	208	Hume	John Law	M	2			Scotch	142 George St, Dumfries
600	209	Hunt	George	M	2			British	London, Ashstead, nr Epsom
604	499	Ilieff	Ilio	M	3	32	Labourer	Bulgarian	Bulgaria
605	501	Ilmakangas	Ida	F	3	27	Servant	Finn	Finland
606	500	Ilmakangas	Pieta Sofia	F	3	25	Servant	Finn	Finland
607	56	Isham	A E (Miss)	F	1			USC	86 Rue de Varenne, Paris
609	505	Ivanoff	Koino	M	3	20	Labourer	Bulgarian	Bulgaria
611	211	Jacobsohn	Sydney S	M	3				7 Pembridge Square, London
614	506	Jardin	Jose Netto	M	3	21	Labourer	Portuguese	Brazil
615	212	Jarvis	John D	M	2	47	Engineer	English	The Crest, Stoneygate, Leicester
616	213	Jefferys	Clifford	M	2	24		English	Rossly, Halfway Banks, Guernsey

Master List No	Old List No	Surname	First Name(s)	Sex	Class	Age	Occupation	Nationality	Last Abode
617	214	Jefferys	Ernest	M	2	22		English	Rossly, Halfway Banks, Guernsey
618	215	Jenkin	Stephen	M	2	32	Miner	American	Nanjivey, St Ives
619	507	Jensen	Hans Peter	M	3	21		Dane	Denmark
620	508	Jensen	Niels R	M	3	48	Farmer	USA	Denmark
621	509	Jensen	Svenst L	M	3	17	Farmer	Dane	Denmark
626	515	Johnson	Jakob Alfred	M	3	34	Labourer	Finnish	Finland
627	512	Johansson	Erik	M	3	20	Labourer	Dane	Denmark
628	510	Johanson	Gustaf	M	3	33		Swede	Sweden
629	514	Johnson	Carl	M	3	32	Labourer	Swede	Sweden
630	511	Johanson	Nils	M	3	30	Labourer	Swede	Sweden
632	513	Johnson	A	M	3			English	Southampton, 8 Kingsley Rd, Millbrook
636	517	Johnsson	Malkolm	M	3	30	Labourer	Swede	Sweden
637	516	Johnson	W	M	3			English	Southampton, 8 Kingsley Rd, Millbrook
638	518	Johnston	A E	M	3	34	Plumber	English	London, 6 Newton Terrace, Paisley
639	520	Johnston	C H	F	3	8	Child	Scotland	London, 6 Newton Terrace, Paisley
640	521	Johnston	William A	M	3	9	Child	Scotland	London, 6 Newton Terrace, Paisley
641	519	Johnston	(Mrs)	F	3	34	Wife	English	London, 6 Newton Terrace, Paisley
642	58	Jones	C C	M	1			USC	c/o Foot, Dorchester or Junction Hotel, Dorchester
643	522	Jonkoff	Lagor	M	3	23	Labourer	Bulgarian	Bale
645	523	Jonsson	Niels	M	3	26	Labourer	Dane	Denmark
646	671	Peter	Anna	F	3	27m	Child	Syria	Syria
648	672	Peter	Mike	M	3	4	Child	Syria	Syria
649	59	Julian	H F	M	1			USC	
651	525	Jussila	Katriina	F	3	20	Servant	Finnish	Finland
652	526	Jussila	Mari	F	3	21	Servant	Finnish	Finland
653	528	Kallio	Nikolai	M	3	17	Labourer	Finland	Finland
654	529	Kalvig	Johannes H	M	3	21	Labourer	Norway	Stavanger
656	216	Kantor	Sehua	M	2	34	Labourer	Russian	c/o WS Line, Leadenhall St, London EC
657	530	Karajic	Milau	M	3	30	Labourer	Switzerland	Basel
659	373	Carlson	Julius	M	3	3	Labourer	Swede	Malmo
660	531	Karlsson	Nils Aug	M	3	22	Farmer	Dane	Copenhagen
661	217	Karnes	T Frank (Mrs)	F	2				
664	532	Kassem	Fared	M	3	18	Farming	Syrian	Syria
665	795	Vassilios	Catavelas	M	3	19	Farmer	Greek	Paris
666	533	Keane	Andy	M	3			Ireland	Queenstown
667	218	Keane	Daniel	M	3				E Ludlow, Limerick
669	534	Keefe	Arthur	M	3	39	Farmer	USA	USA
670	60	Keeping	Edwin Herbert	M	1		M/s to Widener		
671	536	Kelley	James	M	3	44	Labourer	English	London, (W Kelly, Kirk St, Carluke, NB)
674	535	Kelly	James	M	3	19	Painter	Irish	Queenstown
677	61	Kent	Edward A	M	1			USC	Hotel Continental, Paris
678	62	Kenyon	F R	M	1			USC	Hotel de la Tamise, Paris

Master List No	Old List No	Surname	First Name(s)	Sex	Class	Age	Occupation	Nationality	Last Abode
680	537	Khalil	Betros	M	3	25	Farm Labourer	Syrian	Syria
681	538	Khalil	Zahie	F	3	20	Farm Labourer	Syrian	Syria
682	539	Kiernan	John	M	3			Ireland	Queenstown
683	540	Kiernan	Philip	M	3			Ireland	Queenstown
684	541	Kilgannon	Thomas	M	3			Ireland	Queenstown
690	543	Kink	Vincenz	M	3	27		Switzerland	Basel
691	542	Kink	Maria	F	3	22	Maid	Switzerland	Basel
692	219	Kirkland	Chas L	M	2		Minister of Religion	USC	
693	63	Klaber	Herman	M	1				
694	544	Klasen	Gertrud	F	3	1	Child	Swede	Sweden
695	545	Klasen	Hulda K E	F	3	36	housewife	Swede	Sweden
696	220	Klasen	Klas A	M	3	18	Farm Labourer	Denmark	Copenhagen
698	546	Knight	Robert	M	3	39	Fitter	English	Harland & Wolff's man, Belfast
699	547	Kraeff	Thodor	M	3		Labourer	Bulgarian	Bale
702	221	Krins	Geo	M	2			Belgian	
703	222	Kvillner	Johan Henrik	M	3	31	Mechl Engineer	Swedish	Gothenburg, Vattenverket, Trollhattan, Sweden
704	548	Lahoud	Sarkis	M	3	30	Labourer	Syrian	Syria
705	224	Lahtinen	Anna	F	2		Wife	USA	Helsingfors
706	223	Lahtinen	Wm	M	2		Minister of Religion	USC	Helsingfors
707	549	Laitinen	Sofia	F	3	37	Servant	Finnish	Finland
708	550	Laleff	Hristo	M	3	23	Labourer	Bulgarian	Bale
710	551	Lam	Len	M	3	23	Seaman	Chinese	London
711	225	Lamb	John Joseph	M	2			British	Enniskerry, Wood View Cottage, Glencrea
713	552	Lane	Patrick	M	2			Irish	Queenstown
715	226	Laroche	Joseph	M	2				131 Grand Rue Villegrief, Paris
719	554	Larson	Viktor	M	3	29	Labourer	Swede	Sweden
720	553	Larson	Bengt Edvin	M	3	29	Labourer	Swede	Sweden
721	555	Larsson	Edvard	M	3	22	Labourer	Swede	Sweden
726	556	Lefebre	Frances	F	3	39	Wife	France	Havre
727	557	Lefebre	Henry	M	3	4	Child	France	Havre
728	558	Lefebre	Ida	F	3	2	Child	France	Havre
729	559	Lefebre	Jeannie	F	3	6	Child	France	Havre
730	560	Lefebre	Mathilde	F	3	11	Child	France	Havre
732	561	Leinonen	Antti	M	3	23	Labourer	Finland	Finland
734	562	Lemberopoulos	Peter	M	3	30	Labourer	Greece	Marseilles
736	563	Lennon	Denis	M	3			Irish	Queenstown
737	564	Lennon	Mary	F	3			Irish	Queenstown
742	565	Leonard	L	M	3			England	Southampton
744	566	Lester	James	M	3		Dipper	England	West Bromwich, 29 Harwood St
746	227	Levy	Rene T	M	2				Grand Hotel, Paris
748	65	Leroy	E G	M	1			USC	42 Rue le Pelletier, Paris

Master List No	Old List No	Surname	First Name(s)	Sex	Class	Age	Occupation	Nationality	Last Abode
749	228	Leyson	Robert W N	M	2	25	Engineer	Welsh	171 Cromwell Rd, South Kensington, London
750	567	Lievens	Aime Rene	M	3	24	Farmer	Belgium	Antwerp
751	568	Lindahl	Agda	F	3	25	Wife	Denmark	Gothenburg
752	569	Lindblom	August	M	3	45	Labourer	Denmark	Gothenburg
753	66	Lingrey	Edward	M	1				
754	570	Lindell	Edvard B	M	3	36	Labourer	Sweden	Malmo
755	571	Lindell	Elin G	F	3	30	Wife	Sweden	Malmo
758	572	Linehan	Michael	M	3	21	Farm Labourer	Ireland	Kingwilliamstown, c/o P Fitzpatrick
761	573	Ling	Lee	M	3	28		China	
762	805	Wenzel	Linhart	M	3	27	Baker	Austria	Antwerp
763	229	Lingan	John	M	2				
764	574	Lithman	Simon	M	3	20	Baker	Russia	Scotland, c/o Kucher, 17 Drummond St, Edinburgh
765	577	Lobb	Cordelia	F	3	26	Housewife	English	Cornwall, c/o Daniel & Rouse, St Austell
766	575	Lobb	William A	M	3	30	Engineer	English	Cornwall, c/o Daniel & Rouse, St Austell
767	576	Lockyer	Edward	M	3	21	Grocer's Assistant	English	London, 57 Lyall Mews
768	67	Long	Milton C	M	1			USC	Hotel Engadine, Kulm, St Moritz
770	68	Loring	J H	M	1			USC	28 Park Lane, London W
772	230	Louch	Chas	M	2	50	Sadler	British	Regent St, Weston Super Mare
773	578	Lovell	John	M	3	20	Farmer	English	Holsworthy
776	579	Lundahl	John	M	3	51	Labourer	USA	Malmo
780	580	Lyntakoff	Stanko	M	3	44	Labourer	Bulgarian	Bale
781	231	Mack	Mary	F	2	50		English	Bittern Park, Southampton
782	583	MacKay	Geo W	M	3	30	Butler	Scotch	London
786	589	Maenpaa	Matti	F	3	22	Servant	Finnish	Finland
787	69	Maguire	J E	M	1			USC	Kings House, King St, Cheapside, London
788	588	Mahon	Delia	F	3	18		Irish	Ireland c/o Mrs B Walsh, Castlebar
789	599	Meeban	John	M	3			Irish	Queenstown
791	590	Maisner	Simon	M	3	34	Tailor	Russian	London, 29 Houndsditch, EC
792	591	Makinen	Kalle	M	3	29	Labourer	Finnish	Finland
793	232	Malachard	Noel	M	2				c/o T Cook & Son, Paris
794	325	Attala	Malaki	F	3		Servant	Syrian	Syria
795	233	Mallet	Andre	M	2	17			6 Rue Cornmaille, Paris
799	592	Mangen	Mary	F	3			Irish	Ireland
800	234	Mangiavacchi	Emilio	M	2				Paris, (c/o T Cook & Son, Florence)
802	596	Marsh	John Starr	M	3	abt 50	American Sea Post Clerk	American	13 East Park Tce, Southampton
803	593	Mardvissian	Sarkis	M	3	25	Farm Labourer	Syrian	Syria
805	594	Markoff	Marin	M	3	35	Labourer	Bulgarian	Bale
806	595	Markun	Johann	M	3	20	Labourer	Austrian	Austria
807	70	Marvin	D W	M	1			USC	58 Acre Lane, Brixton SW
811	597	Matinoff	Nicola	M	3		Labourer	Bulgarian	Bale
812	237	Matthews	Wm T	M	2			English	Southampton, (Penwithick, St Austell, Cornwall)

Master List No	Old List No	Surname	First Name(s)	Sex	Class	Age	Occupation	Nationality	Last Abode
815	238	Maybery	Frank H	M	2			Brit Colonial	London, (1 Whitecross Rd, Weston Super Mare)
817	71	McCaffry	T	M	1			USC	Hotel Majestic, Nice
819	72	McCarthy	Timothy J	M	1			Irish	Hotel Chatham, Paris
824	239	McCrae	Arthur G	M	2	33	Mining Engineer		Southampton, (c/o Bank of Australasia, Threadneedle St, EC)
825	240	McCrie	James M	M	2			British	Strand Palace Hotel, London
827	581	McEvoy	Michael	M	3			Irish	Ireland
830	582	McGowan	Catherine	F	2			Ireland	Terry, Masbrook, Crossmolina
832	241	McKane	Peter D	M	2	46		English	Highland Vale, Guernsey
833	584	McMahon	Martin	M	3			Ireland	Queenstown
834	585	McNamee	Eileen	F	3	19	Wife	Ireland	London ,(Mr & Mrs O Leary, Parents, Kingston House, Wilton Rd, Salisbury)
835	586	McNamee	Neal	M	3	27	Provision Man	Ireland	London, (Mr & Mrs O Leary, Parents, Kingston House, Wilton Rd, Salisbury)
836	587	McNeill	Bridget	F	3			Irish	Charlesville, Ireland c/o Patrick Hayes, Broadford
837	598	Meanwell	Marion Ogden	F	3	63	Milliner	English	England, c/o W S Hill, Leadenhall St
838	600	Meek	Annie L	F	3	31	Housewife	Irish	Cardiff 89 Windsor Rd, Penarth
843	602	Meo	Alfonso	M	3	48	Musician	Italy	England
844	603	Mernagh	Robert	M	3			Irish	Queenstown
845	242	Meyer	August	M	2			German	26 Kildas Rd, Harrow on Hill, London
846	73	Meyer	Edgar J	M	1			USC	Hotel Majestic, Paris
849	606	Miles	Frank	M	3	23	Engineer	English	Greenwich, 103 King George St
851	74	Millet	Frank D	M	1				Odense, Copenhagen
852	243	Milling	Jacob C	M	2	48	Machine Inspector	Danish	Body recovered and delivered to Green Bay, Wisconsin, USA
855	75	Minehan	W E	M	1		US Medical	USC	Basel
856	607	Mineff	Ivan	M	3	24	Labourer	Bulgarian	Bale
857	608	Minkoff	Lazar	M	3	21	Labourer	Bulgarian	Basel
858	605	Mihoff	Stoytcho	M	3	28	Labourer	Bulgaria	Upland Road, Guernsey
859	244	Mitchell	Henry	M	2	71	Retired	British	Bale
860	604	Mickoff	Mito	M	3	23	Labourer	Bulgarian	Norway
863	609	Moen	Sigurd H	M	3	25	Joiner	Norwegian	c/o Junior Athenaeum Club, Piccadilly W
864	76	Molson	H Markland	M	1			English	21 The Oval, Hackney Road, London
865	235	Mantvila	Joseph	M	2	27	Priest	Russian	Almonds Hotel, Clifford St, London W
868	77	Moore	Clarence	M	1			USC	London, (134 Acre Rd, Kingston on Thames)
869	610	Moore	Leonard Charles	M	3	19	Bricklayer	English	Ireland
871	611	Moran	Daniel J	M	3			Irish	Ireland c/o Jas Barton & Son, Cork
872	612	Moran (alias Dougherty)	James (alias John)	M	3	22		Irish	
873	245	Moraweck	Ernest	M	2		Doctor	USC	Berlin, (c/o Karl Morawick, Hotel Slavia, Brunn, Austria)
874	236	Marshall	Henry	M	2			English	6 Bristol St, Birmingham
875	613	Morley	William	M	3	34	Carpenter	English	London (Lods Bridge, Petworth, Sussex)
876	614	Morrow	Thomas	M	3			Irish	Ireland
881	616	Moussa	Mantoura	F	3	25	Housewife	Syrian	Syria
882	617	Moutal	Rahamin	M	3	28	Traveller	Turk	London, 27 Beauclere Rd, Hammersmith
883	246	Mudd	Thos C	M	2	16		English	Holesworth, Suffolk. (Huntinfield)

Master List No	Old List No	Surname	First Name(s)	Sex	Class	Age	Occupation	Nationality	Last Abode
887	618	Murdlin	Joseph	M	3	22	Chemist	Russian	London
891	620	Myhrman	Oliver	M	3	18	Labourer	Norway	Gothenburg
892	247	Myles	Thos F	M	2			USC	Fermoy
893	621	Naidenoff	Penko	M	3	22	Labourer	Bulgaria	Basel
898	622	Nancarrow	William Henry	M	3	34	Mason	English	Cornwall, c/o Daniel & Rouse, St Austell
899	623	Nankoff	Minko	M	3	32	Labourer	Bulgaria	Bulgaria
900	619	Mustafa	Nasr	M	3	20	Farm Labourer	Syrian	Syria
902	248	Nasser or Nasralla Nicolas		M	1			Turkish	Paris, c/o T Cook & Son
903	78	Natsch	Charles	M	2			USC	
904	624	Naughton	Hannah	F	3			Irish	Queenstown
906	210	Hoffman	Louis	M	2				
908	625	Nenkoff	Christo	M	3	22	Labourer	Bulgaria	Basel
909	249	Nesson	Israel	M	2	26	Electrician	Russian	London
910	79	Newell	A W	M	1			USC	Hotel St James & Albany, Paris
914	250	Nicholls	Joseph Charles	M	2	19	Miner	English	Stemach Villas, St Ives
916	80	Nicholson	A E	M	1			English	Claremont, Shanklin, I W
919	626	Nieminen	Manta	F	3	30	Servant	Finland	Finland
920	627	Niklasen	Sander	M	3		Labourer	Sweden	Hull c/o P Drusdo
921	628	Nilsson	August F	M	3	21	Labourer	Sweden	Copenhagen
924	297	Aijo Nirva	Isak	M	3	41	Labourer	Finnish	Finland
928	251	Norman	Robt Douglas	M	2	28	Electrical Engineer	Scotch	c/o A E G Electric Co, 50 Wellington St, Glasgow
929	630	Nosworthy	Richard C	M	3	20	Labourer	English	Newton Abbot, 11 Fisher Road
931	629	Nofal	Mansour	M	3	20	Journalist	Syrian	Syria
934	631	Nysven	Johan H	M	3	61	Farmer	Norway	Christiania
936	633	O Brien	Thomas	M	3		Labourer	Irish	Queenstown
937	632	O Brien	Denis	M	3	21	Labourer	Irish	Queenstown
938	634	O Connell	Patrick D	M	3		Labourer	Irish	Queenstown
939	636	O Connor	Maurice	M	3		Labourer	Irish	Queenstown
940	635	O Connor	Patrick	M	3		Labourer	Irish	Queenstown
941	637	Odahl	Martin	M	3	23	Labourer	Swede	Sweden
951	639	Olsen	Henry	M	3	28	Donkeyman	Norwegian	Norway
952	638	Olsen	Carl	M	3	42	Labourer	American	Norway
953	640	Olsen	Ole M	M	3	27	Labourer	Norwegian	Norway
954	642	Olsson	Elida	F	3	31	Maiden	Sweden	Copenhagen
955	641	Olson	John	M	3	28	Labourer	Norwegian	Norway
957	304	Andersen	Thor	M	3	20	Labourer	Norway	Christiania
959	643	Oreskovic	Jeko	M	3	20	Farmer	Switzerland	Basel
960	644	Oreskovic	Luka	M	3	23	Farmer	Switzerland	Basel
961	645	Oreskovic	Maria	F	3	20	Farm Hand	Switzerland	Basel
963	646	Osen	Elon	M	3	17	Farm Labourer	Norway	Gothenburg
965	81	Ostby	E C	M	1			USC	Brown Shipley, Pall Mall, London
967	647	O Sullivan	Bridget	F	3	22	Servant	USA	USA

Master List No	Old List No	Surname	First Name(s)	Sex	Class	Age	Occupation	Nationality	Last Abode
968	252	Otter	Richard	M	2	39	Stone Cutter	USC	Southampton, Southwell, Portland, Dorset
969	82	Ovies	S	M	1		Doctor	French	c/o Fauld & Co, 30 Faubourg Poissoniere, Paris
972	253	Pain	Alfred	M	2		Doctor		
974	656	Paulsson	Alma C	F	3	29	Housewife	Sweden	Helsingberg
975	657	Paulsson	Gosta	M	3	2	Child	Sweden	Helsingberg
976	658	Paulsson	Paul	M	3	5	Child	Sweden	Helsingberg
977	659	Paulsson	Stina	F	3	3	Child	Sweden	Helsingberg
978	660	Paulsson	Torborg	M	3	8	Child	Sweden	Helsingberg
979	654	Panula	William	M	3	11m	Child	Finland	Finland
980	649	Panula	Erneste	M	3	17	Labourer	Finland	Finland
981	648	Panula	Eino	M	3	16	Farm Labourer	Finland	Finland
982	650	Panula	Jeko	M	3	18	Labourer	Finland	Finland
983	651	Panula	Maria	F	3	40	Wife	Finland	Finland
984	653	Panula	Urhu	M	3	3	Child	Finland	Finland
985	254	Parker	Clifford R	M	2		Clerk	English	Fernleigh, St Andrews, Guernsey
986	255	Parkes	Frank	M	2	18	Plumber	English	Harland & Wolff's man, Belfast
987	83	Parr	H W.	M	1			English	Harland & Wolff, Belfast
989	84	Partner	Austin	M	1				
990	655	Pasic	Jakob	M	3	21	Farmer	Austrian	Austria
991	684	Potchett	Geo	M	3	19	Shoe Operative	English	England, Hanwick Rd, Wollaston, nr Wellingboro
992	786	Usscher	Pullnent	M	3	16	Plumber	Russian	Paris
993	661	Pavlovic	Stefo	M	3	32	Labourer	Austrian	Austria
994	85	Payne	V	M	1			English	Grand Trunk Rly Co, London
995	662	Peacock	Alfred E	M	3	7m	Infant	English	Southampton Mrs Elkins, 35 Orchard Place
996	664	Peacock	Treasteall (Miss)	F	3	4	Child	English	Southampton Mrs Elkins, 35 Orchard Place
997	663	Peacock	Treasteall (Mrs)	F	3	26	Wife	English	Southampton Mrs Elkins, 35 Orchard Place
998	665	Pearce	Ernest	M	3	32	Farmer	English	England 10 Bedrod Place
1000	86	Pears	Thomas	M	1			English	Mevagissey, Isleworth, Middlesex
1001	680	Pettersen	Olaf	M	3	29	Labourer	Norway	Norway
1002	666	Peduzzi	Joseph	M	3	24	Waiter	Italian	London, 1 Ash Grove, Hackney
1003	667	Pekoniemi	Edvard	M	3	32	Labourer	Finnish	Finland
1004	669	Peltomaker	Nikolai	M	3	25	Labourer	Finland	Finland
1006	87	Penasco	Victor	M	1			Spanish	Hotel Majestic, Paris
1007	256	Pengelly	Fredk	M	2	20	Miner	English	Chilworthy Beams, Gunnislake
1008	670	Perkin	John Henry	M	3	22	Farmer	English	Holsworthy, c/o Hawkins
1009	257	Pernot	Rene	M	2		Chauffeur		12 Rue Lesneur, Paris
1012	258	Peruschitz	Joseph M	M	2		Monk	German	London c/o P Jaricot, St Augustine's College, Ramsgate
1013	673	Peters	Katie	F	3	9	Child	Irish	Ireland c/o P Clark & Co, Cahir, Tipperary
1014	674	Petersen	Marius	M	3	24	Dairyman	Dane	London, 78 West End Rd, Southall
1015	677	Petranes	Matilda	M	3	30	Servant	Austria	Basel
1016	679	Petroff	Nedelco	M	3	19	Labourer	Bulgaria	Bulgaria
1017	678	Petroff	Pentcho	M	3	29	Labourer	Bulgaria	Bulgaria

Master List No	Old List No	Surname	First Name(s)	Sex	Class	Age	Occupation	Nationality	Last Abode
1018	675	Peterson	Johan	M	3	25	Labourer	Sweden	Gothenburg
1019	676	Petersson	Ellen	F	3	18	Wife	Sweden	Gothenburg
1022	259	Phillips	Robert	M	2	45		English	Ilfracombe
1025	681	Plotcharsky	Vasil	M	3	27	Labourer	Bulgarian	Bale
1026	682	Pocruic	Mate	M	3	17	Farmer	Austrian	Austria
1027	683	Pocruic	Tome	M	3	24	Farmer	Austrian	Austria
1028	260	Ponesell	Martin	M	2			Danish	Southampton
1030	88	Porter	Walter Chamberlain	M	1				Kings House, King St, Cheapside, London
1032	261	Pulbaum	Frank	M	2				Luna Park, Paris
1036	685	Radeff	Alexandra	M	3	27	Labourer	Bulgarian	Bale
1037	756	Solvang	Lena Jacobson	M	3	63		Norwegian	Norway
1038	334	Bazi	Rachid	M	3	30	Labourer	Syrian	Syria
1039	686	Reed	Jas Geo	M	3	19	Labourer	Welsh	Cardiff, (Mr Reed, Platform Tavern, Town Quay, Southampton)
1040	262	Reeves	David	M	3	36	Butcher	English	Brighton, (Hayes Lane, Slinfold, Sussex)
1041	687	Rekic	Tido	M	3	38	Carpenter	Austrian	Bale
1044	263	Renouf	Peter Henry	M	2	34	Carpenter	English	Rossly, Halfway Banks, Guernsey
1045	90	Reuchlin	Jonkheer J G	M	1			Dutch	Holland American Line
1047	688	Reynolds	Harold	M	3	21	Baker	English	London 10 Courthill Rd, Lewisham
1049	689	Rice	Albert	M	3		Child	Ireland	Queenstown, W T Kerrigan, The Square, Athlone, Ireland
1050	690	Rice	Arthur	M	3		Child	Ireland	Queenstown, W T Kerrigan, The Square, Athlone, Ireland
1051	691	Rice	Eric	M	3		Child	Ireland	Queenstown, W T Kerrigan, The Square, Athlone, Ireland
1052	692	Rice	Eugene	M	3		Child	Ireland	Queenstown, W T Kerrigan, The Square, Athlone, Ireland
1053	693	Rice	George	M	3		Child	Ireland	Queenstown, W T Kerrigan, The Square, Athlone, Ireland
1054	694	Rice	Margaret	F	3			Ireland	Queenstown, W T Kerrigan, The Square, Athlone, Ireland
1055	264	Richard	Emile	M	2	21	Labourer		St Jean d'Augeleys, Charente, Paris
1060	652	Panula	Sanni	M	2			Finland	Finland
1061	89	Ragheim	Sante	M	1		M/s to White	Finland	
1062	695	Rintaniaki	Matti	M	3	35	Labourer	Finland	Finland
1064	696	Risien	Emma	F	3	58	Hotel Keeper	USA	London, 154 Camden St, Camden Gardens
1065	697	Risien	Samuel	M	3	68	Hotel Keeper	USA	London, 154 Camden St, Camden Gardens
1066	91	Robbins		M	1		M/s to Astor		
1068	698	Robins	Alexander	M	3	50	Mason	USA	Cornwall, c/o Daniel & Rouse, St Austell
1069	699	Robins	Charity	F	1	48	Housewife	USA	Cornwall, c/o Daniel & Rouse, St Austell
1070	92	Roebling	Washington A	M	2			USC	Brown Shipley, Pall Mall, London
1071	265	Rogers	Harry	M	3	18	Waiter	English	Crowndale Cottages, Tavistock
1072	700	Rogers	William John	M	3	29	Miner	Welsh	Pontardawe, c/o Mrs Rogers, Yinsymont Farm, Glais, nr Swansea
1074	705	Rummetvedt	Kristian P	M	3	49	Tailor	Norwegian	Bergen
1075	94	Rood	Hugh R	M	3			USC	Ritz Hotel, London
1076	701	Rosblom	Helene	F	3	41	Wife	Finnish	Finland
1077	703	Rosblom	Salli	F	3	2	Child	Finnish	Finland
1078	702	Rosblom	Viktor	M	3	18	Labourer	Finnish	Finland
1080	93	Rosenshine	G	M	1			USC	17 Faubourg Poissoniere, Paris

Master List No	Old List No	Surname	First Name(s)	Sex	Class	Age	Occupation	Nationality	Last Abode
1081	95	Ross	J Hugo	M	1			USC	Savoy Hotel, London
1085	96	Rothschild	M	M	1			USC	Grand Hotel, Paris
1086	704	Rowse	Richard Henry	M	3	53	Labourer	English	Sittingbourne, 30 New Road
1087	97	Rowe	Alfred	M	1			USC	6 Petersham Place, Gloucester Rd, London
1089	706	Rush	Alfred George T	M	3	17	Porter	English	London, 27 Palace Road, Upper Norwood
1091	707	Ryan	Patrick	M	3			Irish	Queenstown
1092	98	Ryerson	Arthur	M	1			USC	Hotel Langham, Paris
1097	708	Saad	Amin	M	3	30	Farm Labourer	Syria	Syria
1098	709	Saad	Khalil	M	3	25	Farm Labourer	Syrian	Syria
1099	710	Saade	Jean Nasr	M	3	20	Farm Labourer	Syrian	Syria
1101	711	Sadlier	Matt	M	3			Irish	Queenstown
1102	712	Sadowitz	Harry	M	3	17	Fur Cutter	English	London
1103	729	Sather	Simon	M	3	25	Miner	USA	Cape Town
1104	714	Sage	Annie	F	3	44	Wife	English	London, 246 Gladstone Rd, Peterborough
1105	723	Sage	William	M	3	1	Child	English	London, 246 Gladstone Rd, Peterborough
1106	715	Sage	Constance	F	3	7	Child	English	London, 246 Gladstone Rd, Peterborough
1107	716	Sage	Dorothy	F	3	13	Scholar	English	London, 246 Gladstone Rd, Peterborough
1108	717	Sage	Douglas	M	3	18	Baker	English	London, 246 Gladstone Rd, Peterborough
1109	713	Sage	Ada	F	3	9	Child	English	London, 246 Gladstone Rd, Peterborough
1110	718	Sage	Frederick	M	3	16	Assist-Cook	English	London, 246 Gladstone Rd, Peterborough
1111	719	Sage	George	M	3	19	Barman	English	London, 246 Gladstone Rd, Peterborough
1112	720	Sage	John	M	3	44	Tradesman	English	London, 246 Gladstone Rd, Peterborough
1113	721	Sage	Stella	F	3	20	Dressmaker	English	London, 246 Gladstone Rd, Peterborough
1114	722	Sage	Thomas	M	3	4	Child	English	London, 246 Gladstone Rd, Peterborough
1116	724	Salander	Carl	M	3	24	Labourer	Sweden	Gothenburg
1119	725	Salonen	Werner	M	3	29	Labourer	Finland	Finland
1120	726	Samaan	Elias	M	3	18	Labourer	Syria	Syria
1121	727	Samaan	Hanna	M	3	14	Labourer	Syria	Syria
1122	728	Samaan	Youssef	M	3	16	Labourer	Syria	Syria
1127	730	Saundercock	William Henry	M	3	20	Labourer	English	Soton
1128	731	Sawyer	Frederick	M	3	23	Gardener	English	Woolwich, (2 Acres Cottages, Slades Green, Kent)
1129	732	Scanlan	James	M	3			Ireland	Queenstown
1132	270	Smith	Augustus	M	2			Austrian	Berwick St, N London
1133	733	Sdycoff	Todor	M	2	4-	Labourer	Bulgaria	Basel
1134	266	Waddington Sedgwick	Charles Frederick	M	2				London
1137	267	Sharp	Percival	M	2				London
1138	735	Shaughnessy	Patrick	M	3			Irish	Queenstown
1140	736	Shellard	Frederick	M	3	52	Painter	English	Bristol 520 Gloucester Rd, Horfield
1143	737	Shorney	Charles J	M	3	22	Valet	English	Brighton c/o T Cook & Son
1148	99	Silvey	William B	M	1				
1149	739	Simmons	John	M	3	39	Labourer	English	Eng W.W Line, Leadenhall St

222

Master List No	Old List No	Surname	First Name(s)	Sex	Class	Age	Occupation	Nationality	Last Abode
1153	740	Sirayaman	Arsen	M	3	22	Farmer	American	Marseille
1154	741	Sirota	Maurice	M	3	20	Tailor	English	London, 57 Mile End Rd, London E
1155	742	Sivic	Husen	M	3	40	Labourer	Austrian	Bale
1156	738	Sihvola	Antte	M	3	21	Labourer	Finland	Finland
1158	268	Sjostedt	Ernest A	M	2			Swedish	London, (Hjo, Sweden)
1159	743	Skoog	Anna	F	3	43	Labourer	Swede	Sweden
1160	745	Skoog	Harald	M	3	4	Labourer	Swede	Sweden
1161	744	Skoog	Carl	M	3	10	Labourer	Swede	Sweden
1162	746	Skoog	Mabel	F	3	9	Labourer	Swede	Sweden
1163	747	Skoog	Margret	F	3	2	Labourer	Swede	Sweden
1164	748	Skoog	Wm	M	3	39	Labourer	Swede	Sweden
1165	749	Slakenoff	Petco	M	3	42	Labourer	Bulgarian	Bale
1168	269	Slemen	Richard T	M	2	35	Merchant	English	Southampton,(Landrake by St Germans, Cornwall)
1169	751	Slocovski	Selman	M	3	20		Russian	London c/o W.S Line, Leadenhall St
1171	100	Smart	John M	M	1			USC	3 Woodend Cottage, Kildale, via Grosmont, York
1172	752	Smiljanic	Mile	M	3	37	Farm Labourer	Austrian	Basel
1173	101	Smith	J Clinch	M	3			USC	4 Villa Said, Paris
1174	753	Smith	John Richard Jago	M	3	35	British Sea Post Clerk	British	Southampton, 45 Atherley Rd
1175	103	Smith	L P	M	1			English	Reinachs Nephews, London
1178	102	Smith	R W	M	1			British	Queenstown
1179	754	Smyth	Thomas	M	3			English	Porthallow, nr Helston, Cornwall
1183	271	Sobey	Hayden	M	2	25	Quarryman	English	Norway
1184	755	Soholt	Peter	M	3	19	Joiner	Norwegian	Norway
1185	757	Somerton	Francis W	F	3	31	Wife	American	Cheltenham c/o Cook & Son, Cheltenham
1186	758	Spector	Woolf	M	3	23		Russian	London
1191	104	Spencer	W A	M	1			USC	33 Avenue Hy Martin, Paris
1192	759	Spinner	Henry John	M	3	32	Grocer	English	Worcester
1194	760	Staneff	Ivan	M	3	23	Labourer	Bulgarian	Bale
1195	761	Stankovic	Jovan	M	3	33	Labourer	Austrian	Bale
1197	762	Stanley	Ernest Roland	M	3	21	Hotel Porter	English	Swanage
1198	272	Stanton	S Ward	M	2			USC	Paris
1199	105	Stead	W T	M	1			English	5 Smith Square, Westminster
1204	106	Stewart	A A	M	1			USC	Hotel Continental, Paris
1205	273	Stokes	Phillip J	M	2	25	Bricklayer	English	91 Hawstedd Rd, Catford, London
1207	763	Storey	T	M	3			English	
1208	764	Stoytchoff	Ilia	M	3	19	Labourer	Bulgarian	Bale
1209	765	Strandberg	Ida	F	3	19		Swede	Sweden
1211	107	Straus	Isidor	M	1			USC	Hotel Bristol, Paris
1212	108	Straus	(Mrs)	F	1			USC	
1213	766	Strilic	Ivan	M	3	27	Farmer	Austrian	Basel
1214	767	Strom	Elma	F	3	28	Wife	Swede	Sweden

Master List No	Old List No	Surname	First Name(s)	Sex	Class	Age	Occupation	Nationality	Last Abode
1215	768	Strom	Selma	F	3	2	Child	Swede	Sweden
1218	769	Sutehall	Henry	M	3	26	Coach Trimmer	USC	London
1220	109	Sutton	Frederick	M	1			English	
1222	770	Svensson	Johan	M	3	74		Swede	Sweden
1224	771	Svenssen	Olaf	M	3	24	Farmer	Swede	Sweden
1225	274	Swane	Geo	M	2				154 Abbey Road, NW London
1226	275	Sweet	Geo	M	2		Farm Labourer	English	Yeovil
1228	110	Tanssig	Emil	M	1	14		Austrian	Vienna
1233	276	Taylor	Percy Cornelius	M	2			English	9 Fentiman Rd, Clapham, London
1235	111	Thayer	J B	M	1			USC	
1238	772	Theobald	Thomas	M	3	34	Groom	English	Rochester c/o Curtis & Son
1240	773	Thomas	Charles	M	3	31	Dealer	English	Marseille
1241	774	Thomas	John	M	3	34	Dealer	Syrian	Marseille
1242	775	Thomas	Tannous T	M	3	16	Student	Syrian	Marseille
1244	776	Thomson	Alexander	M	3			Scotch	Scotland
1247	777	Thorneycroft	Percival	M	3	36	Labourer	English	London Crundell, 14 Waller St, Penge
1248	778	Tikkanen	Juho	M	3	32	Labourer	Finnish	Finland
1249	779	Tobin	Roger	M	3			English	London
1250	780	Todoroff	Lalio	M	3	23	Labourer	Bulgarian	Bale
1251	781	Tomlin	Ernest Portage	M	3	22	Student	English	London 1 Sanders Rd
1253	783	Torber	Ernest	M	3	41	Gardener	German	London, 112 Walton St, Kensington
1254	784	Torfa	Assad	M	3	20	Farm Hand	Syrian	Syria
1256	782	Toufic	Nakli	M	3	17	Labourer	Syria	Syria
1262	277	Troupiansky	Moses Aaron	M	2	23	Shop Assist.	Russian	London, (African Hotel, Southampton)
1266	785	Turcin	Stefan	M	3	36	Labourer	Austrian	Bale
1269	278	Turpin	Dorothy Ann	F	2	27	Housewife	British	59 Chaddlewood Ave, Plymouth
1270	279	Turpin	Wm John	M	2	29	Carpenter	British	59 Chaddlewood Ave, Plymouth
1271	112	Uruchurtu	M R	M	1			USC	Grand Hotel, Paris
1272	787	Uzelas	Jovo	M	3	17	Farmer	Austrian	Basel
1274	340	Billiard	Austin Van	M	3			USA	London, W Bartlett, 4 Armitage Mansions, Golders Green
1275	341	Billiard	James	M	3		Child	USA	London, W Bartlett, 4 Armitage Mansions, Golders Green
1276	342	Billiard	Walter	M	3		Child	USA	London, W Bartlett, 4 Armitage Mansions, Golders Green
1277	788	Van de Velde	Joseph	M	3	36	Farmer	Belgium	Antwerp
1278	790	Van den Steen	Leon	M	3	28	Farmer	Belgian	Antwerp
1279	113	Van der Hoef	Wyckoff	M	1			USC	5 College Park, E Belfast
1280	502	Impe	Catherine Van	F	3	10	Child	Belgian	Belgium
1281	503	Impe	Jacob Van	M	3	36	Farmer	Belgian	Belgium
1282	504	Impe	Rosalie Van	F	3	30	housewife	Belgian	Belgium
1283	601	Melkebuk	Philemon Van	M	3	23	Farmer	Belgium	Antwerp
1284	789	Van de Walle	Nestor	M	3	28	Merchant	Belgium	Antwerp
1285	796	Vercruysse	Victor	M	3	47	Farmer	Belgium	Antwerp
1286	791	Van der Plancke	Augusta	F	3	18	Servant	Belgian	Antwerp

Master List No	Old List No	Surname	First Name(s)	Sex	Class	Age	Occupation	Nationality	Last Abode
1287	792	Van der Plancke	Emilie	F	3	31	Wife	Belgian	Antwerp
1288	793	Van der Plancke	Jules	M	3	31	Farmer	Belgian	Antwerp
1289	794	Van der Plancke	Leon	M	3	16	Farm Labourer	Belgian	Antwerp
1291	280	Veale	James	M	3			USC	Southampton, Port Navis, Falmouth
1292	804	Wendell	Olof Edvin	M	3	21	Labourer	Swede	Copenhagen
1293	797	Vestrom	Hulda A A	F	3	14	Servant	Swede	Sweden
1294	798	Vook	Janko	M	3	21	Labourer	Austrian	Bale
1295	799	Waelius	Achille	M	3	22	Farm Labourer	Belgium	Antwerp
1297	114	Walker	W Anderson	M	1				Manchester
1300	800	Ware	Frederick	M	3	34	Motor Fitter	English	Greenwich
1301	281	Ware	John Jas	M	2		Builder	English	13 Salthrop Rd, Morley Square, Bishopston, Bristol
1302	282	Ware	Wm T	M	2	23	Blacksmith	English	King Street, Gunnislake
1304	801	Warren	Charles William	M	3	30	Bricklayer	English	Portsmouth
1305	115	Warren	F M	M	1			USC	Paris
1306	283	Watson	Ennis	M	2	18	Electrician	English	Harland & Wolff's man, Belfast
1309	802	Webber	James	M	3	66	Miner	American	Southampton
1311	116	Weir	J	M	1		Colonel in American Army	USC	London
1312	284	Weisz	Leopold	M	2	36		Hungarian	Birmingham, c/o Bromsgrove Guild, Bromsgrove
1320	285	West	E Arthur	M	2	42		English	Bournemouth, (Newhorn, Truro, Cornwall)
1321	453	Georges	Chahini	F	3	66	Wife	Syria	Syria
1322	286	Wheadon	Edward H	M	2		Farmer	English	La Couture, Guernsey
1323	287	Wheeler	Edwin	M	1				Paris, (4 Melcome Rd, Durley Park, Bath)
1325	117	White	Percival W	M	1			English	65 Bridge St, Wednesbury
1326	118	White	Richard F	M	1			English	65 Bridge St, Wednesbury
1327	119	Wick	George D	M	1			USC	
1330	806	Widegrin	Charles	M	3	44	Labourer	Norwegian	Nilsson
1332	120	Widener	George D	M	1			USC	Hotel Ritz, London
1333	121	Widener	Harry	M	1			USC	Hotel Ritz, London
1334	808	Wiklund	Karl Johan	M	3	21	Labourer	Finland	Finland
1335	807	Wiklund	Jakobt Alfred	M	3	21	Labourer	Finland	Finland
1341	803	Weller	Abe	M	3	37	Tailor	Russian	Paris
1342	809	Willey	Edward	M	3	18	Farm Labourer	English	England
1343	122	Williams	Duane	M	1			Canadian	Geneva, Suisse
1345	810	Williams	Harry	M	3		Carman	English	Guernsey
1346	811	Williams	Leslie	M	3	28	Boxer	English	Cardiff Mrs E Williams, 19 Eleanor St, Tonypandy
1348	64	Lambert Williams	Fletcher Fellowes	M	1			USC	6 West Bickerhall Mansions, Gloucester Place, London W
1349	812	Williamson	James Bertram	M	3	35	British Sea Post Clerk	British	93 Clovelly Rd, Southampton
1351	813	Windelot	Einar	M	3	21	Dairyman	Denmark	Cape Town
1352	814	Wirz	Albert	M	3	28	Farmer	Sweden	Basel
1353	815	Wiseman	Philip	M	3	54	Merchant	English	London

Master List No	Old List No	Surname	First Name(s)	Sex	Class	Age	Occupation	Nationality	Last Abode
1354	816	Wittewrongel	Camille	M	3	36	Farmer	Belgium	Antwerp
1358	288	Woodward	John Wesley	M	2			English	The Firs, Windmill Rd, Headington, Oxford
1359	817	Woody	Oscar S	M	3	41	American Sea Post Clerk	American	Parkers Hotel, Southampton
1361	123	Wright	George	M	1				
1363	818	Yazbeck	Antoni	M	3	27	Labourer	Syria	Syria
1366	819	Yousif	Wazli	M	3	25	Farmer	Syrian	Syria
1367	820	Youssef	Gerios	M	3	45	Shoemaker	Syrian	Syria
1368	289	Yrois	Henriette	F	2			French	London (5 Rue des Pyramides, Paris)
1369	821	Zabour	Hileni	F	3	16	Housekeeper	Syrian	Syria
1370	822	Zabour	Tamini	F	3	19	Housekeeper	Syrian	Syria
1371	824	Zakarian	Mapreder	M	3				
1372	823	Zakarian	Artin	M	3	27	Labourer	Syrian	Syria
1373	825	Zimmerman	Leo	M	3	29	Farmer	Swiss	Basel

List of Survivors, RMS *Carpathia*, New York

Master List No	Old List No	Name	Age	Sex	Marital Status	Occupation	Of which country	Nationality	From where travelling	Town/City	Going to
3	1	Abbott, Rosa	36	F	M	Wife	US				Cal, Los Angeles
4											
5	2	Abelseth, Karen	16	F	S	Domestic	Norway	Scand	Norway	Sandmore	
6	3	Abelseth, Olaus	26	M	S	Laborer	Norway	Scand	Norway	Oreskog	Mont, Columbus
7	4	Abelson, Anna	28	F	M	Wife	Russian	Russian	France	Paris	New York
9	5	Abrahamson, August	19	M	S	Sailor	Finland	Finnish	Finland	Dragefgard	NY, Hoboken
10	255	Joseph, Mary	1	F	S	-	US	US	Mich Detroit		
15	7	Aks, Phillip	8m	M	S		Russian	England	London	Va Norfolk	VA, Fredericksburg
16	6	Aks, Leah	21	F	S		Russian	England	London	Va Norfolk	
17	79	Cassam, Nassif	26	M	S	Peddler	Syria	Syria	Syria	Shansh	
22	8	Allan, Elizabeth	29	F	S		US	English			
27	9	Allison, Trevor	*	M	S	Infant	Canada		Canada	Montreal	Que, Montreal
30	10	Anderson, Carla	19	F	S	Domestic	Denmark	Danish	Denmark	Eskildstrup	Den. F-
31	12	Anderson, Harry	42	M	M		USA				
34	464	Wennerstrom, August Edw.	28	M	S	Reporter	Sweden	Scand	Sweden	?stad	Ill Chicago
37	11	Anderson, Erna	16	F	S	Domestic	Finland	Finnish	Finland	NY, New York	
49	13	Angel, Florence	36	F	M	Wife	England	British	Illegible	New York	
61	15	Asplund, Felix	3	M	S		Sweden	Scand	Sweden	Adelfors	Mass, Worcester
63	17	Asplund, John	23	M	S	Carpenter	Sweden	Sweden	Sweden	Oskarsham	Minn, Minneapolis
64	18	Asplund, Lillian	5	F	S		Sweden	Scand	Sweden	Adelfors	Mass, Worcester
65	19	Asplund, Selma	35	F	W		Sweden	Scand	Sweden	Adelfors	Mass, Worcester
67	20	Assaf, Miriam	45	F	S	Domestic	Syria	Syrian	Syria	Kefr Mecheh	Can, Ontario
70	21	Astor, Madeline	19	F	M	Peddler	US	US			
72	22	Aubart, Ninette P.	24	F	M	Married	France	French	France	Paris	France Paris
74	111	Daher or Ajub, Banoora	16	F	S	Housework	Assyria	Assyrian	Assyria	Barnet	Ohio, Columbus
77	23	Backstrom, Maria Matilda	23	F	W	Domestic	Finland	Finnish	Finland	Lovisa	Finland, Stromfors
78	25	Baclini, Jennie	4	F	S		Syria	Syrian	Syria	Schwer	NY, New York
79	24	Baclini, Ilne/Helen	2	F	S		Syria	Syrian	Syria	Schwer	NY, New York
80	27	Baclini, Latifie	24	F	M		Syria	Syrian	Syria	Schwer	NY, New York
81	28	Baclini, Marie	5	F	S		Syria	Syrian	Syria	Schwer	NY, New York
82	29	Badman, Emily	18	F	S	Domestic	England	English	England	Clevedon	NY, Skanteales

Master List No	Old List No	Name	Age	Sex	Marital Status	Occupation	Of which country	Nationality	From where travelling	Town/City	Going to
87	113	Dalls, Mrs. A.	36	F	M	?	Eng	Eng	Eng	Florida	NY, New York
91	31	Barber, Ellen	26	F	S	Lady maid	British	English	England	Stafford	NY, New York
92	32	Barkworth, Algernon Hy.	47	M	S	J.P.er York?	British	English	England	Hessle	Canada, Montreal
97	33	Baxter, Helen Chapub	48	F	M	Wife	Canadian	French	Canada	Montreal	
100	34	Beane, Edward	27	M	M	Bricklayer	US				
101	35	Beane, Ethel	22	F	M	Wife	US				
105	37	Becker, Marion	4	F	S	None	US				
106	36	Becker, Ellen O.	40	F	M	Wife	US				
107	38	Becker, Richd	2	M	S	None	US				
108	39	Becker, Ruth	13	F	S	None	US				
109	40	Beckwith, Rich L.	42	M	M		US				
110	41	Beckwith, Sally M.	42	F	M		US				
111	42	Beesley, Laur—	33	M	?	Schoolmaster	England	English	London	London	
112	43	Behr, Karl	26	M	S	None	US				
114	44	Bentham, Lilian	19	F	S		US				
119	46	Bidois, Rosalie	42	F	M	Astor maid	France	French	New York	New York	NY, New York
120	283	Lee, Bing	32	M	S	Fireman	China	Chinese	Eng	London	Chinamen NY
121	47	Bird, Ellen	29	F	S	Strauss Maid	Gt Britain	English	England	London	NY, NYC
126	45	Bessette, Nellie M.	35	F	S	White's maid	USA				
128	48	Bjornstrom, Stefanson	28	M	M	Diplomatic Service	Sweden	Scand	Stockholm		NY NYC
130	49	Blank, Harry	39	M	S		USA				
131	50	Bonnell, Caroline	30	F	S		USA				
132	51	Bonnell, Elizabeth	62	F	S		USA				
139	52	Boulos, Montoura	35	F	W	-	Syria	Syrian	Syria	Mt. Lebanon	PA
145	53	Bowen, Grace Scott	3-?	F	S		US				
147	54	Bowerman, Elsie	22	F	S	Spinster	Gt Britain	English	England	St. Leonards	NY, NYC
149	55	Bradley, Bridget	20	F	S	Domestic	Ireland	Irish	Ireland	King Williamstown	NY, New York
150	56	Brayton, George A.	34	M	M		US			Montreal	
163	59	Brown, Mildred	20	F	S	Servant	Eng	Eng	Eng		
165	57	Brown, Edith	15	F	S	None	British	English	Africa	Cape Town	Seattle
166	58	Brown, Elizabeth	38	F	M	Wife	British	English	Africa	Cape Town	Seattle
170	60	Dryhl, Miss	30	F	S	Servant	Swedish?	Swedish?	Skara	Rockford, ILL	
172	61	Buckley, Daniel	21	M	S	Laborer	Ireland	Irish	Ireland	King Williamstown	NY, New York
176	62	Burns, Elizabeth M.	39	F	S		USA				
178	63	Buss, Kate	36	F	S	None	British	English	Eng	Sittingbourne	
182	131	Degstrom, Carolina	40	F	M	Wife	US				Cal, San Diego
188	64	Calderhead, Edward P.	42	M	M		USA				
189	65	Caldwell, Albert	26	M	M	Teacher	US				
190	66	Caldwell, Alden	M	M	Child	US					
191	67	Caldwell, Sylvia	26	F	M	Wife	US				
193	68	Cameron, Clear	31	F	S	Maid	Eng	Eng	Eng	New York	

List of Survivors, RMS *Carpathia*, New York

Master List No	Old List No	Name	Age	Sex	Marital Status	Occupation	Of which country	Nationality	From where travelling	Town/City	Going to
197	70	Candee, Helen C.	50	F	M	Widow	USA	US			
202	71	Cardeza, Charlotte	52	F	M		USA				
203	72	Cardeza, Thomas	36	M	S		USA				
213	75	Carter, Lucille P.	32	F	M		US				
214	76	Carter, Lucille P.	14	F	S		US				
215	77	Carter, William E.	35	M	M		US				
216	78	Carter, William T.	9	M	S		US				
219	80	Cassebeer, Eleanor G.	75	F	M		US	USA			
220	81	Cavendish, Julia	25	F	M		USA				
223	82	Chaffee, Carrie	47	F	M		USA				
231	83	Chandauson, Victoria	30	F	S	Maid	France	French	USA	New York	NY Springfield Center
232	87	Cherry, Gladys	44	F	S	None	British	English	England	London	NY, NY City
233	88	Chevre, Paul	48	M	S	Sculptor	France	French	France	Paris	Canada, Montreal
234	89	Chibnall, Edith C.	32	F	M	Married	Gt Britain	English	England	St. Leonards	NY, NYC
235	84	Chang, Chip	48	M	S	Fireman	China	Chinese	Eng	London	Chinamen NY
238	90	Christy, Alice	25	F	W	Widow	Gt Britain	English	England	London	Canada Montreal
239	91	Christy, Julie	28	F	S	Spinster	Gt Britain	English	England	London	Canada Montreal
242	93	Clarke, Mrs. Ada	25	F	M	Wife	England	English	Eng	London	California
244	92	Clark, Virginia M.	22	F	M		USA				
247	94	Cleaver, Alice	19	F	S	Allisons Nurse	Gt Britain	English	England	London	Que, Montreal
250	98	Cohen, Gershan	24	M	S	Compositor	England	Hebrew	England	London	NY, Brooklyn
256	99	Collett, S.		M?	S	Student?	England	English	Eng	London	New York
259	100	Collyer, Charlotte	30	F	M	Wife	England	English	Eng	Hants	Idaho
261	101	Collyer, Marjoria	8	F	S	Child	England	English	Eng	Hants	Idaho
263	102	Compton, Mary E.	64	F	M		USA				
264	103	Compton, Sara R.	39	F	S		USA				
267	104	Connely, Kate	21	F	S	Domestic	Ireland	Irish	Ireland	Curtrasna	NY, New York
271	381	Rogers, Selina	24	F	S	None	British	English	England	Tridge?	Greenwich, Conn
279	105	Corr, Ellen	16	F	S	Domestic	Ireland	Irish	Ireland	Langford	NY, New York
281	107	Coutts, Neville	3	M	S	-	England	English	England	London	NY, Brooklyn
282	108	Coutts, William	9	M	S	-	England	English	England	London	NY, Brooklyn
283	106	Coutts, Minnie T.	36	F	M		Ireland	Irish	England	London	NY, Brooklyn
289	109	Cribb, Laura M.	17	F	S	Domestic	US Citizen	English	England	Dover	NJ, Newark
293	110	Cummings, Florence		F	S	US					
297	112	Dahl, Charles	45	M	S	Carpenter	Norway	Scand	England	London	ND, Fingal
300	114	Daly, Eugene	29	M	S	Mechanic	Ireland	Irish	Ireland	Lieclougher	NY, Brooklyn
301	115	Daly, Marcella	30	F	S	Domestic	Ireland	Irish	Ireland	Athlone	NY, New York
302	116	Daly, Peter Dennis	51	M	S	Merchant	British	Irish	S America, Peru	Lima	S America, Lima
306	117	Daniel, Robert W.	27	M	S		USA				
307	118	Daniels, Sarah	33	F	S	Allison's Maid	Gt Britain	English	England	London	London England

Who Sailed on Titanic?

Master List No	Old List No	Name	Age	Sex	Marital Status	Occupation	Of which country	Nationality	From where travelling	Town/City	Going to
310	122	Davidson, Orian Hays	78	F	M	Married	Canada	English	ill	Montreal	Que, Montreal
314	123	Davies, Agnes	49	F	M	Wife	British	English	St. Ives	Hancock, Mich	
317	124	Davies, John M.	9	M	S	Child	British	English	St. Ives	Hancock, Mich	
321	125	Davis, Mary	28	F	S	None	British	English	London	Tottenville, L.I	
322	126	Davison, Mary	32	F	W	-	England	English	Englannd	Chippenham	Oh, Bedford
325	132	DeMessemaker, Anna	36	F	M	Belgium	German	German	Brabant	Mont, Tampico	Mont, Tampico
326	133	DeMessemaker, William	36	M	M	Ranch Farmer	Belgium	German	Belgium	Brabant	
327	134	Demulder, Theodore	31	M	M	Farmer	Belgium	Belgian	Canton N-	Mich, Detroit	
331	128	Dean, Bertram	2	M	S	-	England	English	England	Peckham	Going back to England
332	129	Dean, Eliza	*	F	S	-		English	England	Peckham	Going back to England
333	130	Dean, Ettie	35	F	W	?	England	English	England	Peckham	Going back to England
334	14	Argena, Genovese	24	F	M	Wife	Italy	Italian	Chicago	Guernsey	NY, Albion
342	155	Duguenin, Joseph	24	M	S	P-cutter	England	English	England	Knocknahur	NY, New York
343	135	Devaney, Margaret	19	F	S	Domestic	Ireland	Irish	Ireland	Calgary, Alberta	Alb, Calgary
345	136	Dick, Albert A	31	M	M	Capitalist	Canada	Scotch	Canada	Calgary, Alberta	Alb, Calgary
346	137	Dick, Vera	20	F	M	Wife	Canada	Scotch	Canada	Calgary, Alberta	
350	138	Dodge, Ruth V.	36	F	M		USA				
351	139	Dodge, Washington	52	M	M		USA		Southampton	New York	
352	140	Dodge, Washington Jr.	4	M	S		USA		Southampton	New York	
354	141	Doling, Ada	34	F	M	Wife	British	English			
355	142	Doling, Elsie	19	F	S	None	British	English			
358	143	Dorkings, Edward A.	19	M	S	Laborer	England	English	England	Liss, Hampshire	IL, Oglesby
359	145	Douglas, Mahla		F	M	US					
360	144	Douglas, Helen Baxter	23	F	S	Wife	Canadian	French	Canada	Montreal	Canada, Montreal
362	146	Dowdell, Elizabeth	27	F	S	Child's tutor	US	NJ, Union Hill			
366	149	Drew, Lulu	34	F	M	Wife	US				
367	150	Drew, Marshall	8	M	S	Child	US				
369	151	Driscoll, Bridget	24	F	S	Domestic	Ireland	Irish	Ireland	Ballydehob	NJ, Jersey City
370	148	Drapkan, Jennie	23	F	S	Boxmaker	Russian	Hebrew	England	London	NY, New York
371	154	Duff-Gordon, Lucy C.	40	F	M	Wife	Gt Britain	Scotch	Scotland	Maryculter	Scotland Marycul
372	153	Duff-Gordon, Cosmo E.	49	M	M	Gent.	Gt Britain	Scotch	Scotland	Maryculter	Scotland Marycul
374	156	Duran, Aswner	27	F	S	Domestic	Spain	Spanish	Spain	Illegible	Havana
375	157	Duran, Florenti	30	F	M	Wife	Spain	Spanish	Spain	Barcelona	Havana
378	158	Dyker, Anna Elizabeth	22	F	W	Housekeeper	US	US	New Haven	Conn, West Haven	
379	159	Earnshaw, Olive P.	25	F		USA					
391	160	Emanuel, Virginia (Ethel)	6	F	S		London	NY, New York			
394	162	Endres, Caroline	38	F	S	England	US				
396	163	Eustas, Elizabeth M.		F	S		US				

230

List of Survivors, RMS *Carpathia*, New York

Master List No	Old List No	Name	Age	Sex	Marital Status	Occupation	Of which country	Nationality	From where travelling	Town/City	Going to
405	152	Drunthorpe, Lizzie	29	F	M	Wife	England	English	Eng	Manchester	Philadelphia
408	164	Finoli, Luigi	39	M		Coachman	US	Italian	Philadelphia	Pa, Philadelphia	
410	165	Flegenheim, Antoinette	48	F	W		US				
416	166	Flynn, J. Irwin	35	M	M		US				
419	86	Cheang, Foo	32	M	S	Fireman	China	Chinese	Eng	London	Chinamen NY
429	167	Fortune, Alice	24	F	S	Spinster	Canada	English	Man	Winnipeg	Man, Winnipeg
431	168	Fortune, Ethel	27	F	S	Spinster	Canada	English	Man	Winnipeg	Man, Winnipeg
432	169	Fortune, Mabel	23	F	S	Spinster	Canada	English	Man	Winnipeg	Man, Winnipeg
434	170	Fortune, Mary	56	F	M	Married	Canada	English	Man	Winnipeg	Man, Winnipeg
437	171	Francatelli, Mabel	30	F	S	Secretary	Gt Britain	England	England	London	England, London
440	172	Franenthal, Clara	40	F	M		USA				
441	173	Franenthal, Henry W.	45	M	M		USA				
442	174	Franenthal, Isaac G.	39	M	M		USA				
443	175	Frolicher, Margaret	48	F	M	Wife	Switzerland	German	Switzerland	Zurich	Switz
444	176	Frolicher, Margaret	22	F	S	Spinster	Switzerland	German	Switzerland	Zurich	Switz Zurich
445	177	Frolicher, Max	61	M	M	Manfs?	Switzerland	German	Switzerland	Zurich	Switz Zurich
450	178	Futrelle, May	40	F	M		USA				
455	179	Garside, E—	34	F	S	Nurse	Eng	Eng	Eng	New York	
461	183	Gibson, Dorothy	22?	F	S		US				
462	184	Gibson, Pauline C.	45	F	M		US				
463	185	Gieger, Amalie	35	F	S	Lady maid	Germany	German	USA	Elkins Park	PA, Elkins Park
472	186	Gilnagh, Kate	17	F		Domestic	Ireland	Irish	Ireland	Rhyne	NY, New York
474	187	Glynn, Mary	19	F	Maid		Ireland	Irish	Ireland	Flagmont	Washington, DC
475	188	Goldenberg, Nella	40	F	M		USA				
476	189	Goldenberg, Samuel	47	M	M		USA				
478	190	Goldsmith, Emily	32	F	-		England	English	England	Kent	Mich, Detroit
480	191	Goldsmith, Frank John Wm.	9	M	-		England	English	England	Kent	Mich, Detroit
490	192	Gracie, Col. Archibald	54	M	M	None	USA Citizen				
491	193	Graham, Edith Alice	55	F	M	None	USA Citizen				
493	194	Graham, Margaret	20	F	S		US				
496	195	Greenfield, Blanch	42	M	M		US				
497	196	Greenfield, William B.	24	M	S		US				
509	197	Hakkarinen, Ellen	24	F	W	Housemaid	Finland	Finnish	Finland	Helsingford	Pa Monessen
512	200	Hamlin, Anna	24	F	M	Wife	US				
513	199	Hamich, Barah	20	M	S		Syria	Syrian	Syria	Hardin	Mich Port Huron
516	198	Hamad, Hassab	27	M	W	Valet	Turkish	Turkish	Egypt	Cairo	New York, NY
520	202	Hansen, Jennie	45	F	W	-	US	WI Racine			
522	203	Harder, Dorothy	21	F	M		USA				
523	204	Harder, George A	25	M	M		USA				
527	205	Harper, Annie	6	F	S	Child	British	English	London	Chicago	
528	206	Harper, Henry S.	49	M	M	None	US				

Master List No	Old List No	Name	Age	Sex	Marital Status	Occupation	Of which country	Nationality	From where travelling	Town/City	Going to
530	207	Harper, Myra H.	49	F	M	None	US				New York
532	208	Harris, Geo.	62?	M	M	Gardener	US				New York
534	209	Harris, Rene W.	32	F	M		USA				
538	210	Harts, Esther	49	F	M	Wife	British	English	Eng	Safford?	
539	211	Harts, Eva	7	F	S	Child	British	English	Eng	Safford?	
542	201	Hamlin, Walter	1	M	S	Child	US				
544	213	Hawksford, Walter James	45	M	M	Export Mgr.	Gt Britain	English	England	Kingston	WI, Bermuda
546	214	Hays, Clara G.	51	F	M	Married	Canada	English	ill	Montreal	Que, Montreal
547	215	Hays, Margaret B.	45	F	S		USA				
550	216	Hedman, Oskar	S	M	S	Realtor	Sweden	Swedish	Sweden	Ragunda	Minn St Paul
551	280	Lang, Hee	24	M	S	Fireman	China	Chinese	Eng	London	Chinamen NY
553	217	Heikkinen, Laina	26	F	S	Servant	Finland	Finnish	Finland	Jyvaskila	Mass Quincy
555	218	Helstrom, Hilda	22	F	S	-	Sweden	Swedish	Sweden	Dom-	Ill Evanston
559	219	Herman, Alice	24	F	S	None	Eng	Eng	Eng	Somerset	New York
560	220	Herman, Jane	48	F	M	Wife	Eng	Eng	Eng	Somerset	New York
561	221	Herman, Katy	24	F	S	None	Eng	Eng	Eng	Somerset	New York
563	222	Hewlett, Mary	-	F	M		US				
572	223	Hirvonen, Helga	22	F	M	Housewife	Finland	Finnish	Finland	Dalhsbruk	Pa Monessen
573	224	Hirvonen, Hildur	2	F	S	-	Finland	Finnish	Finland	Dalhsbruk	Pa Monessen
574	225	Hockings, Eliza	53	F	M	None	British	English	Penzance	Akron, O	
575	226	Hockings, Mary	21	F	S	None	British	English	Penzance	Akron, O	
580	229	Hold, Anna	29	F	M	Wife	US				
586	230	Holverson, Mary A.	35	F	M		US				
587	212	Haver, Homer	40	M	M		US				
588	231	Honkonen, Elina	27	F	S	Domestic	Finland	Finnish	Helsingfors	Helsingfors	Mass Quincy
591	232	Hosono, Masadami	38	M	M	?	England	Japan	Eng	London	Japan
594	233	Howard, Mary	26	F	S	Laundress	England	English	England	Walsham	NY, Carlton Stn
595	234	Hoyt, Frederick	39	M	M		USA				
596	235	Hoyt, Jane	30	F	M		USA				
601	236	Hyman, Abraham	34	M	M	Grocer	England	Hebrew	England	Manchester	Mass, Springfield
602	237	Icard, Amelie	38	F	S	Lady maid	France	French	USA	Cincinnati	Ohio, Cincinnati
603	238	Ilett, Bertha	17	F	S	None	British	England	Eng		
608	239	Ismay, J. Bruce	50	M	M	Ship owner	Gt Britain	English	England	Liverpool	Eng —
610	240	Jacobson, Amy	24	F	M	Married	Gt Britain	English	England	London	Can
612	241	Jalsevec, Ivan	29	M	M	Laborer	Austria	Slovenian	Austria	Topolovic	Ill Galesburg
613	242	Janson, Carl	22	M	S	Carpenter	Sweden	Swedish	Sweden	Korsbergen	Ne Swedeburg
622	244	Jermyn, Annie	22	F	M	Domestic	Ireland	Irish	Ireland	Ballydehob	Mass Lynn
623	245	Jerwan, Mary	23	F	M	Wife	US				
624	248	Johanssen, Brindt	29	M	M	Cook	Norway	Scand	Norway	Haugesund	NY Brooklyn
631	247	Johanson, Oskar	22	M	M	Sailor	Sweden	Swedish	Sweden	Stillingran	Wis Martinooc
633	250	Johnson, Eleanor	*	F	S	-	Sweden	-	Sweden	Jonkoping	Ill St Charles

Master List No	Old List No	Name	Age	Sex	Marital Status	Occupation	Of which country	Nationality	From where travelling	Town/City	Going to
634	249	Johnson, Alice	27	F	M	Housewife	Finland	Finnish	Sweden	Jonkoping	Ill St Charles
635	251	Johnson, Harold	4	M	S	-	Sweden	-	Sweden	Jonkoping	Ill St Charles
644	243	Janson, Karl	25	M	M	RR Brakeman	Sweden	Swedish	Sweden	Killeberg	Minn Camden Stn
646	254	Joseph, Mariana	27	F	M	-	Syria	Syrian	Syria	An Edrhet	Pa Fogelsville
647	252	Joseph, Catherine	24	F	M		Syria	Syrian	Sarol	Mich Detroit	
648	256	Joseph, Michael	4	M	S		US	US	Mich Detroit	Mich Detroit	
650	257	Jousula, Eric	32	M	M	?? worker	Finland	Finnish	Finland	Bove	Pa Monessen
655	274	Kuntor, Miriam	24	F	M	Wife	Russia	Russian	Russia	Boston, Mass	
658	73	Carlson, Einar	21	M	S	Metalworker	Sweden	Swedish	Sweden	Oscarhamm	NY, Brooklyn
662	260	Karoun, Franz	34	M	M	Farmer	Austria	German	Illinois	Galesburg	Ill Galesburg
663	259	Karoun, Annie	4	F	S		Austria	German	Illinois	Galesburg	Ill Galesburg
668	261	Kean, Norah	35	F	S	None	US	Irish	Harrisburg, PA	Harrisburg, PA	Ill Chicago
672	262	Kelly, Annie	17	F	S	Helper	Ireland	Irish	Ireland	Cuilmullagh	New York
673	263	Kelly, Lanery	45	F	M	Widow	Eng	Eng	Eng	London	NY New York
675	264	Kelly, Mary	22	F	S	Domestic	Ireland	Irish	Ireland	Castle Pollard	NY New York
676	265	Kennedy, John	21	M	S	Picture framer	Ireland	Irish	Ireland	Limerick	
679	266	Kenyon, Marion	36	F	M		US				
685	267	Kimball, Edwin N.	45	M	M		USA				
686	268	Kimball, Gertrude P.	42	F	M		USA				
687	269	Kink, Antoine	29	M	M	Storekeeper	Switzerland	German	Switzerland	Zurich	Wis Milwaukee
688	270	Kink, Louisa	26	F	M	-	Austria	German	Switzerland	Zurich	Wis Milwaukee
689	271	Kink, Louisa	4	F	S		Austria	German	Switzerland	Zurich	Wis Milwaukee
700	273	Krikorian, Nishen	27	M	M	Laborer	Asiatic Turkey	Turkish	Asiatic Turkey	Aboshnak	Can Ontario Hamilton
701	272	Koenchen, Emilie	29	F	S	Maid	US		Eng	London	Chinamen NY
709	278	Lam, Ah	37	M	S	Fireman	China	Chinese	Sweden	Karlshamn	NY New York
712	279	Landegren, Aurora	20	F	S	Domestic	Sweden	Scand	Eng	London	Chinamen NY
714	281	Lang, Tang	32	M	S	Fireman	China	Chinese	France	Paris	
716	276	La Roche, Julie	23	F	M	Wife	France	French	Paris	Cap Haitien, Haiti	Cap Haitien, Haiti
717	275	La Roche, Eloise	2	F	S	Child	France	French	Paris	Cap Haitien, Haiti	
718	277	La Roche, Simon	3	M	S	Child	France	French			
724	282	Leader, Alice F.		F	W		USA				
725	481	Zennie, Phillip	21	M	S	Shoemaker	Syria	Syrian	Syria	Tula	NY New York
731	284	Lehman, Bertha	18	F	S	Waitress	Switzerland	English	Germany	Central City	Chicago
733	285	Leitch, Jenet?	29	F	S	None	British	English	Eng	London	
735	286	Lemare, Amelia	34	F	M?	Douglas's Maid	US	French			
743	287	Leroy, Bertha	30	F	S		France	French	USA	Minneapolis	MN Minneapolis
745	288	Lesneur, Gustav	35	M	S	Valet	France				Pa Monessen
756	289	Lindquist, Eina	20	F	S	Laborer	Finland	Finnish	Finland	Dalsbruk	Sweden
757	290	Lindstrom, Sigrid	56	F	M	Married	Sweden	Scand	Sweden	Stockholm	Stockholm

Master List No	Old List No	Name	Age	Sex	Marital Status	Occupation	Of which country	Nationality	From where travelling	Town/City	Going to
771	291	Louch, Alice	43	F	M	Wife	British	English	Eng	Weston S Mare	New York
775	292	Lulic, Nichola	27	M	M	Laborer	Austria	Austrian	Croatia	Ill Chicago	Conn Meridien
777	293	Lunden, Olga	23	F	S	Domestic	Sweden	Scand	USA Conn	Meriden	Cal Los Angeles
778	294	Lundstrom, Edwin	32	M	S	Carpenter	Sweden	Scand	Sweden	Simrishamn	
779	296	Lurette, Elise	58	F	S	Spencer? maid	France	French	France	Paris	France, Paris
783	297	Madigan, Margaret	21	F	S	Servant	Ireland	Irish	Ireland	Askeaton	NY New York
784	298	Madill, Georgette A.	16	F	S		US				
785	299	Madsen, Fritshgof	26	M	M	Sailor	Norway	Scand	Norway	Troughen	NY Brooklyn
796	301	Mallet, Antoine	24	F	M	Wife	France	French	Paris	Montreal	
797	300	Mallet, Andrew	1	M	S	Child	France	French	Paris	Montreal	
798	302	Manion, Margaret	24	F	S	Domestic	Ireland	Irish	Ireland	Loughanboy	NY New York
801	303	Mansa, Hannah	20	F	S	Farmer	Syria	Syrian	Syria	Tripoli	Pa Philadelphia
804	304	Marechal, Pierre	29	M	S	Aviator	French	French	France	Paris	NY, New York
808	306	Marvin, Mary	18	F	M	None	USA Citizen				Michigan City
810	329	Mouselman, Fatima	20	F	S	-	Syria	Syrian	Syria	Ohmon	Canada, Montreal
816	127	De Villiers, Mayne	30	F	M	Wife	Belgian	French	France	Paris	NJ Gutinburg
818	307	McCarthy, Kate	23	F	S	Domestic	Ireland	Irish	Ireland	Ballygusten	NJ Bayonne
820	308	McCormick, Thomas	19	M	S	Bar tender	Ireland	Irish	Ireland	Glenmore	NY New York
821	309	McCoy, Agnes	28	F	S	Domestic	Ireland	Irish	Ireland	Carrickathane	NY New York West
822	310	McCoy, Alice	22	F	S	Domestic	Ireland	Irish	Ireland	Carrickathane West	NY New York
823	311	McCoy, Bernard	21	M	S	Laborer	Ireland	Irish	Ireland	Carrickathane West	
826	312	McDermott, Delia	25	F	S	House maid	Ireland	Irish	Ireland	Knockfarnaught	Mo St Louis
828	313	McGough, James R.	36	M	M		US	Irish	Irish	Leberdale	Ill Chicago
829	315	McGowan, Annie	17	F	S	Domestic	US	Irish	Irish	Carborough	NY New York
831	314	McGovern, Mary	20	F	S	Domestic	Ireland	Irish			
839	317	Mellinger, Mrs. E.	40	F	M	None	England	English	Eng	Wimbledon, Surrey Bellinger, VT	
840	318	Mellinger, Viola	10	F	S	None	England	English	Eng	Wimbledon, Surrey Bellinger, VT	
841	319	Mellon, Wm. J	19	M	M	Salesman	British	English	London	New York	
847	320	Meyer, Leila S.	25	F	M		US				
848	316	Medtsje, Karl	22	M	S	Farmer	Norway	Scand	Norway	Christiania	Ill Chicago
853	321	Minihan, Daisy	27	F	S		USA				
854	322	Minihan, Lillian	38	F	M		USA				
861	324	Mock, Philip	30	M	M		US				
862	323	Mochlare, Ellen	17	F	S	Servant	Ireland	Irish	Ireland	Tycorly	Ill Chicago
866	325	Moore, Beile	28	F	W	Tailoress	Russia	Russian	England	London	Ill Chicago
867	326	Moore, Mayer	7	M	S	-	Russia	Russian	England	London	NY New York
870	327	Moran, Bertha	28	F	S	Collar factory	Ireland	Irish	New York	Troy	NY Troy
877	328	Moss, Albert	29	M	S	Sailor	Norway	Scand	Norway	Bergen	NY New York

Master List No	Old List No	Name	Age	Sex	Marital Status	Occupation	Of which country	Nationality	From where travelling	Town/City	Going to
878	182	George, Yousef (George)	6	M	-		Syria	Syrian	Syria	Mt. Lebanon	Pa
879	180	George, Halim	4	M	-		Syria	Syrian	Syria	Mt. Lebanon	Pa
880	181	George, Mefcorikor Amina	26	-			Syria	Syrian	Syria	Mt. Lebanon	Pa
885	330	Mullen, Kate	20	F	S	Domestic	Ireland	Irish	Ireland	Rhynekilloe	NY New York
886	331	Mulvehill, Bertha	24	F	S	Waitress	Ireland	Irish	Irish	Athlone	RI Providence
888	332	Murphy, Kate	16	F	S	Domestic	Ireland	Irish	Ireland	Aghnacliffe	NY New York
889	333	Murphy, Margaret	21	F	S	Domestic	Ireland	Irish	Ireland	Aghnacliffe	NY New York
890	334	Murphy, Nora	32	F	S	Nurse maid	Ireland	Irish	Ireland	Sallins	NY New York
894	450	Vagil, Adele Jenne	18	F	S	-	Syria	Syrian	Syria	Michonel	NY
895	335	Nakid, Mary	*	F		Laborer	Syria	Syrian	Syria	Zecatia	Conn Waterbury
896	336	Nakid, Salid	20	M		Housewife	Syria	Syrian	Syria	Zecatia	Conn Waterbury
897	337	Nakid, Wadia	20	M		Wife	Syria	Syrian	Syria	Zecatia	Conn Waterbury
901	347	Nussa, Adel	18	F	M		Syria	Syrian	Zahle	OH, Cleveland	
905	228	Hoffman, -opes									
907	227	Hoffman, Lola									
911	339	Newell, Madeleine	31	F	S		USA				
912	340	Newell, Marjory	23	F	S		USA				
913	341	Newsom, Helen M.	19	F	S		US				
917	342	Nichola, Elias	10	M	S		Syria	Syrian	Syria	Hacour	Fl Jacksonville
918	343	Nicholas, Jamile	17		S	Domestic	Syria	Syrian	Syria	Hacour	Fl Jacksonville
922	345	Nilson, Bertha	28	F	S	Domestic	Sweden	Scand	Sweden	Lysvik	MT Missoula
923	338	Nelson, Helminia	22	F	S	Domestic	Sweden	Scand	Sweden	Jonkojan	Ill Joliet
925	349	Nyskanen, John	39	M	M	Miner	Finland	Finnish	Finland	Kivijarvi	VT Graniteville
930	147	Drachstedt, Alfred	22	M	S	Gent.	Germany	German	France	Paris	France, Paris
932	348	Nye, Elizabeth	29	F	M	Wife	British	English	New York	New York	NJ Hackinsack
933	346	Nipten, Anna	24	F	S	Nurse	Sweden	Scand	Sweden	Kisa	NY New York
935	350	O'Brien, Hannah	26	F	W		Ireland	Irish	Ireland	Limerick	NY New York
945	351	O'Dwyer, Nellie	25	F	S	Domestic	Ireland	Irish	Ireland	Limerick City	NY Brooklyn
946	355	Oman, Velin	22		S	Dressmaker	Sweden	Scand	Sweden	Mariestad	Ill Chicago
947	352	O'Keefe, Patrick	21	M	S	Porter	Ireland	Irish	Ireland	? [sic]	NY New York
948	353	O'Leary, Norah	17?	F	S	Domestic	Ireland	Irish	Ireland	King Williamstown	NY New York
950	354	Olsen, Arthur	9	M	M	-	US	US	NY Brooklyn		NY New York
956	246	Johannsen, Oskar	26	M	S	Lumber man	Sweden	Scand	Sweden	Kvismare	Conn New Haven
958	356	Ormond, Fernand	29	M	S	Cotton agent	France	French	France	Havre	France Havre
964	357	Osman, Marya	30	F	S	Domestic	Poland	Polish	Vagovina	Pa Stulton	
966	358	Ostby, Helen	22	F	S		USA				
970	359	Oxenhan, P	22	M	S	Mason	England	English	Eng	London	New York
971	258	Juhan, Padro	26	M	S	Chauffeur	Spain	Spanish	Spain	Barcelona	Havana, Cuba
973	161	Pallaso, Emilio	29	M	S	Sp	Bar-a	Havana			
999	360	Pears, Edith	22	F	M	Married	Gt Britain	English	England	Isleworth	Eng, Isleworth
1005	365	Pinasco, Josefa	22	F	M	Married	Spain	Spanish	Spain	Madrid	Spain Madrid

Master List No	Old List No	Name	Age	Sex	Marital Status	Occupation	Of which country	Nationality	From where travelling	Town/City	Going to
1010	362	Perrault, Annie	30	F	S	Spinster	Canada	English	Que	Montreal	Que, Montreal
1011	363	Person, Ernst	25	M	M	Chauffer	Sweden	Swede	Sweden	Sodermannson	Ill Chicago
1020	361	Penchen, Arthur G.	52	M	M	Major Army	Canada	English	Ont	Toronto	Ont, Toronto
1021	364	Phillips, Alice	21	F	S	None	British	English	Eng	Ilfracombe	N Brighton, PA
1023	305	Marshall, Kate	21	F	M	Wife	England	English	Eng	California	
1024	366	Pinsky, Rosie	24	F	M	Wife	NY	Russian	New York		New York
1029	367	Postalappi, Emilio	30	M	M	Sculptor	Italy	Italian	Italy	Arcisati	
1031	368	Potter, Lily A.	49	F	M		USA				
1033	369	Quick, Jane	33	F	M	Wife	England	English	Eng	Devon	Detroit
1034	370	Quick, Phyllis	8	F	S	Child	England	English	Eng	Devon	Detroit
1035	371	Quick, Winnifred	2	F	S	Child	England	English	Eng	Devon	Detroit
1043	373	Renouf, Lily	30	F	M	Wife	England?	English	Channel Is	Guernsey	New Jersey
1046	372	Renaldo, Enidinacco	28	F	S	Domestic	Spain	Spanish	Puebla Marbella	New York	
1048	374	Rheims, George	36	M	M		US	Norah Kean crossed out and overwritten			
1056	375	Richards, Emily	24	F	M	Wife	British	English	Penzance	Akron, O	Ohio
1057	376	Richards, George	*	M	S	Child	British	English	Penzance	Akron, O	
1058	377	Richards, Wallia	3	M	S	Child	British	English	Penzance	Akron, O	
1059	378	Ridsdale, Lucy	50	F	S	None	Eng	Eng	London	London	
1063	379	Riordan, Hannah	20	F	M	none	Ireland	Irish	Ireland	King Williamstown	NY New York
1067	380	Robert, Elizabeth W.	43	F	M		US				
1079	382	Rosenbaum, Edith L.	32	F	S	Saleswoman	US		England	London	NY New York
1082	383	Roth, Sarah (Mrs. David)	29	F	M		England	English	England	Fife, Scotland	BC, Vancouver
1083	384	Rothes, Noel		F	Lady		Gt Britain	England			
1084	385	Rothschild, Lizzie	42	F	M	None	USA				Del, Wilmington
1088	386	Rugg, Emily	22	F	S		British	English	Eng	Guernsey	NY Troy
1090	387	Ryan, Edward	24	M	S	Chauffeur	Ireland	Irish	Ireland	Emly	
1093	389	Ryerson, Emily Bore Jr.		F	S		US				
1094	388	Ryerson, Emily Bore		F	M		US				
1095	390	Ryerson, John B.					US				
1096	391	Ryerson, Susan P.					US				
1100	392	Saalfeld, Adolphe	47	M	S	?	Gt Britain	German			
1115	400	Segesert, Emma	24	F	S	Maid	Switzerland	Swiss	Paris	France Paris	
1117	393	Salkjilsoik, Anna	21	F	S	Domestic	Norway	Scand	Norway	Halesund	Minn Proctor
1118	418	Soloman, Abram L.	43	M	M		USA				
1123	394	Sandstrom, Agnes	24	F	M	Housewife	Sweden	Scand	Calif	San Francisco	Cal San Francisco
1124	395	Sandstrom, Beatrice	1	F	S		US	US	San Francisco	Cal San Francisco	
1125	396	Sandstrom, Marguerite	4	F	S	-	US	US	San Francisco	Cal San Francisco	
1126	397	Sap, Jules	20	M	S	Laborer	Belgium	Belgian	Belgium	Halle	Mich Detroit
1130	398	Schabert, Emma	35	F	M	Married	Germany	German	Germany	Hamburg	Ger, Hamburg
1131	399	Schurlinch, Jean	29	M	S	Laborer	Belgium	Belgian	Belgium	Kerksken	Mich Detroit
1135	401	Serraplar, Augusta	30	F	S	Ladys Maid	France	French	New York	PA Philadelphia	

Master List No	Old List No	Name	Age	Sex	Marital Status	Occupation	Of which country	Nationality	From where travelling	Town/City	Going to
1142	402	Shine, Ellen	16	F	S	Servant	Ireland	Irish	Ireland	Newmarket	NY New York
1144	403	Shutes, Elizabeth	40	F	S	None	USA Citizen				
1145	404	Silven, Louise	18	F	S	None	Finland	Finn	Russia	Kalumet, Mich	
1146	405	Silverthorne, Spencer V	75?	M	M		USA				
1147	406	Silvey, Alice M.	40	F	M	Married	USA Citizen	US			
1150	407	Simonius, Alfons	56	M	M	Band Pres'd	Switzerland	German	Switzerland	Basle	NY, New York
1151	409	Sincock (niece), M—	24?	F	S	None	illeg	illeg	St. Ives	Hancock, Mich	
1152	408	Simpforen, Anna	30	F	S	Domestic	Finland	Finn	Brighton, Mass	Brighton	
1157	410	Sjoblom, Anna	18	F	S	Domestic	Finland	Scand	Finland	Munsala	Wash Olympia
1167	411	Slayter, Hilda	27	F		None	Canada	English	England	Plymouth	Canada,
1170	412	Sloper, William P.	28	M	s		US				Washington DC
1176	415	Smith, Marion	40	F	S	None	Eng	Eng	Eng	Basingstoke	
1177	413	Smith, Elouise	18	F	M		USA	USA			
1180	414	Smith, Julia	20	F	S	-	Ireland	Irish	Ireland	Potelbara	NY New York
1181	416	Snyder, John	24	M	M		USA	USA			
1182	417	Snyder, Nell	22	F	M		USA	USA			
1187	419	Spedden, Frederick O.	45	M	M		USA	USA			
1188	420	Spedden, Margaretta C.	40	F	M		USA	USA			
1189	421	Spedden, Robert D.	6	M	S		USA	USA			
1190	422	Spence, Eugenie	45	F	M		USA	USA			
1193	423	Stachelin, Max	32	M	M	Director	Switzerland	German	Switzerland	Basle	NY, New York
1196	424	Stanley, Amy	24	F	S	Domestic	England	English	England	Oxford	Conn New Haven
1200	425	Stengel, Annie M.	43	F	M		USA				
1201	426	Stengel, C.E. Henry	54	M	M		USA				
1202	427	Stephenson, Martha E.	F	M			US				
1210	428	Stranden, Yoho	30	M	S	Farmer	Finland	Scand	Finland	Kitee	Minn Duluth
1216	429	Sunderland, Victor	20	M	S	Groom	England	English	England	London E.	Oh Cleveland
1217	430	Sundman, John	44	M	M	Laborer	Finland	Scand	Finland	Munsala	Wyo Cheyenne
1223	431	Svenson, Cervin	14	S	-		US	Scand	Sweden	Halland	SD Beresford
1227	432	Swift, Margaret B.	36	F	W		US				
1231	433	Taylor, Elmer Z.	45	M	M		US				
1232	434	Taylor, Juliet C.	45	F	M		US				
1234	441	Tinglin, Gunner	25	M	S	Fireman	Sweden	Scand	Sweden	Stockholm	Ind Burlington
1236	435	Thayer, John B. Jr	17	M	S		US				
1237	436	Thayer, Marion	39	F	M		US				
1239	437	Thomas, Assid	*	M	S	-	Syria	Syrian	Syria	Pa Wilkes Barre	
1243	438	Thomas, Tamini	21	F	M	-	Syria	Syrian	Syria	Pa Wilkes Barre	
1245	439	Thorne, Gertrude	38	F	W		USA				
1246	440	Toomeycroft, Kate	33	F	W	Dayswork	England	English	England	Maidstone	NY Clinton
1252	442	Toomey, Ellen	50	F	S	Housekeeper	Eng	Ireland	Eng	Indianapolis	
1255	443	Tornkvist, Wm. H.	20	M	S	Sailor	Belgium	German	American Line	Mont Tampico	

Master List No	Old List No	Name	Age	Sex	Marital Status	Occupation	Of which country	Nationality	From where travelling	Town/City	Going to
1257	119	Darwich, Gerges	1?	M	S		Syria	Syrian	Syria	Abuin	Mich, Dowgiac
1258	120	Darwich, Hanna	30	F	M	-	Syria	Syrian	Syria	Abuin	Mich, Dowgiac
1259	121	Darwich, Mariana	10	F	S		Syria	Syrian	Syria	Abuin	Mich, Dowgiac
1261	444	Treubickey, Benoit	33	M	S	Leatherwork	Russia	Russian	England	London	Calif San Francisco
1263	446	Trout, Jessie	27	F	M	None	US	Eng	New York	New York	
1264	445	Trout, Edwina	27	F	S	Domestic	England			New York	
1265	447	Tucker, Gilbert M. Jr	31	M	S		USA				Ohio Ashtabula
1267	448	Turja, Anna Sophia	18	F	S	Domestic	Finland	Scand	Finland	Qulec Prov	Minn Hibbing
1268	449	Turkula, Hedwig	65	F	W		Finland	Scand	Finland	Varna Prov.	
1273	451	Valentine, Augusta	30	F	M	-	US	Name Overwritten with Douglas		Oror	Canada Ontario Hamilton
1290	452	Vartanian, David	20	M	M	Laborer	Asiatic Turkey	Turkish	Turkey		
1296	453	Walcroft, Nellie	35	F	S	Cook	Eng	Eng	Eng	New York	
1298	454	Ward, Annie	40	F	S		USA				
1299	455	Ware, Florence	33	F	M	Wife	British	English	Eng	Bristol	New Britain
1303	456	Warren, Anna	60	F	W		USA				
1307	458	Watt, Bessie	40	F	M	Wife	British	Scotch	Scotland	Aberdeen	Portland, Oregon
1308	457	Watt, Bertha	11	F	S	Child	British	Scotch	Scotland	Aberdeen	Portland, Oregon
1310	459	Webber, Susie	36	F	S	Cook	Eng	Eng	Eng	Conn	
1313	460	Weiz, Mathilde	23	F	M	Wife	France	French		Bromsgrove	Montreal
1314	461	Wells, Addie	29	F	S	Wife	British	English	Haymoor	Akron, O	
1315	462	Wells, Joan	4	F	S	Child	British	English	Haymoor	Akron, O	
1316	463	Wells, Ralph	2	M	S	Child	British	English	Haymoor	Akron, O	
1317	465	West, Ada Mary	33	F	M	Wife	England	English	Eng	Bournemouth	Florida
1318	466	West, Barbara	1	F	S	England	English	Eng	Bournemouth	Florida	
1319	467	West, Constance	4	F	S	England	English	Eng	Bournemouth	Florida	
1321	253	Joseph, Chaneen	40	F	W	Peddler	Syria	Syrian	Syria	Batresne	Ohio Youngstown
1324	468	White, Ella H.	50	F	W	None	USA				
1328	470	Wick, Mary N.	31	F	M		USA				
1329	469	Wick, Mary H.	46	F	M		USA				
1331	471	Widener, Eleanor E.	46	F	M	None	USA Citizen			New York	
1336	472	Wilhelms, Charles	31	M	S	Glass bender	Eng	Eng	Eng	Cornwall	Ohio Akron
1337	473	Wilkes, Ellen	45	F	W	Housewife	England	English	England		
1340	476	Williard, Carstairs			S		US			Harrow	
1344	474	Williams, Charles	23	M	S	?	England	English	Eng		
1347	475	Williams, Richd Norris	21	M	S	Student	US				
1350	477	Wilson, H. Alice	35	F	S		USA	English	London	illeg	
1360	478	Woolmer, Hugh	45	M	W	Coy Director	Gt Britain	English	Eng	Yeovil	
1362	479	Wright, Marion	26	F	S	None	British	English	Eng		Cottage Grove, Oregon

Master List No	Old List No	Name	Age	Sex	Marital Status	Occupation	Of which country	Nationality	From where travelling	Town/City	Going to
1364	480	Yazbeck, Selemie	15	F	W	-	Syria	Syrian	Syria	Hardin	Pa Wilkes Barre

Probable duplicatres

	95	Christy
	96	Christy
	16	Hewlett, Maryt
	97	Jacobson
	30	Bodas, Rosalie
	69	Toomey. Ellen
	74	Balls, A
	26	Valentine, Augusta
	85	Beesley, Lawce

Typed List

Master List No	Old list No	Surname	First name(s)	Class	Master List No	Old list No	Surname	First name(s)	Class
3	252	Abbott	Rosa	2nd cabin	172	330	Buckley	Daniel	Steerage
5	383	Abelseth	Karen	Steerage	176	70	Burns	Elizabeth M	1st cabin
6	382	Abelseth	Olaus	Steerage	178	205	Buss	Kate	2nd cabin
7	195	Abelson	Anna	2nd cabin	182	241	Degstrem	Carolina	2nd cabin
9	411	Abrahamson	August	Steerage	188	47	Calderhead	Edward P	1st cabin
10	338	Joseph	Mary	Steerage	189	253	Caldwell	Albert	2nd cabin
15	402	Aks	Filly	Steerage	190	255	Caldwell	Alden	2nd cabin
16	401	Aks	Leah	Steerage	191	254	Caldwell	Sylvia	2nd cabin
17	421	Cassan	Nassef	Steerage	193	261	Cameron	Clear, Miss	2nd cabin
22	91	Allan	Elizabeth	1st cabin	197	156	Candee	Helen C	1st cabin
27	175	Allison	Trevor	1st cabin	202	38	Cardeza	Charlotte	1st cabin
30	294	Anderson	Carla	Steerage	203	39	Cardeza	Thomas	1st cabin
31	77	Anderson	Harry	1st cabin	213	113	Carter	Lucille P	1st cabin
34	365	Winnerstrom	Aug E	Steerage	214	115	Carter	Lucille P	1st cabin
37	399	Anderson	Anna	Steerage	215	112	Carter	William E	1st cabin
49	227	Angel	Florence	2nd cabin	216	114	Carter	William T	1st cabin
61	441	Asplund	Felix	Steerage	219	85	Cassebeer	Eleanor G	1st cabin
63	378	Asplund	Joh C	Steerage	220	95	Cavendish	Julia	1st cabin
64	440	Asplund	Lillian	Steerage	223	57	Chaffee	Carrie	1st cabin
65	439	Asplund	Selma	Steerage	231	26	Chandauson	Victoria	1st cabin
67	339	Assaf	Miriam	Steerage	232	146	Cherry	Gladys	1st cabin
70	109	Astor	Madeline	1st cabin	233	1	Chevre	Paul	1st cabin
72	12	Aubast	Ninette P	1st cabin	234	7	Chibnall	Edith C	1st cabin
74	361	Ajub	Benora	Steerage	235	448	Chang	Chip	Steerage
77	398	Backstrom	Mary	Steerage	238	235	Christy	....	2nd cabin
78	355	Bakline	Eugene	Steerage	239	236	Christy	....	2nd cabin
79	356	Bakline	Helen	Steerage	242	282	Clarke	Mrs Ada?	2nd cabin
80	353	Bakline	Latife	Steerage	244	31	Clark	Virginia M	1st cabin
81	354	Bakline	Marie	Steerage	247	174	Cleaver	Alice	1st cabin
82	390	Badman	Emily	Steerage	250	408	Cohen	Gosban	Steerage
87	264	Dalls	A, Mrs	2nd cabin	256	273	Cellett	S	2nd cabin
91	158	Barber	Ellen	1st cabin	259	274	Collyer	Charlotte	2nd cabin
92	160	Barkworth	Algernon Hy	1st cabin	261	275	Collyer	Marjorie	2nd cabin
97	161	Baxter	Helen Chaput	1st cabin	263	51	Compton	Mary E	1st cabin
100	243	Beane	Edward	2nd cabin	264	52	Compton	Sara R	1st cabin
101	244	Beane	Ethel, Mrs	2nd cabin	267	460	Connolly	Kate	Steerage
105	178	Becker	Marion	2nd cabin	271	181	Rogers	Selina	2nd cabin
106	176	Becker	Ellen O	2nd cabin	279	328	Corr	Ellen	Steerage
107	179	Becker	Rich'd	2nd cabin	281	453	Coutts	Nevill L	Steerage
108	177	Becker	Ruth	2nd cabin	282	452	Coutts	William	Steerage
109	101	Beckwith	Ridi L	1st cabin	283	451	Coutts	Winnie	Steerage
110	102	Beckwith	Sally M	1st cabin	289	412	Cribb	Laura	Steerage
111	290	Beesley	Laurence	2nd cabin	293	137	Cummings	Florence	1st cabin
112	104	Behr	Karl	1st cabin	297	414	Dalil	Charles	Steerage
114	210	Bentham	Lilian	2nd cabin	300	323	Daly	Eugene	Steerage
119	164	Bedois	Rosalie	1st cabin	301	419	Daly	Marcella	Steerage
120	445	Lee	Berg	Steerage	302	165	Daly	Peter Dennes	1st cabin
121	4	Bird	Ellen	1st cabin	306	82	Daniel	Robert W	1st cabin
126	60	Bessette	Nellie M	1st cabin	307	21	Daniels	Sarah	1st cabin
128	23	Bjornstrom	Stefanson	1st cabin	310	157	Davidson	Orion Hays	1st cabin
130	79	Blank	Henry (Blauk)	1st cabin	314	190	Davies	Agnes	2nd cabin
131	75	Bonnell	Caroline	1st cabin	317	191	Davies	John M	2nd cabin
132	74	Bonnell	Elizabeth	1st cabin	321	208	Davis	Mary	2nd cabin
133	362	Borap	John	Steerage	322	413	Davidson	Mary	Steerage
139	342	Bolos	Martha (Monthia)	Steerage	325	431	Miessmacker	Anna	Steerage
145	126	Bowen	Grace Scott	1st cabin	326	430	Miessmacker	Giullaine (Wiessmacker)	Steerage
147	6	Bowerman	Elsie	1st cabin					
149	333	Bradley	Bridget	Steerage	327	454	De Mulder	Theodor	Steerage
150	128	Brayton	George A	1st cabin	331	396	Dean	Bertram	Steerage
163	262	Brown	Mildred	2nd cabin	332	397	Dean	Gladys	Steerage
166	199	Brown	Elizabeth C	2nd cabin	333	395	Dean	Ettie	Steerage
170	258	Dryhl	D, Miss	2nd cabin	334	232	Argenia	Genovese	2nd cabin

Typed List

Master List No	Old list No	Surname	First name(s)	Class
342	306	Dugennen	Jos	Steerage
343	327	Devaney	Mayoret (Margaret)	Steerage
345	133	Dick	Albert A	1st cabin
346	134	Dick	Vera	1st cabin
350	36	Dodge	Ruth V	1st cabin
351	35	Dodge	Washington	1st cabin
352	37	Dodge	Washington Jr	1st cabin
354	206	Doling	Ada	2nd cabin
355	207	Doling	Elsie	2nd cabin
358	457	Dorkings	Edw A	Steerage
359	116	Douglass	Mahla	1st cabin
360	162	Douglas	Helen Baxter	1st cabin
362	425	Dardell	Eliz	Steerage
366	249	Drew	Lula	2nd cabin
367	250	Drew	Marshall	2nd cabin
369	320	Driscoll	Bridget	Steerage
370	394	Drapkin	Jenie	Steerage
371	17	Duff-Gordon	Lady Lucy C	1st cabin
372	16	Duff-Gordon	Sir Cosmo E	1st cabin
374	228	Duran	Asunees	2nd cabin
375	229	Duran	Florentine	2nd cabin
378	427	Dyker	Eliz	Steerage
379	65	Earnshaw	Olive P	1st cabin
391	426	Emanuel	Ethel	Steerage
394	108	Endres	Caroline	1st cabin
396	135	Eustis	Elizabeth M	1st cabin
405	283	Daunthorpe	Lizzie	2nd cabin
408	442	Finoli	Luigi	Steerage
410	107	Flegenheim	Antoinette	1st cabin
416	138	Flymn	J Irwin	1st cabin
419	449	Cheang	Foo	Steerage
429	171	Fortune	Alice	1st cabin
431	172	Fortune	Ethel	1st cabin
432	173	Fortune	Mabel	1st cabin
434	170	Fortune	Mary	1st cabin
437	139	Francatelli	Mabel	1st cabin
440	50	Frauenthal	Clara	1st cabin
441	49	Frauenthal	Henry W	1st cabin
442	48	Frauenthal	Isaac G	1st cabin
443	9	Frobicher	Margaret	1st cabin
444	10	Frobicher	Margaret	1st cabin
445	8	Frobicher	Max (Frolicher)	1st cabin
450	78	Futrelle	Mary	1st cabin
455	259	Garside	Ethel	2nd cabin
461	99	Gibson	Dorothy	1st cabin
462	98	Gibson	Pauline C	1st cabin
463	149	Gieger	Amalie	1st cabin
472	461	Gallinigh	Kate	Steerage
474	314	Glynn	Mary	Steerage
475	33	Goldenberg	Nella	1st cabin
476	32	Goldenberg	Samuel	1st cabin
478	391	Goldsmith	Emily A	Steerage
480	392	Goldsmith	Frank	Steerage
490	130	Gracie	Col. Archibald	1st cabin
491	142	Graham	Edith	1st cabin
493	143	Graham	Margaret	1st cabin
496	105	Greenfield	Blanche	1st cabin
497	106	Greenfield	William B	1st cabin
509	418	Hokkaranen	Ellen	Steerage
512	248	Hamlin	Master Walter	2nd cabin
513	247	Hamlin	Anna	2nd cabin
516	335	Monbarck	Annie	Steerage
520	432	Hanson	Jenny	Steerage
522	30	Harder	Dorothy	1st cabin
523	29	Harder	George A	1st cabin
527	201	Harper	Annie	2nd cabin
528	120	Harper	Henry S	1st cabin
530	121	Harper	Myra H	1st cabin
532	245	Harris	Geo	2nd cabin
534	59	Harris	Rene W	1st cabin
538	197	Hart	Esther	2nd cabin
539	198	Hart	Eva	2nd cabin
542	147	Hamad	Hassab	1st cabin
544	148	Hawksford	Walter James	1st cabin
546	155	Hays	Clara G	1st cabin
547	66	Hays	Margaret B	1st cabin
550	438	Hedman	Oscar	Steerage
551	447	Lang	Hee	Steerage
553	300	Hakanen	Line	Steerage
555	293	Hillstrom	Hilda M	Steerage
559	271	Herman	Alice	2nd cabin
560	269	Herman	Jane	2nd cabin
561	270	Herman	Kitty	2nd cabin
563	256	Hewlett	Mary	2nd cabin
572	363	Hervonen	Hilda	Steerage
574	188	Hocking	Eliza	2nd cabin
575	189	Hocking	Mary	2nd cabin
580	251	Hold	Annie	2nd cabin
586	93	Holverson	Mary A	1st cabin
587	129	Haven	Horner	1st cabin
588	302	Hankenen	Elina	Steerage
591	281	Hosono	Masadami	2nd cabin
594	389	Howard	Mary	Steerage
595	80	Hoyt	Frederick	1st cabin
596	81	Hoyt	Jane	1st cabin
601	450	Hyman	Abraham	Steerage
602	166	Icard	Amelie	1st cabin
603	222	Ilett	Bertha	2nd cabin
608	11	Ismay	J Bruce	1st cabin
610	237	Jacobson	....	2nd cabin
612	443	Jelsevac	Ivan	Steerage
613	292	Jansson	Carl	Steerage
622	321	Jermyn	Annie	Steerage
623	246	Jerwan	Mary	2nd cabin
624	379	Johansson	Berendt	Steerage
631	416	Johanson	Oscar	Steerage
633	435	Johnson	Eleanore	Steerage
634	434	Johnson	Alice	Steerage
635	436	Johnson	Hawla	Steerage
644	377	Jonsson	Carl	Steerage
646	424	Joseph	Mary	Steerage
647	422	Joseph	Katherine	Steerage
648	423	Joseph	Mogel (Migel)	Steerage
650	305	Jonsela	Erch (Erik)	Steerage
655	194	Kuntor	Miriam	2nd cabin
658	388	Karlsson	Einar	Steerage
662	370	Karun	Franz	Steerage
663	371	Karun	Anna	Steerage
668	220	Kean	Norah	2nd cabin
672	315	Kelly	Annie	Steerage
673	266	Kelly	Lanery, Mrs	2nd cabin
675	322	Kelly	Mary	Steerage
676	463	Kennedy	John	Steerage
679	88	Kenyon	Marion	1st cabin
685	83	Kimball	Edwin N	1st cabin
686	84	Kimball	Gertrude P	1st cabin
687	367	Kuik	Anton	Steerage
688	368	Kuik	Louise	Steerage
689	369	Kuik	Louise	Steerage
700	404	Krikorian	Erich	Steerage
701	92	Koenchen	Emilie	1st cabin
709	444	Lam	Ah	Steerage
712	297	Landegren	Aurora	Steerage
714	446	Lang	Tang	Steerage
716	213	La Roche	Julie	2nd cabin

Who Sailed on Titanic?

Master List No	Old list No	Surname	First name(s)	Class	Master List No	Old list No	Surname	First name(s)	Class
717	215	La Roche	Eloise	2nd cabin	918	347	Nicola	Janile	Steerage
718	214	La Roche	Simon	2nd cabin	922	417	Nelson	Bertha	Steerage
724	86	Leader	Alice F	1st cabin	923	376	Nilsson	Helmeny	Steerage
725	358	Seni	Fabim (Zeeni)	Steerage	925	299	Niskaren	John	Steerage
731	196	Lehman	Bertha	2nd cabin	930	152	Draebstedt	Alfred	1st cabin
733	200	Leitch	Jessie	2nd cabin	932	180	Nye	Elizabeth	2nd cabin
735	240	Lemere	Amelia, Mrs	2nd cabin	933	375	Nysten	Anna	Steerage
743	18	Leroy	Bertha	1st cabin	935	318	O'Brien	Hannah	Steerage
745	3	Lesneur	Gustav	1st cabin	945	319	O'Dwyer	Nellie	Steerage
756	298	Lindgvist	Einar	Steerage	946	295	Otman	Vilm	Steerage
757	14	Lindstrom	Sigrid	1st cabin	947	467	O'Keefe	Patrick	Steerage
771	219	Louch	Alice	2nd cabin	948	309	O'Leary	Norah	Steerage
775	307	Lulu	Nicola	Steerage	950	437	Olsen	Arthur	Steerage
777	366	Lundin	Olga	Steerage	956	385	Johansson	Oscar L	Steerage
778	296	Lindstrom	Inre E	Steerage	958	19	Omond	Fernand	1st cabin
779	168	Lurette	Elise	1st cabin	964	308	Osman	Mara	Steerage
783	312	Madigan	Maggie	Steerage	966	42	Ostby	Helen	1st cabin
784	90	Madill	Georgette A	1st cabin	970	272	Oxenhan	D	2nd cabin
785	381	Frithjof	Mattsen	Steerage	971	224	Juhan	Padro	2nd cabin
796	216	Mallet	Antoine	2nd cabin	973	239	Pallaso	Emilio	2nd cabin
797	217	Mallet	Andrew	2nd cabin	999	5	Pears	Edith	1st cabin
798	359	Hannam	Memi	Steerage	1005	15	Pinasco	Josefa	1st cabin
801	317	Manion	Margt	Steerage	1010	154	Berrault	Annie	1st cabin
804	150	Marechal	Pierre	1st cabin	1011	387	Persson	Ernes	Steerage
808	145	Marvin	Mary	1st cabin	1020	167	Penchen	Arthur G	1st cabin
810	346	Fatnai	Musulman	Steerage	1021	193	Phillips	Alice	2nd cabin
816	163	De Villiers	Mayne	1st cabin	1023	289	Marshall	Kate	2nd cabin
818	466	McCarthy	Katie	Steerage	1024	221	Pinsky	Rosie	2nd cabin
820	326	McCormack	Thomas	Steerage	1029	226	Postalappi	Emilio	2nd cabin
821	329	McCoy	Agnes	Steerage	1031	64	Potter	Lily A	1st cabin
822	468	McCoy	Alice	Steerage	1033	276	Quick	Jane	2nd cabin
823	459	McCoy	Bernard	Steerage	1034	277	Quick	Phyllis	2nd cabin
826	316	McDermott	Delia	Steerage	1035	278	Quick	Winnifred	2nd cabin
828	97	McGough	James R	1st cabin	1043	284	Renouf	Lillie	2nd cabin
829	429	McGowan	Annie	Steerage	1046	230	Reinardo	Enearnacco	2nd cabin
831	464	McGovern	Mary	Steerage	1048	96	Rheims	George	1st cabin
839	279	Mellinger	E, Mrs	2nd cabin	1056	185	Richards	Emily	2nd cabin
840	280	Mellinger	Violet	2nd cabin	1057	186	Richards	George	2nd cabin
841	225	Mellon	Wm J	2nd cabin	1058	187	Richards	Willie	2nd cabin
847	94	Meyer	Leila S	1st cabin	1059	268	Ridsdale	Lucy	2nd cabin
848	380	Medtajo	Carl	Steerage	1063	334	Reardon	Hannah	Steerage
853	56	Minihan	Daisy	1st cabin	1067	89	Robert	Elizabeth W	1st cabin
854	55	Minihan	Lillian	1st cabin	1079	111	Rosenbaum	Edith L	1st cabin
861	110	Mock	Philip	1st cabin	1082	393	Roth	Sarah	Steerage
862	313	Mochlare	Ellen	Steerage	1083	140	Rothes	Noel	1st cabin
866	406	Ucoor	Beile	Steerage	1084	58	Rothschild	Lizzie	1st cabin
867	407	Ucoor	Nicires	Steerage	1088	209	Rugg	Emily	2nd cabin
870	311	Moran	Bertha	Steerage	1090	324	Ryan	Edwd	Steerage
877	386	Moss	Albert	Steerage	1093	124	Ryerson	Emily Bore Jr	1st cabin
878	336	Monbarck	Jurvis	Steerage	1094	122	Ryerson	Emely Bore	1st cabin
880	337	Monbarck	Halim	Steerage	1095	125	Ryerson	John B	1st cabin
885	462	Mullen	Kate	Steerage	1096	123	Ryerson	Susan P	1st cabin
886	420	Mulochill	Bertha	Steerage	1100	2	Saalfeld	Adolphe	1st cabin
888	332	Murphy	Kate	Steerage	1115	13	Segeserr	Emma	1st cabin
889	325	Murphy	Maggie	Steerage	1117	384	Salkjelsork	Anna	Steerage
890	465	Murphy	Norah	Steerage	1118	76	Soloman	Abram L	1st cabin
894	357	Vagib	Adele Nenie	Steerage	1123	372	Sandstrom	Agnes C	Steerage
895	352	Netkan	Marseom (Marsim)	Steerage	1124	374	Sandstrom	Beatrice	Steerage
					1125	373	Sandstrom	Margaret	Steerage
896	350	Netkan	Said	Steerage	1126	456	Sap	Jules	Steerage
897	351	Netkan	Wadai	Steerage	1130	20	Schabert	Emma	1st cabin
901	231	Nussa	Adel	2nd cabin	1131	455	Scheerlinch	Jan	Steerage
905	234	Hoffman	Lopes	2nd cabin	1135	25	Serraplar	Augusta	1st cabin
907	233	Hoffman	Lopo	2nd cabin	1142	310	Shine	Ellen	Steerage
911	44	Newell	Madeleine	1st cabin	1144	144	Shutes	Elizabeth	1st cabin
912	45	Newell	Marjory	1st cabin	1145	211	Silven	Louise	2nd cabin
913	103	Newson	Helen M	1st cabin	1146	34	Silvethorne	Spencer V	1st cabin
917	348	Nicola	Elias	Steerage	1147	169	Silvey	Alice M	1st cabin

Typed List

Master List No	Old list No	Surname	First name(s)	Class	Master List No	Old list No	Surname	First name(s)	Class
1150	153	Simonnis	Alfons	1st cabin	1259	345	Daranarch	Maroam (Mariam)	Steerage
1151	192	Sincock	Maud (Niece)	2nd cabin	1261	410	Trembiskey	Berk	Steerage
1152	223	Simpferen	Anna	2nd cabin	1263	242	Trout	Jessie, Mrs	2nd cabin
1157	364	Sjoblom	Anna	Steerage	1264	238	Trout	Edwin	2nd cabin
1167	159	Slayter	Hilda	1st cabin	1265	63	Tucker	Gilbert M Jr	1st cabin
1170	100	Sloper	William P	1st cabin	1267	301	Turger	Anna	Steerage
1176	265	Smith	Marion	2nd cabin	1268	303	Turkula	Heveg	Steerage
1177	62	Smith	Elouise	1st cabin	1273	22	Valentine	Augusta	1st cabin
1180	331	Smyth	Julia	Steerage	1290	405	Fartaman	David	Steerage
1181	27	Snder/Shyder	John	1st cabin	1296	260	Walcroft	Nellie	2nd cabin
1182	28	Snyder/Shyder	Nell	1st cabin	1298	40	Ward	Annie	1st cabin
1187	67	Spedden	Frederick O	1st cabin	1299	218	Ware	Florence	2nd cabin
1188	68	Spedden	Margaretta C	1st cabin	1303	43	Warren	Anna	1st cabin
1189	69	Spedden	Robert D	1st cabin	1307	202	Watt	Bessie	2nd cabin
1190	46	Spencer	Eugenie	1st cabin	1308	203	Watt	Bertha?	2nd cabin
1193	151	Stachelin	Max	1st cabin	1310	263	Webber	Susie	2nd cabin
1196	400	Stanley	Amy	Steerage	1313	212	Weiz	Mathild	2nd cabin
1200	54	Stengel	Annie M	1st cabin	1314	182	Wells	Addie	2nd cabin
1201	53	Stengel	C E Henry	1st cabin	1315	184	Wells	Joan	2nd cabin
1202	136	Stephenson	Martha E	1st cabin	1316	183	Wells	Ralph	2nd cabin
1210	304	Stranden	Juho	Steerage	1317	286	West	Ada Mary	2nd cabin
1216	458	Sunderland	Victor	Steerage	1318	288	West	Barbara	2nd cabin
1217	415	Sundman	Johan	Steerage	1319	287	West	Constance	2nd cabin
1223	403	Swenson	Servina	Steerage	1321	360	Jousef	Shanien	Steerage
1227	87	Swift	Margaret B	1st cabin	1324	61	White	Ella H	1st cabin
1231	131	Taylor	Elmer Z	1st cabin	1328	73	Wick	Mary N	1st cabin
1232	132	Taylor	Juliet C	1st cabin	1329	72	Wick	Mary H	1st cabin
1234	291	Gunner	Trylen	Steerage	1331	141	Widener	Eleanor E	1st cabin
1236	118	Thayer	John B Jr	1st cabin	1336	257	Whilems	Charles	2nd cabin
1237	127	Thayer	Marion	1st cabin	1337	428	Wilkes	Ellen	Steerage
1239	341	Scunda	Assid	Steerage	1340	119	Willard	Carstairs	1st cabin
1243	340	Scunda	Tamiun	Steerage	1344	285	Williams	Charles	2nd cabin
1245	41	Thorne	Gertrude	1st cabin	1347	117	Williams	Rich'd Norris	1st cabin
1246	409	Thomeycroft	Florence	Steerage	1350	71	Wilson	H Alice	1st cabin
1252	267	Toomey	Ellen	2nd cabin	1360	24	Woolmer	Hugh	1st cabin
1255	433	Tuonquist	Wm H	Steerage	1362	204	Wright	Marion	2nd cabin
1257	344	Daranarch	George	Steerage	1364	349	Yazleick	Salany	Steerage
1258	343	Daranarch	Hanni	Steerage					

Senate Inquiry Exhibit B

Master No	Old No	Passenger's Name	First Name(s)	Title	Class	European Address/Notes	American Address/Notes
1	601	Abbing	Anthony		3rd Class British, Soton		
2	598	Abbot	Eugene		3rd Class British, Soton		Going to Providence, RI
3	599	Abbot	Rosa		3rd Class British, Soton		Going to Providence, RI
4	600	Abbot	Rossmore		3rd Class British, Soton		Going to Providence, RI
5	780	Abelseth	Karen		3rd Class Scan & Cont- Soton		going to Los Angeles, Cal
6	781	Abelsett	Olai		3rd Class Scan & Cont- Soton		going to Minneapolis
7	323	Abelson	Hanna	Mrs	2		Hebrew Shelter and Emigrant Aid Society, 229 East Broadway, New York City
8	324	Abelson	Samson	Mr	2		Hebrew Shelter and Emigrant Aid Society, 229 East Broadway, New York City
9	782	Abrahamson	August		3rd Class Scan & Cont- Soton		
10	1126	Joseph	Mary		3rd Class Cherbourg		
11	841	Dahl	Mauritz		3rd Class Scan & Cont- Soton		
12	602	Adams	J		3rd Class British, Soton		
13	784	Ahlin	Johanna		3rd Class Scan & Cont- Soton		going to Chicago, Ill
14	785	Ahmed	Ali		3rd Class Scan & Cont- Soton		
15	603	Aks	Filly		3rd Class British, Soton		Care of Carrie Greene, 131 College Place, Norfolk, Va
16	604	Aks	Leah		3rd Class British, Soton		Care of Carrie Greene, 131 College Place, Norfolk, Va
17	1108	Cassim	Nassef		3rd Class Cherbourg		going to Fredericksburg, Va
18	523	Oldworth	William	Mr	2	Chauffeur to Mr Carter, first class passenger	
19	605	Alexander	William		3rd Class British, Soton		to Albion, NY
20	786	Alhomaki	Ilmari		3rd Class Scan & Cont- Soton		
21	787	Ali	William		3rd Class Scan & Cont- Soton		
22	1	Allen	Elizabeth Walton	Miss	3rd Class British, Soton	4 South Terrace, Littlehampton	4140 Pendell Boulevard, St Louis Mo
23	606	Allen	William		3rd Class British, Soton		
24	2	Allison	H J	Mr	1	152 Abbey Rd, West Hampstead, London	Montreal, Quebec
25	5	Allison		Miss	1	152 Abbey Rd, West Hampstead, London	Montreal, Quebec
26	3	Allison	H J	Mrs	1	152 Abbey Rd, West Hampstead, London	Montreal, Quebec
27	6	Allison		Master	1	152 Abbey Rd, West Hampstead, London	Montreal, Quebec
28	607	Allum	Owen G		3rd Class British, Soton		to New York City, (father)
29	790	Anderson	Albert		3rd Class Scan & Cont- Soton		
30	795	Anderson	Carla		3rd Class Scan & Cont- Soton		returned on steamship Adriatic, second class
31	8	Anderson	Harry	Mr	1	Waldorf Hotel, London	
32	788	Anderson	Alfreda		3rd Class Scan & Cont- Soton		
33	791	Anderson	Anders		3rd Class Scan & Cont- Soton		
34	1080	Wennerstrom	August		3rd Class Scan & Cont- Soton		going to 7041 Center Avenue, Chicago, Ill

Master No	Old No	Passenger's Name	First Name(s)	Title	Class	European Address/Notes	American Address/Notes
35	797	Anderson	Ebba (child)		3rd Class Scan & Cont- Soton		
36	799	Anderson	Ellis		3rd Class Scan & Cont- Soton		
37	789	Anderson	Erna		3rd Class Scan & Cont- Soton		
38	800	Andersson	Ida		3rd Class Scan & Cont- Soton		
39	796	Anderson	Ingeborg (child)		3rd Class Scan & Cont- Soton		
40	792	Anderson	Samuel		3rd Class Scan & Cont- Soton		
41	793	Anderson	Sigrid (child)		3rd Class Scan & Cont- Soton		
42	798	Anderson	Sigvard (child)		3rd Class Scan & Cont- Soton		
43	801	Andreason	Paul		3rd Class Scan & Cont- Soton		
44	328	Andrew	Frank	Mr	2		Brother is S Alfredo Andrew, New York Ship Building Co, Camden, NJ
45	325	Andrew	Edgar	Edgar	2		
46	9	Andrews	Cornelia I	Miss	1		With sister, 212 East Forty-sixth Street, New York City
47	10	Andrews	Thomas	Mr	1	Care of Harland & Wolff, Belfast	
48	802	Angheloff	Minko		3rd Class Scan & Cont- Soton		
49	326	Angle	W	Mrs	2	1 Mill Street, Warwick, England	
50	327	Angle		Mr	2		
51	11	Appleton	E D	Mrs	1		
52	810	Arnold	Josef		3rd Class Scan & Cont- Soton		
53	811	Arnold	Josephine		3rd Class Scan & Cont- Soton		
54	812	Aronson	Ernest		3rd Class Scan & Cont- Soton		
55	12	Artagaveytia	Ramon	Mr	1		Care of E Metz Green, Consul Uruguay, New York
56	329	Ashby	John	Mr	2		Wife is 517 Synnes Street, West Hoboken, NJ
57	813	Asim	Adola		3rd Class Scan & Cont- Soton		Going to Worcester, Mass
58	803	Asplund	Carl (child)		3rd Class Scan & Cont- Soton		Going to Worcester, Mass
59	804	Asplund	Charles		3rd Class Scan & Cont- Soton		Going to Worcester, Mass
60	806	Asplund	Gustaf (child)		3rd Class Scan & Cont- Soton		Going to Worcester, Mass
61	805	Asplund	Felix (child)		3rd Class Scan & Cont- Soton		Going to Worcester, Mass
62	808	Asplund	Oscar (child)		3rd Class Scan & Cont- Soton		going to friend, Mrs A Engstrom, 212 Fifty-third Street, Brooklyn
63	814	Asplund	Johan		3rd Class Scan & Cont- Soton		Going to Worcester, Mass
64	807	Asplund	Lillian (child)		3rd Class Scan & Cont- Soton		
65	809	Asplund	Selma		3rd Class Scan & Cont- Soton		
66	1118	Gerios	Assaf		3rd Class Cherbourg		
67	1090	Assof	Marian		3rd Class Cherbourg		going to Ottawa, Ontario
68	815	Assam	Ali		3rd Class Scan & Cont- Soton		
69	13	Astor	J J	Col	1		840 5th Avenue, New York City
70	15	Astor	J J	Mrs	1		840 5th Avenue, New York City
71	1167	Steinman	Attalla		3rd Class Cherbourg		
72	17	Aubert	N	Mrs	1		17 Le Seuer Street, Paris
73	816	Augustsan	Albert		3rd Class Scan & Cont- Soton		
74	1099	Banoura	Ayont		3rd Class Cherbourg	going to Youngstown, Ohio	

Master No	Old No	Passenger's Name	First Name(s)	Title	Class	European Address/Notes	American Address/Notes
75	1157	Roufoul	Baccos		3rd Class Cherbourg		
76	817	Backstrom	Karl		3rd Class Scan & Cont- Soton		
77	818	Backstrom	Marie		3rd Class Scan & Cont- Soton	Going back to Finland	
78	1096	Bachini	Eugene		3rd Class Cherbourg	Going to father in New York City	
79	1097	Bachini	Helene		3rd Class Cherbourg	Going to father in New York City	
80	1094	Bachini	Latifa		3rd Class Cherbourg	Going to father in New York City	
81	1095	Bachini	Marie		3rd Class Cherbourg	Going to father in New York City	
82	608	Badman	Emily		3rd Class British, Soton	going to Skaneateles, NY	
83	1098	Badt	Mohamed		3rd Class Cherbourg		
84	330	Bailey	Percy	Mr	2	26 Gwavas Street, Penzance, Cornwall or care of Harry Lutey, 1024 Hefferson Avenue, Akron, Ohio	
85	332	Bambridge	Chas P	Mr	2		
86	819	Balkic	Cerin		3rd Class Scan & Cont- Soton	227 West 125th Street, thence to Jacksonville, Fla	
87	331	Balls	Ada E	Mrs	2	Brother is in Houghton, Mich	
88	333	Banfield	Catherine	Mr	2	20 Grenville Road, Plymouth, England.	
89	1092	Babara	Saude		3rd Class Cherbourg		
90	1093	Babara			3rd Class Cherbourg		
91	64	Cavendish	Maid		1	23 Chesham Place, London	Care of Simpson Crawford Co, New York City
92	19	Barkworth	A H	Mr	1	Tranby House, Hessle, East York	
93	1190	Barry	Julia		3rd Class Queenstown		
94	609	Barton	David		3rd Class British, Soton		
95	334	Bateman	Robert J	Mr	2		
96	20	Baumann	J	Mr	1		
97	21	Baxter	James	Mrs	1		Montreal, Quebec
98	22	Baxter	Quigg	Mr	1		Montreal, Quebec
99	44	Bucknell	Maid		1		
100	335	Beane	Edward	Mr	2		
101	336	Beane	Ethel	Mrs	2		
102	23	Beattie	T	Mr	2		
103	337	Beauchamp	H J	Mr	2		
104	610	Beavan	W T	Mr	3rd Class British, Soton		Care of Mr Morgan, 66 Leonard Street, New York
105	339	Becker	Marion Louise	Miss	2		Care of Thos Cook & Son, Bombay, or Benton Harbor, Mich, or until May 18, Lancaster, Ohio
106	338	Becker	A O	Mrs	2		Care of Thos Cook & Son, Bombay, or Benton Harbor, Mich, or until May 18, Lancaster, Ohio
107	340	Becker	Richard	Master	2		Care of Thos Cook & Son, Bombay, or Benton Harbor, Mich, or until May 18, Lancaster, Ohio
108	341	Becker	Ruth Elizabeth	Miss	2		Care of Thos Cook & Son, Bombay, or Benton Harbor, Mich, or until May 18, Lancaster, Ohio
109	24	Beckwith	R L	Mr	1		Care of McKean, Brewster & Morgan, 40 Wall Street, New York
110	25	Beckwith	R L	Mrs	1		Care of McKean, Brewster & Morgan, 40 Wall Street, New York

Master No	Old No	Passenger's Name	First Name(s)	Title	Class	European Address/Notes	American Address/Notes
111	342	Beesley	L	Mr	2		4 Tetchfield Terrace, London NW, or care Cornell Club, New York City
112	26	Behr	K H	Mr	2		40 Wall Street, New York
113	820	Benson	John		3rd Class Scan & Cont- Soton		
114	343	Bentham	Lilian W	Miss	2		11 Kay Terrace, Rochester, New York
115	821	Berglund	Ivar		3rd Class Scan & Cont- Soton		
116	344	Berreman	W S	Mr	2		
117	1165	Seman	Betros		3rd Class Cherbourg		
118	1100	Bexros	Tannons		3rd Class Cherbourg		
119	16	Astor	Maid		1		840 5th Avenue, New York City
120	614	Bing	Lee		3rd Class British, Soton		
121	283	Straus	Maid		1		
122	822	Berklund	Hans		3rd Class Scan & Cont- Soton		
123	167	Jakob	Birnbaum	Mr	1	11 Rue Membling, Antwerp	
124	27	Bishop	D H	Mr	1		
125	28	Bishop	D H	Mrs	1		
126	307	White	Maid		1		Waldorf-Astoria, New York City
127	823	Bjorkland	Ernst		3rd Class Scan & Cont- Soton		
128	29	Bjornstrom	H Steffenson	Mr	1	See end list	
129	30	Blackwell	Stephen Weart	Mr	1	Brown, Shipley & Co, Son	167 West State Street, Trenton, NJ
130	31	Blank	Henry	Mr	1		Care of Whiteside & Blank, Newark, NJ
131	32	Bonnell	Caroline	Miss	1		Youngstown, Ohio
132	33	Bonnell	Lily	Miss	1		
133	34	Borebank	J J	Mr	1	Carlton Hotel, London	Lodges of the World, Winnipeg
134	824	Bostandyeff	Guentcho	Mr	3rd Class Scan & Cont- Soton		
135	345	Botsford	W H	Mr	2	Care of Thos Cook & Son, London, or father is William B Botsford, 402 West Fifth Street,	Elmira, New York
136	1104	Boulos	Akar		3rd Class Cherbourg		
137	1101	Bontos	Hanna		3rd Class Cherbourg		going to Troy, NY
138	1103	Boulos	Menthora		3rd Class Cherbourg		
139	1102	Boulos	Sultani		3rd Class Cherbourg		
140	1194	Bourke	Cath		3rd Class Queenstown		Going to Ellen Hugh, 66 Ruby Street, Chicago, Ill
141	1193	Bourke	John		3rd Class Queenstown		Going to Ellen Hugh, 66 Ruby Street, Chicago, Ill
142	1197	Burke	Mary		3rd Class Queenstown		going to Ellen Hugh, 66 Ruby Street, Chicago, Ill
143	615	Bowen	David		3rd Class British, Soton		
144	35	Bowen	Solomon	Miss	1		Care of A D Britton, 189 Montague St, Brooklyn, NY
145	346	Bowenur	Elsie	Mr	2	General Post Office, London	
146	36	Bowerman	Jas H	Miss	2	Thorncliff, St Leonards on Sea	
147	347	Bracker	Bridget	Mr	2		
148	1191	Bradley	George		3rd Class Queenstown		
149	39	Brayton	John B	Mr	1	Hotel Metropole, London	Union Trust Building, Los Angeles, Calif
150	37	Brady	Elin	Mr	1		Care of Miss E M Brady, Hotel Wellington, New York City
151	825	Braf			3rd Class Scan & Cont- Soton		

Master No	Old No	Passenger's Name	First Name(s)	Title	Class	European Address/Notes	American Address/Notes
155	38	Brandeis	E	Mr	1		Omaha, Nebr
156	616	Braund	Lewis		3rd Class British, Soton		going to Saskatoon, Canada
157	617	Braund	Owen		3rd Class British, Soton		going to Saskatoon, Canada
158	40	Brewe	Arthur Jackson	Dr	1		
160	348	Brito	Jose de	Mr	2		
161	826	Brobek	Carl		3rd Class Scan & Cont- Soton		
162	618	Brocklebank	William		3rd Class British, Soton		
163	351	Brown	Mildred	Miss	2	152 Abbey Road, London NW	Denver, Colo
164	42	Brown	J M	Mrs	1		
165	349	Brown	E	Miss	2		
166	350	Brown	E C	Mrs	2		Denver, Colo
167	41	Brown	J J	Mrs	1		
168	352	Brown	S	Mr	2		
170	354	Bryhl	Dagmar	Miss	2	Care Oscar Lustig, 511 Pearl Street, Rockford, Ill.; returned to Gothenburg, steamship Baltic, May 9	
171	353	Bryhl	Curt	Mr	2	Brother of Dagmar Bryhl, who survived and returned to Gothenburg, Sweden, on Baltic, May 9.	
172	1192	Buckley	Daniel		3rd Class Queenstown		Going to friends in New York City
173	1195	Buckley	Kath		3rd Class Queenstown		going to Marg Buckley, 71 Mount View Street, Roxbury, Mass
174	43	Bucknell	W	Mrs	1		going to Mrs Burns, 41 Washington Street, Charleston, Mass
175	1196	Burke	Jeremiah		3rd Class Queenstown		Morristown, NJ
176	266	Spedden	Nurse		1		
177	1198	Burns	Mary		1		
178	357	Buss	Kate	Miss	2		Care of Reverend Dalziel, Belmore, L I, thence to San Diego, Cal
179	358	Butler	Reginald	Mr	2		
180	45	Butt	Archibald W	Maj	1		Care of Lewis F Butt, Augusta, Ga
181	355	Byles	T R D	Rev	2		
182	356	Bystrom	Carolina	Mrs	2		1991 Lexington Avenue, New York City
183	827	Cacic	Gego	Mr	3rd Class Scan & Cont- Soton		
184	828	Cacic	Luka		3rd Class Scan & Cont- Soton		
185	830	Calic	Manda		3rd Class Scan & Cont- Soton		
186	829	Cacic	Maria		3rd Class Scan & Cont- Soton		
188	46	Calderhead	E P	Mr	1		Gimbel Bros, New York City
189	359	Caldwell	Albert Francis	Mr	2	2 Upper Montague Street, London, England	
190	360	Caldwell	Alden G	Master	2	2 Upper Montague Street, London, England	
191	361	Caldwell	Sylvia M	Mrs	2	2 Upper Montague Street, London, England	
192	831	Calic	Peter		3rd Class Scan & Cont- Soton		
193	362	Cameron	Clear	Miss	2	Mamaroneck, Conn (?)	
194	363	Campbell	William	Mr	2	Care of Harland & Wolf, Belfast, Ireland	
195	1199	Canavan	Mary		3rd Class Queenstown		
196	1200	Canavan	Pat		3rd Class Queenstown		to sister K Canavan, 1512 Diamond Street, Philadelphia

Master No	Old No	Passenger's Name	First Name(s)	Title	Class	European Address/Notes	American Address/Notes
197	47	Cardell	Churchill	Mrs	1		to P Mullarkey, 7 Hamilton Street, Hartford, Conn
198	619	Cann	Ernest		3rd Class Cherbourg		
199	1106	Caram	Joseph		3rd Class Cherbourg		Care of A Metz Green, consul for Uruguay, New York City
200	1107	Caram	Maria		3rd Class Cherbourg		Care of A Metz Green, consul for Uruguay, New York City
201	364	Carbines	W	Mr	2		
202	48	Cardeza	J W M	Mr	1		
203	50	Cardeza	T D M	Mrs	1		
204	662	Garfirth	John	Mr	3rd Class British, Soton		
205	52	Carlson	Frank	Mr	1		
206	834	Carlsson	August		3rd Class Scan & Cont- Soton		
207	832	Carlson	Carl		3rd Class Scan & Cont- Soton		
208	1202	Car	Jeannie		3rd Class Queenstown		
209	53	Carran	F M	Mr	1		
210	54	Carran	J P	Mr	1		
211	367	Carver	E C	Mrs	2		
212	368	Carver	E C	Rev	2		
213	58	Carter	Lucile	Miss	1		Philadelphia, Pa, Attorneys Winthrop & Stimson, 32 Liberty Street, New York City
214	55	Carter	William E	Mr	1		Philadelphia, Pa, Attorneys Winthrop & Stimson, 32 Liberty Street, New York City
215	56	Carter	William E	Mrs	1		Philadelphia, Pa, Attorneys Winthrop & Stimson, 32 Liberty Street, New York City
216	59	Carter	William T	Master	1		Philadelphia, Pa, Attorneys Winthrop & Stimson, 32 Liberty Street, New York City
217	620	Carver	A	Mr	3rd Class British, Soton	Vaccuum Oil Co, London	
218	60	Case	Howard B	Mr	1		Care of Standard Oil Co, Rochester, NY
219	61	Cassebeer	H A	Mrs	1	50 Rue Vaneau, Paris	
220	62	Cavendish	T W	Mrs	1	23 Chesham Place, London	Care of Simpson Crawford Co, New York City
221	63	Cavendish	T W	Mr	1	23 Chesham Place, London	Care of Simpson Crawford Co, New York City
222	621	Celotti	Francesco		3rd Class British, Soton		
223	66	Chaffee	Herbert F	Mrs	1		Amenia, N Dak
224	65	Chaffee	Herbert	Mr	1		Amenia, N Dak
225	67	Chambers	N C	Mr	1	Royal Mail S P Co, London	Care of W Bruce Cobb, 49 Wall Street,, New York City
226	68	Chambers	N C	Mrs	1	Royal Mail S P Co, London	Care of W Bruce Cobb, 49 Wall Street,, New York City
227	369	Chapman	C	Mr	2	McWheelers, West Droyton, England	
228	370	Chapman	D H	Mr	2	Care of George & George, Leskeard, England	
229	371	Chapman	D H	Mrs	2	Care of George & George, Leskeard, England	
230	1203	Chartens	David		3rd Class Queenstown		going to David Vance, 310 West One hundred and eighth Street, New York
231	241	Ryerson	Maid		1		
232	69	Cherry	Gladys	Miss	1	96 Avenue des Terres, Paris	Care of G S O'Loughlin, 31 Nassau Street, New York City
233	70	Chevre	Paul	Mr	1		Care of E H Fallows, 30 Church Street, New York City

Master No	Old No	Passenger's Name	First Name(s)	Title	Class	European Address/Notes	American Address/Notes
234	71	Chibnall	E M Bowerman	Mrs	1		
235	622	Chip	Chang		1		joining steamship Anetta, Donald Steamship Co
236	72	Chisholm	Robert	Mr	3rd Class British, Soton		
237	623	Christmann	Emil		3rd Class British, Soton		
238	372	Christy	Alice	Mrs	2	Returned to England, Megantic, May 11	
239	373	Christy	Julie	Miss	2	Returned to England, Megantic, May 11	
240	1111	Chronopoulos	Aspostoles		3rd Class Cherbourg		
241	1112	Chronopoulos	Demetris		3rd Class Cherbourg		
242	374	Clarke	Ada Maria	Mrs	2	Returned to England, Celtic, April 25	
243	375	Clarke	Charles V	Mr	2	Colaba-Grange Lane, Netley Abbey, England	
244	73	Clark	Walter M	Mrs	1		Care of Hon W A Clark, 20 Exchange Place, New York
245	74	Clark	Walter M	Mr	1		Care of Hon W A Clark, 20 Exchange Place, New York
247	7	Allison	Nurse	Miss	1		
248	75	Clifford	George Quincy	Mr	1	152 Abbey Rd, West Hampstead, London	Montreal, Quebec
249	835	Coelho	Domingo		3rd Class Scan & Cont- Soton		
250	624	Cohen	Gurshon	Mr	3rd Class British, Soton		
251	1204	Colbert	Patrick	Mr	3rd Class Queenstown		going to an uncle in Brooklyn, NY
252	836	Coleff	Peyo		3rd Class Scan & Cont- Soton		going to Rev Brother Christopher, Sherbrooke, Quebec
253	837	Coleff	Sotio		3rd Class Scan & Cont- Soton		
254	376	Coleridge	R C	Mr	2		
255	377	Collander	Erik	Mr	2	232 Strand, London, W C	Finska, A A
256	378	Collett	Stewart	Mr	2		Care of M E Collett, Port Byron, New York
257	76	Colley	E P	Mr	1	Farmagh, Rathgar, Dublin	Care of Mrs K R Burr, 451 Lexington Ave, NYC
259	379	Collyer	Charlotte	Mrs	2	Mount Hill, Bosingstoke, Hants, England,	or Payette, Idaho
260	380	Collyer	Harvey	Mr	2	Do	
261	381	Collyer	Majorie	Miss	2	Do	
262	79	Compton	A T Jr	Mr	1		Lakewood House, Lakewood, New Jersey
263	77	Compton	A T	Mrs	1		Lakewood House, Lakewood, New Jersey
264	78	Compton	S R	Miss	1		Lakewood House, Lakewood, New Jersey
265	1206	Conlin	Thos H	Mr	3rd Class Queenstown		going to Rosa Conlin, 2238 Fairhill Street, Philadelphia
266	1207	Connaghton	Michel	Mr	3rd Class Queenstown		going to Mrs Horan, 965 De Kalb Avenue, Brooklyn
267	1208	Connolly	Kate	Mrs	3rd Class Queenstown		
268	1205	Conolly	Kate	Miss	3rd Class Queenstown		
269	1209	Connors	Pat	Mr	3rd Class Queenstown		going to J Bunbury, Dobbs Ferry
270	625	Cook	Jacob		3rd Class British, Soton		
271	550	Rogers	Selena	Miss	2		Care of Mrs Bower, 4 East Eighty-ninth Street, New York City
272	838	Cor	Bartol		3rd Class Scan & Cont- Soton		
273	839	Cor	Ivan		3rd Class Scan & Cont- Soton		
274	840	Cor	Ludvik		3rd Class Scan & Cont- Soton		
275	382	Corbett	Irene C	Mrs	2	General Lying-In Hospital, York Road, London	
276	383	Corey	P C	Mrs	2		

Master No	Old No	Passenger's Name	First Name(s)	Title	Class	European Address/Notes	American Address/Notes
277	626	Corn	Harry		3rd Class British, Soton		going to Honer Carr, 38 East Seventy-fifth Street, New York
278	80	Cornell	R C	Mrs	1		
279	1201	Car	Ellen		3rd Class Queenstown		
280	384	Cotterill	Harry	Mr	2	26 Adelaide Street, Penzance, England, or care of Mrs Richards, 457 Rhodes Avenue, Akron, Ohio	
281	629	Coutts	Leslie (child)		3rd Class British, Soton		Going to husband and father in New York
282	628	Coutts	William (child)		3rd Class British, Soton		Going to husband and father in New York
283	627	Coutts	Winnie		3rd Class British, Soton		Going to husband and father in New York
284	630	Coxon	Daniel		3rd Class British, Soton		
285	81	Crafton	John B	Mr	1		Care of H R Crafton, Roachdale, Ind
287	631	Crease	Ernest J		3rd Class British, Soton		going to Cleveland, Ohio
288	632	Cribb	John		3rd Class British, Soton	Victoria Hotel, London	
289	633	Cribb	Alice		3rd Class British, Soton		
290	82	Crosby	Edward G	Mrs	1	Grand Trunk Ry, London SW	Transportation Co, Milwaukee, Wis
291	83	Crosby	Edward G	Mr	1	Grand Trunk Ry, London SW	Transportation Co, Milwaukee, Wis
292	84	Crosby	Harriet	Miss	1	Grand Trunk Ry, London SW	Transportation Co, Milwaukee, Wis
293	85	Cummings	John Bradley	Mrs	1		Care of Hervey, Barber & McKee, 30 Nassau Street, New York
294	86	Cummings	John Bradley	Mr	1	Care of Harland & Wolf, Belfast, Ireland	Care of Hervey, Barber & McKee, 30 Nassau Street, New York
295	385	Cunningham	Alf	Mr	2		
296	1166	Shedid	Daher		3rd Class Cherbourg		going to Fingal, N Dak
297	634	Dahl	Charles		3rd Class British, Soton		Going to Chicago, Ill
298	842	Dahlberg	Gerda		3rd Class Scan & Cont- Soton		
299	843	Dakic	Brankko		3rd Class Scan & Cont- Soton		going to E G Schuktze, 477 Avenue E, Brooklyn, NY
300	1211	Daly	Eugene		3rd Class Queenstown		going to friends at 356 East One hundred and fifty-seventh Street, New York City
301	1210	Daly	Marcella		3rd Class Queenstown		
302	87	Daly	P D	Mr	1		Care of Curtis, Mallet, Prevost & Colt, 30 Broad Street, New York City
303	846	Danbom	Sigrid		3rd Class Scan & Cont- Soton		
304	844	Danbom	Ernest		3rd Class Scan & Cont- Soton		
305	845	Danbom	Gilbert (infant)		3rd Class Scan & Cont- Soton		
306	88	Daniel	Robert W	Mr	1	152 Abbey Rd, West Hampstead, London	328 Chestnut Street, Philadelphia, Pa
307	4	Allison	Maid		1		Montreal, Quebec
308	847	Danoff	Yoto		3rd Class Scan & Cont- Soton		
309	848	Dantchoff	Christo		3rd Class Scan & Cont- Soton		Care of Mr Sparling, Grand Trunk Ry, 200 Broadway, New York City
310	89	Davidson	Thornton	Mrs	1		
311	90	Davidson	Thornton	Mr	1		Care of Mr Sparling, Grand Trunk Ry, 200 Broadway, New York City
312	636	Davies	Alfred		3rd Class British, Soton		

Master No	Old No	Passenger's Name	First Name(s)	Title	Class	European Address/Notes	American Address/Notes
313	389	Davies	Charles	Mr	2		Mohawk, Mich
314	386	Davis	Agnes	Mrs	2		
315	635	Davies	Evan		3rd Class British, Soton		
317	637	Davies	John		3rd Class British, Soton		
318	387	Davis	John M	MasterS			Do
319	638	Davis	Joseph		3rd Class British, Soton	2	
321	388	Davis	M	Miss		29 Fleet Lane, New Gate, London	
322	640	Davison	Mary		3rd Class British, Soton		going to H J Finck, Bedford, Ontario
323	639	Davison	Thomas		3rd Class British, Soton		
325	850	De Messemacker	Emma		3rd Class Scan & Cont- Soton		Going to Tampico, Mont
326	851	De Messemacker	Guillaume		3rd Class Scan & Cont- Soton		Going to Tampico, Mont
327	852	De Mulder	Theo		3rd Class Scan & Cont- Soton		going to e De Clerck, 33 Lessine Street, Detroit
328	1014	Pelsmaker	Alfons de		3rd Class Scan & Cont- Soton		
329	391	Deacon	Percy	Mr	2		
330	641	Dean	Bertram		3rd Class British, Soton	Going to Hume, Mo, but returned steamship Adriatic, May 2	
331	643	Dean	Bertram (child)		3rd Class British, Soton	Going to Hume, Mo, but returned steamship Adriatic, May 2	
332	644	Dean	Vera (infant)		3rd Class British, Soton	Going to Hume, Mo, but returned steamship Adriatic, May 2	
333	642	Dean	Hetty		3rd Class British, Soton	Going to Hume, Mo, but returned steamship Adriatic, May 2	
334	365	Carlo	Sebastiani de	Mrs		Care Branchini, Lucco, Italy	
335	366	Carlo	Sebastiani de	Mr	2	Returned to Italy on Cretie, May 18	
336	849	Delalic	Regzo		3rd Class Scan & Cont- Soton		
337	959	Marinko	Dimitri		3rd Class Scan & Cont- Soton		
338	394	Denbury	Herbert	Mr	2		
339	853	Denkoff	Mitto		3rd Class Scan & Cont- Soton		
340	645	Dennis	Samuel		3rd Class British, Soton		
341	646	Dennis	William		3rd Class British, Soton		
342	650	Dugemin	Joseph		3rd Class British, Soton		
343	1212	Devaney	Margareth		3rd Class Queenstown		going to Albion, NY
344	392	Debsen	William	Mr	2		going to brother in New York
345	92	Dick	A A	Mr	1	Care of Dean & Dawson, Hotel Cecil, London Calgary, Alberta	
346	93	Dick	A A	Mrs	1	Care of Dean & Dawson, Hotel Cecil, London Calgary, Alberta	
347	965	Mirko	Dika		3rd Class Scan & Cont- Soton		
348	854	Dimic	Jovan		3rd Class Scan & Cont- Soton		
349	855	Dintcheff	Valtcho		3rd Class Scan & Cont- Soton		
350	94	Dodge	Washington	Mr	1		San Francisco, Cal: attorney, Nathan Urdaver, 116 Nassau Street, New York City
351	95	Dodge	Washington	Mrs	1		San Francisco, Cal: attorney, Nathan Urdaver, 116 Nassau Street, New York City
352	96	Dodge	Washington	Master	1		San Francisco, Cal: attorney, Nathan Urdaver, 116 Nassau Street, New York City
353	1170	Tannans	Draper		3rd Class Cherbourg		
354	395	Doling	Ada J	Mrs	2	Canute Road, Southampton, England. Returned to England Philadelphia, May 11	

Master No	Old No	Passenger's Name	First Name(s)	Title	Class	European Address/Notes	American Address/Notes
355	396	Doling	Elsie	Miss	2	Canute Road, Southampton, England. Returned to England Philadelphia, May 11	
356	1281	O'Donaghue	Bert		3rd Class Queenstown		
357	1214	Dooley	Patrick		3rd Class Queenstown		going to R Dooley, 142 East Thirty-first Street, New York
358	647	Dorkings	Edward		3rd Class British, Soton		going to Oglesby, Ill
359	98	Douglas	W D	Mrs	1		Minneapolis, Minn
360	97	Douglas	F C	Mrs	1		
361	99	Douglas	W D	Mr	1		Minneapolis, Minn
362	648	Dowdell	Elizabeth		3rd Class British, Soton		going to Union Hill, NJ
363	390	Dawson	William James	Mr	2		
364	1215	Doyle	Elin		3rd Class Queenstown		to Bridget Fox, 123 West Eightieth Street, New York
365	1114	Drazenovic	Josef		3rd Class Cherbourg		
366	398	Drew	James V	Mrs	2	Constantine, Penryn, Cornwall, England	
367	400	Drew	Marshall	Master	2	Constantine, Penryn, Cornwall, England	
368	399	Drew	James V	Mr	2	Constantine, Penryn, Cornwall, England	
369	1216	Driscoll	Bridget		3rd Class Queenstown		
370	649	Drapkin	Jenie		3rd Class British, Soton		
371	129	Gordon	Duff	Lord	1		Care of Lucile (Ltd), 17 West Thirty-sixth Street, New York, (sailed Lusitania, May 8 1912)
372	130	Gordon	Duff	Lady	1		Care of Lucile (Ltd), 17 West Thirty-sixth Street, New York, (sailed Lusitania, May 8 1912)
373	101	Dulles	William C	Mr	1		
374	401	Durand	Asuncion	Miss	2		Care of Monter, Barcelona, or Calle Zulinta, Habana, Cuba
375	402	Durand	Florentina	Miss	2		Care of Monter, Barcelona, or Calle Zulinta, Habana, Cuba
376	1213	Dewan	Frank		3rd Class Queenstown		
377	856	Dyker	Adolf		3rd Class Scan & Cont- Soton		468 Washington, West Haven, Conn
378	857	Dyker	Elizabeth		3rd Class Scan & Cont- Soton		going to mother and father, West Haven, Conn]
379	102	Earnshaw	Boulton	Mrs	1		Care of R B Evans, 1335 Land Title Building, Phil, Pa
381	858	Ecimovic	Joso		3rd Class Scan & Cont- Soton		
382	859	Edwardson	Gustaf		3rd Class Scan & Cont- Soton		
383	403	Eitemiller	G F	Mr	2		Bonnington Hotel, Southampton Row, London, or 29 Webb Avenue, Detroit
384	860	Eklung	Hans		3rd Class Scan & Cont- Soton		going to Bern Eklund, Jerome Junction, Ariz, care of J Bergren
385	861	Ekstrom	Johan		3rd Class Scan & Cont- Soton		
386	1113	Dibo	Elias		3rd Class Cherbourg		
387	1115	Elias	Joseph		3rd Class Cherbourg		
388	1116	Elias	Joseph		3rd Class Cherbourg		
389	1105	Canons	Elias		3rd Class Cherbourg		
390	651	Elsbury	James		3rd Class British, Soton		going to grandparents in New York City
391	652	Emanuel	Ethel (child)		3rd Class British, Soton		
392	1110	Chemat	Emir, Farres		3rd Class Cherbourg		
393	404	Enander	Ingvar	Mr	2		
394	103	Endres	Caroline	Miss	1		Care of D H McIntyre, Punxsutawney, Pa

Master No	Old No	Passenger's Name	First Name(s)	Title	Class	European Address/Notes	American Address/Notes
395	865	Goncalves	Manoel		3rd Class Scan & Cont- Soton		Hotel Belmont, New York City
396	104	Eustis	E M	Miss	1		Care of E G Alsdorf, 40 Wall Street, New York City
397	105	Evans	E	Miss	1		
399	653	Everett	Thomas	Mr	3rd Class British, Soton		
402	405	Fahlstrom	Arne D		2		
403	1218	Farrell	James		3rd Class Queenstown		
404	281	Straus	Manservant		1		
405	408	Faunthorpe	Lizzie	Mrs	2		Care of John Devine, 669 Brooklyn Street, Phil, Pa
406	407	Faunthorpe	Harry	Mr	2		
407	406	Fallbrook	Charles	Mr	2		16 Charles Street, Truro, Cornwall, England, or care of George Filbrook, PO Box 115, Houghton, Mich
408	862	Finoli	Luigi		3rd Class Scan & Cont- Soton		going to 707 Catherine Street, Philadelphia, Pa
409	863	Fischer	Eberhard		3rd Class Scan & Cont- Soton		
410	106	Flegenhein	A.	Mrs	1		
411	1232	Hemming	Norah	Maid	3rd Class Queenstown		Pennsylvania RR Co, Philadelphia, Pa
412	293	Thayer	Maid		1		
414	1221	Flynn	James		3rd Class Queenstown		going to his brother Ant. Flynn, 236 East Fifty-third Street, New York
415	1222	Flynn	John		3rd Class Queenstown		going to 3434 Frazier Street, Oakland, Pittsburgh, Pa
416	107	Flynn	J I	Mr	1		Gimbel Bros, New York City
417	1219	Foley	Joseph		3rd Class Queenstown		going to brother Jer Foley, 252 West One hundred and fifteenth Street, New York
418	1220	Foley	William		3rd Class Queenstown		
419	654	Foo	Cheong		3rd Class British, Soton		
420	655	Ford	Arthur		3rd Class British, Soton		
421	657	Ford	D M Miss		3rd Class British, Soton		
422	658	Ford	E		3rd Class British, Soton		
423	656	Ford	Margaret		3rd Class British, Soton		
424	660	Ford	Maggie (child)		3rd Class British, Soton		
425	659	Ford	M W Y N		3rd Class British, Soton		
426	108	Foreman	B L	Mr	1		306 West Ninety-ninth Street, New York City
429	112	Fortune	Alice	Miss	1	Hotel Metropole, London	29 1/2 Portage Avenue, Winnipeg. Manitoba
430	114	Fortune	Charles	Mr	1	Hotel Metropole, London	29 1/2 Portage Avenue, Winnipeg. Manitoba
431	111	Fortune	Ethel	Miss	1	Hotel Metropole, London	29 1/2 Portage Avenue, Winnipeg. Manitoba
432	113	Fortune	Mabel	Miss	1	Hotel Metropole, London	29 1/2 Portage Avenue, Winnipeg. Manitoba
433	109	Fortune	Mark	Mr	1	Hotel Metropole, London	29 1/2 Portage Avenue, Winnipeg. Manitoba
434	110	Fortune	Mark	Mrs	1	Hotel Metropole, London	29 1/2 Portage Avenue, Winnipeg. Manitoba
435	1223	Fox	Patrick	Mr	3rd Class Queenstown		going to brother Fox, 123 West Eightieth Street, New York
436	409	Fox	Stanley H	Mr	2		Sister is D B Fox, 1250 Astor Street, Chicago, Ill
437	131	Gordon	Maid		1		Care of Lucile (Ltd), 17 West Thirty-sixth Street, New York, (sailed Lusitania, May 8 1912)
438	661	Franklin	Charles	Mr	3rd Class British, Soton	17 Cheapside, E C	
439	115	Franklin	T P	Mr	1		

Master No	Old No	Passenger's Name	First Name(s)	Title	Class	European Address/Notes	American Address/Notes
440	117	Frauenthal	Henry W	Mr	1		
441	118	Frauenthal	Henry W	Mrs	1		
442	116	Frauenthal	T G	Mr	1		
443	119	Frolicher	Marguerite	Miss	1		Care of E J Stehli, 13 West Seventy-Sixth Street, New York City
444	272	Stehli	Max Frolicher	Mr	1	Care of Mr Obersteg, Basel	Care of E J Stehli, 13 West Seventy-sixth Street, New York City
445	273	Stehli	Max Frolicher	Mrs	1		Care of E J Stehli, 13 West Seventy-sixth Street, New York City
446	410	Frost	A	Mr	2	Care of Harland & Wolf, Belfast, Ireland	
447	166	Ismay	Manservant	Mr		30 James Street, Liverpool	
448	411	Funk	Annie	Miss	2	Care of Thos. Cook & Son, London	
449	120	Futrelle	J	Mr	1	44 Gloucester Terrace, Hyde Park, W	Hotel Belmont, New York City
450	121	Futrelle	J	Mrs	1	44 Gloucester Terrace, Hyde Park, W	Hotel Belmont, New York City
451	412	Fyuncy	Jos	Mr	2		
452	413	Gale	Henry	Mr	2		
453	414	Gale	Shadrach	Mr	2		
454	1224	Gallager	Martin		3rd Class Queenstown		going to 296 East One hundred and forty-third Street, New York
455	415	Garside	Alfred	Mr	2		Care Mrs Ellison, 522 Seventy-fifth Street, Brooklyn, NY
456	416	Gaskell	Galovence	Mr	2		
457	417	Gavey	Arthur	Mr	1		Care of Edwin Gee, Lawrence, Mass
458	122	Gee		Mr	1		
459	1120	Gerios	Youssef		3rd Class Cherbourg		
460	1121	Gheorgheff	Stanio		3rd Class Cherbourg		
461	123	Gibson	L	Mrs	1		Care of Curtis, Mallet Prevost & Colt, 30 Broad Street, New York City
462	124	Gibson	D	Miss	1		Care of Curtis, Mallet Prevost & Colt, 30 Broad Street, New York City
463	315	Widener	Maid	Mr	1	57 Avenue Montaigne, Paris	Land Title Building, Philadelphia Pa
464	125	Giglio	Victor	Mr	1		
465	419	Gilbert	William	Mr	2		
466	420	Giles	Edgar	Mr	2	Wheal Unity Road, Pordwen, Cornwall, England	
467	421	Giles	Fred	Mr	2	Wheal Unity Road, Pordwen, Cornwall, England	
468	422	Giles	Ralph	Mr	2	10 Gunderstone Road, West Kensington, England	
469	663	Gilinski	Leslie		3rd Class British, Soton		
470	423	Gill	John	Mr	2	3 Griffin Road, Clevedon, England	
471	424	Gillespie	William	Mr	2		
472	1225	Gilnagh	Katie		3rd Class Queenstown		
473	425	Givard	Hans L	Mr	2		
474	1226	Glynn	Mary		3rd Class Queenstown		going to Washington, DC
475	126	Goldenberg	E L	Mr	1		Do.

Master No	Old No	Passenger's Name	First Name(s)	Title	Class	European Address/Notes	American Address/Notes
476	127	Goldenberg	E L	Mrs	1		
477	128	Goldschmidt	George B	Mr	1		
478	665	Goldsmith	Emily A		3rd Class British, Soton		Going to Mrs Goldsmith's father, Henry Brown, 115 Butternut Street, Detroit, Mich
479	664	Goldsmith	Frank J		3rd Class British, Soton		Going to Mrs Goldsmith's father, Henry Brown, 115 Butternut Street, Detroit, Mich
480	666	Goldsmith	Frank J W		3rd Class British, Soton		Going to Mrs Goldsmith's father, Henry Brown, 115 Butternut Street, Detroit, Mich
481	864	Goldsmith	Nathan		3rd Class Scan & Cont- Soton		
482	668	Goodwin	Augusta		3rd Class British, Soton		
483	670	Goodwin	Charles		3rd Class British, Soton		
484	667	Goodwin	Frederick		3rd Class British, Soton		
485	673	Goodwin	Harold (child)		3rd Class British, Soton		
486	672	Goodwin	Jessie (child)		3rd Class British, Soton		
487	669	Goodwin	Lillian		3rd Class British, Soton		
488	674	Goodwin	Sidney (child)		3rd Class British, Soton		
489	671	Goodwin	William (child)		3rd Class British, Soton		
490	132	Gracie	Archibald	Col	1		Hotel St Loine, Washington Square, New York City
491	134	Graham		Mrs	1	Savoy Hotel, London	Care of I Eaton & Co, 45 East Seventeenth Street, New York City
492	133	Graham	William G	Mr	1		
493	135	Graham	Margaret	Miss	1		
494	675	Green	George		3rd Class British, Soton		
495	427	Greenberg	Samuel	Mr	2		Care of Alexander Wolf, 154 Nasseau Street, New York City
496	136	Greenfield	L D	Mrs	1		
497	137	Greenfield	W B	Mr	1		
498	866	Gronnestad	Daniel		3rd Class Scan & Cont- Soton		going to Regina, Saskatchewan
499	676	Guest	Robert		3rd Class British, Soton		
500	138	Guggenheim	Benjamin	Mr	1		Care of J K McGowan, 165 Broadway, New York
501	868	Gustafson	Alfred		3rd Class Scan & Cont- Soton		to Nielsen & Lundbeck, New York
502	869	Gustafson	Anders		3rd Class Scan & Cont- Soton		
503	870	Gustafson	Johan		3rd Class Scan & Cont- Soton		
504	867	Gustafsen	Gideon		3rd Class Scan & Cont- Soton		
506	871	Haas	Alaisia		3rd Class Scan & Cont- Soton		
507	873	Hagland	Ingvald		3rd Class Scan & Cont- Soton		going to New York, NY
508	874	Hagland	Konrad		3rd Class Scan & Cont- Soton		going to New York, NY
509	876	Hakkurainen	Elin		3rd Class Scan & Cont- Soton		going to Monessen, Pa
510	875	Hakkurainen	Pekka		3rd Class Scan & Cont- Soton		
511	428	Hale	Reginald	Mr	2	Care of Mrs S Hall, Rodney Hoke, near Cheddar, England	
512	430	Hamalainen	infant		2		389 Clay Avenue, Detroit, Mich
513	429	Hamalainen	Anna	Mrs	2		389 Clay Avenue, Detroit, Mich

Master No	Old No	Passenger's Name	First Name(s)	Title	Class	European Address/Notes	American Address/Notes
514	958	Mampe	Leon		3rd Class Scan & Cont- Soton		
515	1122	Hanna	Mansour		3rd Class Cherbourg		
516	1137	Monbarek	Assi		3rd Class Cherbourg		going to Port Huron, Mich
517	878	Hansen	Claus		3rd Class Scan & Cont- Soton		
518	918	Jutel	Henry		3rd Class Scan & Cont- Soton		
519	880	Hansen	Henry		3rd Class Scan & Cont- Soton		
520	879	Hansen	Jenny		3rd Class Scan & Cont- Soton		going to sister in Racine, Wis
521	431	Harbeck	Wm	Mr	2		
522	139	Harder	George A	Mr	1		117 Eighth Avenue, Brooklyn, NY
523	140	Harder	George A	Mrs	1		117 Eighth Avenue, Brooklyn, NY
524	1227	Hagardon	Kate		3rd Class Queenstown		to sister M Hargadon, 133 West One hundred and twenty-sixth Street, New York
525	677	Harknett	Alice		3rd Class British, Soton		
526	678	Harmer	Abraham		3rd Class British, Soton		
527	141	Harper	Henry Sleeper	Mr	1	3 Claude Villa, Denmark Hill, SE, England	
528	143	Harper	Henry Sleeper	Mrs	1	3 Claude Villa, Denmark Hill, SE, returned Celtic Apr 25	
529	432	Harper	John	Mr	2	Almond Hotel, Clifford Street, W	
530	433	Harper	Mina	Miss	2		1716 Massachusetts Avenue, Washington, DC
531	203	Moore	Manservant		1		
532	435	Harris	George	Mr	2		50 Central Park West, New York City
533	144	Harris	Henry B	Mr	1		50 Central Park West, New York City
534	145	Harris	Henry B	Mrs	1		
535	434	Harris	W H	Mr	2	47 Granvill Road, Hoe Street, Walthamston, England	
536	146	Harrison	W H	Mr	2	30 James Street, Liverpool	
537	436	Hart	Benjamin	Mr	2	41 Claredon Street, Pimlico, SW	
538	437	Hart	Esther	Mrs	2	Care of Bloomfield-Slemfold House, Whalebone Road	
539	438	Hart	Eva M	Miss	2	Chadwell Heath, Essex, England, returned on Celtic, Apr 25	
540	1229	Hart	Henry		3rd Class Queenstown		going to John Hart, box 307, Marion, Mass
542	142	Harper	Manservant		1		
543	1129	Kassen	Housseing		3rd Class Cherbourg		
544	148	Hawksford	W J	Mr	1		
545	149	Hays	Charles M	Mr	1	Grand Trunk Ry, London SW	Grand Trunk Ry, Montreal
546	150	Hays	Charles M	Mrs	1	Grand Trunk Ry, London SW	Grand Trunk Ry, Montreal
547	152	Hays	Margaret	Miss	1		304 West Eighty-third Street, New York City
548	153	Head	Christopher	Mr	1		Care of G W Head, Grain Exchange, Winnipeg
549	1230	Healy	Nora		3rd Class Queenstown		going to friends in New York
550	872	Hadman	Oscar		3rd Class Scan & Cont- Soton		going to 414 West First Street, Sioux Falls, S Dak
551	679	Hee	Ling		3rd Class British, Soton		
552	1228	Hagarty	Nora		3rd Class Queenstown		to Mrs Burns, 41 Washington Street, Charlestown, Mass
553	886	Hiekkinen	Laina		3rd Class Scan & Cont- Soton		going to Monessen, Pa
554	881	Heininen	Wendla		3rd Class Scan & Cont- Soton		
555	887	Hillstrom	Hilda		3rd Class Scan & Cont- Soton		going to Evanston, Ill

Master No	Old No	Passenger's Name	First Name(s)	Title	Class	European Address/Notes	American Address/Notes
556	882	Hendekovic	Ignaz		3rd Class Scan & Cont- Soton		going to Iron Mountain, Mich (Olaus Ras)
557	883	Henriksson	Jenny		3rd Class Scan & Cont- Soton		
558	1233	Henery	Delia		3rd Class Queenstown		
559	440	Herman	Alice	Miss	2		Bernardsville, NJ
560	441	Herman	Jane	Miss	2		Do
561	442	Herman	Kate	Miss	2		Do
562	443	Herman	Samuel	Mr	2		
563	444	Hewlett	M D	Mrs	2	Care of Mrs Groves, 6 The Avenue, Brondesbury, England, or Rapid City, S Dak	
564	445	Hickman	Leonard	Mr	2		
565	446	Hickman	Lewis	Mr	2		
566	447	Hickman	Stanley	Mr	2		
567	154	Hilliard	Herbert Henry	Mr	1		Boston, Mass
568	448	Hiesunen	Marsh	Miss	2		
569	155	Hipkins	W E	Mr	1		Avery Scale Co. North Milwaukee, Wis
570	156	Hippach	Ida S	Mrs	1		Hotel Imperial, New York City
571	157	Hippach	Jean	Miss	1		Hotel Imperial, New York City
572	884	Hervonen	Helga		3rd Class Scan & Cont- Soton		going to Monessen, Pa
573	885	Hervonen	Hildwe (child)		3rd Class Scan & Cont- Soton		going to Monessen, Pa
574	449	Hocking	Eliza	Mrs	2	26 St Mary's Street, Penzance, England, or c/o Mrs Emily Richards, 457 Rhodes Avenue, Akron, Ohio	
575	450	Hocking	Nellie	Miss	2	26 St Mary's Street, Penzance, England, or c/o Mrs Emily Richards, 457 Rhodes Avenue, Akron, Ohio	
576	451	Hocking	George	Mr	2	26 St Mary's Street, Penzance, England, or c/o Mrs Emily Richards, 457 Rhodes Avenue, Akron, Ohio	
577	452	Hocking	Saml J	Mr	2	3 Fore Street, Devonport, England	
578	453	Hodges	Henry P	Mr	2		
579	158	Hogeboom	John C	Mrs	1		
580	457	Hold	Annie	Miss	2	630 M Street, Sacramento, Cal	
581	458	Hold	Stephen	Mr	2		
583	888	Holm	John		3rd Class Scan & Cont- Soton		
584	889	Holten	Johan		3rd Class Scan & Cont- Soton		
585	159	Holverson	A O	Mr	1	Piccadilly Hotel, London W	Cluett, Peabody & Co, New York City
586	160	Holverson	A O	Mrs	1	Piccadilly Hotel, London W	Cluett, Peabody & Co, New York City
587	147	Haven	H	Mr	1		
588	877	Hankonen	Eluna	Mr	3rd Class Scan & Cont- Soton		
589	459	Hood	John	Mr	2	going to Indianapolis, Ind	
590	1231	Horgan	Ambrose		3rd Class Queenstown		
591	439	Hasono	M	Mr	2	Imperial Japanese Ry Co, Tokyo, Japan	
592	460	Howard	Benjamin	Mr	2	85 Cheltenham Street, Swindon, England	
593	461	Howard	Ellen T	Mrs	2	85 Cheltenham Street, Swindon, England	
594	680	Hoyt	May		3rd Class British, Soton	going to Jane Hewitt, 1032 Florence Avenue, Albion, NY	
595	161	Hoyt	Frederick M	Mr	1	Care of Brown, Shipley & Co, London	
596	162	Hoyt	Frederick M	Mrs	1	Care of Brown, Shipley & Co, London	

Master No	Old No	Passenger's Name	First Name(s)	Title	Class	European Address/Notes	American Address/Notes
597	163	Hoyt	W F	Mr	1		36 West Thirty-fifth Street, New York City
598	783	Adolf	Humblin		3rd Class Scan & Cont- Soton		
600	462	Hunt	George	Mr	2	The Gardens, Ashstead, Epson	
601	681	Hyman	Abraham		3rd Class British, Soton		going to Springfield, Mass
602	279	Stone	Maid		1		Cincinnati, Ohio
603	393	Decit	Bertha	Miss	2		
604	890	Ilieff	Ylio		3rd Class Scan & Cont- Soton		
605	891	Ilmakangas	Ida		3rd Class Scan & Cont- Soton		
606	892	Ilmakangas	Pista		3rd Class Scan & Cont- Soton		
607	164	Isham	A E	Miss	1		Care of Edward Isham, 26 West Thirty-seventh Street, New York
608	165	Ismay		Mr	1	30 James Street, Liverpool	
609	893	Ivanoff	Kanio		3rd Class Scan & Cont- Soton		
610	463	Jacobsohn	S S	Mrs	2	7 Fembridge Square, London and care F Jones, 73 Apach Road, Josephine Avenue, Buxton	
611	464	Jacobsohn	S S	Mr	2	Returned to England, Megantic, May 11	
612	1179	Yalsevac	Ivan		3rd Class Cherbourg		
613	894	Jansen	Carl		3rd Class Scan & Cont- Soton		
614	896	Jardin	Jose		3rd Class Scan & Cont- Soton		
615	465	Jarvis	J D	Mr	2	The Crest, Stoneygate, Leicester, England	
616	466	Jefferys	Clifford	Mr	2		
617	467	Jefferys	Ernest	Mr	2		
618	469	Jonkin	Stephen	Mr	2		
619	897	Jensen	Hans		3rd Class Scan & Cont- Soton		
620	899	Jensen	Niels		3rd Class Scan & Cont- Soton		
621	898	Jensen	Svenst		3rd Class Scan & Cont- Soton		
622	1234	Jermyn	Annie		3rd Class Queenstown		
623	468	Jervan	A B	Mrs	2		going to sister in Boston, Mass
624	900	Johannessen	Bernt		3rd Class Scan & Cont- Soton		227 West 145th Street, New York City
625	901	Johannessen	Elias		3rd Class Scan & Cont- Soton		going to brother in Brooklyn, NY
626	907	Johnson	Jakob		3rd Class Scan & Cont- Soton		
627	905	Johansson	Erik		3rd Class Scan & Cont- Soton		
628	906	Johansson	Gustav		3rd Class Scan & Cont- Soton		going to Eddy, N Dak
629	895	Janson	Carl		3rd Class Scan & Cont- Soton		going to Sioux Falls, S Dak (414 West First Street)
630	902	Johansen	Nils		3rd Class Scan & Cont- Soton		
631	903	Johanson	Oscar		3rd Class Scan & Cont- Soton		going to 65 Poplar Street, New Haven, Conn
632	683	Johnston	E		3rd Class British, Soton		
633	910	Johnson	Eleanara (infant)		3rd Class Scan & Cont- Soton		going to husband, St Charles, Ill
634	908	Johnson	Elis		3rd Class Scan & Cont- Soton		going to husband, St Charles, Ill
635	909	Johnson	Harold		3rd Class Scan & Cont- Soton		going to husband, St Charles, Ill
636	912	Johnsson	Malkolm		3rd Class Scan & Cont- Soton		going to 814 Seventh Street, Minneapolis, Minn
637	687	Johnstone	W		3rd Class British, Soton		
638	686	Johnstone	A		3rd Class British, Soton		

Master No	Old No	Passenger's Name	First Name(s)	Title	Class	European Address/Notes	American Address/Notes
639	682	Johnston	C (child)		3rd Class British, Soton		
640	684	Johnston	Mrs		3rd Class British, Soton		
641	685	Johnston	William (child)		3rd Class British, Soton		
642	168	Jones	C C	Mr	1		Fillimore Farms, Bennington, Vt
643	913	Jonkoff	Lazor		3rd Class Scan & Cont- Soton		going to Swedeburg, Nebr
644	911	Johnsson	Carl		3rd Class Scan & Cont- Soton		
645	914	Jonsson	Nils		3rd Class Scan & Cont- Soton		
646	1155	Peter	Anna		3rd Class Cherbourg		
647	1153	Peter	Catherine Joseph		3rd Class Cherbourg		
648	1154	Peter	Miki		3rd Class Cherbourg		
649	169	Julian	H F	Mr	1		Care of G W Shepherd, 30 Church Street, New York
650	917	Jussila	Erik		3rd Class Scan & Cont- Soton		Monessen, Pa
651	915	Jussila	Katrina		3rd Class Scan & Cont- Soton		
652	916	Jussila	Mari		3rd Class Scan & Cont- Soton		
653	919	Kallio	Nikolai		3rd Class Scan & Cont- Soton		going to Roland, Iowa
654	920	Kalvig	Johannes		3rd Class Scan & Cont- Soton		Care of Lieberman, 1314 Brook Avenue, Bronx, NY
655	470	Kantor	S	Mrs	2		Care of Lieberman, 1314 Brook Avenue, Bronx, NY
656	471	Kantor		Mr	2		
657	921	Karajic	Milan		3rd Class Scan & Cont- Soton		going to 447 Bergen Street, Brooklyn, NY
658	922	Karlson	Einar		3rd Class Scan & Cont- Soton		
659	833	Carlson	Julius		3rd Class Scan & Cont- Soton		
660	923	Karlson	Nils		3rd Class Scan & Cont- Soton		
661	472	Karnes	J F	Mrs	2		Care of Mrs Lavely, North Water Street, Kittanning, Pa
662	1127	Karun	Franz		3rd Class Cherbourg		
663	1128	Karun	Anna		3rd Class Cherbourg		
664	1130	Kassein	Fared		3rd Class Cherbourg		
665	1178	Vassilios	Catavelas		3rd Class Cherbourg		
666	1238	Keane	Andy		3rd Class Queenstown		John Keane, 162 Melrose Street, Auburndale, Mass
667	473	Keane	Daniel	Mr	2		Father (?) of Nora Keane, who survived and went to Harrisburg, Pa
668	474	Keane	Nora A	Miss	2		Harrisburg, Pa
669	688	Keefe	Arthur		3rd Class British, Soton		
670	313	Widener	Manservant		1		Land Title Building, Philadelphia Pa
671	689	Kelly	James		3rd Class British, Soton		
672	1236	Kelly	Annie K		3rd Class Queenstown		going to Chicago, Ill
673	475	Kelly	F	Mrs	2	31 Bedford Place, Russell Square, London, England, or 68 West Seventy-first Street, New York City	
674	1235	Kelly	James		3rd Class Queenstown		going to friends in New York
675	1237	Kelly	Mary		3rd Class Queenstown		going to 29 Perry Street, New York, NY
676	1239	Kennedy	John		3rd Class Queenstown		512 Delavan Avenue, Buffalo, NY
677	170	Kent	Edward A	Mr	1		Care of J Kenyon, Southington, Conn
678	171	Kenyon	F R	Mr	1		Care of J Kenyon, Southington, Conn
679	172	Kenyon	F R	Mrs	1		

Master No	Old No	Passenger's Name	First Name(s)	Title	Class	European Address/Notes	American Address/Notes
680	1131	Khalil	Betros		3rd Class Cherbourg		
681	1132	Khalil	Lahie		3rd Class Cherbourg		
682	1241	Kierman	John		3rd Class Queenstown		
683	1242	Kierman	Phillip		3rd Class Queenstown		
684	1240	Kilgannon	Thomas		3rd Class Queenstown		going to 449 West Fifty-ninth Street, New York
685	173	Kimball	E N	Mr	1		c/o McKean, Brewster & Morgan, 40 Wall Street, NYC
686	174	Kimball	E N	Mrs	1		c/o McKean, Brewster & Morgan, 40 Wall Street, NYC
687	925	Kink	Anton		3rd Class Scan & Cont- Soton		Going to uncle in Milwaukee, Wis
688	926	Kink	Louise		3rd Class Scan & Cont- Soton		Going to uncle in Milwaukee, Wis
689	927	Kink	Louise (child)		3rd Class Scan & Cont- Soton		Going to uncle in Milwaukee, Wis
690	929	Kink	Vincenz		3rd Class Scan & Cont- Soton		
691	928	Kink	Maria		3rd Class Scan & Cont- Soton		
692	476	Kirkland	Charles Leonard	Rev	2		Care of D S Netter, 441 Market Street, Philadelphia, Pa
693	175	Klaber	Herman	Mr	1		
694	932	Klasson	Gertrud (child)		3rd Class Scan & Cont- Soton		
695	931	Klasson	Hilda (child)		3rd Class Scan & Cont- Soton		
696	930	Klasson	Klas		3rd Class Scan & Cont- Soton		
698	477	Knight	R	Mr	2	Care of Harland & Wolf, Belfast, Ireland	
699	1133	Kraeff	Theodor		3rd Class Cherbourg		
700	1134	Krikorean	Nichan		3rd Class Cherbourg		going to Yarmouth, Nova Scotia
701	228	Robert	Maid	Mr-	1		4140 Pendell Boulevard, St Louis
703	566	Svillner	Johan Henrik		2	4 South Terrace, Littlehampton	
704	1164	Sarkis	Lahond		3rd Class Cherbourg		
705	478	Lahlenen	Wm	Mr	2		Brother is C Albert Sylvan, Hancock, Mich
706	479	Lahlenen	Wm	Mrs	2		going to New York City
707	933	Laitinen	Sofia		3rd Class Scan & Cont- Soton		
708	934	Laleff	Kristo		3rd Class Scan & Cont- Soton		
709	690	Lam	Ah	Mr	3rd Class British, Soton		
710	691	Lam	Len	Mr	3rd Class British, Soton		
711	480	Lamb	J J		2		joing steamship Anetta of Donaldson Steamship Co
712	935	Landegren	Aurora		3rd Class Scan & Cont- Soton		going to New York City
713	1243	Lane	Patrick		3rd Class Queenstown		to O'Mahony, Hotel Webster, West Forty-fifth Street, NYC
714	692	Lang	Fang		3rd Class British, Soton		joing steamship Anetta of Donaldson Steamship Co
715	482	Laroche	Joseph	Mr	2	131 Grand Rue, Villegnif	
716	483	Laroche	Joseph	Mrs	2	Do	
717	484	Laroche	Louise	Miss	2	Do	
718	485	Laroche	Semorine	Miss	2	Do	
719	936	Larson	Viktor		3rd Class Scan & Cont- Soton		going to New York City
720	937	Larsson	Bengt		3rd Class Scan & Cont- Soton		going to 70 Smith Street, Harford, Conn
721	938	Lasson	Edward		3rd Class Scan & Cont- Soton		going to 70 Smith Street, Hartford, Conn
724	177	Leader	F A	Mrs	1		
725	1189	Zen ni	Filip		3rd Class Cherbourg		going to Cincinnati, Ohio

Master No	Old No	Passenger's Name	First Name(s)	Title	Class	European Address/Notes	American Address/Notes
726	939	Lefebre	Frances		3rd Class Scan & Cont- Soton		Going to Mystic, Iowa
727	940	Lefebre	Henry (child)		3rd Class Scan & Cont- Soton		Going to Mystic, Iowa
728	941	Lefebre	Ida (child)		3rd Class Scan & Cont- Soton		Going to Mystic, Iowa
729	942	Lefebre	Jeanne (child)		3rd Class Scan & Cont- Soton		Going to Mystic, Iowa
730	943	Lefebre	Mathilde (child)		3rd Class Scan & Cont- Soton		Going to Mystic, Iowa
731	486	Lehman	Bertha	Miss	2		c/o Jos Lehman, 171 West Ninety-fifth Street
732	944	Leionnen	Antti		3rd Class Scan & Cont- Soton		
733	488	Leisch	Dessie	Miss	2	3 Claude Villa, Denmark Hill, S E, returned Celtic Apr 25	
734	1135	Lemberopoulos	Peter		3rd Class Cherbourg		
735	481	Lemon	A	Mrs	2		Care of Linnix, 2236 Austin Avenue, Chicago, Ill
736	1244	Lemon	Denis		3rd Class Queenstown		
737	1245	Lemon	Mary		3rd Class Queenstown		
742	693	Leonard	L		3rd Class British, Soton		
743	100	Douglas	Maid		1		Minneapolis, Minn
744	694	Lester	James		3rd Class British, Soton		
745	51	Cardeza	Manservant		1		
746	489	Levy	R J	Mr	2	Grand Hotel, Paris	
748	178	Lewy	E G	Mr	2		Lewy Bros. Co, State and Adams Streets, Chicago, Ill
749	490	Leyson	R W	Mr	2	171 Cromwell Road, South Kensington, London	
750	1087	Zievens	Rene		3rd Class Scan & Cont- Soton		
751	948	Lindhal	Agda		3rd Class Scan & Cont- Soton	to mother, 20 Woodruff Street, Saranac Lake, NY	
752	945	Lindablom	August		3rd Class Scan & Cont- Soton	to Nichols Avenue, route No 13, Starford, Conn	
753	182	Lingrey	Edward	Mr	1		
754	946	Lindell	Edvard		3rd Class Scan & Cont- Soton		
755	947	Lindell	Elin		3rd Class Scan & Cont- Soton		
756	949	Lindqvist	Vino		3rd Class Scan & Cont- Soton		
757	179	Lindstroem	J	Mrs	1	going to Monessen, Pa	
758	1246	Linehan	Michel		3rd Class Queenstown		
759	180	Lines	Ernest H	Mrs	1		c/o Krauthoff, Harmon & Mathewson, 55 Wall Street, NYC
760	181	Lines	Mary C	Miss			c/o Krauthoff, Harmon & Mathewson, 55 Wall Street, NYC
761	695	Ling	Lee		3rd Class British, Soton		
762	1081	Wenzel	Zinhart		3rd Class Scan & Cont- Soton	joining steamship Anetta of Donaldson Steamship Co	
763	491	Lingan	John	Mr	2		
764	696	Lithman	Simon		3rd Class British, Soton		
765	697	Lobb	Cordelia		3rd Class British, Soton		
766	698	Lobb	William		3rd Class British, Soton		
767	699	Lockyer	Edward		3rd Class British, Soton	going to Ontario, NY	
768	183	Long	Milton C	Mr	1		
769	184	Longley	Gretchen F	Miss	1		Springfield, Mass
770	185	Loring	J H	Mr	1	28 Park Lane, London W	
771	492	Louch	Alice A	Mrs	2	Returned to England, Celtic Apr 25	Care of Thos Plunkett, 49 Broadway, New York City
772	493	Louch	Charles	Mr	2	Regent St, Weston-super-Mare, England	

Master No	Old No	Passenger's Name	First Name(s)	Title	Class	European Address/Notes	American Address/Notes
773	700	Lovell	John		3rd Class British, Soton		going to Chicago, Ill
775	950	Lulic	Nicola		3rd Class Scan & Cont- Soton		
776	951	Lundall	John		3rd Class Scan & Cont- Soton		going to sister in New York
777	952	Lundin	Olga		3rd Class Scan & Cont- Soton		going to brother in Chicago, Ill
778	953	Lundstrom	Edwin		3rd Class Scan & Cont- Soton		Care of J C Tiedeman, St George's Church, New York
779	269	Spencer	Maid		1		
780	954	Lyntakoff	Stanko		3rd Class Scan & Cont- Soton		
781	497	Mack	Mary	Mrs	2		
782	701	MacKay	George		3rd Class British, Soton		going to friends in New York
783	1247	Madigan	Maggie		3rd Class Queenstown		4140 Pendell Boulevard, St Louis, Mo
784	186	Madill	Georgette Alexandra	Miss	1	4 So Terrace, Littlehampton	
785	955	Madsen	Fridjof		3rd Class Scan & Cont- Soton		going to Brooklyn to join a ship
786	956	Maenpaa	Matti		3rd Class Scan & Cont- Soton		
787	187	Maguire	J E	Mr	1		
788	1260	McMahon	D		3rd Class Queenstown		
789	1262	Mechan	John		3rd Class Queenstown		to Nora Meehan, 4745 Indiana Avenue, Chicago, Ill
790	235	Rothes	Maid		1		Ritz Carlton Hotel, New York City
791	702	Maisner	Simon		3rd Class British, Soton		
792	957	Makinen	Kalle		3rd Class Scan & Cont- Soton		
793	501	Malachard	Noel	Mr	2		
794	1091	Attala	Malaka		3rd Class Cherbourg		
795	498	Mallet	A	Mr	2	6 Rue Cornmaile, Paris	
796	499	Mallet	A	Mrs	2	Returns to France	
797	500	Mallet	Andre	Master	2	Returns to France	
798	1123	Hanna	Meme		3rd Class Cherbourg		
799	1249	Mangan	Mary		3rd Class Queenstown		to brother Ed Mangan, 1848 Lincoln Avenue, Chicago
800	503	Mangeavacche	Emilio	Mr	2	Thos Cook & Son, London, or care of Miss Jennie Zuckerman, 1814 Clinton Avenue, Bronx, New York City	
801	1248	Mannion	Margareth		3rd Class Queenstown	going to sister in New York	
803	1163	Sarkis	Mardirosian		3rd Class Cherbourg		
804	188	Marechal	Pierre	Mr	1		
805	960	Markoff	Maria		3rd Class Scan & Cont- Soton		
806	1125	Johann	Markin		3rd Class Cherbourg		
807	189	Marvin	D W	Mr	1	58 Acre Lane, Brixton SW	
808	190	Marvin	D W	Mrs	1	58 Acre Lane, Brixton SW	
810	1142	Muselman	Fatima		3rd Class Cherbourg		going to Michigan City, Ind
811	1136	Malinoff	Nicola		3rd Class Cherbourg		
812	507	Matthews	W J	Mr	2	Penwithick, St Anstell, Cornwall, England	
815	508	Maybery	Frank H	Mr	2	1 Whitecross Road, Weston Super-Mare, England	
816	91	de Villiers	B	Mrs	1	111 Rue Farder, Brussels.	
817	191	McCaffry	T	Mr	1		Vancouver, British Columbia

Master No	Old No	Passenger's Name	First Name(s)	Title	Class	European Address/Notes	American Address/Notes
818	1250	McCarthy	Katie		3rd Class Queenstown		going to Mrs P J Murray, 231 East Fiftieth Street, City
819	192	McCarthy	Timothy J	Mr	1		
820	1254	McCormack	Thomas		3rd Class Queenstown		going to friends in New York
821	1251	McCoy	Agnes		3rd Class Queenstown		Going to 267 St Marks Avenue, Brooklyn
822	1252	McCoy	Alice		3rd Class Queenstown		Going to 267 St Marks Avenue, Brooklyn
823	1253	McCoy	Bernard		3rd Class Queenstown		Going to 267 St Marks Avenue, Brooklyn
824	494	McCrae	Arthur G	Mr	2		
825	495	McCrie	J M	Mr	2	Care Bank of Australasia, 4 Threadneedle Street, SE	
826	1255	McDermott	Delia		3rd Class Queenstown		Wife is 503 North Sixteenth Street, Sarina, Ont
827	1256	McElroy	Michel		3rd Class Queenstown		going to St Louis, Mo
828	193	McGough	J R	Mr	1		Gimbel Bros, New York City
829	1259	McGowan	Annie		3rd Class Queenstown		going to aunt in Chicago, Ill
830	1258	McGowan	Kath		3rd Class Queenstown		to 3241 North Ashland Avenue, Chicago, Ill
831	1257	McGovern	Mary		3rd Class Queenstown		going to friends in New York
832	496	McKane	Peter D	Mr	2		
833	1261	McMahon	Martin		3rd Class Queenstown		going to 415 West Fifty-third Street, New York
834	703	McNamee	Eileen		3rd Class British, Soton		
835	704	McNamee	Neal		3rd Class British, Soton		
836	1285	O'Neill	Bridget		3rd Class Queenstown		
837	705	Meanwell	Marian		3rd Class British, Soton		
838	706	Meek	Annie		3rd Class British, Soton		
839	510	Mellenger	Elizabeth	Mrs	2		Care of Mrs C C Jones, Bennington, Vt
840	511	Mellenger	child		2		Care of Mrs C C Jones, Bennington, Vt
841	509	Mellers	Wm	Mr	2		Richmond Country Club, Dongan Hills, Long Island, NY
843	707	Meo	Alfonso		3rd Class British, Soton		
844	1263	Mernagh	Robert	Mr	3rd Class Queenstown	26 St Kindas Road, Harron Road, England	going to M Mernagh, West Street, Chicago, Ill
845	512	Meyer	August	Mr	2		
846	194	Meyer	Edgar J	Mr	1		Care of Saks & Co, New York City
847	195	Meyer	Edgar J	Mrs	1		Care of Saks & Co, New York City
848	962	Midtsjo	Carl		3rd Class Scan & Cont- Soton		going to Chicago, Ill
849	708	Miles	Frank		3rd Class British, Soton		
850	196	Millet	Frank D	Mr	1		
851	513	Milling	Jacob E	Mr	2		
853	199	Minahan	Daisy	Miss	1	Savoy Hotel, London	Fond du Lac, Wis
854	197	Minahan	W E	Mrs	1	Savoy Hotel, London	Fond du Lac, Wis
855	198	Minahan	W E	Dr	1	Savoy Hotel, London	Fond du Lac, Wis
856	963	Mineff	Ivan		3rd Class Scan & Cont- Soton		
857	964	Minkoff	Lazar		3rd Class Scan & Cont- Soton		
858	1055	Stoytcho	Mikoff		3rd Class Scan & Cont- Soton		
859	514	Mitchell	Henry	Mr	2		
860	966	Mitkoff	Mitto		3rd Class Scan & Cont- Soton		
861	200	Mock	Philip E	Mr	1		Care of Curtis, Mallet, Prevost & Colt, 30 Broad Street,

Master No	Old No	Passenger's Name	First Name(s)	Title	Class	European Address/Notes	American Address/Notes
862	1264	Mocklare	Ellie		3rd Class Queenstown		New York City
863	967	Moen	Sigurd		3rd Class Scan & Cont- Soton		going to friends in New York
864	201	Molsom	H Markland	Mr	1	Junior Athenaeum Club, Picadilly, W	Montreal, Quebec
865	502	Manevila	Joseph	Mr	2	21 The Oval, Hackney Road, N E, England	
866	709	Moor	Beile		3rd Class British, Soton		
867	710	Moor	Meier		3rd Class British, Soton		
868	202	Moore	Clarence	Mr	1	Almond Hotel, Clifford Street, W	1716 Massachusetts Avenue, Washington, DC
869	711	Moore	Leonard		3rd Class British, Soton		
870	1266	Moran	Bertha		3rd Class Queenstown		going to 1226 Shakespeare Avenue, New York, NY
871	1267	Morgan	Daniel J		3rd Class Queenstown		going to 22 Dow Street, Troy, NY
872	1265	Moran	James		3rd Class Queenstown		
873	504	Maraweck	E	Dr	2		Brother is A H Maraweck, care of Pacific Phone and Telegraph Co, San Francisco, Cal
874	505	Marshall	Henry	Mr	2		
875	712	Morley	William		3rd Class British, Soton		
876	1268	Morrow	Thos		3rd Class Queenstown		
877	968	Moss	Albert		3rd Class Scan & Cont- Soton		to brother Waddell Morros, Gleichen, Alba, Canada
878	1139	Moncarek	Genios (child)		3rd Class Cherbourg		going to Philadelphia to join steamer
879	1140	Moncarek	Halim (child)		3rd Class Cherbourg		Going to Wilkes-Barra, Pa
880	1138	Moncarek	Hanna		3rd Class Cherbourg		Going to Wilkes-Barra, Pa
881	1141	Mousea	Mantoura		3rd Class Cherbourg		Going to Wilkes-Barra, Pa
882	713	Moutal	Rahamin		3rd Class British, Soton		
883	515	Mudd	Thos C	Mr	2		
885	1269	Mullen	Katie		3rd Class Queenstown		going to Mrs P J Murray, 231 East Fiftieth, New York
886	1270	Mulvihill	Bertha		3rd Class Queenstown		going to sister in Providence, RI
887	714	Murdlin	Joseph		3rd Class British, Soton		
888	1273	Murphy	Kate		3rd Class Queenstown		going to 2238 Fairhill Street, Philadelphia, Pa
889	1272	Murphy	Mary		3rd Class Queenstown		going to 2238 Fairhill Street, Philadelphia, Pa
890	1271	Murphy	Norah		3rd Class Queenstown		going to Mrs P J Murray, 231 East Fiftieth, New York
891	969	Myhrman	Oliver		3rd Class Scan & Cont- Soton		
892	516	Myles	T F	Mr	2		
893	971	Naidenoff	Penko		3rd Class Cherbourg		
894	1150	Odele	Najib, Jene		3rd Class Cherbourg		
895	1145	Naked	Maria		3rd Class Cherbourg		Going to Waterbury, Conn
896	1143	Naked	Said		3rd Class Cherbourg		Going to Waterbury, Conn
897	1144	Naked	Waika		3rd Class Cherbourg		Going to Waterbury, Conn
898	715	Nancarrow	Joseph		3rd Class British, Soton		
899	973	Nankoff	Minko		3rd Class Scan & Cont- Soton		
900	1146	Nasr	Mustafa		3rd Class Cherbourg		Care of Thos Cook & Sons, London; 652 Bolivia Road, Cleveland, Ohio
901	518	Nasser	Nicolas	Mrs	2		

Master No	Old No	Passenger's Name	First Name(s)	Title	Class	European Address/Notes	American Address/Notes
902	517	Nasser	Nicolas	Mr	2		Care of Thos Cook & Sons, London; 652 Bolivia Road, Cleveland, Ohio
903	204	Natsch	Charles	Mr	1		
904	1274	Naughton	Hannah		3rd Class Queenstown		going to P Naughton, 433 West Thirty-third Street, New York
905	454	Hoffman		Master	2		Children, care of Miss Hays, 304 West Eighty-third Street
906	455	Hoffman		Master	2		Children, care of Miss Hays, 304 West Eighty-third Street
907	456	Hoffman		Mr	2	Care of Thos. Cook, Monte Carlo	
908	975	Nenkoff	Christo		3rd Class Scan & Cont- Soton		
909	519	Nesson	I	Mr	2		
910	205	Newell	A W	Mr	1		
911	207	Newell	Madeline	Miss	1		Care of Bureau of University Navel, Boston, Mass
912	206	Newell	Alice	Miss	1		Care of Bureau of University Navel, Boston, Mass
913	208	Newsom	Helen	Miss	1		Care of Bureau of University Navel, Boston, Mass
914	520	Nicholls	Joseph C	Mr	2		c/o McKean, Brewster & Morgan, 40 Wall Street, NYC
916	209	Nicholson	A S	Mr	1		Care of Mrs E M Cory, 1 Greenwood Avenue, Brooklyn, NY
917	1148	Nicola	Elias (child)		3rd Class Cherbourg		Going to friends in New York
918	1147	Nicola	Jamila		3rd Class Cherbourg		Going to friends in New York
919	976	Nieminen	Manta		3rd Class Scan & Cont- Soton		
920	716	Niklasen	Sander		3rd Class British, Soton		
921	977	Nilson	August		3rd Class Scan & Cont- Soton		
922	982	Nelson	Bertha		3rd Class Scan & Cont- Soton		going to Missoula, Mont, 533 East Trent Street
923	978	Nilson	Helmina		3rd Class Scan & Cont- Soton		going to Joliet, Ill, care of Edward Sander
924	979	Nirva	Isak		3rd Class Scan & Cont- Soton		
925	980	Nyskanen	John		3rd Class Scan & Cont- Soton		going to Graniteville, Vt
928	521	Norman	Robt D	Mr	2	A E G Electric Co, 50 Wellington Street, Glasgow	
929	717	Nosworthy	Richard		3rd Class British, Soton		
930	397	Drashsledt	von	Baron	2 (saved as first class)		
931	1149	Norel	Mansouer		3rd Class Cherbourg		
932	522	Nye	Elizabeth	Mrs	2	Salvation Army, London	
933	970	Nyster	Anna		3rd Class Scan & Cont- Soton		
934	981	Nyoven	Johan		3rd Class Scan & Cont- Soton		
935	1277	O'Brien	Hannah		3rd Class Queenstown		going to cousin in New York City
936	1276	O'Brien	Thomas		3rd Class Queenstown		
937	1275	O'Brien	Denis		3rd Class Queenstown		going to friend in Brooklyn, NY
938	1279	O'Connell	Pat D		3rd Class Queenstown		
939	1278	O'Connor	Maurice		3rd Class Queenstown		
940	1280	O'Connor	Pat		3rd Class Queenstown		to Michael O'Connor, 539 East Seventy-second Street, NY
941	983	Odahl	Martin		3rd Class Scan & Cont- Soton		going to Peoria, Ill
945	1282	O'Dwyer	Nellie		3rd Class Queenstown		going to cousin in New York City
946	984	Olman	Velin		3rd Class Scan & Cont- Soton		going to Chicago, Ill

Master No	Old No	Passenger's Name	First Name(s)	Title	Class	European Address/Notes	American Address/Notes
947	1283	O'Keefe	Pat		3rd Class Queenstown		going to J Phelan, 416 West Thirty-eighth Street
948	1284	O'Leary	Norah		3rd Class Queenstown		
949	221	Penasco	Maid		1		Care of Mrs F Garcia, 6 East 58th Street, New York City. Sail La Provence, May 9
950	985	Olsen	Arthur		3rd Class Scan & Cont- Soton		going to stepmother in Brooklyn, NY
951	987	Olsen	Henry		3rd Class Scan & Cont- Soton		
952	986	Olsen	Carl		3rd Class Scan & Cont- Soton		
953	988	Olsen	Ole		3rd Class Scan & Cont- Soton		going to Moose Jaw, Saskatchewan
954	991	Olsen	Elida		3rd Class Scan & Cont- Soton		
955	990	Olson	John		3rd Class Scan & Cont- Soton		
956	904	Johanson	Oscar		3rd Class Scan & Cont- Soton		going to Detroit, Mich
957	794	Anderson	Thor		3rd Class Scan & Cont- Soton		
958	210	Omont	F	Mr	1		
959	994	Oreskovic	Teko		3rd Class Scan & Cont- Soton		
960	992	Oreskovic	Luka		3rd Class Scan & Cont- Soton		
961	993	Oreskovic	Maria		3rd Class Scan & Cont- Soton		
963	989	Olson	Elen		3rd Class Scan & Cont- Soton		going to Mitchell, S Dak
964	995	Osman	Mara		3rd Class Scan & Cont- Soton		going to Steelton, Pa
965	211	Ostby	E C	Mr	1		Providence, RI
966	212	Ostby	Helen R	Miss	1		Providence, RI
967	1286	O'Sullivan	Bridget		3rd Class Queenstown		
968	524	Otter	Richard	M-	2	Care of Herbert Green, Southwell, Portland, Dorset	
969	213	Ovies	S	M-	1		Care of H B Claflin Co, New York City, Mr J M Menendez
970	525	Oxenham	T	Mr	2	86 South Street, Ponders End, N, England	
971	526	Paard	Julian	Mr	2	Care of Montes, Barcelona, or Calle Zuleieta, Habana, Cuba	
972	527	Pain	D A		2		
973	528	Pallas	Emilio	Mr	2	Do	
974	1007	Paulsson	Alma		3rd Class Scan & Cont- Soton		Going to husband, Nils Paulsson, 159 West Erie Street, Chicago, Ill
975	1008	Paulsson	Gosta (child)		3rd Class Scan & Cont- Soton		Going to husband, Nils Paulsson, 159 West Erie Street, Chicago, Ill
976	1009	Paulsson	Paul (child)		3rd Class Scan & Cont- Soton		Going to husband, Nils Paulsson, 159 West Erie Street, Chicago, Ill
977	1010	Paulsson	Stina (child)		3rd Class Scan & Cont- Soton		Going to husband, Nils Paulsson, 159 West Erie Street, Chicago, Ill
978	1011	Paulsson	Torberg (child)		3rd Class Scan & Cont- Soton		Going to husband, Nils Paulsson, 159 West Erie Street, Chicago, Ill
979	1004	Panula	William (infant)		3rd Class Scan & Cont- Soton		
980	999	Panula	Erneste		3rd Class Scan & Cont- Soton		
981	998	Panula	Eina		3rd Class Scan & Cont- Soton		
982	1000	Panula	Juha		3rd Class Scan & Cont- Soton		
983	1001	Panula	Maria		3rd Class Scan & Cont- Soton		

Master No	Old No	Passenger's Name	First Name(s)	Title	Class	European Address/Notes	American Address/Notes
984	1003	Panula	Urhu (child)		3rd Class Scan & Cont- Soton		
985	529	Parker	Clifford R	Mr	2		
986	530	Parks	Frank	Mr	2	Care of Harland & Wolf, Belfast, Ireland	
987	214	Parr	M H W	Mr	1	85 Abingdon Road, Kensington, -W or Deer Lodge, Mont	
988	531	Parrish	L D	Mrs	2		
989	215	Partner	Austin	Mr	2	Care of Meyers & Robertson, 11 Copthall Court, London EC	Care of Barrow, Wade & Guthrie, 25 Broad Street, New York City
990	1005	Pasic	Jakob		3rd Class Scan & Cont- Soton		
991	725	Potchett	George		3rd Class British, Soton		
992	1176	Usher	Baulmer		3rd Class Cherbourg		
993	1012	Pavlovic	Stefo		3rd Class Scan & Cont- Soton		
994	216	Payne	V	Mr	1	Grand Trunk Ry, London SW	Grand Trunk Ry, Montreal
995	718	Peacock	Alfred (infant)		3rd Class British, Soton		
996	719	Peacock	Treasteall		3rd Class British, Soton		
997	720	Peacock	Treasteall (child)		3rd Class British, Soton		
998	721	Pearce	Ernest		3rd Class British, Soton		
999	217	Pears	Thomas	Mrs	1	Inevagissey, Isleworth, NW	Care of Walter Janvier, 417 Canal Street, New York City
1000	218	Pears	Thomas	Mr	1	Inevagissey, Isleworth, NW	Care of Walter Janvier, 417 Canal Street, New York City
1001	1019	Petersen	Olaf		3rd Class Scan & Cont- Soton		
1002	722	Peauzzi	Joseph		3rd Class British, Soton		
1003	1013	Pekonemi	E		3rd Class Scan & Cont- Soton		
1004	1015	Peltomaki	Miholai		3rd Class Scan & Cont- Soton		
1005	219	Penasco	Victor	Mrs	1		Care of Mrs F Garcia, 6 East 58th Street, New York City. Sail La Provence, May 9
1006	220	Penasco	Victor	Mr	1		Care of Mrs F Garcia, 6 East 58th Street, New York City. Sail La Provence, May 9
1008	723	Perkin	John		3rd Class British, Soton		
1009	487	Leinot	Rene	Mr	2	12 Rue Lesueur, Paris	
1010	151	Hays	Maid		Grand Trunk Ry, London SW	Grand Trunk Ry, Montreal	
1011	1016	Person	Ernest		3rd Class Scan & Cont- Soton		
1012	532	Permschitz	P Joseph M	Rev	2	Care of P Jaricot, St Augustine's College, Rainsgate, England	going to 3546 La Salle Avenue, Chicago, Ill
1013	1287	Peters	Katie		3rd Class Queenstown		supposed to go to Mrs Egan, 243 East Forty-fifth Street, New York
1014	724	Peterson	Marius		3rd Class British, Soton		
1015	1020	Petranec	Matilda		3rd Class Scan & Cont- Soton		
1016	974	Nedelio	Petroff		3rd Class Scan & Cont- Soton		
1017	1006	Pastcho	Petroff		3rd Class Scan & Cont- Soton		
1018	1018	Peterson	John		3rd Class Scan & Cont- Soton		going to Claus Ras, 805 East Second Street, Iron Mount, Mich
1019	1017	Peterson	Ellen		3rd Class Scan & Cont- Soton		
1020	222	Peuchen	Arthur	Maj	1	Savoy Hotel, London W	Toronto, Ontario
1021	533	Phillips	Alice	Miss	2		700 Thirteenth Street, New Brighton, Beaver County, Pa

Master No	Old No	Passenger's Name	First Name(s)	Title	Class	European Address/Notes	American Address/Notes
1022	534	Phillips	Robert	Mr	2		Father of Alice Phillips, who survived and went to 700 Thirteenth Street, New Brighton, Beaver Co.,Pa
1023	506	Marshall	Kate	Mrs	2	7 New Street, Birmingham, England. Returned Celtic, Apr 25	
1024	535	Pinsky	Rosa	Miss	2		
1025	1025	Plotcharsky	Vasil		3rd Class Scan & Cont- Soton		
1026	996	Macruic	Mate		3rd Class Scan & Cont- Soton		
1027	997	Pacruic	Tame		3rd Class Scan & Cont- Soton		
1028	536	Ponesell	Martin	Mr	2		
1029	537	Portaluppi	Emilio	Mr	2		
1030	223	Porter	Walter Chamberlain				Care of R B Evans, 1335 Land Title Building, Philadelphia, Pa
1031	224	Porter	Thomas Jr	Mrs	1	Milford, N H	
						1	
1032	538	Pulbaum	Frank	Mr	2	Luna Park, Paris	
1033	539	Quick	Jane	Mrs	2		
1034	540	Quick	Phyllis	Miss	2		
1035	541	Quick	W V	Miss	2		
1036	1026	Randeff	Alexandre		3rd Class Scan & Cont- Soton		
1037	1052	Solvang	Lena		3rd Class Scan & Cont- Soton		
1038	1156	Raihed	Razi		3rd Class Cherbourg		going to Centerville, S Dak
1039	727	Reed	James		3rd Class British, Soton		
1040	542	Reeves	David	M-	2		
1041	924	Kekic	Tido		3rd Class Scan & Cont- Soton		
1043	543	Renouf	Lillie	Miss	2		
1044	544	Renouf	Peter H Y	Mr	2		Care of Holland-America Line, 39 Broadway, New York City
1045	225	Reuchlin	Jonkheer J G	Mr	1		
1046	545	Reynolds	E	Miss	2		
1047	728	Reynolds	Harold		3rd Class British, Soton		
1048	226	Rheims	George	Mr	1	42 Rue de Paradis, Paris	
1049	1289	Rice	Albert (child)		3rd Class Queenstown		Going to Spokane, Wash., care of Mrs T Coleman, East 1922 Columbia Avenue
1050	1292	Rice	Arthur (child)		3rd Class Queenstown		Going to Spokane, Wash., care of Mrs T Coleman, East 1922 Columbia Avenue
1051	1291	Rice	Eric (child)		3rd Class Queenstown		Going to Spokane, Wash., care of Mrs T Coleman, East 1922 Columbia Avenue
1052	1293	Rice	Eugene (child)		3rd Class Queenstown		Going to Spokane, Wash., care of Mrs T Coleman, East 1922 Columbia Avenue
1053	1290	Rice	George (child)		3rd Class Queenstown		Going to Spokane, Wash., care of Mrs T Coleman, East 1922 Columbia Avenue
1054	1288	Rice	Margaret		3rd Class Queenstown		Going to Spokane, Wash., care of Mrs T Coleman, East 1922 Columbia Avenue
1055	546	Richard	Emile	Mr	2	St Dean d'Angeleys, Charente, France	

Master No	Old No	Passenger's Name	First Name(s)	Title	Class	European Address/Notes	American Address/Notes
1056	547	Richards	Emily	Mrs	2	26 St Marys Street, Penzance, England, or care of Mrs Emily Richards,	457 Rhodes Avenue, Akron, Ohio
1057	418	George	William Rand S	Master	2	26 St Marys Street, Penzance, England, or care of Mrs Emily Richards,	457 Rhodes Avenue, Akron, Ohio
1059	548	Ridsdale	Lucy	Miss		8 Quebec Street, Montague Square, London, or 1117 —— Street, Marietta, Ohio	
1060	1002	Panula	Sanni		3rd Class Scan & Cont- Soton		Waldorf-Astoria, New York City
1061	308	White	Matti		1		going to friends in New York
1062	1027	Rintamaki	Hannah		3rd Class Scan & Cont- Soton		
1063	1294	Riordan	Emma		3rd Class Queenstown		
1064	729	Risien	Samuel		3rd Class British, Soton		
1065	730	Risien			3rd Class British, Soton		
1066	14	Astor	Manservant		1		840 5th Avenue, New York City
1067	227	Robins	Edward S	Mrs	1	4 South Terrace, Littlehampton	
1068	731	Robins	Alexander		3rd Class British, Soton		4140 Pendell Boulevard, St Louis
1069	732	Roebling	Charity		3rd Class British, Soton		Trenton, NJ
1070	229	Roebling	Washington A 2d	Mr	1		Uncle is Fred Adams, 49 Oxford Street, Lee Park, Wilkes-Barre, Pa
1071	549	Rogers	Harry	Mr	2		
1072	733	Rogers	William		3rd Class British, Soton		
1073	230	Rolmane	C	Mr	1		235 West 107th Street, New York City
1074	1031	Runnestvet	Kristian		3rd Class Scan & Cont- Soton		
1075	231	Rood	Hugh R	Mr	1	Ritz Hotel, London, W	
1076	1028	Rosblon	Helen		3rd Class Scan & Cont- Soton		
1077	1029	Rosblon	Sally (child)		3rd Class Scan & Cont- Soton		
1078	1030	Rosblon	Viktor		3rd Class Scan & Cont- Soton		
1079	232	Rosenbaum	G	Miss	1		
1080	295	Thorne		Mr	1		
1081	233	Ross	J Hugo	Mr	3rd Class British, Soton	Savoy Hotel, London	going to New York City
1082	726	Rath	Sarah		1		Ritz Carlton Hotel, New York City
1083	234	Rothes	the Countess of	Mrs	1		753 West End Avenue, New York City
1084	236	Rothschild	M	Mr	1		753 West End Avenue, New York City
1085	237	Rothschild	M		1		
1086	734	Rouse	Richard H	Mr	3rd Class British, Soton	6 Petersham Place, Gloucester Road, W	Care of Knox & Co, 17 Battery Place, New York City
1087	238	Rowe	Alfred	Miss	1		119 South Van Buren Street, Wilmington, Del
1088	551	Rugg	Emily		2		
1089	735	Rush	Alfred	Mr	3rd Class British, Soton		going to sister in Troy, NY
1090	1296	Ryan	Edw		3rd Class Queenstown		going to 1503 Hoe Avenue, Bronx, NY
1091	1295	Ryan	Patrick		3rd Class Queenstown		Care of G S O'Loughlin, 31 Nassau Street, New York City
1092	239	Ryerson	Arthur	Mr	1		Care of G S O'Loughlin, 31 Nassau Street, New York City
1093	242	Ryerson	Arthur	Miss	1		Care of G S O'Loughlin, 31 Nassau Street, New York City
1094	240	Ryerson		Mrs	1		Care of G S O'Loughlin, 31 Nassau Street, New York City
1095	243	Ryerson		Miss	1		Care of G S O'Loughlin, 31 Nassau Street, New York City

Master No	Old No	Passenger's Name	First Name(s)	Title	Class	European Address/Notes	American Address/Notes
1096	244	Ryerson	Amin	Master	1		Care of G S O'Loughlin, 31 Nassau Street, New York City
1097	1158	Saad	Amin		3rd Class Cherbourg		
1098	1159	Saad	Khalil		3rd Class Cherbourg		
1099	1124	Jean Nassr	Saade		3rd Class Cherbourg		
1100	245	Saalfeld	Adolphe		1	Victoria Park, Manchester	Hotel Astor, New York City (sails Cedric May 16)
1101	1297	Sadlier	Matt	Mr	3rd Class Queenstown		going to Thos Sadlier, R F D. 3 Lakewood, NJ
1102	736	Sadowitz	Harry		3rd Class British, Soton		going to Providence, RI
1103	748	Sather	Simon		3rd Class British, Soton		
1104	738	Sage	Annie		3rd Class British, Soton		
1105	744	Sage	William (child)		3rd Class British, Soton		
1106	746	Sage	Constance (child)		3rd Class British, Soton		
1107	743	Sage	Dorothy		3rd Class British, Soton		
1108	741	Sage	Douglas		3rd Class British, Soton		
1109	745	Sage	Ada (child)		3rd Class British, Soton		
1110	742	Sage	Frederick		3rd Class British, Soton		
1111	740	Sage	George		3rd Class British, Soton		
1112	737	Sage	John		3rd Class British, Soton		
1113	739	Sage	Stella		3rd Class British, Soton		
1114	747	Sage	Thomas (child)		3rd Class British, Soton		
1115	18	Aubert	Maid		1		17 Le Seuer Street, Paris
1116	1032	Salander	Carl		3rd Class Scan & Cont- Soton		going to Red Wing, Minn
1117	1033	Saljilsvik	Anna		3rd Class Scan & Cont- Soton		going to Proctor, Minn
1118	246	Saloman	A L	Mr	1		
1119	1034	Salonen	Werner		3rd Class Scan & Cont- Soton		
1120	1161	Samaan	Elias		3rd Class Cherbourg		
1121	1160	Samaan	Hanna		3rd Class Cherbourg		
1122	1162	Samaan	Jouseef		3rd Class Cherbourg		
1123	1035	Sandstrom	Agnes		3rd Class Scan & Cont- Soton		Going to husband and father in San Francisco
1124	1036	Sandstrom	Beatrice (child)		3rd Class Scan & Cont- Soton		Going to husband and father in San Francisco
1125	1037	Sandstrom	Margretha (child)		3rd Class Scan & Cont- Soton		Going to husband and father in San Francisco
1126	1053	Sop	Jules		3rd Class Scan & Cont- Soton		going to E De Clerck, 33 Lessine Street, Detroit, Mich
1127	749	Saundercock	W H		3rd Class British, Soton		
1128	750	Sawyer	Frederick		3rd Class British, Soton		
1129	1298	Scanlan	James		3rd Class Queenstown		going to Kate Scanlon, the Plaze, New York
1130	247	Schabert	Paul	Mrs	1		Curtis, Wallet, Prevost & Colt, 30 Broad Street, New York
1131	1039	Sheerlinck	Jean		3rd Class Scan & Cont- Soton		going to E De Clerck, 33 Lessine Street, Detroit
1132	561	Smith	A	Mr	2	11 Berwick Street, London	
1133	1038	Sdycoff	Todor		3rd Class Scan & Cont- Soton		
1134	552	Sedgwick	C F W	Mr	2	68 Ampthill Road, Aigleurith, Liverpool, England	Philadelphia, Pa. Attorneys Winthrop & Stimson,
1135	57	Carter	Maid		1		32 Liberty Street, New York City
1136	248	Seward	Frederic K	Mr	1	Savoy Hotel, London WC	

Master No	Old No	Passenger's Name	First Name(s)	Title	Class	European Address/Notes	American Address/Notes
1137	554	Sharp	Percival	Mr	2		going to sister, 1509 Lexington Avenue, New York
1138	1299	Shaughnesay	Pat		3rd Class Queenstown		
1139	1182	Youssef	Brahim		3rd Class Cherbourg		
1140	752	Shellard	Frederick		3rd Class British, Soton		
1141	555	Shelley	J	Mrs	2	85 Abingdon Road, Kensington, -W	or Deer Lodge, Mont
1142	1300	Shine	Ellen		3rd Class Queenstown		
1143	753	Shorney	Charles		3rd Class British, Soton	going to brother in New York	
1144	249	Shutes	E W	Miss	1		168 West One hundred and twentieth Street, NYC
1145	556	Silven	Lyyli	Miss	2		Care of Calvert Sylvan, Hancock, Mich
1146	250	Silverthorne		Mr	1		St Louis, Mo
1147	251	Silvey	William B	Mrs	1		Care of Mrs S Deshler, 1811 Wyoming Avenue, DC
1148	252	Silvey	William B	Mr	1		Care of Mrs S Deshler, 1811 Wyoming Avenue, DC
1149	754	Simmons	John	Mr	3rd Class British, Soton		
1150	253	Simonius	Oberst Alfons	Mr	1		Ritz-Carlton Hotel, New York City
1151	557	Sincock	Maude	Miss	2		Hancock, Mich
1152	553	Senkkonen	Anna	Miss	2		Brighton, Mass
1153	1151	Orsen	Sirayaman		3rd Class Cherbourg		
1154	751	Serata	Maurice		3rd Class British, Soton		
1155	1041	Sivic	Hnsen		3rd Class Scan & Cont- Soton		
1156	1040	Sihvola	Antti		3rd Class Scan & Cont- Soton		
1157	1042	Sjoblon	Anna		3rd Class Scan & Cont- Soton		
1158	558	Sjostedt	E A	Mr	2	Hjo, Sweden	to father, care of Gab. Gustafson, Olympia, Wash
1159	1043	Skoog	Anna		3rd Class Scan & Cont- Soton		Going to uncle, Olaus Ras, 802 East Second Street, Iron Mountain
1160	1045	Skoog	Harold (child)		3rd Class Scan & Cont- Soton		Going to uncle, Olaus Ras, 802 East Second Street, Iron Mountain
1161	1044	Skoog	Carl (child)		3rd Class Scan & Cont- Soton		Going to uncle, Olaus Ras, 802 East Second Street, Iron Mountain
1162	1046	Skoog	Mabel (child)		3rd Class Scan & Cont- Soton		Going to uncle, Olaus Ras, 802 East Second Street, Iron Mountain
1163	1047	Skoog	Margret (child)		3rd Class Scan & Cont- Soton		Going to uncle, Olaus Ras, 802 East Second Street, Iron Mountain
1164	1048	Skoog	William		3rd Class Scan & Cont- Soton		Going to uncle, Olaus Ras, 802 East Second Street, Iron Mountain
1165	1049	Slabenoff	Petco		3rd Class Scan & Cont- Soton		
1167	559	Slayter	H M	Miss	2		Moon Island, near Vancouver, British Columbia
1168	560	Slemen	Richard J	Mr	2	Landrake St, Germans, Cornwall, England	
1169	755	Slocovski	Selman		3rd Class British, Soton		
1170	254	Sloper	William T	Mr	1	Waldorf Hotel, London W	
1171	255	Smart	John M	Mr	1		
1172	1050	Smiljanic	Mile		3rd Class Scan & Cont- Soton		
1173	256	Smith	J Clinch	Mr	1		Care of C S Butler, 32 Nassau Street, New York City

Master No	Old No	Passenger's Name	First Name(s)	Title	Class	European Address/Notes	American Address/Notes
1175	258	Smith	L P	Mr	1		Huntingdon, W Va
1176	562	Smith	Marion	Miss	2		Care of Mrs Kelly, 68 West Seventy-first Street, NYC
1177	259	Smith	L P	Mrs	1		Huntingdon, W Va
1178	257	Smith	R W	Mr	1		Care of Ford & Lyon, Fitchburg, Mass
1179	1217	Emmeth	Thomas		3rd Class Queenstown		
1180	1301	Smyth	Julia		3rd Class Queenstown		going to friends in New York
1181	260	Snyder	John	Mr	1		Minneapolis, Minn
1182	261	Snyder	John	Mrs	1		Minneapolis, Minn
1183	563	Sobey	Hayden	Mr	2		Port Hallow, near Helston, Cornwall, England. Intended going to Houghton, Mich
1184	1051	Soholp	Peter		3rd Class Scan & Cont- Soton		
1185	756	Somerton	F W		3rd Class British, Soton		
1186	757	Spector	Woolf		3rd Class British, Soton		
1187	262	Spedden	Frederick O	Mr	1		Morristown, NJ
1188	263	Spedden	Frederick O	Mrs	1		Morristown, NJ
1189	265	Spedden	R Douglas	Master	1		Morristown, NJ
1190	267	Spencer	W A	Mrs	1		Care of J C Tiedeman, St George's Church, New York
1191	268	Spencer	W A	Mr	1		Care of J C Tiedeman, St George's Church, New York
1192	758	Spinner	Henry		3rd Class British, Soton		
1193	270	Stahelin	Max	Dr	1		Ritz Hotel, New York City.
1194	1054	Staneff	Ivan		3rd Class Scan & Cont- Soton		
1195	1168	Stankovic	Jovan		3rd Class Cherbourg		
1196	759	Stanley	Amy		3rd Class British, Soton		going to Grace French, 310 Prospect Street, New Haven, Conn
1197	760	Stanley	E R		3rd Class British, Soton		
1198	564	Stanton	S Ward	Mr	2	Thos Cook & Son, London and Paris	
1199	271	Stead	W T	Mr	1	5 Smith Square, Westminster, London SW	
1200	274	Stengel	C E H	Mr	1		13 Astor Place, New York City
1201	275	Stengel	C E H	Mrs	1		South Broad Street, Newark, NJ
1202	276	Stephenson	W B	Mrs	1		South Broad Street, Newark, NJ
1204	277	Stewart	A A	Mr	1		
1205	565	Stokes	Philip J	Mr	2		Uncle is Philip O'Grady, Kewanee, Ill
1206	278	Stone	George	Mrs	1		Cincinnati, Ohio
1207	761	Storey	T		3rd Class British, Soton		
1208	1056	Stoytehoff	Ilia		3rd Class Scan & Cont- Soton		
1209	1057	Strandberg	Ida		3rd Class Scan & Cont- Soton		going to New York, NY. (Finnish Steamship Co Agency)
1210	1058	Stranden	Jako		3rd Class Scan & Cont- Soton		going to Graniteville, VT
1211	280	Straus	Isidor	Mr	1		Care of R H Macy & Co, New York City
1212	282	Straus	Isidor	Mrs	1		Care of R H Macy & Co, New York City
1213	1059	Strilic	Ivan		3rd Class Scan & Cont- Soton		
1214	1060	Strom	Elma		3rd Class Scan & Cont- Soton		3905 Grapevine Street, Indiana Harbor, Ind
1215	1061	Strom	Selma (child)		3rd Class Scan & Cont- Soton		3905 Grapevine Street, Indiana Harbor, Ind
1217	1062	Sundman	John		3rd Class Scan & Cont- Soton		Going to Cheyenne, Wyo

Master No	Old No	Passenger's Name	First Name(s)	Title	Class	European Address/Notes	American Address/Notes
1218	762	Sutehall	Henry		3rd Class British, Soton		
1220	284	Sutton	Frederick	Mr			Care of Mrs E C Sutton, Haddonfield, NJ
1222	1063	Svensson	John		3rd Class Scan & Cont- Soton		
1223	1064	Svensson	Servin		3rd Class Scan & Cont- Soton		going to Alcester (Beresford), S Dak
1225	567	Swane	George	Mr	2		
1226	568	Sweet	George	Mr	2		
1227	285	Swift	Frederick Joel		1	154 Abbey Road, London NW	
1228	286	Taussig	Emil	Mr	1		
1229	288	Taussig	Ruth	Miss	1		
1230	287	Taussig	Emil	Mrs	1		
1231	289	Taylor	E Z	Mr	1	Whitehall Hotel, Bloomsburg Square, WC	
1232	290	Taylor	E Z	Mrs	1	Whitehall Hotel, Bloomsburg Square, WC	
1234	1067	Tonglin	Gunner		3rd Class Scan & Cont- Soton		to Erick Morberg, 502 South Marshall, Burlington, Iowa
1235	291	Thayer	J B	Mr	1		Pennsylvania RR Co, Philadelphia, Pa
1236	294	Thayer	J B jr	Mr	1		Pennsylvania RR Co, Philadelphia, Pa
1237	292	Thayer	J B	Mrs	1		Pennsylvania RR Co, Philadelphia, Pa
1238	763	Theobald	Thomas		3rd Class British, Soton		
1239	1173	Thomas	Assad (infant)		3rd Class Cherbourg		
1240	1171	Thomas	Charles		3rd Class Cherbourg		Going to Yarmouth, Nova Scotia
1241	1174	Thomas	John		3rd Class Cherbourg		
1242	1169	Thomas	Thomas		3rd Class Cherbourg		
1243	1172	Thomas	Tamin		3rd Class Cherbourg		Going to Yarmouth, Nova Scotia
1244	764	Thomson	Alex		3rd Class British, Soton		
1245	296	Thorne	G	Mrs	1		
1246	765	Thorneycroft	Florence		3rd Class British, Soton		going to Clinton, NY
1247	766	Thorneycroft	Percival		3rd Class British, Soton		going to Clinton, NY
1248	1065	Tikkanen	Juho		3rd Class Scan & Cont- Soton		
1249	1302	Tobin	Roger		3rd Class Queenstown		to Mrs Egan, 243 East Forty-fifth Street, New York
1250	1066	Todoroff	Lalio		3rd Class Scan & Cont- Soton		
1251	767	Tomlin	Ernest		3rd Class British, Soton		
1252	569	Toomey	Ellen	Miss	2		Care of Mrs Bridget Hannery, 119 Bates Street, Indianapolis, Ind
1253	768	Torber	Ernest		3rd Class British, Soton		
1254	1117	Forfa	Assad		3rd Class Cherbourg		
1255	770	Tunquist	W		3rd Class British, Soton		
1256	1175	Toutik	Nakle		3rd Class Cherbourg		
1257	1185	Youssef	Georges (child)		3rd Class Cherbourg		
1258	1185	Youssef	Hanne		3rd Class Cherbourg		
1259	1184	Youssef	Marian (child)		3rd Class Cherbourg		
1261	769	Trembisky	Berk		3rd Class British, Soton		
1262	571	Troupeansky	Moses Aaron	Mr	2	African Hotel, Southampton	
1263	570	Trent	Jessie	Mrs	2		to J G Grossman, 13 South High Street, Columbus, Ohio

Master No	Old No	Passenger's Name	First Name(s)	Title	Class	European Address/Notes	American Address/Notes
1264	572	Trout	E C	Miss	2		Auburndale, Mass
1265	297	Tucker	G M jr	Mr	1		
1266	1068	Turcin	Stefan		3rd Class Scan & Cont- Soton		
1267	1069	Turgo	Anna		3rd Class Scan & Cont- Soton		going to Ashtabula, Ohio
1268	1070	Turkula	Hedwig		3rd Class Scan & Cont- Soton		going to Hibbing, Minn
1269	573	Turpin	D A	Mrs	2	Plymouth, England	
1270	574	Turpin	William J	Mr	2	59 Chaddlewood Avenue	
1271	298	Uruchurtu	M R	Mr	1		Care of R R Uruchurtu, Mexico City, Mexico
1272	1071	Uzelas	Joso		3rd Class Scan & Cont- Soton		
1274	611	Billiard	A van		3rd Class British, Soton		
1275	612	Billiard	James (child)		3rd Class British, Soton		
1276	613	Billiard	Walter (child)		3rd Class British, Soton		
1277	1076	Vande Velde	Joseph		3rd Class Scan & Cont- Soton		
1279	299	Van der Hoef	Wyckoff	Mr	1		109 Joralemon Street, Brooklyn, NY
1280	1073	Van Impe	Catharine (child)		3rd Class Scan & Cont- Soton		
1281	1074	Van Impe	Jacob		3rd Class Scan & Cont- Soton		
1282	1075	Van Impe	Rosalie		3rd Class Scan & Cont- Soton		
1283	961	Melkebuk	Philemon		3rd Class Scan & Cont- Soton		
1284	972	Nandewalle	Nestor		3rd Class Scan & Cont- Soton		
1285	1077	Vereruysse	Victor		3rd Class Scan & Cont- Soton		
1286	1021	Planke	Augusta Vander		3rd Class Scan & Cont- Soton		
1287	1022	Planke	Emilie Vander		3rd Class Scan & Cont- Soton		
1288	1023	Planke	Jules Vander		3rd Class Scan & Cont- Soton		
1289	1024	Planke	Leon Vander		3rd Class Scan & Cont- Soton		
1290	1177	Vartanian	David		3rd Class Cherbourg		going to Brantford, Ontario
1291	575	Veale	James	Mr	2	Care of B Veale, Port Navis, Falmouth, England	
1292	1079	Wendal	Olof		3rd Class Scan & Cont- Soton		
1293	1082	Westrom	Holda		3rd Class Scan & Cont- Soton		
1294	1078	Vook	Janko		3rd Class Scan & Cont- Soton		
1295	1072	Vaclens	Adulle		3rd Class Scan & Cont- Soton		
1296	579	Watcroft	Nellie	Miss	2		Mamaroneck, Conn (?)
1297	300	Walker	W Anderson		1		East Orange, NJ
1298	49	Cardeza	Maid		1		
1299	576	Ware	F L	Mrs	2		186 South Main Street, New Britain, Conn
1300	771	Ware	Frederick		3rd Class British, Soton		
1301	577	Ware	John J	Mr	2	Care of H J Long, 13 Salthrope Road, Moreley Square, Bishopston, Bristol, England	
1302	578	Ware	William J	Mr	2	Care of H J Long, 13 Salthrope Road, Moreley Square, Bishopston, Bristol, England	
1303	301	Warren	F M	Mrs	1		
1304	772	Warren	Charles		3rd Class British, Soton		
1305	302	Warren	F M	Mr	1		
1306	580	Watson	E	Mr	2	Care of Harland & Wolf, Belfast, Ireland	
1307	582	Watt	Bessie	Miss	2	Care of Mrs Ballantyne, 2 Gorst Road, Wandsworth, England, thence to Portland, Oreg, care of W Watt	

Who Sailed on Titanic?

Master No	Old No	Passenger's Name	First Name(s)	Title	Class	European Address/Notes	American Address/Notes
1308	581	Watt	Bertha	Miss	2		Care of Mrs Ballantyne, 2 Gorst Road, Wandsworth, England, thence to Portland, Oreg, care of W Watt
1309	773	Webber	James	Mr	3rd Class British, Soton		
1310	583	Webber	Susie	Miss	2		61 Heath Street, Harford, Conn
1311	303	Weir	J	Mr	1	Care of Mrs Carter, 6 Howe Street, Edinburgh	
1312	584	Weitz	L	Mr	2	Care of Bronsgrove Guild, Bronsgrove, Worcestershire, England, or care of Bronsgrove Guild, Bank of Toronto Building, Montreal	
1313	585	Weitz	L	Mrs	2	Care of Bronsgrove Guild, Bronsgrove, Worcestershire, England, or care of Bronsgrove Guild, Bank of Toronto Building, Montreal	
1314	586	Wells	A D	Mrs	2		270 Arch Street, Akron, Ohio
1315	587	Wells	Joan	Miss	2		Do
1316	588	Wells	Ralph	Master	2		Do
1317	589	West	E A	Mrs	2	Newborn–Truro, Cornwall, England	
1318	592	West	P J	Miss	2	Returned to England per Celtic, Apr 25	
1319	591	West	E M	Miss	2	Returned to England per Celtic, Apr 25	
1320	590	West	E A	Mr	2	Returned to England per Celtic, Apr 25	
1321	1109	Chanini	Georges		3rd Class Cherbourg		
1322	593	Wheaton	Edward W	Mr	2		
1323	594	Wheeler	Edwin	Mr	2		
1324	306	White	J Stuart	Mrs	1	Mr Vanderbilt's servant	
1325	304	White	Percival W	Mr	1		Winchendon Springs, Mass
1326	305	White	Richard F	Mr	1		Winchendon Springs, Mass
1327	309	Wick	George D	Mr	1		Youngstown, Ohio
1328	311	Wick	Mary	Miss	1		Youngstown, Ohio
1329	310	Wick	George D	Mrs	1		Youngstown, Ohio
1330	1083	Widegrin	Charles	Mr	3rd Class Scan & Cont- Soton		
1331	312	Widener	George D	Mrs	1		Land Title Building, Philadelphia Pa
1332	314	Widener	George D	Mr	1		Land Title Building, Philadelphia Pa
1333	316	Widener	Harry	Mr	1		Land Title Building, Philadelphia Pa
1334	1084	Wiklund	Carl	Mr	3rd Class Scan & Cont- Soton		
1336	595	Wilhelms	Charles	Mr	2		
1337	774	Wilkes	Ellen	Mrs	3rd Class British, Soton		
1340	317	Willard	Constance	Miss	1		going to son in Akron, Ohio
1341	1089	Abi	Weller		3rd Class Cherbourg		Care of J W Moffit, Duluth, Minn
1342	775	Willey	Edward	Mr	3rd Class British, Soton		going to wife, 1330 South Halstead Street, Chicago, Ill
1343	318	Williams	Duane	Mr	1		Care of Alex Williams, Philadelphia Club, Philadelphia, Pa
1344	596	Williams	C	Mr	2		
1345	776	Williams	Harry	Mr	3rd Class British, Soton		
1346	777	Williams	Leslie	Mr	3rd Class British, Soton		
1347	319	Williams	R M Jr	Mr	1		Care of Alex Williams, Philadelphia Club, Philadelphia, Pa
1348	176	Lambert-Williams	Fletcher Fellows	Mr	1	6 W Bickerhall Mansions, Gloucester Place, London W	
1350	264	Spedden	Maid		1		Morristown, NJ

276

Master No	Old No	Passenger's Name	First Name(s)	Title	Class	European Address/Notes	American Address/Notes
1351	778	Windelov	Einar		3rd Class British, Soton		
1352	1085	Wirz	Albert		3rd Class Scan & Cont- Soton		
1353	779	Wiseman	Philip		3rd Class British, Soton		
1354	1086	Wittenrougee	Camille		3rd Class Scan & Cont- Soton		
1360	320	Woolner	Hugh	Mr	1		Care of I Jackerman, Polhemus Printing Co, 121 Fulton Street, New York
1361	321	Wright	George	Mr	1		Cottage Grove, Oregon
1362	597	Wright	Marion	Miss	2		going to Wilkes-Barre, Pa
1363	1180	Yazbeck	Antoni		3rd Class Cherbourg		234 West 44th Street, New York City
1364	1181	Yazbeck	Salini		3rd Class Cherbourg		
1365	322	Young	Marie	Miss	1		
1367	1119	Gerios	Joussef		3rd Class Cherbourg		
1368	426	Grais	H	Miss	2	Alliance Hotel, Southampton	
1369	1187	Zabour	Hilien		3rd Class Cherbourg		
1370	1186	Zabour	Tamini		3rd Class Cherbourg		
1371	1188	Zakarian	Mapri der		3rd Class Cherbourg		
1372	1152	Ortin	Lakarian		3rd Class Cherbourg		
1373	1088	Zummermann	Leo		3rd Class Scan & Cont- Soton		

CAVE LIST

Master List No	Old list No	Cabin	Surname	Title	First name(s)
22	1	B5	Allen	Miss	Elizabeth Walton
24	3	C22/26	Allison	Mrs	H J
25	5	C22/26	Allison	Miss	
26	2	C22/26	Allison	Mr	H J
27	6	C22/26	Allison	Master	
31	8	E12	Anderson	Mr	Harry
46	9	D7	Andrews	Miss	Cornelia I
47	10	D7	Andrews	Mr	Thomas
51	11	C101/2	Appleton	Mrs	E D
72	12	B35	Aubert	Mrs	N
91	47	C46	Cavendish	Maid	
92	14	A23	Barkworth	Mr	A H
97	15	B58/60	Baxter	Mrs	James
98	16	B58/60	Baxter	Mr	Quigg
99	33	D15	Buckell	Maid	
102	17	C6	Beattie	Mr	T
109	18	D35	Beckwith	Mr	R L
110	19	D35	Beckwith	Mrs	R L
112	20	C148	Behr	Mr	K H
121	218	C55/57/97	Straus	Maid	
123	131		Jakob	Mr	Birnbaum
124	21	B49	Bishop	Mr	D H
125	22	B49	Bishop	Mrs	D H
126	238	C32/99-1/120-1	White	Maid	
129	23	T	Blackwell	Mr	Stephen Weart
130	24	A31	Blank	Mr	Henry
131	25	C7	Bonnell	Miss	Caroline
132	26	C103/1	Bonnell	Miss	Lily
134	27	D22/1	Borebank	Mr	J J
147	28	E33	Bowerman	Miss	Elsie
151	29	A21/1	Brady	Mr	John B
155	30	B10	Brandeis	Mr	E
164	31	C101/1	Brown	Mrs	J M
174	32	D15	Buckell	Mrs	W
176	204	E34/36/40-1	Spedden	Nurse	
180	34	B88	Butt	Major	Archibald W
188	35	E24/3	Calderhead	Mr	E P
202	36	B51/58/53/101	Cardeza	Mrs	J W M
203	37	B51/58/53/101	Cardeza	Mr	T D M
213	40	B96/98	Carter	Miss	Lucile
214	41	B96/98	Carter	Mr	William E
215	42	B96/98	Carter	Mrs	William E
216	43	B96/98	Carter	Master	William T
218	44		Case	Mr	Howard B
220	46	C46	Cavendish	Mrs	T W
221	45	C46	Cavendish	Mr	T W
223	49	E81	Chaffee	Mrs	Herbert F
224	48	E81	Chaffee	Mr	Herbert F
232	50	C37	Cherry	Miss	Gladys
233	51	A9	Chevre	Mr	Paul
234	52	E33	Chibnall	Mrs	E M Bowerman
236	53		Chisholm	Mr	Robert
238	54		Christy	Mrs	Alice Frances
239	55		Christy	Miss	Juli
244	57	C89	Clark	Mrs	Walter M
245	56	C89	Clark	Mr	Walter M
247	7	C22/26	Allison	Nurse	
248	58	C110	Clifford	Mr	George Quincy
257	59	E58	Colley	Mr	E P
262	61	E45/49/52	Compton	Mr	A T jnr
263	60	E45/49/52	Compton	Mrs	A T
264	62	E45/49/52	Compton	Miss	S R
278	63	C101/3	Cornell	Mrs	..C

Master List No	Old list No	Cabin	Surname	Title	First name(s)
286	64	C182/1	Craig	Mr	Norman C, K.C., M.P
290	66	B22	Crosby	Mrs	Edward G
291	65	B22	Crosby	Mr	Edward G
302	67	E17	Daly	Mr	P D
307	4	C22/26	Allison	Maid	
310	69	B71	Davidson	Mrs	Thornton
311	68	B71	Davidson	Mr	Thornton
345	71	B20	Dick	Mr	A A
346	72	B20	Dick	Mrs	A A
350	74	A34	Dodge	Mrs	Washington
351	73	A34	Dodge	Mr	Washington
352	75	A34	Dodge	Master	Washington
359	77	C86	Douglas	Mr	W D
360	76	B60	Douglas	Mrs	F C
361	78	C86	Douglas	Mrs	W D
371	161	A16/20/E36	Morgan	Mrs	
372	160	A16/20/E36	Morgan	Mr	
373	80	A18	Dulles	Mr	William C
379	81	C53	Earnshaw	Mrs	Boulton
380	82	D31	Eastman	Miss	Anne K
394	83	C45	Endres	Miss	Caroline
396	84	D20	Eustis	Miss	E M
397	85	A29	Evans	Miss	E
404	217	C55/57/97	Straus	Manservant	
412	229		Thayer	Maid	
416	86	E25/3	Flynn	Mr	J L
426	87	C111	Foreman	M	B L
429	88	C23/25/27	Fortune	Miss	Alice
430	89	C23/25/27	Fortune	Mr	Charles
431	90	C23/25/27	Fortune	Miss	Ethel
432	91	C23/25/27	Fortune	Miss	Mabel
433	92	C23/25/27	Fortune	Mr	Mark
434	93	C23/25/27	Fortune	Mrs	Mark
437	162	A16/20/E36	Morgan	Maid	
439	94	D34/3	Franklin	Mr	T P
442	95	D40	Frauenthal	Mr	T G
443	96	B39	Frolicher	Miss	Marguerite
444	211	B41	Stehli	Mrs	Max Frolicher
445	210	B41	Stehli	Mr	Max Frolicher
458	97	E63	Gee	Mr	Arthur
463	244	C80/82/D44	Widener	Maid	
464	98	C92	Giglo	Mr	Victor
475	100	A5	Goldenberg	Mrs	E L
476	99	C92	Goldenberg	Mr	E L
477	101	C51	Goldschmidt	Mr	George B
490	102	C42	Gracie	Colonel	Archibald
491	104	C91/125	Graham	Mrs	William G
492	105	D10/12	Graham	Mr	
493	103	C91/C125	Graham	Miss	Margaret
496	106	D10/12	Greenfield	Mrs	L D
497	107	B84	Greenfield	Mr	W B
500	108	B84	Guggenheim	Mr	Benjamin
522	110	E50	Harder	Mrs	George A
523	109	E50	Harder	Mr	George A
528	111	D33	Harper	Mr	Henry Sleeper
530	112	D33	Harper	Mrs	Henry Sleeper
533	114	C83	Harris	Mr	Henry B
534	115	C83	Harris	Mrs	Henry B
542	113	D33	Harper	Manservant	
544	116	D45	Hawksford	Mr	W J
545	117	B69/73/24	Hays	Mr	Charles M
546	118	B69/73/24	Hays	Mrs	Charles M
547	119	B69/73/24	Hays	Miss	Margaret
548	121	B11	Head	Mr	Christopher
567	122	E46	Hilliard	Mr	Herbert Henry
569	123	C39	Hipkins	Mr	W E
570	125	B18	Hippach	Miss	Jean
571	124	B18	Hippach	Mrs	Ida S

Who Sailed on Titanic?

Master List No	Old list No	Cabin	Surname	Title	First name(s)
579	126	D11	Hogeboom	Mrs	John C
582	127		Holden	Rev	J Stuart
595	128	C98	Hoyt	Mr	Frederick M
596	129	C98	Hoyt	Mrs	Frederick M
602	214	B28	Stone	Maid	
607	130	C49	Isham	Miss	A E
649	132	E60	Julian	Mr	H F
670	243	C80/82/D44	Widener	Manservant	
677	133	B37	Kent	Mr	Edward A
678	134	D21	Kenyon	Mr	F R
679	135	D21	Kenyon	Mrs	F R
685	136	D19	Kimball	Mr	E N
686	137	D19	Kimball	Mrs	E N
693	138	C124	Klaber	Mr	Herman
701	184	B3	Robert	Maid	
723	140	E37/1	Lawrence	Mr	Arthur
724	141	D17/3	Leader	Mrs	F A
743	79	C86	Douglas	Maid	
745	39	B51/58/53/101	Cardeza	Manservant	
747	142	D31	Lewis	Mrs	Charlton T
759	144	D28	Lines	Miss	Mary C
760	143	D28	Lines	Mrs	Ernest H
768	145	D6	Long	Mr	Milton C
769	146	D9	Longley	Miss	Gretchen F
779	207	B76/80-1	Spencer	Maid	
784	147	B5	Madill	Miss	Georgette Alexandra
787	148	C108	Maguire	Mr	J E
790	189	C37	Rothes	Maid	
804	149	C47	Marechal	Mr	Pierre
807	150	D30	Marvin	Mr	D W
808	151	D30	Marvin	Mrs	D W
816	70	C90	de Villiers	Mrs	B
817	152	C6	McCaffry	Mr	T
819	153	E46	McCarthy	Mr	Timothy J
828	154	E25/1	McGough	Mr	J R
851	155	E38	Millet	Mr	Frank D
853	156	C78	Minahan	Miss	Daisy
854	158	C78	Minahan	Mrs	W E
855	157	C78	Minahan	Dr	W E
864	159	C30	Molsom	Mr	H Markland
903	163	C118	Natsch	Mr	Charles
910	164	D48/36	Newell	Mr	A W
911	166	D48/36	Newell	Miss	Madeline
912	165	D48/36	Newell	Miss	Alice
913	167	D47	Newsom	Miss	Helen
949	178	C65/109-1	Penasco	Maid	
965	168	B30/36	Ostby	Mr	E C
966	169	B30/36	Ostby	Miss	Helen R
969	170	D43	Ovies	Mr	S
987	171		Parr	Mr	M H W
989	172	C142	Partner	Mr	Austin
994	173		Payne	Mr	V
999	175	C2	Pears	Mrs	Thomas
1000	174	C2	Pears	Mr	Thomas
1005	177	C65/109-1	Penasco	Mrs	Victor
1006	176	C65/C109-1	Penasco	Mr	Victor
1010	120	C54	Hays	Maid	
1020	179	C104	Peuchen	Major	Arthur
1030	180	C110	Porter	Mr	Walter Chamberlain
1031	181	C50	Potter	Mrs	Thomas, jnr
1045	182		Reuchlin	Mr	Jonkheer J G
1061	239	C32/99-1/120-1	White	Manservant	
1067	183	B3	Robert	Mrs	Elizabeth Walton
1070	185	A24	Roebling	M Washington A	
1075	186	A32	Rood	Mr	Hugh R
1081	187	A10	Ross	Mr	J Hugo
1083	188	C37	Rothes	Countess	
1100	190	C106	Saalfeld	Mr	Adolphe

Cave List

Master List No	Old list No	Cabin	Surname	Title	First name(s)
1115	13	B35	Aubert	Maid	
1144	191	C125	Shutes	Miss	E W
1146	192	E24/1	Silverthorne	Mr	
1147	194	E44	Silvey	Mrs	William B
1148	193	E44	Silvey	Mr	William B
1150	195	A26	Simonius	Mr	Oberst Alfons
1173	197	A19	Smith	Mr	J Clinch
1178	196	A7	Smith	Mr	R W
1181	198	-45	Snyder	Mr	John
1182	199	-45	Snyder	Mrs	John
1187	200	E34/36/40-1	Spedden	Mr	Frederick O
1188	201	E34/36/40-1	Spedden	Mrs	Frederick O
1189	202	E34/36/40-1	Spedden	Master	R Douglas
1190	206	B76/80-1	Spencer	Mrs	W A
1191	205	B76/80-1	Spencer	Mr	W A
1193	208	B50	Stahelin	Mr	Max
1199	209		Stead	Mr	W T
1202	212	D20	Stephenson	Mrs	W B
1206	213	B28	Stone	Mrs	George M
1211	215	C55/57/97	Straus	Mr	Isidor
1212	216	C55/57/97	Straus	Mrs	Isidor
1220	219	D50	Sutton	Mr	Frederick
1227	220	D17/1	Swift	Mrs	Frederick Joel
1228	221	E67/68-1	Taussig	Mr	Emil
1229	223	E67/68-1	Taussig	Miss	Ruth
1230	222	E67/68-1	Taussig	Mrs	Emil
1231	224	C126	Taylor	Mr	E Z
1232	225	C126	Taylor	Mrs	E Z
1235	226		Thayer	Mr	J B
1236	228		Thayer	Mr	J B jnr
1237	227		Thayer	Mrs	J B
1265	230	C53	Tucker	Mr	G M jnr
1279	231	B19	Van der Hoef	Mr	Wickof
1297	232	D46	Walker	Mr	W Anderson
1298	38	B51/58/53/101	Cardeza	Maid	
1303	234	D37	Warren	Mrs	F M
1305	233	D37	Warren	Mr	F M
1324	235	D26	White	Mrs	J Stuart
1325	236	D26	White	Mr	Percival W
1326	237	C32/99-1/120-1	White	Mr	Richard F
1331	241	C80/82/D44	Widener	Mrs	George D
1332	240	C80/82/D44	Widener	Mr	George D
1333	242	C80/82/D44	Widener	Mr	Harry
1348	139	C128	Lambert Williams	Mr	Fletcher Fellowes
1350	203	E34/36/40-1	Spedden	Maid	
1356	245	D82	Wood	Mr	Frank P
1357	246	D82	Wood	Mrs	Frank P
1360	247	C52	Woolner	Mr	Hugh
1365	248	C32	Young	Miss	Marie

Inbound to Halifax

Master List No	Old List No	Surname	Name (s)	Sex	Age	Marital Status	Ever Been to Canada	Read
67	7	Assaf	Mar	F	45	S	to nephew	N
163	4	Brown	Mildred	F	20	S		
700	5	Krikorian		M	27	M	to uncle	Y
796	1	Mallet	Antoine	F	24	W	to friend	Y
797	2	Mallet	Andre	M	2	S		N
916	8	Yarred	Jumilah M	F	17	S	to mother	N
917	9	Yarred	Elias	M	10	S	to mother	Y
1290	6	Vartanian	David	M	20	M	to cousin	Y
1313	3	Weisz	Matilda	F	33	W	to friend	Y

Write	Country of Birth	Race	Post Office	Province	Occupation	Last permanent Residence
N	Syria	Syrian	Ottawa	Ontario	Domestic	
	England	English	Montreal	Quebec	Domestic	
Y	Turkey	Armenian	Brantford	Ontario	Labourer	
Y	France	French	Montreal	Quebec		Montreal
N	France	French	Montreal	Quebec		
N	Turkey	Syrian	Yarmouth	N.S	Domestic	
Y	Turkey	Syrian	Yarmouth	N.S		
Y	Turkey	Armenian	St Catherines	Ontario	Labourer	
Y	France	French	Montreal	Quebec		

List of Bodies Identified and Disposition of Same

Master List No	Old list No	Surname	Name(s)	Ref	Disposition	Class	Remarks
4	83	Abbott	Rossmore	190	Buried at sea	3rd/Southampton	
11	84	Adahl	Mauritz	72	Buried at sea	3rd/Southampton	
12	85	Adams	John	103	Buried at sea	3rd/Southampton	
21	86	Ale	Wm.	79	Mt. Olivet, Halifax NS	3rd/Southampton	
26	33	Allison	H.J.	135	Fwd'd to Montreal c/o G.E. Clark	1st/Southampton	
28	87	Allum	Owen G.	259	Fwd'd May 4th, Boston to connect w/ ARABIC, Liverpool May 7th	3rd/Southampton	Instructions, NY Office, wire May 2nd
29	88	Anderson	Mr.	260	Fairview, Halifax NS	3rd/Southampton	later identified from effects
55	29	Artagaveytia	Ramon	22	claimed / Alfred Metz Green-Uraguayan Consul-fwd'd S.A. via NY	1st/Cherbourg	
58	90	Asplund	Carl	142	fwd'd Mrs. Selma Asplund, Worcester, MA, May 3rd.	3rd/Southampton	
69	30	Astor	J.J.	124	Del. To Mr. N. Biddle-fwd'd to NY May 1st	1st/Cherbourg	
95	61	Bateman	R.J. [Rev]	174	Fwd'd May 6th to Mrs. R.J.Bateman, Jacksonville, FL	2nd/Southampton	fwd'd in accordance wire from Mrs. Bateman, May 2nd.
96	32	Birnbaum	Jacob	148	Fwd'd May 3rd. Joachim Birnbaum, Red Star Line pier 60, NY city	1st/Cherbourg?	instructions NY Office, wire, May 2nd
129	34	Blackwell	Stephen W.	241	Fairview, Halifax NS	1st/Southampton	instructions NY office, wire, April 29th
155	31	Brandeis	Emil	208	Fwd'd to Mrs. Brandeis, Omaha NE May 2nd.	1st/Cherbourg	
173	78	Buckley	Katherine	299	Fwd'd to Boston, May 3rd.	3rd/Queenstown	fwd'd at request of sister Margaret, 71Montview Rd. Roxbury, MA-letter April 29th-Boston office
179	62	Butler	Reginald	97	Fairview, Halifax NS	2nd/Southampton	claimed by brothers from Calumet MI
181	63	Carbines	Wm.	18	Fwd'd May 10th, to St. Ives Eng. Via NY-request of brothers	2nd/Southampton	instructions, NY Office, wire May 1st
220	35	Cavendish	Tyrell W.	172	Fwd'd May 3rd. C/o Simpson, Crawford & co., to Mrs. Cavendish	1st/Southampton	instructions, NY Office, wire May 1st
227	64	Chapman	Chas. H.	130	Fwd'd May 2nd. C/o J.J. Griffin,2282 7th Ave., NY	2nd/Southampton	
228	65	Chapman	John H.	17	Fairview, Halifax NS	2nd/Southampton	
269	79	Connors	Patrick	171	Buried at sea	3rd/Queenstown	
291	36	Crosby	E.G.	269	Del. To Howard G. Kelley, V.P., G.T. Ry., to Milwaukee May 3rd.	1st/Southampton	
296	75	Schedid	Nihl	9	Fwd'd May 4th, to Mrs. Schedid, Mt. Carmel, PA	3rd/Cherbourg	instructions NY office, wire May 2nd
304	92	Danbom	E. Gilbert	197	Fwd'd to Alfred Danbom, Stanton IA, May 3rd.	3rd/Southampton	instructions, NY Office, letter April 30th.
335	59	Del Carlo	Sebastiano	295	Fwd'd to Boston April 30th - shipment Italy CRETIC, May 18th	2nd/ ??:	

List of Bodies Identified and Disposition of Same

Master List No	Old list No	Surname	Name(s)	Ref	Disposition	Class	Remarks
361	27	Douglas	Walter D.	62	Fwd'd May 1st to G.C.Douglas (son) Minneapolis MN	1st/??	instructions, NY Office, wire April 29th.
365	71	Drazenire	Yosip	51	Buried at sea	3rd/Cherbourg	
373	28	Dulles	W.C.	133	Fwd'd to R.R.Bringhurst Phila. PA, May 1st.	1st/??	
399	93	Everett	Thos. James	187	Fairview, Halifax NS	3rd/Southampton	
403	80	Farrell	James	58	Buried at sea	3rd/Queenstown	
406	66	Faunthorpe	Harry	286	Fwd'd to Mrs. Faunthorpe c/o Wm. Stringfield, Phila. PA	2nd/Southampton	instructions NY office, wire May 3rd
436	67	Fox	Stanley H.	236	Fwd'd May 3rd. Rochester, NY, to widow	2nd/Southampton	order of Mrs. Emma Fox
451	60	Fynney	Joseph J.	322	Del. to Mr. Hoseason, CNSS Co., to be taken to Montreal	2nd/???	
458	3	Gee	Arthur	275	Fwd'd to New York May 9th, to Liverpool per BALTIC	1st	instructions NY office, wire May 6th
459	72	Gerios	Youssef	312	Mt. Olivet, Halifax NS	3rd/Cherbourg	
468	37	Giles	Ralph	297	Fairview, Halifax NS	2nd	
469	94	Gilinski	Leslie	27	Buried at sea	3rd/Southampton	
470	38	Gill	John W.	155	Buried at sea	2nd	
473	39	Givard	Hans Christiansen	305	Fairview, Halifax NS	2nd	
492	4	Graham	Geo. E.	147	Fwd'd April 30th Toronto, care of T. Eaton & Co.; Matthews, undertaker escort	1st	
495	40	Greenberg	S.	19	Fwd'd May 3rd to Mrs. Greenberg, Bronx, NY City	2nd	
502	69	Gustafsson	Anders Wilhelm	98	Buried at sea	3rd	
511	41	Hale	Reg.	75	Buried at sea	2nd	
519	91	Damgaard	Henry	69	Buried at sea	3rd/Southampton	coroner note: Shown on list as Henry Damsgaarden
521	42	Harbeck	W.H.	35	Fwd'd May 4th to Mrs. Harbeck, 733 Michigan St., Toledo, OH	2nd	
536	5	Harrison	W.H.	110	Fairview, Halifax NS	1st	
545	6	Hays	Charles M.	307	Delivered to Mr. Howard G. Kelley, VP G.T. Rly., taken to Montreal	1st	
556	95	Henderkovic	Tozni	306	Mt. Olivet, Halifax NS	3rd/Southampton	
565	43	Hickman	Leonard [see comments]	256	Fwd'd May 4th to Honeyman, c/o Simpson, undertaker, Neepawa MB	2nd	Leonard corrected to Lewis, by hand
578	44	Hodges	Henry P.	149	Fairview, Halifax NS	2nd	
585	7	Holverson	A.O.	38	Delivered to H.T. Holverson, Alexandria MN, & fwd'd May 1st to NY	1st	
598	96	Humblen	Adolph	129	Buried at sea	3rd/Southampton	
626	97	Johanssen	Jacob Alfred	143	Fairview, Halifax NS	3rd/Southampton	
627	98	Johansson	Eric	156	Buried at sea	3rd/Southampton	
628	99	Johansson	Gustaf Joel	285	Fairview, Halifax NS	3rd/Southampton	
636	100	Johnson	Malkolm Joakim	37	Fairview, Halifax NS	3rd/Southampton	
642	8	Jones	C.C.	80	Delivered to Dr. James H. Donnelly, May 1st for fwd'ing to Bennington VT	1st	
656	46	Kantor	Cenai	283	Fwd'd to 1735 Madison Ave., NY, c/o Speiler	2nd	
665	77	Vassilios	Catavelas	58	Buried at sea	3rd/Cherbourg	
670	122	Keeping	Edwin	45	Buried at sea	Servant	
671	81	Kelly	James	70	Buried at sea	3rd/Queenstown	
677	9	Kent	Edward A.	258	Delivered May 1st, to H.K. White of Boston, for shipment to Buffalo NY	1st	
703	47	Kvillner	Henrik	165	Fairview, Halifax NS	2nd	
734	76	Semperopolis	Petril	196	Mt. Olivet, Halifax NS	3rd/Cherbourg	

Master List No	Old list No	Surname	Name(s)	Ref	Disposition	Class	Remarks
749	48	Leyson	Robert W. Norman	108	Buried at sea	2nd	wire from Rud Linhart, May 6th and NY office May 2nd
762	101	Linhart	H.Wenzel	298	Mt. Olivet, Halifax NS	3rd/Southampton	
767	102	Lockyer	Edward	153	Buried at sea	3rd/Southampton	letters from C.L. Long April 23rd & 24th, father's instructions
768	10	Long	Milton C.	126	Fwd'd to Springfield, MA, April 30th, c/o J.H. Shepherd	1st	
772	49	Louch	Chas.	121	Buried at sea	2nd	
781	51	Mack	Mrs.	52	Buried at sea	2nd	
798	73	Hanna	Merne	188	Mt. Olivet, Halifax NS	3rd/Cherbourg	
799	82	Mangan	Mary	61	Buried at sea	3rd/Queenstown	
802	1	March	John S.	225	Fwd'd to Newark NJ, May 3rd, c/o Smith & Smith, undertakers	?	crew? Mail clerk - instructions NY office letter, April 30th
817	11	McCaffry	Thomas	292	Delivered to E.E. Code, May 2nd, for fwd'ing to Montreal	1st	
819	12	McCarthy	Timothy J.	175	Delivered to Mr. J.V. Finn, April 30th for fwd'ing to Boston	1st	
824	50	McCrae	Arthur Gordon	209	Fairview, Halifax NS	2nd	wire from E.D. Upham, Denver, May 10th
834	103	McNamee	Mrs. N.	53	Buried at sea	3rd/Southampton	
843	104	Martino	A. Meo	201	Fairview, Halifax NS	3rd/Southampton	on list as Meo, Alphonso - closer exam., of effects = Martino, A. Meo
851	13	Millet	Frank D.	249	Delivered, May 1st, to Mr. Loverling Hill, for fwd'ing to Boston	1st	instructions NY office, wire May 4th. Ashes to be sent to Clausen, Copenhagen
852	52	Milling	F.C. (or J.C.)	271	Fwd'd, May 6th to Boston, for cremation	2nd	
855	14	Minahan	Dr. W.E.	230	Delivered May 2nd, to V.J. Minahan, Green Bay WI	1st	instructions NY office, wire April 29th, and V.J. Minahan's wire, same date.
863	105	Moen	Sigurd H.	309	Fwd'd to NY, May 10th, for shipment to Norway by S-A-Line	3rd/Southampton	instructions NY office, May 10th
902	53	Nasser	Nicholas	43	Fwd'd May 3rd, to J.J. Cronin, undertaker, Brooklyn NY	2nd	instructions NY office, wire April 29th
906	45	Hoffman	Louis M.	15	Hebrew Cemetery, Halifax, NS	2nd	
910	15	Newell	A.W.	122	Fwd'd to Boston, May 1st, per wire from Mrs. Mary A. Newell	1st	later identified from effects by Carbines bros., of Calumet MI
914	54	Nicholls	J.C.	101	Buried at sea	2nd	instructions NY office, wire May 4th
916	16	Nicholson	A.S.	263	Fwd'd May 6th, to F.E. Campbell, 214 West 23rd St., NY	1st	
928	55	Norman	Robert D.	287	Fairview, Halifax NS	2nd	
931	74	Novel	Mansor	181	Buried at sea	3rd/Cherbourg	
951	106	Olsen	Henry	173	Buried at sea	3rd/Southampton	
957	89	Anderson	Thos.	89	Buried at sea	3rd/Southampton	
965	17	Ostby	Engelhart C.	234	Delivered to David Sutherland, for fwd'ing to Providence RI	1st	letter of H.W. Ostby, April 24th
969	18	Ovies	Servando	189	Mt. Olivet, Halifax NS	1st	indentified by J.A. Rodrigue of Rodrigue & Co., Havana Cuba

List of Bodies Identified and Disposition of Same

Master List No	Old list No	Surname	Name(s)	Ref	Disposition	Class	Remarks
974	107	Paulsson	Alma Cornelia	206	Fairview, Halifax NS	3rd/Southampton	buried by crew of CS Mackay-Bennett, by special request
975	124	Paullsson	[baby]	4	Fairview, Halifax NS	3rd/Southampton	
989	19	Partner	Austin	166	Fwd'd to NY, May 7th, for shipment per MINNEHAHA, sailing May 11th	1st	instructions NY office, wire May 1st
1030	20	Porter	Walter Chamberlain	207	Delivered to Mr. E. Sessions, April 30th for fwd'ing to Worcester MA	1st	instructions of widow on MONTMAGNY
1047	110	Reynolds	Harold	327	Fairview, Halifax NS	3rd/Southampton	
1061	123	Ringhini	Sante	232	Fwd'd to NY May 11th, escort, F.W. Wender, for widow	Servant	request of Mrs. J. Stuart White, NY. (Mrs. White's manservant)
1068	108	Robins	A.,	119	Fwd'd May 4th, to Yonkers NY	3rd/Southampton	request of Mrs. Curtin (daughter), 24 Garfield St., Yonkers NY
1069	109	Robins	Mrs. A.	7	Fwd'd May 4th, to Yonkers NY	3rd/Southampton	request of Mrs. Curtin (daughter), 24 Garfield St., Yonkers NY
1080	21	Rosenshine	George	16	Delivered to A.A. Rosenshine, for fwd'ing to NY	1st	
1087	22	Rowe	Alfred	109	Fwd'd May 4th, from Halifax per EMPRESS OF BRITAIN, to Liverpool	1st	instructions NY office, wire May 3rd
1103	112	Sather	Simon	32	Fairview, Halifax NS	3rd/Southampton	
1105	111	Sage	William	67	Buried at sea	3rd/Southampton	
1128	113	Sawyer	Frederick	284	Fairview, Halifax NS	3rd/Southampton	
1205	56	Stokes	Philip Joseph	81	Buried at sea	2nd	
1207	114	Storey	Thomas	261	Fairview, Halifax NS	3rd/Southampton	
1211	23	Straus	Isador	96	Delivered to Mr. M. Rothchild, and fwd'd May 1st, to NY	1st	instructions of Mr. P.S. Straus, NY
1212	24	Sutton	Fred	46	Buried at sea	1st	
1225	57	Swane	George	294	Fairview, Halifax NS	2nd	
1238	115	Theobald	Thomas	176	Buried at sea	3rd/Southampton	
1251	116	Tomlin	Ernest Portage	50	Buried at sea	3rd/Southampton	
1274	117	Van Billiard	Austin	255	Fwd'd May 4th, to North Wales Depot, PA	3rd/Southampton	instructions NY office, wire May 2nd; later identified from effects, instructions NY office, wire May 2nd
1276	118	Van Billiard	W.	1	Fwd'd May 4th, to North Wales Depot, PA	3rd/Southampton	
1279	25	Van der	Wyckoff	245	Delivered to Mr. D.C. Chauncey for fwd'ing to NY	1st	instructions NY office, letter April 26th
1295	68	Wailens	Achille	140	Fairview, Halifax NS	2nd?	
1312	58	Weisz	Leopold	293	Fwd'd to E. Armstrong & Co. Montreal	2nd	instructions Montreal office, wire April 30th
1326	26	White	R. Fraser	169	Delivered to F.A. Smith, fwd'd April 30th, to Boston MA	1st	instructions from mother
1335	119	Wiklund	Jacob Alfred	314	Fairview, Halifax NS	3rd/Southampton	
1346	120	Williams	Leslie	14	Buried at sea	3rd/Southampton	
1352	121	Wirz	Albert	131	Fwd'd May 8th, to Mrs. T.M. Brown, Beloit WI	3rd/Southampton	instructions NY office, wire May 7th
1359	2	Woody	O.S.	167	Buried at sea	?	Not on crew list-probably mail clerk
1371	70	Der Zacarian	Maurpre	304	Fairview, Halifax NS	3rd/Cherbourg	buried Halifax, request of brother

Appendix 2

Captain Edward John Smith, Service Record 1875-1912

Captain's Service Record – Edward John Smith
Born Hanley, Staffordshire 1850.
Passed: Liverpool 1875, Certificate No 14102

Ship Name	O.N.	Voyage	Dest.	Crew List Location (where known)
Arzilla	46615	26.05.75	NA	NMM
Senator Weber	51475	28.09.75	US	MHA
Lizzie Fennell	64485	09.05.76	SP	MHA
		22.05.77	NA	MHA
		11.03.78		MHA
		31.07.78		MHA
		09.12.78		PRO
		14.08.79		PRO
Coptic (s)	84164	10.03.82	C	
		29.08.82	NP	
		11.11.82		
		20.01.83		
Britannic (s)	69368	28.02.84	US	
		11.06.84		
		25.09.84		
		04.12.84		NMM
		08.01.85		NMM
		19.03.85		NMM
		16.07.85		NMM
Republic (s)	65907	23.07.85	US	NMM
		03.12.85		
		07.01.86		
		15.04.86		
		03.11.86		
		20.01.87		
		21.04.87		
		19.05.87		
Britannic (s)	69368	24.08.87	US	
		19.10.87		
		14.12.87		
		29.02.88		
Baltic (s)	65877	04.04.88	US	
		05.05.88		
Britannic (s)	69368	20.06.88	US	
		12.09.88		
Cufic (s)	93825	08.12.88	US	Liverpool CRO
Republic (s)	65907	16.01.89	US	

Appendix 2

Ship Name	O.N.	Voyage	Dest.	Crew List Location (where known)
Celtic (s)	65979	10.04.89	For	
		07.05.89	US	
		29.07.89		
Adriatic (s)	65925	23.10.89	US	
Coptic (s)	84164	12.12.89	Aus	
Adriatic (s)	65925	24.12.90	US	
		17.01.91		
Runic (s)	93837	26.03.91	For	Liverpool CRO
Britannic (s)	69368	27.05.91	US	
		19.08.91		
		08.12.91		
		13.01.92		
		03.05.92		
		02.08.92		
		21.12.92		
		18.01.93		
		08.05.93		
Adriatic (s)	65925	03.06.93	For	
Britannic (s)	69368	05.07.93	US	
		03.10.93		
		27.12.93		
		30.01.94		
		22.05.94		
		13.08.94		
		10.12.94		
		07.01.95		
		01.04.95		
Germanic (s)	70932	14.05.95	US	NMM
Majestic (s)	97763	06.07.95	US	PRO
		29.10.95		PRO
		28.12.95		PRO
		30.01.96		PRO
		18.04.96		PRO
		05.09.96		PRO & Liv CRO
		28.12.96		Liverpool CRO
		26.01.97		Liverpool CRO
		15.04.97		Liverpool CRO
		21.07.97		Liverpool CRO
		13.10.97		Liverpool CRO
		14.12.97		Liverpool CRO
		10.01.98		PRO & Liv CRO
		01.04.98		PRO & Liv CRO
		03.08.98		PRO & Liv CRO
		22.12.98		Liverpool CRO
		21.01.99		Liverpool CRO
		15.04.99		Liverpool CRO
		05.08.99		Liverpool CRO

Who Sailed on Titanic?

Ship Name	O.N.	Voyage	Dest.	Crew List Location (where known)
		09.12.99		Liverpool CRO
		07.02.00	Cp	Liverpool CRO
		22.05.00	US	Liverpool CRO
		12.09.00		Liverpool CRO
		01.12.00		Liverpool CRO
		05.01.01		Liverpool CRO
		28.05.01		Liverpool CRO
		24.08.01		Liverpool CRO
		14.12.01		Liverpool CRO
		23.03.02		Liverpool CRO
		14.06.02		Liverpool CRO
		22.08.02		Liverpool CRO
		11.11.02		Liverpool CRO
Germanic (s)	70938	30.12.02	US	
		30.01.03		
		01.05.03		
Majestic (s)	97763	12.05.03	US	
		31.07.03		
		19.12.03		
		16.01.04		
		12.03.04		
		03.06.04		
Baltic (s)	118101	27.06.04	US	
		28.08.04		
		17.10.04		
		12.12.04		
		13.01.05		
		11.03.05		
		06.05.05		
		11.07.05		
		30.09.05		
		25.11.05		
		01.01.06		
		26.02.06		
		18.05.06		
		14.07.06		
		05.10.06		
		04.12.06		
		26.01.07		
		25.03.07		
Adriatic (s)	124061	06.05.07	US	PRO
		27.06.07		PRO
		23.09.07		PRO
		13.12.07		PRO
		10.01.08		MHA
		07.03.08		MHA
		29.05.08		MHA

Appendix 2

Ship Name	O.N.	Voyage	Dest.	Crew List Location (where known)
		25.07.08		MHA
		22.09.08		MHA
		18.11.08		MHA
		20.01.09		
		13.04.09		
		04.06.09		
		28.09.09		
		19.11.09		
		28.12.09		
		21.01.10		
		18.04.10		
		08.07.10		
		06.09.10		
		29.11.10		
		28.02.11		MHA
		28.04.11		MHA
Olympic (s)	131346	13.06.11	US	PRO
		12.07.11		PRO
		09.08.11		PRO
		30.08.11		PRO
		20.09.11		PRO
		19.12.11	US	PRO
		10.01.12		PRO
		05.02.12		PRO
		13.03.12		PRO
Titanic (s)	131428	10.04.12		PRO

Key: O.N. – vessel's official number as shown in Lloyd's Register of Shipping; MHA – Maritime History Archive, Memorial University, St John, Newfoundland; NMM – National Maritime Museum, Greenwich, London; Liverpool CRO – Liverpool City Record Office, Merseyside; PRO – Public Record Office, Kew

Note: These crew list references are the most likely locations extracted from BT99 Class List held at the Public Record Office in Kew, England, the publications listing the holdings of the Maritime History Archive, Memorial University, St John, Newfoundland, Canada and those held in County Record Offices. There is some overlap within the holdings. Researchers wishing to view the documents would be wise to contact the relevant archive before travelling.

Appendix 3

Possibilities for Further Research

Sources for Further Research
Passenger Lists in Britain, United States and Canada
Many families cherish a story passed down the generations about a relative's brush with death – they were booked to sail on *Titanic* but due to illness, lost baggage or travel problems they were forced to take another ship. Research frequently reveals that the true voyage took place weeks, months or even years later and the fondly remembered story proves to be nothing but a small slice of excitement invented to enliven what had in fact been an uneventful Atlantic crossing.

On the other hand, for some passengers the story may have been true. George Vanderbilt, his wife and daughter apparently had a last minute change of plan and sailed a week earlier on the *Olympic*. Elias Johannessen's appendicitis almost certainly saved his life. Reverend Stuart Holden's wife fell ill so he cancelled his ticket.

Beware of stories suggesting that there was no room on the ship. *Titanic* was under booked in all classes. Likewise, be sceptical of stories suggesting that having just missed *Titanic's* departure (usually for reasons beyond their control) they instead went immediately to Liverpool and took a ship for Canada. Except in a few cases where the shipping line had been responsible for a person being unable to board *Titanic* or any other ship for that matter, all the responsibility for making and paying for a new booking would have fallen upon the unfortunate passenger. The problems involved in changing ports, purchasing new tickets and rearranging travel plans for a new destination within a few days makes this scenario extremely unlikely.

A second popular story is that a family, while at sea on board another ship 'saw *Titanic*'. For anyone attempting to locate records of an ancestor's sea crossing this (if the story is true) is a significant clue.

If those concerned left Liverpool, Glasgow or one of the Irish east coast ports on 2 April, or were inbound to those ports on that day, then it is possible that they may have seen *Titanic* during her sea trials. They could also have seen her on her way from Belfast up the English Channel to the Solent and Southampton Water between 2 April and midnight on 3/4 April when she arrived at Southampton. Anyone who was aboard the *Olympic* on the voyage leaving Southampton in the afternoon of 3 April would have had an excellent view of *Titanic* off Portland, Dorset, when the two ships passed.

Titanic left Southampton on 10 April, reached Cherbourg that evening, and Queenstown in the middle of the following day. She was at sea for little more than four days in total. In theory, anyone in the vicinity of the western end of the English Channel or St George's Channel could have seen her on 10 and 11 April as could anyone on board ship in the Atlantic from later on 11 April to the evening of 14 April going in either direction. She could have passed slower ships also heading for New York, but the most likely way anyone would have seen her is if they were travelling in the opposite direction towards Britain or northern Europe, on 11 or 12 April.

If, after carefully rationalising the story in light of the information in this book, there is real reason to suspect that the story may be true, then it is wise to conduct a search of the Board of Trade's British passenger lists for all the ships leaving or arriving within a week or two of *Titanic's* departure.

Appendix 3

PRO reference numbers for boxes containing passenger lists for vessels inbound or outbound during April 1912 are as follows:

Port	Outbound	Inbound
Belfast		BT26/511
Bristol	BT27/742	BT26/511
Cardiff	BT27/743	BT26/512
Dover	BT27/743	BT26/512
Glasgow	BT27/744	BT26/744
Liverpool	BT27/751, 752, 753	BT26/517, 518; 525 joint Queenstown
London	BT27/768, 769	BT26/532
Plymouth	BT27/776	BT26/537
Queenstown	BT27/776	BT26/538
Southampton	BT27/780A	BT26/540
Swansea	BT27/784	

Notes for Researching in British passenger lists 1890–1960

British Board of Trade passenger lists are held at the Public Record Office, Ruskin Avenue, Kew, England; Tel 0208 876 3444; website http://www.pro.gov.uk

British lists, with the exception of *Titanic's*, have not been filmed. Many of them are in a fragile condition and searching them is very time consuming. There are no indexes of names, and many of the lists are handwritten. Rarely are they alphabetical. The information given on the lists varies throughout the period but can include age, occupation, and (after 1920) last address in the United Kingdom. Inbound lists are similar but after 1920 the address shown is the proposed address in the UK. They do not show the last address prior to joining the ship.

When planning a visit to the Public Record Office to search passenger lists, it is important to know as closely as possible the date of arrival or departure. Because the lists are arranged chronologically by port, it may require a search of three or more ports even if the date of departure is known. As a guide, searching one year's passenger lists for ships heading for New York from Liverpool will take more than one day.

The only finding aids of any kind are the Registers of Passenger Lists in BT32 covering the period 1906–50. They are small books arranged in month order and then by port with inbound and outbound shown separately, listing the ship names for which passenger lists were received during each month. Dates of sailing are shown at certain periods during the series but in general the dates given are those of the receipt of the passenger list by the Board of Trade. The origin (for inbound) and destination (for outbound) are not given. They are of very limited value, because they were originally compiled for the Board of Trade's use and were never intended to be used as a finding aid. They are only useful if a ship name is known but not a port, or if a ship name is known but not the month of arrival. If a ship name is not known, these registers are of no help whatsoever.

United States Passenger Manifests

Anyone contemplating a search in the British records should bear in mind that a search may be more fruitful in the corresponding American arrival records. Most of the records have been filmed and there are extensive indexes which may be searched by name or by soundex. The films may be available through the Family History Centres maintained by the Church of Latter Day Saints (the Mormons). A full description and explanation of the records held in the US archives is outside the scope of this book and readers wishing to undertake research in those records should contact the National Archives in Washington, D.C., at 700 Pennsylvania Avenue, NW, Washington D.C., 20408-0001. Tel 202-501-5400 or visit the website at http://www.ins.usdoj.gov/graphics/aboutins/history/immrecs/passlist.htm

If all the relevant information is known, then archives staff are able to conduct a search on behalf of a researcher. Some records have been filmed and have recently been put online. If an immigrant passed through Ellis Island information may be found at http://www.ellisislandrecords.org

Canadian Passenger Lists
Some records of Canadian arrivals are also being filmed and may be available through LDS Family History Centres. Records not yet available may in some cases be available directly through the Canadian National Archives. An in-depth discussion of Canadian passenger records is outside the scope of this book but readers are advised to contact the National Archives of Canada at 395 Wellington Street, Ottawa, Ontario, K1A 0N3

Readers with access to the internet may like to visit http://www.theshipslist.com where the subject of locating and searching passenger lists from these and other countries is discussed and explained.

Researching 20th century British Master Mariners
Appendix 2 lists the service record of Captain Edward J. Smith. For those researching other 20th century Master Mariners, the following information explains what may be found.

The filmed volumes of Lloyd's Captains' Registers found in large archives worldwide are frequently cited as the main, if not the only source, for tracing the career of a Master Mariner. In fact, they are just one of the sources available and they do have limitations. The purpose of the following list is not to explain the reasons for and methods of compiling information at each source, but to list the main sources available for anyone wishing to trace Master Mariners. It is not an exhaustive list. Where there is overlap you should check all sources. Remember also that most Masters and Mates will have seen service as ordinary seamen or apprentices before gaining their certificate.

Records of the Registrar General of Shipping & Seamen:
1845–1921
BT122-128 – Registers of Certificates of Competency and Service, Masters and Mates
                Home & Foreign Trade
Series of six registers in several volumes indexed by BT127 with key.
1845–94
BT127 –   Indexes to Registers of Certificates of Competency and Service, Masters and
                Mates, Home & Foreign Trade
1910–30
BT352 –   Indexes To Certificates of Competency – Masters, Mates, Engineers and
                Fishing Officers, Home and Foreign Trade
1913–35
BT318 –   Registers of Examinations for Certificates of Masters, Mates and Engineers
                – Returns of Passings and Failures
1917–68
BT317 –   Registers of Masters and Mates Certificates, Passings and Renewal

Lloyd's Captains' Registers
1851–1947 Series of Registers each in several volumes predominantly listing men employed

in the foreign trade. The earliest date available is 1869 which has been printed and published on microfiche. This is readily available in libraries and for purchase. Although this contains retrospective details to 1851, it officially contains the details only of those Masters in service in 1869 though there are isolated entries where the man is known to have died, and the information had not yet been transmitted.

Note that these registers can contain a wealth of information about individual voyages and also some biographical information about each man. Original Lloyd's Captains' Registers are at the Guildhall Library, Manuscripts Department, Aldermanbury, London EC2P 2EJ. http://ihr.sas.ac.uk/gh

20th century Crew Logs and Crew Agreements of British Registered Ships
The Merchant Shipping Act of 1835 required crew lists and related documents to be filed with the Register Office of Merchant Seamen (now the RGSS). There were different types of crew list, dependant on the particular voyage. In addition to information relating to the voyages, it may be possible to identify the seaman's ticket number, his place of birth and age, the capacity in which he is now employed, the last ship in which he served, and the place and date of joining and leaving the ship. All records up to 1860 are filed at the Public Record Office.

When the system began, it was important to know the port at which the ship was registered. After 1857 the system changed. Ships were given an official number on registration and the documents were filed accordingly in numerical order.

After 1861, the documents have been scattered between archives. The PRO holds 10 per cent of all Crew lists from 1861–1938, and 1951–89 in BT99. The National Maritime Museum holds the remaining 90% for 1861, 1862 and all for years ending in 5 except 1945, up to 1972. Certain County Record Offices and other archives hold many crew agreements for vessels registered in ports within their area, for the years 1863–1912. The Registry of Shipping and Seamen holds all Crew lists 1939–50, and those from 1990 to the present day. For 1972–89 all apart from those held at the PRO and those for 1975 and 1985 at the NMM, have been destroyed.

Almost all other records are held at the Maritime History Archive at the Memorial University of Newfoundland for the period 1863–1972.

The main exception is the class of records in BT100 – documents relating to celebrated ships, those vessels considered to be 'famous' such as the *Great Eastern*, *Lusitania* and of course *Titanic*, are held at the PRO in the class Agreements and Crew Lists, Series III – Celebrated Ships.

The Mercantile Marine Act of 1850 laid out rules requiring masters of all British registered ships to keep an Official Log Book for every voyage. The information contained in these varies and as you may expect, the earliest ones include much less information than 20th century examples. In general, they will all include such information as births and deaths on board, illness, disciplinary issues, conduct of crew, including notes of desertion, and anything else of significance taking place on board a ship during the period of the voyage or voyages. Home Trade ships were required to deposit the log half-yearly and Foreign Trade ships after each return voyage, with the Registry of Shipping & Seamen. These records begin to appear around 1852, but relatively few remain for the early years. Any containing a note of a birth, death or marriage at sea should have been retained but in reality that is no guarantee that you will find the one you need.

They are filed with the Agreements and Crew Lists, except for the period 1902–19, when there is a separate class in BT165 at the Public Record Office in Kew, England containing all surviving logs from that period.

Births, Marriages and Deaths at Sea
They are held at the Public Record Office in Kew, England, in the following series of records:

1. BT158 Births, Deaths and Marriages of Passengers At Sea 1854–90. These have been filmed and may consequently be available through your LDS library. Note that marriages were recorded only up to 1883 and births only up to 1887.
2. BT159 Registers of Deaths of British Nationals at Sea 1875–88.
2a BT160 Registers of Births of British Nationals at Sea 1875–91. These have also been filmed and may be available through your LDS library. These registers also include deaths of seamen.
3. BT334 Registers and Indexes of Births, Deaths and Marriages of Passengers and Seamen at Sea, 1891–1972. In an ideal situation, all these entries should appear in the GRO Marine Registers but in practice there are many omissions as records were not always forwarded. The GRO Marine Registers themselves began much earlier than the BT records mentioned above but again there are many omissions in the early years. As stated, marriage records are not recorded in the Marine Registers. It will be seen therefore that in order to search for a record of an event at sea, it may be necessary to search all of the above sources. Recognise also that until the Registration Act of 1874, Masters were not required by law to notify the RGSS of births and deaths on board and, although the events should have been entered into the log, this was not always done.

If after extensive searching in all the above sources you are still unable to confirm the birth, marriage or death of your ancestor as expected, you may have to consider whether this story was just a romantic notion. Always check the normal GRO registers of birth, marriage or death if you are unsuccessful in the marine registers – you could be surprised.

The text from which these extracts are taken were written and published by the author of this book as private tutorials for personal use. They are now also available in their entirety to those with internet access at the Mariners' website at http://www.mariners-L.freeserve.co.uk

Bibliography

Cameron, *Titanic, Belfast's Own*, Wolfhound Press, 1998

Booth & Coughlan, *Titanic, Signals of Disaster*, White Star, 1993

Cork Examiner, April 1912, *Irish Examiner* Image Library, Cork, Ireland

Destrais, Gerard, *Le Titanic à Cherbourg*

Eaton, John P., and Haas, Charles A., *Titanic – Destination Disaster*, Patrick Stephens, 1997

Eaton, John P., and Haas, Charles A., *Titanic – Triumph & Tragedy*, Patrick Stephens, 1992

Evans, Nicholas J., 'Indirect Passage from Europe. Transmigration via the UK, 1836-1914', *Journal for Maritime Research*, Greenwich, June 2001

Gardiner, Robin, and Van der Vat, Dan, *The Riddle of the Titanic*, Orion, 1998

Gracie, Col Archibald, *Titanic, A Survivor's Story*, Sutton, 1985

Hyslop, Donald, Forsyth, Alistair, and Jemima, Sheila, *Titanic Voices*, Sutton, 1997

Marriott, Leo, *Titanic*, PRC Publishing, 1997

McCluskie, Tom, *Anatomy of the Titanic*, PRC Publishing, 1998

Mersey, Lord, Proceedings on Formal Investigation into the Loss of the SS *Titanic*, HMSO, 1912

Moody, *Southampton's Railways*, Atlantic, 1997

Ruffman, *Titanic Remembered*, Formac, 1999

Sebak, Per Kristian, *Titanic, 31 Norwegian Destinies*, Genesis, 1998

Spence, *Victorian & Edwardian Railways*, Batsford, 1975

Taylor, *The Distant Magnet*, Eyre & Spottiswoode, 1971

United States' Senate, Report of Hearings, US Government Printing Office, 1912

Philip Hind (ed, 2001), Encyclopedia Titanica http://www.encyclopedia-titanica.org

Acknowledgements

I thought it would be a simple task, to acknowledge all those who have helped me in some way with this book. I soon discovered that the list was almost endless and I am very sorry that through constraints of space, some people could not be mentioned by name. If I have not included your name and you feel I really should have done, please accept my sincerest apologies for the oversight – do call me and tell me how you feel. That way at least I will feel as bad about it as you do.

Appreciation and thanks to a group of friends, without whom this project would never have begun: most of all to Sue Swiggum and Marian Smith. It has changed a lot from what we originally planned, but without their help in transcribing, photocopying and above all their constant encouragement, I should never have started writing it. Secondly, to Mary Ingham and Nick Evans who, over numerous cups of coffee in the Public Record Office's cafeteria, finally succeeded in persuading me that there really was room for another *Titanic* book, and have continued to badger me until I have finally finished it. Thank you for the help and support, and to Nick, for the generous access to all of his own research material. Grateful thanks, too, to Michael Palmer in California, who patiently read the whole manuscript twice over, and who, with heavy use of a red pen, finally succeeded in dragging my text into some semblance of grammatical order.

Thanks also to John Carr, PRO Kew; Neil Staples, RGSS; Louise Weymouth and Gordon Bussey of the Marconi Museum and Archives; the staff of Southampton City Archives, Merseyside Maritime Museum and Southampton City Library; to Per Kristian Sebak for his help, and permission to use some of his research; to Ted Finch for shipping fleet research; to Bob Bracken, Hermann Soeldner and Lester Mitcham, without whose generous help I would not have the complete copies of the Contract Ticket List; to Sue and Gery Swiggum for giving up their valuable spare time in trekking out to take photos; to the writers of a multitude of books and websites who have confirmed or refuted what I thought I knew, and in the course of doing so have greatly added to my knowledge and understanding. They are too numerous to mention with one outstanding exception – the many contributors to the 'Encyclopedia Titanica' internet website at http://www.encyclopedia-titanica.org The astounding amount of valuable research has opened the doors and enabled me to complete my own comparisons of some of the trickiest names on each of the lists. I am indebted to the editor Philip Hind for his kind permission to use some of the latest names from the website in the Master List.

I would also like thank everyone at Ian Allan Publishing who have brought this whole project to fruition; thank you too to anyone else I have ever phoned or emailed with a *Titanic* question, and to all those friends who have read a few chapters and given me their opinions, good or bad.

But the biggest thanks of all to my long suffering family: to David, who has had to cook his own dinners for six months as well as scan images, retouch photos and read the manuscript umpteen times; to our son Matthew, who worked all manner of magic on my computerised data, and to our other five children, Sarah, Alex, Victoria, Jessica and Penny, who have all been abandoned in Woking, while I have been sitting here by the sea, writing.

Debbie Beavis
Broadstairs, 2002

Index